THE ROUGH GUIDE TO

# Hip-Hop

by Peter Shapiro

**ROUGH GUIDES**

**Rough Guides online**
www.roughguides.com

## Rough Guides Credits

**Editing:** Matt Milton
**Series editor:** Mark Ellingham
**Picture research (second edition)**: Matt Milton and Sarah Cummins
**Proofreading**: Neil Foxlee
**Design**: Daniel May and Duncan Clark
**Layout**: Matt Milton and Link Hall
**Production**: Julia Bovis

## Picture Credits

**Mike Lewis**: 7, 26, 28, 32, 34, 56, 59, 63, 65, 66, 84, 87, 92, 97, 100, 101, 127, 145, 153, 191, 199, 201, 204, 232, 318, 323. **Ninja Tune/Big Dada:** 10, 11, 45, 46, 47, 53, 67, 143, 211, 220, 221. **Warp Records** 9, 13. **Michael Linssen/Redferns** 69, 338. **George Chin/Redferns** 188. **George Desota/Redferns** 226. **Ebet Roberts/Redferns** 326. **Mario Castellamos** 177. **Ray Burmiston** 283. **Roadrunner Records** 17. **Matt Milton** 265, 266. **Anthony Barboza** 162. **Battle Axe Records** 54

The graffiti font used in all Feature Box titles is 08 Underground, used by kind permission of its designer, Johan Waldenström.

## Publishing Information

This second edition published April 2005 by Rough Guides Ltd, 80 Strand, London WC2R 0RL.

**Distributed by the Penguin Group**
Penguin Books Ltd, 80 Strand, London WC2R 0RL.
Penguin Putnam, Inc. 375 Hudson Street, NY 10014, USA
Penguin Books Australia Ltd, 487 Maroondah Highway, PO Box 257, Ringwood, Victoria 3134, Australia
Penguin Books Canada Ltd, 10 Alcorn Avenue, Toronto, Ontario, Canada M4V 1E4
Penguin Books (NZ) Ltd, 182–190 Wairau Road, Auckland 10, New Zealand

Printed in Italy by LegoPrint S.p.A

416 pp
A catalogue record for this book is available from the British Library
ISBN 1-84353-263-8

# Contents

Introduction                     iv

## A–Z              **1–398**

Hip-hop slang            399

How hip-hop came to be     400–401

Books, magazines and websites    402–403

## Feature boxes

| | | | |
|---|---|---|---|
| African hip-hop | 3 | Gangsta rap | 178 |
| B-boying (breakdancing) | 359 | Go-go | 156 |
| Beefs | 169 | Graffiti | 160 |
| The booming system | 395 | Hip-hop and fashion | 182 |
| Breakbeats | 378 | Hip-hop and Islam | 391 |
| British hip-hop | 45 | Hip-hop and the movies | 288 |
| Canadian hip-hop | 52 | Hip-hop video | 306 |
| Christian rap | 298 | The human beatbox | 324 |
| The Dirty South | 293 | Miami Bass | 342 |
| DJing/turntablism | 99 | The mixtape | 332 |
| Dough on plastic | 312 | Rap-Rock | 278 |
| East Coast vs. West Coast | 285 | Reggaetón | 315 |
| Electro | 120 | Roots of the DAISY age | 310 |
| French hip-hop | 141 | White rappers | 174 |

## A note on recordings

Recommended recordings are preceded by a symbol: ☉ for an album on CD, and ⓞ for vinyl. Most classic hip-hop vinyl albums have been reissued on CD, and many have been re-pressed on vinyl several times.

# Introduction

Hip-hop may be all about the lyrical flow, but it has never been about simplistic linear narratives or smooth, continuous progressions. Like the music itself, hip-hop's history has been characterized by cut and chopped segues, ludicrous leaps of imagination and "wildstyle" flights of fancy and derring-do. To constrain hip-hop culture within the framework of chronology almost seems sacreligious.

There are certainly plenty of hip-hop creation myths – the lore and legends of prime movers such as **Kool DJ Herc**, **Grandmaster Flash** and **Afrika Bambaataa**. But the real "godfather" of hip-hop might very well have been some guy called **Robert Moses** – an unelected New York City official who exerted tyrannical control over the Big Apple's city planning in the 1950s and '60s. One of Moses' pet projects was the **Cross-Bronx Expressway**. Built in the early 1960s, it became Route One for white flight from the city to the exclusive suburbs of Westchester County and Connecticut. In order to build this fifteen-mile stretch of road, several thousand people were displaced, and large sections of the Bronx were levelled. This destroyed communities, necessitated the construction of ugly, modern housing developments and left large portions of the Bronx nothing but crumbling tenements and rubble.

With New York City bankrupt, and beholden to the bond-holders who imposed austerity programmes on the city, the Bronx became a brutal place to live. The first generation of post-CBE children in the Bronx tried to piece together bits from this urban scrap-heap. Like carrion crows or hunter-gatherers, they picked through the debris and created their own sense of community, finding vehicles for self-expression from cultural ready-mades, ephemera, trash and aerosol cans.

"If you can make it there, you'll make it anywhere", goes New York's anthem, and the ultimate dream was to make it "all-city": to have your name known from Staten Island to Manhattan, from Van Cortlandt Park to Rockaway Beach. Eventually, the local reps of early folk heroes such as graffiti-writer **Taki 183** and **Kool DJ Herc** spread beyond 183rd Street and Sedgwick Avenue. Hip-hop's first-wave pioneers became Johnny Appleseeds planting the hip-hop virus throughout the five boroughs, until eventually it went not only all-city, but all-world.

The *Rough Guide to Hip-Hop* follows hip-hop culture in all of its aspects, both musical (DJing and MCing) and visual (graffiti and b-boying or breakdancing), from its origins as the urban folk culture of the mid-'70s Bronx to its present status as the most important and biggest selling genre in modern music. Following hip-hop's basic tenet of competition, *The Rough Guide to Hip-Hop* is a comprehensive reference guide, but it is an opinionated one and, hopefully, will spark as many debates and cause as many beefs as it quashes.

## Acknowledgements

Thanks to everyone at Rough Guides, Mike Lewis, Pooh Daddy, YT, Michael Schenker, and most of all thanks to my wife Rachael, who is more inspirational than all the CDs and 12"s mentioned in this book put together.

# Above The Law

Maybe even more than its questionable moral framework, the biggest problem with gangsta rap was the uniformity of its sound. You can make the same criticism of any of hip-hop's subgenres, but the signature sounds of gangsta rap and G-Funk are so set in stone that it's impossible for anyone but the originators to rise above the merely formulaic. This was always the thing that dogged Above the Law, the quartet of **Cold 187um** (aka Big Hutch and/or Gregory Hutchison), **KMG** (Kevin Dulley), **Go Mack** (Arthur Goodman) and **DJ Total K-Oss** (Anthony Stewart), which formed in the late 1980s in Pomona, California.

The group's debut album, *Livin' Like Hustlers* (1990), featured production from Dr. Dre, but it didn't really stand out from the deluge of gangsta rap product pouring out of the West Coast at the time. The one exception was the song "Murder Rap", a disorientating mix of the whining synth effect from the *Ironside* and *Five Fingers of Death* themes, a Chuck D sample, a chopped and stretched "Funky Drummer" beat, and raps

that resembled the East Coast far more than the laidback drawl of Cali.

After N.W.A.'s split, and the feud between Dr. Dre and Eazy-E, Above the Law stayed with Eazy's Ruthless label – Cold 187um produced the group's second album, *Black Mafia Life* (1993). Even though Hutch is the son of jazz vibraphonist **Bobby Hutcherson**, his admittedly warm and breezy production couldn't keep the pace set by Dr. Dre on *The Chronic*, and tracks like "V.S.O.P." sounded wholly derivative of Dre's G-Funk blueprint. "Pimpology 101", however, with its seriously fat Ohio Players sample and laidback jazzy feel, sounded so consummately G-Funk it lent a bit of credence to the rumours that it was actually Cold 187um who originally invented the G-Funk sound. *Uncle Sam's Curse* (1994) attempted to add a political element to their tales of hustling and bad sex. It wasn't entirely convincing, but "Black Superman", thanks to its interpolation from funk band **Kleer**, was at least super-funky.

An odd move to the unsuitable home of **Tommy Boy** records for *Time Will Reveal* (1996) arguably scuppered what was perhaps their best album. The live instrumentation leant the album a warm and laidback feel, but Tommy Boy's East Coast rep and an overall bad timing – G-Funk was a genre whose best days were long behind it – meant that the album got lost. *Legends* (1998) and *Forever Rich Thugs* (1999) were little more than paint-by-numbers post-G-Funk and were utterly ignorable.

**Big Hutch** went solo on 1999's *Executive Decisions*, which didn't add anything to the predictable Above the Law formula, and suffered because he didn't have KMG as a foil. Soon after this release, Hutch was picked to run Death Row's production, and he worked on Death Row's vault-raiding releases such as 2Pac's *Until the End of Time*, Tha Dogg Pound's *2002* and Snoop's *Dead Man Walkin'*. After problems with the label, though, Above the Law released *Diary of a Drug Dealer* (2002) on their own label. The title proved sadly appropriate, as around this time DJ K-Oss was arrested on drug possession charges, which threw the group's status into limbo. Big Hutch's second solo album, *Live From the Ghetto* (2004), didn't make matters any clearer.

**Time Will Reveal**
Tommy Boy, 1996

Hip-hop had moved on, and largely left G-Funk for dead, but this album was Above the Law's most consistent in a career of following the lead of others. The lyrics are utterly clichéd, but Cold 187um's production and use of live instrumentation is uniformly excellent – simultaneously warmer and dirtier than run-of-the-mill G-Funk.

# Aceyalone

♢ See *Freestyle Fellowship*

# Aesop Rock

♢ See *Def Jux records*

# Afrika Bambaataa

The moral guardians who think that hip-hop is nothing but a negative force need to take a look at the life of Kevin Donovan. In fact, if it wasn't for hip-hop, and Donovan's influence upon it, New York might very well be the anarchic hell envisioned by John Carpenter in his film, *Escape From New York*.

Once the leader of the Big Apple's most notorious street gang, the Black Spades, Donovan, inspired by the sight of Africans fighting the British imperialist overlords in the wretched film *Zulu*, renamed himself Afrika Bambaataa and turned his gang into the **Zulu Nation**, an organisation dedicated to urban survival through peaceful means. With their party promotions and b-boy battles, the Zulu Nation gave disenfranchised kids in The Bronx – and soon, all of New York and beyond – a sense of belonging and success that they had previously only found in the violent street gangs that ruled New York during the early 1970s.

While Bambaataa would be a hip-hop figurehead for this fact alone, his legendary reputation was cemented by his role in some of the most epochal records in hip-hop history. When he graduated from high school, Bambaataa was given a set of turntables by

# AFRICAN HiP-HOP

Hip-hop has ancestral echoes in the griots and praise singers of Africa, so it should come as no surprise that, despite having an awesomely deep musical tradition of its own, Africa has been quick to adopt hip-hop as its own. However, its distance from the source has meant that Africa, like every other foreign outpost of hip-hop, is often little more than a pale imitator of the US original.

Hip-hop has existed in Africa since the mid-1980s, but the music's hardcore urbanism and comparative rhythmic simplicity was largely alien to Africa's musical cultures, based as they are on complex, syncopated rhythms and profound melodies. The growth of African reggae throughout the 1980s and early 1990s, however, helped open previously antagonistic ears, as did the airy, warm sounds of G-Funk.

While the most famous, and probably best, African rapper is **MC Solaar,** whose parents brought him from Senegal to Paris as a baby, Africa's first significant hip-hop crew was Senegal's **Positive Black Soul**, which formed in 1989. Rather than aping American styles, the duo of Doug E. Tee and Awadi blend traditional and popular Senegalese music with hip-hop beats and rhymes. Their *Salaam* album (1996) was the first African hip-hop record to be released by a major Western label, but more important was their *New York-Paris-Dakar* (1997) project which featured collaborations with KRS-One and Supernatural, an album finally made available in the West by the Night & Day label in 2003. Although their goal of uniting hip-hop with their country's ancient musical traditions is laudable, and a few Senegalese crews have followed suit (**Abass Abass**, **Gokh-Bi System**, **Daara J**), most of their countrymen (**Pee Froiss**, **BMG 44**, **V.A.**) try to imitate the latest American styles – an almost impossible feat given the poorly-equipped state of most African studios and the extravagant production values of popular American rap.

But every once in a while this approach yields good results. One of the best in this vein is Kenyan crew **Kalamashaka**'s "Ni Wakati", which echoes both the positivity and the rage of hip-hop's golden age, with its Malcolm X sample and Ennio Morricone-style moodiness. While the hip-hop crews from the francophone African countries benefit from a couple of degrees of linguistic separation from the US original, the hip-hop from the anglophone African nations is more often hampered by its shared tongue. South Africa's **Prophets of Da City** (active since the mid-1980s) have styles that sound alarmingly like Del Tha Funky Homosapien, while Gambia's **Da Fugitivz** exhibit the overwrought dramatics of 2Pac.

In Ghana, where the indigenous highlife music was supplanted in the 1980s by the Afrobeat, Juju and Fuji that came from Nigeria, a hybrid form called hiplife has since become big news. Kicked off by the Ghanaian-born but American-raised Reggie Rockstone, hiplife blends the tropical lilt of highlife with the beats of hip-hop and has become something of an underground phenomenon in the UK.

## VARIOUS ARTISTS

### ⊙ Africa Raps
Trikont, 2002

The German Trikont label specialises in musical scholarship of the most aracane kind, and this trawl through the cassette stalls of Dakar's Sandaga Market doesn't disappoint. This collection mostly features Dakar, currently Africa's hip-hop capital, with some sidetrips into neighbouring Gambia and Mali. The big names (Positive Black Soul, Da Brains) shine, but so do obscure artists like Senegal's Abass Abass and Mali's rather wonderful Tata Pound.

### ⊙ The Rough Guide To African Rap
World Music Network, 2004

Put all thoughts of synergistic cross-promotion out of your heads: the first pan-African hip-hop collection on the Western market is quite simply an excellent compilation, regardless of the name in the title. There are a few dated recordings, and some of the production is pretty interna-

tional sounding, but with tracks such as Reggie Rockstone's Fela-sampling "Eye Mo De Anna" and Tanzania's X Plastaz' "Msimu Kwa Msimu" (Swahili female MCing over a Bollywood sample), you can't go too far wrong.

No, it's not The Village People – or an outtake from *The Warriors* movie – but Afrika Bambaataa (centre) and posse, taking a break from creating the template for the next twenty years' worth of popular music.

his mother and, with a prodigious record collection, he was soon given the honorific title **"Master of Records"**. You can hear the Master of Records at work on *Death Mix* (1983), a less-than-legal copy of a tape of Bambaataa playing a party at the James Monroe High School in the Bronx, released on Winley Records (apparently without his consent). Featuring MCs advertising the next party over incredibly rough and primitive cutting and scratching by Bambaataa and Jazzy Jay – and the most dire fidelity since Edison's cylinders – *Death Mix* is hip-hop's equivalent of cave painting.

Bambaataa's first appearance on wax was the similarly ancient-sounding live recording "Zulu Nation Throwdown" (1980), also released by former doo-wop impresario Paul Winley. Far more important, however, was his first single for **Tommy Boy**, "Jazzy Sensation" (1981), made with the **Jazzy 5**. Ironically, "Jazzy Sensation" was the closest Bam would get to "pure" hip-hop during his studio career. After the infectious group energy and Sugar Hill-style street funk of "Jazzy Sensation", Bambaataa would remake hip-hop in the image of his favourite group – the German techno pioneers **Kraftwerk**. Exploiting the surreal popularity of Düsseldorf's performing showroom dummies at New York discos and block parties, Bambaataa, keyboardist John Robie and producer Arthur Baker welded the melody of Kraftwerk's "Trans-Europe Express" to the synth-bass of Kraftwerk's "Numbers" and the percussion from Captain Sky's "Super

Sperm" to create the song that taught the world that machines could be just as funky as James Brown. Bambaataa & Soulsonic Force's **"Planet Rock"** (1982) was the Rosetta Stone of electro and one of the most important records of the last quarter century.

They followed "Planet Rock" with the almost as good "Looking For The Perfect Beat" (1982) and "Renegades of Funk" (1983). These three early hip-hop masterpieces were included on his very late first album *Planet Rock: The Album* (1986). However, in the lag between his singles and the album, Bam hooked up with **James Brown** for the *Unity Pts. 1-6* EP (1984) – which contained the title track and so-so versions of every b-boy's favourite Godfather song, "Give It Up Or Turn It Loose" – and with Bill Laswell, as Shango, for *Shango Funk Theology* (1984), which included a cover of Sly Stone's "Thank You Falettinme Be Mice Elf Agin". An even stranger cover could be found on Bambaataa's second Tommy Boy album, *Beware (The Funk Is Everywhere)* (1986): an electro-shocked version of **The MC5**'s "Kick Out The Jams".

Ever since, Bambaataa has been working with ex-members of P-Funk, remixing "Planet Rock" about 100 times, and forging links with the rave generation that "Planet Rock" helped spawn. This was borne out in 2001 when Bambaataa contributed a mix to the **United DJs of America** series of dance music compilations. *Electro Funk Breakdown* was a strange mix of schlocky 'nu' electro, Southern Bass and British big beat.

⊙ **Looking For The Perfect Beat: 1980-1985**
Tommy Boy, 2001

Finally, after spending the better part of two decades being ignored by the reissue industry, Bambaataa's legacy gets preserved with something like the respect it deserves. Shame about the lack of liner notes, though.

# Afu-Ra

Ever since he appeared on Jeru the Damaja's "Mental Stamina" with a clumsy catalogue of multi-syllabic "abstract" metaphors, Afu-Ra (aka Aaron Phillip) has somehow carved a steady career out of a rather pedestrian flow and some of

the weakest similes in the game. Proving once again that it's not what you know but who you know, Afu-Ra's friends have kept him laced with rich beats that help you forget the poverty of his mic skills.

His first release outside of Jeru's patronage was "Whirlwind Thru Cities" (1998), an absolutely classic New York beat courtesy of **DJ Premier** and **DJ Roach**. The mournful, off-key piano and horn samples on top of drums with that characteristic Premo swing made "Whirlwind" an instant hit among hip-hop cognoscenti. Afu-Ra's charmless, wit-less rhymes just about managed not to lose the momentum. "Defeat" (1999) was more of the same, a problem only compounded by *Body Of The Life Force* (2000), which included both

singles. "Bigacts, Littleacts" had GZA giving Afu some personality training, and on "D&D Soundclash" his rhymes were rendered gratifyingly irrelevant in the face of a sick Beatminerz production.

There are no lines as truly awful as "steppin' on them like they was doormats" (from *Body*'s "All That"), but *Life Force Radio* (2002) wasn't exactly a huge improvement. Although the beats (from Premier, Easy Mo Bee and **Curt Cazal**), in fact, are probably better than on *Body of the Life Force*. However, Afu-Ra's charisma-free rapping just isn't worth the bother. Here's hoping they release an instrumental version.

Unsurprisingly, Afu-Ra's crew, the **Perverted Monks**, couldn't improve things much on *Afu-Ra Presents Perverted Monks* (2004), an album that got far more play in Europe than it did in the US.

### ◉ Life Force Radio
Koch International, 2002

Since you're not buying an Afu-Ra album for lyrical flights of fancy or well-timed punchlines, this one wins out slightly because the beats are a notch better. After a few listens, Afu's meat-and-potatoes rapping becomes wallpaper and you can just concentrate on stellar beats like DJ Premier's "Blvd.", Easy Mo Bee's "Hip Hop" and "Perverted Monks", and Curt Cazal's "1, 2, 3".

# Akinyele

One of the all-time great rappers made his recording debut on Main Source's posse cut "Live at the Barbecue". So did Akinyele Adams, of Lefrak City, Queens. With his trademark basso-shift at the end of every rhyme, Akinyele didn't embarrass himself on "Live at the Barbecue" – the first appearance on wax of a certain rapper called **Nas** – but it quickly became clear that he didn't have any other ideas.

In the event, Akinyele recorded his first solo album before Nas did – 1993's *Vagina Diner*. Despite some nifty **Large Professor** beats, the album showed that not only was Akinyele a one-trick pony in the flow department, he also had only one thing on his mind: sex. And when his thoughts on the subject were so vacuous and grotesque, the end results were never going to be very pretty. The one good thing about the album was that it introduced **DJ Rob Swift** (of the X-Men/X-Ecutioners) to the world beyond DMC competitions.

With its crushing bassline and chantable single entendres, "Put it in Your Mouth" (1996) was that year's blowjob anthem of choice in the clubs. Of course, with lines like "I'll be like Herbie Hand-you-a-cock" it was probably the worst song dedicated to fellatio since N.W.A.'s "Just Don't Bite It". *Aktapuss: The Soundtrack* (1999) was structured like a blaxploitation flick, but with dumb parodies like "Pussy Makes the World Go Round" it was more tedious than a bad porno movie.

Although he managed to talk about guns as well as hoochies on *Anakonda* (2001), unbelievably stupid lines like "pushing your wig back like some bitch on chemotherapy" just continued to lower expectations. Shockingly, however, *Live At The Barbecue – Unreleased Hits* (2004), which was a collection of tracks left on the cutting-room floor, was by far his best album. Displaying more range and humour than any of his legit releases, *Live at the Barbecue* showcases a rapper with personality, if not consummate skills. It makes you wonder what could've been.

### ◉ Live At The Barbecue
Eastern Conference, 2004

Beats from Large Professor, Buckwild, Dr Butcher, Rob Swift and CJ Moore, and a guest appearance from Kool G Rap make this an enticing prospect. But it's Akinyele himself, with genuinely funny lines like "I'm so pro-black I don't even pick the cotton out of aspirins", who steals the show.

# Tha Alkaholiks/ Likwit Crew

Given their name and SoCal origins, it should come as no surprise that Tha Alkaholiks are protégés of legendary partier and St. Ides pitch-man **King Tee**. Tash (Rico Smith), J-Ro (James Robinson) and E-Swift (Eric Brooks) made their vinyl debut on King Tee's *Tha Triflin' Album* (1993), on the stellar song "I Got It Bad Y'all".

Tha Alkaholiks' debut album, *21 & Over*

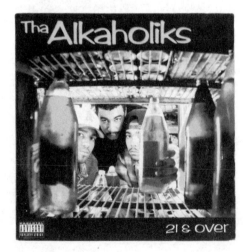

The Alkaholiks engage in a spot of backgammon dahn their local boozer.

(1993), was a collection of good old-fashioned party rhymes and stoner anthems. "Hooked on gin and tonic like ya mama's hooked on phonics", as they described themselves, the Liks cold rocked the party with drunken juvenilia and, in the G-Funk era, it was one of the more refreshing sounds in hip-hop. "Make Room" was an enormous, floor-filling single, with wailing James Brown horns and booming beats that sounded far more East Coast than LA in style, while "Likwit" was simply fat by anyone's standards. As if to fully prove their funk credentials, the album's most stupid moment, "Only When I'm Drunk", featured **J-Ro** actually burping on beat.

The group somehow managed to avoid becoming a one-joke act and on *Coast II Coast* (1995) they matured without losing their sense of fun. While the **Diamond D**-produced "Let It Out" covered old territory (admittedly very well), tracks like "Flashback" and "WLIX" saw the group reminisce about hip-hop's glory days as if they were elder statesmen.

There were no signs of the Liks checking into the Betty Ford clinic on *Likwidation*

(1997) as the inevitable collabo with **Ol' Dirty Bastard**, "Hip Hop Drunkies", proved. However, the joy was no longer there. Both "Killin' It", with **Xzibit**, and "All Night" (a collection of old school party rhymes over a Stevie Wonder Moog riff), may have had knockout production, but Tash and J-Ro sounded ornery and tired.

Tha Alkaholiks' Likwit Crew (Defari, Lootpack and Barbershop MCs), however, kept the momentum going with a collection of superb underground releases. **Defari**'s "Bionic" and, in particular, "People's Choice" (both 1997) found the schoolteacher-turned-rapper laying down the blueprint of an alternative LA style that would later be picked up by groups like **Dilated Peoples**. His slept-on *Focused Daily* (1999) album was a collection of classic flows and undiluted beats such as "Likwit Connection" and "Keep it on the Rise". Lootpack's *Soundpieces* (1999) followed suit with devastating tracks like "The Anthem", "Whenimondamic" and "The Long Awaited".

Meanwhile, Tash's solo album, *Rap Life* (1999), managed to do what the Liks hadn't been able to as a group for some time –

7

actually sound like he was having fun. **Catashtrophe**, as he restyled himself, didn't exactly break any boundaries, but his album was inebriating all the same. However, when the whole group reunited in 2001 as Tha Liks for *X.O. Experience*, the stick-to-the-formula hangover had really kicked in. Even a Neptunes-produced single, "Best U Can", couldn't cure the buzzkill. J-Ro evidently thought that dissing former crew member Xzibit was the best medicine, but 2003's "Look Out (The X Homie)" (2003), with its dull beat and lame insults, remained solely the preserve of the mixtape DJs.

⊙ **21 & Over**
Loud, 1993

It may have been nothing but "party and bullshit" – complete with shout-outs to their favourite brands of malt liquor – but at least they didn't overstay their welcome or throw up on your sofa.

# All Natural/ Family Tree

Despite Chicago's long and proud musical history, it still remains a backwater in the hip-hop world. With the exception of **Common**, it has failed to produce a major artist of note. It does have a fairly active underground scene though, much of it centred around All Natural – the duo of **Capital D** (Dave Kelly) and **Tone B Nimble** (Tony Fields).

The two got together as students in the mid-1990s and released their first single, "Writer's Block", in 1997. The record was Capital D's impression of the lives of the people on one city block in Chicago, and it remains one of hip-hop's great narrative poems. Their debut album, *No Additives, No Preservatives* (1998), however, could have maybe used some steroids, growth hormones and modified corn syrup, because, while everything was present and correct, it was all a bit flat. Both the MCs and the producers could have done with a personality transplant. It was originally released with a book by Capital D called *Fresh Air*, which was a collection of comics, poetry, short stories and essays about hip-hop culture.

*Second Nature* (2001) was released on arch-indie label **Thrill Jockey** – a combination to make you throw up in your backpack, if you were bored silly of underground hip-hop's dull ersatz Premier loops. But, although All Nat didn't exactly make you run out and pick up all those **People Under The Stairs** or **J Rawls** 12"s you missed, at least they didn't try to rhyme on top of the dry Prog noodling that Thrill Jockey specialized in. On the other hand, anyone who names a track after Strunk and White's subeditor's bible, *Elements Of Style*, has got to be worthy of your ears. There were no dangling participles or modifiers in Capital D's Rakim-influenced raps, and he had more going for him than just good grammar. He "loves the old skool but won't reverse" and is "ugly on point like Sam Cassell". The best track, "Uncle Sam", featured Atmosphere's **Slug** trading extended metaphors with Capital D about their crazy uncles, Sam and Tom. Disappointingly, the song "Godspeed" wasn't a shout-out to everyone's favourite Quebecois art rock merchants.

Capital D & The Molemen's *Writer's Block* (2002) was the All Natural debut single writ large in concept album form. Sort of like Diamond D crossed with Studs Terkel, Capital D chronicled the dreams, aspirations and difficulties of living in the inner city to beats reeking of underground classicism. Like much of his work, it was an album to admire rather than like, live with and cherish.

All Natural's **Family Tree Crew** – Iomos Marad, Daily Planet, Mr. Greenweedz, Rita J and Dug Infinite – released a series of 12"s of varying quality, most of which were collected on *Planting Seeds* (2001), and more appeared on *Tree House Rock* (2003). **Iomos Marad**'s *Deep Rooted* (2003) featured some of the Molemen's finest production yet, while Daily Planet's *Team Daily* (2003) was something of an underground all-star get-together, with **Dug Infinite** and J Rawls manning the boards, and El Da Sensei and Medaphor guesting on the mic.

**CAPITAL D & THE MOLEMEN**

⊙ **Writer's Block**
All Natural, 2002

The story of a single block in Chicago, the album tries to live up to hip-hop's self-image as ghetto

They may be All Natural, but that fleece and that ski-jacket look distinctly polyurethane/cotton/nylon blend.

communiqué, only without all the self-aggrandizement and self-congratulatory bullshit that goes along with it these days. Its aims are laudable, but it doesn't quite succeed because the beats are rather stale, and Capital D isn't entirely compelling on the mic. Still, this is the most impressive album dangling from All Natural's Family Tree.

# Anticon records

Over the course of some thirty albums, several boutique EPs, more guest appearances than Busta Rhymes and innumerable MP3s, the core of the Anticon collective (Dose One, Jel, Why?, Alias, Odd Nosdam, Passage, The Pedestrian and Sole) and their "co-worker cousins" (The Bomarr Monk, Controller 7, DJ Mayonnaise, Matth, Moodswing9, Telephone Jim Jesus, Sage Francis, Sixtoo and Buck 65) have taken hip-hop's hunter-gatherer aesthetic to its logical extreme.

On any given Anticon records track, absurdist, stream-of-consciousness non-sequiturs might wrestle for space in the mix with diary entries, quotations from former Supreme Court justices, an impromptu chorus of "Row, Row, Row Your Boat", observations on the golden age of MGM Studios and "Dear John" letters to rappers who let them down. While hip-hop's producers have always been scavengers, Anticon records often sound as if they have been found at the bottom of a trash heap, buried beneath not just the expected needle fluff and static but a patina of encrusted muck, with strange details such as fairground sounds and **Tortoise** basslines accumulated like bits of chewing gum; the edges smoothed out like sea glass, eroded by salt, wind and the SP1200 sampler.

Their references to "art" and their desire to expand generic boundaries have got Anticon into lots of trouble with a large portion of the hip-hop community. They are persona non grata in the mainstream hip-hop media, the objects of scorn on internet message boards, and the targets of backbiting and smear campaigns, often from the very parts of the independent hip-hop scene that nurtured their talents. Perhaps inevitably, their

cLOUDDEAD: (from right–left) Dose One, Why?, and the back of Odd Nosdam's head.

music gets derided as "Prog HipHop" and "unlistenable noise". However, unlike the Rick Wakemans and Keith Emersons of this world, or the legions of nerd boys in the "intelligent dance brigade", Anticon's roster has no messianic self-belief in its own genius. Yes, they are trying to push boundaries, but they're not making any grandiose claims for themselves and how they're making hip-hop better; they're not "giving you what you need" as certain boho hip-hop groups claim about their own music. They might plead for people to think or feel a bit more every once in a while, but that's about as far as their preachiness goes. No one in the crew was in the music academy studying Bach arpeggios two years ago before deciding to become a DJ to get the chicks. Anticon is simply a group of sensitive, intelligent, painfully self-aware young men trying to express themselves the only way they know how. And that way is through beats and rhymes, even if the rhymes don't always rhyme and are more likely to namedrop Zeus than Versace, and the beats are shaky and ramshackle, like Rube

Goldberg contraptions held together by masking tape and rubber bands.

Dealing with the excesses of popular culture was not the modus operandi of prog-rock but that of punk and post-punk. And, just as rock was in the mid-1970s, hip-hop is now twentysomething and is equally in need of a kick up the butt. So it's conceivable that 26 June 1998 just might become a date as significant as the day **The New York Dolls** wandered into Malcolm McLaren's King's Road boutique. For it was on this day that MCs **Dose One**, **Alias**, **Sole** and **Slug** (from Atmosphere) and producers **Jel**, **Ant** (Atmosphere), **Mayonnaise**, **Moodswing9** and **Abilities** (part of The Rhymesayers crew with Slug and Ant) travelled from Cincinnati, Ohio, Portland, Maine and the suburbs of Chicago to gather in Slug's living room in Minneapolis to produce one of the true classics of DIY hip-hop: **Deep Puddle Dynamics**'s *The Taste Of Rain ... Why Kneel* (2000). Although it's probably more "conventional" than the music that's since been made under the Anticon banner, the album has all the

Anticon trademarks: completely naked, unashamed self-analysis; shifting points of view; quotations from both KRS-One and Oliver Wendell Holmes; beats as likely to induce nausea as head-nodding; hooks like "I took a dip last week through the liquid that gathered/Near the tip of that peak that exists in my matter/I taught myself to survive without my feet on the ground/I never felt so alive as when I drowned"; an earnestness that's sometimes cringeworthy but more often thoroughly disarming, and occasionally breathtaking.

Minus Slug, Ant and Abilities, the participants moved out to the Bay Area and formed the Anticon label. The new label's first release was *Anticon: Music For The Advancement Of HipHop* (1999). The title may have been a scandal, very much like "intelligent dance" and fuel for the "Prog" fire, but the music was often extraordinary, even if the best track came from an outsider. Slug, despite being a key participant in Deep Puddle Dynamics, remained in Minnesota to concentrate on his group Atmosphere. Nevertheless, his "Nothing But Sunshine" anchored the compilation with its Jurassic 5/Scarface's "My Block"-style piano riff and lines like, "Now when my mother died, I had to take it in stride/There ain't no room for pride in watchin' your father cry/And dad made it until maybe a year later/When they found his suicide inside of a grain elevator."

The most striking thing about the album was the brutal honesty, the unremitting self-critical gaze at the rapper's psyche, and the seeming total lack of separation between art and life. Along with other vitriolic navel gazers such as Eminem, El-P and the Emo-rock brigade, Anticon (especially Sole, Alias and Dose One on his album with Boom Bip, *Circle* (2000)) are part of a growing trend in which performers are abandoning characters and detached first-person narration in favour of baring their souls like latter-day James Taylors. However, it's not just class and delivery that differentiates "shrink rap" from its singer-songwriter

Beatmaker Sixtoo, one of Anticon's "co-worker cousins", and friends, gettin' busy in the studio in studiously Anticonian fashion: music for the advancement of hip-hop indeed.

forebears, but the rage and willingness to pick over and dwell on the minutiae of neuroses. Yes, it's therapeutic, but it's closer in spirit to E.S.T. or regression therapy than the polite confessionals of "Sweet Baby James" and his trust-fund buddies.

Both Dose One and Sole got their start on the underground battling scene (Dose lost the 1997 Scribble Jam to a then-unknown Eminem), but with their battling days over they began shadow boxing with themselves – Sole in particular. His *Bottle Of Humans* (2000) album featured eerie, elegaic, minor-key string settings through which Sole wandered sort of like Allen Ginsberg (reincarnated as a red-head goy from Maine) walking around an art shtetl rapping the Kaddish for his own self-loathing. On records like *Hemispheres* (1998), Greenthink's *Blindfold* (1999), Them's *Them* (1999) and Themselves' *The No Music* (2002), Dose One displays one of music's utterly unique voices – something like a wise-cracking Jewish duck reincarnated as Percy Bysshe Shelley, or a beatnik Marge Simpson after assertiveness training.

The biggest "stars" Anticon has produced are probably cLOUDDEAD – Dose One, Why? and Odd Nosdam – whose records have been released on Mush and Big Dada, but not, paradoxically, on Anticon. On their self-titled debut of 2001, Dose One and Why?'s impressionistic reveries are delivered in off-the-wall cadences that don't exactly ride the beat, such as it is, but reinforce the musical

dream-state created by Odd Nosdam's production – an opiated palette of drawn-out (and washed-out) synths, decaying whirligigs, backwards grinding organs, drifting textures that wouldn't be out of place on a Labradford album, Richard Pryor samples, scratch squiggles and punch-drunk beats. The follow-up, *Ten* (2004), was more of the same.

### VARIOUS ARTISTS

**The Anticon Label Sampler 1999–2004**
Anticon, 2004

Comprising a song from every single Anticon album that had then been released, this 80-minute mix is one of the essential documents of hip-hop's avant-garde. Included are a love song to a chicken, the musings of God as she looks down at all the shit she's created, and an ode to a hospital. And that's just the accessible stuff.

# Antipop Consortium

As they themselves said, Antipop Consortium "rock like Kilimanjaro": wise, graceful, difficult forces of nature inscribing an imposing, geometrical challenge to all comers on hip-hop's horizon. Their motto was "disturb the equilibrium" and their complex, tongue-twisting lyrics influenced by Pharoah Monche, and forbidding electro-shocked beats made for anything but run-of-the-mill hip-hop. **Priest**, **Beans** and **M Sayyid** are MC Eschers twisting trompe l'oreille verbal mazes out of stairways to the nebulae, while producer **Earl Blaize** provides them with a suitably "warped geometry" in which they can defy the laws of physics.

Beans and Priest were performance poets/MCs on the Big Apple's "jazz not jazz" circuit in the early 1990s, often sharing the stage at venues such as Giant Step and the Nuyorican Poets Cafe. They were both members of **Shä-Key**'s Vibe Khameleons and contributed tracks to her 1994 album, *A Head Nädda's Journey To Adidi Skizm*, alongside people like Rahzel and J-Live. Working on the album, they met producer/engineer Earl Blaize, and

anticon label sampler: 1999 - 2004

Antipop Consortium. They really need to move into a bigger apartment.

eventually ran into *Urb* magazine scribe and Survival Research Labs alumnus M Sayyid at the Rap Meets Poetry nights at the Fez Bar in Manhattan. Their initial releases were cassettes, under the name "Consortium", released on the Anti-Pop label. Quickly the group became known as the Anti-Pop Consortium and released the mind-boggling "Disorientation" 12" (1997) with Apani B Fly MC of the **Polyrhythm Addicts**. Featuring one of the craziest synth lines ever and lyrics like "High priest,

extracurricular illustrator/Fuck a president, nominate Priest for dictator/Separate you like binary fission/Envision division of good and evil", "Disorientation" lived up to the group's motto and hailed them as one of the most talented crews in the underground.

In 1999 they collaborated with DJ Vadim ("through the mail, Unabomber style") on the superb, self-titled *Isolationist* album before dropping their debut album proper, *Tragic Epilogue* (2000). Despite the album's complexity and resolutely sci-fi beats, Anti-Pop were anything but anti-hip-hop. They had the fundamentals down, particularly a collection of some of the most inspirational disses in years: "Knowing your marble-mouthed Marlon Brando mumbles would never humble the tag-team Tony Atlas", "Your world is flat/Hah hah, you fell off/Hoping the laws of gravity will bring you back to earth" and "On the daily I'm facing more clowns than a John Wayne Gacy painting".

After an EP, *Diagnol Ryme Garganchula 2.0* (2000), released under the name Tripinnacle and a Japanese-only album, *Shopping Carts Crashing* (2001), the group dropped a hyphen, and the Antipop Consortium signed to electronica label Warp. *The Ends Against The Middle* (2001) was an EP of doodles and sketches, ideas written in the margins and not necessarily followed through all the way: a chugging freakazoid bop with wah-wah called "Dystopian Disco Force"; Bernard Parmegiani playing ping-pong with the Phantom of the Opera and a ring modulator on "Pit"; and "Perpendicular", their version of *Tubular Bells*. The production was John Foxx and Steve Strange without the make-up.

*Arrhythmia* (2002) featured occasionally stunning production from Earl Blaize, but more often than not, the group sounded less focused and less inspired, often settling for one-liners like "spraying freeon on Celine Dion" rather than the extended metaphors of their first album. Perhaps it was the sound of the group fracturing and going in different directions, because soon after the record's release Antipop broke up.

**Beans**, who had previously released the "Nude Paper" 12" in 2000, was the first member with a solo album, *Tomorrow Right Now* (2003), a slightly more accessible, bouncier effort than the APC records. *Antipop Vs. Matthew Shipp* (2003) was a posthumous release that teamed APC with jazz pianist **Matthew Shipp** and bassist **William Hooker**. "Hip-hop is the new jazz" is an assertion that has been bandied about for years, but usually only because bohos

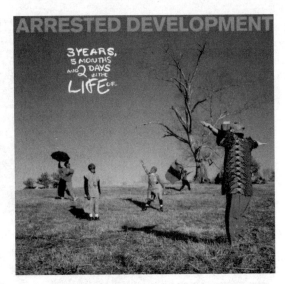

were sampling Grant Green records. This, however, was one of the few records that viewed jazz as a process, not just a sound, and it provided a fitting memorial to one of hip-hop's most challenging groups.

**Tragic Epilogue**
75 Ark, 2000

While it certainly doesn't meet you more than half-way, this isn't as forbidding as many other experimental hip-hop albums. There's lots of dense wordplay, wordflow and dystopian sci-fi weirdness – to be sure – but the album is ultimately sculptural, more about negative space and creating sonic shapes than information overload. As Sayyid says on "9.99", "You paint the picture".

# Arrested Development

Never has a group meant so much to the larger music community, and so little to the community that they came from, than Arrested Development. Formed in 1988 in Atlanta by rapper Speech and DJ Headliner, the group burst onto the scene in 1992 with an album that was hailed as a classic by the mainstream music press, MTV and the National Academy of Recording Arts & Sciences... and virtually ignored by diehard hip-hop fans. The truth is that neither reaction was entirely justified. *3 Years, 5 Months & 2 Days In The Life Of...*

was by no means a work of genius, it's just that its positivity and adherence to the musical values of the old guard meant that rock critics felt that they could latch onto it in the face of changing musical paradigms. But nor was Arrested Development a group of tree-hugging hippies without any skills. Of course, the fact that the group had a "spiritual advisor" (Baba Oje) proved which side the scales were tipped.

Speech and Headliner had previously worked together in **Secret Society**, a group that had more street-appeal, but they soon changed tack to a more Afrocentric direction upon exposure to Public Enemy and Sly Stone. Their debut album (named after the length of time it took the group to get a recording contract) was filled with warm, just-about-funky grooves that were closer to classic soul than to hip-hop, but the sound, unlike their sources, hasn't dated well. Singles like "Tennessee" (an admittedly moving depiction of an African-American's complex relationship with Dixie) and the anti-gangsta "People Everyday" (note: the single version – i.e. the decent version – isn't on the album) have stood the test of time OK, but the rest of the record sounds even worse than it did when it was released: feel-goodism and liberal guilt-tripping of the smuggest, most pompous, insufferable sort.

*Unplugged* (1993) was a quickie cash-in sponsored by MTV, and deserved the comparative boycott it was greeted with. *Zingalamaduni* (1994) was a catastrophic commercial failure, a reaction that its tepid grooves and cloyingly aphoristic lyrics deserved. The group broke up soon afterward, with singer Dionne Farris scoring a hit with "I Know" from *Wild Seed – Wild Flower* (1995), but just as quickly fading into obscurity. Speech, meanwhile, released a few utterly ignorable solo albums – *Speech* (1996), *Hoopla* (1999) and *Spiritual People* (2002) – plus a couple more in Japan.

⊙ **The Best Of Arrested Development**
EMI, 1998

The only reason to go for this over *3 Years, 5 Months & 2 Days In The Life Of...* is that this has the single version of "People Everyday" (which is the one you want). If you're scared of hip-hop and all that it means, you need this. Otherwise, stick to your De La Soul albums.

# Artifacts

Coming out of "New Jeruzalem" (or Newark, New Jersey) in the mid-1990s, the Artifacts helped set the parameters and mindset of much of the underground hip-hop that was to follow in their wake. Comprised of former graff writers **Tame One** and **El Da Sensai**, the Artifacts gave their DJ some (**DJ Kaos** was his name) and wrote homages to the burners in the train yards, at a time when rappers' egos and standard music biz promotional practices were threatening to destroy the cultural aspects of hip-hop (MCing, DJing, graffiti and breakdancing).

The Artifacts first appeared on "Do Ya Wanna Hear It" (1993), a collaboration with the Nubian Crackers. The group got widespread exposure on the East Coast with "Wrong Side Of Da Tracks" (1994). With the oft-sampled line, "I'm out to bomb like Vietnam", on top of a **Grover Washington Jr.** loop, "Wrong Side of Da Tracks" was a tribute to aerosol culture that managed to find some space on the airwaves for itself when Biggie and Tupac were running things. *Between a Rock and a Hard Place* (1994) followed a similar blueprint, with crunching drums and catchy horn loops, particularly on the singles "C'mon Wit Da Get Down", which featured a pre-stardom **Busta Rhymes** as well as some of the first sightings of now classic breaks from David Axelrod and Galt McDermot, and "Dynamite Soul", with Timbaland's favourite rapper **Mad Skillz**.

The mellow but eerily insistent "Art of Facts" followed in 1996, preceding their second album, *That's Them* (1997). The sequel to "Wrong Side. . . ", "Return to Da Wrongside", sported a killer Bennie Maupin sample and "Collaboration of Mics" featured Lords Finesse and Jamar, but the album was a bit too one-dimensional. After a single as the **Brick City Kids** ("Brick City Kids/What What") for Rawkus in 1997, Tame One and El Da Sensai, like Journey, went their separate ways.

Tame One has since appeared on tracks from Fatal Hussein and Redman and worked with his Boom Skwad posse. He has also dropped two solo joints, "In Ya Area"

(1998) and "Trife Type Tymez" (1999) on his Boom Skwad label. In 2003 he released his first solo album, *When Rappers Attack*, on High & Mighty's Eastern Conference label. The following year he hooked up with shock rapper Cage for the **Leak Bros.** project, which sounded like a slightly funkier than usual Def Jux record.

El Da Sensei, meanwhile, has become something of a hired gun on the underground scene, working with everyone from Organized Konfusion and Mike Zoot (on Sensai's "Frontline" single of 1998) to Norway's Tommy Tee and the UK's Creators. In 2002 he finally released his debut solo album, *Relax, Relate, Release*, which featured appearances from such "undie" stalwarts as Zoot, Pharoahe Monch, Sadat X, J-Live and Asheru, but it suffered from lightweight, unfocused production.

⊙ **Between A Rock And A Hard Place**
Big Beat/Atlantic, 1994

From its appreciation of graffiti to its prescient crate-digging archaeology (David Axelrod, Galt McDermot), this is a classic of the underground '90s aesthetic.

# Atmosphere

What is it about Minneapolis that makes guys so obsessed with the minutiae of sex? Ever since Prince went off the deep end, fellow Twin Cities resident **Slug** (aka Sean Daley) has picked up his mantle as music's most prolific chronicler of coitus.

The only difference is that in **Prince**'s lyrics he'd be bird-dogging brides on their way to get married, and running into women masturbating in hotel hallways. Slug dwells on the aftermath, the frustrations, the break-ups, the anger, the bitterness of running into an ex... and a woman with tattooed hands who masturbates in front of him ("The Woman With The Tattooed Hands").

Slug's **Rhymesayers** crew began as a high school affiliation with locals like Stress (Siddiq Ali), Spawn (Derek Turner), MC Musab, Phull Surkle, The Dynospectrum and The Micranots. Working in various permutations, they released a series of

tapes called **Headshots** throughout the mid-1990s that are something of a cause célèbre on the underground scene and go for ridiculous money on eBay when they turn up. The most famous of these tapes are probably volumes six and seven, *Industrial Warfare* (1998), which introduced **Eyedea & Abilities**, and *Se7en* (1999), which was Slug under his Sept Sev Sev alias.

Hooking up with producer **Ant** (Anthony Davis), Slug formed Atmosphere with **Spawn** and released *Overcast!* (1997). An awkward combination of the b-boy bravado of the early Headshots tapes with the introspection that would set Slug apart from most of his peers, *Overcast!* was the sound of a group finding its feet. Spawn doesn't really contribute very much, but the glimpses of Slug's future sound are pretty extraordinary: "Scapegoat" ("It's stick up kids/It's Christian conservative terrorists/It's porno flicks/It's the East Coast/No, it's the West Coast/It's public schools/It's asbestos... It's everything you be/But it ain't me motherfucker, it ain't me") and "God's Bathroom Floor", a narrative of a drug overdose.

With Atmosphere reduced to a duo of Slug and Ant, *Lucy Ford: The Atmosphere EPs* (2000) collected two EPs that, along with the first Anticon releases, mark the birth of what would unfortunately become known as "emo-rap" (as terms go, "shrink rap" is much better). "Nothing But Sunshine" was an extraordinary narrative of a fucked-up adolescence, a sardonically-titled, morbid tale recounting the suicide of its protagonist's parents.

Lucy Ford (yes, it's as bad a Satan reference as Louis Cypher in *Angel Heart*) reappears on *God Loves Ugly* (2002). "Fuck You Lucy" finds Slug exorcising the demons of a crappy childhood at the same time as he wrings his hands over his string of failed relationships. While Ant had shifted his production style a bit, particularly on the reggae-ish "Blamegame" and the almost radio-friendly "Modern Man's Hustle", Slug's flow had grown thin with increased exposure, even though his lyrical skill was a strong as ever.

*Seven's Travels* (2003) was the group's

first for punk titans Epitaph and the move to a rock label seemed to rub off on Slug. *Seven's Travels* was filled with groupie tales, and even if Slug was more intelligent and more sensitive than Mark Farner or Steven Tyler, a groupie tale is a groupie tale. Slug's gift for narrative was still apparent, though, particularly on "Always Coming Back Home to You", and Ant's production was as good a reconciliation between underground grime and mainstream shine as you could hope for. As an added bonus, the traditional Atmosphere hidden track

is an ode to the Midwest that goes, "If you know that this is where you wanna raise your kids/Say 'Shhhh'… If the playground is clear of stems and syringes/If there's only one store in your town that sells 12-inches/Say 'Shhhh'".

**Lucy Ford: The Atmosphere EPs**
Rhymesayers, 2000

Call it "emo-rap", "shrink rap", "punk-ass sissy shit", or whatever you want, but the fact is that this one of the most creative hip-hop albums of the new century.

Atmosphere's Slug (foreground) and Sole bring da (emotional) pain.

# Audio Two

The duo of **Milk Dee** and **Gizmo** is in this book for one reason: one of the greatest singles, hip-hop or otherwise, of all time. A supercharged blast of noyze, "Top Billin'" (1987) was everything hip-hop was supposed to be about: drum machines that rumbled and screeched like the A-train, blunt cuts from Giz, a sample from **Stetsasonic**'s "Go Brooklyn 1" in the background and a rap from Milk that was all pumped-up b-boy attitude. Perhaps even better than the original mix was **Clark Kent**'s remix, which introduced both the Jimmy Castor "Going way back" intro and the piano riff from Rick James's "Mary Jane". If Milk has a vocal resemblance to a certain female MC, it's not surprising: **MC Lyte** was Milk and Giz's half-sister. In fact, the whole family initially recorded for dad Nat Robinson's First Priority label.

"Top Billin'" anchored their debut album, *What More Can I Say?* (1988), which took its name from the hook from "Top Billin'". Although much of the album attempted to recapture the hit's energy burst to little effect, *What More Can I Say?* did have some fine, disorientating production from Stetsasonic's **Daddy-O**, the inspired lunacy of "I Like Cherries" and the funny follow-up single, "Hickeys Around My Neck". *I Don't Care* (1990) was more of the same,

only differentiated by a semi-classic in "Get Your Mother Off the Crack" and, disappointingly, the reprehensible gay-bashing of "Whatcha Lookin' At".

By this time, hip-hop had largely passed the duo by, while their half-sis borrowed Milk's rhyming style and it took her to hip-hop stardom. The group split in 1992 and Milk released a solo album, *Never Dated* (1994), for American Recordings. The album's title wasn't entirely accurate, but it had a few moments where Milk almost re-ignited the flame of "Top Billin'", especially the stoopid fresh duet with the Beastie Boys' **Ad Rock**.

Ten years later, out of nowhere, Milk Dee turned up as the brains behind Staten Island punk doo-wopper **Eamon**. With spare production not entirely unreminiscent of "Top Billin'" from Milk Dee, "F*ck it (I Don't Want You Back)" (2003) turned Eamon into an urban novelty sensation. The album, *I Don't Want You Back*, also featured two guest raps from Milk, neither of which will go down in hip-hop lore.

**What More Can I Say?**
First Priority, 1988

A pretty typical album from the period (i.e. two great cuts and a lot of lame filler), but its high point, "Top Billin'" is one of the genre's apexes.

# AZ

AZ the Visualiza (aka Anthony Cruz) first came to attention on **Nas**'s "Life's a Bitch" talking about "Schwepervesence street ghetto essence" and "Keepin' it real/Packin' steel/Gettin' high/Cause life's a bitch then you die". AZ's laconic flow, echoes of **Kool G Rap**, and slight warble gave his lyrics a poignancy that prevented him from being totally outshone by rap's chosen one.

On his own, however, AZ is a bit one-dimensional and he doesn't have the lyrical skill of his mentor to fully explore the contradictions of the "trife life" that he chronicles. AZ's debut album, *Doe Or Die* (1995), presaged Nas's move into the mafioso posturing that has since dogged his career. Not quite the full-on celebration that he would soon indulge in as part of **The Firm**, *Doe Or Die* nevertheless abandoned the journalistic voice that made *Illmatic* such a masterpiece in favour of a less nuanced cataloguing of street trauma. The one exception was "Mo Money, Mo Murder 'Homicide'", which featured a verse from Nas and was reminiscent of the best of his stunning *Illmatic* album.

After participating in the ill-fated The Firm project (see Nas entry), AZ released *Pieces of a Man* (1998), which seemingly sank without a trace. Despite some fine beats from The Trackmasters and L.E.S., and occasionally better lyrics than his debut (particularly on "What's the Deal"), the album suffered from a crippling lack of marketing and is something of a lost classic. *S.O.S.A. (Save Our Streets AZ)* (2000) was a controversial, independent release that was heavily bootlegged and found AZ reinvigorated by some gritty underground beats, especially "I Don't Give a Fuck Now" and "Problems".

"Problems", based on a proto-**Kanye West** DeBarge sample, reappeared on *Nine Lives* (2001) – the best track on an otherwise lacklustre record that tried too hard for commercial success. *Aziatic* (2002), however, was the rapprochement with the mainstream that AZ had long sought. "Once

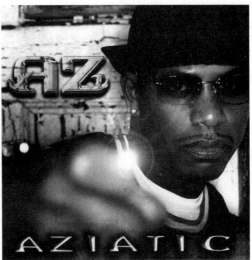

Again" chopped up the theme song from 1970s sitcom *Welcome Back Kotter* to great effect as AZ told his life story, while "The Essence" was a duet with Nas that had the two MCs trading compliments and grooming tips.

**Aziatic**
Motown, 2002

His true talent may be for Kool G Rap-style gritty crime rap, but this commercially-minded crossover attempt showcases AZ's considerable rapping skills better than any of his other albums. Never a thinking man's rapper or an aesthete's favourite, AZ was more of a formalist on the mic and the upwardly mobile production values here suit his meat-and-potatoes style.

# ⊙ B-Boy records

Formed by Big Jack Allen and Chill Bill Kamarra in 1986, B-Boy Records represented the last gasp of the drum machine in New York hip-hop. Manifestoes of pure sensation featuring enormous drum kicks, gratuitous vocoders, primitive, blurting horn samples and incredibly unpolished scratching, B-Boy's releases were some of the last records to approach hip-hop as pure noise, to realise that, as **Jewel T** declared, "the walls of Jericho can't take [their] scenario". Like punk, the attitude *was* the meaning: an audacity born of exploited technology and new-found voices.

B-Boy is most famous for unleashing **KRS-One** and **Boogie Down Productions** on the world. Indeed, BDP's extraordinary "South Bronx" was the label's first release. As awesome as BDP's spare, chilling drum-machine geometry was, however, the target of "South Bronx" – the pioneering sampling production of Marley Marl for his Queensbridge **Juice Crew** – was winning the overall war, and hip-hop was rapidly shifting to this more fleshed-out sound. BDP and the rest of the B-Boy artists reacted against this "softening" influence by getting sparser, gruffer and more angular in their production style. Records like **The Brothers'** (Akiem, Narkim and DJ Supreme) "I Got Rhythm", **Wax Master Torey**'s "Duck Season" and Jewel T's "I Like It Loud" (all 1987) simply exploded from the speakers, with shotgun snares, jackhammer kicks and not much else apart from assertive voices buzzing with puffed-up b-boy attitude. The BDP releases aside, the best of these records was **Levi 167**'s "Something Fresh To Swing To" (1987): a punishing drum beat buffeted by metallic

Doin' Damage

gusts that sound like the DJ is scratching with buzzsaw blades. Castle D's "Just Saying Fresh Rhymes" (1987), meanwhile, is an early, if not the earliest, precursor of gothic hip-hop. Its eerie keyboard line and ticking hi-hat pattern was the direct ancestor of the West Coast creep beat.

When the sampler did creep into the B-Boy aesthetic, it was used in much the same way as the drum machines – with all the finesse of a frustrated child trying to jam a square peg into a round hole. Records like The Busy Boys' "Classical" and **Cold Crush Brothers**' "Feel the Horns" (both 1987) sliced up James Brown with jagged, rusted corrugated knives, while Sparky D's "Throwdown" (1987) used Boz Scaggs' "Lowdown" as a half-hearted afterthought to round out the slightly thin beat. By 1988, though, the B-Boy stable seemed to make peace with the Akai and **JVC FORCE**'s "Strong Island" rode its Freda Payne sample to become one of the most kinetic records in hip-hop history. Unfortunately, soon after this landmark release the label folded amidst recriminations from KRS-One and problems with the law.

## VARIOUS ARTISTS

**The Best Of B-Boy Records**
Landspeed, 2002

While much of the B-Boy catalogue has been reissued on vinyl, this is relatively easy to find and is a pretty faultless collection of hits and obscurities.

# ◎ Bad Boy records

P. Diddy (né Sean "Puffy" Combs) might provide irrefutable proof of Freud's famous equation between shit and gold. But if someone's going to trade in hip-hop's cultural capital for multi-million dollar success, better Cream Puff than Vanilla Ice. Writing new lyrics to all of your favourite hits, **P. Diddy** is hip-hop's Weird Al Yankovic – just replace Al's humour with a messianic belief in his own greatness (Puff once released an industry-only showcase disc called *Puffy Combs: Changing the Sound of Popular Music*). Making a mockery of hip-hop's much vaunted skills culture, Puff Daddy has amassed a fortune from a stable of talent-deficient MCs, turning rock critic Lester Bangs' "attitude-is-everything" dictum into a Nietzschean will to power.

Before he became the only hip-hop mogul who could rival such legends as his future paymaster Clive Davis, or Walter Yetnikoff, Combs was a kid from money earnin' Mount Vernon, New York, who started promoting parties while attending Howard University in Washington DC. On the recommendation of childhood friend Heavy D, Combs landed a gig as an intern at Andre Harrell's Uptown Records. At the same time he was promoting a series of successful parties called "Daddy's House" at Manhattan's Red Zone club. At the end of 1991, he organised a charity basketball game which went horribly wrong, as nine people were trampled to death in a scramble to get inside.

A year later he emerged as the brains behind both the "Queen of Hip-Hop Soul" **Mary J Blige** and chief "boot-knockers" **Jodeci**. In order to get his acts played in both the jeeps and the bedrooms, Puffy almost invented the art of street promotion, hiring teams of kids to sticker anything stationary in New York and litter the club scene with flyers. As a result, he was promoted to vice president of A&R at Uptown. While still in that position, he conceived his **Bad Boy Entertainment** label, and was fired for insubordination by Harrell.

Bad Boy became an imprint of Arista and immediately ruled the streets of New York with **Craig Mack**'s "Flava In Ya Ear" (1994). Mack, who had previously recorded MC EZ & Troup's "Get Retarded" (1989), brought things back to the old school with his B-Boy cold flow and corny jokes on his underrated album, *Project: Funk The World* (1994). Mack's album was released on the same day as Notorious BIG's *Ready To Die* (see Notorious BIG entry) and, although it went gold, Mack quickly took a back seat to Bad Boy's plans. Mack left the label, released the dire *Operation: Get Down* (1997), and became the butt of jokes from every comedian on BET (Black Entertainment Television). He returned in 2000, though, riding a loop of Frank Sinatra's "High Hopes", courtesy of **45 King**, on the massive "Wooden Horse". Mack was welcomed back into the fold in 2002 when he appeared on the remix of **G. Dep**'s "Special Delivery", featured on the *We Invented The Remix* (a title of typical Combsian understatement) album.

Unfortunately for hip-hop fans, Bad Boy had debuted with its two best artists, and it was all downhill from there. After some r&b projects – Biggie's former wife **Faith Evans**, 112 and Total – and Biggie's weaker *Life After Death* (1997), Puff Daddy & the Family released the mind-bogglingly awful *No Way Out* (1997), which somehow managed to go seven times platinum on the back of the Police-sampling "I'll Be Missing You" tribute to Biggie. Believe it or not, it took a whole team of behind-the-sceners like producer Derric "D-Dot" Angelettie and ghost writer Sauce Money to make the song as execrable as it was – perish the thought of what it would've been like without their input. Even worse was the collected oeuvre of sidekick **Mase** – *Harlem World* (1997), *Double Up* (1999) and *Mase Presents Harlem World – The Movement* (1999) – who rapped like a deer caught in the headlights. Even though your kid sister could freak a beat better than

Mase, he too sold several million records. Unfortunately, despite retiring in 1999 to devote his life to God, he staged a comeback in 2004.

After being responsible, in one way or another, for a staggering 40% of Billboard number ones in 1997, Puff relocated Daddy's House to the exclusive beach community of the Hamptons so he could live by the sea, like his magic dragon namesake, and bum-rush the upper echelons of American "society". It soon started to go wrong, however. After their gold debut, *Money, Power And Respect* (1998), **The LOX** split from Bad Boy very publicly, with their "Let The LOX Go"

campaign, and defected to Ruff Ryders Records. One month later, P. Diddy's hit-making equations failed him on his sprawling *Forever* (1999) album, which sold several million less than his debut.

**Black Rob**'s much-delayed *Life Story* (2000) and its hit single, "Whoa!" seemed to steady the ship, but with Puff in legal trouble (not for the first time) over an incident in a New York club, Bad Boy's CEO was living up to his label's name and Puffy threatened to go up in smoke. Somehow, however, he managed to land on his feet after being acquitted of all charges. With Black Rob and G. Dep in tow, Diddy unleashed *The Saga Continues* (2001). It by and large ditched the karaoke machine in favour of a team of producers (one track has 17 writers' credits and – count 'em – 21 different publishing companies). These included the scene's current supernovas, **The Neptunes**, alongside absolute no-names borrowing liberally from more famous producers' trademark styles (what – the video really cost so much that he couldn't afford to hire **Rockwilder** himself?). Of course, that's not to say that the ghosts of AM radio of yore were totally exorcised – you were still haunted by memories of The Alan Parsons Project and Chuck Mangione. However, by far and away the best track, "Bad Boy For Life", featured a killer original guitar riff that pointed out a possible future where Combs wouldn't be bragging about writing cheques rather than rhymes.

## VARIOUS ARTISTS

⊙ **Bad Boy's 10th Anniversary: The Hits**
Bad Boy, 2004

It's got nowhere near all of the label's hits, but if you can't get enough of Puff and Mase mumbling and stumbling their way through the karaoke machine of your local pub, this is the least painful way to do it.

# Rob Base & DJ E-Z Rock

Robert Ginyard (aka Rob Base) and Rodney Bryce (aka DJ E-Z Rock) might have started their careers as ten-year-olds in Harlem, but they will forever be remembered for one single that they released in 1988. Named the greatest single of all time by *Spin* magazine in 1989, **"It Takes Two"** was an enormous club hit that ranks as one of the most breathtakingly immediate records ever made by someone who was not James Brown. Of course, the part of the record that grabbed you by the seat of your pants was a loop of a trademark JB yelp and grunt that electrified it with Brownian motion. The loop (as well as the beat and the vocal hook) was taken from Lyn Collins' 1972 single "Think (About It)", which was Brown's most influential outside production. Along with **Eric B. & Rakim**'s "I Know You Got Soul", "It Takes Two" foregrounded Brown's disembodied shrieks and chopped-

up beats as the main elements in a chaotic urban soundscape that helped make "Brother Rapp" an unavoidable presence in hip-hop.

While Base and E-Z Rock made Brown's energy positively bionic on "It Takes Two", their debut album *It Takes Two* (1988) was filled with Base's straightforward raps layered on top of even more straightforward samples. "Joy and Pain" was a respectable follow-up in commercial terms (if not artistically), but **Maze** and Frankie Beverly later sued the duo for failing to clear the sample or for crediting the large chunk of the lyrics that the duo borrowed from the Maze song of the same name.

Base's follow-up, *The Incredible Base* (1989), ditched E-Z Rock, but followed the same format of simple cadences and familiar samples. Anticipating the Puff Daddy formula by a decade, Base laid tired rhymes over obvious samples of The Gap Band, Marvin Gaye and Edwin Starr. Reunited with E-Z Rock, Base tried to recapture the electricity and success of "It Takes Two" on *Break Of Dawn* (1994), with predictably lame results.

⊙ **It Takes Two**
Profile, 1988

Most of the album is unembarrassing, although very dated, pop-rap; the title track, however, is one of the truly great hip-hop singles and the only reason Rob Base and DJ E-Z Rock are in this book.

# Beanie Sigel

According to his official bio, the erstwhile Dwight Grant paid no dues – he went straight from the cipher to the studio. Perhaps this explains why the Philadelphian rapper's flow and rhymes are so one-dimensional. He first came to attention with cameos on "Reservoir Dogs" from **Jay-Z**'s *Vol. 2... Hard Knock Life* (1998) and **The Roots**' *Adrenaline* (1998), both of which offered ample evidence of his rather pedestrian rhyming skills. His verse on "Reservoir Dogs" rhymed, in succession: "walkin'", "sparkin'", "sparklin'", "auction", "hawkin'" and "margin". The rhyme scheme displayed on "Adrenaline" was AAAA, AAAA, AAAA followed by AAAA, including thirteen lines in a row which ended in either "them" or "'em". Ogden Nash he ain't.

**The Reason**
Roc-A-Fella, 2001

Neither particularly charismatic nor skilful, Beanie Sigel is hard to digest over the course of an entire album. But Beanie's rhyme skills are slightly better here than on his debut, and the production is tighter.

Nevertheless, Jay-Z tapped him for his Roc-A-Fella empire.

On his first solo album, *The Truth* (2000), Beanie Mac was totally overshadowed by the bonus Jay-Z cut, "Anything", the Oliver-sampling follow-up to "Hard Knock Life" which was left off the American version of *Vol. 3*. Sigel's rhyming could barely sustain a minute-long cameo, let alone an entire album, no matter how good the beats were (and here they were pretty good).

The production was even better on *The Reason* (2001), particularly on the seriously funky "Get Down" and "Beanie (Mack Bitch)". Sigel even managed to change his rhyme schemes to something like AAAABBB – impressive growth. But collaborations with **Scarface** (the Hallmark-card-awful "Mom Praying"), Daz Dillinger and Kurupt (the N.W.A. rip-off "Gangsta Gangsta") and Memphis Bleek (an ill-advised cover of EPMD's "So Whatcha Sayin'") lose any momentum that Beanie built on his own.

A team-up with protégé **Freeway**, "Roc the Mic", from the *State Property* soundtrack (2002), was his best track yet, largely thanks to the beat's great choppy guitar. But Beanie had improved yet again, actually managing to inject some humour into his rhymes: "Come on don't test I kid/I firebomb cribs like Left Eye did/Notorious like that Bed-Stuy kid/B.I.G. or small you can get it/Dead wrong, like tryin to brawl a strong-armed midget". Legal problems, however, temporarily stalled Beanie's career soon afterwards, with his fate still undecided at press time.

# Beastie Boys

In the liner notes to the cassette *New York Thrash* (1982), the crucial document of New York hardcore punk, compiler Tim Sommer wrote, "Beastie Boys, brief stars somewhere in the fall, nutty, fun and a bit bizarre, unfortunately dissolving before they could reach their full promise". Doh! OK, so it's unfair to single out Sommer's howler: not even John Landau would have realised that these young, drunk and stupid high school kids were the future of popular music.

Formed in May 1981, when bassist Adam Yauch joined the **Young Aborigines** – a punk group comprising vocalist Mike Diamond, drummer Kate Schellenbach and guitarist John Berry – the first incarnation of the Beastie Boys was inspired by Black Flag and Bad Brains to up the tempo of punk rock into masturbatory blurts of teen angst. Their *Polly Wog Stew* EP (1982) included such gems of breathless energy as the 23-second "Riot Fight", the 57-second "Beastie" and the positively epic one-minute-and-20-second account of an ambush on a punk rock doorman "Egg Raid on Mojo". Soon after the EP was released, Berry left and was replaced by former member of the **Young And The Useless**, Adam Horovitz.

The following year, the group released "Cooky Puss" (1983), a recording of a series of phony phone calls to various franchises of the Carvel ice-cream store chain. The record blew up on New York college radio to such an extent that a portion of it was actually used in a British Airways commercial, prompting the group to sue. The Beasties soon started to get into hip-hop. They hooked up with college DJ and NYU student Rick Rubin, and Schellenbach gradually faded out of the picture.

Young, drunk and stoopid, the Beasties were now known as **MCA** (Yauch), **Mike D**

(Diamond) and **King Ad-Rock** (Horovitz) and ran around in matching red sweat suits and Puma Clydes. With Rubin producing and releasing the results on his new Def Jam label, they released the *Rock Hard* EP (1984) which featured John Bonham drums and Angus Young guitar riffs. More rock-rap, Pro-Wrestling shenanigans were to be found on "She's On It" (1985) from the Krush Groove soundtrack. Somehow, they got themselves the opening slot on Madonna's Like A Virgin tour and offended a nation of pre-teens with their Dictators-set-to-a-drum-machine routines. When singles like "It's A New Style" and "Hold It Now, Hit It" (both 1986) came out, however, they began to apply their Jewish wiseguy schtick ("If I play guitar it'd be Jimmy Page/The girlies that I like are under age") to more conventional hip-hop beats.

They may have seemed like a joke, but *License To Ill* (1986) became the multi-platinum soundtrack to every frat party from Hilo to Harvard. Tracks like "Fight For Your Right (To Party)" and "No Sleep 'til Brooklyn" were intended as parodies of Neanderthal rock, but they were so perfect that, like other pop burlesquers Steely Dan and Chic, the Beasties ended up becoming what they were poking fun at. Nevertheless, it was a helluva lot of fun.

With their drunken stage antics and ques-

tionable sexual politics, the three stooges became media pariahs. Retreating from the spotlight and splitting from Def Jam, they relocated to LA to record *Paul's Boutique* (1989) with the **Dust Brothers**. A Salvation Army store of the mind, *Paul's Boutique* was one of the high watermarks of the sampling era. The throwaway references to White Castle and Led Zeppelin on the first album were now a dense collage of namechecks, allusions and "B-Boy Bouillabaisse", enhanced by the Dust Brothers' thrift-store clutter style of production.

The Beasties were inspired by the Dust Brothers to become dedicated crate-diggers, but their growing affection for groups like **The Meters** ultimately led them to pick up their instruments again. *Check Your Head* (1992) fused laidback late-1960s funk with arena-rock-sized fuzzy grooves and hardcore textures, creating the blueprint for skate and snowboard music in the process. *Ill Communication* (1994) was more of the same. "Sabotage" is the definitive song of this part of their career and its accompanying video, directed by Spike Jonze, is one of the defining documents of the 1990s. During this time, with their reformed attitude, attempts to free Tibet, occasionally great magazine *Grand Royal* and clothing line, the Beasties had become the darlings of the music and lifestyle press, principally because just about every editor and writer wanted to be them.

After some fairly pointless EPs and vault-raiding exercises, *Hello Nasty* (1998) found the former class clowns revisiting the old school they had once terrorised. "Intergalactic" and "Body Movin'" were retro-electro reminiscences crafted with the help of the superlative turntable skills of new **DJ Mix Master Mike**, but their ears remained open enough to include some bossa nova on "I Don't Know". Now established elder statesmen, the Beastie Boys had miraculously maintained the longest viable career in hip-hop. This was put in jeopardy in 2001, when their Grand Royal label went bankrupt and its assets were auctioned on eBay. However, led by their faith in both the Dalai Lama and hip-hop they returned in 2004, like paunchy, middle-aged rock 'n' roll survivors, with *To The Five Boroughs*, a politically-charged, if lyrically and musically uninspired, love letter to New York. Unfortunately, like the Catskills comedians they always threatened to become, their punchlines had grown as flat as stale matzoh.

⊙ **License To III**
Def Jam, 1986

Disproves Dean Warner's pronouncement that "young, drunk and stupid is no way to go through life" as this album pretty much created the blueprint for mainstream American rock in the 1990s.

⊙ **Paul's Boutique**
Capitol, 1989

With its dizzying sample collages and endless pop culture referencing, this is the white *It Takes A Nation Of Millions To Hold Us Back*.

⊙ **The Sounds Of Science**
Grand Royal, 1999

A 42-track, double-disc compilation that chronicles their journey: from acne-ridden hardcore pranksters to obnoxious frat-punks to lovable wiseguys, and finally to mellow, mantra-reciting media darlings.

# Beatnuts

Among the finest producers in the biz, the Beatnuts' sound was the logical progression from Pete Rock. Both melodic and head-snapping, the beats constructed by Psycho Les (Lester Fernandez) and JuJu (Jerry Timeo) defined the state of the art of New York hip-hop in the mid-1990s. Like most of the best producers, before getting into production the Corona, Queens duo were aspiring DJs and as teenagers they ran in a clique with the X-ecutioners' **Rob Swift**. After stockpiling a massive record collection at the tail-end of the golden age of sampling, Les and JuJu began their careers as producers with **Chi-Ali**'s "Age Ain't Nothin' But A Number" (1991). Running with the Native Tongues, they soon produced tracks for Monie Love, the Jungle Brothers, Artifacts, Pete Nice and Kurious.

Joining forces with MC **Fashion** (aka Al Tariq aka Bertony Smalls), the Beatnuts released the *Intoxicated Demons* EP in 1993. Sounding like the funkiest frat party you never attended, *Intoxicated Demons'* best tracks – "Reign of the Tec", "Psycho Dwarf" and "No Equal" – combined cutting-edge, jazzy production from the labs with the rudest, crudest lyrics from the gutter. *Beatnuts* (1994) was more of the same: tracks about oral sex and fried chicken, jump-around party anthems, gratuitous gunplay, scintillating beats and loops and a **Das-EFX** diss thrown in for good measure.

Despite their prodigious mixing-desk skills, the Beatnuts remained a strictly underground concern until their 1997 album, *Stone Crazy*. Fashion left the group, but he was replaced by numerous cameo appearances from various MCs. The album's shining moment was the ridiculously catchy **"Off The Books"**, which featured Big Punisher on the mic. Still, as hot as Pun's verse was, it was the flute riff that propelled the track into the charts. The rest of *Stone Crazy* was similarly loopy and established Les and JuJu as the finest East Coast knob-twiddlers this side of DJ Premier.

Unfortunately, *A Musical Massacre* (1999) sounded stale in comparison. The lead single, "Watch Out Now", was a blatant attempt to recreate the success of "Off the Books", while the rest of the album

Psycho Les and Juju are The Beatnuts – can they kick it? It appears they can.

just sounded like everything else that was around. Of course, when they did actually feel like challenging themselves, the beats were as bumping as ever.

*Take It Or Squeeze It* (2001) followed suit with more breezy, beach-party beats. Les and Juju's ability to tame Afro-Cuban poly-rhythms to fit the constraints of hip-hop once made them unique, but by now their fire had been stolen by the cyber-salsa piano of **Swizz Beatz**. *The Beatnuts Present: The Originators* (2002) found them plowing the same field yet again, refusing to get out of their rut or respond to anything around them.

**Classic Nuts**
Relativity, 2002

Lyrically, this greatest hits collection isn't exactly appropriate for school children, but it is a lesson in beatsmanship, with Afro-Cuban percussion parts chopped into head-nodding patterns, model organ loops, and guitar-fuzz driving choruses.

# Benzino

Raymond Scott's (aka Ray Benzino and/or Ray Dog) association with *The Source* publisher and CEO David

Mays has dogged his career for the better part of a decade, and it's likely it always will. There were two incidents: the first was in 1994, when Mays allegedly tried to sneak an article about Benzino's group, **The Almighty RSO**, into the magazine without anyone on the editorial staff knowing; and the second was in 2001 when it emerged that Benzino had secretly become co-owner of *The Source* with Mays, which explained why such a mediocre rapper got so much attention in the magazine, and why he was able to attract such stellar guest stars on his albums.

Along with fellow Bostonians E Devious, Tony Rhome, Big T and DJ Def Jeff, Scott (aka **Ray Dog**) formed The Almighty RSO ("Rock Shit On") in 1983. Early singles like "The Greatest Show On Earth" (1985) and "The Almighty RSO Crew 12-Inch Bomb" (1987) were very much in the Boston vein of **TDS Mob**, but the group would really attract attention when they adopted a gangster pose in 1990 and signed to Tommy Boy. Both "Shoot A Muthafucka In A Minute" and "One In The Chamba" were held back from release due to new member **Rock** being stabbed in a club, and then the record companies' unease after the furore over Body Count's "Cop Killer" (see Ice-T entry). The group then signed to RCA and released the so-so *Revenge Of Da Badd Boyz* EP (1994), which featured the fairly hot "Hellbound (The RSO Saga Part 2)". *Doomsday: Forever RSO* (1996) had the minor hit "You Could Be My Boo" (a shameless rip-off of Method Man and Mary J Blige's "You're All I Need To Get By") which had Faith Evans on the chorus. Even this early (although it's been reported that he was a partner in *The Source* from 1995), Scott showed his knack for snagging high-calibre guest stars, with appearances from Evans, Mobb Deep and **Eightball & MJG**.

Benzino, Devious (now Antonio Twice Thou) and Def Jeff (now Jeff 2X) regrouped as **Made Men** in 1999 for *CLE: Classic Limited Edition*. The gangsters of old had had a jiggy make-over, and you could tell they didn't know what they were talking about from the get-go. Dropping "stoking skins in the Ramada" as proof of your high-class credentials is pretty desperate, even in a rhyme. Guests here included Master P, Mase, The Lox, Montell Jordan, Big Pun, Daz Dillinger, Kurupt and Monifah.

While still a part of the Hangmen 3 production team with Jeff 2X and JB, Benzino went solo on *The Benzino Project* (2001). The production is top-rate, particularly on two Teddy Riley numbers – "Bootee" and "Figadoh" – but the rapping is uninspired and Benzino is outshined by Snoop Dogg, Black Rob, Raekwon, Foxy Brown, Bobby Brown, Scarface, Prodigy, Cormega, Pink and even P. Diddy.

After fewer sales than most Christian rock albums, Motown dropped Benzino and he quickly released a pointless remix album which didn't create any more interest. Frustrated, he lashed out at the easiest target around – **Eminem**. "Pull Your Skirt Up" (from the very mediocre 2003 album *Redemption*) called Eminem "the hood ornament on the machine's car", but Eminem destroyed him on "Nail In The Coffin" ("If you was really selling coke/Then what

the fuck you stop for dummy?/If you slew some crack, you'd make a lot more money than you do from rap") and "The Sauce". Benzino hit back with "Die Another Day", which called Eminem "the rap David Duke, the rap Hitler/The culture-stealer, niggas ain't wit' ya'" but really nobody cared.

**Doomsday: Forever RSO**
Rap-a-Lot, 1996

"You Could Be My Boo" was a minor hit, there were some star turns from Mobb Deep and Eightball & MJG, and some OK mic skills. In essence, this sucks less than most Benzino projects – even if the production was uninspired at best.

# Big Daddy Kane

King Asiatic Nobody's Equal is just that: perhaps the most complete MC ever. No one has managed to match Big Daddy Kane's combination of fierce battle rhymes, smooth lover's rap and Five Percent knowledge. Jiggy long before Puffy ever got busy, as intimidating as Rakim, dropping Muslim science on huns before King Sun, and as funny as Chris Rock, Kane not only destroyed the mic device, he also ghost wrote rhymes for **Roxanne Shanté** and Biz Markie.

Antonio M Hardy was introduced to the

Juice Crew by Biz in 1986 and made his debut the following year with "Raw". With **Marley Marl**'s killer production, based on Lyn Collins' "Mama Feelgood", "Raw" must have given the Bomb Squad a few ideas. Even so, Kane stole the show with nimble battle rhymes like "Rulin' and schoolin' MCs that I'm duellin'/Watch 'em all take a fall as I sit there coolin'/On my throne with a bronze microphone/Mmm, God bless a child that can hold his own".

If it hadn't been released in 1988, perhaps hip-hop's greatest year, *Long Live the Kane* would have been hailed as one of the greatest hip-hop albums ever. Although it was over-shadowed by Public Enemy, Boogie Down Productions and NWA, *Long Live the Kane* was nearly perfect. "Ain't No Half Steppin'" saw Kane slow the tempo, but remain as fero-cious as he was on "Raw", while "Wrath of Kane" found Kane stomping MCs like they were roaches, on top of a beat that would have had most rappers hyperventilating after the second bar. While the rhymes were almost uniformly b-boy boasts, the cover hinted at Kane's future direction. Decked out in his "fresh Cameo cut", cloaked in a toga and gold rope chain, with three female minions feeding him grapes, Kane started to think of himself as a ladies' man.

It's a *Big Daddy Thing* (1989) found Kane distancing himself from Marley Marl's hard funk production, towards a glossy *GQ* sheen. The album's biggest hit, "I Get the Job Done" (1989), featured fan-tastic New Jack beats from **Teddy Riley** and Kane still in impressive form, but the lover-man schtick was just lame, and only made worse by tracks like "Pimpin' Ain't Easy". He started to wear designer suits in his vid-eos, sipping champagne and macking, and, although he contributed a fiery verse to **Public Enemy**'s "Burn Hollywood Burn", by his next album, *Taste of Chocolate* (1990), he was duetting with **Barry White**.

Although he envisioned himself carousing in a penthouse like Teddy Pendergrass, rub-bing his girl down with essential oils, *Prince of Darkness* (1991) and *Looks Like a Job For Big Daddy Kane* (1993) were treated like street trash by the hip-hop audience. Instead of changing his image for *Daddy's Home* (1994), he spent his time posing nude for

*Playgirl* and **Madonna**'s *Sex* book and total-ly played himself out. *Veteranz Day* (1998) wasn't as horrific as it could have been, but it wasn't anywhere near as pretty as Big Daddy thought he was.

The Mack returned to form with a couple of underground singles in the new millen-nium. "Flame On" (2001) was a smoking cut-up of "I Shot the Sheriff" that found Kane spitting lines like "Your shit is milk, huh?/Well I'm lactose intolerant" with the old grace. "The Man, The Icon" (2002) was less convincing, if only because he was wast-ing his breath on dissing Wyclef, something even schmucks like Ja Rule and Fabolous could do with ease.

⊙ **Long Live the Kane**
Cold Chillin', 1988

With Kane still hungry, and Marley Marl at the peak of his powers, this is one of the true greats.

# Big L

◊ See *Diggin' In The Crates*

# Big Punisher

The history books will remember Big Punisher as the first solo Latino rapper to go platinum, but hip-hop heads will honour Pun as one of the funniest, most nimble MCs of the 1990s.

Born Christopher Rios in November 1971, he started rapping at the end of the

'80s under the name Big Moon Dog. With future members of his Terror Squad crew, Triple Seis and Cuban Link, the renamed Pun caught the attention of Diggin' In The Crates Crew's **Fat Joe** who introduced Pun on "Firewater", the b-side to his "Envy" single from his *Jealous One's Envy* (1996) album. After matching **Raekwon** word for word on that track, Pun quickly became a fixture on the underground mixtape circuit.

It was Pun's verse on The Beatnuts' "Off The Books" in 1997, however, that really turned heads. Riding the track's flute hook, Pun spryly dropped rhymes like, "It's all love, but love's got a thin line/And Pun's got a big nine/Respect crime, but not when it reflect mine" and "My cream's fat/I smoke the greenest grass/My bitch got the meanest ass". His first single, "You Ain't A Killer" appeared on the *Soul In A Hole* (1998) soundtrack, but it was his second that made him a star. A massive summertime hit with its piano stabs and chorus from R&B singer **Joe**, Pun's "Still Not A Player (Remix)" saw him take over the title of "overweight lover" from Heavy D: "I'm not a player, I just fuck a lot".

"Still Not A Player" anchored Pun's debut album, *Capital Punishment* (1998). Although his rhyme skills were evident throughout (particularly on "Twinz", with its superlative couplet, "Dead in the middle of Little Italy/ Little did we know that we riddled a middle man who didn't know diddly"), the production was too slick, and pandered to hip-hop's pop contingent. It achieved its aims, though: *Capital Punishment* has sold some two million copies.

Along with Fat Joe, Cuban Link, Triple Seis, Armageddon and Prospect, Pun released the equally commercially-minded *Terror Squad: The Album* (1999). By this time, though, Pun's health was becoming a serious issue. On February 7, 2000, Pun suffered a heart attack while staying at a hotel in upstate New York and died later that day. The cause was said to be health problems resulting from his obesity: at the time of his death, he weighed a reported 698 pounds (50 stone). He had completed *Yeeah Baby!* (2000) weeks before his death and it was released two months later. There were a couple of hardcore head-nodders like "New York Giants" and "We

Don't Care", but the out-of-place guitars on "Leather Face", the too-obvious "It's So Hard" with **Donnell Jones**, and the Simple Minds interpolation on "Don't You (Forget About Me)" meant that the album wasn't the memorial he deserved.

*Endangered Species* (2001), a greatest hits compilation, wasn't either. While his hits, as well as guest appearances, are here, so too are unreleased material that should have remained that way, and some awkward remixes of Ricky Martin's "Livin' La Vida Loca".

⊙ **Capital Punishment**
Loud, 1998

"Still Not A Player" allowed him to nuzzle up to Jennifer Lopez, but there are enough bangers like "Dream Shatterer" to make this worthwhile, even to player-haters.

# Biz Markie

The clown prince of hip-hop, the one and only Biz Markie (Marcel Hall) may have been a pudgy guy in an ill-fitting T-shirt, but unlike the Fat Boys, "The Diabolical" Biz Markie was no novelty act. Biz's comedic talent was only one aspect of his formidable armoury.

For one thing, Biz Mark was a formidable beatboxer, as he proved on his first wax appearance, **Roxanne Shanté**'s "The Def Fresh Crew" (1986). The human SP1200 backed Shanté's ferocious rap with a symphony of Bronx cheers and an imitation of

a cat food commercial, and on the flip, "Biz Beats", he created one of the truly great saliva solos in hip-hop history.

Biz Mark was also a fine MC with perhaps the most engaging personality of any mic spitter. Just like Shanté, most of his rhymes were written by **Big Daddy Kane**, but it was the Biz's delivery, rather than the words that mattered. The human orchestra's first single, "Make the Music With Your Mouth Biz" of 1986, featured not only Biz's beatboxing, but it also introduced his singular, drunken rhyming style over a crashing drum beat and an **Isaac Hayes** piano snippet. With its killer production (based on Steve Miller's "Fly Like an Eagle"), 1987's "Nobody Beats the Biz" had a title parodying an advert for New York electronics chain The Wiz, and Biz dropping the immortal, and much imitated, line, "Reagan is the prez, but I voted for Shirley Chisholm" (the first African-American woman elected to the US Congress, and the first to campaign for the presidency).

*Going Off* (1988) was his debut album. It included his singles and remains a classic. Riding the beat from James Brown's "Papa Don't Take No Mess", "The Vapors"

was a savage and funny attack on jealous neighbours, with lyrics that could've been written by Leiber and Stoller. "Something for the Radio" was another instant classic, but the landmark cut was probably "Pickin' Boogers". While hip-hop was turning hardcore and political, Biz was rapping about flipping snot into other people's lunch, over the groove from Graham Central Station's "The Jam".

*The Biz Never Sleeps* (1989) saw Biz take over production duties from Marley Marl. While Biz has a record collection that is probably equalled only by Afrika Bambaataa (according to legend, Biz had to buy a second house just to store his records), his mixing-deck skills couldn't match Marl's. Nevertheless, the album had the absurd and hilarious "Just a Friend", which found Biz singing like a dying swan – on the radio it was the perfect antidote to the narcissism of Bobby Brown and his ilk.

*I Need A Haircut* (1991) was again produced by the Biz. While he dug deep in his crates on tracks like "Check It Out", the album became more famous for his failure to dig deep enough. He was sued by **Gilbert O'Sullivan** for his use of "Alone

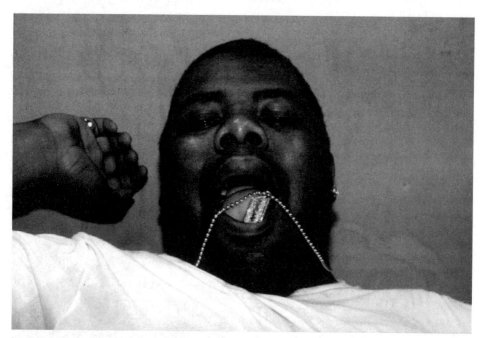

Secrets of the Biz Markie school of dope beatboxing, lesson one: every morning, after flossing, Biz has a quick gargle with his old school gold chain.

# Black-Eyed Peas

Coming out of the LA live scene like some Sunset Strip metal band (complete with long hair and scarves), the Black Eyed Peas made their rep with their high-energy, stage-diving performances years before they ever got a record contract. Perhaps because of their rock-like dues-paying and "progressive hip-hop" mentality, Will.I.Am, Appl D App and Taboo were, along with Jurassic 5, the toast of hip-hop tourists in 1998.

With live instruments, thrift-store garb and anti-gangsta lyrics, their debut album *Behind the Front* (1998) was a cause célèbre among European dance mags. The breakthrough track was "Fallin' Up", a plea for peace in hip-hop's intercoastal rivalry. "Karma" interpolated the chorus of Blondie's "One Way Or Another" to warn gangsta rappers that there "Ain't no runnin' from karma". While their level-headed lyrics attracted pacifists, hippies and people who didn't understand metaphor, it was their warm, mellow production that really got heads turning. "Clap Your Hands" sampled both **The Meters** and Inner Circle to re-create an old school block-party vibe, while "What it Is" swiped a lick from Tom Browne's "Funkin' For Jamaica". There were also plenty of acoustic guitars and basslines that were as warm and fuzzy as a Guatemalan sweater. It wasn't all jazzience and Brazilian percussion though: they also sampled **Laid Back**'s lost '80s classic, "White Horse", and made like Frankie Valli on the discoed-up "Joints & Jams".

Following the same blueprint but without any inspiration or passion, the title of *Bridging the Gap* (2000) seemed to indicate the only place that would play such insipid hip-hop. Bringing new member Fergie (a former girlfriend of one of **N'Sync**) into the fold, BEP changed from faux boho clothes horses to bona fide pop stars with *Elephunk* (2003). Thanks to Fergie's past, Justin Timberlake appeared on the chorus of "Where Is The Love?", helping the

Again (Naturally)" and Judge Kevin Duff ruled that sampling was theft under copyright law. Biz was threatened with time in the slammer and hip-hop's golden age of sampladelia was over. *All Samples Cleared* (1993) may have featured production by Large Professor, but it was largely comprised of obvious samples and uninspired raps. Biz basically traded on his cartoon persona and showed up in cameo appearances for the likes of the **Beastie Boys** singing "Benny And The Jets" and **Handsome Boy Modeling School** singing "Night Fever".

The singles "Turn Tha Party Out" and "Tear Shit Up", in 2001 and 2002 respectively, found Biz returning to recording in his own right. Neither single was exactly a return to the golden age, but they were endearing pieces of nostalgic fluff. Unfortunately, *Weekend Warrior* (2003), which was sabotaged by piracy and sample clearance problems, was simply diabolical, particularly when Biz tried to trade dancehall licks with Elephant Man.

**Going Off**
Cold Chillin', 1988

With Marley Marl's stellar production and Biz's inspired lunacy, this is damn near a perfect album.

Black-Eyed Peas, way back in their boho coffee shop days, before Timberlake-related chart success..

track to become a British number one single. The follow-up, "Shut Up", was one of the most execrable pop songs in a year of shouty, tone-deaf execrable pop songs. Nevertheless, the group had become part of the pop firmament, so much so that even the US started to listen, and the National Basketball Association chose the group to spearhead their 2004 ad campaign.

**Behind the Front**
Interscope, 1998

With Interscope running scared from anything gangsta-ish, the Black Eyed Peas capitalised with this pleasant, harmless album.

# Black Moon/ Bootcamp Clik

As is typical of the cities' histories, in the early/mid-1990s LA rap made everyday violence cinematic and ultra-stylised, while New York hip-hop presented it raw and unmediated. Emphasising pure skills, dusty samples and murderous metaphors, Black Moon represented the grim inverse of Dr Dre's well polished G-Funk.

The trio of Buckshot, 5Ft. Excellerator and DJ Evil Dee exploded on to the scene with their debut single, "Who Got The Props?" in 1993. On top of a deceptively mellow Fender Rhodes loop from **Da Beatminerz** production team (Evil Dee and his brother Mr Walt), Buckshot Shorty "sounded like an automatic" as he delivered this deliriously combative anthem to "Crooklyn, better known as Brooklyn". *Enta Da Stage* (1993) featured more gun-clapping lyrics

and denuded smooth soul samples on "How Many MCs?", "Black Smif-N-Wessun", "Son Get Wrec" and "Slave". A Barry White-heavy remix of "I Got Cha Opin" found the group breaking through to mainstream radio, but aside from an unauthorised collection of b-sides and freestyles, *Diggin' In Dah Vaults* (1996), the group wouldn't be heard from again until the so-so *War Zone* (1999), credited to Buckshot, 5Ft. and Evil Dee rather than Black Moon.

In the meantime, however, Buckshot (with Dru Ha) started the Duck Down label and management team. Part of Buckshot's Boot Camp Clik, **Smif-N-Wessun** (the duo of MCs Tek and Steele) followed in Black Moon's orbit with the magnificently moody "Bucktown" in 1994. *Dah Shinin'* (1995) was similarly slow and dusty, seething with menace and punctuated by blasts of rudebwoy reggae — an absolute underground classic. After being forced to change their name by the Smith and Wesson gun company, Tek and Steele re-emerged as **Da Cocoa Brovaz** on the surprisingly good *Rude Awakening* (1998) which featured a stunning collaboration with reggae deejay Eek-A-Mouse on "Off the Wall".

The Boot Camp Clik continued to come kicking with **Heltah Skeltah** (Rock and Ruck) and the **Originoo Gun Clappaz** (Starang Wondah, Louieville Sluggah and Top Dawg Da Big Kahuna). With new Beatminer Baby Paul behind the boards, Heltah Skeltah and OGC's "Leflaur Leflah Eshkoshka" of 1996) introduced the "Fab Five" on top of a serene synth loop in 1996. Heltah Skeltah's *Nocturnal* (1996) was an overlooked album of weeded beats and laid-back flows, while *Magnum Force* (1999) suffered from awkward and moneygrubbing collaborations with the likes of **Tha Dogg Pound**. OGC's *Da Storm* (1996) was similarly slept on, which was hard to believe with the fire of "Wild Cowboys in Bucktown" and "Hurricane Starang". Their *M-Pire Shrikez Back* (1999), however, suffered from the absence of Da Beatminerz, stranding the OGC's hardcore styles in a morass of sterile live instrumentation.

In 2001, Da Beatminerz decided to record their own album. Since none of them could rap, they called in a bunch of favours from people like Diamond, Talib Kweli, Busta Rhymes, Naughty By Nature, Pete Rock, Rass Kass, Heather B and more on *Brace 4 Impak* (2001). Not only did the album suffer from a lack of a coherent personality, it also found the Minerz sacrificing their trademark crackling production in favour of a more commercial sound that ended up pleasing nobody.

Boot Camp Clik's *Chosen Few* (2002), however, was a return to form for the entire crew. It wasn't anything new, but it covered old ground with some panache on classic New York style bash-ups such as "Whoop His Ass" and "Welcome to Bucktown USA".

**Enta Da Stage**
Wreck/Nervous, 1993
Buckshot's thuggery matched with Da Beatminerz basement beats make this gritty, dusty, nasty New York hip-hop at its best.

**Boot Camp Clik's Greatest Hits: Basic Training**
Priority, 2000
Pretty much all the grime and gunplay you'd want from Black Moon, Heltah Skeltah, OGC and Smif-N-Wessun.

# Black Rob

⟡ See *Bad Boy*

# Black Sheep

Less earnest, and funnier than their brethren and sistren, Black Sheep were the smart alecks and, indeed, the black sheep of the Native Tongues. **Dres** (Andreus Titus) and **Mista Lawnge** (William McLean) first got together in the mid-80s in North Carolina. Moving back to New York, where they were both originally from, the duo hooked up with the Jungle Brothers, with whom they toured, before releasing their debut.

*A Wolf In Sheep's Clothing* (1991) was a big hit on the college radio circuit, thanks largely to the monstrous remix of "The Choice Is Yours" – one of the most sure-fire dancefloor cuts in hip-hop history. The rest of the album was almost as good.

There was comedy aplenty on tracks like "Flavor Of The Month", "Similak Child", "Strobelite Honey" and "U Mean I'm Not", a great gangsta parody in which the narrator kills his sister for using his toothbrush. The midtempo, jazzy production perfectly suited Dres's slightly astringent voice.

*Non-Fiction* (1994) ditched the humour of the first album in favour of an autobiography of sorts that retold Dres's and Mista Lawnge's journey from North Carolina to the Big Apple. Nowhere near as good as their debut, *Non-Fiction* is perhaps only notable for bringing Black Sheep into the most one-sided wax war in the annals of hip-hop. After MC Hammer dissed the album, they responded with "Ha", the B-side to "Without a Doubt". If you're only attracting the attention of "the funky headhunter", as Hammer was then unconvincingly styling himself, you know you're in trouble, and Black Sheep split soon afterwards.

Dres re-emerged in 1998 with "Pardon Me", a complete change of pace that found him ditching his instantly identifiable sound of old for a rather faceless hardcore New York-style flow. *Sure Shot Redemption* (1999) followed in a similar fashion – it tried on lots of different styles and felt comfortable in none of them.

🔘 **A Wolf in Sheep's Clothing**
Mercury, 1991

Back in the days when you could still be funny without being soft, and take the piss out of people without risking your neck, this album took all the liberties that a more innocent time allowed. Enough skills for the hardcore, enough humour and Afrocentrism for the avant-garde, and enough

jump around anthems for the college kids. With a more well-rounded vision, this could have been an album for the ages.

# Kurtis Blow

Grandmaster Flash may have a bigger significance nowadays, but Kurtis Blow was hip-hop's biggest early star. Curtis Walker was a mobile DJ, who was turned on to rapping by DJ Hollywood. Basing his smooth style almost entirely on Hollywood's, Kurtis Blow was spotted at an MC battle at the Hotel Diplomat by former *Billboard* magazine writers Rocky Ford and J.B. Moore, who were persuaded by Blow's manager, Russell Simmons, to let him record a song they had loosely written, "Christmas Rappin'". Released at the end of 1979, "Christmas Rappin'" followed the formula of "Rapper's Delight" by apeing the "Good Times" bassline and Nile Rodgers' chicken-scratch disco guitar, but it surpassed the Sugar Hill Gang's magnum opus with better rhymes and a hefty dose of seasonal cheer.

"Christmas Rappin'" moved crazy numbers and Blow became the first rapper on a major label when he signed to Mercury. "Christmas Rappin'" reached #30 on the UK pop charts and Simmons sweet-talked a place for Blow on **Blondie**'s European tour. When he returned from Europe in 1980 Blow released one of the greatest singles in hip-hop history, "The Breaks". Complete with timbale breaks from **Jimmy Delgado** and spacey keyboard lines, "The Breaks" was a quantum leap from

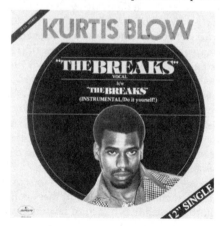

"Christmas Rappin'" in terms of musicality, but it was its lyrical sophistication that really set the record apart. Bringing hip-hop out of the party and into the outside world, Blow rapped couplets like "If your woman steps out with another man/And she runs off with him to Japan" and "And you borrowed money from the mob/And yesterday you lost your job/Well these are the breaks". Of course, there was also plenty of "Just do it, just do it, just do it, do it, do it", but it only added to the atmosphere and "The Breaks" became hip-hop's first certified gold single.

"The Breaks" anchored Blow's first album, *Kurtis Blow* (1980). Although *Kurtis Blow* had more developed social commentary in the form of "Hard Times", Blow, like all early hip-hop artists, was a singles artist. All of his albums have acres of filler and awkward, straight r&b tracks. While "Rockin'", a 1981 single, was OK, it wouldn't be until 1983 that Blow would have another artistic or commercial success. Featuring Washington DC go-go artists EU, "Party Time" was a tribal percussion throwdown that briefly ruled the East Coast.

However, a group featuring an MC named Run, who at one point went by the name of "The Son of Kurtis Blow" and was Kurtis's DJ, soon emerged and made the old school redundant overnight. Unlike his contemporaries, Blow did manage to have a couple of hits during the **Run DMC** era. "Basketball" was omnipresent in blacktops across New York from the Boogie Down to the 'burbs in 1984, while the joyous but poignant "If I Ruled the World" (1985) from the *Krush Groove* soundtrack would eventually be the basis for Nas's "If I Ruled The World (Imagine That)". There was also the drum-machine symphony "AJ Scratch" (1984) – an ode to Blow's DJ – but by this time Blow was more of a producer than an artist, working with the Disco 3 (aka the **Fat Boys**), the Fearless Four, and Dr. Jeckyl & Mr. Hyde.

Blow continued to turn out eminently forgettable albums until he called it a day after

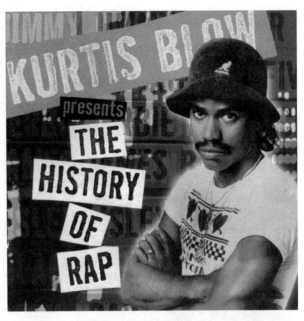

the very optimistically titled *Back By Popular Demand* (1988). He now lives in LA, where he hosts an old school radio show, and compiled the three-volume *Kurtis Blow Presents The History Of Hip-Hop* series for Rhino in 1997.

**Best of Kurtis Blow**
Mercury, 1994

Smooth and suave, but definitely party-hearty, this is definitive early hip-hop.

# Bone Crusher

Like so many others, Wayne Hardnett's introduction to hip-hop came from the Fresh Fest tour in 1985. He began breakdancing and DJing soon afterwards, and with the emergence of fellow Atlanta rappers like MC Shy-D and Raheem he started rapping soon afterwards. In 1993 he started calling himself Bone Crusher and hooked up with Baby B and Bizar and formed Lyrical Giants. After a deal went sour with **Erick Sermon**'s Def Squad, the group bounced around the South showing up on records by OutKast, Too $hort and Youngbloodz doing hooks that had been written by Bone Crusher.

In 1998 they hooked up with **Lil' John** and recorded a few outrageously rowdy sin-

Bone Crusher – just when you thought it was safe to go back into the aerobics class...

gles like "F*@ck Nigga" and "Brave Shirts" that introduced Lil' John's combination of Miami Bass with New Orleans bounce and electro echoes. Crusher added his hyper, shouted vocals to **Reese & Bigalow**'s "Neva Sked", which was a big hit down South in 2002. Bone rerecorded the single with keyboardist/producer Avery Johnson, Killer Mike and TI for his self-released *Bone Crusher And His Industry Friends* (2002).

The album came to the attention of Jermaine Dupri, who signed Crusher to his So So Def label. Yet another version of "Never Scared" (2003) became a huge hit and was the bedrock of his *AttenCHUN!* (2003) album. Although "Never Scared" had undeniable appeal as a one-off single, a whole album of Bone Crusher's drill-sergeant delivery was too much to bear, particularly when he had no skills to speak of and nothing to say. "Fat Man Stomp" was another monster lead single in 2003, but expectations for *Vainglorious* (2004) were lowered with each passing month that it was delayed.

# Bone Thugs-n-Harmony

It's a wonder no one thought of it sooner: combine gangsta realness with smooth vocal group harmonies, throw in some triple-time, tongue-twisting rhymes for good measure and sell more than ten million records. Cleveland's Bone Thugs-N-Harmony's multi-platinum style was allegedly devised when one of these former drug dealers, **Krayzie Bone** (Anthony Henderson), was in prison for shooting his fellow thug Wish Bone (Byron McCane).

When he got out of the pen, Krayzie, along with Wish (who evidently doesn't bear grudges), Layzie Bone (Steven Howse), Flesh-N-Bone (Stanley Howse) and Bizzie Bone (Charles Scruggs) formed a group called **Bone Enterprises** and combined the smooth music to which real gangsters listen when they need to escape with the titillating tales of guns and drugs that people not living the life love to listen to.

Relocating to LA in 1993, the group renamed themselves Bone Thugs-N-Harmony and caught the ear of **Eazy E**, who signed them to his Ruthless Records label and hooked them up with production whiz DJ U-Neek, who helped craft the group's multi-platinum sound. Their debut release, the eight-track *Creepin On Ah Come Up* EP (1994), eventually sold three million copies. The fairly standard Dr. Dre-style funk production was fleshed out with their G-Funk barbershop harmonies and largely indecipherable raps about the game, revenge murders and Ouija boards. The breakthrough

single was "Thuggish Ruggish Bone", which introduced the world to their sing-song, rapid-fire rhyming style.

*E. 1999 Eternal* (1995) knocked **Michael Jackson**'s *HIStory* off the top of the American pop charts. Its contradictory mix of dead-homie sentimentality and unrepentant violence had replaced Jackson's racial/sexual ambiguity as the split-personality pop pose of choice. Beginning with the muezzin incantation of "Da Introduction" and moving through the graceful brutality of "Mo' Murda" and "Die Die Die", *E. 1999 Eternal* envisioned a world that wasn't all that different from a ghettocentric heavy metal, a vibe that was only enhanced by the skull iconography, supernatural shtick and Biblical doomsday verses. Elsewhere, though, the album was less schlocky: "1st Of Tha Month" catalogued the creative ends to which you could put your welfare cheque, while the huge hit "Tha Crossroads" (built on a sample of the **Isley Brothers**' "Make You Say it Again Girl"), was a saccharine, but ultimately effective, eulogy of their label boss who had died of AIDS a few months earlier.

With some seven million sales behind them, the group went about empire-building. They started their own label, **Mo Thugs Records**, which debuted with the platinum *Mo Thugs Family Scriptures* (1996). 1998's sequel, *Mo Thugs Chapter II: Family Reunion*, included what was probably hip-hop's second ever country song (after Disco Four's "Country Rock Rap"), "Ghetto Cowboy", which spent seven weeks on top of Billboard's rap chart.

*The Art Of War* (1997) was a double album that showed the group had, predictably, run out of ideas, but Americans still bought a couple of million copies of the damn thing. The group's solo albums were generally mind-bogglingly awful. The title of Bizzy Bone's *Heaven'z Movie* (1998) was an invitation for a kicking from wags, and the album was notable only for "Thugz Cry" which was a pretty savage attack on Eazy E's widow, Tomica Woods-Wright, who had taken over **Ruthless**. Krayzie Bone's *Thug Mentality 1999* (1999) was a 32-track epic of indo smoking, disses (directed at Twista and Three-6 Mafia) and more indo smoking, which had Krayzie's light-speed patter matching the speed of a machine gun's rat-a-tat-tat-tat, only to hit with the force of a ten-cent water pistol.

*BTNHResurrection* (2000) was another endurance test, but the rapid-fire snares, stuttering kicks, "Little Red Corvette" interpolations and occasionally funny lyrics ("I was trying to call my dick, but it couldn't hear me" on "Ecstasy") made it less of an ordeal than their previous record. The same old same old *Thug World Order* (2002) was ostensibly a Bone-Thugs-n-Harmony album, but all the skits acting as commercials for each member's forthcoming solo albums suggested otherwise.

⊙ **The Collection, Vol. 1**
Ruthless, 1998

Their style is singularly annoying, but DJ Uneek's production, and the amazingly garish "Tha Crossroads" eventually crawl under your skin. There's also a cover of NWA's "Fuck Tha Police" for completists, if there are any.

# Boo-Yaa T.R.I.B.E.

L os Angeles' Boo-Yaa T.R.I.B.E. ("Too Rough International Boo-Yaa Empire") are something like the West Coast equivalent of the long-lost **Ghetto Brothers**, a group of New York Latino gang menbers who played a searing hybrid of rock, soul and salsa in the early 1970s. The six brothers Devoux (Godfather Rock Te, Ganxsta Ridd, Don L, Rosco, EKA and OMB) started out playing gospel songs in their Samoan father's church in LA.

They soon graduated to Slade and Kleer covers before becoming pop lockers and gang-bangers (the group's name was taken from the slang for the discharge of a sawed-off). After spending some time in Japan with a sumo-wrestler cousin, the brothers refocused on music and found themselves opening for James Brown in LA in 1986.

In 1988 they recorded their debut single, "Coming Hard to America" which landed them an appearance on a **Club Nouveau** track. Signed to 4th & Broadway, Boo-Yaa released the underrated *New Funky Nation* (1990). The album was notable for its compelling mix of live instrumentation (played by the group) and samples courtesy of producers Joe "The Butcher" Nicolo and the

Dust Brothers. The sound was reminiscent of mid-1970s LA Chicano funk of War and Mandrill, with some ruminations on gang banging thrown in for good-measure.

A proposed second album, *Good Times Bad Times*, was never released because it was primarily concerned with the killings of two Samoan brothers who were allegedly shot in the back by the LAPD, and was scheduled for release at the time of the "Cop Killer" controversy (see Ice-T entry). Some of the material showed up on *Doomsday* (1994), which was similar in style to their debut but much harder in tone and attack. *Occupation Hazardous* (1995) continued the darker thread, but musically they seemed to have run out of ideas.

With guest appearances from no-marks like **Yukmouth** and **Layzie Bone**, *Mafia Lifestyle* (2000) seemed to suggest that Boo-Yaa had become a straight-up gangsta group, without much time for nuance or contradiction. For *West Koasta Nostra* (2003), Boo-Yaa largely ditched the instruments in favour of production from West Coast underground legend DJ Battlecat. While Boo-Yaa come correct with lots of bile directed at the industry, the album was most notable for the stellar guest appearances from Kurupt, Mack 10, WC, Knoc-Turn'al, B-Real and **Eminem**.

⊙ **New Funky Nation**
4th & Broadway, 1990

Tracks like "Psyko Funk" intimated that Boo-Yaa were affiliated to the Piru Bloods gang, and gave a hint of their fantastic live show. But although they embraced the gangsta style, they also had enough experience to reveal its contradictions.

# Boogie Down Productions

F ormed by DJ Scott La Rock and KRS-One at a South Bronx homeless shelter, Boogie Down Productions were hip-hop's militant minimalists. BDP's music was characterized by rhythms so sparse that there was rarely anything resembling a hook. This kind of spartan rigour mirrored the rigid but confused ideology of

KRS-One (Knowledge Rules Supreme Over Nearly Everyone). Undeniably one of hip-hop's greatest MCs, the self-styled "Blastmaster" is, like most important figures in the music's history, a bundle of contradictions: he was an articulate spokesperson against black-on-black violence, yet he made his battle rhymes flesh when he physically threw **PM Dawn** off a stage; he railed against materialism and the commercialisation of hip-hop, but then did a commercial for Sprite.

BDP's first album, *Criminal Minded* (1987), avoided any political commitment, instead concerning itself with reasserting the Bronx as hip-hop's home. BDP's first single, "South Bronx" (1986), was an attack on MC Shan's "The Bridge" and the Juice Crew, who were claiming that Queensbridge was where hip-hop was at. BDP eventually won hip-hop's second most famous battle with the awesome "The Bridge Is Over" which interpolated both **Billy Joel** and some Kingston dancehall chatter. The album's clipped drum-machine beats and bleak samples were constructed with the help of the Ultramagnetic MCs' **Ced Gee** and were a brutal response to what KRS-One and Scott La Rock considered the "sweetening" of hip hop.

The first track on the follow-up, *By All Means Necessary* (1988), indicated BDP's future direction, in the wake of the murder of Scott La Rock by an unknown assassin in August 1987. From here on in, BDP would pioneer politically conscious rap, alongside Public Enemy. The album's title and cover art explicitly referenced **Malcolm X**, and BDP were largely responsible for the resurgence of his teachings in the hip-hop community. "Stop The Violence" was KRS-One's response to the death of his friend and musical conspirator, and introduced his oft-used trope of drug peddling as a metaphor for the abuses by the white power structure.

The **Weldon Irvine**-sampling "My Philosophy" introduced KRS-One as hip-hop's teacher. His songs frequently descended into pedagogy, but still had occasional moments of brilliance. He founded the Stop the Violence Movement, which released "Self-Destruction" in 1989, an all-

star jam featuring BDP, PE, Stetsasonic and Kool Moe Dee. *Ghetto Music: The Blueprint Of Hip-Hop* was released the same year, and featured BDP's most austere music yet. It also featured some of KRS-One's best songs: "Who Protects Us From You?" and "You Must Learn". But his pedantic tone started to take over and *Edutainment* (1990) frequently devolved into lecturing. After a remarkably decent live album, *Live Hardcore Worldwide* (1991), *Sex And Violence* (1992) suffered from the fall-out from his divorce from **Ms. Melodie** and declined into grotesque sexism.

KRS-One's first album under his own name, *Return Of The Boom Bap* (1994), was not only a return to form, but a stylistic leap as well. While not abandoning the stark arrangements of old, he successfully incorporated the rhythmic innovations of hip-hop's new school to make a record of brooding funk, with "Sound of the Police" being the standout. This pattern continued on *KRS-One* (1995), which featured "MC's Act Like They Don't Know", an excellent collaboration with the one and only **DJ Premier**, who at this point could even have rescued The Backstreet Boys's street cred. The minimalism was gone entirely by the time of *I Got Next* (1997), which featured the excellent "Step Into My World (Rapture)", a reworking of Blondie's "Rapture" and The Mohawks' "Champ".

*Maximum Strength* (1998) was an uncomfortable mismatch of the Blastmaster's stentorian roar with contemporary, lightweight beats, but by this point KRS had become an A&R exec at Reprise and was concentrating most of his efforts on his earnest Temple of Hip-Hop project. *Sneak Attack* (2001) was like that moment when you first notice that your mum or dad has suddenly, seemingly out of nowhere, acquired jowls. KRS-One had had more than his share of mediocre records in the past, but he'd always had a voice and style that compelled you to listen. Here, however, he just sounded like he was waiting for his enshrinement in his Temple of Hip-Hop and just biding time until Vegas came calling.

Instead, it was God that came calling. *Spiritual Minded* (2002) was a straight-up gospel album from a guy who used to skewer scripture instead of spout it. All the KRS-One hallmarks are here – the stentorian delivery, the minimal production – but hearing him churn out bland platitudes to his maker was just damned depressing.

Thankfully, *D.I.G.I.T.A.L.* (2004), a collection of rare B-sides and unreleased tracks from KRS-One's salad days, served as a welcome reminder of both his greatness and his pig-headedness.

**Criminal Minded**
B-Boy, 1987

One of hip-hop's towering monuments. Its rhythmic minimalism and fierce tribalism stripped hip-hop to its purest essence.

**A Retrospective**
Zomba, 2000

Not perfect, but a good to place to start to get the breadth of KRS-One's vision. Includes both BDP and solo tracks.

# Brand Nubian

One of the first hip-hop singles to engage with the Jamaican dancehall, Masters of Ceremony's "Sexy" (1987) was a sizable underground hit and the best track on the group's underrated *Dynamite* (1988) album. The lead raggamuffin on "Sexy" and tracks like "Cracked Out" and "Master Move" was Grand Puba (Maxwell Dixon), who would soon leave the group and found Brand Nubian with his New Rochelle, New York homeboys Derek X (Derek Murphy), Lord Jamar (Lorenzo Dechalus) and DJ Alamo.

Their first album, *One For All* (1990), was a masterpiece of sound (one of the best examples of the freedom allowed by sampling technology, loose, free-flowing rhymes and funky fresh flows), but it was let down by scabrous Five Percent rhetoric and lyrical hypocrisy. "Slow Down" was ample proof of hip-hop's redemptive powers (it turned the ignorance-is-bliss hippy bullshit of Edie Brickell and the New Bohemians' "What I Am" into a dark, moody groove), but its cautionary tale of drug abuse soon turned into an irritating, all-too-predictable indictment of skeezers. Picking up where **Trouble Funk** left off, "Drop the Bomb" was a fine, black nationalist anthem, but Brand Nubian just as often ignored Muslim teachings and fucked everything in sight.

Grand Puba and Alamo left the following year to make Puba's *Reel to Reel* (1992). While the album highlighted Puba's dextrous flow on a bunch of so-so party jams, *Reel to Reel* is perhaps most notable for one of the first (if not *the* first) Tommy Hilfiger shout-out in hip-hop: "Girbauds hanging baggy, Hilfiger on the top" from "360° (What Goes Around)". *2000* (1995) had even less substance – most of it was taken up

BOOGIE DOWN PRODUCTIONS
BY ALL MEANS NECESSARY

with Puba's flirtations with r&b.

With DJ Sincere replacing Alamo, and Derek X becoming Sadat X, Brand Nubian continued with *In God We Trust* (1992). The album featured was more hardcore, both in sound and sentiment, particularly on the hot but loathsome "Punks Jump Up to Get Beat Down" and the more overt Five Percent rhetoric on tracks like "Allah and Justice" and "Meaning of the 5%". *Everything Is Everything* (1994) found the group struggling in a changing hip-hop climate. They eschewed East Coast block-rockers in favour of West Coast rollers and an atrocious **Simply Red** interpolation on "Hold On".

After Sadat X's spaghetti western set in the Harlem badlands, *Wild Cowboys* (1996), the original Brand Nubian reunited for *Foundation* (1998), easily their best album. There were still disgraceful platitudes and the older-than-Fatback's "King Tim III" hip-hop chestnut – "girls didn't want nothing to do with me until I got a record deal" type of thing – but as far as non-playa-hating mainstream hip-hop goes, this was about as good as it got while Puff Daddy was still running things. "The Return" was one of those killer laidback funk grooves that DJ Premier seemed to churn out by the ton without even getting out of bed, while "Back Up Off the Wall" sounded like it was constructed out of a Chopin nocturne.

Unfortunately, the album didn't really get anywhere and Grand Puba and Sadat X concentrated on solo projects. Puba sounded well behind the times on his *Understand This* (2001) album for that refuge of over the hill rappers, the Koch International label. Sadat X released a couple of rather pro forma singles, the best of which was probably "The Great Dot X" (2001), a rather unpleasant sex boast, but at least it was funky. Lord Jamar, meanwhile, landed a role on the HBO prison drama *Oz*. In 2003 Brand Nubian signed with Babygrande Records and a new album was expected at press time.

◉ **Foundation**
Arista, 1998

Brand Nubian's rhymes won't blow anyone's mind, but even the dodgy Five Percent rhetoric sounds positively liberatory compared to Mase's drivel from the time.

# Busta Rhymes

In the age of "keeping it real", how is it that one of hip-hop's biggest stars is a hyper-active court jester, a whirling dervish harlequin, the Tasmanian devil with a sore throat? Busta Rhymes (né Trevor Smith) is certainly hip-hop's most personable and charismatic star, but he is more than just the clown prince of hip-hop.

With his ridiculous energy levels, dancehall-inspired rhyming style, outrageous videos, Five Percent Nation (an off-shoot of the Nation of Islam) beliefs and obsession with the apocalypse, Busa-Bus is hip-hop's most contradictory personality this side of Tupac, and thus its most iconic presence.

Busta first came to attention in the early '90s as a member of the **Leaders of the New School** with Charlie Brown, Dinco D and Cut Monitor Milo. Their debut album, *A Future Without a Past* (1991), took the terminology of old and new schools literally and the record was divided into "Homeroom", "Lunchroom" and "Afterschool" sessions (you could get away with stuff like that back then). Despite this, lifting routines from the Cold Crush Brothers and rhymes like "Causing aggravation, I'll never pause/Pushing out spit balls with plastic straws", *A Future Without a Past* managed to make such schoolboy antics very agreeable, due largely to production by the **Bomb Squad**'s Eric Sadler and an irrepressible group energy on tracks like "Case of the PTA" and "International Zone Coaster".

"Case of the PTA" was a minor hit, but it was a show-stealing cameo on **A Tribe Called Quest**'s "Scenario" that made Busta a star. His lion roar soon popped up on tracks by everyone, and the Leaders' second album, *T.I.M.E. The Inner Mind's Eye* (1993), suffered from both group dissension and the changing times. The group disbanded later that year, minutes before a scheduled TV appearance.

After more guest appearances than anyone aside from Big Pun, Busta's solo career finally took off with his double-platinum debut album, *The Coming* (1996) and its massive single, "Woo-Hah!! Got You All in Check". Built on a loop from

Galt McDermot's "Space", "Woo-Hah!!" had great production, but it was dominated by Busta's personality (though definitely not his rhymes). Elsewhere, with help from EPMD's DJ Scratch, "Do My Thing" was similarly cartoonish, while "Keep it Movin'" was a reunion of the LONS.

*When Disaster Strikes* (1997) was equally successful and featured another anthem in the form of the awesome "Put Your Hands Where My Eyes Can See". "Turn it Up/ Fire it Up" found Busta riding the **Knight Rider** theme to the top of the charts in 1998. *Extinction Level Event* (1999) had the ultimate harbinger of millennial apocalyspe: Busta collaborating with both Ozzy Osbourne for a version of Black Sabbath's "Iron Man", and with Janet Jackson on the lame, Timbaland-biting "What's it Gonna Be?!"

After introducing his **Flipmode Squad** (Rah Digga, Lord Have Mercy, Spliff Star, Rampage and Baby Sham) on "Cha Cha Cha" (1998) and then over-exposing them, he actually found time to record his fourth album, *Anarchy* (2000), which suffered from Busta being unable to change his flow one iota and the world not ending. Meanwhile, the remaining Leaders of the New School, who hadn't been heard from since the group broke up, attempted a comeback with *That's How Life B* (1999), but sadly, they remained unheard by just about everyone.

On *Genesis* (2001), Busta was rejuvenated by a change of labels (from Elektra to J), particularly on the singles – "Break Ya Neck" and the irresistible "Pass the Courvoisier" – but instead of being one-dimensional, the album was all over the place, with beats by everyone from Dr Dre to **Pete Rock** to Just Blaze causing just too many personality changes. *It Ain't Safe No More* (2002) was more of the same, with Busta shifting from "That's why we thinkin' that it's better to ball/While the devil be sittin' and watchin'/Plottin' how to murder us all" to the tired sex/club rap "Make it Clap" and back again, but without any killer singles to compensate. "Light That Ass On Fire", his contribution to the Neptunes' showcase album, *Clones*, was impressive. A party track built upon a stark, minimal beat that wouldn't have sounded out of place on *Paid In Full*, it had more instances of the word "ass" crammed into it than any song in recorded history.

### BUSTA RHYMES

⊙ **Total Devastation: The Best Of Busta Rhymes**
Rhino, 2001

It's possible that this well-chosen greatest hits collection will be too unrelenting for some, but you don't listen to Busta Rhymes for subtlety or quiet reflection. You listen to get the party moving and to get carried away by his madcap energy.

# BRITISH HIP-HOP

Despite the fact that the UK has produced one of hip-hop's most revered MCs (**Slick Rick**), the British music press will never tire of bemoaning the state of its homegrown hip-hop. Ignored by record companies, journalists, shops and record buyers in favour of their American brethren, and dance music, UK hip-hop artists have survived in a state of not-so-benign neglect for so long that any attention, positive or negative, comes as a relief. Part of the problem is that the Brits just can't see when they have a good thing. **Monie Love**, who had worked with **MC Mell 'O'** and **DJ Pogo**, didn't receive any acclaim until she hooked up with Queen Latifah on "Ladies First" (1989). **Derek B**'s "Rock the Beat" (1988), while viewed as something of a joke in its home country, became a crucial part of the New Orleans bounce aesthetic when its drum beat was fused with The Showboys' "Drag Rap", helping Louisiana labels No Limit and Cash Money go multi-platinum. As an A&R man at the Music of Life label, Derek B helped sign the **Demon Boyz** (Mike J and Darren). Many people accused Das EFX of borrowing their raggamuffin-inspired, motor-mouth deliveries.

Of course, prescience isn't always a blessing. The Cookie Crew's "Rok Da House" (1987) is generally credited as being the first hip-house track – not an achievement to be proud of. The Wee Papa Girl Rappers' rap version of George Michael's "Faith" (1988) didn't lend the scene any credibility either. The Cookie Crew, Wee Papa Girl Rappers and the She-Rockers, all all-female groups, unfortunately established Brit-hop's identity as a novelty genre despite the best efforts of the Afrocentric **Overlord X**, the hardcore **Hijack**, the symphonic First Down and the East End gangsta style of the **London Posse**. Comprised of Rodney P and Bionic, the London Posse were perhaps the first UK hip-hop crew to attempt to rhyme in a style that wasn't consciously imitating American flavours on their *Gangster Chronicles* album (1990). **Rodney P** later showed up alongside Roots Manuva, Phi-Life Cypher and the Scratch Perverts' Tony Vegas on DJ Skitz's fine rallying cry for UK hip-hop, "Fingerprints of the Gods" (1998). Despite excellent production, the single was dragged down by the MCs trying perhaps a little too hard: "Just like Man United relying on Schmeichel". Nevertheless, the track featured the artists who would help take Brit-hop ever so slightly out of the dark ages.

South London's **Roots Manuva** (Rodney Smith) had previously worked with North London stalwarts **Blak Twang** before releasing his *Brand New Second Hand* album (1999) on the best British hip-hop label, the avantist Big Dada. Like many Brit MCs, his flow has got as much to do with Barrington Levy and Capleton as it does with Method Man and Rakim, but, unlike too many Limey MCs, he understands how to attack a beat with effective cadences. *Run Come Save Me* (2001) was even better, if more challenging. The album was more or less equally divided between slightly askew club tracks like "Witness (1 Hope)" and dark, experimental tracks like "Sinny Sinny Sin" where Roots Manuva confronted his strict, ultra-religious father.

**Phi-Life Cypher**, on the other hand, are the most mellifluous, flowing British MCs around, best sampled on their *Earth Rulers* EP (2000). Where most MCs who speak the Queen's English go for a kind of gothic Busta Rhymes bluster because of their Caribbean origins, or simply because they can't rap, Phi-Life could pass muster among the Rotten Apple's purists.

Separated by a common language, the UK hip-hop scene has made its most impact on American heads

DJ Vadim, Russo-London beatmaker extraordinaire.

Roots Manuva, free of baggage, makin' tracks. And getting in an early bid for the Cary Grant role, should anyone decide to remake *North By Northwest*.

in the realm of turntablism. The Scratch Perverts – Tony Vegas, Prime Cuts, First Rate, Mr Thing and Harry Love – were one of the world's most formidable DJ crews, winning numerous ITF and DMC competitions. Unlike many of his turntablist brethren, **Jeep Beat Collective**'s The Ruf wasn't interested in defending the turntable's status as a musical instrument, or in tearing apart syntax with lightning-speed juxtapositions and improbably named scratches. Instead, on his excellent *Repossessed Wildstyles* (1998) and *Technics Chainsaw Massacre* (1999) albums he slowed down the pace of the cuts, broke out some party tricks and packed his collages full of hooks and mnemonic devices.

In order to break through the language barrier, many British producers worked with Yankee MCs. The Creators (Si and Juliano) provided beats for

MCs such as Mos Def, El Da Sensai and Mike Zoot on their very fine *The Weight* album (2000); The Next Men (Baloo and Search) delivered a smooth, Wes-Montgomery-on-quaaludes EP, *Break the Mould* (1999), that fell somewhere between Shawn J Period and Pete Rock, with Grap Luva, Soulson and Red Cloud; **DJ Vadim** teamed up with Iriscience from Dilated Peoples, Sarah Jones and the great British beatboxer **Killa Kela** on his excellent *USSR: Life From the other Side* album (1999), and with New York's brilliant avant-garde MC trio, Anti-Pop Consortium, for The Isolationist's *Isolationist* (1999).

The second album from Roots Manuva's Big Dada labelmates **New Flesh** (lyricists Toastie Taylor and Juice Aleem, and DJ/producer Part 2), *Understanding* (2002), was perhaps the perfect British hip-hop album. A blend of dancehall, twisted r&b, UK

New Flesh: Toastie Taylor (Trinidad), Juice Aleem (Birmingham) and Part 2 (Yorkshire).

garage and anything but straightforward hip-hop, *Understanding* was an eloquent summation of the UK's position as a crossroads of the Afro-Caribbean diaspora.

## ROOTS MANUVA

**Roots Manuva – Run Come Save Me**
Big Dada, 2001

With production that sounds like Darkchild caught in one of dub producer Scientist's loops, this is one of the most fully realised statements of British hip-hop.

## THE CREATORS

**The Weight**
Bad Magic, 2000

They may be cheating by using American guest MCs, but the 100% British production is smoking.

## NEW FLESH

**Understanding**
Big Dada, 2002

Courtesy of often astounding production, and MCs who can actually attack a beat with grace, this is an experimental and challenging album that never sacrifices groove or hooks.

## DJ WOODY

**Bangers & Mash**
Woodwurk, 2004

An excellent mix of Brit-hop obscurities from the era of Hijack, London Posse and Krispy 3.

# Camp Lo

Nostalgia is one of those old world paradigms that hip-hop was supposed to wipe off the face of the earth with one flip of the cross-fader. However, as hip-hop became more and more like business as usual, misty-eyed reminiscing has become more and more prevalent. If hip-hop nostalgia had an acceptable face it was Camp Lo, the Bronx duo of **Sonny Cheeba** and **Geechie Suede**.

Their 1970s fixation first came to public attention with the single "Coolie High", which evoked big afros and brothers in leather jackets sweet-talking Foxy Browns across 110th Street. The blaxploitation vibe was writ large on Camp Lo's debut album *Uptown Saturday Night* (1997). From the cover, which aped the sleeve of **Marvin Gaye**'s *I Want You*, to

the **Skull Snaps** and **Isaac Hayes** samples, *Uptown Saturday Night* was a complete appropriation of the cool of the decade that taste forgot. "Luchini (aka This Is It)" rode the smooth horns from **Dynasty**'s "Adventures In The Land Of Music" to hip-hop bliss. Even though they fancied themselves as "Casanova Brown levitatin' jiggy in dashikis", they weren't rapping about anything all that different from posers like **Ma$e**, it's just that their vision of jiggy paradise was a lot more inclusive than Diddy's mercenary capitalism.

After numerous label problems, they seemingly disappeared off the face of the earth, only to return in 2001 on their own Dymon Crook label with "Trouble Man" and "Cookers". *Let's Do It Again* (2002) was another collection of extravagant lifestyle shoots set in retro and exotic locales, but by this point it was a lot less fresh than their debut.

**Uptown Saturday Night**
Profile, 1997

The only difference between Camp Lo's debut and P. Diddy's lifestyle of the rich and shameless schtick was that Geechie and Cheeba were clinking champagne flutes in Spanish Harlem with Willie Dynamite, instead of in the Hamptons with their stockbrokers.

# Cam'ron / Diplomats

Cameron Giles had been a promising American Football player – an all-city guard at Manhattan Center High School in New York, where his teammate was one Mason Bertha, but bad grades and a hamstring injury ended his sporting career. He soon turned to rap, and his old teammate, who was now going by the name of **Ma$e**, hooked him up with **Notorious BIG** and his partner Lance "Un" Rivera. After several appearances on some of DJ Clue's mixtapes, Cam'ron dropped ".357" (1998), which became a big street hit in New York on the strength of its sample of the *Magnum PI* theme tune.

"Horse & Carriage" (1998) followed and did even better, thanks to its hot production from Trackmasters, based on **Bill Withers**'s "Who Is He And What

Is He To You?", but no thanks to the nauseating Ma$e on the hook. Cam'ron's laidback flow (not that dissimilar to Ma$e's, though at least Cam'ron could enunciate) on top of similarly styled pop-street production dominated *Confessions of Fire* (1998), but apart from the two singles Cam'ron didn't display a lot of flair.

The much-delayed *SDE (Sports, Drugs, Entertainment)* (2000) showed a harder, more streetwise Cam'ron, but the production, mostly from Digga, failed to follow suit with far too obvious samples of The Police's "Roxanne" and Edwin Starr's "War". The album also introduced his rather odious **Diplomats** (aka Dip Set) crew: Freaky Zeeky, Jimmy Jones and Juelz Santana.

*Come Home With Me* (2002) followed Cam'ron's shift of allegiances to the Roc-A-Fella label. With the new label came a change in production style, and beats from **Just Blaze**, Kanye West and DR Period set him off much better than the sub-Puffy pap of old. "Oh Boy" was a massive radio hit, thanks to its sped-up sample of **Rose Royce**, while "Welcome to New York City" was a collaboration with **Jay-Z** over a firing beat from Just Blaze.

Unfortunately, Come Home With Me also marked the beginning of Cam's bizarre desire to remake rap classics that really shouldn't be remade. "Live My Life (Leave Me Alone)" used the same beat as 2Pac's "Ambitionz Az A Ridah". This pattern was repeasted ad nauseam on The Diplomats truly awful two-disc turkey *Diplomatic Immunity* (2003) where they included "Bout It Bout It Pt. III" with Master P and a remake of Starship's "We Built This City". Almost every single track featured the sped-up sample schtick that was the only reason anyone listened to "Oh Boy", and to make matters worse the Dip Set compared themselves repeatedly to the Taliban and Al Qaeda – which is just plain idiotic.

For some reason people bought into this shit and Cam started to make like a mogul, buying liquor stores in Harlem,

introducing a range of cologne and starting a car service. *Purple Haze* (2004) was more of the same, with a remake of Cyndi Lauper's "Girls Just Wanna Have Fun" and more samples at 78rpm. At least the guy dressed well.

⦿ **Come Home With Me**
Roc-A-Fella, 2002

At the time, "Oh Boy" was fairly irresistible (even if the sped-up sample thing was already getting old), but now that the gimmick's been used a thousand times it's just boring. So is the rest of the album, but it's got more shine than any of his other records.

# Canibus

Once hailed as the second coming, Canibus has been relegated to a footnote in hip-hop history. He is doomed to be remembered only for his battle with **LL Cool J** and the subsequent bomb of a debut LP that basically destroyed his career. The sad fact is that, when he's on top of his game, Canibus is absolutely ferocious on the mic and coulda, shoulda been a contender.

Canibus was born Germaine Williams in Jamaica and spent much of his youth globetrotting, as his mother's job entailed that she change location all the time. Spending more time with his games than with any constantly shifting group of friends, the introspective Williams was a natural rhymer when he was introduced to hip-hop. Part of a crew called **THEM**

(The Heralds of Extreme Metaphors), Canibus soon attracted the attention of Charles Suitt of Group Home Records, who made him general manager of the label. After some mixtape appearances, his wax debut was a verse on **Ras Kass**' "Uni-4-orm" in 1997, but it was his extended cameo on **The Lost Boyz**' "Beasts From The East" that really turned heads. Filled with lyrics like "A hundred times nicer than the best is/Twice as African as KRS is/Who want to test this?/Fuck y'all, you don't impress me and no can test me/An MC so ill I got AIDS scared to catch me", Canibus's extraordinary two-and-a-half minutes had hip-hop heads going crazy.

More appearances, on Wyclef's "Gone Til November" remix, and Common's "Making a Name for Ourselves", kept the momentum up, until a fateful meeting with LL Cool J at LA's Hit Factory studios. Cool James had asked Canibus to contribute a verse to "4, 3, 2, 1" on his upcoming *Phenomenon* album. Canibus's rhyme apparently made a passing reference to LL's tattoo of a microphone, which Ladies Love didn't take too kindly to for some reason, and wrote a verse that attacked Canibus. Canibus responded with "Second Round KO" (1998), his first single, which declared, "You don't want me to shine/But you study my rhyme/Then you lace your vocals over mine/That's a bitch move/Something only a homo rapper would do". It was an intense record – not even a novelty appearance from Mike Tyson could destroy its momentum.

Unfortunately, the album *Can-I-Bus* (1998) could, and did. The driving fury of his previous records was gone. In its place was a collection of almost laidback beats that suited his flow and venom not one iota. Canibus placed the blame squarely on producer **Wyclef**. Yes, the beats sucked, but the fact is that there were too many story raps (Canibus had never shown any narrative streak previously) and preachy anti-gun tales, and almost none of the spit and fire that had made him an underground star.

The production was definitely better

# CANADIAN HIP-HOP

Although "iced out" has a very different meaning in the Great White North, Canadian MCs don't exactly situate their raps in the tundra or brag about shooting caribou instead of five-O. Hip-hop north of the 49th parallel inevitably lies in the shadow of the music made across the border, but this distance from the centre of the hip-hop community has allowed Canada to develop a number of artists who don't have to depend on the Canadian content law to get radio airplay, and who have broadened hip-hop's sonic frontiers.

The first Canuck MC that anyone in the wider world ever heard of was Toronto's **Maestro Fresh Wes**. Long before "T dot O" became common parlance in indie hip-hop circles, Wes and his Vision Crew were representing the 416 area. Wearing tie, tail and fade, Wes dropped "Let Your Backbone Slide" in 1989, which became a fairly sizeable radio hit on the strength of Wes's linguistics. His debut album, *Symphony In Effect* (1990), sold over 200,000 copies in Canada (double platinum in Canadian money). After a dud of a second album, however, Wes moved to Brooklyn and released *Naah, Dis Kid Can't Be From Canada* (1994), which set Wes's dated rhyme style against contemporary production from Showbiz, making Wes seem more awkward than a mountie in Bed-Stuy.

The Dream Warriors, a duo of West Indian immigrants – King Lou and Capital Q – had been around since 1988, but burst on the scene in 1991 at the height of the jazz hip-hop thing with "My Definition of a Boombastic Jazz Style". Sampling an old game-show theme tune, "My Definition" and its follow-up – the equally quirky "Wash Your Face in My Sink" – remade hip-hop as a beatnik carnival, perfect for slumming indie kids and acid jazz fashionistas. The sound world displayed on *And Now The Legacy Begins* (1991) was undeniably impressive, but their rhyming skills left a bit to be desired, a fact only temporarily remedied by their excellent collaboration with **Gang Starr**, "I've Lost My Ignorance" (1992). Like similar artists, from Digable Planets to Disposable Heroes of Hiphoprisy, Dream Warriors couldn't escape the coffee shop vibe, even when their core audience had moved on as well, and *Subliminal Simulation* (1994) was just dire. They disappeared for the rest of

the decade, only to emerge on trip-hoppers The Herbaliser's *Very Mercenary* album (1999).

**Kwest Tha Madd Lad** took the opposite route: sex-obsessed juvenilia. Kwest's *This Is My First Album* (1996) had some amusing lines, but, due to delays, the tracks were two years old and really sounded it by the time the album was released. A better display of Kwest's skills can be heard on "Bathroom Cipher" from *Lyricist Lounge Volume One* (1998), where he rips freestyles with Hazadous, IG Off, Thirstin Howl III and J-Treds.

With such high-profile commercial failures, the Canadian scene has been sustaining itself on the underground. Despite local success for the likes of **Thrust** and **Michie Mee**, one of the few Canadian rappers to be signed to a major label is **Choclair**, who debuted in 1995 with "Twenty-One Years". Word filtered down to New York, where DJ Premier included it on his *New York Reality Check 101* (1997) compilation and scratched up Choclair's vocals from his second single, "Just a Second" (1996), on Gang Starr's "You Know My Steez". His debut album, *Ice Cold* (1999), however, was overwhelmed by his somewhat monomanical obsession with booty. Far better was a collaborative single with **Frankenstein**, **Kardinal Offishall** and **Marvel** – "Internal Affairs" (1999).

Those artists (with the exception of Frankenstein), along with **Solitair**, **Saukrates**, **YLooK**, **Jully Black** and **Afrolistic**, comprise Toronto's **Circle Crew**. The dancehall-inspired **Kardinal Offishall**'s *Eye & I* (1997) included the indie anthem, "On Wid Da Show", but this seriously (and deservingly) hyped MC's best track is "Ghetto" (1999), which features gems like, "You know you're ghetto when your stuck inside a jail/And them Jordans on your feet's costin' more than your bail". Saukrates, on the other hand, sounded monotonous and anachronistic on *The Underground Tapes* (1999). While the Circle Crew run T-O, **Frankenstein** got heads nodding with his instrumental *UV EP* (1999), released on his own Knowledge of Self label, and **Ghetto Concepts** rocked the shores of Lake Ontario with "Precious Moments" (1999).

Across the country in Vancouver, **The Rascalz** (Red 1, Misfit, Kemo and Dedos) blew up with the trans-continental collaboration "Northern Touch"

(1998). Along with Choclair, Thrust, Kardinal Offishall and Checkmate, The Rascalz spat battle rhymes over a slamming track that was like a jiggier version of EPMD's "So Watcha Sayin'". The Pacific Coast's best, however, are **Swollen Members**. They might have the worst name in the biz, but Madchild and Prevail are two of the most innovative artists in hip-hop. They debuted with the *Swollen Members* EP (1998), which featured the magnificently moody "Paradise Lost", a dense fog of dark strings and nails-across-a-blackboard scratching, courtesy of **Mixmaster Mike**. At the drop of a Kangol, the epic *Balance* (1999) moved from fizzing, twisted dubscapes with stream-of-consciousness sci-fi metaphors to huge, piano-fuelled jump-up anthems, and brought a new range of expression to the Aleister-Crowley-adept wing of hip-hop. While lines like

"Mischievous elves cringe at my introduction" suggested that the MCs not only "drink with Dionysus" but also listened to a lot of Ronnie James Dio, the horror-show imagery was tempered by classic boasts like "Even Van Gogh looked at me and said 'You're one piece of work'/So I said 'Lend me an ear cause I'm the state of the art'" which elevated *Balance* above the merely cartoonish. *Bad Dreams* (2001) was essentially a backpacker's all-star album, with appearances from **Chali 2Na**, Evidence, DJ Babu, Joey Chavez, Planet Asia, DJ Revolution and **Moka Only**, among others. Tracks like "Full Contact" and "Take It Back", while expanding the Members' stylistic range, nonetheless heard them succumbing to the monotonous stab/cadence pattern that afflicts so much West Coast rap. *Monsters In The Closet* (2002) was a collection of B-sides

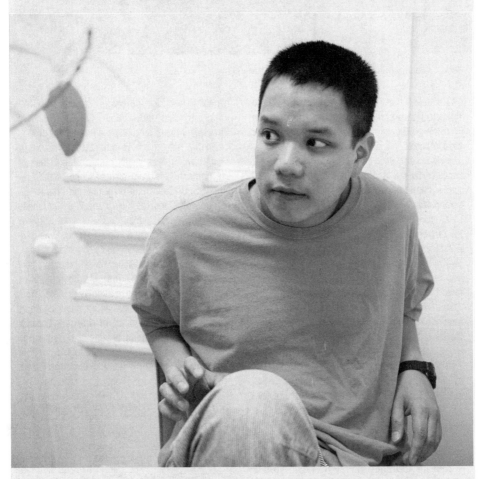

Kid Koala always demands eucalyptus leaves as part of his rider.

Top Canadian sword-'n'-sorcerer MCs Swollen Members.

and outtakes that mostly showed them to be in thrall to Kool Keith, although the collaboration with **Nelly Furtado**, "Breath", sounded like their bid for Murder Inc.-style success.

In Montreal, where aspiring hip-hoppers are shackled by the language barrier, the city's best and brightest have mastered the art of turntablism instead. Fifteen-year-old **DJ A-Trak** won the DMC world mixing championship in 1997, and laced **Obscure Disorder**'s "Lyrically Exposed" (1998) with some of the wildest array of crabs and flares ever heard on a conventional hip-hop record. Meanwhile, media fave **Kid Koala** even rocked a little Genesis on his superlative *ScratchCratchRatchAtch* (1997) bootleg mixtape, which felt like one of those chase scenes that closes an episode of the *Benny Hill Show*. His *Carpal Tunnel Syndrome* album (2000) was proof that, where most turntablists are out to wow you with their prowess behind the decks, Kid Koala impresses you with sheer force of personality. His album *Some Of My Best Friends Are DJs* (2003) was similarly quirky, although the mostly jazz sources lent the album a more downbeat quality.

With the growing synergy between hip-hop and dancehall, **Kardinal Offishall** has parlayed his ability to bridge the two genres into cult stardom. His major-label debut, *Quest for Fire: Firestarter Vol. 1* (2001), was uneven, but featured the stellar space-age anthem "Bakardi Slang", which was a minor hit on both sides of the border. The album also had one of the first sightings of Sean Paul on a hip-hop album – a hideous harbinger of the future. The Neptunes-produced "Belly Dancer" of 2003, with Kardinal Offishall's most yard-centric styles yet, was perhaps the best track in hip-hop's "orientalist" fad.

Canada's healthy distance from hip-hop business as usual was epitomised by the debut album by **K-OS** (aka Kheaven Brereton), *Exit* (2002). Cellos were almost as prevalent as drum machines, and, like most of the best Canuck hip-hop, the ghosts of reggae haunted all of the album's nooks and crannies. In fact, K-OS's approach was often more like that of a dancehall singjay than a rapper.

### SWOLLEN MEMBERS

**Balance**
Battle Axe/Jazz Fudge, 1999
Quite simply one of the best indie hip-hop albums of the century's close.

and more suited to his style on *2000 BC* (2000), but this only shone the spotlight on Canibus's deficiencies as an MC. Canibus is pretty monotonal and he can really only function when he's in overdrive. Even on these thuggish beats, he gets so overamped that he loses the rhythm, and the beat becomes superfluous to his words.

*"C" True Hollywood Stories* (2001) was yet another brick of an album, based on the television show of just about the same name. The concept was daring and potentially very interesting: on "U Didn't Care" Canibus raps in the persona of Stan, the obsessive fan **Eminem** created in his song of the same name, creating a sequel of sorts by rescuing Stan from the river in which he drowned at the song's climax and turning him into a great rapper. A wonderful idea, but the execution is so shocking that you can't help but feel that it was merely an attention-getting tactic.

*Mic Club: The Curriculum* (2002) had Canibus's most literate, thoughtful rhymes, but again the production let him down. The "Stan" schtick seemed to have worked, though, because Eminem replied with the song "Canibitch". On "Dr. C PhD" Canibus in turn responded, "You better run for the pacifier/Tie you up and drown you in the saliva quagmire/Till your oxygen expires and your lungs dry up/'Cause you said Bis ain't dope, you a damn liar".

(•) **Mic Club: The Curriculum**
Mic Club, 2002

Most of this album is Canibus doing what he does best: getting pissed off and venting spleen on the mic. The production ain't great, but Canibus generally ignores the beat anyway, so it's kind of irrelevant. Still, you're better off seeking out one of his legions of mixtapes, where propriety and the record label lawyers can't bother him.

# Cannibal Ox

◊ See *Def Jux records*

# Capone-n-Noreaga

R enaming their Big Apple environment after Middle East trouble spots – Lefrak City (Iraq), Queensbridge (Kuwait),and Brooklyn (Baghdad) – Kiam "Capone" Holley and Victor "Noreaga" Santiago, Jr. have taken Chuck D's pronouncement that "rap is black people's CNN" more literally than anyone else. With a street reportage style similar to their neighbours Nas and Mobb Deep, C-N-N are the Christiane Amanpour and Wolf Blitzer of the Queens housing projects.

The two met while they were both serving time at the Collins Correctional Facility in upstate New York. After Capone was released, he started working with Tragedy the Intelligent Hoodlum and, when Noreaga got out six months later, they recorded the single "LA, LA" in 1995 with **Tragedy** and **Mobb Deep**, a response to **Tha Dogg Pound**'s "New York, New York". Anchored by the fearsome "T.O.N.Y." and the very Mobb Deep-like "Halfway Thugs", the duo's debut *The War Report* (1997) quickly became a classic of the stark, grim, chillingly hopeless sound of New York thug rap.

Soon after the album came out, though, Capone was arrested for a parole violation and was sent back to prison for another two years. Severing ties with Tragedy (and releasing the savage "Halfway Thugs, Pt. II" to mark the occasion in 1998), Noreaga went solo with *N.O.R.E.* (1998). Standing, apparently, for "Niggas On the Run Eatin'", N.O.R.E. was a hungrier, more commercially savvy album than C-N-N's debut. The title track and "Superthug" featured bouncing synth stabs, lush production (by the Trackmasters and the Neptunes), absurdist rhymes ("Run laps around the English Channel/Neptunes, I got a cocker spaniel") and a catchphrase ("Whut?! Whut?!") that took over New York and helped make the album gold. "Body In A Trunk", a collaboration with **Nas**, and the album's urban gothic production didn't hurt either.

*Melvin Flynt Da Hustler* (1999) was an album in which Noreaga came across as a sort of composite of *Hustler* (and *Rap*

Noreaga looks up from the void...

*Pages*) magazine publisher **Larry Flynt** and the Melvin Udall character from the Jack Nicholson movie *As Good As it Gets*. It was meant to unveil a new facet of Noreaga's persona, but it was the same old routine without the hooks.

Capone was released from prison in 1999, and the two joined forces again for *The Reunion* (2000). Much anticipated, the album was a damp squib, with Noreaga's forceful solo personality unable to gel again with his old partner in crime. The two parted ways once more and Noreaga released *God's Favorite* in 2002. The album was packed with guest appearances and superstar producers (The Neptunes, Swizz Beatz, EZ Elpee and Irv Gotti), but it's notable only for the super-sexy club anthem "Nothin'", one of the Neptunes' finest moments, and the skidding, metal-on-metal boast beatdown "Nahmeanuheard".

**The War Report**
Penalty, 1997

Raw, gritty, and grimy from start to finish – the sound of two street kids with absolutely nothing to lose.

# Cash Money records

New Orleans is the cradle of modern popular music, but if you look at almost any history of the Crescent City's long and illustrious music scene it will tell you that today New Orleans is nothing but a museum for old styles like zydeco, swamp pop, dixieland, Mardi Gras chants, cajun fiddle breakdowns and street funk. With the success of the Cash Money and No Limit record labels, however, that notion has been shown up as the middle-class fantasy it is.

**Cash Money** is the leading purveyor of that peculiar sub-genre of hip-hop native to New Orleans called **Bounce**. Although it now encompasses drum machine versions of local Mardi Gras rhythms, Bounce was kick-started by a group from Queens, New York, called **The Showboys**. The scattershot drums and the weird, digital-xylophone break of The Showboys' 1986 single, "Drag Rap" (aka "Triggerman"), was a huge hit down south, and budding MCs from the Magnolia

Projects in New Orleans' Third Ward would rhyme over the top of it. Instead of trying to match the rapid-fire beats, the rappers would use that molasses-slow Nworlins drawl made famous by such lazy soul singers as **Lee Dorsey** and Alvin Robinson. One of these MCs was **Terius "Juvenile" Gray**, whose "Bounce for the Juvenile" (1993) was a huge local hit when it appeared on DJ Jimi's *It's Jimi* album, which also featured another proto-Bounce hit, "Where Dey At".

In 1995 Juvenile recorded *Being Myself* for New York-based Warlock Records, but it went nowhere and Juvenile quit music temporarily to work on an oil rig. In 1996, however, he hooked up with the Cash Money label, who had been releasing New Orleans rap by groups like UNLV (whose "Sixth & Barone" and "Drag 'Em in the River" were the label's first hits), Pimp Daddy and B.G. (aka Christopher Dorsey) since 1991. In 1996 Cash Money reorganised itself around Juvenile and a trio of man-childs – 16 year-old **B.G.**, 15 year-old **Dwayne "Lil' Wayne" Carter** and 16 year-old **Tab "Turk" Virgil** – who had all been through more before the age of 20 than any person should go through in an entire life. With this first-hand knowledge of the dark side and a youthful, infectious *esprit de corps*, Cash Money quickly moved from being a local concern to one of the biggest labels on the hip-hop landscape.

The other ingredient in their transformation was producer **Mannie Fresh**. Like that other supernova producer, **Swizz Beatz**, Fresh created a seemingly endless storehouse of recoiling beats that were simultaneously old school and futuristic. And, just like Swizz Beatz, he claimed it took him about 15 minutes to come up with a beat. Cash Money's breakthrough track was Juvenile's "Ha" from his triple platinum *400 Degreez* (1998) album. "Ha" had great production – skittering snares and hi-hats, bizarre basslines ricocheting around the mix – but you couldn't understand a word Juvenile said: he rapped like he had a jar of peanut butter stuck in all those gold teeth. Called an "off-the-porch flow", Juvenile's impact was like Snoop Doggy Dogg's

in 1992: a completely original sound that took everyone by surprise. The mix of shine and grime continued on Juvenile's *G-Code: Live By It – Die By It* (2000) with tracks like "Take Them 5" and "Never Had Shit", which brought age-old Big Uneasy concerns into the present. However, "U Understand" was a discouraging novelty – a boring Mannie Fresh beat – that didn't bode well for the future.

Fresh was on top form, though, on B.G.'s *Chopper City In The Ghetto* (1999). Tracks like "Thuggin'" and "Trigga Play" may have chronicled the smokin' of fools with forensic detail, over menacing beats reminiscent of Dr. Dre's heyday, but the best track here was "Bling Bling", a 'hood fantasy so garish that it viewed the world as one big **Pen & Pixel** album cover. *Guerrilla Warfare* (1999) by **The Hot Boy$** (the Cash Money supergroup, featuring everyone on the label), followed a similar agenda and showed that the Mannie Fresh assembly line was still operating with maximum efficiency.

By the following year, though, Fresh wasn't really bouncin' no more. An endless slew of albums like *Baller Blockin'*, by **Cash Money Millionaires** (yet another label supergroup featuring whoever happened to be in the studio that day), B.G.'s *Checkmate*, Lil' Wayne's *Lights Out*, *I Got That Work*, by The **Big Tymers** (Fresh and label CEO Bryan "Baby" Williams) (all 2000) and Juvenile's

*Project English* (2001) flattened all of Fresh's fizz. As the spotlight started to shine on other southern cities, Fresh went back to the lab and fine-tuned his sound slightly on albums like Lil' Wayne's *500 Degreez* and The Big Tymers' *Hood Rich* (both 2002). Both were mildly entertaining, but nothing to match the crunktastic sounds coming from the rest of the region.

Juvenile had been complaining very publicly about Cash Money's business dealings, and when he released a compilation of up-and-coming rappers on Orpheus Records in 2002, it looked like he had flown the coop. However, *Juve The Great* appeared in 2003 and was the best Cash Money album in a while, looking like it might reinvigorate the label's flagging energy and boost their dwindling bank accounts.

### JUVENILE

**400 Degreez**
Cash Money, 1998

The lyrics are nothing to write home about, but the flow and the beats are as hot as the album's title.

### VARIOUS ARTISTS

**Cash Money Records Platinum Hits Vol. 1**
Cash Money, 2002

Featuring Juvenile's "Ha" and "Back That Azz Up", B.G.'s "Bling Bling" and The Big Tymers' "#1 Stunnas", this has all the records that changed both the lexicon and the bounce of hip-hop.

# Cash Money & Marvelous

In the mid-1980s, enterprising DJs from Philadelphia looking to make a name for themselves in a hip-hop world ruled by New York invented turntable techniques that would turn the City of Brotherly Love into the centre of DJing excellence. **Transformer scratching** (clicking the fader on and off while moving a block of sound – a riff or a short verbal phrase – across the stylus) was invented by **DJ Spinbad**, but perfected by Cash Money, perhaps the best DJ to ever come out of Philly's fertile environs. As well as perfecting transforming, Cash Money's main advance was to make scratching more rhythmic, with techniques such as the shiver and the stutter.

Under the name **Dr. Funkenstein**, Cash Money recorded the seminal early scratch record "Scratchin' To The Funk" (1985), but he would really make a name for himself a couple of years later. With his arsenal of skills, Cash Money won both the New Musical Seminar Battle for World Supremacy in 1987 and the DMC Championship in 1988, a feat duplicated only by **DJ Cheese** and **DJ Noise**. In 1987, Cash Money hooked up with Philly MC Marvelous. Although Marvelous was nowhere near the equal of "the brother with the green eyes", the duo were responsible for some solid, if not great, moments. Signing to New York's **Sleeping Bag** records in 1988, they released the occasionally funny single "All The Ugly People Be Quiet".

The humour was writ large on their only album, *Where's The Party At?* (1988), which has dated better than similarly-styled albums from the era. The album's highlight was undoubtedly the Cash Money showcase, "The Music Maker". An electric mash-up of the **Beastie Boys**, Art of Noise, James Brown, Eric B. & Rakim, **Batman** and some very 1980s horn stabs, "The Music Maker" made turntablism's weird science as infectious and as party-rocking as any Rob Base or LL Cool J

DJ Cash Money and an ugly person being quiet.

track.

The demise of Sleeping Bag in 1990 drained the duo's momentum, but they re-emerged in 1993 with a classic single, "Mighty Hard Rocker", for Warlock. With Bomb Squad-style horn squeals and chunky breaks, "Mighty Hard Rocker" may have been passé when it was released, but for those who weren't fashion-conscious, its huge beats and Marvelous's simple rhymes made the party jump. Concentrating too much on the DJ, and with boasts that wouldn't scare an old lady, Cash Money & Marvelous were anathema to the current scene, but with the renewed interest in turntable skills towards the end of the decade, Cash Money re-emerged with a large dose of his deck prowess, *Old School Need Ta Learn Plot II* (1997).

🔘 **Where's the Party At?**
Sleeping Bag, 1988

If you can find it, this is a fine example of what the non-conscious, non-gangsta hip-hop of the golden age was like.

# Chill Rob G

Born Robert Frazier, Chill Rob G came to prominence as a member of the Flavor Unit alongside **Queen Latifah**, Latee, Lakim Shabazz, Apache and **Lord Alibaski** in the late 1980s. With a flow that managed to be both declamatory and nimble, Chill Rob was probably the best of the Flavor Unit's MCs. Unfortunately, despite his mic skills, Rob's main claim to fame outside the circles of hardcore hip-hop fiends came as the result of a couple of European hacks, **Snap!**, who borrowed his vocals.

Working with producer the **45 King**, Rob released a handful of classic singles for the **Wild Pitch** label: "The Court Is Now In Session", "Wild Pitch", "Let Me Show You" and "Let the Words Flow". All of these were collected on Rob's only full-length, *Ride the Rhythm* (1989). "The Court Is Now In Session" found Rob "puttin' heads to bed" over a fierce 45 King beat constructed from **Graham Central Station**'s "The Jam" and a piercing, siren horn loop from Maceo & the Macks' "Soul Power '74". The 45 King pulled out more rabbits from his Kangol hat on "Ride the Rhythm", "Motivation"

and the **Kool & the Gang**-juiced "Let Me Show You". "Let The Words Flow" featured Rob's stentorian voice rhyming at the speed of thought over a loop of **The Police**'s "Voices Inside My Head".

German-based dance producers Benito Benites and John Garrett Virgo III (aka Snap!) took the one word version of "Let the Words Flow" and layered it over a **Jocelyn Brown** sample to create the massive hit "The Power". Both Wild Pitch and Chill Rob G objected to the track and Snap! remade "The Power" with a terrible rap by **Turbo B**, while Rob released his own version in 1990. Of course, it was Snap!'s version that was the worldwide hit, and Chill Rob quickly faded into obscurity, releasing a single in 1996 that went nowhere.

He briefly re-emerged in 2002 as a guest rapper on a couple of tracks ("Bullshit" and "Imagine That") on the *In the Red* album from British production duo **DSP**.

⊙ **Ride the Rhythm**
Wild Pitch, 1989
With classic b-boy beat science from the 45 King and assertive raps from Chill Rob G, this is an undeservedly overlooked album. (Later versions also included "The Power".)

# Chingy

Oh great, just what the world needed – another **Nelly**. Like Nelly, Chingy is from St Louis and has only one song, one cadence and one gimmick. Unlike Nelly, though, he has no cha-

risma aside from pronouncing words that rhyme with "air". Like "urr". Of course, in the new millennium this was the stuff that careers were based on.

Chingy grew up in the Walnut Park section of St Louis and almost chose the name **Thugsy** before settling on Chingy. Almost as soon as he started bubbling on the St Louis rap scene, Chingy was picked to tour with Nelly in 2002, where he was noticed by **Ludacris** and signed to his Disturbing Tha Peace imprint. His debut single, "Right Thurr" (2003), became the pop-rap sensation of the year. It wasn't hard to see why – the percolating beat, constructed of oscillating synths and syncopated handclaps, gave a bit of substance to Chingy's bludgeoning pronunciation gimmick.

Inevitably, Chingy's limited style, cadence and vocabulary couldn't sustain an entire album and, even at 60 minutes (almost an EP in the rap world these days), *Jackpot* (2003) felt way too long. The remarkably dirty (for an album largely targeted at a teen audience) "Holidae In" featured **Snoop** and Ludacris sleepwalking through the track, but still schooling Chingy. As if his one gimmick didn't spell it out clearly enough, the **Track Starz**' production – all sing-songy hooks, playground synths and Neptunes-lite rhythms – lets you know that no one saw Chingy as anything more than a novelty artist.

⊙ **Jackpot**
Capitol, 2003
Chingy exploded onto the scene with "Right Thurr" – a single that was about as catchy as they come. Of course, you can't base an entire album on funny pronunciation. But that's the beauty of pop-rap – you can just buy the single.

# Chino XL

Hip-hop has no shortage of arrogant "muhfuhs" who will talk trash about anything and everything that moves, and would diss their own mother if it fitted into their rhyme. But the nastiest, most shocking, and wittiest of them all just might be Chino XL.

Derrick Barbosa was the nephew of P-

Funk's phantom of the opera keyboard-player, **Bernie Worrell**, and as a kid spent a lot of time on tour with George Clinton's gang of merry pranksters. He grew up in East Orange, New Jersey, where in the late 1980s he formed **Art of Origin** with Kern Chandler (aka **Kaoz**). The group signed to Rick Rubin's Def American and released two singles, "No Slow Rollin'" in 1992 and "Unration-Al" in 1993, which are widely considered to be the precursors of horrorcore, with their dark occult images and sounds.

Nothing really happened with the singles, and the group broke up in 1994. Chino XL stayed with Rubin's label and released the album *Here to Save You All* (1996). One of the album's opening lyrical gambits was "Now Everlast will never last with no ghetto pass/Leave you breathin' hard like bitches at Lamaze class", and that pretty much let you know what the entire album was like. Throughout the entire album "the king of ill lines and punchlines" drops quotable rhyme after quotable rhyme with no holds barred: "Your career is George Burns/I can't believe you ain't dead yet"; "Can't be productive when your partner's just a lazy bitch/Leaves you feeling frustrated like you're signed to Wild Pitch"; "Avoid battling me like I'm Eazy E's blood samples", and so on. The production, by **Kutmasta Kurt**, DJ Homicide and Bird, is content to just sit in the background and let Chino shine.

After problems with both American and Warner Bros., Chino wasn't heard from, apart from his legendary appearances on **Sway & Tech**'s "Wake Up Show", until 2001, when he dropped *I Told You So* on the indie Metro Records. The album begins with a skit in which an automated telephone operator asks if we'd prefer to hear Chino XL "dissing everybody", "speak intelligently as a strong eloquent black man on the issues of today" or "discourse on how inner city urban job loss resulted from the shift of the US economy from a primarily industrial to a service economy". The caller obviously selects option one. While Chino delivers plenty of classic lines ("Don't even blink, and turn your voice down a decibel/Or start lookin' for a studio that's wheel-chair-accessible" and "I hate to end this off on a bad note like SWV live"), he didn't really name names like he did first time around. The unrepentant glee he used to show had been replaced by the hard-bitten anger of someone that's been burned.

Aside from numerous acting roles in straight-to-video films, Chino re-recorded a previously shelved album, *Poison Pen*, which was released by Activate in 2004, and was involved in a couple of tracks on the long-promised *Four Horsemen* record with **Canibus**, Ras Kass, Killah Priest and Kurupt.

⊙ **Here to Save You All**
**American, 1996**

Quincy Jones refused to clear a sample because of Chino's lyrics, the lawyers had to excise a rhyme about Monie Love and chlamydia, but that didn't save OJ Simpson, Whitney Houston, Tupac, Arthur Ashe, Liberace or any of the cast of thousands who get lambasted by Chino on this rip-roaring romp through some of the choicest battle rhymes in hip-hop history.

# Chubb Rock

Born Richard Simpson in Jamaica, Chubb Rock brought the Kingston dancehall's love of deep, stentorian voices to hip-hop. After dropping out of college, he hooked up with his cousin **Hitman Howie Tee** and made the instantly forgettable *Chubb Rock Featuring Hitman Howie Tee* (1988). Somehow he managed to hang on to his recording contract and released the excellent single "Caught Up" (1989). Based on a sample from **Inner Life**'s disco classic "Caught Up (In A One Night Love Affair), "Caught Up" highlighted Chubb's rhythmic flexibility and made him one of the most popular rappers of the era.

"Caught Up" was the lead cut on his very fine album *And The Winner Is...* (1989). "Ya Bad Chubbs" found Chubb spitting on top of the beat from **Lyn Collins**' "Think", while on "And The Winner Is... (The Grammys)" Chubb lectured the **National Academy of Recording Arts and Sciences** on hip-hop history.

In 1990 Chubb and Howie Tee continued their disco sampling with the classic "Treat 'Em Right". With string stabs and a chorus from **First Choice**'s "Love Thang", "Treat 'Em Right" was an exhilarating whirlwind – Chubb's baritone moving at something approaching light speed, but never losing sight of the groove. *The One* (1991) followed and, while it couldn't maintain the high standards of *And The Winner Is...*, it featured a couple of excellent cuts in the form of the anti-drug "Night Scene" and the number one rap hit "The Chubbster".

*I Gotta Get Mine Yo!* (1992) saw Chubb stagnating and getting left behind, although it did feature a moody and apocalyptic prayer for peace, "Lost in the Storm". Chubb Rock was definitely a product of the late 1980s, and he wasn't to be heard from again until he released the surprisingly decent comeback album, *The Mind* in 1997. With production now handled by Easy Mo Bee and KRS-One, *The Mind* ditched the light-hearted rhymes of old and followed where "Lost in the Storm" left off.

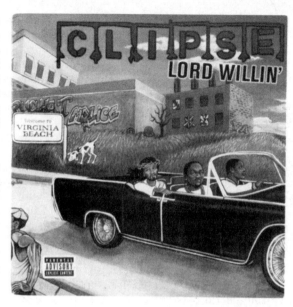

⊙ **And The Winner Is...**
Select, 1989

Fast, furious, funny, and with great production — what more could you want from a hip-hop album?

# The Clipse

Sure, hip-hop is mostly about who you know rather than what you know, but once you've had the door opened for you, you've got to have the skills to stay there. **Pusha T** and **Malice**, brothers from New York transplanted to the new r&b/hip-hop capital of Virginia, might have been long-time friends of über-producers **The Neptunes**, but their street reportage is just about compelling enough not to need their Midas touch.

The Clipse first came to attention in 1999 with "The Funeral", a New York-style track with a from-beyond-the-grave rap. After some problems with Elektra, they ditched an already recorded album,

signed with The Neptunes' fledgling **Star Track** imprint and recorded the album *Lord Willin'* (2002). Unlike just about every other hip-hop album of the period, *Lord Willin'* was produced entirely by The Neptunes. There were no outsiders used for the club track, the r&b crossover, the radio jam, the quiet storm move, the West Coast slow-roller... nothin'. This fact alone gave it a leg up on the competition, and when the beats were as good as those on *Lord Willin'* it was something special. The lead single, "Grindin'", was simply an all-time classic: utterly menacing kick drums punctuated by snares that sounded like stalactites dropping on your head, Pusha injecting a bit of humour into the drug-dealing tale with lines like "Call me subwoofer 'cause I pump base like that".

The album was more than just one titanic single, however. The semi-autobiographical "Young Boy" was funky like **Ernie Shavers** in denim overalls, while the street documentary of "Virginia" showed that the Old Dominion wasn't just for lovers.

Pusha T and Malice subsequently appeared on numerous tracks and remixes: **Mad Skillz**' VA version of "The Symphony", "Crew Deep" (2003), **Kelis**'s "Milkshake" remix (2003) and **E-40**'s super-hot "Quarterbackin'" (2003). "Blaze Of Glory", their contribution to the compilation *Neptunes' Present: Clones* (2003), was one of its highlights: a refined and more subtle take on "Grindin'"'s bare-bones simplicity.

**Lord Willin'**
Star Track/Arista, 2002

The production is so good that even Jadakiss doesn't drop the ball when he appears on "I'm Not You". Pusha T and Malice more than hold their own, though, with their hustlin' rhymes and novel nasal flows.

# cLOUDdead

◊ See *Anticon*

# Cold Crush Brothers

They weren't the first hip-hop crew to make a record, but unless you lived on Sedgewick Ave. in The Bronx in 1978, the **Cold Crush Brothers**' rhymes were the first ones you ever heard. When Sugarhill's **Sylvia Robinson** first heard Henry "Big Bank Hank" Jackson rapping along to a tape in a New Jersey pizzeria, it was a tape of a Cold Crush Brothers show that he was listening to. When **Big Bank Hank** and the rest of the Sugar Hill Gang recorded "Rapper's Delight", they borrowed liberally from Cold Crush Brother **Grandmaster Caz**'s book of rhymes. Although they laid the foundation for all subsequent hip-hop MCs, Caz, **DJ Charlie Chase**, Tony Tone, JDL, the **Almighty Kay-Gee** and Easy AD have never really made a record that lives up to their reputation. Nevertheless, the Cold Crush Brothers remain one of the most legendary crews in hip-hop history.

Despite their contribution to making hip-hop a commercial force, Cold Crush would have to wait until 1982 to make their first record, "Weekend", for the Elite label. Most people's introduction to Cold Crush, however, was in Charlie Ahearn's 1983 film, *Wild Style*. With lines like "Charlie Chase as cute as can be/You'd

Grandmaster Caz cold crushin'.

sell your soul to the devil to play like me", their first appearance during the basketball court battle with their old foes, the **Fantastic Five**, might not have been awe-inspiring, but they had charisma to spare. That charisma came to the fore on their awesome performance at the South Bronx's Dixie club. One of the definitive old school documents, their five-minute live showcase in the movie was simply electric and influenced all hip-hop live shows that followed. Very few have managed to match it.

Apart from their contributions to the **Wild Style** soundtrack, Cold Crush's best record was "Fresh, Wild, Fly and Bold" (1984). Featuring huge drum machines and electro blips, "Fresh, Wild, Fly and Bold" was packed with b-boy energy. The only problem was that, by the time it came out, Run DMC and LL Cool J were making the old school ancient history. Soon afterwards, Caz left the crew and released a few solo records for Tuff City, such as "The Judge" (1987) and "The Hitman" (1990), which showed that Caz was able to make the transition in rap styles better than any of his contemporaries. Meanwhile, Kay-Gee and Tony Tone continued the Cold Crush Brothers as a duo, and recorded *Troopers* (1988) for B-Boy Records.

With old school nostalgia running rampant in the late 1990s, some legendary Cold Crush performances have been released. *The Cold Crush Brothers All The Way Live in '82* (1994) on Tuff City and *Cold Crush Brothers Vs. The Fantastic Romantic 5* (1998) both captured Cold Crush at the height of their powers and are well worth searching out.

**All The Way Live In '82**
Tuff City, 1994

Long before the advent of the DAT, the Cold Crush did it all the way live and better than anyone else, no matter how much technology the big names might have today.

# Common (Sense)

Hip-hop may have its Grandmasters, Lords, Kings and Big Daddies, but one of its biggest talents has taken a rather more run-of-the-mill name. Common Sense (Lonnie Rashied Lynn) burst out of the hip-hop backwater of Chicago at the beginning of the 1990s with a nasal, b-boy cold flow and one of the smoothest deliveries around. His debut album, *Can I Borrow a Dollar?* (1992), may be the work of an MC who had yet to find his identity, but it had enough pure skills and lateral thinking on display to let heads know that Common wasn't as workaday as his name. Although "Heidi Hoe" had production by **The Beatnuts**, the highlight was undoubtedly "Soul By The Pound", a serious head-nodder that had Common claiming he was "fatter than heavy metal and harder than punk rock".

By the time of his second album, *Resurrection* (1994), the laidback keyboards of the debut had developed into a fully-fledged jazz aesthetic and Common Sense had become as conscious as his mic name. "I Used To Love H.E.R." was a dazzling extended metaphor that viewed hip-hop as an unfaithful lover, and instigated a beef with **Ice Cube**. On tracks

Common talking sense.

like "Resurrection", "Watermelon" ("I stand out like a nigga on a hockey team") and "Sum Shit I Wrote", meanwhile, the callow rhymes of the first album had become a warm and funny style that seemed to have faith in hip-hop's sacrament that wordplay can transform one's surroundings. He was so confident in his abilities that on "Pop's Rap" he invited his father to drop some knowledge.

Losing his "Sense", a rechristened Common's *One Day It'll All Make Sense* (1997), unfortunately, failed to build on the foundation of *Resurrection*. All the elements were there — particularly on "Retrospect For Life", a duet with **Lauryn Hill** which found him meditating on responsibility, the value of life and abortion — but they didn't come together. Far better were his indie singles of 1999. On "Like They Used to Say/1-9-9-9", Common dropped a Gil-Scott-Heron-thinking-he's-Billy-Dee-Williams flow over **Dug Infinite**'s easy listening motif, while on "Car Horn", **45 King**'s loping, off-kilter shuffle remembered the days when funky meant greasy and stinky, rather than the polish of David Axelrod

or Jeff Lorber.

*Like Water For Chocolate* (2000) was hailed in many quarters as a masterpiece, but it was suffocated by its relentless bohemianism. The production (by **Jay Dee**, D'Angelo, ?uestlove, James Poyser and **DJ Premier**) was often staggering, but, like Common's rhymes, it was impressive rather than likeable.

*Electric Circus* (2002) was more of the same, despite the presence of **The Neptunes** (on "I Got A Right Ta") to knock Common out of his cosmic torpor. Tracks like "Star*69 (PS With Love)" and "Aquarius" (both performed with r&b singer **Bilal**) were straight-up quiet storm ballads – Common trying to come across like an empyrean **Barry White** – while tracks like "Soul Power" were simply messy.

◉ **Resurrection**
Relativity, 1994

Before he became all smug in his daishikis and knit caps, Common released this mesmerising, infectious album that never sacrificed hooks for intelligence.

Co Flow's DJ Mr Len, stoking the fire in which you burn slow.

# Company Flow

Exploding out of Brooklyn with the wildest beats and illest rhymes, screaming that they were "independent as fuck", **Company Flow** was the most original hip-hop crew around. Unlike too many "independent" hip-hop artists, who are merely minor league MCs waiting for a major label break, **El-P** (Jamie Meline), DJ **Mr. Len** (Leonard Smythe) and **Bigg Juss** created uncompromising, extremely challenging hip-hop that wouldn't know jiggy if **Lil' Kim** came up and shook her thing in its face.

Co Flow began when Mr. Len met El-P while he was DJing at his 18th birthday party. The following year El-P and Len released the single "Juvenile Techniques" (1993) as Company Flow. With Bigg Juss coming on board, the *Funcrusher* EP (1995) followed on the group's own Official Recordings label. It would be the "8 Steps To Perfection/Vital Nerve" single in 1996, however, that would establish Company Flow as the voice of the underground. On "8 Steps To Perfection", a smooth 1970s soul string part straight out of **Dr. Dre**'s repertoire got dissolved and acid-washed into an attenuated blur,

while El-P bragged that he was "the third gunner on the grassy knoll" and that he had "manners like Bruce Banner when he's stressed". "Vital Nerve", meanwhile, was a savage battle rhyme that managed to be both brutally minimal and viciously funky.

After 1997's brilliant "Info Kill" single, the group signed to indie titans Rawkus and released the devastating *Funcrusher Plus* (1997) album. Hearkening back to the raw, old school productions of **Schooly D**, Run DMC and Audio Two, Funcrusher Plus was filled with stale, musty atmospheres that were punctuated by what sounded like shards of metal. Its tracks were so disjointed that they felt like the nightmares in *The Manchurian Candidate* movie and its scratching lay somewhere between the battle scars of the **X-Ecutioners** and the switchblade slashes of **DJ Code Money**. As shown by the stunning "Last Good Sleep" (that rarest of things in hip-hop, a track that not only confronts misogyny, but also admits to weakness and failure), their emotional palette extended beyond their egos. While Big Juss pierced vital nerves with brutal funk, the William Gibson and Philip K Dick-inspired El-P described himself thus: "Triple felon MC minus the melanin/ When I bomb I talk with the shit to make Baby Jessica jump back in the well again."

Even with all of the science on display, Co Flow didn't neglect the groove. They had enough sense to keep things down to earth, quoting professional wrestlers, and specialising in the one-line mini-epiphanies that are hip-hop's raison d'être: "My shit is like *War And Peace*, yours is just the Cliff Notes" and "Fuckin' with your theology like Darwinism in the Bible Belt". Just for good measure, *Funcrusher Plus* also included the mind-boggling track from the **Indelible MCs** (Co Flow with **J-Treds** and **The Juggaknots**), "The Fire In Which You Burn".

The *End To End Burners* EP (1998) was another disorientating body blow to hip-hop syntax. As El-P rapped on "Krazy Kings Too", sounding like he was trapped in one of his own loops, "Kid, I feel asphyxiated/I wear the city air like wet leather/Alarmed that the populace dwells so closely together". The *Little Johnny From The Hospital* (1999) instrumental album attempted to shift paradigms once again. Trying to recreate the feeling of the mid-1980s, when hip-hop was a gruff, assertive challenge of sheer attitude, by using aggressive drum machines, wayward video game noises and punitive basslines, El-P's soundworld was abrasive and menacing, where hip-hop's traditional funk snippets became de-funked, or "funcrushed". Like the **Bomb Squad**, **George Clinton** and **Miles Davis**, Company Flow rearranged and reinterpreted James Brown's original bitches' brew in a bubbling cauldron of seething funk.

Inevitably, all this intensity was too much and El-P and Mr. Len split (Bigg Juss had left the group after *End To End Burners*). While El-P went on to set up

Big Juss, former Co Flow MC, now psychotic-alien-collaborator, and concoctor of Black Mamba Serums.

the equally forbidding **Definitive Jux** label, which released extraordinary albums from El-P, Cannibal Ox, Mr. Lif and Aesop Rock, Mr. Len released *Pity the Fool...* (2001), a dark, moody album that just about managed to allow a few cracks of light to puncture the hardcore veneer. Bigg Juss, meanwhile, formed his own **Sub Verse** label, releasing records like **KMD**'s controversial *Black Bastards* album, **Scienz of Life**'s *Coming Forth By Day* and his own *Plantation Rhymes* EP. Teaming up with underground Californian rapper **Orko Eloheim** (aka Orko the Sycotik Alien) as **NMS** (Nephilim Modulation Systems), Bigg Juss released *Woe To Thee O Land Whose King Is A Child* (2003), a sci-fi concept album about living in George W. Bush's "Amerikkka". A magnum opus that he had been all the while working and re-working emerged in 2004 as *Black Mamba Serums V2.0*, an album on Big Dada records that veered from the timely hysteria of "Suburban Nightmare Texas Size New World Order" to the homespun bathos of "No Dessert Til You Eat Your Vegetables".

( • ) **Funcrusher Plus**
Official/Rawkus, 1997

Dropping the most inspirational sucker MC disses since Roxanne Shanté over the harshest beats since Schooly D, this was not only hip-hop classicism of the most brutal kind, but the most original since Public Enemy.

# Coolio

Long before he made his fantastic voyage to the top of the pop charts, Coolio (né Artis Ivey) was a reformed basehead who joined up with **WC** and **DJ Crazy Toones** to form **WC and the MAAD Circle**. The group's debut album, *Ain't A Damn Thing Changed* (1991), was a classic slice of West Coast hardcore funk that tempered its gangsta-isms with biting social commentary.

After working with the LA hip-hop collective **40 Thievz**, Coolio went solo and recorded *It Takes A Thief* (1994) with **DJ Brian "The Wino" Dobbs**. At the peak of G-Funk, "Fantastic Voyage", which liberally sampled **Lakeside**'s funk-lite masterpiece of the same name, smoothed out the LA sound with more streamlined beats and a light-hearted fantasy of the good life. Its sense of humour, focus on the lighter side of the gangsta lifestyle and inclusivity pushed "Fantastic Voyage" to number three on the US pop chart. *It Takes a Thief* wasn't all about the good times, however, as tracks like "County Line" catalogued the degradations of poverty and welfare.

Although Coolio's vision darkened considerably on his follow-up album, *Gangsta's Paradise* (1995) was an even bigger success. The title track, which also featured on the soundtrack to the **Michelle Pfieffer** movie *Dangerous Minds*, was one of the year's biggest pop hits, reaching number one worldwide and staying on the charts for some 40 weeks. Based on a reworking of **Stevie Wonder**'s "Pastime Paradise" and making it sinister with slashing strings and a perilously deep bassline, "Gangsta's Paradise" proved that pop-rap didn't have to be as cartoonish as Jazzy Jeff and the Fresh Prince, or as mindless as Tone Loc. While *Gangsta's Paradise* also included decent tracks like "Too Hot" and "Kinda High, Kinda Drunk", it featured lame covers of **Smokey Robinson**'s "Cruisin'" and Billy Paul's "A Thing Goin' On" that threatened to undo any respectability the be-dreaded one had earned with the title track.

Following the blueprint of "Cruisin'" rather than "Gangsta's Paradise", *My Soul* (1997) failed to build on Coolio's artistic and commercial success. Coolio tried to be a Hollywood player with an acting role in the straight-to-video *Tyrone*, but all he proved was that he was no Will Smith. When radio and MTV fully embraced **Jay-Z**'s pottymouth and **DMX**'s bark, it seemed unlikely that Coolio would recapture his commercial pre-eminence – which was proven by the reception granted to *El Cool Magnifico* (2002), a tragic album that found the former prince of the mainstream desperately trying to catch up to a world that had completely changed.

Coolio. He no longer lives in a gangsta's paradise.

(•) **Fantastic Voyage: The Greatest Hits**
Tommy Boy, 2001

Featuring the title track, "Too Hot", "Gangsta's Paradise" and "1,2,3,4 (Sumpin' New)", this is about as catchy as hip-hop gets.

# Cormega

Queensbridge rapper Cormega first came up alongside **Nas** in the early 1990s but, while his former friend became one of hip-hop's greatest MCs, Cormega's career has taken more twists and turns than that of Nick Cassavetes. First, a bid in prison stalled his career (Nas's song "One Love" was dedicated to him). When Cormega was released, he appeared on "Affirmative Action" (1996) with Nas, Foxy Brown and AZ, and the hip-hop supergroup **The Firm** was born.

However, Cormega was left off **Foxy Brown**'s B-side "La Firmillia" in 1996, and, when the time came to record The Firm's album, Cormega was ditched in favour of the rapper **Nature** for reasons unknown. Cormega released the rugged but not entirely devastating diss track "Fuck Nas and Nature" in response in 1997. Cormega's scheduled Def Jam album, *The Testament*, was endlessly delayed and only a few tracks have ever emerged (on 1998's Def Jam compilation called *Survival of the Illest*). More label troubles ensued and the only Cormega track to get a major release during this period was "Who Can I Trust?" with **The Hot Boys** from *Violator: The Album* (1999).

Cormega finally released an album in 2001, *The Realness*. Despite his smooth voice, it was evident that Mega was certainly no halfway crook. His hustling tales were vivid and unflinching, as were his disses of Nas: "Who's tale you tellin'? Are you frail or felon?/Was you making sales or watching niggas selling?/You exploit niggas' lives in your rhymes and then avoid 'em/You never felt the moisture in the air from coke boiling".

Given his history, it was entirely possible that this would be his only album, so *Hustler/Rapper* (2002), a collection of freestyles, sketches and half-finished tracks was rush-released to capitalise on *The Realness*. After an attempted reconciliation with Nas on "The Bridge 2001", Cormega came back firing darts at him again on *The True Meaning* (2002): "I was never jealous of you, in fact I was proud of you/I smiled when I heard you on 'Live At The Barbeque'/I respect you as an artist though I'm no longer fond of you/I gave you love from the

heart unlike the people surroundin' you". The beats this time around were from **Alchemist**, Hangmen 3, DR Period, Hi-Tek and **Buckwild** and were stronger than on his debut.

*Legal Hustle* (2004) was a disappointment. There were way too many guest appearances (from **Large Professor**, MOP, Ghostface, Kurupt, Jayo Felony, AZ, Tony Touch and the female **MC Doña**). The production was tired, uninspired and nowhere near as good as *True Meaning*, particularly on "Beautiful Mind", which was a straight jack of the **Isaac Hayes** piano from "Make the Music With Your Mouth Biz".

**● True Meaning**
Legal Hustle/Landspeed, 2002

On his second album, Cormega shows the skills, especially his exquisite breath control, that make him a favourite of the purists. Excellent production and a smaller chip on his shoulder than he had on his debut make this the choice item in Cormega's unjustifiably small catalogue.

# The Coup

Politics and music often make strange bedfellows, but along with **Public Enemy** and **Boogie Down Productions**, The Coup, from Oakland, California, have managed that all too rare feat of making

political hip-hop that is also great hip-hop. One of the reasons that they succeed where so many others fail is that they walk it like they talk it: **MC Boots Riley** has been a community activist since he was in high school, while the group's other MC, **E-Roc**, is a union organiser. On the symbolic front, **DJ Pam the Funkstress** is one of the most visible female DJs in hip-hop, working with **Saafir** and the **Conscious Daughters** as well as The Coup.

Boots formed The Coup in 1990 after joining the **Mau Mau Rhythm Collective**, an organisation that used hip-hop to address community and political issues. The group's debut EP, *The Coup: The EP*, was released in 1991 without much fanfare on Polemic Records. Signing to Wild Pitch, The Coup's message should have reached the masses but, by this time, the label was on its last legs. *Kill My Landlord* (1993) mixed didacticism with rolling, East Bay funk, as revolutionary tracks like "Dig It" and "Not Yet Free" moved both asses and minds by combining the politics of **Paris** with the rubbery funk of **E-40**.

1994's *Genocide And Juice* was a gangsta parody that, with cameos from Spice 1 and E-40, was probably too close to its subject matter to be really effective. Biting tracks like "Fat Cats, Bigga Fish", though, made their intentions clear. Wild Pitch dissolved soon after *Genocide And Juice* was released, however, and the group members returned to community activism, with Boots founding the **Young Comrades**, a youth group that protests against the racism of the Oakland police.

In 1999 The Coup returned with perhaps their best album, *Steal This Album*. Boots' flow had gotten progressively less stentorian and more typical of that Cali drawl, but instead of being a sell-out move, it was really a clever strategy to get the group's message across. Tracks like "Me And Jesus The Pimp In A '79 Granada Last Night" might sound on a cursory listen like your average bitch-slapping, mack tale (even though details like "His name was Jesus/Slapped a ho to pieces with his plastic prosthesis" let you know that this was out of the ordinary), but The Coup subverted the genre conventions and made

it a moving, scary tale that was every bit the equal of Funkadelic's "Cosmic Slop". Unlike most politically motivated crews, The Coup didn't sacrifice pleasure for the message: there's humour, someone pissin' on George Washington's grave and production that is shockingly lush, consider-

ing it comes from such guerrilla operatives. **Karl Marx** was probably turning in his grave.

The original cover of *Party Music* (2001) might have cheered him up, though – attacking as it did the prime symbol of global capitalism. However, the FBI weren't too happy about it. Completed in June 2001 but not released, the startlingly prescient cover showed Boots and Pam in front of an exploding World Trade Center, with Boots pressing the button on a detonator. Of course, after September 11th, there was a huge furore over the image, after it was circulated on the Internet. The album was finally released with a cocktail glass on the cover, an image which made absolutely no sense whatsoever, considering the incendiary political comment found inside. Even though the mostly live instrumentation gave the album a warm feel, the message of tracks like "5 Million Ways To Kill A CEO" and "Ghetto Manifesto" was utterly unmistakable.

⦿ **Steal This Album**
Dogday, 1999

With blaxploitation beats, clever rhymes and well thought-out politics, revolution hasn't sounded this good since the glory days of Public Enemy.

# Crash Crew

From Harlem's Lincoln Projects, Crash Crew were one of the greatest, if most undersung, of the old school groups. **EK Mike C**, **La Shubee**, **G-Man**, **Barry Bistro**, **Reggie Reg** and **DJ Darryl C** first got together at a talent show in 1977 when they were all 15 or 16 years old. They started promoting parties around Harlem and along with **Treacherous Three** and **Fearless Four**, they became one of Manhattan's biggest crews. Using a lot of harmonies in their routines, the group had a unique sound that fleshed out their very typical old school rhymes.

Crash Crew's first record came out under the name of **Disco Dave and the Force of Five MCs**. "High Power Rap" (1980) was one of the high-water marks of old school hip-hop. The record has been sampled and borrowed from dozens of times (Beastie Boys' "Hey Ladies", LL Cool J's "Jinglin' Baby", and Jay-Z's "Girls, Girls, Girls" for starters). Released on the group's friends' Mike & Dave Records, "High Power Rap" was a studio recreation of a routine they used to do live on top of the break from **Freedom**'s "Get Up and Dance". A few months later, **Grandmaster Flash & the Furious Five**'s "Freedom" used the same break and there was a mild beef between the two crews.

Disco Dave and DJ Darryl C also appeared on the Boogie Boys featuring Kool Ski and Kid Delight's "Rappin' Ain't No Thing" (1981), another oft-sampled ("We are willin'") rarity on Mike & Dave, but, right around this time, **Sugar Hill** signed the Crash Crew in order to quell the beef with the **Furious Five**. Their first record on Sugar Hill was "We Want to Rock" (1981), but it was "Breaking Bells (Take Me To The Mardi Gras)" (1982) that was more notable. With its fusion of **Bob James**' "Take Me To The Mardi Gras" break and electro-shocked drum machine programming, the record was effectively a bridge between the old school's first phase and the new drum-machine phase. Also from this period was the promo-only "Scratching" (1982), a fearsome performance from the Sugar Hill house band on the groove from **Magic Disco Machine**'s "Scratchin'".

"We Are Known As Emcees (We Turn The Party Out)" (1983) was more drum-machine madness and was the best example of the group's harmonizing style. "On The Radio" (1983) followed in similar style on Sugar Hill subsidary Bay City, but by this point Sugar Hill was struggling and the group was growing dissatisfied. "Here We Are" (1984) was the group's last record for Sugar Hill before they left. In 1985 the group hooked up with a young **Teddy Riley** and recorded "Crash Crew's Back", but the record, along with a re-recorded version of "High Power Rap", wasn't released until 1987. By this point, however, most of the group had quit rap, several of them becoming police officers.

**We Are Emcees**
Sequel, 2001

Part of Sequel's Sugar Hill reissue series, this compiles pretty much everything the group recorded for Sugar Hill. It's an essential old school document. The only bummer is that "High Power Rap" only appears here in a shortened demo version. If you can't afford a couple of hundred bucks for the original, it's on *Harlem World: The Sound of the Big Apple Rappin'* (Heroes & Villains, 2001).

# Crucial Conflict

One of the most ridiculous gimmicks in rap somehow didn't sink Chicago's Crucial Conflict. Instead, the usual industry shenanigans did. Rewriting G-Funk as a bizarre black cowboy music they called **RODEO** (Rhymes Of Dirty English Organisation), **Wildstyle**, **Cold Hard**, **NEVER** and **Kilo** viewed the West Side of Chicago as the Wild West, complete with Death Valley, barn dances, marauding injuns and gun fights. Their oater imagery didn't stop with their music either: they all sported Native American braids and denim overalls, and their signature dance steps (sort of like bucking a bronco) were called "giddy-up".

The group's debut album, *The Final Tic* (1996), went gold on the strength of "Hay", one of hip-hop's great odes to the kind bud. Slowing down the West Coast sound to a crawl, but with all sorts of percussion bouncing around underneath, "Hay" sounded as disarmingly disorienting as what they rapped about. Elsewhere, though, their rapid-fire rhymes had people accusing them of stealing **Bone Thugs-N-Harmony**'s style. These comparisons would dog their career.

Despite going gold, the group had little to show for it, due to not understanding how the industry worked, and their follow-up suffered because of it. **Good Side Bad Side** (1998) showed the group struggling unsuccessfully to both shake off any Bone Thugs resemblance, and to come to grips with a post-G-Funk world that had now embraced the sound of **Timbaland**, the producer who managed to give the South's percussion (which Crucial Conflict borrowed) a spit shine. *The Call Of The Wild* (2001) failed to rectify the problems, and almost nobody heard it.

⊙ **The Final Tic**
Palla/Universal, 1996

The fact is that RODEO ain't all that different from what was coming out of both the West and the South, but on "Hay" they managed to concoct a sound that was original and intoxicating.

# Cypress Hill

Rapping about *la vida loca* long before it became a mainstream concern, LA hip-hop's multi-racial group of vatos, Cypress Hill, changed the face of hip-hop in the early 1990s. Enjoying and endorsing cannabis at a time when the inner city was still reeling from crack, Cypress Hill combined the **Bomb Squad**'s production sound with a West Coast pimp roll to produce a dusty, blunted style. As one of their songs put it, "stoned is the way of the walk".

**Lawrence Muggerud** was a relocated New Yorker who had gotten his start with LA crew **7A3**, which had a moderate hit with a hip-hop remake of Queen's "We Will Rock You" (1987). When they dissolved, DJ Muggs and 7A3 rapper **B-Real** (Louis Freese) hooked up with former DVX hypeman **Sen Dog** (Senen

Reyes) and formed Cypress Hill in 1989. Their eponymous debut album of 1991 attempted to remake **Cheech and Chong**'s *Up In Smoke* for barrio dwellers who came strapped with both a gat and a one-hitter. But where Cheech and Chong were just dopey, Cypresss Hill were sardonic and menacing: Muggs' production was murkier than month-old bongwater and B-Real's nasal whine was cartoonish, biting and full of "just don't give a fuck" attitude all at the same time, as he rapped nursery rhymes about killing cops. Tracks like "How I Could Just Kill A Man" and "Hand On The Pump" were dripping with both THC and casual violence.

*Black Sunday* (1993) was a self-confessed rushed follow-up to their double platinum debut. While its Mary-Jane-and-glocks schlock didn't break any new ground, it did feature the massive single "Insane in the Membrane", and it pushed their sound into the paranoiac realm that inevitably comes with massive marijuana intake. *Cypress Hill III: Temples of Boom* (1995) continued their journey into the heart of darkness, with brooding atmospheres and creeping beats creating a kind of gangsta psychedelia. There were no moments of abandon where the crowd could throw their hands in the air – with the exception of the fittingly-titled "Throw Your Set In The Air". Even the **Ice Cube** diss "No Rest For The Wicked", couldn't lift the vibe of this discomfiting gangsta critique.

After a three-year lay-off, which found Muggs producing *The Soul Assassins* (1997) compilation, *Cypress Hill IV* (1998) signalled the group retreating into the caricatures that they always threatened to become. *Los Grandes Éxitos en Español* (1999) was a somewhat artistically pointless, if perhaps culturally significant, greatest hits album done entirely in Spanish. The album also marked the arrival of percussionist Eric Bobo as fully-fledged member of the group after appearing on their tours. *Skull & Bones* (2000) was one half vintage (or generic) Cypress Hill, one half **Kid Rock/Limp Bizkit** rap-rock brio. The *Skull* disc was all eerie pianos, Latino lingo, zooted beats and their trademark, jump-around war chants. The *Bones* disc featured a wailing cameo from **Fear Factory** guitarist Dino Cazares dishing out the thrash on "Get Out Of My Head", while "Dust" was pure heavy metal rowdiness.

*Live at the Fillmore* (2000) continued to please their skater demographic with more rap-rock hysterics. With bludgeoning power chords (courtesy of members of rock band **SX-10**) turning already rowdy tracks like "A To The K" and "(Rock) Superstar" into mosh-pit marauders, *Live at the Fillmore* was one of the most intense, energetic live albums not just in hip-hop history (which wouldn't be difficult), but in recorded music, period.

*Stoned Raiders* (2001) continued where the previous two albums left off, although with diminishing returns, sounding like Cypress were trying to get high off the resin residue left in their bongs. Apart from the collaboration with reggaeton sensation Tego Calderón, "Latin Thugs", *Till Death Do Us Part* (2004) was even more of a buzzkill.

**Cypress Hill**
Ruffhouse/Columbia, 1991

Inventing blunted hip-hop with one broad stroke, making in-roads into the Beastie Boys/Lollapalooza crowd, managing to be both experimental and populist at the same time, this is one of the true classics of hip-hop.

# dälek

An MC who names himself after the robots from **Dr Who**, an album title demonstrating an etymological link between blackness and death – on a record label better known for its punk acts – yup, this is underground hip-hop of the most extreme kind. **dälek** (Will Brooks) and partner **Oktopus** (Alap Momin) met in the mid-1990s at William Patterson College in New Jersey, where they collaborated on making the beats that would eventually be used on the album **Negro Necro Nekros** (1998).

With the turntable skills of **DJ Rek** added, *Negro Necro Nekros* was released on the Gern Blandsten label, and the punk connection could be heard in the gritty, industrial rhythms, the nine minutes of feedback ("Praise Be The Man"), the **William Burroughs** samples and dälek's intense, unhead-noddable rhymes. dälek's combination of noise and beat inevitably attracted the attention of British feedback aesthete **Kevin Martin**, who invited them to remix and tour with his group **Techno Animal**. The Matador 12" "Megaton/Classical Homicide" (2000) bore the fruit of this match made in unholy heaven. In 2001 dälek guested on the debut album from like-mind and labelmate **MC Oddateee**, entitled *Steely Darkglasses*, a set with production from Oktopus that combined the craziness of Kool Keith with the jazziness of the Hieroglyphics.

*From Filthy Tongues Of Griots And Gods* (2002) was another pairing for dälek with an underground rock maverick and his label – in this case, ex-Faith No More frontman **Mike Patton**, on his Ipecac imprint. Where *Negro Necro Nekros* often sought after the beauty in grime, this album just wallowed in the industrial muck and was not nearly as compelling. dälek traded in the crunch for the glitch on *Ruin It* (2002), a remix swap shop with blippy electronica prankster **Kid606**.

dälek's grab-bag of sounds often sounded like nothing so much as the Krautrock legends **Faust**, on their *Faust Tapes* album, and so it came as little surprise that dälek collaborated with the group on *Derbe Respect, Alder* (2004). Essentially Faust jams that had been treated and rapped over by dälek, *Derbe Respect, Alder* was often unrelentingly bleak, but at its best it was potent, paranoid political music of the highest order.

◉ **Negro Necro Nekros**
Gern Blandsten, 1998

It's not for everyone, but underground aesthetes will appreciate the disorientating collages, aggressive feedback and dälek's spooky and imagistic lyrics. The were moments of light, however – especially on "Images Of .44 Casings", a poetic meta-rap of grim beauty.

# Dana Dane

D ana McCleese's rap career started when he befriended a British expatriate by the name of Ricky Walters at the LaGuardia High School of Music & Arts. The two became known as the **Kangol Crew** and performed at various park jams and battles throughout the city. While MC Ricky D hooked up with **Doug E Fresh** in 1984 and would soon become known to the world as **Slick Rick**, Dana Dane borrowed his friend's quasi-English accent, but has stayed in his shadow ever since.

"Nightmares" was released on Profile in 1985, due to its producer, Sam Jacobs, playing in the band that played at the bar mitzvah of the brother of label head Cory Robbins. Released a few months after Slick Rick's "La-Di-Da-Di", "Nightmares" was almost a carbon copy with the Queen's English raps and the long narrative about troublesome females. The only difference was that "Nightmares" replaced Doug E Fresh's human beatboxing with a *Munsters* keyboard riff.

1986's "Delancey Street", a tale about

Dana Dane getting robbed by three women on the Lower East Side, wasn't as big a hit, but was less reliant on Slick Rick's style. Ironically, Dana Dane was perhaps the bigger star of the two at this point in their careers, and his *Dana Dame With Fame* (1987), recorded largely with Hurby "Love Bug" Azor, was "Nightmares" writ large, with plenty of novelty tracks like "Cinderfella Dana Dane" keeping the album firmly in that goofy style that characterised many early rap albums.

*Dana Dane 4 Ever* (1990) was released three years later and, compared to everyone else, Dana Dane sounded like he was rapping in a time machine. Producer **Clark Kent** did the best he could, but Dane's lighthearted, comedic raps sounded positively archaic compared to **Public Enemy**, N.W.A., BDP, **De La Soul** and the new school. Needless to say, *Rollin' Wit Dana Dane* (1995), in which he tried to come off hardcore, was utterly ridiculous, despite some solid production from **DJ Battlecat**.

Dana Dane couldn't take the hint, however, and he continued to release singles that no one was interested in, like "Let Me Do My Thing" (1999). A duet with **Slick Rick** ("Pimpin' Ain't Easy (The Godfather Theme)") from the *WWF Aggression* (2000) album was slightly more interesting, but only because of Rick's appearance. Bizarrely, Dana turned up on underground rapper **Thirstin Howl III**'s album *Skillitary* (2004).

◉ **The Best of Dana Dane**
BMG, 2002

You certainly don't need anything other than his first album, but this is easier to find, and Dana, sporting white argyle socks, a beret and clear Cazals, looks great on the cover.

# Das EFX

D as EFX, the duo of **Krazy Drayz** (Andre Weston) and **Skoob** (Willie Hines), started rapping together at Virginia State University in 1988. Performing at a talent contest, they were discovered by **EPMD**, who served as judges. Even though the group didn't win, EPMD still invited them to join their **Hit Squad** and got them a deal with East West. Although they attracted the most fame out of the bunch for their highly idiosyncratic stiggedy-stuttering, diggedy-dancehall-inspired mic styles, it was their lyrics, packed with pop culture references, which were actually far more appealing.

On *Dead Serious* (1992) they talked about giving **Sinead O'Connor** her crew cut, rhymed "Trapper John MD" with "Marcus Welby" and even made a phrase like "shiver me timbers" sound funky. Tracks like "They Want EFX" and "Mic Checka" blew up thanks to their gimmicky delivery, which sounded like nothing else on the American hip-hop scene, and rock-solid production from EPMD. Their album eventually went platinum and attracted scorn from the UK scene, who accused them of biting the **Demon Boyz**'s style, something the Demon Boyz addressed on "Glimmity Glammity" (1992), which used the beat from "They Want EFX".

Whatever the origins of their style, Das EFX were quickly revealed as a one-trick pony. *Straight Up Sewaside* (1993) followed in the exact same style, but lyrics like "I'm next G, heavens to Betsy, I sting like Pepsi/Or Coca Cola-swola" and "I bake that ass like Betty Crocker" just didn't cut it. *Hold It Down* (1995) went nowhere (partially abetted by their siding with Parrish Smith during EPMD's feud) and *Generation EFX* (1998) was a most unwelcome comeback. On *How We Do* (2003) Drayz and Skoob ditched their trademark technique in favour of straight-up New York-style rapping, but the results were not pretty.

⦿ **Dead Serious**
East West, 1992

It's possible that the ubiquitous Sean Paul and Beenie Man may now have opened up younger ears to their raggamuffin-inspired rhyming style, but this album has not aged well. Nevertheless it's their best, and "They Want EFX" and "Mic Checka" still sound pretty good.

# David Banner

Although he hasn't had any Hulk-outs like his comic-book namesake, the mild-mannered, community-oriented **David Banner** burst out of Jackson, Mississippi in 2003 and quickly became a "crunk" superhero. Although he seemed to come out of nowhere to most people north of the Mason-Dixon Line, he'd been bubbling under down South with his group **Crooked Lettaz** for some time.

Named after the schoolyard mnemonic for their home state ("M-I-Crooked letter-Crooked letter-I…"), Crooked Lettaz stayed in keeping with Mississippi's musical traditions by offering a bluesy take on the 'pimp trick gangster clique' clichés of the Dirty South. Consisting of Banner, Kamikaze, Veil and Phinga Print, Crooked Lettaz released their only album, *Grey Skies*, in 1999. Flipping the script like OutKast, "Pimp Shit" was actually about the hustling perpetrated by the **Illuminati**, while on "It's Ours", **Kamikaze** rapped "I bust the same sad story, over mandatory blunts and the liquor/I'm thinkin' back to them ancient times when we was once the victors/In them wars fought on the shores of the Barbary coasts". The album's best track, though, was "Get Crunk", a creeping, menacing, but anthemic reworking of **Run-DMC**'s "Rock Box".

Banner's first solo album, *Them Firewater Boyz* (2000), was more of a Dirty South variety show with guest appearances from UGK's **Pimp C**, Jazze Pha, Young Bleed, Boo, Noreaga, Ras Kass, Devin the Dude and **Thug Addict**. The production wasn't great, but on the severely uptempo tracks like the title track, "Firewater", "Spazz Out", "Twerk Something" and "Trill", the breathtaking pace blew away any reservations you might have had. Despite *Them Firewater Boyz*'s lacklustre beats, Banner gained notoriety as a producer, especially for the striking **George Winston**-style piano on **Trick Daddy**'s "Thug Holiday" (2002).

Although less nuanced than OutKast, *Mississippi: The Album* (2003) was an exploration of a Southern playa's schizophrenic lifestyle. Reflective tracks like the great "Cadillac On 22's", "Mississippi" and "Fast Life" rubbed up against hyper, unrepentant pimp and (strip) club tracks such as "Like A Pimp", "F*** 'Em" and "Might Getcha". Banner moves back and forth between these extremes with ease and with numerous different styles and flows. *Mississippi: The Screwed & Chopped Album* (2003) found Banner and **Swishahouse**'s Michael Watts giving the entire record the **DJ Screw** treatment. It's strictly for those fond of sippin' on "sizzyrup", even if a few of the tracks are worth listening to in isolation, especially "Cadillacs On 22s", which is somehow more poignant when dragged through the musical molasses.

After the success of the *Mississippi* album, *MTA2: Baptized in Dirty Water* (2003) followed in rapid succession. Banner didn't produce as many tracks this time around and the album definitely had a rushed feel. The *Screwed & Chopped* version (2004), however, was better than its 2003 prototype, with more interesting effects used, and you could finally understand what **Twista** and **Busta Rhymes** were rapping about on the "Like A Pimp" remix.

**Mississippi: The Album**
Universal, 2003

Perhaps it's not a great album, but it's as close as anything from the South has got, this side of OutKast. The club tracks are uniformly jumpin' and menacin' in true Southern style, while songs like "Mississippi" put everything in perspective: "We from a place where dem boys still pimpin' dem hoes/We from a place Cadillacs still ridin' on vogues/We from a place and my soul still don't feel free/Where a flag means more to me – Mississippi!"

# Dayton Family

Not sure if **Michael Moore** would approve of his hometowners' attitude and lifestyle, but he sure would recognise where it comes from. The Dayton Family, consisting of **Bootleg** (Ira Dorsey), **Shoestring** (Raheen Peterson) and **Matt Hinkle**, grew up on Dayton Avenue in Flint, Michigan, one of the most notorious streets in the US. Never strangers to the

backseat of a cop car, their situation wasn't helped at all when in 1991 the group released a five-song cassette that included a song called "Fuck Being Indicted", naming officers on the Flint police force who had given them grief.

Numerous incarcerations and run-ins with the law later, the Dayton Family released *What's On My Mind* (1995) on a small Atlanta indie label. Gritty and nasty (there are no moments of ghetto-fabulous redemption on their records), the Dayton Family represented the flip side of G-Funk, even if they copped much of its sound (as well as that of the **Geto Boys**). "If I was livin' in those days I would have stuck up Capone," Bootleg rapped on "Dope Dayton Ave." and you believed him.

*FBI* (1996) was released on Relativity and the improved production values (courtesy of **Steve Pitts**) improved matters no end. Instead of **Dr. Dre**'s trademark high-pitched synth whines, Pitts' keyboard riffs were eerie and downbeat, lending a musical menace to the already bone-chilling raps of Bootleg and Shoestring. Bootleg recorded his verses during a two-week leave from prison, and his incarceration put the group on hold for the next three years.

Bootleg emerged first with his solo album, *Death Before Dishonesty* (1999), which suffered from too many guest rapper appearances and the strange decision to include singers on some of the hooks – a move that was guaranteed to displease his hardcore legion of fans. Shoestring followed later in the year with his own solo album, *Representin' Till The World Ends* (1999), which was released, oddly, on **Tommy Boy**.

Neither of these projects did anything much and the two rappers signed to **Esham**'s Overcore label, where they were much more at home. Both Shoestring's *Cross Addicted* (2001) and Bootleg's *Hated By Many, Loved By Few* (2001) were returns to form, on which they weren't rubbing up awkwardly with major-label glitz. The Dayton Family's *Welcome To The Dopehouse* (2002) continued where Bootleg's last solo album left off, in that it had more of a Dirty South electro feel and the MCs used more of a double-time cadence.

**FBI**
Relativity, 1996

No cars, no jewellery, no drunken parties, almost no women – just straight-up violence and drug dealing. Even with Steve Pitts' fine production, it's not an easy listen, but if you like your hardcore uncut like a snuff flick, then this is the music for you.

# dead prez

Khnum Olugbala got his first taste of revolution as a sixth-grader in Shadeville, Florida. Already an aspiring rapper, his history teacher suggested that he should write a rhyme about African-American history for Black History month. During his performance in front of the entire school, he said "to hell with Uncle Sam" and the school's white principal turned his mic off. His fellow students reacted by rioting.

Several years later Olugbala, now called **Stic.man**, formed dead prez with his brother **Mutulu** (aka M1). Signed to Loud, they recorded "Food, Clothes and Shelter" for a label sampler in 1997, before appearing on Big Pun's *Capital Punishment* album in 1998. Unlike most albums by current politically minded groups, their incendiary debut album, *Let's Get Free* (2000), was neither anachronistic nor directed only at the legion of "backpackers" who seem to be the only people who care about politics in hip-hop anymore. Stic and M1, with help from production duo **Hedrush**, laced the record with contemporary beats (even "getting crunk" on a couple of tracks), hoping to insinuate notoriously apolitical black radio with their message. To a large degree it worked, and proved that shiny things and blinging musical digitalia didn't have to be a guilty pleasure.

Unfortunately, it appeared that politics was a guilty pleasure for their label, as they were promptly dropped. *Turn Off The Radio: The Mixtape Vol. 1* (2002), released under the name of **DPZ**, was eventually released on the indie label Landspeed. Although there were too many gangsta/bling parodies, *Turn Off The Radio* was perhaps more forceful because they took more musical chances and weren't apeing radio rap, except on the awful r&b tear-jerker "BIG Respect". *Turn Off The Radio Mixtape Vol. 2: Get Free Or Die Tryin'* (2003) was far less interesting, and highlighted their deficiencies as rappers – even Onyx's washed-up **Fredro Starr** outpunched M1 and Stic with his sterling couplet "I done broke every rule in the good book/Trust me, I've memorized the Anarchist Cookbook".

The title of their third album, *RBG: Revolutionary But Gangsta* (2004), laid out the group's contradictions succinctly – how else to categorise a group that puts a single on the soundtrack to the movie *2 Fast 2 Furious* and then fantasizes about a police-station drive-by? Of course, "RBG" also stands for "red, black and green" – then again they have the ultimate flosser **Jay-Z** on the remix of "Hell Yeah". The music was also less fiery than on their previous records, opting for a richer, lusher, more gangsta feel.

**Let's Get Free**
Loud, 2000

Long before Stic succumbed to the scourge of creative rappers (dating Erykah Badu), dead prez teamed up with such talents as turntablist Mista Sinista, bassist Melvin Gibbs and überproducer Kanye West (for the remix of "It's Bigger Than Hip-Hop") for this exciting album that got over on more than just its politics.

# Death Row records

Shady connections to organized crime, questionable business practices, beat-downs, lavish expense accounts: the Death Row story was business as usual for the music industry. Nevertheless, as the most prominent proponent of that media bête noire, 'gangsta rap', the record label acquired a notoriety that belied the normality of such practices in the industry. From the lyrics of the label's artists right down to founder **Suge Knight**'s garish red

jacket and the label's logo (a hooded man sitting in an electric chair), everything Death Row did was designed to inflame a racist media and the white establishment. However, even if you're trying to side-step the devil, if you play with fire, you're gonna get burned.

Death Row was formed in 1991 when Knight, an ex-football-player turned body-guard, and a gang of similarly propor-tioned, lead-pipe-wielding men alleged-ly "persuaded" Ruthless Records owner **Eazy-E** to release Dr. Dre from his con-tract with the company. Knight negoti-ated an unprecedented contract with the Interscope label that allowed Death Row almost complete autonomy and owner-ship of the master tapes. The Death Row era actually began with a song that was released on Epic, Dr. Dre's title track from the *Deep Cover* soundtrack (1992), which featured **Snoop Doggy Dogg**. Snoop's Southern gothic drawl introduced a new style to hip-hop, while Dre's stream-lined P-Funk was irresistible. The sound, dubbed G-Funk, was all over Dre's *The Chronic* album (1992), which achieved pop music's ultimate triumph of making rage and alienation sound sexy and cool and appealing.

Snoop's *Doggystyle* (1993) followed in a similar, if less sophisticated style, and Death Row found it had sold eight million copies of its first two albums. The *Above*

the *Rim* soundtrack (1994) and **Tha Dogg Pound**'s (Kurupt and Dat Nigga Daz) unredeemably gratuitous *Dogg Food* (1995) both went multi-plati-num as well. Those whining synths and Parliament samples were every-where – Cali was ruling the hip-hop world. The East Coast came up with its own cartoon CEO, **Sean "Puffy" Combs**, who attempted to replace G-Funk with his karaoke hits. The rivalry between the two appeared to have extended beyond the market-place when Knight dissed Combs at *The Source* magazine's music awards in 1995.

In 1995, rapper **Tupac Shakur** signed a four-page, handwritten con-tract with Knight, in exchange for Knight's posting the bail money Shakur needed while he was in jail on a rape charge. Tupac released his *All Eyez On Me* (1996) album a few months after being released. The double album went seven times platinum, but the label was in trouble: Dre wanted out; Snoop was in court on a murder charge; Knight was involved in numerous court cases; and the East Coast-West Coast beef was alarmingly transcending the realm of metaphor.

The inevitable results of this embrace of gangsta glamour were realised in September 1996, when Tupac was mur-dered in Las Vegas. Suge Knight, who had symbolised a kind of "fuck you", independ-ent black capitalism, was incarcerated and forced to sell his master discs. Nevertheless, Death Row continued to release records: **Lady of Rage**'s much delayed *Necessary Roughness* (1997), Tha Dogg Pound's *West Coast Aftershock* (1998) and *Suge Knight Represents: Chronic 2000* (1999). Extricating themselves from Death Row, **Dat Nigga Daz** and **Kurupt** both released solo albums, most notably Kurupt's *The Streetz Iz A Mutha* (2000), which featured the brutal diss cut "Calling Out Names". A rumoured deal with former Ku Klux Klan mem-ber and Louisiana politician **David Duke** only made the Death Row saga even more bizarre, yet nonetheless one utterly typical of the wider music biz.

In 2001, after Knight was released from

prison, the label started trading again, but under the name of **Tha Row**. *Dysfunktional Family* (2003) was the soundtrack to the **Eddie Griffin** movie of the same name, but the album was as unworkable as its title suggested. There was some old blood present – R&B crooners **Danny Boy** and **Michel'le**, and a back-in-the-fold **Kurupt** – but the album was mostly given over to new signees like **Eastwood**, Crooked I, Spider and **Skippa** who were nowhere near as talented as the old guard. The most noteworthy track was the first appearance of **Lisa "Left Eye" Lopes**' rap alterego N.I.N.A.

Kurupt's *Against The Grain* (2004) was the first album of all-new material released by the label in years, but it was hardly worth the wait – the same old gangsta clichés with slightly newer beats and, surprise, surprise... a Tupac sample.

**Death Row Greatest Hits**
Death Row, 1996

Not the greatest selection (too many lame remixes, and where the hell is "Dre Day"?) and filled with Suge's venom (the inclusion of Ice Cube's "No Vaseline" and J-Flex's "Who Been There, Who Done That?"), but still the best available label overview.

# Def Jam records

" **M** usical myth-seeking people of the universe, this is yours". With these words the biggest label in hip-hop history began its 15-year reign. **T La Rock & Jazzy Jay**'s "It's Yours" (1984) was the first record to feature the Def Jam logo, although it was actually released on **Arthur Baker**'s Partytime label. It was an amazing record – the densest rhymes this side of **Rammellzee Vs K-Rob**'s "Beat Bop", production from **Rick Rubin** that sounded like Stockhausen and was almost as unfunky – but a strange beginning for such a commercial juggernaut.

It was **Afrika Bambaataa**'s associate Jazzy Jay who first introduced Def Jam founders Rubin and **Russell**

**Simmons**, who at the time was running Rush Artistic Management, overseeing the careers of **Kurtis Blow** and **Run DMC** (Jazzy Jay's "Def Jam/Cold Chillin' In The Spot" (1985) featured Russell Simmons showing why he wasn't a rapper himself). Made in Rubin's dorm room at New York University, the first proper Def Jam record, **LL Cool J**'s "I Need A Beat" (1984), sold 100,000 copies and firmly established the label as a force.

In 1985 Def Jam signed a distribution deal with CBS, becoming the first label to be backed by major-label money, and immediately knocking all competition out of the water. Of course, having LL Cool J, the **Beastie Boys** and **Public Enemy** on the roster didn't hinder Def Jam from becoming the genre's most important and successful label. Even such artistic disasters as smoove loverman Oran "Juice" Jones couldn't stop the Def Jam steamroller.

Although Rubin and Simmons brought hip-hop into the mainstream, they also held it down on the underground with **Original Concept**'s "Knowledge Me/Can U Feel It" (1986), introducing the world to future *Yo MTV Raps!* frontman **Dr. Dre**. While Rubin was getting more into heavy metal, Def Jam continued to innovate in hip-hop by putting out **Slick Rick**, stealing **EPMD** away from Fresh and forming **3rd Bass** from two distinct entities. **MC Serch**, Prime Minister Pete Nice and Sam Sever released the classic *The Cactus Album*

(1989) which proved that white men could funk on tracks like the Beasties-dissing "Gas Face", "Steppin' to the AM" and "Product Of The Environment". Unfortunately, their *Derelicts Of Dialect* (1992) couldn't keep up the momentum, with easy disses of **Vanilla Ice** and, ironically, overly commercial production.

Although Rubin left the label after a feud with Simmons' right hand man **Lyor Cohen**, who soon became the label's CEO, Def Jam didn't miss a beat with **Redman**, Onyx, Warren G, Montell Jordan (the 1990s version of Oran "Juice" Jones) and **Method Man**. Feeling like he couldn't miss, Simmons diversified into fashion with his **Phat Farm** line, film and TV projects and an ad agency. Even though the **Def Comedy Jam** and *The Nutty Professor* had Simmons looking elsewhere, hip-hop acts like **Foxy Brown**, Ja Rule, Jay-Z and **DMX** and link-ups with Jay-Z's **Roc-a-Fella** and Irv Gotti's The Inc. labels championed the thug/Cristal aesthetic and continued to pay his rent.

With Dixie becoming an ever-greater force in hip-hop, Def Jam moved south of the Mason-Dixon Line with its **Def Jam South** imprint, responsible for the likes of **Ludacris**, Chingy and the surprising revival of **Scarface** (who just happened to be the head of the imprint).

Even with all the cash lining the pockets of Simmons and Cohen, they kept their ears to the streets. In 2003 they signed mixtape cult hero **Joe Budden** – long a fixture on tapes from DJ Clue and Kay Slay. With its stuttering chorus and anthemic horns, his collaboration with producer **Just Blaze**, "Pump It Up" was one of 2003's best and biggest singles. His self-titled debut album couldn't quite sustain the momentum, but it was a solid piece of work nevertheless.

---

**VARIOUS ARTISTS**

 **The Def Jam Music Group 10th Anniversary Box Set**
Def Jam, 1995

Hip-hop heads will own most of this already, but this 59-track overview of the label's first ten years is pretty unimpeachable (aside from the random programming).

# ⊙ Definitive Jux records

As his previous group, **Company Flow**, was splitting from the Rawkus label, and was in the process of breaking up, rapper and producer **El-P** started the Def Jux label. The label debuted with the *Def Jux Presents...* EP (2000), which featured three Company Flow tracks, two tracks from **Cannibal Ox** and a track each from **Aesop Rock** and RJD2. While Co Flow was as crazy avant as ever ("I get my swerve on like a narcoleptic race car driver on the autobahn in monsoon season" – wooh!), the EP's stars were the label's other acts – particularly Cannibal Ox.

Can Ox lived up to the promise those two tracks showed on the remarkable *The Cold Vein* (2001) album. Bloody, dirty, intense (*really* intense), intimidating, tremulous, claustrophobic, but ultimately as inspiring as the sun rising over the Empire State Building, *The Cold Vein* was the album that tried to save independent hip-hop from its own worst instincts. Unlike underground university grads like **Anti-Pop Consortium** or the roster of Anticon records, Cannibal Ox's **Vordul Megilah** and **Vast Aire** weren't arty cats out to wow you with artifice, nor were they beat-diggers out to wow you with their dusty artifacts. Instead, *The Cold Vein* united the street corner and the dorm room, the cipher and the poetry slam, the backpacker and the gat-packer seamlessly, without even trying.

*Labor Days* (2001) was the fourth album of Lower East Side blues from Big Apple fabulist **Aesop Rock** (he had previously recorded *Music for Earth Worms* (1998), *Appleseed* (1999) and *Float* (2000) for various labels). There was no trademark dystopic/dyspeptic production from the Def Jux label boss; instead, Aesop and producer **Blockhead** constructed airier, sing-songy, string-heavy, "Knight Rider meets Zamfir" beats, that eschewed El-P's claustrophobia in favour of a 'voices in your head' paranoia. Aesop sounded like a combination of **Del The Funky Homosapien** and **Dose One**, mixing a slightly rigid, stentorian authority with a nasal, shmendrick neurosis. His rhymes were similarly balanced: one half **Woody Allen** (in Bergman mode, but stealing lines from the Wu-Tang Clan) collaborating with Samuel Delany on an abstract blaxploitation flick (about commuters, female artists and transcending the city); one half **Rammellzee** trading insults with the counterman at Katz's Deli.

Boston rapper **Mr Lif** had previously released the excellent *Enter the Colossus EP* (2000) on Def Jux, but really had heads turning with the *Emergency Rations* EP (2002), a paranoid, deeply committed rumination on the state of the nation

Three Def Jukies (left to right): Aesop Rock, El-P and Mr Lif.

after 9/11. *I Phantom* (2002) was a full-length that was no less political, but its focus on working-class heroes made both his raps and the production less claustrophobic.

The beats on **El-P**'s solo debut album, *Fantastic Damage* (2002) weren't block-rockin' so much as knock-your-block-off. There were grooves buried in there, but they sounded as if they had been compressed in a trash compactor and taken out to a landfill in Staten Island to be shat on by seagulls and gnawed on by rats. The album had the biotic odour of the locker room: you could imagine **Henry Rollins**, Norman Mailer, Robert Anton Wilson and **Philip K Dick** doing bench presses to *Fantastic Damage*. However, trapped beneath the unremitting torrent of largely untranslatable code and forbidding urban gothic grime was a touching, vulnerable humanity that elevated *Fantastic Damage* beyond the preserve of survivalist *Star Wars* geeks who play *Magic: The Gathering*.

After some choice words from Def Jam's legal department, Def Jux was forced to change its name to **Definitive Jux** – no doubt those hundreds of thousands of people picking up *The Cold Vein* had meant to buy that **Cadillac Tah** joint instead. No matter, the label kept producing great records – **RJD2**'s *Deadringer*

Rjd2 Deadringer

De La Soul: 3 is the magic number.

(2002) and *RJD2* (2004), **Aesop Rock**'s *Bazooka Tooth* (2003) – and not so great records – **MURS**' *The End of the Beginning* (2002) and *3:16 The Ninth Edition* (2004).

**Cannibal Ox** broke up in 2003, with Vast Aire going on to release an uneven solo album, *Look Ma, No Hands* (2004) on the Chocolate Industries label.

## CANNIBAL OX

**The Cold Vein**
Def Jux, 2001

Vast Aire, who "flow[ed] like arachnids on water spouts", is the star, delivering the most vivid descriptions of urban heartbreak and survivalism since Richard Wright: "You were a stillborn baby/ Your mother didn't want you, but you were still born/Boy meets world, of course his pops is gone/ What you figure?/That chalky outline on the ground is a father figure?" This is only intensified by El-P's production: a wasteland of percussive rubble and biting, steely synth winds, stinging guitars, punch-drunk rhythms and even the odd, strangely anthemic, chorus of Valkyries.

## EL-P

**Fantastic Damage**
Definitive Jux, 2002

A thoroughly uncompromising album full of contradictions, but all the more fascinating for it.

"Stepfather Factory" may not be as staggeringly brilliant, shocking or moving as "Last Good Sleep" from *Funcrusher Plus*, but as an examination of capitalism, sex and family life it has no peers. (Apart from perhaps the Stones's "(I Can't Get No) Satisfaction" and X-Ray Spex's "Oh Bondage, Up Yours".)

# De La Soul

Like their fellow suburban Long Islanders **Public Enemy**, Eric B & Rakim and EPMD, Amityville's De La Soul remade hip-hop in their own image. With their elliptical lyrics, in-jokes and lush samplescapes, De La Soul expanded hip-hop's emotional palette by introducing an almost pastoral quality to an urban grid of chopped-up drum breaks and soundbite raps.

De La Soul's debut album, *Three Feet High And Rising* (1989), saw **Posdnous** (Kelvin Mercer), **Trugoy the Dove** (David Jolicoeur) and **Pacemaster Mase** (Vincent Mason) create what they called the **D.A.I.S.Y. Age** ("Da Inner Sound Y'all"), its flower imagery reflecting their un-macho approach and their arty, suburban roots. Produced by **Prince Paul** from

Stetsasonic, the album was a dense collage of samples that ranged from "A Little Bit Of Soap" by The Jarmels, through Steely Dan, to French-language instructional tapes. Featuring cameos from other members of the Native Tongue posse (**Jungle Brothers**, **A Tribe Called Quest** and **Queen Latifah**) and a mellow, inclusive feel, *Three Feet High And Rising* fostered a communitarian spirit that was in sharp contrast to the "go for yours" mentality of standard hip-hop.

In a pattern that would become all-too familiar among independent hip-hop crews, when the singles "Me, Myself and I" and "The Magic Number" crossed over to the mainstream, the hip-hop community took De La Soul's popularity with a white audience as proof that they were soft. De La Soul were out to regain their stret cred with their 1991 follow-up – the dark, angry and frustrated *De La Soul Is Dead*. The album was populated with insider jokes aimed at black radio, **Sylvester Stallone**, fast-food restaurant employees and American chat-show host **Arsenio Hall**. Amid the unpleasant vibe, there was some great music: an exposé of sexual abuse, "Millie Pulled A Pistol On Santa"; "A Roller Skating Jam Named 'Saturdays'" which sampled **Chic** and Frankie Valli; "Bitties In The BK Lounge" (a dozens game set to music); and the uplifting "Keepin' The Faith". Ultimately, though, the album wasn't the masterpiece it could and should have been, because of its pre-occupation with pop's worst subject – the burdens of fame.

Their obsession with the fine distinctions between crossing over and selling out continued on their third release, *Buhloone Mindstate* (1993). On both "Eye Patch" and "Patti Dooke", De La Soul declared, "It might blow up, but it won't go pop", re-affirming their commitment to the streets. Despite brilliant soundbites like "I'll make you lost like high school history" and "Fuck being hard, Posdnous is complicated", *Buhloone* was even more wilfully obscurantist than its predecessors. The skits were filled with a venomous black humour and the music was a langourous elegy to the blues, which heightened the mainstream-damning references to hip-hop history (they quoted everyone from **Melle Mel** to **Public Enemy**).

The band returned with *Stakes Is High* (1996), distilling the frustrations of the previous two albums into a collection of bone-jarringly blunt, minimalist sketches. Both the title track and "The Bizness" revolved around two-note basslines and snapping snares, creating bleak attacks on lame rappers and institutionalised racism. Once again, De La Soul had managed to change their flow and their style – not to move with the times, but to stay ahead of them.

However, when they released the first part of the sprawling three-CD project, *Art Official Intelligence* (2000), the group seemed shackled by label expectations. While tracks like "Oooh!" (with Redman on the hook) and "Foolin'" were good radio records, *Mosaic Thump*, the first chapter of the three-part project, lacked direction and was caught in the digital mire.

**Oscar Goldman** would not have been very happy with *Bionix* (2001), the second instalment of the *Art Official Intelligence* triptych. De La Soul were neither better, faster nor stronger. Where they once created paradigms and set agendas, De La were left wondering how to stay relevant when everyone, even the critics who used to keep them afloat, had accepted the mainstream ideology. Where their records were once characterised by

humour, playfulness and a fingerpainting creativity, *Bionix* was characterised by paint-by-numbers production, lines like "That pussy stank, smellier than Africans in Africa" and included a collaboration with a very over-the-hill Slick Rick. The one bright spot was "Held Down", which brought **Al Green** into the 21st century, but with a message that the good reverend would never preach: "They were looking for God, but found religion instead". "Held Down" may have shone like a beacon, but the rest of *Bionix* was dull and monochrome. Someone needs to rebuild them.

### ◉ Three Feet High And Rising
Tommy Boy, 1989

A landmark record in the history of hip-hop. Their surreal humour and light-heartedness works perfectly with the disjointed artistry of the music to create an album that inherits George Clinton's mantle of politico-socio-sexual funk.

### ◉ De La Soul Is Dead
Tommy Boy, 1991

A good record, pulled down by its obsession with the problems of success. The rich, sample-based grooves keep the jokes from falling flat.

### ◉ Buhloone Mind State
Tommy Boy, 1993

Lacking the hooks of the previous releases, this is dark, cryptic and occasionally nasty. There are some great moments, but it takes a lot of patience to get there.

# Devin the Dude

With his group, **Odd Squad** (which also featured DJ Screw), Devin Copeland was one of the pioneers of second-wave Houston rap. The experience of their album *Fadanuf Fa Erybody!* (1994) was like spending the evening sitting on a couch talking shit about girls with your stoner friends from college while listening to **The Five Stairsteps**. Evidently not even Houston was ready for it, because it promptly went out of print.

Devin the Dude kept soldiering on though, as part of **Scarface**'s Facemob, who released *The Other Side Of The Law* in 1996. Going solo in 1998, Devin released *The Dude* album the same year. The weed was a bit stronger this time around, though, and the mood wasn't as silly. The sex raps were uglier – more like a malt-liquor hangover than a harmless case of the munchies. Nevertheless, Devin attracted the attention of **Dr. Dre** who had him rap a verse on "Fuck You" in 1999. Another guest appearance, on **De La Soul**'s "Baby Phat" in 2001, had his stock rising considerably.

*Just Tryin' Ta Live* (2002) found Devin smoking the kind bud again, getting silly and reflective in equal measure. With **DJ Premier** going back to his Texas roots with a stunning jacuzzi of a jazz guitar beat, "Doobie Ashtray" was a wistful tale of a down-on-his-luck stoner: "You probably don't have a big ol' house on the hill/But if you did, just imagine how it would feel/If your phone got disconnected, no cash, and your gas cut off/And the gal that you had that was helping just stepped the fuck off/What's really fucked up is now you're just normal". "Lacville '79" was an ode to his broken-down "hooptie", while "Who's That Man, Mama?" was a pretty funny ode to his penis. There was even a vocodered alien named **Zeldar** rapping the merits of weed on the album's first track. The follow-up, *II The Extreme*, came in 2004 in a similar style, and there were rumours of an Odd Squad reunion album in the near future.

Cool like dat: jazz hepcats Digable Planets.

🔘 **Just Tryin' Ta Live**
Rap-A-Lot, 2002

Wine, women, song and weed have inspired countless rap albums, most of them pretty ugly. While this certainly has its unpleasant moments, it also has plenty of charm that doesn't require a bongful of indo to appreciate.

# Digable Planets

Formed in 1991 while studying in Washington DC, the Digable Planets picked up where **A Tribe Called Quest**'s *Low End Theory* left off and took bebop hip-hop into new areas of abstraction and quirkiness. Instead of leaving their jazziness in the production, **Butterfly,**

**digable planets**
reachin' (a new refutation of time and space)

**Doodlebug** and **Ladybug** inflected their raps with beatnik slanguage and hipster-isms, briefly becoming the house band of the black bohemian intelligentsia in the process.

The group's first album, *Reachin' (A New Refutation Of Time And Space)* (1993), was a big crossover hit among those who got into hip-hop during its sampladelic golden age, but were now scared off by **Dr. Dre**'s amorality. Based around a sample from **Art Blakey & the Jazz Messengers**, "Rebirth Of Slick (Cool Like Dat)" fingerpopped its way into the pop consciousness with boho flows and mellow, mellifluous swing. The album wasn't all grainy, thrift-store appeal, though. It also had bite: "La Femme Fetal" worked a soundbite from the **Last Poets** into the mix as the Planets spun a pro-choice yarn that didn't hold back on the political content.

Riding black style politics for all they were worth, *Blowout Comb* (1994) brought a streetwise nationalism to the fore. Utilising cryptic phrases (such as "makin' bacon" for the hip-hop stock subject of killing cops), the lyrics may have been as oblique as those on *Reachin'*, but it was no longer wordplay for wordplay's sake. Like just about every other group whose success came from a kinder, gentler form of hip-hop, the Digable Planets ditched their pop appeal in an attempt to become more street. Unsurprisingly, it didn't work and

*Blowout Comb* precipitated the group's quick slide into obscurity.

While the group has faded into memory, their DJ, **Silkworm**, rechristened himself **King Britt** and was a big presence on the dance-music scene, thanks to his work with **Josh Wink** on their Ovum Recordings label. Working with the cream of the Philly scene (including bassist **Jamaaladeen Tacuma**, keyboardist James Poyser and wordsmith **Ursula Rucker**) as Sylk 130, he released *When The Funk Hits The Fan* (1998), a jazzy, boho concept album about the day in the life of a teenaged DJ in 1977.

**Ishmael Butler** (aka Butterfly) meanwhile re-emerged in 2003 as part of **Cherrywine**, a live instrmental hip-hop band. Their debut album, *Bright Black* (2003), was a dull, ponderous mix of sub-Q-Tip/Roots boho jazziness. Craig Irving (aka Doodlebug) has resurfaced under the name **Cee Knowledge**. With his band, the **Cosmic Funk Orchestra**, he has pursued a similar, live funk/soul/jam band aesthetic, and has released collaborations with Roy Ayers and members of **Sun Ra**'s Arkestra (on a cover of Ra's "Space Is The Place").

⊙ **Reachin' (A New Refutation Of Time And Space)**
Pendulum/EMI, 1994

Unfortunately, beyond their initial crossover success, the group couldn't keep on doing what the title suggested (reachin', that is). But this remains a fine album of unconventional hip-hop, if very much marked by the climate in which it was released.

# Diggin' In The Crates

Naming themselves after the science of record-collecting, New York's Diggin' in the Crates crew have it held it down for hip-hop purists since 1990. The crew's linchpin DJ/producer **Diamond D** (Joe Kirkland), who had worked with **Jazzy Jay** since the early days, first appeared on wax as part of Ultimate Force with **MC Master Rob** (who "had more hair on his chest than Chuck Norris") on the blues-guitar-based "I'm Not Playing" (1989). DITC started taking shape the following year when **Lord Finesse** (Robert Hall) asked Diamond to work on beats for his *Funky Technician* album (1990). With fellow residents of The Bronx's Forrest housing projects DJ/producer **Showbiz** (Rodney Lemay) and MC **AG** (aka Andre the Giant, aka Andre Barnes), Diamond helped make *Funky Technician* one of the most "butter" albums of the early 1990s.

After working on Lord Finesse's album, Showbiz and AG teamed up again for the legendary *Can I Get A Soul Clap* EP (1991). With the title cut and "Party Groove", the EP was a classic of raw Bronx rhymes teamed with dusty but motorvating production. The vibe was writ large on *Runaway Slave* (1992), which, in addition to cuts from the EP, featured the smoking "Fat Pockets" and the jazz cut-ups of "Silence Tha Lambs". Their *Goodfellas: The Medicine* album (1995), however, suffered from an identity crisis and, aside from the hot "Next Level", couldn't sustain the duo's momentum.

In 1992 Diamond took to the mic for *Stunts, Blunts & Hip Hop*. He couldn't match the skills of either Finesse or AG, but Diamond's simplified rhyme-style nonetheless helped make *Stunts* a classic. His streamlined vocal rhythm allowed him, and co-producers **45 King**, **Large Professor**, **Showbiz** and **Q-Tip** to make a club-friendly but complex collection of slamming beats. "Best Kept Secret" and "A View From The Underground" introduced **Fat Joe** (Joseph Cartagena), while "Comments From Big L And Showbiz" featured the wax debut of **Big L** (Lamont Coleman). Although his mic technique had improved, Diamond succumbed to the trend for more melodic, less loopy production on his delayed follow-up, *Passion, Hatred And Infidelity* (1997).

**Fat Joe** released the fairly mediocre *Represent* (1993) (which included the hit "Flow Joe") and *Jealous One's Envy* (1995), but his thug life Darwinism was at its best on *Don Cartagena* (1998). *Jealous Ones Still Envy (JOSE)* (2001) and *Loyalty* (2002) were nothing but a series of diminishing returns. Big L, meanwhile, made a name for himself with scene-stealing guest appearances on Lord Finesse's "Yes You May (Remix)" (1992) and Show & AG's "Represent" (1994). His debut album, *Lifestylez Ov Da Poor & Dangerous* (1995), was a rugged affair that burst to light on "MVP" and the posse cuts "8 Iz Enuff" and "Da Graveyard".

"8 Iz Enuff" was produced by **Buckwild** (Anthony Best) who had previously been Finesse's tour DJ. Buck had also produced **OC**'s (Omar Credle) underground anthem "Time's Up" (1994). OC had debuted on **Organized Konfusion**'s "Fudge Pudge" (1991) and Buck helped produce their *Stress: The Extinction Agenda* (1994). OC's own debut album, *Word Life* (1994), marked the emergence of one of indie hip-hop's greatest, most reflective, most commanding MCs, and aligned DITC with the underground.

Loved on the streets but ignored by

consumers, DITC focused on the independent scene and started their own DITC label in 1997 with the posse cut, "Day One", which featured OC, Fat Joe, Big L and Diamond spitting to a Diamond-encrusted beat. Although DITC remained a largely cult phenomenon, Fat Joe was awarded the ultimate accord: he had a sandwich (grilled turkey, fried eggs and American cheese) named after him at New York's Stage deli. Meanwhile, Big L torched the underground with "Ebonics" (1998) which saw him play the slang teacher like **Wide Boy Awake**. On February 15, 1999, however, Big L was gunned down in Harlem and the posthumous collection of his rhymes, *The Big Picture* (2000), reveals how much New York hip-hop will miss his presence.

As a group, DITC signed to Tommy Boy and released *Diggin' In The Crates* (2000), largely a compilation of tracks they had released on their label, but featuring new cuts like the smoking **Premier**-produced "Thick". It failed to generate much excitement, though, as even most New York purists had moved on from the style that DITC had been pushing for so long.

Bon Appetit (2001) was OC's attempt at rectifying the situation by indulging in flossing rhymes and glittery production. He didn't convince anyone. Diamond's *Grown Man Talk* (2003), meanwhile, went the other direction by resolutely sticking to the old and familiar, but boring everyone to tears.

---

**SHOWBIZ AND AG**

⊙ **Runaway Slave**
Payday, 1992

No-nonsense, true school Bronx hip-hop at its finest.

---

**OC**

⊙ **Word Life**
Wild Pitch, 1994

Both deep and hard-knock, his debut album showed that OC is one of the most complete MCs around.

# Digital Underground

Exploding out of the Bay Area with the utterly amazing "Doowutchyalike" (1989), Digital Underground brought **George Clinton**'s Parliafunkadelicment thang back to the public consciousness. At the outset of their career, ringleader **Shock G** (and his alter ego Humpty Hump), **Money B**, **DJ Fuze** and **Chopmaster J** made some of the most delicious, party-rocking hip-hop ever, only to get paralyzed by formula.

It may have introduced a new, funkier sound into hip-hop, but "Doowutchyalike" was everything old school hip-hop was about: jokey, cornball rhymes that had one object and one object only, to cold rock a party. With stoopid fresh lines like "Help yourself to a cracker with a spread of cheddar cheese/Have a neckbone, you don't have to say please" on top of some serious handclaps and P-Funk punctuation, "Doowutchyalike" was the year's most irresistible single.

*Sex Packets* (1990) was thoroughly Clintonian in its conception: the album was based around a putative narrative in which a mad scientist unleashes a drug that causes those who ingest it to have wet dreams. The music was equally rooted in

the **P-Funk** Mothership. With its grinding bassline, numerous Parliament samples and hilarious rhymes like "Crazy, wack, funky/ People say, 'You look like MC Hammer on crack Humpty'", "The Humpty Dance" was even better than "Do-owutchyalike" and is undoubtedly the greatest dance craze that never was. The bizarre sense of humour and Parliamentarianism continued on "Freaks Of The Industry" which highlighted the mic skills of **Money B**.

*This Is An EP Release* (1990) was a bit short on new material with two remixes of tracks from *Sex Packets* including a great reworking of "The Way We Swing". Of the new tracks, "Same Song" was the most notable, not only for its bumping rhythm, but also for marking the vinyl debut of one **Tupac Shakur**. *Sons Of The P* (1991) had more P-Funk stylings, but it didn't have the same effervescence of the debut. However, the album's best track, "No Nose Job", was exactly what George Clinton should have been singing about in the 1990s: a funny, clever, cartoonish critique of black people who want to switch.

Money B and DJ Fuze formed the DU offshoot **Raw Fusion** in 1991 and released *Live From the Styleetron*, an underrated album that blended speeded-up dancehall beats with hip-hop, and featured the great "Throw Your Hands In The Air". Raw Fusion's follow-up, *Hoochified Funk* (1994), however, was as stale as the main band had become by this point.

Digital Underground's *Body Hat Syndrome* (1993) was another concept album about sex and prophylactics, but it was nowhere near as inspired as *Sex Packets*. It was perhaps notable only for the debut of the rapper **Saafir**. *Future Rhythm* (1996) continued the losing streak with abominable cyber-sex cover art and equally abysmal music. *Who Got The Gravy?* (1998) found Shock G and Money B teaming up with such East Coasters as **Biz Markie**, **Big Pun** and **KRS-One** in an effort to regain some momentum. While it was a significant improvement on the previous couple of releases, it still didn't make enough noise to register on the radar of public consciousness.

⊙ **Sex Packets**
Tommy Boy, 1990

It might not be as great as its inspiration, but Shock G and crew don't embarrass themselves on what may be hip-hop's best party album.

# Dilated Peoples

Perhaps the sensation of the hip-hop underground, LA's **Dilated Peoples** eschew any geographical stylistic boundaries in favour of a kind of hip-hop purity. Indie hip-hop scenesters continually go on about staying true to the culture, but nothing epitomises this more than Dilated Peoples' commitment to unadulterated mic and turntable skills. A member of the World Famous Beat Junkies, **DJ Babu** (Chris Oroc) "is so nice he don't slice, he severs", while MCs **Evidence** (Michael Perretta) and **Iriscience** (Rakaa Taylor) pop your eardrums with cutting battle rhymes and detailed strings of images.

Evidence and Iriscience were both graffiti artists who dropped the aerosol in favour of mics in 1992. The duo became Dilated Peoples in 1994 and soon inked a deal with the Epic-distributed Immortal Records due to their affiliation with House of Pain's **DJ Lethal**. Their first wax appearance was "End Of The Time" which was featured on *The Next Chapter* compilation (1996). The Peoples finished recording their debut album, *Imagery, Battle Hymns And Political Poetry,*

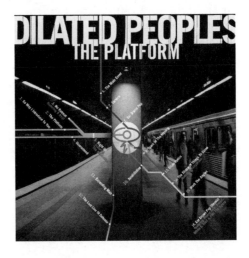

Dilated Peoples (left-right): Evidence, Iriscience and DJ Babu.

but Epic dropped Immortal Records and the album has never seen the light of day.

Undeterred, Evidence and Iriscience appeared on **Defari**'s "Bionic" in 1997, which was released on Bay Area DJ **Beni B**'s ABB Records. Always Bigger and Better then released the singles which are responsible for Dilated's formidable rep. "Third Degree" featured both Defari and Babu's first cuts with the group. 1998's "Work the Angles", though, was the breakthrough and it remains the closest thing the 1990s' underground got to an anthem. Produced by Evidence, "Work The Angles" had the scything guitar stabs that characterise their sound, cadences that only emphasised the track's head-nodding factor, and the most outrageous scratching ever to feature on a non-DJ track. On the flipside, "Main Event" had Evidence "spray[ing] rain on your parade" over a beat by **Alchemist**, and "Triple Optics" was Iriscience's fresh spin on hip-hop's evergreen "third eye" metaphor.

Evidence and Iriscience laced "After the Heat" (1998) by **Joey Chavez** (who had produced some of their unreleased album), before releasing the equally superb *Re-Work The Angles* EP (1999). They then signed to Capitol and their debut album, *The Platform*, finally dropped half-way through 2000. Although it suffered slightly from cadences that were too similar, *The Platform* highlighted why hip-hop sucked so much in the new millennium. In an iced-out world, no one cared much about skills anymore, a sorry state made all the more obvious by Dilated's excellent live shows, which were always punctuated by Evidence's stagedives during "Work The Angles".

With its echoes of the '62 Mets and '77 Blue Jays, *Expansion Team* (2001) probably wasn't the most accurate title for a group who had become leading lights of the underground hip-hop scene. In order to combat the cadence problem of the first album, the group invited a host of guest producers and MCs including **Da Beatminerz**, Juju from **The Beatnuts**, Alchemist, Black Thought, Tha Liks, **Defari**, and the guy who had largely invented the stab pattern the underground seemed to be impaled on, **DJ Premier**. While the strategy paid some dividends and made *Expansion Team* a

more well-rounded record, it focused the spotlight on the group's other fatal flaw: neither Evidence nor Rakaa had enough microphone charisma to sustain an entire album, no matter how many guests showed up.

*Neighborhood Watch* (2004) was undone not by an over-reliance on guest appearances, but by an over-reliance on one producer, the seemingly overworked Alchemist. Instead of the flows being monotonous, this time around it was the production that wore the listener down. Maybe next album they'll finally get the mix right.

**The Platform**
Capitol, 2000

This features "Work The Angles", "Main Event" and "Triple Optics". As Iriscience says, it moves like "John Coltrane pushing a blue train".

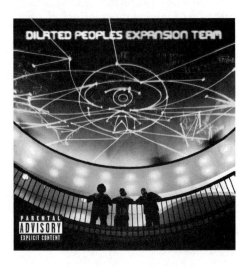

# Disposable Heroes of Hiphoprisy / Spearhead

Michael Franti and Rono Tse first started to harangue against the evils of capitalism in the late 1980s as part of San Franciscan industrial tape loopers, **The Beatnigs**. Unlike similar bands with a gaggle of percussionists playing circular saws, The Beatnigs' rants always had a touch of **Gil Scott-Heron** about them, particularly when dubmeister **Adrian Sherwood** remixed what seemed to be their only song, "Television".

Tiring of the metal-on-metal clangour of The Beatnigs, Franti and Tse left to form **Disposable Heroes of Hiphoprisy** in 1990. "Television" reappeared on *Hypocrisy Is the Greatest Luxury* (1992) as "Television: The Drug of the Nation", a decent enough rabble-rousing single for the committed, but an irritating lecture for everyone else. Ironically, the embrace of hip-hop made their music less pleasurable and more pedantic. The fact that Mark Pistel, of leaden *sturm und drang* beatsmiths **Consolidated**, produced the album didn't help.

Perhaps the Disposables' most convincing work – and one unquestionably congruent with hip-hop's aesthetics – had no lyrical input from Franti whatsoever. On *Spare Ass Annie (And Other Tales)* (1993), the words were provided instead by **William Burroughs**, the originator of the cut-up technique, reading selections from his oeuvre over music that Franti and Tse had put together.

Franti's next project, **Spearhead**, tried to make the political personal. *Home* (1994) was more about domestic politics, about day-to-day life, about... gulp... love. The album was produced by **Joe "The Butcher" Nicolo** and his real hip-hop sensibility – beats that actually swung – introduced a hint of humanity into Franti's stridency. He even said, "I am deadly serious about us havin' fun".

Fun and warmth were less in evidence on *Chocolate Supa Highway* (1997). Sounding like Franti had listened to **Tricky**'s *Maxinquaye* one too many times, the album was buried in a funk murk that dragged more than it signified. Where *Chocolate Supa Highway* tapped into **Sly Stone**'s dark period, *Stay Human* (2001) explicitly echoed his early, hippy, uplifting vibe. Except that Sly never framed any of his albums with fictional accounts of the trial of a San Francisco activist – which pretty much destroyed the groove Spearhead built up throughout the album. *Everyone Deserves Music* (2003) was largely produced by reggae titans Sly & Robbie, who never let Franti's worst instincts take over. Except in the lyrics, that is. Franti still sings stuff like "We can bomb the world to pieces/But we can't bomb it into peace".

**Home**
Capitol, 1994

Knocked off his soapbox by the warm music created by luminaries like Vernon Reid, Scott Storch and Charlie Hunter, *Home* is Franti's most humanistic, most listenable album.

# Divine Styler

One of hip-hop's most celebrated mystery figures, Divine Styler has forged a path that is pretty much unique in the music's history. Part of Divine Styler's originality comes from the fact that he's a Brooklynite who came to prominence as a member of **Ice-T**'s West Coast **Rhyme Syndicate** posse. His geographical non-alignment encouraged him to pursue his own unique, personal muse – even if he takes no more than a handful of people with him.

His 1989 debut album, *Word Power*, was a dense paean to Islam that explored the coded complexities of mysticism a good couple of years before the Five Percent Nation faction rose to prominence in hip-hop. Although musically similar to the **Native Tongues** albums of the same era, Styler's wordplay and bizarre stream-of-consciousness conceptual drift on tracks like "Divine Stylistics" staked out new territory, and was the first equation in Styler's so-called "ill black calculus".

The follow up, *Spiral Walls Containing Autumns Of Light* (1992), was as psychedelic as its title, and saw Divine playing most of the live instruments himself. Against a forbidding wall of noise constructed from atonal synth squall and feedback guitar that at times recalled fusioneers like **Herbie Hancock** and **Larry Young**, Divine called himself "Your blackest fathom", delved even further into the mystical depths of Islam and made his flow even more dervish-like.

Then, unless you count working with **House of Pain** on their third album as keeping in circulation, he more or less vanished. His disappearance from the scene prompted a fanzine called *In Search of Divine Styler*, and Divine became an object of hip-hop trainspotters' fascination. In 1997, Divine made the pilgrimage to Mecca, and the experience renewed his faith both in Allah and in music. El Hadji Divine Styler released the brilliant 12" single "Before Mecca" soon after he returned, which set the stage for his comeback album, *Word Power 2 – Directrix* (1999).

His return was marked by a muezzin calling the faithful to prayer and, after an instrumental and spoken-word invocation, Divine started to "refine the myth". Where most MCs who praise Allah couch their beliefs in scabrous rhetoric and arcane numerology, Divine's raps were filled with the kind of twisted images and labyrinthine logic that made you want to take the time to unravel his metaphors rather than leaving them for the adepts.

In fact, unlike his Five Percent Nation peers, Divine's most pious tracks were the most accessible. The rough, bruising synth lines and knock-your-wind-out drum beats cohered into a kind of futuristic gothic symphony. Notwithstanding his impressive dedication to language, Divine didn't forget that Allah created noise before he made the word.

**Word Power 2 – Directrix**
DTX/Mo' Wax, 1999/2000

"Logos" may be a Christian concept, but with his lyrical originality — and crucially, equally original production — Divine Styler tried to make the word of God flesh.

# DJ Assault

Ghetto-tech pioneer **DJ Assault** (aka Craig Adams) attracted attention because of song titles like "Ass-N-Titties", "Asses Jigglin'", "Big Bootie Hoes and Sluts Too" and "Sex On The Beach". The truth is, though, that Assault is one of the finest DJs in the Detroit light-speed cut-up tradition started by **Jeff Mills** (in his radio mixes as The Wizard), and his productions combine Motor City scatology and electro-funk in equal measure.

A native Michigander, Craig Adams attended university in **Atlanta**, and when he returned to Detroit he combined the techno of his hometown with the booty bass of the South to create ghetto-tech. He hooked up with **Ade' MH Mainor** in 1996 ("DJ Assault" was a duo up until 2000) and the pair started the Electrofunk label, releasing the *Terrortec* EP in 1996. It was with the mixtape series *Straight Up Detroit Shit*, though, that Assault really started to make a name. Rifling through 100 songs in 60 minutes, Assault speeded up soul classics, the minimal techno of Berlin's Basic Channel label, and gratuitous uncleared samples, to match the ferocious pace of his own productions. Not for the easily offended, the *Straight Up Detroit Shit* mixes were nonetheless responsible for some of the wildest, most delirious music of the 1990s.

*Belle Isle Tech* (1997) was a two-disc set, one half of which was devoted to the duo's less-than-inspiring rapping. The second, however, was an extraordinary mix of some of their previous 12"s, such as "Terrortec", "Return of Terrortec" and "Ass-N-Titties". The lyrics were pretty grotesque, but they were so fratboy puerile they were hard to take seriously, and the headlong rush of the album – party music of the highest order – rendered them easily ignorable. The album was eventually reissued on **Mo' Wax** two years later.

More 12"s and mixes followed, most notable of which was probably *Off The Chain For The Y2K* (2000). *Jefferson Ave.* (2001) followed the duo's split, with Assault's pedestrian sleaze-rap skills to the fore.

⊙ **Straight Up Detroit Shit Volume 5**
Electrofunk, 1998

Everything popular music is supposed to be: lubricious, frenzied, scandalous and truly exciting. It is not for the easily offended, however, even if there is no parental advisory sticker to warn you.

# DJ Clue

Before **DJ Clue** (Ernesto Shaw) hit the scene in the early 1990s, mixtapes were of two varieties. One was the blend tape where a DJ would lay a rap acapella over a classic r&b beat; the other was the mix, where a DJ would create a mix of the hot rap tracks. In order to distinguish himself, Clue created the modern mixtape: a collection of vocals recorded especially for the tape – new verses over hot beats and records that no one else has.

Although he had been making tapes since about 1991, it was in 1994 that he really made a name for himself. He put the original, unreleased version of **Notorious BIG**'s "One More Chance" on a tape, and it blew up. The move was extraordinarily bold – it prompted a threat from Biggie himself – but the gamble worked. Clue was instantly the biggest mixtape name in New York. Soon it became de rigueur for an aspiring rapper from New York to spit some rhymes on a Clue mixtape.

With Clue's rep so huge, **Roc-A-Fella**

signed him to create legit mixes. *The Professional* (1998) had an impressive roster of talent: **Nas**, Jay-Z, Mobb Deep, **EPMD**, Raekwon, Big Pun, Noreaga, Canibus, **Cam'ron** and more. His partnership with **Duro** as the **No Question** production team kept him busy putting together beats for the likes of **Jay-Z**, Lil' Mo and B2K.

With all the unsigned rappers passing through his studio to record verses, it was perhaps inevitable that Clue would start his own label. He kicked off his Desert Storm imprint in 2001 with the first album by **Fabolous**. But Clue still kept releasing mixtapes, both official and illicit: *Backstage* and *The Professional, Pt. 2* (both 2000) and his *Hate Me Now* series.

⊙ **The Professional, Pt. 2**
Roc-A-Fella, 2000

Although Clue's tapes are more of an entrepreneurial exercise than a traditional mixtape, they have their own pleasures. Here, Nas, relieved from commercial pressures, relives his glory days with "Live from the Bridge", and Mobb Deep follow suit with "The Best of Queens".

# DJ Jazzy Jeff & the Fresh Prince

The Philadelphia duo of **DJ Jazzy Jeff** (not to be confused with the Funky Four's Jazzy Jeff) and Fresh Prince are responsible for one of hip-hop's best trends and one of its worst. As a deck technician, DJ Jazzy Jeff (Jeffrey Townes) was almost without peer in the 1980s: his development of the "transformer scratch" and invention of the "chirp scratch" helped propel the art of DJing from the ground zero of Flash's backspins to the current "hamster-style" state of the art. On the other hand, the **Fresh Prince** (Will Smith) was the first rapper to become a TV and movie star, thus beginning the trend of rappers as entertainers rather than musicians.

The two got together in 1985 in South Philly, and they landed a record contract after Jeff won the New Music Seminar **DJ Battle for World Supremacy** in 1986.

Originally released on the Word Up label, *Rock The House* (1987) featured the poptastic, *I Dream of Jeanie*-sampling "Girls Ain't Nothing But Trouble" alongside more radical, proto-turntablist fare from Jeff, like the awesome "Touch of Jazz".

*He's The DJ, I'm The Rapper* (1988) had more turntable antics from Jeff, but it was dominated by crossover material like "Parents Just Don't Understand". The album went triple-platinum and clinched the duo the first rap Grammy. *And In This Corner* (1989) was even more of a grasp at pop stardom, and hit with the pretty dire "I Think I Can Beat Mike Tyson". *Homebase* (1991) followed suit with more suburbia-friendly hip-hop, but they reached rock bottom with the scandalously bad "Boom! Shake the Room" from *Code Red* (1993).

By this time, though, Smith was starring in TV sitcom **The Fresh Prince of Bel-Air,** and he began his movie career with *Six Degrees of Separation*. Several box-office smashes later, Smith deigned to bless the mic again on the *Men in Black* soundtrack with a pointless remake of **Patrice Rushen**'s "Forget Me Nots", the theme song "Men in Black" (1997). Smith got jiggy wit' it on *Big Willie Style* (1997), selling five million and becoming one of the biggest stars on the planet. *Willennium* (1999) had more ghostwritten rhymes and obvious samples, and it too went multi-platinum. *Born to Reign* (2002) included the hit theme song to **Men in Black II**, but found Smith bidding for more "artistic" success – a move that is almost always doomed to failure. To add insult to injury, it was a copy-protected CD, giving yet another reason not to buy it.

In 2002 Jazzy Jeff attempted to emerge from Smith's shadow with his own album, *The Magnificent*. While there were some exciting moments – particularly "Break It Down" with **J-Live**, and "We Live In Philly", a nod to **Roy Ayers**'s "We Live In Brooklyn, Baby" featuring **Jill Scott** – the album was too stylistically broad to really cohere. It was nice to have the more talented member of the duo back, though.

◉ **Rock The House**
Jive, 1987

Not even Puffy would touch it nowadays, but "Girls Ain't Nothing But Trouble" was fine, breezy pop way back when, and there was plenty of Jeff on the decks to make this their least cringeworthy release.

DJ Jazzy Jeff, in a rare moment of abulia, forgets what a record is.

# DJ Magic Mike

Back when he was still sporting a white dweeb's version of the high-top fade haircut, and a good few years before he would become the rock-rap saviour of the MTV generation, no less an authority than **Kid Rock** called DJ Magic Mike "the Puff Daddy of Miami Bass music". It may have been a back-handed compliment, but it gets to the very heart of the universal appeal of Magic Mike's brand of **Bass**. Emphasising old school breakbeats rather than rigid 808 drum-machine programming, Magic

Mike's records allow people who don't frequent booty clubs, or cruise south Florida's strip malls in neon-lit sports utility vehicles, to experience the visceral excitement, momentum, speed and catharsis of Bass music. Pulling rabbits out of hats with his sampler, Magic Mike was the undisputed king of Bass during the 1990s, notching up four gold albums and one platinum album.

Born in Orlando, Florida, the erstwhile Michael Hampton shared his name with one of **Funkadelic**'s guitarists, so it was perhaps written in the stars that he would spend his childhood, not as a mouseketeer at **Walt Disney World** (which was just down the road) but as a funkateer in Uncle Jam's army – listening to P-Funk and early **Prince** albums like *For You* and *Dirty Mind* inspired Mike to become a DJ at the tender age of twelve.

The Magic man started performing tricks on the wheels of steel a year later, at an eighth-grade school dance. Originally just a mixer and a selecter, Mike was inspired to learn how to scratch by UTFO's "Roxanne, Roxanne" and later by the group's DJ, **Mixmaster Ice**. While "escaping Orlando" in New York in 1986, he started listening to DJs like **Cash Money** and **Jazzy Jeff**, adding transforming to his armoury of turntable skills and becoming one of the fastest DJs on earth.

Back in Orlando in 1987, Mike teamed up with **Beatmaster Clay D** to produce a couple of singles for the duo of MC **Cool Rock** and **MC Chaszey Chess**, the first being "Creep Dog", for the Vision Records imprint. Mike's production on the mean, moody low-roller "Boot The Booty" epitomized the Bass sound, and introduced the world to the immortal phrase "Ain't nothin' but tutti frutti, get on the floor if you got that booty". After doing a couple of records with one of Bass's most influential MCs, Shy D, Mike hooked up with a struggling local alternative label called Cheetah in 1988. Almost despite themselves, his first two singles for Cheetah, "Magic Mike Cutz the Record" and "Drop the Bass", were huge hits on the Bass scene.

They anchored Mike's debut album, *DJ Magic Mike And The Royal Posse* (1989), which would eventually break out of Florida and sell more than a million copies. By the time Mike recorded his second album, *Bass Is The Name Of The Game* (1990), his style had moved away from the 808 beats that dominated Bass music towards a cut-and-scratch style reminiscent of **Master Ace on 45.**

After further gold records with *Vicious Bass* (1991) and *Ain't No Doubt About It* (1992), Mike took a more low-profile approach and let other Bass producers make some money during the mid-to-late 1990s. He moved away from straight Bass on *Magic's Kingdom* (2000) by including a few r&b and Southern-fried rap tracks.

**⊙ Cheetah's Bassest Hits**
Cheetah, 1993

None of his greatest hits compilations include his best record, "Magic Mike Cutz the Record", except for the remade version on Mo' Wax's *The Journey* (1999). This does have all the best of his other work, though, and makes a fitting introduction to the fastest DJ this side of Jeff Mills.

# DJ Quik

Although **David Blake** had connections with the Tree Top Piru Bloods street gang, and left the "c" out of his mic-name because it represented the Crips, DJ Quik is less of a gangsta rapper than he is a continuation of the traditions of street-corner signifying and filthy party comedy of **Rudy Ray Moore** and **Redd Foxx**. As a producer, Quik was one of the first Left Coasters to develop the rolling version of the P-Funk. Despite his mixing-board chops, Quik will probably always be associated with what may be hip-hop's most devastating series of diss records: his battle with **MC Eiht**.

After lacing LA underground mix tapes for a couple of years, Quik emerged with *Quik Is The Name* (1991). "Tonite" was a top fifty single about the pleasures of "getting bent" and playing cee-lo that rode a huge synth/vocoder groove from funk

# DJING-TURNTABLISM

There are DJs and then there are DJs. Radio, club and mixtape DJs such as **Funkmaster Flex**, Kid Capri, Tony Touch, DJ Clue, Ron G, Doo Wop, Kayslay, Eclipse and **Tim Westwood** serve their function, but it's the logic of the cut and scratch that really separates hip-hop from disco. Of course, hip-hop DJing is more than just dragging a record back and forth across a stylus or segueing two tracks together nice and smooth. Hip-hop is a lot like the British class-system: it's not so much what you say that matters, but how you say it. This is as true of the DJ as it is of the MC and graffiti tagger. What great DJs recognise is that the best music is a complete triumph of style over substance; everything's been said already, so why bother listening unless the speaker's got some serious moxie. In fact, the DJ's style is the very substance of turntablism. All of which serves to explain hip-hop's infatuation with kung-fu flicks: when everyone is using the same basic materials, style – whether it's drunken boxing and Shaolin shadow boxing or flaring and beat juggling – becomes all important.

Long before **Kool DJ Herc** started manipulating two copies of the same record to elongate the beat, the first piece of music to envision the turntable as a musical instrument was **John Cage**'s *Imaginary Landscape No. 1* (1939) which was written to be performed in a studio by a pianist, a Chinese cymbal player and two turntablists playing Victor frequency records, taking advantage of the turntable's ability to switch gears from 33 1/3 to 78 in order to manipulate recordings of constant tones. While several composers took up Cage's challenge by scoring pieces for other apparatuses of electronic reproduction like the radio and microphone, the possibilities of the turntable as an instrument in its own right lay dormant until Kool Herc transplanted the Jamaican sound system to the Bronx in the early 1970s.

Herc's breakbeat style laid the foundations for hip-hop, but it was another DJ, **Grandwizard Theodore**, who created its signature flourish in 1977 or 1978. Purely by accident, Theodore stumbled across scratching when he was practicing in his bedroom and had his attention diverted and rubbed the record across the stylus. You can hear Theodore scratching it up on "Can I Get a Soul Clap" (1982), but the two most vital documents of early hip-hop DJing are Grandmaster Flash's "The Adventures of Grandmaster Flash on the Wheels of

Steel" (1981) and Afrika Bambaataa's *Death Mix* (1983) (see entries).

While Flash and Bamabaataa were using the turntable to explore repetition, alter rhythm and create the instrumental stabs and punch phasing that would come to characterise the sound of hip-hop, **Grandmixer DST** was busy cutting "real" musicians on their own turf. His scratching on **Herbie Hancock**'s 1983 single, "Rockit" makes it perhaps the most influential DJ track of them all — even more than "Wheels of Steel", it established the DJ as the star of the record, even if he wasn't the frontman. Compared to "Rockit", **West Street Mob**'s "Break Dancin' – Electric Boogie" (1983) was a savage punk negation. Only DJ Code Money's brutalist record mangling on Schooly D's early records can match the cheese-grater note shredding of "Break Dancin'". As great as "Break Dancin'" was, though, it also highlighted the limited tonal range of scratching, which was in danger of becoming a short-lived fad – like human beatboxing – until the emergence of Code Money's DJ brethren from Philadelphia in the mid-1980s.

Despite New York's continued pre-eminence in the hip-hop world, scratch DJing was modernised 90 miles down the road in Philadelphia. Denizens of the City of Brotherly Love were creating the climate for the return of the DJ by inventing what was termed transformer scratching. Developed by DJs **Spinbad**, **Cash Money** and **DJ Jazzy Jeff** , transforming was basically clicking the fader on and off while moving a block of sound (a riff or a short verbal phrase) across the stylus. Expanding the tonal as well as rhythmic possibilities of scratching, the transformer scratch epitomised the chopped-up aesthetic of hip-hop culture.

The only problem the Philly DJs faced was a matter of timing. Hip-hop was starting to become big money, and the cult of personality was beginning to take over. Hip-hop became very much at the service of the rapper, and Cash Money and DJ Jazzy Jeff were saddled with B-list rappers such as Marvelous and the Fresh Prince and were accorded perhaps one track on an album to get busy (check tracks like DJ Jazzy Jeff's "A Touch of Jazz" (1987), "Jazzy's in the House" (1988), and Cash Money's "The Music Maker" (1988)). Other crucial DJ tracks from this period include **Tuff Crew**'s DJ Detonator's "Behold the Detonator" and "Soul Food" (both 1989), **Gang Starr's** "DJ Premier in Deep Concentration" (1989) and 2 Live Crew's "Mr Mixx on the Mix!" (1986) and "Megamix 2" (1989).

With turntable chops so awesome that they've been banned from the competitions that are the lifeblood of the turntablist scene, **Q-Bert** and his **Invisbl Skratch Piklz** crew (Apollo, Mix Master Mike, Shortkut and DJ Disk) heralded the return of the DJ as a self-contained one-man band. Emerging as a force in 1992, by taking the DMC World DJ Championship away from the odious DJ Dave from Germany (who, as John Carluccio's excellent film *Battle Sounds* showed, actually air scratched and did handstands on a moving turntable). The Skratch Piklz brought turntablism back to the basics of scratching and cutting, and away from the grandstanding showmanship that it had largely become. Where Flash and Herc created hip-hop out of the syncretic readymade of the breakbeat, on his *Demolition Pumpkin Squeeze Musik* mixtape (1994) Q-Bert colonised and infested the break with his

One-time Beastie DJ Mixmaster Mike on the wheels of steel.

scratches and blocks of viral noise, creating true adventures on the wheels of steel through fantastic **George Lucas**-style soundscapes where the scratches sounded like the shape-shifting video game charcters of Q-Bert's imagination.

The emergence of crews like the Skratch Piklz, the **X-ecutioners** and the **Beat Junkies** dovetailed with the developing independent hip-hop movement to establish a flourishing "real" hip-hop culture that stood in opposition to the crass materialism, stupid violence and talentlessness of what they disparagingly called "Rap". Originally released in 1995, Return of the *DJ Vol. 1* was amazingly the first album to be devoted exclusively to the hip-hop DJ. Picking up on an idea from Q-Bert (and John Cage) who used to play tunes like "Mary Had a Little Lamb" on the turntable by manipulating a recording of a pure tone with

the pitch control lever, X-ecutioner **Rob Swift**'s "Rob Gets Busy" used the pitch control adjustment on the Technics to mutate the Moog riff from **The J.B.s'** "Blow Your Head" before embarking on an exposition of the beat-juggling techniques developed by **Steve D** in 1990. The Skratch Piklz showed off their battery of flare and crab scratches on "Invasion of the Octopus People", while **Mixmaster Mike** invoked the ghosts of **Double Dee & Steinksi** on "Terrorwrist". It wasn't all excitement and flash, though. Peanut Butter Wolf's "The Chronicles (I Will Always Love H.E.R.)" was a melancholic journey through hip-hop's short history that showed both how much had been gained and how much had been lost.

On vinyl, DJs such as **DJ Disk** (*Ancient Termites* (1999)), **DJ Faust** (*Man or Myth?* (1998)), **Kid Koala** (*Carpal Tunnel Syndrome*

Beat Junkie DJ Babu wrecks it on the ones-and-twos.

(2000) and *Some Of My Best Friends Are DJs* (2003)) and **DJ Quest** (with the turntable/ live instrument improv group **Live Human** on *Monostereosis* (1999) and *Elefish Jellyphant* (2000)) continued to push the boundaries with records that pushed the art form into new realms of expressivity and abstraction.

**Return of the DJ**
Bomb Hip-Hop, 1995
Although all three volumes of this ground-breaking series are worth picking up, this is the record that almost single-handedly resurrected the art of the DJ.

band **Kleer.** Quik drawled fast and furious on the title track, which was based on snippets from **Brass Construction** and **Cameo**, while "Born And Raised in Compton" sampled **Isaac Hayes** over a slamming kick-drum.

*Way 2 Fonky* (1992) followed *Quik Is The Name* as a gold album largely thanks to the fearsome single, "Jus Lyke Compton". *Way 2 Fonky* also escalated his wax war with MC Eiht on the title track and "Tha Last Word", which also responded to **Tim Dog**'s Compton-baiting. However, *Way 2 Fonky* made no advances on his debut's sound,

and the only growth was in the number of pussy references.

Reeling under the sheer weight of Eiht's "Def Wish" records, Quik released the absolutely savage song "Dollars & Sense" in 1994 after hooking up with Death Row's **Suge Knight**. Based on the groove of Brick's "Dazz", "Dollars & Sense" was merciless in its slander of Eiht: "'E-I-H-T' now should I continue?/Yeah, you left out the 'G' cause the G ain't in you". The battle continued on *Safe & Sound* (1995) with "Let You Havit", but the vast majority of the album was taken up with pseudo-comic tracks about his prowess in bed that wouldn't have made anyone in the locker room laugh, and flaccid, back-in-the-day reminiscing like "Summer Breeze".

*Rhythm-al-ism* (1999) was a major progression in production (Quik played most of the keyboard, bass and drum parts himself). The fuller, warmer sound apparently had its effect on the lyrics too: on "You'z a Ganxta" Quik made peace with Eiht in the fallout from the deaths of **Tupac** and **Biggie**. Of course, the old macking lyrics like "Hand in Hand" were there too, but the beats were so good that you didn't mind. *Balance & Options* (2000) followed too quickly on the heels of Rhythm-al-ism, with a brace of uninspired covers of Eazy-E and **Digital Underground** tracks. The only bright spot was a collaboration with **Raphael Saadiq**, "Well", which was the most tasteful and moving meeting of hip-hop and R&B in a long, long time.

With the South quickly supplanting the West Coast as hip-hop's second home, Quik hooked up with **Eightball & MJG** and produced their "Buck Bounce" single in 2001. Moving away from the stale G-Funk he'd been pushing for years, "Buck Bounce" paved the way for the surprising *Under Tha Influence* (2002). Over an acoustic guitar, Quik rapped "So I put on my game face, go back to the same place/Only to realise that y'all ain't got the same taste". Gone indeed were the whining synths and vocoders; they were replaced by bouncing string and pianos that followed slightly strange rhythmical paths, proving that Quik was something more than the genre toady everyone had him pegged as.

⊙ **The Best Of DJ Quik – Da Finale**
Arista, 2002

Including everything from "Born And Raised in Compton" and "Tonite" to Under Tha Influence's "Trouble", this is a convincing portrait of the young G-Funker as an artist.

# DJ Shadow

Of all the people who have been inspired by the original hip-hop cut-ups of **Grandmaster Flash** and **Double Dee & Steinski**, no one, with the possible exception of **Coldcut**, has taken the cut 'n' paste aesthetic as far as DJ Shadow. Growing up as an isolated hip-hop junkie in suburban Davis, California, allowed Josh Davis to take the music in any direction he wanted without the constrictions of having to "keep it real". Hip-hop became the music of his fantasies, and the largely instrumental beat collages that he would soon make were all characterised by a bleary, dreamy quality.

Shadow's first release was an explicit update of **Double Dee & Steinski**'s "Lesson Mixes", entitled "Lesson 4", which appeared on the b-side of a single by **The Lifers' Group**, a hip-hop crew comprised of ex-cons, in 1991. "The Legitimate Mix" was another mind-boggling sampladelic collage hidden away on the b-side of a lame record – this time, **Zimbabwe Legit**'s eponymous EP – that really made beat heads take notice in 1992. It established not only his skills with the sampler, but on the decks as well, with a flurry of transformer scratches.

"The Legitimate Mix" prompted **Mo' Wax**'s head honcho, James Lavelle, to sign Shadow, and the immediate result was the stunning collage from the vinyl dustbin, "In/Flux" (1993). Like its source material (obscure 1970s soul records), "In/Flux" was a gloomy meditation on a society in transition that didn't mope and was never dragged down by its heavy vibes. Equally impressive was his debut for his own **Solesides** label, "Entropy" (1993), which was a 17-minute discourse on why hip-hop culture was dying.

His next release on Mo' Wax, "Lost and Found" (1994), plunged further into the depths of the sampler. Largely built around one of the decade's most inspired feats of beat archaeology (the martial drums from **U2**'s "Sunday Bloody Sunday") and keyed on a deceptively loony spoken-word sample about being true to yourself, "Lost and Found" showed that downtempo beat collage could be more than the aural equivalent of bong water. "What Does Your Soul Look Like?" (1995) was another beat suite about self-actualisation, but perhaps not quite as effective as his earlier efforts.

During this time, Shadow was also producing records by members of his **Solesides** crew – **Blackalicious** and the MCs who would soon become **Latyrx** – but his forte would remain the largely instrumental compositions with which he made his name. "Midnight In A Perfect World" (1996), one of those rare tracks that sounded exactly like the utopia they described (a dusty record shop cluttered with undiscovered breaks), was his most emotive track yet. *Endtroducing...* (1996) may not have had his two best tracks, but it was still an often blinding album that suggested that, despite the money, hip-hop did not suck in 1996 (as one of the album's tracks claimed).

While Shadow kept a low profile in 1997 and 1998 (aside from his production of Latyrx's excellent debut album and **UNKLE**'s dead duck of a debut, *Psyence Fiction*), Invisbl Skratch Pikl **Q-Bert**'s "Dog Sled Camel Race" (1997) was a remarkable display of turntable skills that transformed some of Shadow's greatest beats out of Morpheus' realm and into a scratch orgy of Dionysian excess. "Dog Sled Camel Race" also appeared on *Pre-Emptive Strike* (1998), a collection of his singles.

Shadow produced the bulk of his Quannum crew's often startling showcase album, *Spectrum* (1999), before focusing on his own *The Private Press* (2002). It was a laudable effort to move instrumental hip-hop out of the twin cul-de-sacs of slapstick thrills 'n' spills and morose stoner nod, and it definitely had its moments – the monstrous grooves of "Walkie Talkie" and "Right Thing/GDMFSOB", and the melancholy psychedelia of "Six Days". But the album also suffered from a sense of defeat, from the sense that everything with a turntable and a sampler had already been done.

⊙ **Endtroducing...**
Mo' Wax, 1996

An album that proved that trip-hop (or instrumental hip-hop, or blunted beats, or whatever else you want to call it) wasn't just an excuse for bohemians to drop out. Shadow showed that an entire universe could be created out of a crate of records and a sampler.

# DMX/Ruff Ryders

Along with Jay-Z, DMX and his Ruff Ryders crew ruled hip-hop at the end of the millennium. DMX may not be the best rapper in the world, but he performed a feat that all sentient human beings have to respect: he knocked **Garth Brooks** off the top of the American pop chart twice within a year. About as far away from Brooks' clean and corporate image as you could possibly be, DMX's satanic verses and over-the-top delivery remake hip-hop as **heavy metal**.

With his un-nuanced pitbull bark that is as unsubtle as, and not all that different from, the growl from the bowels of hell of **Napalm Death**'s Lee Dorian, DMX (aka Earl Simmons) was a legend on New York mixtapes for years before he finally signed a record deal. Instead of metal's raging guitars, DMX's hellhound snarl is surrounded by the metallic polyrhythms of producer **Swizz Beatz**, who made the Casio futurism of Timbaland even shinier, and sometimes even wilder. It might seem like an odd match, but by making a hideous, amoral, hopeless vision of the world as catchy as the **Spice Girls**, the pairing of DMX's brutal, future-gothic lyrics and Swizz's state-of-the-art pop craftsmanship is scarier than the blackest of black metal.

Knocking hip-hop out of its Wu-Tang

piano loop and Puffy karaoke machine stupor, DMX's debut album, *It's Dark And Hell Is Hot* (1998), was little short of a sensation. On the back of the street anthem "Get At Me Dog", it entered the US charts at number One and went double-platinum in a few weeks. Seven months later, *Flesh Of My Flesh, Blood Of My Blood* (1998) did the same. Like his metal brethren, DMX terrorized motorists and pedestrians alike with his gang of motorcycle fiends in his videos and concerts (à la Judas Priest), and he appeared on the sleeve of *Flesh of My Flesh, Blood of My Blood* covered in blood – **Marilyn Manson** even made a guest appearance on "The Omen".

On his best tracks, such as "Get At Me Dog" (from *It's Dark*) and "What's My Name" (from 1999's *...And Then There Was X*), DMX is all bluster, like a wolf growling and panting at its cornered prey. With his asthmatic growl, Doberman tenacity when he attacks a beat, his collection of attack dogs and tales of death and pain, DMX tried to be hip-hop's Cerberus guarding the gates of hell. But where Cerberus had three heads (and presumably three different barks), DMX has got only one voice, one flow and one gimmick.

His posse, the **Ruff Ryders**, attempted to remedy this on the album *Ryde Or Die* (1999), with appearances from **Eve**, **Drag-on**, and Bad Boy exiles The LOX, with cameos from Jay-Z, Big Pun and **Juvenile**. Featuring the salsa-flavoured "What Ya Want" (which made Eve the biggest thing since striped toothpaste), the intense synth riffs of "Platinum Plus" and the impossibly weird "Bugout", Ryde or Die was really a production showcase for Swizz Beatz. Similarly, while Eve wasn't half bad on *Ruff Ryders' First Lady* (1999), it was the beats that made the record: the foghorn bombast of "Scenario 2000", the relentlessly catchy acoustic guitars of "Gotta Man", the Michael Nyman-style piano of "Philly, Philly" and the slip-sliding-away funk of "Ain't Got No Dough". The Ruff Ryders' biggest coup, though, was tempting **The LOX** away from an ailing Bad Boy for the *We Are The Streets* (2000) album. It's true, however, that, for all of The Ruff Ryders' commercial acumen, the two best

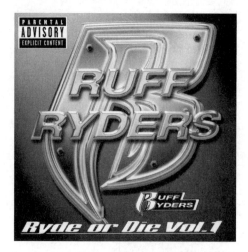

beats came from outsiders: **DJ Premier** on "Recognize" and **Timbaland** on "Ryde Or Die, Bitch".

*The Great Depression* (2001) was DMX's fourth album in three years and it really sounded like it. His bellow, towering paranoia and death complex had become just too much, and when matched to the bludgeoning, relentlessly staccato, sing-song beat of "Who We Be" it was frankly unbearable. Thankfully, by this time DMX was spending most of his time trading blows on the silver screen with **Steven Seagal**. *Grand Champ* (2003) hopefully convinced him that he should stay there.

*Ryde or Die, Vols. 2* and *3* (2000, 2001) were not so much posse albums as they were production showcases for Swizz and his disciples. While Eve, DMX, Drag-On and Jadakiss all showed up, *Vol. 2* was dominated by the appearances from **Snoop Dogg**, Method Man and Busta Rhymes. *Vol. 3* had a srong Southern presence with **Bubba Sparxxx**, Ludacris and Petey Pablo; tracks like "Dirrty", with Pablo stealing a chorus from **Beenie Man** over Swizz's ricocheting synth comets, and "They Ain't Ready", with **Jadakiss** and Bubba Sparxxx stealing more dancefloor cadences on the chorus, showed that the Ryders' commercial slump had more to do with our overfamiliarity with the rappers than the production, which was still occasionally dazzling.

Which is probably why Swizz Beatz decided to go it alone on *Swizz Beatz Presents GHETTO Stories* (2002). While it was that rarest of things – a hip-hop album with only one producer – the cast of thousands (including **Metallica**) made it seem just as faceless as every other commercially minded hip-hop album of the day.

## RUFF RYDERS

⦿ **Ryde or Die**
Ruff Ryders/Interscope, 1999

DMX is pretty hard to take over the course of a whole album, so this collection of insane beats from Swizz Beatz is the one to go for. Just try not to listen to the lyrics.

# The D.O.C.

Born Trey Curry in Dallas, Texas, The D.O.C. was poised to become one of hip-hop's biggest stars at the end of the 1980s. Signed to Eazy-E's Ruthless Records at the time of **N.W.A.**'s breakthrough, The D.O.C. was probably the best pure MC in the extended crew. Along with **Masta Ace** and **Ice Cube**, The D.O.C. could ride the fast beats prevalent at the time better than anyone and, at any tempo, he had an authoritative voice and enunciation that would've made Rex Harrison proud.

His debut album, *No One Can Do It Better* (1989), was a huge hit and proved that the West Coast wasn't just about pulling gats and bitch-slapping hoes. Produced by **Dr. Dre**, *No One Can Do It Better* featured killer cuts such as the intense "Portrait Of A Masterpiece" (which taught the **Chemical Brothers** a trick or ten), the classic Cali roller "It's Funky Enough" (which featured The D.O.C. dropping some Jamaican-flavoured rhymes), "The Formula" and the stellar "Grand Finale".

At the top of his game, however, The D.O.C. was, tragically, involved in a car accident that crushed his larynx. Despite this setback, he still managed to ghost-write lyrics for N.W.A.'s *Efil4Zaggin* (1991) and Dr. Dre's

*The Chronic* (1992), and he made brief cameos on both *The Chronic* and **Snoop Dogg**'s *Doggystyle*. Shortly afterwards, he split with Death Row in a dispute over money, and recorded an ill-advised comeback album. Brave though it was, *Helter Skelter* (1996) was a pretty awful album.

Over really tired beats, The D.O.C. rapped like 1950s rock 'n' roll singer **Clarence "Frogman" Henry**, except that it wasn't meant to be funny.

Nonetheless, The D.O.C. continues to pen lyrics for other MCs, and has worked with Tha Dogg Pound's Kurupt, Snoop and Dr. Dre.

⦿ **No One Can Do It Better**
Ruthless, 1989

Even with high-quality appearances from most of N.W.A., The D.O.C.'s mic skills get pretty damn near close to living up to the album's title.

# Tha Dogg Pound

Dat Nigga Daz (Delmar Arnaud) and Kurupt (Ricardo Brown) contributed verses to both *The Chronic* and *Doggystyle* before coming together as a duo at the behest of the **Death Row** brain trust. They were named Tha Dogg Pound to capitalize on Snoop's larger-than-

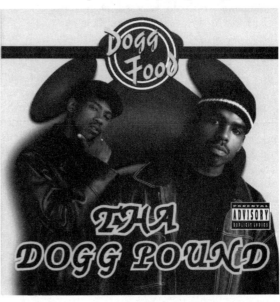

DEATH ROW PRESENTS...
Tha Dogg Pound
2002

life profile and recorded the frightening "What Would U Do?" for the *Murder Was The Case* soundtrack (1994).

Whatever effect their name may have had on the record-buying public, the group's best marketing ploy came courtesy of **C Delores Tucker**, who singled out Tha Dogg Pound's as yet unreleased *Dogg Food* album as the target of her moral outrage campaign against gangsta rap. She attacked Tha Dogg Pound with such singlemindedness that she must have been on **Suge Knight**'s payroll because – duh! – her criticism only drove anticipation for the album to breaking-point.

When it was finally released, *Dogg Food* (1995) went double-platinum. This certainly wasn't down to the music, which was resolutely second-tier gangsta and pretty unredeemable (apart from "New York, New York"). But even their Big Apple barbs were pretty feeble.

Soon after the album's release, Death Row fell into disarray and Tha Dogg Pound broke up, with Daz (now calling himself **Daz Dillinger**) sticking with the sinking ship, and Kurupt opting for his own A&M imprint, Antra. Daz's solo album, *Retaliation, Revenge And Get Back* (1998), was released just as Death Row hit rock bottom, and it sounded like it too. Even the cream of the West Coast (**Kurupt**, Snoop, Too $hort, 2Pac, MC Eiht, WC, Nate Dogg and **B-Legit**) couldn't prevent the album from sounding at least three years out of date. Meanwhile, Kurupt's solo effort, *Kuruption!* (1998), was a double-album divided into East and West Coast discs, when no one was interested in even one.

Kurupt's *Tha Streetz Iz A Mutha* (1999) was perhaps more notable, if only for "Callin' Out Names", which was exactly what he did: "Buckshot, Noreaga, Jigga – cool/Canibus, Wu-Tang, my niggas – cool/Def Squad and Def Jam, but fuck Ja Rule". *Space Boogie: Smoke Oddessey* (2001) was another sprawling, all-over-the-place album that featured laughable crossover attempts with **Limp Bizkit**, Everlast and r&b crooner **Jon B**. When the mainstream didn't come knockin', Kurupt went out to Hollywood, and landed roles in *Hollywood Homicide* and *Dark Blue*.

Daz, meanwhile, formed his own label, **DPG**, and released *RAW* (2000), which felt like a hastily cobbled together hash of tracks sitting in the vault. A hookup with Northern California's entrepreneur of haphazard gangsta clichés, **JT the Bigga Figga**, didn't do anything to change that impression. With Suge Knight holding the rights to The Dogg Pound name, Daz and Kurupt – who had continued to work on each other's records – reunited as DPG for entitled *Dillinger & Young Gotti* (2001), which featured yet more low-budget gangsta retreads. After Death Row put out the bottom-feeding, vault-raiding *2002* (2001) album, Kurupt and Daz seemed to have reunited once again for *The Last Of Tha Pound* (2004), but it was really just a collection of old Death Row rejects that had been remixed, and some darts aimed at **Suge Knight**.

Despite these attacks, Kurupt was scheduled to drop his long-delayed *Against the Grain* album for Death Row in 2004.

**Dogg Food**
Death Row, 1995

None of their records are any good, so you might as well plump for the hit. The production, mostly from Daz and DJ Pooh, is a fine imitation of Dre's G-Funk, but Daz and Kurupt are just plain lazy and, even worse, uncharismatic on the mic.

# Double Dee & Steinski

Probably the greatest and most important artists you've never heard of, **Double Dee & Steinski** took hip-hop's cut 'n' paste logic to its furthest possible extremes and ushered in the era of sampladelia. Picking up where "The Adventures Of Grandmaster Flash On The Wheels Of Steel" left off, studio engineer **Doug DiFranco** and advertising jingle producer **Steve Stein** diced and spliced break-beats, song snippets, movie fragments and mass-media soundbites into audio collages that were potent critiques of the information society, but were also as exciting as any James Brown song.

The winner of a contest held by Tommy Boy for mastermixes of **G.L.O.B.E. & Whiz Kid**'s 1983 single "Play That Beat Mr. DJ", Double Dee & Steinski's "The Payoff Mix" (1984) became an enormous cult hit in New York by virtue of its prescient reading of sampling as the modern equivalent of the call-and-response that characterised African-American music. Despite the fact that you couldn't hear the joins or edits, however, "The Payoff Mix" was not the product of sampling technology, but the result of endless hours in the studio literally cutting and pasting tape together. It encompassed **Spoonie Gee**, "Soul Power" chants courtesy of Bobby Byrd, **Funky Four Plus One More**'s "It's The Joint", the World Famous Supreme Team radio show, **Incredible Bongo Band**'s "Apache", Culture Club, **Little Richard**, exercise routines, dialogue from **Humphrey Bogart**, Herbie Hancock's "Rockit", **The Supremes**' "Stop in the Name of Love", Grandmaster Flash, **Chic** and about 100 other things, not to mention "Play That Beat Mr. DJ". "The

Payoff Mix" remains one of the most audacious records ever made.

Following its success, DiFranco and Stein applied their mastermixing touch to the "hardest working man in showbusiness" on "Lesson Two: The James Brown Mix" (1984). A few years before **Eric B. & Rakim** heralded the age of hip-hop's JB idolatry, Double Dee & Steinski recognised the Godfather of Soul as the progenitor of hip-hop. Another promiscuous mixture of sounds, "Lesson Two: The James Brown Mix" sandwiched Mr. Please-Please's greatest hits with to **Bugs Bunny**, Dirty Harry, Junior's "Mama Used to Say", **Sly Stone**, "Double Dutch Bus" and G.L.O.B.E. & Whiz Kid.

"Lesson Three: The History of HipHop" (1985) appeared with the other two on an EP that was scheduled for release by Tommy Boy, but was blocked by corporate copyright robber-barons who demanded compensation for the samples. With an info-slipstream comprised of snippets from **Herman Kelly & Life**'s "Dance To The Drummer's Beat", **Dennis Coffey**'s "Scorpio", "Starski Live At The Disco Fever", the B-movie *Mars Needs Women*, original cut 'n' paster **Dickie Goodman**, a late-night talk-show announcer, Baby Huey, **Newcleus**, Kraftwerk, Lauren Bacall, **Groucho Marx**, and human beatboxing courtesy of the Fat Boys, "Lesson Three" was as mind-boggling as the first two and was a perfect summation of hip-hop culture.

Although the multinational greed merchants at the record labels put a halt to the duo's multi-textual nefariousness, Steinski continued his guerilla media pranks while DiFranco returned to engineering. Credited to **Steinski & Mass Media**, "The Motorcade Sped On" (1987) was a stunning comment on the assassination

DOUBLE DEE
&
STEINSKI
Mastermixes

Produced by:
Double Dee &
Steinski
Engineered by:
Double Dee
For Promotional Use Only
Not For Sale

Side A
33 1/3 RPM
DDS-001A
5:20

The Payoff Mix
(Mastermix of G.L.O.B.E. and Whizkid's
"Play that beat, Mr. D.J.")
Courtesy Tommy Boy Records
To contact Double Dee & Steinski,
call 212-789-8578 or 212-836-0633

of President Kennedy. A cut-up of the news coverage with beats, a snippet of **Bob James**' "Mardi Gras" and **Queen** thrown in for good measure, "The Motorcade Sped On" held a mirror up to the face of post-modernism with its utterly ambiguous flurry of signifiers.

Far less nebulous was the post-**Gulf War** call to arms, "It's Up to You" (1992), which was a lot funnier and less facile than most left-wing Bush bashing. After contributing to the *Producers for Bob* (1993) project, which consisted of cut 'n' paste artists having their way with speeches emanating from The Church of the Sub-Genius (a spoof fundamentalist Christian religious organization), Stein continued to write music for adverts, produced an excellent radio show for New Jersey's WFMU station, and contributed an ode to the sex manual for Coldcut's *Let Us Play* album in 1997.

"NY, NY" emerged in 2001 on **Freddy Fresh**'s Howlin' label, part of which would re-appear on Steinski's excellent mixtape *Nothing to Fear* (2002). Steinski's *Sugar Hill Mix: Burning Out Of Control* (2003) firmly established Steinski as the undisputed king of the cut-up.

## VARIOUS ARTISTS

⊙ **No Rights Given Or Implied: The Original Samplers**
Bond Street, 1992

Given the litigiousness of copyright owners, none of Double Dee & Steinski's work is easy to find. This brilliant compilation (which includes all the "Lesson Mixes" as well as "The Motorcade Sped On" and "It's Up to You") is probably the easiest to track down.

# Dr. Dre

" **S** even days a week, he's on call/ To get the party people off the wall". He may not be the best or most consistent (that's **DJ Premier**), the most historically important (that's **Marley Marl**) or the most radical (that's the **Bomb Squad**), but Dr. Dre is certainly the most influential producer in hip-hop. From practically inventing high energy, West

Coast electro-funk with the **World Class Wreckin' Cru** (and starting the "Cabbage Patch" dance craze in the process), to creating the blueprint for gangsta rap with **N.W.A.** to birthing G-Funk as a solo artist, Dr. Dre has started more mini-epochs in popular music than anyone this side of James Brown.

Andre Young was born in Compton, California in 1965 and attended Centennial High where he caught the music bug at block parties and all-ages clubs like Eve's After Dark. After wowing the crowd with a DJ set at Eve's, Dre was invited by the club's owner, **Alonzo Williams**, to join his crew of DJs and rappers, the World Class Wreckin' Cru. Along with **DJ Yella**, the Unknown DJ, **Cli-N-Tel** and **Lonzo**, Dre was responsible for such uptempo (125-plus bpm) electro-funk tracks as "World Class", "Juice" and Cli-N-Tel's ode to Dre, "Surgery", in 1984 and 1985. After one album, *Rapped In Silence* (1986), the WCWC disbanded and Dre and DJ Yella hooked up with Stereo Crew MC Ice Cube, MC Ren and Eazy-E to form **Niggaz With Attitude.**

With N.W.A., Dre produced some of the most powerful music ever made: *Straight Outta Compton* (1989) screamed out of the speakers with a sonic rage that matched the lyrics, while *Efil4zaggin* (1991) began the trend for whiny synths and P-Funk beats that Dre would perfect on *The Chronic*. During this time, Dre also found time to produce records for **The DOC** and the "We're All In The Same Gang" (1990) single.

Extricated from his contract with Eazy-E's Ruthless label by Death Row CEO **Suge Knight**, Dre changed the world with what could have been just another throwaway track from a movie soundtrack. Over a beat more menacing and askew than anything trip-hop would come up with in five years of ripping it off, "Deep Cover" (1992) introduced **Snoop Doggy Dogg** drawling, "It's 1-8-7 on an undercover cop", in a Deep South accent that exuded a fearsome casual violence. *The Chronic* (1992) was even more frightening. It took the oft-stated truism that real gangsters listen to the smoothest music as its starting point, and forensically explored the tension between

The doctor will see you now...

the two meanings of the word "chilling". *The Chronic*'s languid pace, lazy drawls and laidback beats surrounded tales of horrific but matter-of-fact violence, and its insouciance was simultaneously bloodcurdling and seductive. The album dominated hiphop: "Nuthin' But A G Thang" and "Dre Day" both went top ten; the album sold four million copies; it created more "wiggas" than **Muddy Waters** ever did; and it more or less ended hip-hop's sampling era by demonstrating the potency of live basslines, Moog hooks and **Leon Haywood**, Isaac Hayes and **Donny Hathaway** interpolations.

After the Death Row label got itself into trouble, Dre formed his own label,

**Aftermath** and released the disappointing *Dr. Dre Presents ... The Aftermath* (1996) which saw Dre backing away from G-Funk. The album's one great moment was actually the preposterous video for "Been There, Done That".

He foisted **Eminem** on the world, and then returned with *Dr. Dre 2001* (2000). Almost a decade after *The Chronic*, Dre hadn't moved an inch. The misogyny was worse than ever; the mercenary capitalism, which was contextualized by the LA riots in 1991 on *The Chronic*, was now just grotesque and dumb, even if things haven't changed much; and the music was a garish imitation of past glories. Compared to producers like **Swizz Beatz**, who took Dre's

ghetto symphonies to new levels of grandeur with shimmering synth lines, sleek beats and salsa touches, Dre's work on 2001 sounded as archaic as his World Class Wreckin' Cru records did when *Straight Outta Compton* dropped.

Nevertheless, the album was huge and Dre started to pop up everywhere again. His post-2001 productions – **Xzibit**'s "X" and "U Know", **Mary J Blige**'s "Family Affair", **Eve**'s "Let Me Blow Ya Mind", **Truth Hurts**' "Addictive" and, oh yeah, some guy called **Eminem** – were far better and far funkier than the ones on his album, and indicated that, once again, the doctor was always on call.

⊙ **The Chronic**
Death Row/Interscope, 1992

So effortlessly funky, it's no wonder that this was the most influential hip-hop album of the 1990s.

# Jermaine Dupri/ So So Def

Making hits is almost in Jermaine Dupri's blood: his father, Michael Mauldin, is an ex-musician who managed **Arrested Development** before he was appointed president of Sony's black music division. As a kid, Dupri danced for both **UTFO** and **Whodini**; by the age of 14

he had produced his first record – **Silk Tymes Leather**'s instantly forgettable debut.

Dupri made his name, though, as the svengali behind the teenage novelty rap sensation **Kriss Kross**. Pulling the strings that made **Daddy Mack** and **Mack Daddy** "Jump", Dupri was behind the pop sensation of 1992, with their debut album, *Totally Krossed Out*, producing three top twenty singles. When Kriss Kross's balls and voices dropped, however, Dupri shifted focus to another under-age r&b sensation, **Usher**, for whom he produced the enormous "You Make Me Wanna..." in 1997.

In the meantime, Dupri discovered Shawntae Harris (aka **Da Brat**) and signed her to his So So Def label. Her debut album, *Funkdafied* (1994), was the first album by a female rapper to go platinum. On the title cut, *Funkdafied* proved itself a more upwardly mobile take on Dr. Dre's G-Funk, with smoother synth riffs, bongo patterns stolen from crosstown producers **Organized Noize**, lusher production values, Da Brat's flow (complete with "Brat-a-tat-tat" catchphrase) and a more refined taste in product placements (Moët being the tipple of choice, rather than Tanqueray).

*Anuthatantrum* (1996) was largely more of the same, except not as funky. While Da Brat cameoed on just about every single Dupri production, she wouldn't release another album until *Unrestricted* (2000), which saw her toss away her trademark baggy camouflage trousers in favour of make-up and cleavage. The music had had a make-over too: with **Timbaland** triggers, flamenco guitar and r&b collaborations replacing the rolling funk.

Not content with having carved out a large chunk of the r&b and pop-rap markets, Dupri launched the **So So Def Bass Allstars** to bring the Atlanta Bass sound to the mainstream. He was also behind the **Ghost Town DJs**' summer hit, "My Boo" (1996). Dupri's real motivation, however, seemed to be imitating Bad Boy. He not only dragged in **Notorious BIG** for "The

Dirty B-Side" (1994), the flip of Da Brat's "Funkdafied", and gave shout-outs to Puffy's enterprise, he even rapped like Puffy on his debut album as an artist, *Life In 1472* (1998). On "Money Ain't A Thing" Dupri stumbled and mumbled just like **Puff Daddy** and Mase — he even pronounced his "r"s with a New York accent. Astutely, he called in **Jay-Z** to act as his Biggie-like crutch and the track blew up, with Jigga dropping gleaming jewels like, "It's all basic/I've been spending 100s since they had small faces".

There were even rumours circulating that Dupri was trying to lure Ma$e away from Bad Boy, before Ma$e ended up retiring from the rap game (sadly temporarily, it would transpire). With Bad Boy struggling, Dupri set about emulating that other high-profile ghetto-preneur, **Master P**, when he started his own sports management agency. Had Dupri announced he was planning on opening a chain of So So

Once Da Brat, always Da Brat.

Def supermarkets, you wouldn't have been surprised in the least.

Rather than compete with Wal-Mart, however, Dupri peddled more kid-hop in the form of pre-teen MC **Lil' Bow Wow**'s *Beware of Dog* (2000), which featured "Bounce With Me" – the "Jump" for the "noughties" – and went multi-platinum. *Doggy Bag* (2001) was more of the same formulaic, button-pushing pop-rap, and it gave wags ample opportunity to razz on the title.

Dupri's own *Instructions* (2001) was among the more reprehensible albums in a long and inglorious history of reprehensible albums in hip-hop: nothing but Dupri and guests rapping about how to become a playa. The answer: sit around and collect loot by ripping off every other commer-

cially successful rapper and producer.

Dupri's So So Def label followed his instructions to the letter on St. Louis teenager **J-Kwon**'s monstrous debut single "Tipsy" (2003). Over the top of a beat (by the **TrackBoyz**) that was a zeitgeist-copping meeting of **The Clipse**'s "Grindin'" and **Lil' Jon**-style crunk, the underaged J-Kwon rapped about the pleasures of getting your drink on in the club. *Hood Hop* (2004) was a typical Dupri cash-in: repeat the formula of the hit single ad infinitum, capitalize on the kid's charm while he's still young and too dumb to know any better, then and ditch him as soon as he starts shaving.

**⊙ Da Brat – Funkdafied**
Columbia, 1994

Slick G-Funk retooled for a tomboy, this is the most bearable entry in Dupri's secondhand hit parade.

# E-40 & The Click

Long before wannabe playas were sipping on Hennessy and champagne, gamers were chilling with jugs of cheap Californian Burgundy. What Puffy is to Cristal, **E-40** is to Carlo Rossi. The poet laureate of big-ballin', shot-callin' "Yay Area" (Bay Area) hustlin', **Earl Stevens** is the Charlie Hustle of the Hall of Game: one of the great playas, but one who has never received the respect he deserves. E-40 is one of hip-hop's singular performers – he's brought more phrases into popular usage than anyone since **Noah Webster** (he's even published his own dictionary – the *Dictionary Book of Slang*) and his phrasing and flow has influenced everyone from OutKast's **Big Boi** to Blackalicious's **Gift of Gab**. But, due to his NoCal locale, he has largely been ignored by the New York-centric hip-hop media. He's one of those MCs who, in his own singular parlance, you either smell or you don't.

E-40 first came to attention as part of **The Click**, a group made up of himself, his sister **Suga-T**, his brother **D-Shot** and his cousin **B-Legit**. Following the lead of Too $hort, they started their own company,

Sick Wid' It, and hawked tapes out of the trunk of their car on their home turf of Vallejo, California. Before this, E-40, B-Legit and D-Shot started performing as students at Grambling State University in Louisiana, and the transplanted Southern drawl became a large part of the group's charm. The *Less Side* EP (1990) was their first widely available release, but it was E-40's *Federal* (1992) album and his bizarre rhyming style on tracks like "Carlo Rossi", "Mr. Flamboyant", "Drought Season" and "Federal" that really got the clique noticed, and it officially sold 200,000 copies.

E-40's real breakthrough, though, was *The Mailman* EP (1993). "Practice Lookin' Hard" was a hilarious exposé of the playa poseur, while "Captain Save A Hoe" was the best example of the stuttering, drawling, light-speed combo-flow of **Forty Fonzarelli** (as he styled himself), and his penchant for inventing words. As a result of the huge success of *The Mailman*, Jive licensed Sick Wid' It and distributed their product internationally.

*In a Major Way* (1995) went gold as E-40 tightened up his synth-funk and gave the people exactly what they wanted on the cheeky duet with **Suga-T**, "Sprinkle Me". The Click's *Game Related* (1995) followed, with more expertly crafted street tales and the best hip-hop drinking song since **N.W.A.**'s "Eightball", "Hurricane". E-40's *Hall Of Game* (1996) was a slight depar-

ture, featuring the hit "Rappers' Ball" with **Too $hort** and **K-Ci** from Jodeci on which E-40 revealed his philosophy: "I don't freestyle, I don't rap for free".

*The Element Of Surprise* (1998) was E-40's best since *The Mailman* and featured classic West Coast funk courtesy of producers **Ant Banks** and **Tone Capone**. "Hope I Don't Back" found 40 bragging about his success and praying he wouldn't have to go back to hustling, while "Lieutenant Roastabotch" was a classic battle-of-the-sexes rhyme with **Silk E**. *Charlie Hustle: The Blueprint Of A Self-Made Millionaire* (1999) found E-Freezy getting more autobiographical, but instead of the hunger and humour that he used to sling, here he just sounded complacent and bloated.

But, by this time, seemingly everyone wanted in on a bit of that Charlie Hustle magic, and his albums became little more than series of cameos. *Loyalty and Betrayal* (2000), *Grit & Grind* (2002) and *Breakin' News* (2003) featured appearances from **Ice Cube**, Pastor Troy, Eightball, Nate Dogg, **Fabolous**, Bun B and the like. Not that these records didn't have their high points – particularly "Rep Yo City" (from *Grit & Grind*) with **Petey Pablo**, Bun B and Eightball, and "Quarterbackin'" (from *Breakin' News*), a superb imitation **Neptunes** production that found E-40 trading hustling rhymes with **The Clipse**.

**The Mailman**
Sick Wid' It, 1993

With its humour, newly-minted slanguage and synth-funk, this is an absolute classic of "Yay Area" hip-hop.

# Eazy-E

See *N.W.A.*

# ED OG & The Bulldogs

Typically of Boston's unprepossessing hip-hop scene, its most famous MC will permanently be associated with Brooklyn. But while **Guru** had to leave "Beantown" for New York to gain fame with Gang Starr, **Ed OG and The Bulldogs** managed to garner a rep without ever having to set foot outside of Roxbury. That said, however, Ed OG and gang still owed their career to the New York-based production team and radio DJs the **Awesome Two** (Special K and Teddy Ted), who produced their debut album and broke their hits on their influential show on WHBI.

*Life Of A Kid In The Ghetto* (1991) probably couldn't have been made in any other year than 1991. The album's naïvety was just about the last gasp of hip-hop's "golden age" before its wide-eyed optimism got blown away by Cypress Hill and Dr. Dre. On their biggest hit, "I Got to Have It", Ed OG (**Edward Anderson**) told us that "The Bulldogs" was an acronym for "Black United Leaders Living Directly On Groovin' Sounds" — you can't get any more early 1990s than that. Come to think of it, you can't get any more late 1980s than that.

Despite such silliness, "I Got To Have It" was based on an irresistible, chopped-up loop of the human metronome **Hamilton Bohannon**, and a killer horn riff that would be swiped by other producers and would later play a key role in X-Ecutioner Rob Swift's beat-juggling routine. *Life of a Kid In The Ghetto* also featured the irritat-ingly self-righteous "Be a Father to Your Child" (naturally a favourite of *Yo! MTV Raps*, in its moralistic days) and "Bug-A-Boo", which would later be revisited by Destiny's Child.

While they were behind the times when they released *Life Of A Kid In The Ghetto*, they were hopelessly outdated on *Roxbury 02119* (1994). Despite production by **Diamond D** and **Prince Rakeem** (aka the RZA), *Roxbury 02119* found Ed OG desperately trying to sound hard and failing miserably. Tracks like "Skinny Dip (Got it Goin' On)" were laughable, with Ed claiming his *nom de mic* was an acronym for "Every Day Other Girls". The only cut with any redeeming features was "Love Comes And Goes", a paean to victims of random street violence, including Ed's father.

After a few years laying really low, Ed OG returned with "Just Because" (1998) on the Mass In Action label. With production by **DJ Spinna** and Joe Mansefield, "Let's Be Realistic/Better Than Before" (1999) found Ed sounding comfortable with the sonics of the late 1990s underground. His third album, *All Said And Done* (2000), followed a similar formula, with tracks from **DJ Premier**, Pete Rock, Spinna and **Dialect**.

Premier and Pete Rock showed up again for *The Truth Hurts* (2001), along with fellow Bostonian **Guru**, Black Thought from The Roots and **Tajai** and **Casual** from the Hieroglyphics crew. Ed continued to prove himself more than capable of holding his own with other underground MCs in terms of technique. His lyrics ("Ed OG is to rapping what Pedro is to pitching" – yeesh), however, left something to be desired. *Wishful Thinking* (2003), mostly produced by **DJ Supreme One**, fared better because of a more consistent production style and the sharpening of Ed's wit ("Everything I write is a masterpiece/You're gettin' raped by your label like Catholic priests").

**Life Of A Kid In The Ghetto**
Mercury, 1991

The ungainly lyrics and self-righteous politics sound impossibly corny now, but the production makes the album worthwhile.

# Edan

Hip-hop's built-in mythology doesn't leave a lot of room for irreverence. While magazines like *Ego Trip*, *Life Sucks Die* and *Fat Lace* have managed to skewer hip-hop pretence at the same time as they celebrate those same postures, musicians themselves have rarely managed the same feat. **Prince Paul** springs immediately to mind, but no one else aside from a 20-something punk prankster from Boston called Edan the Humble Magnificent.

Edan Portnoy grew up in Baltimore where he developed a taste for the curse words of **N.W.A.**. He soon started collecting rare hip-hop records and went to Boston's Berklee School of Music, in an attempt to turn his record collection into gold. Dropping out, he started selling mixtapes and making his own tracks. In 1999 he released "Sing It Shitface" on Biscuithead Records. More singles like "Rapperfection" (2000), "Drop Some Smooth Lyrics" (2001) and "Rap Beautician" (2002) followed on his own **Humble Mag** record label.

Most of these early singles were collected on *Primitive Plus* (2002). At first glance, Edan seemed like the worst kind of indie MC: he imitated **Greg Nice** on "Emcees Smoke Crack", pastiched the **Ultramagnetic MCs** on "Ultra '88", dropped more names

than **Nigel Dempster** and refused to admit that **Big Daddy Kane** ever fell off. However, what immediately set Edan apart from the legions of old school carrion crows was his sense of humour: the bonus track at the end of *Primitive Plus* was a dead-on mockery of hip-hop love songs such as LL Cool J's "I Need Love" with Edan cooing lines like "I just want to make friends with MCs/Buy them ice cream/Take 'em to the park... Let's go walk around and talk about each other's problems".

What really made Edan special, though, was that the guy had hooks: the ultra-nasal "MCs smoke crack, I smoke aluminum" was as memorable a catchphrase as independent hip-hop had come up with since **Dilated Peoples**' "Work The Angles". Wipe away the lo-fi production, do away with the skills showcases, and you've got a born entertainer who would be just as comfortable in the **Borscht Belt** as he would at **Skribble Jam**.

The album was followed by two wonderful examples of insane hip-hop archaeology that revealed the depths of Edan's crates: *Fast Rap* (2002) and *The Sound Of The Funky Drummer* (2004). "I See Colours" (2004) rocked a loop of the old children's song "I Can Sing A Rainbow" and offered a fittingly delirious preview of his *Beauty And The Beat* (2004) album.

★EDAN★ I SEE COLOURS 12"

**Primitive Plus**
Lewis, 2002

The hip-hop underground's old school fetishism isn't always very pretty – as if deep crates and knowledge somehow make up for a lack of skills. While Edan could tell you what colour shoelaces Paul C was wearing when he did Super Lover Cee and Casanova Rud's "Do The James", on this album the old school veneration was more along the lines of "I farted in the fishbowl/And then I played pinball with Zev Love X and Percee P and Stezo/Yo, this is a number one record".

# Egyptian Lover

Long before it was the home of gangsta rap and **G-Funk**, Los Angeles played host to a small but vibrant and prolific scene of electro-funkateers who blended their raps with large doses of "Planet Rock" and P-Funk. One of the prime movers of this scene was **Greg Broussard**, aka Egyptian Lover.

The Egyptian Lover got his start as part of Rodger Clayton's **Uncle Jamm's Army**, a crew of DJs who played parties throughout LA. Along with a certain **Ice-T** and Chris "The Glove" Taylor, Egyptian Lover made an appearance in the 1983 breakdance documentary *Breaking and Entering*. He collaborated with those three on the soundtrack, which is an extremely sought-after collector's item. He released his first single, "Egypt, Egypt" (1984) on Clayton's Freak Beat Records and then set up his own Egyptian Empire label.

The overwrought, faintly Germanic vocals, vague sci-fi, future primitivist concepts and clipped drum-machine programming of "Egypt, Egypt" and "My House (On the Nile)" (1984) were closer to the proto-techno style of Detroit's Cybotron than it was to either the East Coast electro style or the more straightforward electro-funk of **World Class Wreckin' Cru** et al. "What Is A DJ If He Can't Scratch?" (the flip of "Egypt, Egypt"), however, was a demand for traditional hip-hop vir-

tues even as he was helping to banish the DJ with his synths and drum machines. "Girls" (1984) rewrote the homo-eroticism of **Kraftwerk**'s "Tour De France" for homies from South Central who, even though they were wearing make-up and spangled jackets (this *was* the early 1980s...), liked eyeing up the hoochies in biker shorts. All of Egyptian Lover's early singles were collected on his great debut album, *On The Nile* (1984).

Egyptian Lover's sophomore album, *One Track Mind* (1986), suffered from his **Prince** fetish taking centre-stage over his hip-hop leanings. Nevertheless, two of the album's singles, "The Lover" and "Freak-A-Holic", were bigger hits than any of his previous records. That same year, he introduced longtime LA hip-hop stalwart **Rodney O** on their duet, "These Are My Beats" (1986), which featured Rodney rapping over the kind of bassline that would become the stock in trade of Berlin's now legendary techno label, **Basic Channel**. Rodney O was to team up with DJ **Joe Cooley** for one of the records that would shift LA hip-hop out of the electro-hop style and closer to the gangsta sound that would give it fame a few years later. "Everlasting Bass" (1986), again released on Egyptian Empire, sported a slowed-down interpolation of **Barry White** and a really deep, slow, rolling rhythm that sounded like an impala on a creep-up.

With all the changes that were taking place in LA hip-hop, Egyptian Lover's *Filthy* (1988) sounded hopelessly out of date, even if it did have some decent dance tracks, in the form of "DSLs" and "Overdose". Egyptian Lover disappeared until 1992, when he produced Rodney O & Joe Cooley's response to **Tim Dog**'s "Fuck Compton", *Fuck New York* (1992). He reconfigured "Egypt, Egypt" for the rave scene as "Egypt Rave '93" (1993) and released "Bounce That Bootie" (1994) a year later. A few more albums have emerged from the Lover's camp, but they have become increasingly irrelevant to the hip-hop scene.

**On the Nile**
Egyptian Empire, 1984

Aside from the proclamations of "What Is A DJ If He Can't Scratch?", this doesn't sound very much like hip-hop as we know it. Nevertheless, it's one of the definitive documents of early LA electro-hop. "Egypt, Egypt", "Girls" and "My House (On the Nile)" are all electro classics and will move your feet even if they don't get your head nodding.

# Eightball & MJG

If anyone made the Dirty South dirty it was **Eightball & MJG**. Before Eightball & MJG (aka **Premro Smith** and **Marlon Jermaine Goodwin**) hit the scene, Southern hip-hop was the source of endless laughs for heads from the two coasts. As soon as Eightball & MJG started telling their Southern-fried gangsta tales on top of the scattershot drum machine beats that characterised Memphis's **Gangsta Walk** dance, however, the South finally rose again and players from Atlanta to Winston-Salem got their swerve on. The entire US was "'bout it, 'bout it", as rapper Cam'ron put it.

Smith and Goodwin are childhood friends from the crack-ravaged Orange Mound neighbourhood of Memphis, who started rapping in high school. In 1991 they released the *Listen to the Lyrics* tape, which was a big hit in their hometown. They soon came to the attention of **Suave House** CEO, Tony Draper, who signed the duo and persuaded them to relocate to his home base in Houston, where they recorded *Comin' Out Hard* (1993). Filled with brutal vignettes from the street like "9 Little Millimeta Boys", and rhyme after rhyme of pimp exploits like "Mr. Big", *Comin' Out Hard* proved that the South wasn't all Miami Bass soft porn, or corny pre-teens who wore their clothes backwards (see Jermaine Dupri entry).

*On The Outside Looking In* (1994) featured more tales of the M.E.M.P.H.I.S. (Making Easy Money Pimping Hoes In Style) lifestyle, with the anthemic "Lay It

Down" being the highlight. They really made a virtue of their Southern drawls on *On Top Of The World* (1995), however. With no airplay whatsoever, the group did most of the promotion themselves, driving across the country below the Mason-Dixon Line, and *On Top of the World* debuted in the Top 10 of *Billboard*'s album chart and at number two on the R&B chart. The album's more sophisticated approach was epitomised by "Space Age Pimpin'", which housed their mackin' philosophy in the bluesy funk that the **Organized Noize** production crew would make their stock in trade.

MJG and Eightball reinforced their commercial clout with two solo albums, *No More Glory* (1997) and *Lost* (1998) (a triple CD), which went gold and double platinum respectively. They re-emerged in 1999 with *In Our Lifetime Vol. 1*, which featured both reminiscing ("Paid Dues" with **Cee-Lo** from Goodie Mob) and "crime pays" tales like "Armed Robbery" (a consummate example of the archetypal Southern beat, with a bit of *Mission Impossible* thrown in for good measure). With the exception of the typewriter-like synth stutters of the DJ Quik-produced "Buck Bounce", *Space Age 4 Eva* (2000) suffered, perversely, from improved production values – the spacey haze of old was replaced with glitz and shine. A state of affairs that was only compounded by the duo's strange move to **Bad Boy** for 2004's *Living Legends*, an album with a more menacing, less pimped-out feel. The album's lead single, "You Don't Want Drama", had a crude synth riff and lyrics like "Overheat 'em, really mistreat 'em/ Let's Rodney King 'em and over-beat 'em".

**In Our Lifetime Vol. 1**
Suave House, 1999

They may sound like Compton's Most Wanted with exaggerated drawls, but these guys are Southern pioneers. This is their most thoughtful and well-produced album.

# El Da Sensei

See *Artifacts*

# EI-P

◊ See *Company Flow*; see also *Def Jux*

# Missy Elliott

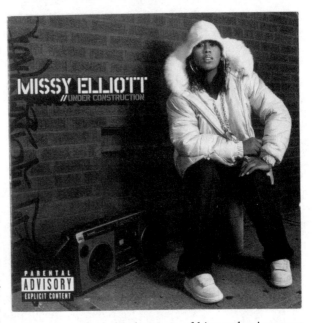

Missy "Misdemeanor" Elliott is the closest thing r&b has had to an iconic presence since **Prince** and **Michael Jackson** fell off. It's not just the eye-boggling, gargantuan rubbish bag she wears in "The Rain" video, though. With the possible exceptions of **Mary J. Blige** and **Lauryn Hill**, every other female r&b act has traditionally been putty in the producer's hands. Elliott, on the other hand, is clearly her own woman. Showing why hip-hop has more or less killed off soul music, Elliott is pure attitude. She'd be buried in the back row of the church choir, and she wouldn't be welcome in most hip-hop ciphers either, but she's upfront and in your face in an age when no one but the fiercest gangsta rapper has got any 'tude to speak of.

Elliott was originally part of a vocal group called **Sista** that was signed to Jodeci member **DeVante Swing**'s label. She soon hooked up with Swing associate

Timbaland as part of his production crew Da Bassment. She first came to prominence with her rap on the Bad Boy remix of Gina Thompson's "The Things That You Do" (1996), but it was her debut album, *Supa Dupa Fly* (1997), and her extraordinary wardrobe in her videos that set her on the road to doing Gap ads with **Madonna**. With Missy playing the bold superhero up front, and Timbaland the brainy producer who's got her back, the pair was a tag team that could have competed with the Road Warriors and the Freebirds. Their submission hold was the track that made Elliott a star, "The Rain (Supa Dupa Fly)". With a sample of the weirdest r&b track (until Timbaland came along), **Ann Peebles'** "I Can't Stand The Rain", a freaky, off-kilter bassline and Missy rapping lines like "Beep, beep, who's got the keys to the jeep/Vrrrroom", "The Rain" was the most crunching calling-card since wrestler Ric Flair's figure-four leg lock.

While the album *Da Real World* (1999) was just as good, Elliott was fast becoming the premier singles artist of her generation. "She's A Bitch", "Hot Boyz" and "All N My Grill" dominated urban radio with their combination of Timbaland's digital breakbeat freakery and Elliott's take-no-prisoners persona. *Miss E… So Addictive* (2001) followed with one of the most important singles of the new millennium, "Get Ur Freak On". The track's tabla and zither beat inaugurated the fad of hip-hop orientalism and launched a hundred records that used a similar beat (or sampled Asha Bhosle). "One Minute Man" and "Lick Shots" weren't bad either.

*Under Construction* (2002), Elliott's love letter to hip-hop, featured another stone-cold classic in "Work It", an energising take on the drums from Blondie's "Heart of Glass" with dentist-drill synth stabs, *Ironside*-like siren effects, elephant noises and Elliott speaking in tongues because she's so horny. *This Is Not a Test!* (2003), however, found Timbaland and herself in a holding pattern. Perhaps making her third album in three years had sapped her creative juices, or maybe the rest of the world had finally caught up with Timbaland.

**Supa Dupa Fly**
Elektra, 1997

Although the inevitable greatest hits package will be your best bet, you can't really go wrong with any of Elliott's albums (except for maybe *This Is Not A Test*). There isn't a producer currently working in hip-hop or r&b who hasn't lifted ideas off this album. Elliott's strong personality, taking the place of the usual r&b singer eye candy, is much, much more than the icing on the cake.

# Eminem

His views on bow hunting have yet to be recorded, but **Eminem** is nevertheless the leading contender to inherit Ted Nugent's title of "Motor City Madman". Born **Marshall Mathers**, Eminem grew up on the east side of Detroit in a predominantly black neighbourhood. Of course, it's no small

# ELECTRO

History is littered with "important" records, but few are truly as epochal as **Afrika Bambaataa & Soulsonic Force**'s "Planet Rock" (1982). Testament to the most bizarre musical union since Hawaiian slide guitars found their way to the Mississippi Delta, "Planet Rock" was the ultimate result of the bizarre popularity among America's urban black communities of Kraftwerk's **Trans-Europe Express** and **Autobahn** albums. By taking the melody from "Trans-Europe Express" and welding it to the bottom end of "Numbers", Afrika Bambaataa imagined what the Teutonic man-machines would sound like if they had Afros and fat-laced Adidas shell-toes.

Teaching the world that drum machines and video games could be funky, "Planet Rock" single-handedly kick-started the **electro** movement of the early '80s. With **Planet Patrol**'s "Play at Your Own Risk" (1982) and **Jonzun Crew**'s "Pack Jam" (1982) and "Space Cowboy" (1983), Bam's label Tommy Boy fully jumped on the electro bandwagon. Sugar Hill managed to briefly keep pace with **Reggie Griffin**'s Prince-meets-**Cabaret Voltaire** track, "Mirda Rock" (1982), but Sugar Hill was quickly supplanted by Tommy Boy as hip-hop's leading label.

Much of the best electro action, however, was happening on the margins. **Man Parrish**'s "Hip Hop Bee Bop (Don't Stop)" (1982) was Kraftwerk in dub. Probably the most original electro record after "Planet Rock" itself, and a favorite of body-lockers the world over, the echoing synth shimmers and *Computer World*-era basslines of "Hip Hop Bee Bop" made it sound like an early Tears for Fears B-side being mercilessly cut to death by Grandmaster Flash. Even so, it affirmed Kraftwerk's glacial electronics as the new sound of urban cool, and pointed the way for such dance-dub classics as The Peech Boys' "Don't Make Me Wait".

**Tyrone Brunson** capitalised on a bizarre dance craze with "The Smurf" (1982), while **Hashim** (**Jerry Calliste** and **Aldo Marin**) evoked some kind of imaginary cyberdelic casbah on the amazing "Al-Naafiysh (The Soul)" (1983). Calliste was also part of the **Imperial Brothers** whose "We Come to Dub" (1983) does for hiccoughs, sneezes and belches what "Planet Rock" did for drum machines. Calliste was a mainstay on New York's Cutting Records label, and he also had a hand in cult classics by the **Hi-Fidelity Three** like "B Boys Breakdance" and "Never Satisfied" (both 1983).

irony that the main contribution to hip-hop of America's largest city with a predominantly African-American population has been a string of melanin- and skills- deficient rappers such as **Kid Rock**, **Insane Clown Posse** and the like. Eminem, however, has a lot more going for him than some recycled Aerosmith riffs and secondhand Kiss make-up.

Mathers began rapping in high school, and he quickly acquired a rep for his freestyling abilities. In 1995 he released a single with fellow Detroit MC **Proof** on a tiny local label, which led to the *Infinite* (1996) album on the Web Entertainment label. While *Infinite* showcased Eminem's abundant wit and rhyming ability, it was a muddled effort in a very different, more positive style than

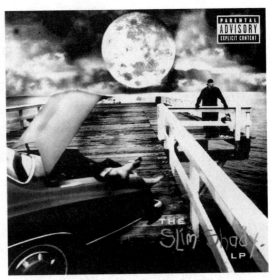

the one that has made him famous.

On the *Slim Shady* EP (1997), however, Eminem got his license to ill, and on the

Coming on like an old soul band that had stumbled across one of their kids' vocoders, **Newcleus** "made the girls go wikki-wikki" with "Jam On Revenge" (1984). **Whodini** went with the new trend on "Magic's Wand" (1982), while real old school cats like Bernie Worrell and Last Poet Jalal Nuriddin got electrified on records on the Celluloid label. Even soul collector Aaron Fuchs, who owned the Tuff City label, got into the act with **Davy DMX**, who emphasised the sub-genre's debt to European ideas with a British female rapper on classics like "One for The Treble" and "DMX Will Rock" (both 1984).

With the ascendency of Run DMC and their much harder drum-machine matrix, however, electro quickly died out on the East Coast, despite the best efforts of **Mantronix** and master tape-editors the **Latin Rascals** and **Chep Nunez**. On the West Coast, though, things were different. With **Egyptian Lover**, **World Class Wreckin' Cru**, **Knights of the Turntable** and **The Unknown DJ**, electro-funk kept Californian poppers and lockers rocking well into the mid-1980s with party jams that eschewed the East Coast's Orwellian alienation and darkness. The same was true in Miami, where mid-1980s electro records like Debbie Deb's "When I Hear Music" and **Pretty Tony**'s "Jam The Box" (both 1984) kept the South Beach shaking till the early hours. By the follow-

THIS LP FEATURES 'HIP HOP BE BOP (DON'T STOP)'

**MAN PARRISH**
**MAN PARRISH**
**MAN PARRISH**
**MAN PARRISH**
**MAN PARRISH**

ing year, however, MC Ade's "Bass Rock Express" was heralding the distinct 808 bass-bin sound of Miami Bass.

**VARIOUS ARTISTS**

**Street Jams: Electric Funk Vols. 1-4**
Rhino, 1992

An excellent series, providing an overview of all the styles from New York to Miami to Detroit to Los Angeles.

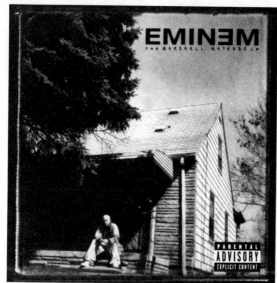

extraordinarily nihilistic "Just The Two Of Us" (in which he talks to his daughter while her mother's corpse is in the trunk of the car they're driving) and "Just Don't Give A Fuck", he displayed the awesome skills and stoopidly mordant worldview that would win him multi-platinum sales on his next release.

After becoming a favourite on LA's *Wake Up Show*, Eminem signed to Aftermath records and worked with **Dr. Dre** for *The Slim Shady LP* (1999). Built on a kiddie-park calliope keyboard and a sing-song bassline, "My Name Is" featured lines like "Got pissed off and ripped Pamela Lee's tits off/And smacked her so hard it knocked her clothes backwards like Kriss Kross" and "You know you blew up when women rush the stands and try to touch your hands like some screaming Usher fans" and became one of the singles of the year. The second single, "Guilty Conscience", was based on that scene in the movie **Animal House** where Tom Hulce's conscience and id battle it out, with Dr. Dre playing the conscience, setting up Eminem's "You're gonna take advice from someone who slapped Dee Barnes?" line. Aside from the three Dre tracks, though, the production couldn't match Eminem's gratuitously offensive wordplay, and made *The Slim Shady LP* feel too much like a novelty record.

Eminem was at his best, however, on indie singles like "Any Man" (1999) which featured on Rawkus's *Soundbombing II* compilation. Produced by **Da Beatminerz**, "Any Man"'s simple, raw and head-nodding beats suited Eminem's flow and rhymes ("I'll strike a still pose and hit you with some ill flows/ That don't even make sense like dykes using dildos/So reach in your billfolds for ten ducats/To pick up this Slim Shady shit that's on Rawkus/Sumtin', sumtin', sumtin', sumtin', I get weeded/My daughter scribbled over that rhyme, I couldn't read it") far better than those on *The Slim Shady LP*.

With beats from Dre, **45 King**, F.B.T. and Eminem himself, *The Marshall Mathers LP* (2000) didn't improve the production any (their cartoonish quality still deadened the impact of both his rhymes and his flow), but Eminem's growing self-consciousness made the album compellingly disturbing. There was a trend for rappers claiming that they weren't role models in the early 1990s, but Eminem's response to the moral panic surrounding him and **Marilyn Manson** was to get all broody, and to hurl invective at Middle America. He talks about raping his mother, he adopts the persona of an obsessed fan whose letters he doesn't respond to, and avers "There's a Slim Shady in all of us". The first single, "The Real Slim Shady" was the only light relief. If the beats had been better, this would have been hip-hop's *There's a Riot Goin' On*.

A similar fate befell *The Eminem Show* (2002) – released after Eminem's surprisingly good semi-autobiographical performance in the film *8 Mile* – which mostly explored the media circus surrounding his rise to superstardom. The beats once again emphasised the playground, wise-ass nature of Eminem's delivery, undercutting the often fairly robust political invective found on the album. When he wasn't attacking the hypocrisy of **Lynne Cheney** (the wife of Vice President Dick Cheney), castigating his ex-wife or baiting the press about his homophobia, the album was either hopelessly mawkish ("Cleaning Out My Closet") or plain stupid ("Drips").

Eminem's penchant for sing-song juvenilia was writ large on the records he made with his shock-rap crew **D12** (Peter S Bizarre, Kon Artis, Swifty McVay, Proof and Kuniva). After debuting with the incendiary "Shit On You" ("I'm responsible for killing John Candy/Got JonBenet Ramsay in my '98 Camry") which stole a page from fellow Motowner **Esham**, D12 dropped *Devil's Night* (2001), a foul-smelling brew of splatter rhymes, boasts of ugly sex and wanton pharmaceutical abuse – one strictly for the death metal crowd. *D12 World* (2004) was more of the same horror-flick imagery and scatology, punctuated by Eminem bleating about his feud with **Benzino**. Em returned to the fray towards the end of that year with a new single "Mosh". A slow processional march, its release coincided with the run-up to the 2004 presidential election, and its lyrics urged his legions of fans to make use of their vote to oust George Bush. The song had a narcissistic, messianic self-importance, but did at least feature the couplet "we're responsible for this monster, this coward/who we have empowered". It was swiftly followed by the album *Encore*. The beats followed his now tried-and-tested formula, leaving only the clattering, camera-shutter percussion of "My 1st Single" and the Cypress-Hill-meets-*Nutcracker*

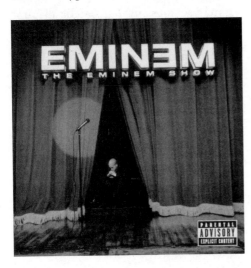

*Suite* riff of "Big Weenie" to frame his grandstanding with any panache.

⊙ **The Slim Shady LP**
Aftermath, 1999

Despite uneven production, the high points make this the most cathartic, teenage angst cartoon since Slayer's *Reign in Blood*.

# 💿 Enjoy Records

Sugar Hill may have been first, the biggest and most powerful of the early hip-hop labels, but Enjoy was just as important. Unlike Sugar Hill, which had a high "novelty" factor, Enjoy released records by established crews who had been rockin' parties for years without having to borrow **Grandmaster Caz**'s notebook.

Enjoy was founded by longtime record man and one-time doo-wop impresario Bobby Robinson. In the late 1970s he was turned on to the hip-hop phenomenon by his nephew Gabriel Jackson, who persuaded him to sign both **Funky Four Plus One** and **Grandmaster Flash & the Furious Five**. Based on Cheryl Lynn's "Got to Be Real", Funky Four Plus One's dynamic 14-minute epic "Rappin' And Rocking The House" (1979) was the label's first release. It was topped a month later by the Furious Five's singular "Superrappin'" (1979), another ten-minute-plus epic that featured the best vocal interplay on any early hip-hop record, on top of a monstrous, Chic-influenced, heavily syncopated groove courtesy of house percussionist **Pumpkin**.

Unfortunately for Robinson, both crews signed with Sugar Hill soon afterwards. Nevertheless, in **The Treacherous Three** he still had one of the greatest old school crews. They debuted, with Gabriel Jackson (who was now calling himself **Spoonie Gee**) on "Love Rap/New Rap Language" (1980), an epochal single that laid the roots for the new school with its more plain-speech style of MCing, as opposed to the declamatory, theatrical style common in the early days. Singles such as "The Body Rock" and "At the Party" in 1980, and "Feel the Heartbeat" in 1981 followed, before the

Treacherous Three also skipped across Harlem to Sugar Hill.

Despite losing their best artists, Enjoy kept releasing classics, from **The Disco Four**'s "Move to the Groove" and **Kool Kyle the Starchild**'s "Do You Like That Funky Beat" in 1980, to Kyle's fantastic version of Jimmy Bo Horne's "Is it In?" – "It's Rockin' Time" in 1981 – **Fearless Four**'s "Rockin' It" (1982) and **Masterdon Committee**'s "Funk Box Party" (1982). Although he once again showed his prescience by signing **Doug E Fresh** for 1984's "Just Having Fun", his timing was once again off, and Fresh quickly left. Robinson struggled on for the next few years, releasing a trickle of so-so 12"s. Enjoy finally shut its doors after releasing Most Wanted's "Good Ole Days" in 1988.

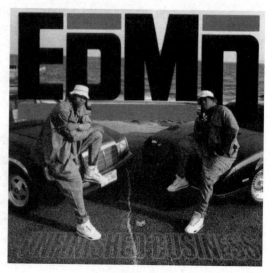

### VARIOUS ARTISTS

**The Best of Enjoy Records**
Hot Productions, 1989

With great grooves, courtesy of a band led by drummer Pumpkin and percussionist Pooche Costello, and a roster that included the best of the old school crews, Enjoy released some of the best records of the early hip-hop period. Most of Enjoy's best moments – including "Superrappin'", "The New Rap Language", "Feel the Heartbeat" and "Funk Box Party" – are included here.

# EPMD

Childhood friends **Erick Sermon** and **Parrish Smith** represented hip-hop in its purest form: they were neighbourhood kids made good, with no other aim than to find fresh beats and get paid. No strict aesthetic sensibilities or political agendas for **EPMD** (Erick and Parrish Making Dollars) – instead they were self-proclaimed "locksmiths with the key to fame".

Their debut album, *Strictly Business* (1988), remains one of the funkiest hip-hop albums ever made. Unlike the majority of MCs at the time, who hyperventilated or yelled to get their words across, Erick and Parrish (along with Rakim) originated the laid-back rapping style. EPMD relished

in the sound of their plain speech — they made an art out of their New York accents and Erick's cottonmouth flow. Making jeep beats for the booming car audio systems that dominated New York's urban soundscape during the time, "You Gots 2 Chill" and "It's My Thing" were grounded by woofer-destroying sub-bass and samples of **Zapp**'s "More Bounce To The Ounce" and The Whole Darn Family's "7 Minutes Of Funk", while the title track sampled Eric Clapton's "I Shot The Sheriff" to create a rhythmic juggernaut. The album also introduced one of hip-hop's most enduring slang dick references: 'bozack'.

*Unfinished Business* (1989) was slightly less accomplished, but followed the same formula to good effect. With its moody guitar sample and Funkadelic-inspired chorus, "So What Cha Sayin'" became their signature tune, while "Please Listen To My Demo" practically introduced back-in-the-day nostalgic reminiscing to hip-hop. *Business As Usual* (1990) did just what it said on the cover, but, as Karl Marx would surely have told them, business as usual leads to over-production. There were highlights, though: "Rampage", a collaboration with **LL Cool J**, which played on the differences between Erick's mealy-mouthed style and Cool J's *My Fair Lady* elocution for all they were worth, and "Hardcore", which featured a hot cameo from one of the members of EPMD's Hit Squad posse, **Redman**.

*Business Never Personal* (1992) built on the foundations of "So Whatcha Sayin'" and "Get the Bozack" by concentrating on a tougher, darker, tenser music filled with hard-hitting guitar samples and brutal metaphors. Epitomising the new approach was the awesome collaboration with Redman and fellow Hit Squad member K-Solo, "Headbanger". After the album, however, Erick and Parrish split on extremely unfriendly terms. During their split, Parrish's PMD Records struggled, while Erick struck gold with his Def Squad crew. It included Redman and **Keith Murray**, who both appeared on Erick's rather good, seriously blunted 1995 solo project, *Double Or Nothing*.

In 1997 though, Erick and Parrish started making dollars together again with a surprisingly decent comeback record, *Back In Business*. Based on a killer loop from **The Meters**' "Just Kissed My Baby", "Never Seen Before" was the highlight and announced the duo's return with a raw take on the Jay-Z skitter style. Then, although they claimed that the title of their follow-up, *Out of Business* (1999), referred to the end of the millennium, it was hard to shake the feeling that this was their final goodbye. Still, tracks like "Pioneers" and "Symphony 2000" showed that, unlike almost all of their contemporaries from the 1980s, Erick and Parrish could cut it

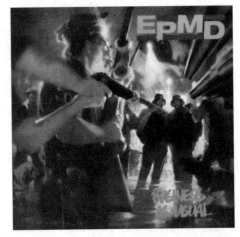

with the new styles. Sermon's *Def Squad Presents Erick Onassis* (2000) highlighted the group's timelessness, featuring a collaboration from beyond the grave with **Eazy-E**, trans-coastal cuts with DJ Quik and **Xzibit**, and straight-up, who-cares-where-you're-from bangers.

Sermon's 2001 single "Music" was perhaps the best thing he's ever done – an absolutely stunning "duet" with **Marvin Gaye** and a testament of faith in the power of music that managed to be both moving and banging in the same breath. The album *Music* (2001) carried on in the same mood, though tracks like "The Sermon" (with **R. Kelly**) attempted to follow the same formula but ended up being simply cloying.

The same pattern ruined *React* (2002). The title track was a super-hot club track with Redman which rode a sample of Indian film singer **Asha Bhosle**, but the rest of the album was nothing but pro-forma Sermon talking shit with his mush-mouth over stale beats – or trying to recapture the magic of "Music" (as on "Love Iz" where he turns the same trick with Al Green's "Love and Happiness"). *Chilltown, New York* (2004) moved away from the club bangers altogether, in favour of a sound that recalled the Big Apple circa 1993. It was a move that appealed to the purists, but was a tad boring for everyone else.

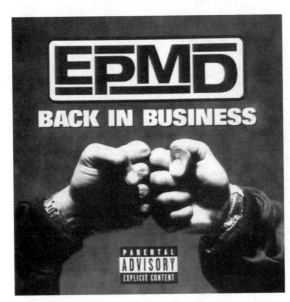

**BUSINESS NEVER PERSONAL**

PMD, meanwhile, disappeared underground for a while, hooking up with DJ Honda, **Kut Master Kurt** and Big Noyd. He returned in 2003 with *The Awakening*, an album that suffered from lacklustre beats and Parrish's one-dimensional flow.

⊙ **Strictly Business**
Priority, 1988

Their debut album was probably responsible for introducing one of hip-hop's most enduring concerns — the dialectic between the rough and the smooth.

# Eric B & Rakim

Hip-hop may have been "Run's House" throughout most of the 1980s, but **Eric B & Rakim** definitely jumped the fence and sprayed their musk around the backyard. When hip-hop made its artistic and commercial breakthrough in the mid-late 1980s, the genre's focus had shifted from New York's mean streets to the suburban enclave of Long Island. The duo of **Eric Barrier** (turntables) and **William 'Rakim' Griffin** (vocals) heralded this paradigm shift in 1986 with their debut single, "Eric B Is President". With its stark minimalism and dub-like sound effects, courtesy of producer Marley Marl, "Eric B Is President" was a staggering experiment in sound manipulation. It also introduced Rakim's thoroughly original and influential rapping style: calm, level, never missing a beat, and as incisive as a surgeon. The opening lines – "I came in the door, I said it before/I never let the mic magnetize me no more" – displayed Rakim's unique lyrical vision: almost 'meta-rapping'. "Eric B" was followed by the even more minimal "My Melody" (1986), which was little more than a kick-drum beat, whomping sub-bass and Rakim's brutal sucker-MC diss.

The landmark *Paid In Full* (1987) followed and became one of the two or three most influential hip-hop albums ever. On first listen, the album seemed like it was loaded with filler, but the instrumental tracks, which show off Eric B's fearsome turntable skills, were passionate defences of the concept of the DJ as a self-sufficient band. The album's austere minimalism was an expression of the duo's formalist rigour. Hip-hop was now a science with its own internal logic. Aside from "Eric B Is President", the highlights were "I Know You Got Soul" and the title track. With a

Rakim letting the mic magnetize him once more.

rhythm track sampled from James Brown, "I Know You Got Soul" was single-handedly responsible for hip-hop's cult of the Godfather of Soul. As Stetsasonic put it, 'To tell the truth, James Brown was old/ 'Til Eric and Rak came out with "I Know You Got Soul"'. "Paid In Full" was the duo at their most melodic, and introduced what has become hip-hop's central trope: "get[ting] some dead presidents" – i.e. making money. The track precipitated a heap of remixes, with Coldcut's stunning "Seven Minutes Of Madness" being the most notable. Although Eric and Rakim hated it, its sampling of Yemenite vocalist **Ofra Haza** was one of the boldest collages of sound and timbre ever committed to vinyl.

*Follow the Leader* (1988) saw the duo refine their ascetics, fleshing it out but retaining the music's raw ferocity. "Microphone Fiend" was based on what sounded like Santa's sleigh bells, and a guitar sample with an almost terrifying trebly quality, while "Lyrics of Fury"'s sample, from **The Eagles**, evidenced hip-hop's ability to redeem almost anything. Meanwhile, Rakim appeared to be taking the implied

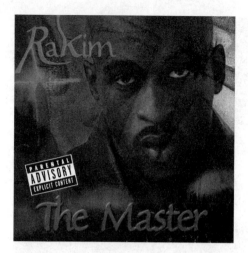

studiousness and complexity of the debut album's track title "Chinese Arithmetic", and putting it into practice: his lyrics were a series of cryptic axioms, bon mots, wordplay and pure flow that redefined the art of the MC. Eric B & Rakim did it the other way around from their sampladelic peers – all the complexity was in the lyrics, not the music.

Their next album, *Let The Rhythm Hit 'Em* (1990), was an attempt to rekindle the magical simplicity of their debut album. However, with the exception of "Let The Rhythm Hit 'Em", which did exactly that, the record was a fairly dull rehash of a style that was already an antique in hip-hop's world of hyper-speed stylistic innovations. Eric and Rak's final album, *Don't Sweat The Technique* (1992), managed to blend the high points of the first two plates. The hard rhythm but smooth groove of the title track was representative of the entire album's scope. Its commercial failure, however, suggested that hip-hop had left the duo behind and, after a year of inactivity, they split.

Eric B recorded a poorly received self-titled solo album that went nowhere in 1995. Rakim waited until 1997 to drop his solo album, *The 18th Letter*, which was solid, if nowhere near his earlier brilliance. *The Master* (1999) was more of the same, but the dream-team collaborations with **DJ Premier** just about lived up to the names on the marquee. Since then, however, Rakim has seemingly been content with guest appearances, most notable on **Truth**

Hurts' splendid "Addictive" (2002).

⊙ **Paid In Full — The Platinum Years**
4th & Broadway, 1999
The absolutely essential debut album, plus a bonus CD of remixes including Coldcut's awesome "Seven Minutes of Madness".

# Esham/NATAS

On his track "Still Don't Give A…" Eminem boasts that he's "a cross between Manson, **Esham** and Ozzy" — a claim that severely undersells Detroit legend Esham, the personification of evil on the microphone. The kind of guy that would make Cradle of Filth shit their bondage trousers, **Esham Smith** takes the funk out of hip-hop, reshaping its pimp strut into the ominous, relentless creeping of **Michael Myers**. He calls his black-metal schtick "acid rap" and his splatter patter has influenced everyone from horrorcore artists the **Flatlinerz** to Motown neighbours Kid Rock, Insane Clown Posse, Kottonmouth Kingz and Eminem. But whatever you think of his sales pitch, you've got to admire his work rate: in his first ten years as a recording artists, he put out twelve albums and five EPs.

Picking up on ideas from the **Geto Boys**, Esham released his first, self-produced cassette himself – *Boomin 1990* (1990), which has since been reissued as *Boomin Words From Hell*. Picking up on ideas from **Guns 'N Roses**, he released the influential Black Sabbath-sampling *Judgement Day Vols 1 And 2* (1992). After the *Helterskkelter* EP (1992), Esham released the outrageous *KKKill The Fetus* (1993). On "Symptoms of Insanity" he talked about cutting the head off his dog and throwing it in a bucket – if animal rights weren't exactly top of his priorities, at least he was pro-choice. Although it was the sonic equivalent of a grade-D **Dario Argento** movie bootleg, the cruddy sound and depressive heavy-metal samples made it somewhat compelling.

With **TNT** and **Mastamind**, Esham formed **NATAS** (which allegedly stands for "Nation Ahead of Time and Space") and released *Life After Death* (1993), an album that continued Esham's penchant for sampling the Beastie Boys, borrowing tricks from Slick Rick, and dropping really lame sex raps. Their *Blaz4me* (1994) album contained such acid rap classics as "Boo Yah" and "Stay True To Your City". *Doubelievengod* (1995) was all doom-and-gloom oscillator synths, Notorious BIG disses, a nice riff on a Gil Scott-Heron lyric ("We Almost Lost Detroit") and the unbelievably crass line "I'm the nigger that raped the bitch that Tupac went to jail for" on "Torture".

Meanwhile, Esham had released *Closed Casket* (1994) on New York's Warlock label, but returned to his own Gothom-Overcore label for *Dead Flowerz* (1995), an altogether G-Funkier album than previous releases. *Bruce Wayne Gothom City 1987* (1996) found Esham flossing like it was 1998, with a sound not entirely dissimilar to **Dr. Dre** circa 1999, particularly on the shout-out to Michigan's favourite bank, "Comerica".

NATAS returned in 1997 with *Multikillionaire*, on which they "wrote their rhymes in blood" and quoted Sam Raimi's *Candyman* movie. Esham's *Mail Dominance* (1999) was slightly more tuneful, even sampling **Walter Murphy**'s disco kitsch classic "A Fifth Of Beethoven". NATAS's *Wicket World Wide.Com* (1999) was housed in a Hieronymous Bosch-style sleeve, took one of its hooks from the theme from *Kojak*, and tried to cast a black magic spell on you on "Levitation", but the production was grinding and irritating, highlighting just how bad their raps were.

Esham's *Tongues* (2001) contained the potentially interesting/frightening collaboration with Kool Keith, "All Night Everyday", but Keith just highlighted that Esham was all chills and no skills. *Repentance* (2003) *was* truly frightening: Esham had joined forces with Detroit's

"BOOTLEG" (FROM THE LOST VAULT)-VOL.1

cartoon clowns Insane Clown Posse, and the results were predictably disastrous.

**"Bootleg" (From The Lost Vault) Vol. 1**
Overcore/TVT, 2000

Featuring tracks from *Boomin Words From Hell* to *Mail Dominance*, this collection functions as Esham's gravest hits.

# Eve

More than merely a roughneck sex symbol, Eve is one of the few female MCs this side of **Roxanne Shanté** and **MC Lyte** who can brag, boast and diss like the big boys. Neither slutty like Lil' Kim nor tomboyish like Da Brat's initial persona, Eve presents the most well-rounded female image in rap.

Born **Eve Jihan Jeffers** in Philadelphia, Eve first came to attention on the *Bulworth* soundtrack with "Eve of Destruction" (1998). She was signed to Dr. Dre's After math at the time, but the label was in flux and Eve was let go. She soon hooked up with **DMX** and his **Ruff Ryders** crew, and recorded the salsa-flavoured "What Ya Want" for the *Ryde Or Die Vol. 1* (1999) compilation.

At the time, there was no stopping the Ruff Ryders, and Eve's debut album, *Let There Be Eve... Ruff Ryder's First Lady*

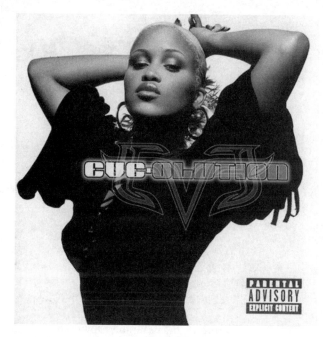

(1999), entered the US charts at number one, the first time that a female rapper had accomplished such a feat. The album eventually went double platinum, and it was easy to see why.

Eve's responses on the battle of sexes cut with **Drag-On**, "Let's Talk About", would make Jenna Jameson blush, and she more than held her own on the posse cut "Scenario 2000" with DMX, **The LOX** and Drag-On. It did her rep no harm, however, that she had **Swizz Beatz**'s production to work with. While Eve herself wasn't half bad, it was the beats that really *made* the record: the foghorn bombast of "Scenario 2000", the relentlessly catchy acoustic guitars of "Gotta Man", the **Michael Nyman**-esque piano of "Philly, Philly" and the slip-sliding-away funk of "Ain't Got No Dough".

*Scorpion* (2001) found Eve sounding even more confident. The **Teflon**-produced "Who's That Girl?" featured a ridiculously catchy hook and boasts like "I'm

the thrill in your life, breath of fresh air/Little boys hang me on their wall, I grow 'em chest hair", while the stellar "Let Me Blow Ya Mind" staged a reunion between Eve and **Dr. Dre**. This time around, though, Eve is the clear star, as the majority of the album's production wasn't up to the standard of the debut.

In 2002 Eve started to appear in movies, with roles in *XXX* and *Barbershop*. Perhaps inevitably, then, *Eve-Olution* (2002) was more of a high-gloss r&b album than a straight-up rap album. "Gangsta Lovin'" featured the former "pitbull in a skirt" duetting with **Alicia Keys** on top of a sample of Yarbrough & Peoples' "Don't Stop the Music", while she tried to rewrite **Prince** on "Irresistible Chick" (a cover of a 1983 Prince B-side, "Irresistible Bitch"). It seemed Eve had also run out of things to say. But, with her incursion into the world of fashion (teaming up with designer Marc Ecko to produce a line called Fetish), it probably didn't matter much.

**Let There Be Eve... Ruff Ryder's First Lady**
Interscope, 1999
All of her albums have their weak points, but this is probably the most consistent. Ballbreaker, sexpot, compassionate sister... it was all here on one of the few rap albums to transcend gender stereotypes. Some of Swizz Beatz's finest work didn't hurt either.

# Everlast

◊ See *House Of Pains*

# Fabolous

With a real name as prosaic as John Jackson, it's understandable that Fabolous wanted to big up his status a little bit. But the grandiosity of Jackson's chosen *nom de mic* just invites ridicule and haters, particularly when his rap style is so laconic and monotone that it sounds as if he can't be bothered to get his ass off the chaise longue.

Fabolous was just starting to make a name for himself on the streets, when he passed through **DJ Clue**'s studio to drop a couple of verses on his latest mixtape. Instead of letting someone else make money off of his "discovery" like he'd been doing for the better part of the past decade, Clue decided that Fabolous could be the linchpin of his new **Desert Storm** label. Clue put Fabolous on the remix of **Lil' Mo**'s 2001 track, "Superwoman", which had both the streets and the charts buzzing. Fabolous' "I Can't Deny It" (2001) was the perfect hip-hop demographic-stretcher: it stole its hook from **2Pac**, it had Nate Dogg crooning on it,

and it was produced by Rick Rock (A-list beatmaker of choice for Jay-Z, Xzibit and others). Further contributions from **Timbaland**, The Neptunes and DJ Envy helped make up for Clue and Duro's lacklustre production on Fab's debut album, *Ghetto Fabolous* (2001). But if anyone really took the shine off the record it was Fabolous himself, with lines like "I keep a lethal weapon like Mel Gibson" – dude, that wasn't cool even in 1987.

*Street Dreams* (2003) was even more blasé and tired. Fabolous is not just flat, monotonous and repetitive, he's also clumsy: "Y'all hustlers can't eat fit meals, and it feels something like when it's Ramadan". On the first album he was out-rapped by Ja Rule, but here he achieved the all-time low of being schooled by **P Diddy**. On *More Street Dreams Pt. 2: The Mixtape* (2003) Fabolous unwittingly but aptly described his style: "The flow is so sick, sooner or later these niggas gonna need barf bags, bigger than golf bags". He wasn't kidding.

El Faboloshus shows us his bling.

⊙ **Ghetto Fabolous**
Desert Storm/Elektra, 2001

"Faboloso" is anything but. Unfortunately, that doesn't seem to mean much to the Hot 97 crowd who seem to buy his records by the dozen. It's not just that Fabolous flosses so much that your gums will bleed, it's that he does it with no skill, wit or verve.

# Fat Boys

B efore they became the rotund court jesters of hip-hop, **Prince Markie Dee, Kool Rock-ski** and **Darren "Buffy" Robinson** (aka The Human

Beatbox) were a trio of Brooklynites called the **Disco 3**. In 1983 they entered a rap contest at Radio City Music Hall and won first prize, a contract with Sutra Records, due in large part to Buffy's skill at human beatboxing, which he had started doing in 1981 while in junior high.

The Disco 3's first record was 1984's "Fat Boys/Human Beatbox" single, which was produced by **Kurtis Blow**. Other than setting up the microphones, it's unclear what Blow did on "Human Beatbox", because the record consists of Markie Dee and Kool Rock-ski dropping some invigorating old school rhymes over the top of Buffy creating beats out of raspberries and Bronx cheers. "Human Beatbox" has since become one of the most sampled hip-hop records, thanks to Buffy's trademark rhythmic hyperventilating. Aside from giving the group their future name, "Fat Boys" was notable for another stellar beatboxing solo by Buffy, and great mechano-dub production from Blow.

With a combined weight that would intimidate any World Wrestling Entertainment tag-team, it was inevitable that the Disco 3 would change their name to the **Fat Boys**. Mugging for the cameras with mountains of food in their publicity photos, the Fat Boys would soon make eating the subject of just about every one of their songs that wasn't a cover of a rock standard. "Jailhouse Rap" (1984), their first single under their new name, again featured sublime early 1980s production from Blow and a moment of narrative genius when Kool Rock-ski gets sent to jail for stiffing Burger King.

"The Fat Boys Are Back" (1985) was more of the same, but with less inspired production. "All You Can Eat" (1985) followed suit, and their novelty image grew with their appearance in the movie *Krush Groove*, stuffing their faces to its dulcet tones. Somehow, the group managed to stay commercially viable and even starred in their own movie, the so-bad-it's-really-bad *Disorderlies*, in 1987. The film provided the group with a number twelve hit, a shockingly awful cover of The Surfaris' "Wipeout" with The Beach Boys. *Crushin'* (1987), which included "Wipeout", went

platinum and broke into the album chart top ten. As if that wasn't surreal enough, they collaborated with 1960s rock 'n' roller **Chubby Checker** on a version of his "The Twist" in 1988, which managed to reach number 16. A version of "Louie Louie" in 1988 managed to dent the lower reaches of the pop chart, but Prince Markie Dee soon left to pursue an ill-advised solo career. While his own records went nowhere, he did go on to work with **Father MC** and **Mary J Blige**. Meanwhile, Kool Rock-ski and Buffy (now calling himself Buff Daddy – is this where Sean Combs took his name from?) reunited for 1991's *Mack Daddy*, a pretty woeful attempt at keeping up with the times, featuring lots of sub-Public Enemy-style production.

In 1995, Robinson died of a cardiac arrest. He was 28.

**All Meat, No Fillah! The Best Of The Fat Boys**
Rhino, 1997
A collection of 18 Fat Boys' songs is pure gluttony, but then they would've wanted it that way.

# Fat Joe

See *Diggin' In The Crates*

# Fearless Four

From St Nicholas Terrace in Harlem, the Fearless Four were protégés of neighbours the **Treacherous Three**. Formed as the **Houserockers Crew**, by The Devastating Tito (Tito Jones), DLB (Caryl Barksdale), Mike and DJ Master OC (Oscar Rodriguez), the group became the Fearless Four when Ski the Great Peso (Mitchell Grant) joined. After recording the devastating old school classic "Rap Attack" in 1980 with the Family Four, the Mighty Mike C (Michael Clee) joined, and the crew was known for a time as the **Fearless Five**. Mike Ski soon left and another DJ, Krazy Eddie (Eddie Thompson), joined before the group signed to Bobby Robinson's **Enjoy** label.

The group's first single, "It's Magic",

came out in 1982, and was based on **Cat Stevens**' bizarre foray into electronic music, "If Dog Was a Doughnut". One of the best old school productions, the same year's "Rockin' It" was a startling fusion of the riff from Kraftwerk's "Man Machine" and "King of the Beat" Pumpkin's array of congas and cowbells. The MCs weren't bad either. **Master OC** and Pumpkin produced two excellent singles by Fantasy Three, "It's Your Rock" and "Biters in the City", both from 1983.

Fearless Four became the first rap group to sign to a major label. Their first record for Elektra was the Gary Numan-sampling dud "Just Rock" (1983), which strangely featured a remix by disco DJ **Larry Levan**. They justified Elektra's faith, though, with the fine post-"The Message" track, "Problems of the World Today" in 1983, which showed off the group's harmonizing to good effect over absolutely monstrous kick drums, care of producer Davy DMX.

More harmonizing was featured on 1984's "Dedication", released on Tuff City. By this point, the group had been superseded by the new wave ushered in by **Run DMC**, and only released one more single together – 1987's "After Tonight". The **Mighty Mike C** released the slightly desperate "I'm Stupid Fresh" in 1986, and the Great Peso had some solo joints before working on DJ Easy Lee's old school reunion, *Raiders Of The Lost Art* (1994). Master OC, meanwhile, had a couple of almost-hits with **Krazy Eddie** – "Masters Of The Scratch" and "Private Lessons" in 1984 and 1985 – worked with both Cold Crush's Charlie Chase (Bambi & Freeze's "Let Us Entertain You") and Grandmaster Flash ("At The Party") in 1985, before producing the embryonic **Naughty By Nature** crew, New Style (1989's "Scuffin' Those Knees").

🔘 **Rockin' It**
Enjoy, 1982

An original copy of this 12" would hit you hard, but this oft-sampled early electro gem has been compiled on CD loads of times – *The Best Of Enjoy Records* (Hot Productions) also includes "It's Magic", and is a great collection anyway. "Planet Rock" may have been first, and totally electronic, but "Rockin' It" remains a stone-cold classic, and was a softer rapprochement between video game funk and the pre-school's Latin percussion breaks.

# Field Mob

**B**oondox (Darion Crawford) and **Kalage** (Shawn Johnson) first met each other in high school in Albany, Georgia, a city of 100,000 in rural south Georgia. After MC-battling each other for days on end with no clear winner, they decided to join forces. Naming themselves after their neighbourhood the Field, Field Mob released their debut single, "Project Dreamz", in 1999.

Signing to MCA, the duo released *613: From Ashy to Classy* (2000). Constrained by both the pedestrian production of **Ole-E and Pop** and their largely callow rhymes, Field Mob came across as strictly amateurish. Some originality, sensitivity and intelligence shone through on a couple of tracks, however. "Channel 613, Part 1" was **Slick Rick**'s "Children's Story" rewritten through the prism of reality shows, while "Crutch" was touching and funny at the same time: "I was so broke, my wet dreams were about eating a meal".

*From Tha Roota To The Toota* (2002) was a quantum leap forward. The album's centrepiece was the extraordinary "Nothing 2 Lose", a plea for freedom that connected its subject matter – slavery – with the modern form of the blues – hip-hop – without being mawkish or preachy. "KAN (Kuntry Ass Niggahs)" was **Dirty South** crunk as reimagined by the **Bomb Squad**, while "Betty Rocker" had some "hayseed" playing a banjo over some mega 808 beats, and "Sick Of Being Lonely" was one of the best Southern rewrites of **G-Funk** yet. The album garnered the group numerous Grammy nominations, and put them at the top of the heap of the Southern invasion of hip-hop.

⦿ **From Tha Roota To Tha Toota**
MCA, 2002

This is among the best Southern rap albums not to come from the Dungeon Family camp for two reasons. First and foremost, Boondox and Kalage had improved enormously as rappers since their debut, moving from lazy, careless groupie tales to more complex narratives of poverty and strife. Secondly, the production from ET3 (OutKast), Mannie Fresh and Jazze Pha managed to blend backwoods feel and inner-city steel with aplomb.

# 50 Cent

In many ways, 50 Cent was the second coming of 2Pac. He burst onto the scene in 2003 with a ready-made violent mythology, he totally blurred the lines between gangsta art and gangsta life (no wonder Eminem signed him), and he had, if not movie-star looks, then a movie-star body (all the pecs and tattoos he could manage). The only thing missing was the evident self-loathing. As Eminem said, in describing him, "Take some Big and some Pac/And you mix them up in a pot/Sprinkle a little Big L on top/What the fuck you got?"

Curtis Jackson was born in Jamaica, Queens and lost his mother at age eight when a drug deal went wrong. He soon went into the crack trade himself, until one too many trips to jail encouraged him to focus on rap instead. After a deal with **Jam Master Jay**'s JMJ label amounted to nought, he hooked up with the Trackmasters, who produced his planned debut *Power Of The Dollar*. The album was preceded by the single "How To Rob" (1999), a comedic shopping list of platinum-selling rappers and singers that 50 planned to stick-up, including **Bobby Brown**, Ol' Dirty Bastard and Big Punisher. The track was pretty damn funny, but thoroughly savage: "I'm about to stick Bobby for some of that Whitney money"; "I'd rob ODB, but that'd be a waste of time"; "I'll rob Pun without a gun, snatch his piece then run/This nigga weigh 400 pounds, how he gonna catch me son?"; and "Run up on Timbaland and Missy with the pound/Like 'You, gimme the cash, put the hot dog down'". Even though the song's chorus said "This ain't serious", people in the industry did not take kindly to his naming names. So much so that, on May 24, 2000, he was shot nine times while sitting in the passenger seat of a car that was parked in his neighbourhood. Soon afterwards, Columbia shelved *Power of the Dollar*, some say because they wanted nothing to do with 50, others because the album had already been bootlegged to death.

When 50 recovered (with his voice now a sort of slur, due to his having been shot in the jaw), he appeared on seemingly every mixtape in New York, openly mocking all the allegedly fake gangstas and flossers, especially Ja Rule, who was from the same neighbourhood ("Scream murder! I don't believe you"). The most crucial of these was perhaps "The Realest" from DJ Whoo Kid's *Max Payne 2* (2002) tape – basically a duet with Biggie from beyond the grave that was so huge on the streets in New York that radio programmers were forced to add the track to their rotations. These appearances generated huge hype, and a bidding war ensued for his services, which was won by **Eminem** and **Dr. Dre**. Around this time, *Guess Who's Back?* (2002), a collection of unreleased tracks from *Power of the Dollar* and mixtape verses was released on the none-more-independent Full Clip label. It was far from the best-sounding record ever released, but it convincingly captured 50 Cent at his rawest, most bragadocious.

50's "Wanksta" single of 2002 – written in ignorance of the title's connotations in terms of UK slang – continued in the vein of calling out fake thugs, and its appearance on the *Eight Mile* soundtrack created even more anticipation for his debut album proper. "In Da Club" (2003), a classic Dre synth strut, quickly went to number one and ushered in *Get Rich Or Die Tryin'* (2003) as the fastest-selling debut album of all-time. It was a good record, but the Dre/Eminem commercial juggernaut behind him seemed to take away some of his venom – which was always his most appealing aspect.

50's **G-Unit** crew (Lloyd Banks, an incarcerated Tony Yayo and Young Buck) inevitably rode in on his coat-tails for *Beg For Mercy* (2003), an insultingly shallow album, of which the only redeeming feature was the beats, from producers such as Dr. Dre, Scott Storch, Hi-Tek and No ID. Lloyd Banks' solo album, *Hungry for More* (2004), failed to convince that the G-Unit was anything but a bunch of arriviste punks.

**Guess Who's Back?**
Full Clip, 2002

In between calling out "wankstas" and plain-talking trash to everyone who crosses his path, 50 Cent lays out his philosophy of life, "The only excuse for being broke is being in jail". On this collection of unreleased songs, freestyles and mixtape tracks, 50 Cent is the brashest, most combative, thuggest cat around. As long as you're not caught in the crossfire, it's still one of the most impressive sounds in hip-hop.

# Flipmode Squad

◊ See *Busta Rhymes*

# ◎ Fondle 'Em records

Founded by radio host and sneaker-collector extraordinaire **Bobbito Garcia** in 1995, Fondle 'Em was the premier underground hip-hop label of the mid-to-late 1990s. The label was started as a joke, but from such humble origins often emerges genius. Indeed, the loose, free-association feel of most Fondle 'Em releases, the spare beats and the MCs' willingness to say absolutely anything made Fondle 'Em records a refreshing relief from the increasingly formulaic mainstream hip-hop of the time.

**Kool Keith** and **Godfather Don** were recording some promos for the Stretch Armstrong radio show on New York's WKCR FM, which was hosted by Bobbito, and Bobbito decided to release the fairly ridiculous results and extend them into a real session. While *The Cenobites* EP (1995) had its comic moments like "Kick A Dope Verse" ("I eat a knish and then I fart" being typical of its lines), and the stoopid, surreal travelogue "Mommy", "You're Late" featured hardcore battle raps from Keith, Don and underground legend **Percee P.**

The 1996 self-titled EP from **The Juggaknots** (Breezly Bruin and Buddy Slim) might not have had the personality of The Cenobites record but, with the chilling sex and murder rap "I'm Gonna

The original cover for KMD's *Black Bastards* album, shelved until Fondle 'Em stepped in.

Kill U", and the father-son racism chat "Clear Blue Skies", it was equally impressive. **The Arsonists** (Q-Unique, Jise One, Freestyle, Swel Boogie and D-Stroy), meanwhile, went straight for A Tribe Called Quest-style jazzy funk on 1996's "The Session". Mr Live's "Relax Y'self", from the same year, featured some of Earl Blaize's earliest production – sadly not in the style that made his work for Antipop Consortium so good. **Siah and Yashua Da PoED**'s *The Visualz* EP, also 1996, centred around the extraordinary 11-minute epic, "A Day Like Any Other", with its bucolic, *Alice In Wonderland*-style fantasy lyrics. **Lord Sear**'s "Alcoholic Vibes" (1997) was a really lame rap, but set to one of the most outrageous beats you'll ever hear.

Fondle 'Em's real coup, though, was hooking up with Zev Love X of KMD, who had reincarnated himself as **MF Doom**. Aside from Doom's stellar *Operation Doomsday* (1999) album, Fondle 'Em released tracks from the shelved KMD album, *Black Bastards*, and unreleased cuts from Doom's deceased brother Subroc. Further contributions from MF Grimm, Ohio's MHz crew and Scienz of Life ensured the label's rep as a showcase for the cream of the underground.

The label soon folded, though, and left underground hip-hop without a standard-bearer. El-P's Def Jux label picked up the pieces in 2001, with both an excellent compilation and a self-titled tribute record by The **Fondle 'Em Fossils** that featured MF Doom, Q-Unique and El-P among others.

⊙ **Farewell to Fondle 'Em**
Def Jux, 2001

Bobbito closed down Fondle 'Em in 2000, and most of its releases promptly became wallet-challenging martyrs to eBay. Many, though not all, of the label's best moments are preserved on this excellent compilation from El-P's Def Jux label. The highlight just might be the wheelchair-bound – the result of receiving ten gunshot wounds as a result on his life – MF Grimm's monologue, where he asks a dead friend to ask God questions such as "Why'd You let Indians get used and abused?/Why'd You let Hitler crucify all the Jews?"

# The 45 King

Preferring these days to go by the name of **The 45 King** rather than DJ Mark the 45 King as he was once known, **Mark James** was one of the producers responsible for bringing hip-hop out of its drum-machine doldrums in the late 1980s. Looping up old James Brown and Kool & the Gang records for rappers like Queen Latifah, **Lakim Shabazz** and Chill Rob G, the 45 King, along with Marley Marl, was instrumental in leading hip-hop into its sampladelic age.

The 45 King began his journey through the intricacies of old school funk at the dawn of hip-hop. As the record boy for the Funky Four (before they became Funky Four Plus One), he had a rare insight into the clandestine, arcane world of breakbeats, where records like "Catch A Groove" by Juice and "Scratching" by the Disco Magic Machine – records that

were rare to the point of non-existence – acquired a mystical aura because of their crowd-moving capabilities. The 45 King's first production, after a somewhat less-than-productive stint as a DJ, was a demo for **MC Marky Fresh** that was picked up by Kiss FM's DJ Red Alert.

It wouldn't be until 1986, and the arrival of the Flavor Unit posse, that the 45 King would get noticed, though. The Flavor Unit was a crew of Jersey-based MCs – Latee, Lakim Shabazz, Queen Latifah, Chill Rob G, Apache and Lord Alibaski – that were organised around the 45 King. Latee's bass-heavy, Lyn Collins-sampling "This Cut's Got Flavor" single of 1986, on the Wild Pitch label, was the crew's breakout track. The sparseness of "This Cut's Got Flavor" gave way to the classically funky stylings of Latee's "No Tricks" of 1987, Lakim Shabazz's under-rated album *Pure Righteousness* (1988), **Chill Rob G**'s "Court Is In Session" and "The Power", from 1989 and 1990, and Queen Latifah's *All Hail the Queen* (1989).

In 1990, the 45 King recorded a solo album for Aaron Fuchs' Tuff City label that would yield the track which will be forever associated with his name. With a slowed-down horn riff from **Marva Whitney**'s "Unwind Yourself" and an enormous drum loop, "The 900 Number" remains one of hip-hop's greatest and funkiest instrumental tracks. It has since become the unofficial theme song for *Yo! MTV Raps*, soundtracked a beer commercial, and pushed **DJ Kool**, who based his club tune "Let Me Clear My Throat" on it, into the American pop charts. "The 900 Number" was the lead track on his first solo album, *45 Kingdom*, which also featured reconstructions of old school beats from The Honey Drippers, The Soul Searchers and Kool & the Gang.

*45 Kingdom* was followed up by the almost as good *Lost Breakbeats* (1991), but soon afterwards the 45 King receded from public view, largely because of his addiction to angel dust. However, with the re-release of *Lost Breakbeats* in 1997 by British label Ultimate Dilemma, and DJ Kool's "Let Me Clear My Throat" hit, the 45 King started his comeback, which hit its apex in 1998 with his production of Jay-Z's *Annie*-sampling "Hard Knock Life". He even managed to make **Craig Mack** cool again with a beat based around Frank Sinatra's "High Hopes" on 2000's "Wooden Horse".

His rehabilitation was complete when he stumbled across a song by then-unknown singer-songwriter **Dido** being played on the TV, sampled it and put it on one of his mixtapes. The tape made its way to **Eminem**, who loved the beat,

and turned it into the stalker anthem "Stan" (2000).

**⊙ 45 Kingdom**
Tuff City, 1990

Consisting of nothing but looped beats, breakbeat albums are never an easy listen, but this, featuring "The 900 Number", is not only the best of the 45 King's breakbeat albums, but quite simply one of the best ever.

# Foxy Brown

Taking her stage name from a 1970s blaxploitation flick, **Inga Fung Marchand** has attracted as much notoriety and as many drooling admirers as Pam Grier's original **Foxy Brown**. She made a name for herself as a 14 year-old prodigy at New York's legendary freestyle showcase Lyricist Lounge, calling herself Big Shorty, but really attracted attention on the remix of LL Cool J's "I Shot Ya" in 1995. She exploded into the big time as Jay-Z's distaff foil on 1996's "Ain't No Nigga", pandering to Jigga's mercenary sexism with lines like "From Dolce & Gabana to H. Bendel/I ring your bells/So who the player?/I still keep you in the illest gators". As a member of **The Firm** with Nas, AZ and Nature, Foxy Brown gave new meaning to the notion of standing by your man: "I'm married to The Firm, boo, you gotta understand I'll die for them/Give me a chair and I'll fry for them".

Calling herself "the ill na na with the slanted eyes" (she is part-Chinese), Foxy's debut album, *Ill Na Na* (1996), was the composite portrait of the hip-hop diva, and promptly won itself platinum sales. Unsurprisingly, as is true of almost any woman in hip-hop and R&B who isn't **Lauryn Hill**, she attracted criticisms of materialism, being degrading to women with her overt sexuality, and having her rhymes ghostwritten by both **Jay-Z** and **Nas**. While all of the above may or not be true, *Ill Na Na* was state-of-the-art jigginess.

Beginning with the classic couplet, "Rhyme or crime, let's get it on/MCs

THE 45 KING PRESENTS
The Flavor Unit

Kelly) featuring appearances from dance-hall dons Spragga Benz and Baby Cham.

**◉ Ill Na Na**
Def Jam, 1996

The sleek production by the Trackmasters makes Foxy Brown's blinging pipedreams really come to life.

# Freestyle Fellowship

Ever since LA producers stopped making silly little electro-funk tunes, the style most people associate with Angeleno hip-hop has been unapologetically gangsta – the sound of glocks, drop-tops, smashing St Ides bottles, sirens and whirring police-chopper blades. But while the popular face of LA hip-hop was defined by nihilism, a group of aspiring MCs and poets dodged the crossfire at open mic nights at a cafe fittingly called the Good Life.

Coming together as the **Freestyle Fellowship**, many of these MCs – **Aceyalone**, **Mikah Nine**, **P.E.A.C.E.**, **J Sumbi** and **Self Jupiter** – released what many people consider the Holy Grail of underground hip-hop, *To Whom it May Concern* (1991). While **A Tribe Called Quest** and Gang Starr were remaking hip-hop in Donald Byrd's image and calling it "jazz", the Freestyle Fellowship sounded as if they were attempting to graft the vocalese of Lambert, Hendricks and Ross onto one of **Ornette Coleman**'s harmolodic jams. Bionically scatting, creating narrative sequences with non-planar geometry, scattering syntax like ashes on the sea, the Freestyle Fellowship "took rap music to its threshold of enlightenment".

The trouble was, barely anyone was listening, and J Sumbi left the fold before they recorded *Inner City Griots* (1993). Picking up where *To Whom It May Concern* left off, the group continued to shred text like **Fawn Hall**, but the experimentation was now as musical as it was verbal, allowing it to avoid sounding like merely a tongue-twisting cutting session.

want to eat me, but it's Ramadan", "Hot Spot" introduced her second album, *Chyna Doll* (1999). Although it wasn't quite the litany of designer apparel that *Ill Na Na* was, *Chyna Doll* was nonetheless more of the same, except that she strangely didn't sound as confident as on her debut.

*Broken Silence* (2001) was yet another extended shopping list and, while it has been said that **Laurence Olivier** could read the phone book and make it compelling, "Fox Boogie" was no longer similarly charismatic, even if there were the odd zingers like "Y'all only nice behind mics like Pippen". The production, though, was pretty state-of-the-art, with "Hood Scriptures" anticipating the "orientalist" fad in hip-hop beats by a year or so, and "Oh Yeah", "Run Dem" and "Tables Will Turn" (the last two with production from the king of Kingston, Dave 'Rudeboy'

Aceyalone's showcase, "Cornbread", took hip-hop as far out into poetic realms as it had ever been, and it would take years for radical MCs like Antipop Consortium, Deep Puddle Dynamics and Mike Ladd to pick up its mantle.

Aside from a devoted cult following, most of the hip-hop community wanted to revoke their poetic licence, and the group unfortunately obliged by breaking up in 1994. Along with Abstract Rude, Aceyalone showed up at the **Project Blowed** nights, which replaced the Good Life as the headquarters of LA's free-stylers. The *Project Blowed* (1994) album was another collection of skewed dynamics, scatted vocals and all manner of lyrical phantasmagoria. Acey's solo album, *All Balls Don't Bounce* (1995) paled next to the Fellowship's collective efforts, but still won over hearts and (open) minds on tracks like "Arhythmaticulas" and "Knownots". His *Accepted Eclectic* (2000) was the most conventional album he ever made, but the melancholic "I Neva Knew" and the steamy "Bounce" prevented this from being a totally retrograde step.

In 1999 the Fellowship reunited with an earlier producer of theirs, OD, on "Can You Find The Level Of Difficulty in This?" which, despite its title, was catchier than anything they had previously done, but still filled with potent, challenging imagery. The single was recorded for the *Shockadoom* album which was recorded in 1998 but not released until 2002, but the four-year delay couldn't dampen the compelling group dynamics. *Temptations* (2001), however, suffered from dull, lifeless production – "No Hooks No Chorus" indeed.

**Self Jupiter**'s *Hard Hat Area* (2001) at least had some sterling drum-machine programming, courtesy of Omid, to flesh out the tongue-twisting. **Mikah Nine**'s *Timetable* (2001) was a so-so, heavily jazzy solo album, while *A Work In Progress* (2003) was simply awful – electronic production does not suit him at all, particularly when he's copping moves from P-Funk and parodying gangsta rappers.

Aceyalone's *Love And Hate* (2003) fared far better thanks to varied production from **RJD2**, El-P, J-Roc and regular beat-smith PMG. "Lost Your Mind" featured the brightest groove that Acey had ever rapped over, while on "City Of Shit" Acey and El-P bring the best out of each other and temper each other's worst instincts. RJD2 also appeared on Project Blowed's *The Good Brothers* (2003), delivering a heavy but funky track on which Acey and Raaka Iriscience expand their rhythmic horizons. Unfortunately, the best track here was "Give it Here", which stole a page from The Neptunes production manual – not a promising sign for the underground.

⊙ **Inner City Griots**
4th & Broadway, 1993

If Ornette Coleman had been a wordsmith, he would have sounded like this.

# Freeway

Beanie Sigel's mate from Philly, the City of Brotherly Love, **Freeway** made his debut on "1-900-Hustler" from Jay-Z's *Dynasty Roc la Familia* (2000) album, dishing out advice to buyers and sellers alike: "First things first, watch what you say out your mouth/When you talkin' on the phone to hustlers/Never play the house, think drought, keep heat in the couch/When you sittin' in the presence of customers".

Freeway's high-pitched voice made it sound like he was just learning which was the business end of a gat, but his arrest for drug dealing in 2000 suggested otherwise. He re-emerged in 2002 with a couple of verses on **Beanie Sigel**'s "Roc The Mic" (from the *State Property* album), but truly made a name for himself with "Line 'Em Up". Actually, anyone could have made a name for themselves rhyming on top of **Just Blaze**'s head-splitting funk-rock beat, but Freeway's thugged-out menace was thoroughly appropriate.

*Philadelphia Freeway* (2003) featured more state-of-the-art production, courtesy of Just Blaze, **Kanye West**, Ruggedness and Black Key, and more so-so rapping from Freeway. It's not that Freeway was bad, just that he had one topic – hustling – and the same theme with the same delivery over the course of an album gets pretty tiresome – something that all the guest appearances (**Nelly**, Snoop Dogg, Nate Dogg, **Jay-Z**, Mariah Carey and Faith Evans) couldn't cover up. A cameo on **Mark Ronson**'s "Ooh Wee" smash in 2003 followed before he decided, as rappers inevitably tend to, to wheel on his crew, known as **Ice City**. "U Talk It I Live It" in 2004 featured lyrics like "When I was chillin' in the park with bitches/You was home alone havin' to wash some dishes", while the flip, "The Sure Shot", was ostensibly a remake of Gang Starr's "Dwyck".

⊙ **Philadelphia Freeway**
Roc-A-Fella, 2003

As monotonous rappers go, there are far worse than Freeway. At least his voice manages to convey a sense of excitement as he recounts his up-to-no-good life story, even if he tells it over and over again. What isn't monotonous is the stellar production from the Roc-A-Fella all-stars.

# Doug E Fresh

Although he called himself "the world's greatest entertainer", the sad truth is that **Doug E Fresh** is a workmanlike rapper at best. His reputation basically rests on one truly inspired single, "The Show/La-Di-Da-Di" of 1985. While the former **Douglas Davis** claimed that he invented human beatboxing on his first single, "The Original Human Beat Box" (1984) (a claim disputed by both Biz Markie and the Fat Boys' Darren Robinson), one undeniable fact is that "The Show" might have been truly inspired, but it wasn't exactly original. The record's keyboard hook and beatboxing previously appeared on the Bad Boys' "Bad Boys", which was released a few months prior to Doug's disc.

"The Show", however, was the far superior record. Fresh's beatboxing was often mind-boggling, while the scratch of Cold Crush Brothers' "Punk Rock" (the "Oh

# FRENCH HIP-HOP

*Les banlieues* may translate as "the suburbs", but the French have a very different understanding of the 'burbs from the British or Americans. Neighbourhoods like 93 Seine Saint Denis, Sarcelle's and 92 Haut de Seine, on the outskirts of Paris, are characterised by bad housing, heavy-handed policing, lack of opportunity and a population of disillusioned immigrant families. In other words, prime hip-hop territory. With a large portion of France's urban populace living in *les banlieues*, France has the second-largest hip-hop industry in the world. Of course, it also has the concomitant controversy: gangster business practices, run-ins with club-owners, the police and the racist *Front National*, and – in the 19802 – groups being banned from performing. The French hip-hop industry is so well-developed it even has its own Will Smith, who raps over Elton John samples – **Yannick**.

The first French-*language* hip-hop record was "Une Sale Histoire" (1982) by **Fab Five Freddy** and **B-Side**. That same year graffiti took France by storm, with exhibitions by Rammellzee and Jean-Michel Basquiat, and Dee Nasty set up the

country's first hip-hop radio show. In 1984 **Dee Nasty** put out the first French hip-hop record, *Paname City Rapping*, himself, because no label wanted anything to do with it. However, in the early days French hip-hop was largely imitative of American records, and most MCs rapped in English. One clue as to how backward the French hip-hop scene was then was that the

*paradisiaque*
**mc★solaar**

most famous early French hip-hop record was produced by **Henri Belolo** and **Jacques Morali,** the men behind The Village People – Break Machine's "Street Dance" (1984).

He may be persona non grata on the "real" hip-hop scene now, but **MC Solaar** was the person who changed French hip-hop from a tiny, specialised cult into the voice of French youth. His debut album, *Qui Sème Le Vent Récolte le Tempo* (1991), was probably the biggest-selling, and most important, hip-hop album released outside the US. Riding **Jimmy Jay** and Boom Bass's jazzy beats, Solaar unleashed lines like, "Ses hématomes étaient plus grandes que le sein de Samantha Fox" ("bruises bigger than Sam Fox's tits"), and showed that French was hip-hop's second language. The album produced four French top ten singles, including the title track and "Victime de la Mode". Solaar's best single, however, was to be found on his second album, *Prose Combat* (1993). "Nouveau Western" rode a loop from **Serge Gainsbourg**'s "Bonnie and Clyde" and had Solaar comparing the Wild West with America's cultural imperialism. Unfortunately, ever since Solaar became a pop star, he's followed trends instead of setting them. Though even on his lame gangsta tracks, such as "Illico Presto", he still finds space to

namecheck Umberto Eco.

Solaar was introduced on the legendary *Rapattitude* (1989) compilation. *Rapattitude* also launched the careers of **Kool Shen** and **Joey Starr** who make up France's most potent act, **NTM** (Nique Ta Mère — "Fuck Your Mother"). Their "Je Rappe" track on *Rapattitude* showed very little of the controversy that would surround the band. But on their debut album, *Authentik* (1991), they claimed they were committing "la sodomie verbale" and attracted more than a few raised eyebrows. However, worse was to come: after the release of *J'Appuie sur la Gâchette* (1993) they were sent to jail for inciting their audience to kill cops. *Paris Sous les Bombes* (1995) was less aggressive, but still full of rage, and it sold 400,000 copies. *Supreme NTM* (1998) was even bigger, with the ragga-tinged "Ma Benz" and the head-nodder "That's My People". Kool Shen and Joey Starr are both fine producers, responsible for outside projects like **Sniper** (Joey Starr) and the super group IV My People (Kool Shen, neighbour **Busta Flex**, the excellent lyricist Noxea and Serum).

From the Secteur A production house, **Ministère A.M.E.R.** introduced today's biggest stars in the early 1990s: Doc Gynéco, Stomy

Grand Dadaistes TTC show off their ACME guns'n'bling, *Who Framed Roger Rabbit*-style.

Bugsy and Passi. All of the above have had platinum-selling albums, with Stomy Bugsy being the closest thing to a French equivalent of **Tupac**. Other Secteur A stars include Ärsenik, Pit Baccardi and Hamed Daye. Tracks like Ärsenik's Sly Stone-interpolating "Affaires de Familles", Daye's "L'An D1000" and Bugsy's "Mon Papa À Moi Est Un Gangster" may be little better than received G-Funk, but the **Secteur A** live album, *Live At Olympia* (1998), could show their American brethren a thing or two about taking it to the stage.

From Marseille, **IAM** and their awesome MC/producer **Akhenaton** went double platinum

in 1998 with their hit "Indepenza". Also from Marseille are **Le 3ème Oeil** who have mastered the melancholy piano loop even better than RZA, and Fonky Family, who looped The Beatles on their hit "Si Je Les Avais Écoutés" (1999).

Newcomers like **113**, whose "Truc de Fou" (1998) sampled a Malian guitar bands, and Bisso Na Bisso, who rocked on top of a groove fashioned out of Senegalese mbalax, Congolese soukous and Jamaican dancehall on their self-titled debut single (1998), have made compelling fusions of the traditions of the Maghreb and sub-Saharan Africa with modern technology. The purest hip-hop experience, however, may be offered by **Saian Supa Crew**. Their album, **KLR** (1999), sounded like Dadaists Tristan Tzara and Richard Huelsenback trading rhymes with **Jurassic 5**. They don't have a DJ – instead Sly and Leeroy beatbox all the scratches and sound effects, giving it an "open mic night at the Cabaret Voltaire" feel. The album's best moment was the amazing beatboxed version of Anita Ward's "Ring My Bell".

A similarly unique take on hip-hop was offered by TTC (who have teamed up with like minds such as Dose One and Hi-Tek). The title of *Ceci N'est Pas Un Disque* (2002) referenced Belgian surrealist René Magritte, and the album's sounds, rhymes and cadences were as crazed as that might lead you to expect. French hip-hop: *toi-meme, tu sais.*

## MC SOLAAR

⊙ **Prose Combat**
Island, 1993

Perhaps the easiest to find of his albums, this features French hip-hop's greatest moment, "Nouveau Western".

## SAIAN SUPA CREW

⊙ **KLR**
Source, 1999

The cadences and the beats sound like everyone from Missy Elliott to Busta Rhymes to The Pharcyde, but as a distillation of every major sub-genre of 1990s hip-hop, it's a lot of fun, even if your French isn't sharp enough to keep pace.

my God!") became one of hip-hop's signature devices. "The Show" was that rarest of records: a disposable novelty single with so much energy and sonic daring that it has remained a standard ever since. While the A-side highlighted Fresh's beatboxing skills, the flip belonged to a guy called **MC Ricky D** – even though he rapped over a background made entirely of Fresh's raspberry percussion. "La-Di-Da-Di" was a dirty, braggadocious story about a guy with gold teeth wearing Gucci underwear, filled with street-corner signifying and an ending to the story that was absolutely scandalous at the time. With his British accent, MC Ricky D introduced at least three hip-hop stock phrases on "La-Di-Da-Di". It was immediately obvious that Ricky D was a star in his own right, so he went off on his own and became Slick Rick.

Fresh's debut album, *Oh My God!* (1986), failed to live up to his great single. Not only were his raps mediocre at best, but he had found God and couldn't resist singing about it. The follow-up album, *The World's Greatest Entertainer* (1988), didn't even come close to living up to the title, but it

did at least tone down the proselytising. Paradoxically, however, the album's best track, "Keep Risin' to the Top", was a shout-out to the big guy in the sky that became a big hit.

Perhaps inevitably, Fresh faded from the limelight and made his comeback on **Hammer**'s Bust It label with *Doin' What I Gotta Do* (1992), and he tried one more time with **Puff Daddy** on the surprisingly tolerable *Play* (1995). A throwback to the halcyon days of the old school, it had sing-along, call-and-response choruses

'Scuse me Doug E... 'Scuse me Doug E... 'Scuse me Doug E. Fresh you're awn... ah, those were the days...

and plenty of party-hearty lyrics.

**Greatest Hits Vol. 1**
Bust It/Capitol, 1996

All you need to know is that it's got "The Show" and "La-Di-Da-Di" on it.

# Fugees

Aside from maybe Hootie & the Blowfish, the **Fugees** were the biggest pop group of the 1990s. Forming in South Orange, New Jersey in 1989, vocalist **Lauryn Hill**, multi-instrumentalist **Nel Wyclef Jean** and his cousin, keyboardist **Prakazrel Michel**, parlayed their warm grooves and gentle politics into a global market-share Michael Jackson would have been envious of in his heyday.

Their first album, *Blunted on Reality* (1994), was a rugged set that attempted to shed light on the political situation in Haiti, from where Wyclef and Pras are refugees (hence the name). It was a laudable effort, although it lacked personality, coming to life only on "Vocab" and the remix of "Mona Lisa".

The group took over production for the second album and the ensuing blend of Caribbean lilt, alterna-rap and supperclub soul became a worldwide phenomenon. Sporting a cover based on the posters for *The Godfather*, *The Score* (1996) got the kind of respect and success that John Gotti could only have dreamed about. To date, the album has sold over 18 million copies worldwide. Which is fairly remarkable considering that, aside from the massive singles "Killing Me Softly" (a cover of the Roberta Flack song), "Ready or Not" and "Fu-Gee-La", and the cover of Bob Marley's "No Woman, No Cry", *The Score* was a dark, downtempo album. It was politicized, talking about Newt Gingrich sucking dick. And it was littered with soundbites from a Kingston dancehall, wafting vapour trails from an East Harlem air shaft, and samples of doo-wop group The Flamingos.

While Hill stole the show with her rich vocals and not-bad mic skills, Wyclef's solo album, *The Carnival* (1997) showed that she didn't have a monopoly on the

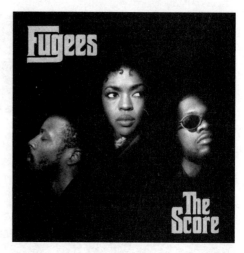

group's talent. Nowhere near as good as *The Score*, *The Carnival* had Clef collaborating with the Neville Brothers and Celia Cruz and not embarrassing himself. He'd save that for his duet with Bono, "New Day" (1999). *Ecleftic: Two Sides Of A Book* (2000), however, showed that *The Carnival* was a fluke: the cast of star guests included Kenny Rogers, and "However You Want It" proves that Canibus was right to blame Clef for the failure of his album. After appearing on a record by one of the guys from East 17 (?!?), Wyclef continued his desperate demographic gerrymandering with *Masquerade* (2002). As if duetting with Kenny Rogers wasn't odd enough, you really had to wonder just who he was trying to appeal to when he roped in Tom Jones for a rendition of "What's New Pussycat?" Surely he hadn't sunk so far that he had to appeal to the hen-party crowd?

Pras's *Ghetto Supastar* (1998) album had him living up to his Dirty Cash alias, by including ten-plus minutes of celebrity endorsements from the likes of Elton John, Sting and, of course, Donald Trump. The album was eventually turned into a movie, *Turn it Up*, in 2000, but by this point everyone had forgotten who he was. Except, that is, for Hollywood casting agents, who have kept him in polyester and beer with roles in *Go For Broke* and *Higher Ed*.

The real solo career action, however, was to be found on Hill's *The Miseducation of Lauryn Hill* (1998). Looking back to 1960s and 1970s soul's age-old virtues, referencing 1970s sitcoms, reminiscing about mid-1980s hip-hop, dabbling in reggae and dancehall, and digging in the crates like the best 1990s beat-freaks, *The Miseducation of Lauryn Hill* was the black bohemian equivalent of a Beastie Boys album, but from a woman's point of view. Replacing the wise-cracks and cheap laughs of the Beasties with a sense of personal triumph (which, granted, did occasionally creep into self-righteousness), Hill made the ultimate crossover album of the hip-hop era.

Unfortunately, she followed it up with the ultimate car-crash of an album. *MTV Unplugged No. 2.0* (2002) was two discs of Hill rambling on in twisted Oprah-speak platitudes and rasping her way through original songs about the political climate and how terrible fame was. She said that her old songs were nothing but lies – never a way to keep fans – and that she was now all about "reality". The 1990s brought us a whole rash of stars whining about the celebrity spotlight (everyone from George Michael to Eminem), but this was the least fun, the least insightful, most full-of-itself record in a singularly ignominious genre.

the album's message more potently than the lyrics, turning clichés into words that hit like the gospel truth.

**The Miseducation Of Lauryn Hill**
Ruffhouse/Columbia, 1998

It's not perfect, but, at its best, the soaring music — the string stabs, the uplifting drums, the motivational scratches, the grain of her voice — transmits

# Fu-Schnickens

F rom the Times Square cinemas that fired the imagination of the early hip-hoppers by showing **Shaw Brothers** chop-sockie movies on 24-hour loops, to Aaliyah co-starring with **Jet Li**, kung fu has had a long history in hip-hop culture. A year or so before the **Wu-Tang** emerged with their Shaolin mysticism, East Flatbush's Fu-Schnickens leapt onto the scene like a hopping golden vampire, with martial arts references (and garb), TV-show song titles, ragga rhymes and other pop culture trash, all cobbled together to make up their comedic, disposable worldview.

**Chip Fu** (Roderick Roachford), **Poc Fu** (Lennox Maturine) and **Moc Fu** (J Jones) all grew up together in Brooklyn. After a performance at Howard University in Washington DC, they were signed by Jive, who released their debut single "Ring the Alarm", a hip-hop reworking of **Tenor Saw**'s dancehall classic of the same name, in 1992. *FU Don't Take It Personal* (1992) featured production from **A Tribe Called Quest** and **Dres** from Black Sheep, and was a semi-classic of that jump-around, frat-party-friendly hip-hop of the early 1990s, thanks to the shouted hooks of tracks like "La Schmoove" and "True Fuschnick".

The mosh-pit building theatrics continued on 1993's "What's Up Doc?!? (Can We Rock?)" single, a big hit that marked the mic debut of basketball superstar **Shaquille O'Neal**. The kung-fu schtick was gone for *Nervous Breakdown* (1994), but their high-energy rapping wasn't. The trouble was, the rapid-fire stream of cartoonish exclamations had grown pretty stale by this point, and the group quickly faded into obscurity.

● **Greatest Hits**
Jive, 1995

What on earth is a group with two so-so albums doing with a greatest hits package? Well, this is one time you can thank corporate greed, because it spares you from buying two albums packed with filler, cutting straight to the good stuff. The drill-hammer beats and scattershot rhyming get pretty wearying pretty quickly, but in small doses it's unreservedly good fun.

# Funkdoobiest

Protégés of **DJ Muggs** and part of his Soul Assassins clique, Funkdoobiest represented the less interesting side of Cypress Hill's fusion of Cheech & Chong and los Vatos Locos. The trio of **Son Doobie** (Jason Vasquez), **Tomahawk Funk** (Tyrone Pachenco) and **DJ Ralph M** (Ralph Medrano) formed in 1990 and first appeared on "Stoned Is the Way Of The Walk" (1991) from Cypress Hill's debut album.

Further cameos on tracks by **House of Pain** and **Paris** preceded their debut album, *Which Doobie U B?* (1993). Son Doobie's flow was reminiscent of Everlast's and (consequently?) Muggs constructed him beats that had the same tempo and feel. Doobie's lyrical concerns – getting high, cartoons and porn flicks – didn't add anything to the English lexicon, but tracks like "Bow Wow Wow" ("Jump Around" with more bass), "The Funkiest" ("Jump Around" with more bass) and "Wopbabalubop" (**Little Richard** meets B Real) were pleasing enough party jams.

*Brothas Doobie* (1995) found Muggs giving the group smoother, less dirty beats at the same time that Son Doobie was getting progressively filthier. "Rock On" more or less did what its title promised, and "Dedicated" was a heartfelt shout-out to Son Doobie's dead homies, but mostly this album was about the "Superhoes" – probably because Son Doobie had starred in a porn film that year, *Son Doobie: Porn King*. For *The Troubleshooters* (1998), Funkdoobiest ditched Muggs and brought in such titular troubleshooters as **Da Beatminerz** and DJ Rectangle to get them out of their stoner rut. The problem, however, wasn't Muggs so much as it was Son Doobie's single cadence, something that was only highlighted by the various production strategies on offer here.

Funkdoobiest broke up soon afterwards, with Son Doobie going on to host a radio show in LA and then, strangely, hooking up with Canadian rappers **Swollen Members** (must've been their name that appealed to him). He appeared on their *Bad Dreams* (2001) album, and then released his solo album, *Funk Superhero* (2003), on their Battle Axe label.

**Which Doobie U B?**
Epic, 1993

DJ Muggs' not-so secret technique – West Coast flows over East Coast beats – is in full effect on this enjoyable album. The problem is, just about every track sounds exactly the same: stack "Freak Mode", "Which Doobie U B" and "Bow Wow Wow" back to back and see if you can tell the difference.

# Funkmaster Flex

The biggest DJ on the biggest radio station in the biggest radio market in the world will always have some degree of power in the music industry. When that radio station is a hip-hop station in the city that invented hip-hop and which still, to a large degree, lives and breathes it like no other, it's no wonder that Funkmaster Flex is one of the biggest players in the game.

**Aston Taylor** was born in the Bronx, the son of a soundsystem DJ who had played house parties and dances in Jamaica. At age 19, Flex was one-time B-Boy and KISS-FM DJ **Chuck Chillout**'s record boy. According to legend, one day Chuck was late and KISS's program director let Flex spin for five minutes. Three hours later, a star was born. Flex soon moved to WBLS where he filled in for DJ Red Alert. During this time, Flex was also becoming the most popular club DJ in New York. When HOT

97 decided that they were going to take over the airwaves, they chose Flex as their man. He didn't disappoint – he's been rated the number one DJ ever since.

By the mid-1990s, Flex's show was beamed to radio stations across the US, and he was signed by Loud for a series of mixtapes, *60 Minutes Of Funk* (1995, 1997, 1998, 2000), the first to be released by a major label. The tapes were a mixture of classic tracks, whatever was hot on the streets, exclusive freestyles, and irritating shout-outs, with glittering arrays of stars. The problem with a Flex mixtape is that you could never tell whether he was simply a slavish follower of fashion or whether he was setting the trends.

While all of the *60 Minutes Of Funk* series was strictly A-list, not even **Robert Altman** could have mustered the star power of *The Tunnel* (1999): **Nas**, Jay-Z, DMX and the Ruff Ryders, **Eminem**, Snoop Dogg, LL Cool J, Method Man, Mary J Blige, the Cash Money Millionaires, **Raekwon**, Erick Sermon, Prodigy, Kool G Rap, Redman and Capone-N-Noreaga. Flex even pulled the coup of having hip-hop's two martyrs on the album, in the form of a live Biggie 'n' 2Pac freestyle from 1993. None of his subsequent mixtapes could match it, but that hasn't stopped him from retaining his position at the top of the hip-hop heap.

⊙ **The Tunnel**
Def Jam, 1999

The A-list star personnel is simply sensational, even if they don't all live up to their reputations. Despite having just about every supernova in the hip-hop firmament, the album's real treat is the freestyle between Biggie and 2Pac, which was a simultaneously joyous and depressing reminder of simpler, better times. By the way, Biggie absolutely slays him.

# Funky Four Plus One

L argely consigned to history, Funky Four Plus One were one of the great old school crews. Their rhymes and *esprit de corps* were every bit the equal of the Furious Five and Cold Crush Crew; they were the first crew to include a woman; and they were the first crew to feature two DJs (not that you can tell that from their records).

DJs **Breakout** and **Baron** began doing parties together in the mid-1970s as the Brothers Disco with MCs like **KK Rockwell** and Busy Bee. Busy Bee soon left and **Keith Keith**, **Sha Rock** and **Raheim** joined the crew, making them the Funky Four MCs. In 1978 Rahiem joined the Furious Five and Sha Rock left the crew. They were replaced by **Lil' Rodney Cee** and **Jazzy Jeff** (no, not that Jazzy Jeff) from the Magnificent 7. With their two DJs and their **Mighty Mighty Sasquatch** soundsystem, the Funky Four became the most popular crew in the north Bronx.

In 1979 Sha Rock joined again, making them The Funky Four Plus One More. They were approached by Bobby Robinson of **Enjoy Records** and made the remark-

able 14-minute "Rappin' And Rocking The House" (1979) in one take while rehearsing in a garage. With Pumpkin & Friends playing an ultra-percussive extended jam on the rhythm from **Cheryl Lynn**'s "Got to Be Real", the Funky Four dropped some classic old school rhymes with incredible finesse, but it was Sha Rock and her sparkling mic personality that really made the record.

The following year the group moved to Sugarhill and recorded "That's The Joint" (1981), a re-worked version of "Rappin' And Rocking The House" that featured a sublime interaction between a complex arrangement and party-rockin' rhymes.

In 1981 KK and Lil' Rodney Cee left the group to form **Double Trouble**, and later appeared on the *Wildstyle* soundtrack (1983). Sha Rock, calling herself Lil Sha Rap, appeared with the Hypnotizing 3 on the legendary *Live Convention '81* (1981). But a slimmed down Funky Four with Sha Rock, Jazzy Jeff and Keith Keith continued to release records for Sugarhill: 1982's "Do You Wanna Rock?" and "Feel It" and "King Heroin" in 1983. After "King Heroin", the group broke up for good, with Sha Rock forming **Us Girls** with Lisa Lee and Debbie D for a small part in **Beat Street**, while Jazzy Jeff signed with Jive and released "King Heroin 85" in, unsurprisingly, 1985, before suing the label after they signed DJ Jazzy Jeff and the Fresh Prince.

⊙ **That's the Joint**
Sequel, 2000

Funky Four Plus One recorded just about enough material for Sequel to squeeze out this 13-track retrospective. A monstrous version of a groove lifted from the girl funk band Taste Of Honey, "That's The Joint" was their best record – perhaps the greatest old school track not recorded by Grandmaster Flash & the Furious Five or Afrika Bambaataa.

# g

## Warren G

If Dr. Dre is the mad scientist, Snoop Dogg the mischievous but loveable Dennis the Menace and Tupac the smooth-talking lothario, Dr. Dre's half-brother **Warren Griffin III** is G-Funk's boy next door. His subject matter doesn't stray that far from the gangsta blueprint, but where his compatriots relish the contradictions between their laidback music

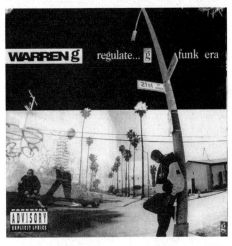

and hard lyrics, **Warren G** relaxes in his cushiony synths and takes being smooth as an end in itself.

Warren started rapping in a group called **213** (named after their city's area code) with childhood friend **Snoop** and **Nate Dogg** in Long Beach, California. He produced a track for **MC Breed**, but really got noticed with Mista Grimm's "Indosmoke" (1993). Riding a similar groove to his half-brother, Warren crafted a jazzier version of the G-Thang, complete with keyboard noodling, for fellow Los Angeles Borough of Compton resident Grimm, who kept asking "Are you high yet?" The track appeared on the *Poetic Justice* soundtrack and got Warren signed to Chris Lighty's new label Violator.

Warren's multi-platinum *Regulate... G-Funk Era* (1994) album was announced with one of the singles of the decade, "Regulate". Using a big chunk of ex-Doobie Brother **Michael McDonald**'s "I Keep Forgettin' (Every Time You're Near)", "Regulate" managed to combine G-Funk's bounce with an almost MOR quality, making it a sure-fire crossover hit. It wasn't just a marketing strategy, though; "Regulate" had an affective, melancholy fatalism similar to **Ice Cube**'s "Dead Homiez". The follow-up single, "This DJ", followed the same formula, but was a little more obvious and simplistic. The rest of the album didn't reach the same heights, but it was easy on the ears nevertheless.

*Take A Look Over Your Shoulder* (1997) tried to be a soundtrack for a summer jam in the LBC, but it was as airheaded and lazy as its ambition. Even though he proved that he couldn't spell on *Regulate*'s "What's Next" ("What's next, what's next, what N-X-E-T?"), here his remedial rhyme skills were glaringly obvious. The beats were similarly smoothed out on *I Want It All* (1999). Despite the presence of an all-star team of MCs including Snoop, **Slick Rick**, Mack 10, Eve, Drag-On and **Crucial Conflict** – and a reunion of **213** on "Game Don't Wait" – the closest *I Want it All* came to rocking the streets was when its title track was used as a warm-up song in football stadiums.

You could sense the desperation in his next project from the title on down. *Return Of The Regulator* (2001) was one of those projects – like Kiss donning the make-up again or *Frampton Comes Alive II* – that just reeked of someone who knew his days were numbered and needed a little extra cash for the retirement fund. "Yo' Sassy Ways" witnessed another reunion of 213, but failed as anything other than a history lesson – the same could be said of the rest of the album.

In 2004 Warren G, Nate Dogg and Snoop finally recorded a 213 album, *The Hard*

*Way*. Of course, by this time, Long Beach had changed its area code twice, and *The Hard Way*, with tracks like "Long Beach Is A Motherfucker" (the first song they ever did) and the reminiscing "Back In The Day", was as musty as the 1951 edition of the Encyclopedia Britannica in your school library.

Regulate... G-Funk Era
Violator/RAL, 1994

The perfect middle ground between Coolio and Dr. Dre.

# Gang Starr

They've never had any moments that shook the world like Run DMC or Public Enemy, never really blown people's minds like De La Soul or Eric B & Rakim, never turned their uncompromising vision into platinum sales, like A Tribe Called Quest or Wu-Tang Clan, but the duo of **DJ Premier** (**Christopher Martin**) and **Guru** (**Keith Elam**) is unquestionably one of the greatest groups in hip-hop history. Unlike all of their peers, **Gang Starr** are consistent: they've never made an unqualified masterpiece of an album, but they've never made a duff one either. As Guru almost said, "They've got discipline and they use it a lot". Primo and Guru aren't mere professionals, however. They might not have an overarching vision that draws outsiders in, but they're the embodiment of the hip-hop purist's creed: it's the skills, stupid.

WARREN G
I WANT IT ALL

DJ Premier (left - paying sartorial homage to Missy Elliott in NASA radiation suit), and Guru (right).

Gang Starr started off life in Boston as a trio of Guru, **Damo-D Ski** and **DJ 12B Down**. The group made a few singles like "Bust a Move" and "Gusto" in 1987, with the 45 King producing, before the group split, leaving Guru in New York trying to maintain a career in the music biz. Guru hooked up with the Wild Pitch label, who passed him a demo of DJ Premier, who had previously been in a Houston, Texas crew called Inner Circle Posse. The two hit it off and in 1988 recorded "Manifest", an infectious combination of James Brown's "Bring it Up (Hipster's Avenue)", Dizzy Gillespie's "A Night In Tunisia" and Guru's readymade battle rhymes. "Manifest" featured along with the trend-setting "Jazz Thing" on *No More Mr Nice Guy* (1989). While the album is justly celebrated as the album that brought jazziness into hip-hop, it was a pure hip-hop track that stood out. "DJ Premier In Deep Concentration" was more than just a collection of Mach 1 scratches to display Premier's deck dexterity – it was an emotive sound assemblage that took in **Kool & the Gang**'s "Summer Madness", Double Trouble's "Double Trouble", Billy Stewart's ululation from "Summertime" and the buzzing horn hook from Freda Payne's "Unhooked Generation". Of course, the scratching was pretty ace too, with one scratch sampled by Sonz of a Loop Da Loop Era at the beginning of the Hardcore classic "Far Out". It was the loop of the piano intro from "Summer Madness", though, that made the track the best turntable montage since "Wheels Of Steel". Undoubtedly influencing **DJ Shadow** and Peanut Butter Wolf, Premier was able to incorporate a sense of melancholy into a genre normally associated with content-free thrills and spills.

*No More Mr Nice Guy* had nice moments but it never quite came together. *Step In The Arena* (1990), however, was a great leap forward, not just for the group, but for all of hip-hop and beat-based music. With the background details of "Execution Of A Chump", the smoking loops of "Who's Gonna Take The Weight", the

hop, while Premier firmly estab-lished himself as the greatest pro-ducer in hip-hop with his work on Jeru The Damaja's *The Sun Rises In The East*, Nas's *Illmatic* and Notorious BIG's *Ready to Die*. Gang Starr returned in 1994 with *Hard to Earn*, which found Primo perfect-ing his symphonies of dissonance on "Speak Ya Clout" and giving a masterclass on the chopped beat on "Code of the Streets", which also featured Guru at his most eloquent.

With their 1997 single, "You Know My Steez", Premier flipped the script once more, working magic with a guitar loop from Joe Simon's "Drowning In The Sea Of Love". Simultaneously leaping from the speakers and wallowing in melancholy, "You Know My Steez" was a lesson in economy and the art of stab-bing. *Moment of Truth* (1998) followed in a similar style, with clipped guitar phrases rocketing out from all angles. Amazingly, it was Gang Starr's first gold album.

Premier launched his Year Round label in 2002 with NYG'z's "Giantz Ta This", a seriously hardcore rumination on the eternal "Seven Minutes Of Funk" beat – a perfect teaser for Gang Starr's *The Ownerz* (2003). Their sixth studio album found the group as angry as they had ever been, with a reinvigorated Guru spicing up his meat-and-potatoes lyrics. While it was time to disarm the "Militia" (variations of this track's idea had appeared on several

string stabs of "Check The Technique", the keyboard peals of "Say Your Prayers" (which must have given Dr. Dre an idea or two) and the beat psychedelia of "Beyond Comprehension", Primo had dived head first into his Akai S950 sampler and emerged on the other side as one of the best producers in hip-hop. Guru, too, had developed, combining book-smart bat-tle rhymes with street-smart tales of the inner city to become one of hip-hop's best content providers. The key track was "Just To Get A Rep": Premier instantly became an object of cult fascination by sampling Jean-Jacques Perrey's then-obscure, Moog funk masterpiece "EVA", while Guru estab-lished himself as a street chronicler of rare sensitivity.

*Daily Operation* (1992) at first sounded like a retreat from the radicalism of *Step In The Arena*, but it was really just Premier redefining the sound of hip-hop. With the sampladelic age ending, Premier threw out much of its sonic baggage, leaving his now trademark, neck-snapping kicks to do all of the damage, with some action going on in the mid-range and not much else (check out "Take It Personal"). That said, the whirling strings of "Soliloquy Of Chaos" filled the entire sound-field and established a mini-genre of askew, orches-tral hip-hop.

In 1993 Guru released his **Jazzmatazz** project, explicitly uniting live jazz and hip-

albums – here appearing in its third install-
ment), and there were too many celebrity
walk-ons, they were still as consistent as
ever sixteen years into their career .

**Full Clip - A Decade Of Gang Starr**
Noo Trybe/Virgin, 1999

It's short on the group's weirder moments (where's
"Deep Concentration"?), but this double-CD collection offers conclusive proof that Primo and Guru
are the finest exponents of pure hip-hop.

# Genius

◊ See *Wu-Tang Clan*

# Geto Boys

Along with N.W.A. and Ice-T,
Houston, Texas's **Geto Boys**
are hip-hop's true OGs. Just
like LA's original gangstas, the Geto
Boys put not just Houston, but all of
the US south of the Mason-Dixon
Line on the rap map. But where Cali's
jheri-curled MCs hid behind the
"reality rap" label, the Geto Boys had
no pretences about representing anything other than their own demented
imaginations.

Under the auspices of James "Lil J"
Smith's newly formed Rap-a-Lot label,
the **Ghetto Boys** released "Car Freaks"
(1987), a track about girls, such as
L'Trimm, sweating guys with nice
rides. The Ghetto Boys — **Juke Box**,

**Ready Red**, **Johnny C**, **Raheem** and dancer **Bushwick Bill** (Bushwick, Brooklyn-
raised **Richard Shaw**) — then released
*Making Trouble* (1988), a lame rip-off of
Run DMC (they even sported Homburgs,
black clothing and gold medallions on the
sleeve art).

With Lil J wanting the group to pursue a more violent direction, Juke Box,
Johnny C and Raheem all left the group.
Renaming themsleves the Geto Boys, a
new line-up of Bill, Red, **DJ Akshen**
(aka **Scarface**, Brad Jordan) and **Willie
D** recorded *Grip It! On That Other Level*
(1989) for a mere $2500. With tracks like
the industry-bashing, Curtis Mayfield and
"Apache"-sampling remake of "Do it Like
A G.O." ("Motherfuck the KKK/Wearing
dresses and shit, what the fuck, is they
gay?") which had previously appeared on
Willie D's *Controversy* (1989) album and
the over-the-top "Mind Of A Lunatic"
("Had sex with the corpse before I left
her/And drew my name on the wall like
'Helter Skelter'"), *Grip It! On That Other
Level* eventually went gold and made the
industry take note of regional rap.

**Rick Rubin** liked the album so much
that he offered Rap-a-Lot a distribution
deal, but Geffen balked at distributing an
album that talked about necrophilia, and
*The Geto Boys* (1990) attracted a storm of
controversy. Essentially an updated version of *Grip It!*, *The Geto Boys* added the

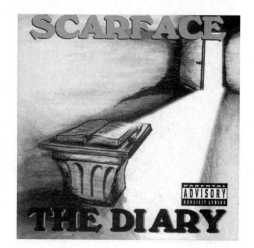

splatter rap "Assassins" and Bill's savage solo turn, "Size Ain't", and attracted the full wrath of Tipper Gore's PMRC who, of course, missed the irony that tracks like "Do it Like a G.O." attacked the hypocritical, racist society whose values Gore was so stringently trying to uphold.

The cover of *We Can't Be Stopped* (1991) was the Geto Boys' most outrageous statement yet: it featured Bill on a hospital gurney with his eye shot out talking on a mobile phone. With production from John Bido, *We Can't Be Stopped* featured the stunning "Mind Playing Tricks On Me". Based on a moody guitar riff from **Isaac Hayes**' *Three Tough Guys* soundtrack, "Mind Playing Tricks on Me" was the paranoid flipside to all the nuts-grabbing gangsta poses, and it went platinum on the back of heavy MTV rotation. Elsewhere, on tracks like "Chuckie" and "Gota Let Your Nuts Hang" they were up to their usual shenanigans.

With the success going to his head, Willie D left the group to pursue a solo career and was replaced by Convicts' **Big Mike** on *Till Death Do Us Part* (1993).

Aside from the compelling "Six Feet Deep" and "Crooked Officer", *Till Death Do Us Part* was a sterile rip-off of *The Chronic* formula. The group then split and released mostly weak solo albums, with the exception of Scarface who shone on the **Marvin Gaye**-sampling "A Minute To Pray And A Second To Die" from *Mr. Scarface Is Back* (1991) and "I Seen a Man Die" from *The Diary* (1994). No longer content with spilling fake blood from Dario Argento's

## GO-GO

If hip-hop hadn't been invented in New York, and had been played by a live band instead of DJs, it probably would have sounded like go-go, a musical phenomenon unique to **Washington DC** that weds funk and hip-hop. Just like early hip-hop, go-go focuses on Latin-flavoured percussion breaks and vocals which are little more than exhortations to the crowd to get down and jam.

The symbiosis between hip-hop and go-go goes back to 1974 when **Chuck Brown and the Soul Searchers**, the godfathers of go-go, released *Salt Of The Earth*. The album featured "Ashley's Roachclip", which became one of the all-time classic hip-hop breaks, sampled by everyone from 2 Live Crew to Eric B & Rakim. The same album also featured "Blow Your Whistle", a track that overlaid the rhythm of Grover Washington Jr.'s "Mr Magic" with percussion breaks inspired by Chuck Brown's tenure in a group called Los Latinos. This combination of

a slow funk groove with congas and cowbells became go-go. In 1979 Brown recorded what would be go-go's calling card, "Bustin' Loose", and pretty soon this became the dominant sound in DC.

**Trouble Funk**, a group that had formed in the 1960s as the Trouble Band, soon supplanted the Soul Searchers as the biggest go-go band. Their first single was 1980's "E Flat Boogie", but they really blew up when they signed to **Sugar Hill** in 1982. "Drop The Bomb" was quite simply one of the funkiest records ever, with its Parliament rhythms and keyboards combined with cowbells, while "Pump Me Up", from the same year, had percussion that was like the Mau-Maus marching up the Potomac.

Other major early groups included **EU** (Experience Unlimited), Rare Essence, Redds and the Boys, **Mass Extension**, Junk Yard Band and **Hot Cold Sweat**. There was a brief vogue for go-go in Britain in the mid-1980s, and EU had a

props department, Scarface became the thinking and feeling man's thug with his reflections on the consequences of the hustler's lifestyle.

The Geto Boys reconvened for the so-so *The Resurrection* (1996), but Bushwick Bill left amidst a lawsuit with Rap-a-Lot. Willie D and Scarface carried on as a duo on the tired *Da Good, Da Bad & Da Ugly* (1998).

In 2000 Scarface was picked to run the new Def Jam South imprint. His success

was repaid with *The Fix* (2002), a star-studded album that brought Scarface back to prominence. He continued to humanise the gangsta lifestyle with the weepy "My Block", while "Guess Who's Back" featured **Jay-Z** getting nice over a mournful Kanye West beat.

## SCARFACE

⊙ **Mr. Scarface Is Back**
Rap-a-Lot, 1991

Scarface is easily the best rapper in the group and he shines on his solo debut.

## GETO BOYS

⊙ **Uncut Dope**
Rap-a-Lot, 1992

The best moments from *The Geto Boys* and *We Can't Be Stopped* – an essential document of no-holds-barred splatter rap.

# Ghostface Killah

◊ See *Wu-Tang Clan*

---

moderate hit with "Da Butt" in 1989 thanks to its appearance in **Spike Lee**'s movie *School Daze*. But go-go never really made it out of DC, despite the increasing influence of hip-hop in

the music, as can be heard on **Rare Essence**'s "Body Snatchers" (1996) or **Backyard Band**'s cover of OutKast's "Ms Jackson" (2000).

## VARIOUS ARTISTS

⊙ **Meet Me at the Go-Go**
Sanctuary, 2003

Perhaps not the best (seek out *Go-Go Crankin'* which was released on 4th & Broadway in 1985) mainstream compilation of go-go, but certainly the most readily available. This features classics like Trouble Funk's "E Flat Boogie" and "Let's Get Small", Chuck Brown and the Soul Searchers' "We Need Some Money" and Hot, Cold Sweat's "Meet Me At The Go-Go" as well as obscurities like Arkade Funk's awesome "Tilt" and Ski Bone's "Take It To The Top".

## TROUBLE FUNK

⊙ **Live**
American/Infinite Zero, 1996

A reissue of quite possibly the greatest live album ever made. Originally released on TTED in 1981, this four-track double album is basically just one long jam. But unlike the soporific extended jams of, say, the Grateful Dead, this is pure intensity from the get-go.

# The Goats

With their left-wing politics, use of live musicians and multiracial make-up, Philadelphia's **The Goats** were probably doomed from their inception to be the hip-hop group that it was OK for the indie rock kids to like. And while it is true that their brand of hip-hop was focused more on beats to make you jump around than head-nod, **Madd, Swayzack, OaTie Kato, Rucyl, Love** and DJ **1Take Willie** had enough skills to escape the "backpacker" ghetto.

The Goats' first album, *Tricks Of The Shade* (1992), was co-produced by Schooly D producer **Joe "The Butcher" Nicolo**, who ensured that there was plenty of boom and DJ Code Money-style scratches to go along with the righteous politics. The lead track, "Typical American", was an explosion of enormous drum breaks, an undeniable sing-along chorus and high speed rhymes like "Pie à la mode/The ghettoes will explode/While you sit pigeon-toed at a diamond commode". With skits like "Columbus' Boat Ride", "Leonard Peltier in a Cage" and "Noriega's Coke Stand" nestled in a narrative that followed the two fictional protagonists **Chicken Little** and **Hangerhead** around a nightmarish freak show in search of the mother who abandoned them at birth, it became clear that *Tricks Of The Shade* was a concept album about the state of the union. The politics might have been facile, but with the flowing deliveries of Madd, Swayzack and OaTie Kato and the chops of the live band, the album became something more than a funky feel-good session for self-righteous and complacent liberal white folk.

1994's *No Goats No Glory*, however, moved away from the lyrical flag-burning in an attempt to be accepted by the hard-core hip-hop market. While it was by no means *just* the politics that made them so enjoyable first time around, by excising the content in favour of style, they lost a large part of their personality.

After the group disbanded, Oatie (now travelling under the name MC Uh-Oh) founded **Incognegro** with DJ Smoove, Gungi Brain and former **Bad Brains** drummer Chuck Treece. Signing to Philly's thrash metal/hardcore label CHord, they released a self-titled album in 1999 that included a Hammond organ-heavy cover of **The Clash**'s "Brand New Cadillac" as well as the more breezy "Sunny Days" and "Keepin' It Lovely".

**Tricks Of The Shade**
Columbia/Ruffhouse, 1992

A funny, scathing critique of Amerikkka that doesn't sacrifice beats and skills for the message.

# Godfather Don

↻ See *Fondle 'Em records*

# Goodie Mob

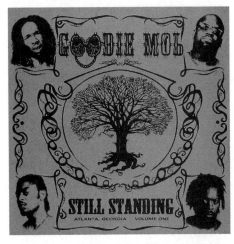

Comprising **Thomas "Cee-lo" Callaway, Robert "T-Mo" Barrett, Willie "Khujo" Knighton** and **Cameron "Big Gipp" Gipp**, Goodie Mob (Good Die Mostly Over Bullshit) make fellow Dungeon Family members OutKast's allusions to politics utterly explicit. Their world is full of dark conspiracies, people peering through windows, a system designed to keep the masses down, and smoking dank just to get away from it all.

Their debut album, *Soul Food* (1995), was released at the height of the "murder music" trend and its paranoia and brutal imagery fit in perfectly. Dubbing **Louis Armstrong** into ghetto hell, the conspiracy-obsessed "Cell Therapy" sounded like an old plantation work chant with Casio drums replacing rhythmic handclaps. "Dirty South" was superficially an anthem of regional pride, but the video featured a young girl drawing a Confederate flag, making obvious the real meaning of living in Dixie.

The follow-up album, *Still Standing* (1998), was similarly contrary, a kind of G-Funk in reverse: smooth guitars running backwards, synths that whimpered instead of whining, and songs about people not dancing any more. On *World Party* (1999), however, their uncompromising vision had been replaced by a sharper, more contemporary electronic sound. And lyrics such as "The world would be a better place to live if there were less queers". Ugly mis-steps aside, though, *World Party* managed to maintain the Mob's playfulness on tracks like "What it Ain't (Ghetto Enuff)" (with labelmates **TLC**), "Get Rich To This" and "Chain Swang". With occasionally great, state-of-the-art prodcution and a couple of superb radio songs, *World Party* was the sort of compromise fans would have to settle for in an apolitical age.

The album took its toll on the group, however, and in 2002 **Cee-Lo** went solo on *Cee-Lo Green and His Perfect Imperfections*. The production, mostly by Cee-Lo himself, was rather amazing – laying a mysterious voodoo juju on the "crunk" style of the moment – but the singing was mostly by Cee-Lo as well, and it wore really thin really fast, as did his gratuitous weirdness (he even sounded like **Dose One** on "One for the Road").

In June 2002 **Khujo** was in a car accident that resulted in one of his legs being amputated, but the group (without Cee-Lo) decided to soldier on regardless. They released the *One Monkey Don't Stop No Show* album, an apparent reference to Cee-Lo, in 2004. Like Cee-Lo's second album, *Cee-Lo Is The Soul Machine*, from the same year, it suffered from trying too hard to sound current, to keep up with the crunk trend that was taking over hip-hop.

⊙ **Soul Food**
LaFace, 1995

One of hip-hop's most underrated gems. The album's cybernetic spirituals perfectly encapsulated the new South: the sound of both the high-tech industries that made the region boom and the pernicious ghosts of old hovering around every corner and in every tree.

# Grand Daddy IU

Grand Daddy IU might have been the first rapper to wear spats and get away with it. Very much in the **Big Daddy Kane** mould – his flow was similar, but more laid-back and without the resonance or venom – IU was both a suave ladykiller and a devastating MC torcher.

The Strong Island MC was discovered by **Biz Markie**, who then produced his debut album, *Smooth Assassin* (1990). A slept-on classic, the album featured tracks like "Something New", based on a loop from **James and Bobby Purify**'s "I'm Your Puppet" and had memorable put-downs like "You're cold booty, softer than Cottonelle", the mean slow-roller "Mass Destruction" and the smoking "This Is A Record". His smooth side sometimes got the better of him, as on "Sugar Free", which was in a wretched early r&b crossover style, before they really got the formula right. Biz's beats and IU's rhymes were in the definitive **Cold Chillin'** label style, except probably a year too late for the album to make much of an impact.

It took him four years to release another album, *Lead Pipe* (1994), and by that time the predominant style had changed so much that IU couldn't keep up. The super-amped thug chorus of the early 1990s East Coast was pretty much the diametric opposite of the style that had made IU's debut so enjoyable. In the meantime, however, IU had gone into production, and he came up with a couple of gems for Roxanne Shanté: "Big Mama" (1990) and "Dance to This" (1992).

Aside from an appearance on **Big L**'s *Lifestylez Ov Da Poor And Dangerous* (1995),

# GRAFFITI

Although humans have been painting walls since the beginning of time, in New York and Philadelphia in the late 1960s and early 1970s the word was made fresh. The early graffiti writers knew their Bible, and knew that if the word made the world, then the word could change it.

Dreaming a little bigger than the guys who wrote "Joey-n-Stacy 2gether 4ever" or "For a good time call Vicki..." in the stalls of the men's room at Howard Johnson's, early graff heroes like **Top Cat**, **Cornbread**, **Tracy 168** and **Taki 183** imagined what their names would look like up in lights,

IU pretty much disappeared until his re-emergence (of sorts) on "Face Down" with **Vakill** and **The Molemen** in 1998. He produced a track for KRS-One's *The Sneak Attack* (2001), dropped into **Sway and Tech**'s show for a freestyle or two and showed up on a couple of mixtapes with **Capone-N-Noreaga** and Nature, but as *Lead Pipe* had already proved, his best days were behind him.

⊙ **Smooth Assassin**
Cold Chillin', 1990

An advertising tag line would probably read "If you like Big Daddy Kane, you'll love Grand Daddy IU" but there's enough individuality on this album to make it recommendable for more than just those times when you can't find *Long Live The Kane*. IU is smooth, doesn't rush anything and has a devastating line or two.

# Grandmaster Flash & the Furious Five

Grandwizard Theodore may have invented scratching, but it wouldn't mean a thing without the swing developed by **Grandmaster Flash** (**Joseph**

and proceeded to make that dream a reality, albeit on concrete with Rust-Oleum spraypaint and magic markers.

Granted, gangs in Chicago had scrawled territorial messages to mark their turf in the early 1960s. True, Philly's Top Cat and Cornbread had most likely invented the idea of the tag – the graff writer's signature – and its concomitant, manifest-destiny will to scrawl it bigger, broader and farther out than anyone else. But it was in New York that **graffiti** really took off. The arrogance of New Yorkers (who believe that the city is a universe unto itself, and that the world is a microcosm of Gotham City, not the other way around), conspired with the inter-borough transit system to make graffiti the ticket to fame. Take your name or your nickname, add the number of the street you live on, bomb the number 4 IRT and boom, your name is known from Van Cortlandt Park to Flatbush. Graff may have predated hip-hop – as a *musical* form – by a few years, but writing was the essence of hip-hop culture. Who, with the most limited of materials, could make the most ghetto-fabulous style? Who could "go all-city" with the flyest colours and the deffest technique? Who could make the letters flow like a fountain?

The earliest tags were basic block letters with the scantiest of flourishes. Writers soon progressed on to bubble letters, and then to what Tracy 168 dubbed "Wildstyle": mad, abstract geometry that would have MC Escher and Kasimir Malevich scratching their heads; Jackson Pollock drips; and crazy calligraphy that could put both 14th-century monks and Japanese Kenji artists to shame. New York being practically a lawless financial ruin in the mid-1970s, writers like **Dondi**, **Futura 2000**, **Daze**, **Blade**, **Lee**, **Zephyr**, **Rammellzee**, **Crash**, **Kel**, **NOC 167** and **Lady Pink** became public enemies number one, and the Manhattan Transit Authority spent the equivalent of the gross domestic product of many Third World countries trying to halt the "menace".

Eventually, though, graff became both mainstream (among the 1980s art set who were after a bit of authentic rough) and marginalised (in its original milieu). **Jean-Michel Basquiat**, with his "SAMO" tag, soon became the darling of the art world, **Beat Street** brought writing, breakdancing and rapping to Hollywood, and the subway burner soon became less important and less meaningful. Hip-hop was big money by the mid-1980s – who cared about pissing off the MTA and getting known in Far Rockaway when you could make a record and have the whole world sing your name? With 'zines like the **International Graffiti Times** and **Can Control**, and eventually videotapes, websites and **Mo' Wax** album covers, graffiti became domesticated – a thing not a process. Nevertheless, the art of eye-shocking still gives people a buzz and, whether it's daubed on a freight train in Kansas, a highway underpass in Tokyo or a canvas in some highfalutin' art college in London, the painterly emissions of cans of Krylon will always have a certain frisson.

To hear tales of tags, burners and wildstyles on chromium oxide, check out The Artifacts' "Wrong Side Of Da Tracks" (*Between A Rock And A Hard Place*) and Company Flow's "Lune TNS" (*Funcrusher Plus*).

The past is another country: they wear things differently there. (Especially Grandmaster Flash & the Furious Five).

Saddler). The sound of a record being rubbed across a stylus is hip-hop's equivalent of the guitar solo — the climactic moment of intensity and skill that everyone wants to emulate — but the techniques developed by Grandmaster Flash are more like hip-hop's riffs — the less flashy facets, but the genre's very foundations.

Inspired by **Pete DJ Jones**, Flash brought DJing to a new level of sophistication by introducing the techniques of backspinning and cutting. Flash was the pioneer of the cross-fader, cutting back and forth between records, slicing and dicing them, and overloading the mixer's channels with brilliant, arrogant noise. With his phonographic flights of fancy, Flash truly made DJing something other than just spinning records and proved that the audio montage could be more than just the smart-ass shenanigans of the Dickie Goodmans and Bill Buchanans of the hip-hop world.

Of course, Flash had more than just his turntable skills going for him. He had

the **Furious Five**, one of the best of the old school MC troupes. With **Melle Mel** (Melvin Glover), **Cowboy** (Keith Wiggins), **Kidd Creole** (Danny Glover), **Rahiem** (Guy WIlliams) and **Mr Ness** (Eddie Morris), Flash signed to Enjoy records in 1979 and released "Superappin'" (1979). Although it blew "Rapper's Delight" out of the water, and featured a verse that would later show up on the epochal "The Message", "Superappin'" and its follow-up, "Super Rappin' No 2" (1980), didn't get anywhere near the attention that those interlopers of the Sugar Hill Gang received. So Flash and the Five defected to Sugar Hill.

Their first release for their new label was the effervescent party jam "Freedom" (1980), which looped the kazoo intro and the trumpet bridge of Freedom's "Get Up And Dance".

The group's early records had emphasised the MCs at the expense of Flash's deck skills, but "The Adventures of

GRANDMASTER FLASH
& THE FURIOUS FIVE

THE MESSAGE

Grandmaster Flash On The Wheels of Steel" (1981) redressed the balance and exposed the world outside of the Bronx to the art of the DJ. A collage of the Sugar Hill Gang's "8th Wonder", **Queen**'s "Another One Bites the Dust", **Blondie**'s "Rapture", Chic's "Good Times", The Sequence & Spoonie Gee's "Monster Jam", Grandmaster Flash & the Furious Five's "Birthday Party", The Incredible Bongo Band's "Apache", a **Flash Gordon** record and a mock children's story from an album called *Singers, Talkers, Players, Swingers & Doers* by The Hellers, "Wheels Of Steel" was recorded live on the decks. If Flash messed up, he erased everything and started from scratch, and he nailed it on the fourth or fifth take. Of course, "Wheels Of Steel" was more than just a simple collage — it was a cut-up that was *on beat* for the track's full seven minutes.

Flash showed that, despite its normal usage, the turntable was also a percussion instrument with a tonal range and expressive capability as musical as that of drums, woodblocks and marimbas. As audacious, assertive and aggressive as anything coming from downtown New York's art-punk fringe (check the vicious scratch that served as the bridge from the children's story to "Birthday Party"), "Wheels of Steel" was (and remains) hip-hop's greatest feat of derring-do.

Flash had changed the face of music with "Wheels of Steel", but the Furious Five changed the face of hip-hop with "The Message" (1982) – without Flash, who hated the record. Before "The Message", hip-hop rhymes had been all about partying, call-and-response chants of "yes yes y'all", and battling fellow MCs. "The Message" (written by Melle Mel and **Duke Bootee**) was, by contrast, a devastating blast of social realism filled with rage ("Don't push me 'cause I'm close to the edge") and dislocation (the other-worldly space-age synthesizer dub production).

While the group continued to release landmarks like "Flash to the Beat", "It's Nasty (Genius Of Love)" and "Scorpio" (all 1982), "The Message" had driven a rift into the Furious Five. After recording the awesome "White Lines (Don't Do It)" (1983), which was really a Melle Mel solo turn, the group split. **Raheim** and **Kidd Creole** stayed with Flash and Melle Mel, **Ness** and **Cowboy** went out on their own. Melle Mel's group stayed with Sugar Hill, Flash signed to Elektra, but neither troupe could survive in Run DMC's new school age. They reunited in 1988, and proved how old they were by recording a version of **Steppenwolf**'s "Magic Carpet Ride" with the rock band's singer John Kay.

As epochal a DJ as Grandmaster Flash was, it wouldn't be until 2002 that someone would devote a whole album to "the disco dream of the mean machine, the Darth Vader of the slide fader" and his turntable exploits. And then, wouldn't you know it, two came along at once. *The Official Adventures of Grandmaster Flash* was a strange, sometimes ill-fitting conglomeration – Flash repeated his old routines interspersed with tiny little snippets of 1979 and 1982 appearances at the **T-Connection** and **Disco Convention** and full-length old school classics such as **Babe Ruth**'s "The Mexican".

Nevertheless, it did offer some insights as to what those old block parties might have been like. "Flash Tears The Roof Off" finds Flash delaying the climax for even longer than **Dr Funkenstein** did on the Parliament albums, teasing us with the intro to "Give

Up The Funk (Tear the Roof Off The Sucker)" before unleashing a prolonged wave of "Apache" congas and deracinated synths, that lasts roughly eight minutes, until Flash finally delivers the goods and allows the P-Funk to groove. *Essential Mix: Classic Edition* was a less revelatory mix of 1980s synth jams from **D Train**, Maze and Nu Shooz.

⊙ **Adventures On The Wheels of Steel**
Sequel/Sugar Hill, 1999

An essential three-CD collection of all of Flash and the Furious Five's work for Sugar Hill.

# Grandmixer D.ST

**B**orn **Derek Showard**, **Grandmixer D.ST** is one of the greatest DJs in the history of hip-hop. Expanding on the innovations of Grandmaster Flash and Grand Wizard Theodore, D.ST (his name comes from his graffiti tag, which is short for "Delancey Street") basically helped make turntablism what it is today. D.ST elevated scratch DJing from a rather primitive technique to a rhythmic art form as complex as a school of octopuses playing Latin polyrhythms.

D.ST was originally one of the **Zulu Nation** DJs with Bambaataa and **Whiz Kid** in the late 1970s. He really came to prominence, though, when he won the New Music Seminar DJ battle in 1982. This led him to working with producer/bassist/agent provocateur Bill Laswell, who had been commissioned by French label **Celluloid** to produce five hip-hop records. His first single, "Grandmixer Cuts It Up" (1982), didn't highlight his deck skills, but it was a pretty amazing example of the early 1980s videogame soundscape metamorphosing onto vinyl.

Becoming the Dizzy Gillespie to **Grandwizard Theodore**'s Louis Armstrong, D.ST made the turntable into the electric guitar of the next decade, with his scratch-ing on **Herbie Hancock**'s 1983 single, "Rockit". "Rockit" only reached number 71 on the American charts, but its moderate crossover success (and heavy airplay on MTV) meant that it is one of the most influential hip-hop tracks ever. Cited by nearly every turntablist as the reason they started DJing, "Rockit" – even more than Grandmaster Flash's "Wheels Of Steel" – established the DJ as the star of the record, even if he wasn't the frontman. Produced by Laswell, "Rockit" was a dense assemblage of Fairlight keyboards, Oberheim DMX drum machines and vocoders that managed to move with a dexterity that belied its rump of steel electronic skin. However much detail might be packed into it, everything was subordinate to D.ST's scratching — it's what you listened to and what you listened for. Making the case for hip-hop being the new jazz far better than any **Roy Ayers**-sampling Pete Rock production, D.ST approached his solo as if he was playing at a bebop cutting session at Minton's Playhouse in the 1940s. Nearly as in your face as "Wheels Of Steel", D.ST's violent interjections of scratching (according to David Toop, he was using a record of Balinese gamelan) serve to trash Hancock, as if telling him to go back to the 1970s because "this is our time now".

While Grandmaster Flash and Afrika Bamabaataa were using the turntable to explore repetition, alter rhythm and create the instrumental stabs and punch-phrasing that would come to characterise the sound of hip-hop, Grandmixer D.ST was continuing to explore the outer reaches of turntable science. "Crazy Cuts" (1984) may have reprised a lot of his scratching from "Rockit", but the new passages showed just how rhythmically inventive he was. "Mega-Mix II (Why Is it Fresh?)" (1984) was the kind of turntable throwdown that wouldn't be heard until DJs like **Cash Money** and **Spinbad** invented the transforming technique. D.ST was also featured on records such as **Time Zone**'s "The Wildstyle", Last Poet **Jalaluddin Mansur Nuriddin**'s "Mean Machine" and records by **Material** and **Manu Dibango**.

D.ST (now renamed DXT) has continued to work to with Laswell and appears on many of his nefarious projects. Particularly noteworthy are his contributions to 1996's *Altered Beats* compilation.

**Rockit**
Columbia, 1983

Probably the most influential DJ track of them all, this showcases D.ST's jaw-dropping turntable skills years before this kind of scratching became commonplace.

# Grand Puba

◊ See *Brand Nubian*

# Group Home

L il Dap and Melachi the Nutcracker made their first appearance on **Gang Starr**'s "I'm the Man" from the *Daily*

*Operation* (1992) album, and then two years later on "Speak Ya Clout" and "Words From The Nutcracker" from *Hard To Earn* (1994). The verses weren't terribly memorable, but their workaday rhymes had a ruggedly solid feel that appealed to the East Coast underground.

*Livin' Proof* (1995) was produced almost entirely by **DJ Premier** and **Guru**, and Premier's basic, but thoroughly neck-snapping, beats laid the foundations for an entire cottage industry of copyists. The spare production framed Dap and Melachi's elementary raps perfectly, and made the album something of an underground classic. Three tracks in particular stood out: "Livin' Proof" with its chilling **Ramsey Lewis** sample, the elegaic "Supa Star" which featured some of Premier's best-ever work, and the menacing "Tha Realness".

Despite its evident quality, the album got lost in the fray, particularly with the **Wu-Tang Clan**'s solo albums coming out around the time and redefining East Coast hip-hop. Group Home's next album, *A Tear For The Ghetto*, wasn't released until 1999 and by then everyone had forgotten about them. Premier only produced one track. Not a great deal has been heard of them since. Lil Dap released the weak "Brooklyn Zone" single in 2001, and appeared on a few underground records such as **Shabazz the Disciple**'s "Thieves In The Night" remix (2002) and French DJ **Mehdi**'s "About Me" (2002).

**Livin' Proof**
Payday, 1995

Lil Dap and Melachi the Nutcracker won't wow you with their street observations, but they're solid enough on the mic. What will wow you, though, is Premier's devastating production. It's nothing terribly new, but he nails every New York convention on the head.

# Hammer

**S**tanley Kirk Burrell was an entertainer first and foremost, a businessman second and a hip-hop artist somewhere down on the list below dancer and corporate toy — if Berry Gordy had still been around, he would have signed him on the spot. A former batboy for the Oakland A's baseball team, Burrell earned his mic name from his resemblance to baseball legend "Hammerin'" Hank Aaron. With money he borrowed from some of the A's, **MC Hammer** started his own record label, Bust It, and released a couple of records by himself and Oaktown's **3-5-7** that garnered enough local attention to get him signed to Capitol.

*Let's Get It Started* (1988) was his major label debut. With production by Felton Pilate from **Con Funk Shun**, *Let's Get It Started* inaugurated the formula that would make Hammer the biggest rap star in the world: lots of obvious, pre-digested samples from **Parliament**, James Brown and **The Jacksons**, simple rhythms that your grandmother could rap over with-

out stumbling and plenty of "Hammer time" breaks so that he could show off his footwork and balloon trousers during live shows and videos.

*Please Hammer Don't Hurt 'Em* (1990) picked up on the momentum that his debut generated and became the (then) biggest-selling rap album ever. The **Rick James**-sampling "U Can't Touch This" is the single everyone remembers, but the **Chi-Lites** cover "Have You Seen Her" and the **Prince**-sampling "Pray" were bigger hits. After 21 weeks on top of *Billboard*'s album chart, Hammer was everywhere: ads for Taco Bell, Pepsi and Kentucky Fried Chicken, a Saturday-morning cartoon show called *Hammerman* and even a Mattel doll.

*Too Legit To Quit* (1991) was typical music-biz overkill: even if people weren't already sick of the guy, the corporate hype machine ensured that the album wouldn't live up to expectations. The album was as lame as ever, but you had to admire the gargantuan proportions of the title track (maybe he should have hooked up with **Keith Emerson**) and, though they won't admit it, those old enough still remember the hand signals from the "Too Legit To Quit" video.

With **Dr. Dre** ruling the charts, Hammer went gangsta on *The Funky Headhunter* (1994) and, remarkably, people bought the damn thing. The album went gold and the **George Clinton**-sampling "Pumps and a Bump" made the Top 40, but the sight of a former Christian rap artist (he was in a group called the **Holy Ghost Boys**) putting out G-Funk was laughable.

*V Inside Out* (1995) saw him return to his MC Hammer moniker, but his name change couldn't help him revisit past glories or trick the record-buying public into thinking that this was "Hammer time" all over again. After several greatest hits packages, embarassing bankruptcy proceedings and an abortive return to Christian rap, MC Hammer returned with the post-9/11 cash-in attempt, *Active Duty* (2001), on his own World Hit label.

**Please Hammer Don't Hurt 'Em**
Capitol, 1990

Hey kid, you wanna hear where P Diddy got all his ideas?

# Heavy D

eavy D (Dwight Myers) is probably the only rapper who has been able to maintain a resolutely pop career without being hounded out of the industry by either fickle tastes or hip-hop's hardcore element. Perhaps it's because Myers *is* part of the industry – he replaced **Andre Harrell** as the boss of Uptown Records and was a vice-president at Universal – and no one wants to front on someone with so much power. But more likely it's that the self-styled "overweight lover" has an engaging microphone personality that manages to stay on just the right side of novelty.

Havey D formed **Heavy D & the Boyz** in the mid-1980s in Mount Vernon, New York with schoolmates **Trouble T-Roy**, **Eddie F** and **G-Whiz**. Harrell, who was working at Def Jam at the time, wanted to sign the group, but Russell Simmons thought the group would go nowhere and passed. When Harrell formed Uptown in

1987, though, he signed them and *Living Large* (1987) went gold on the strength of a string of hits that were produced by **Marley Marl** and Harrell and blended easy pop appeal, playfulness and surprisingly on-point mic skills: "Mr. Big Stuff", "The Overweight Lover's In The House" and "Chunky But Funky".

*Big Tyme* (1989) featured an all-star cast (Marley Marl, **Q-Tip**, Big Daddy Kane) and another hit in the form of "We Got Our Own Thang" and a serviceable reworking of **Zapp**'s "More Bounce to the Ounce" in the form of "More Bounce". Heavy's breakthrough, though, was 1991's cover of the O'Jays/Third World classic, "Now That We Found Love". With **Aaron Hall** singing the chorus with an unbearable, overwrought melisma, Heav's version combined just about every form of black music that was selling at the time – hip-hop, swingbeat, house and Jamaican dancehall – in an undeniable assault on the pop charts. "Now That We Found Love" anchored *Peaceful Journey* (1991) along with his other hit, "Is It Good To You".

*Blue Funk* (1993) saw Heavy moving in a more hardcore direction with darker, more menacing production, although his subject matter would always stay focused on girls. "Who's the Man?" found the Heavster brushing off his critics and playa haters to the refrains of **Steve Miller**'s "Fly Like an Eagle" and **Cypress Hill**'s "How I Could Just Kill A Man". *Nuttin' But Love* (1994) returned Heav to his playful pop roots. "Got Me Waiting" rode a **Luther Vandross** sample into the US Top 30, while the title track found the unlikely loverman convincing just enough people to reach the lower reaches of the Top 40.

*Waterbed Hev* (1997) was overinflated with r&b, and was as lame as its title's reference to the original genius of love, **Waterbed Kev**. *Heavy* (1999), though, was a more prepossessing blend of the latest sounds. "You Know" featured **Cee-Lo** from the Goodie Mob and was a decent blend of the Big Apple with the Dirty South, while "On Point", with **Big Pun** and Eightball, was produced by **Erick**

**Sermon** and had so much weight that it crushed you into submission. After a quiet period, in 2002 Heavy came down from his high-rise office to produce "Guns & Roses" for Jay-Z's *The Blueprint 2: The Gift & the Curse.*

**Heavy Hitz**
MCA, 2000).

Featuring pretty much all of Heavy D's hits, this collection traces the blueprint of all subsequent pop rap. Its charming innocence overcomes its lightweight nature.

# BEEFS

Hip-hop's raison d'être is the "battle" – a ferocious display of one-upmanship between DJs, MCs, b-boys and graffiti artists where each participant tries to come up with the most outlandish flourish, the most original stylization or the most damning insult. Its fierce competitive nature – its echoes of **Clint Eastwood** and **Lee Van Cleef** meeting face to face at the big gundown – was precisely why it appealed to kids left to fend for themselves in the lawlessness of the ghost towns of The Bronx.

While battling had existed since the earliest days of hip-hop – with crews like the **L Brothers**, Herculords, Cold Crush Brothers and **Fantastic 5** going toe to toe on the stages of uptown discos and Bronx boîtes – the rhyme wars largely consisted of the routines that the crews already had down cold (i.e. there wasn't that much original material). That all changed on New Year's Eve 1981 when the Treacherous 3's **Kool Moe Dee** was in a contest with Chief Rocker Busy Bee Starski. After Busy Bee went through his usual routine, Moe Dee, who showed up late, stormed the stage and started impersonating Busy Bee before launching into an unprecedented improvised verbal attack: "Now to bite a nigga's name [the "Starski" was appropriated from Lovebug Starski] is some lowdown shit/If you was money, man, you'd be counterfeit." The crowd went berserk and a new paradigm was born. Battles were no longer simply competition, they were now personal. "Beef" was now the main constituent of the hip-hop diet.

The first beef to make it to record was probably the "Roxanne" saga that was instigated by **Roxanne Shanté** when she answered UTFO's diss "Roxanne Roxanne" (1984) with "Roxanne's Revenge" (1985). Soon afterwards, **The Real Roxanne** and **Sparky D** entered the fray, and then so did (The Real) Roxanne's parents, her sister and her analyst – one Clarence "Blowfly" Reid

even felt he had to have his say on the matter, on "Blowfly Meets Roxanne". If there was one early wax war that elevated the art of beef from brisket to porterhouse, it was the battle of "The Bridge", which pitted Marley Marl's Queensbridge-based **Juice Crew** against the South Bronx's **Boogie Down Productions**. After the Juice Crew claimed hip-hop dominance for arriviste Queens on MC Shan's "The Bridge" single of 1986, BDP came in and saved the day for the birthplace of hip-hop on tracks like "South Bronx" (1986) and "The Bridge Is Over" (1987).

However, the most savage battles have been fought out west, with feuds between **Dr. Dre** and **Eazy E** – Dre's "Fuck Wit Dre Day" (1992), Eazy E's *It's On Dr. Dre 187um Killa* (1993) – **N.W.A.** and **Ice Cube** – N.W.A.'s "100 Miles and Runnin'" (1990), Cube's "No Vaseline" (1991) – and **Pooh Man** and **Ant Banks** – Pooh's "Bring it to 'Em" (1993), Ant Banks' "Fuckin' Wit Banks" (1994) – breaking out into skirmishes worthy of the **Jerry Springer Show**. Perhaps the longest and most brutal diss match (West Coast or otherwise) was between **MC Eiht** and **DJ Quik**, which lasted for eight years until Quik made peace on "You'z A Gangsta" (1998).

The intervening years have seen no let-up in the verbal sparring, with memorable battles between LL Cool J and Canibus, Eminem and Cage, Jay-Z and Nas, and Nas and Cormega.

## VARIOUS ARTISTS

**Beats, Rhymes and Battles**
Relativity, 2001

Compiled by DJ Red Alert, this collection provides a thumbnail sketch of the most important wax wars of the '80s. Both the Roxanne and "The Show" (Salt-N-Pepa's retort to Doug E Fresh's "The Show") sagas are here, as well as the duels between BDP and Marley Marl's Juice Crew, LL Cool J and Kool Moe Dee and MC Lyte and Antoinette.

# Heltah Skeltah

◊ See *Black Moon*

# Hieroglyphics

One of the underground's most beloved crews, the **Hieroglyphics'** story could be the blueprint of hip-hop's standard cautionary tale – if it weren't for the legions of groups who preceded them down the same path. From offering a bright and breezy alternative to the doom and gloom of G-Funk, to retreating to a dark, paranoid, interior pose, to learning lessons from their **Bay Area** forbears and taking their music directly to the people and the means of production into their own hands, the Hieroglyphics represent what seems to be the only path available to hip-hop crews who don't make records that get played on HOT 97.

The Hieroglyphics first gained attention when Ice Cube's cousin, **Del tha Funkée Homosapien**, made a phone-in appearance on *Amerikkka's Most Wanted* saying "Fuck radio", and ghost wrote some rhymes for Cube associate Yo-Yo. It was his debut single, "Mistadobalina" (1991), though, that was the real breakthrough. With its samples of Parliament and James Brown, "Mistadobalina" was an infectious, crowd-pleasing, sing-along tale of hip-hop fakes. *I Wish My Brother George Was*

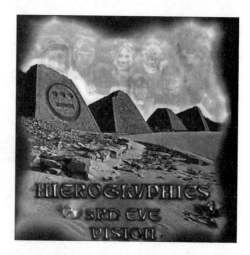

*Here* (1991) continued in the same vein, with bubbly funk underpinning eccentric rhymes on tracks like "Dr. Bombay" and "Ahonetwo, Ahonetwo".

The East Oakland-based **Souls of Mischief** (**Tajai**, **Opio**, **Phesto** and **A Plus**) made their debut on Del's "Burnt", which was the B-side of "Mistadobalina". According to legend, however, it was a Hieroglyphics showcase at an industry convention that got S.O.M., **Extra Prolific** and **Casual** signed to Jive. S.O.M.'s debut, *'93 'Til Infinity* (1993), was an absolute classic: hazy like a sweet daydream, but with torrents of words that proved they weren't just hiding behind their **Freddie Hubbard** samples. Casual's *Fear Itself* (1993) was more spotty, but harder: tracks like "This Is How We Rip Shit" and "Thoughts Of The Thoughtful" proved that West Coast MCs could battle as well as drawl gangsta fantasies.

By the time of Del's *No Need For Alarm* (1993), however, things were starting to look a little bleak. Plagued by hip-hop's number one killer – crossing over to white music critics and indie kids – the Hieroglyphics sound grew darker and more insular. Extra Prolifics' *Like It Should Be* (1994) was just plain tedious, while S.O.M.'s *No Man's Land* (1995) found them wrestling with their image and trying to prove that they were hard.

Unsurprisingly, the Hieros found themselves without contracts, and taking after **Too $hort** and **E-40**, they launched their own website (www.hieroglyphics.

com) and their own label, **Hieroglyphic Imperium**. Long before MP3 files became the biggest thing since coloured vinyl, the Hieros were attracting ridiculous numbers of hits and shifting crazy units through the Internet. The Hieroglyphics' *Third Eye Vision* (1998) was a huge underground hit and announced the crew's re-emergence after Del had devoted himself to study-ing Japanese and Tajai had graduated from Stanford with a degree in anthro-pology.

S.O.M.'s *Focus* (1999) didn't create the buzz *Third Eye Vision* had, but it proved that they were as tight as ever. Del's *Both Sides Of The Brain* (2000) showed that he was the only

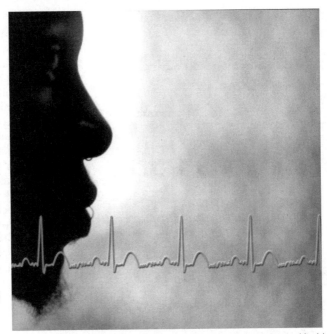

Del dwells in the shadows both on the cover and inside his magnificently deranged *Both Sides Of The Brain* album.

rapper who could almost out-weird **Kool Keith**. With strings of bizarre images and gruesome metaphors, Del "eviscerates your mental state" as he "spits the wickedness" and "surgically removes you from his tes-tes" (?!!). Light years away from the crowd-pleasing funk of "Mistadobalina", Del and guest producers **Casual**, **Domino**, **El-P**, **Prince Paul**, **Khaos Unique** and **A-Plus** sur-rounded his brutal science fiction with the crazy, Company Flow-influenced beats his new world-view demanded.

Teaming up with producer **Dan the Automator** and boy-wonder turntablist **Kid Koala**, Del continued the dystopian sci-fi vibe on *Deltron 3030* (2000). The album was one of the few successful attempts to create some kind of political discourse in music in the 21st century. "Virus" was the great anarchist, nihilist, fantasy anti-anthem the times cried out for: over a slowly insist-ent, slightly psychopathic beat – with an eerie guitar pattern and gnawing scratching – that made you think that he just might be sick enough to do it, Del rapped "I wanna devise a virus to bring dire straits to your environment/Crush corporations with a

mild touch/Trash your whole computer system and revert you to papyrus".

Souls of Mischief's *Trilogy: Conflict, Climax, Resolution* (2000) was more murky, dank funk, but was by and large too devoid of Del's political engagement to make it signify beyond the confines of the diehard independent hip-hop faithful. Casual's *He Think He Raw* (2001) displayed the same penchant for battle rhymes that his debut did, but the unfocused, paint-by-num-bers beats were not suitable frames. In 2001 longtime Hiero affiliate Pep Love finally released his own album, *Ascension*, which featured plenty of clever lyrics and impassioned hectoring, but again was let down by production that could have been phoned in.

The full crew got back together for *Full Circle* (2003), a sprawling album that was occasionally impressive, but just as often stumbled over its ambitions. Tracks like "Classic", which flips some baroque chamber music into a hot groove, or "Let it Roll", which rocked a **Björk** interpo-lation, featured production that set off the MCs perfectly, but the more 'organ-ic' instrumentation on tracks like "Full

Circle" and "Make Your Move" tried too hard to be ingratiating.

## SOULS OF MISCHIEF

⊙ **'93 'Til Infinity**
Jive, 1993

That rarest of things: a jazzy, bohemian album that didn't sound like it was infatuated with its own magnificence.

## DELTRON 3030

⊙ **Deltron 3030**
75 Ark, 2000

Paranoid, claustrophobic, political and more than a little touched, this summed up the times perfectly.

# High & Mighty

Underground stalwarts **Mr Eon** (Eric Meltzer) and **Mighty Mi** (Milo Berger) grew up together in Philadelphia and got their first taste of hip-hop fame as part of a high school group called **The Freshman 3**. The two eventually moved to New York, called themselves The High & Mighty and started their own label, **Eastern Conference Records**.

The label's first release was "Hands On

Experience" (1996), a cheeky ode to masturbation that was a big underground hit. "Open Mic Night" (1997) was a more typical declaration of skills, but it firmly established the duo as a major presence on the non-corporate hip-hop scene. Eastern Conference continued to release solid "backpacker" records (the backpack being the urban hardcore hip-hop geek's tribal fashion accessory of choice), such as the **Smut Peddlers'** (Eon and **Cage**) "One By One" (1998) and **Madd Skillz**'s Slick Rick cover, "Lick The Balls" (1998), as High & Mighty hooked up with Rawkus records for "B-Boy Document" (1998), a funky throwdown with **Mos Def**, **Mike Zoot** and **El-P**.

Rawkus released the duo's debut album, *Home Field Advantage* (1999), a more than competent collection of no-frills rap. There were great lines aplenty ("Heads pretend they're hard, their favourite movie is Lucas"; "I cruise around town naked pumpin' James Brown"; "I'm flabbergasted on two tabs of acid/Threw my baby's mother in the hatchback and latched it"), except they were mostly from the legion of guest MCs. Although shouting out both pornographer **Al Goldstein** and former president **Bill Clinton** as "smut peddlers

for life" was pretty damn funny. Sounding like a less hyper Redman, Eon was a fine pointman – he wouldn't make too many turnovers, but he would never make the cutting pass either. Mighty Mi's production was similar but with a little more flair – the Andrew Toney to Eon's Mo Cheeks. In layman's terms, they made consummate fun, straightforward hip-hop, but could surprise you every so often nonetheless.

The Smut Peddlers' *Porn Again* (2001) had a bit more personality, but the **Larry Flynt** rhymes were a little one-

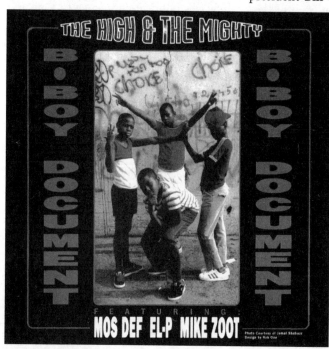

dimensional, even if a gem like "You little kids playin' the critics hard/Go back to your other hobby – Pokemon cards" cropped up every once in a while. High & Mighty's extended EP, *Air Force I* (2002), didn't expand their parameters very much, but the humour in couplets like "Don't fuck with Eon and J-Zone last/That's like Edward Scissorhands wiping his own ass" suggested that there was potential under the generally run-of-the-mill style.

"I'm that idiot still dissecting *Critical Beatdown*," Eon rapped on *The Highlite Zone* (2003), and some of Ultramagnetic MC **Kool Keith**'s inspired lunacy seemed to have rubbed off on him. There was way too much nostalgia on show, but tracks like "Fast Food Nation" (an indictment of junk food culture) and "Take it Off" (an indictment of rappers wearing throwback jerseys) displayed a newfound venom that hit with more force than any of the usual underground cry-babies.

**The Highlite Zone**
Eastern Conference, 2003

Sure, they replicate routines from Jazzy Jeff & the Fresh Prince, swipe hooks from De La Soul and Poor Righteous Teachers and lift beats from Eric B & Rakim, but the retro vibe doesn't feel as if they're acting as the moral guardians of hip-hop. When they do call out MCs for wearing throwbacks and knowing their history, at least they do it with panache and style: "Lady in pink, dog, you ain't hip-hop/'96 couldn't get a job in Nike sweatshops/ Get your free kicks from your stylist guy". It may not be an Earl The Pearl fade-away, but it's not a Billy Paultz double-dribble either.

# House Of Pain

Although they are known primarily for their first, massive hit, the greatest frat party anthem since "Louie Louie", **Erik "Everlast" Schrody**, **Leor "DJ Lethal" Dimant** and **Danny Boy O'Connor** had a rep on the LA hip-hop underground scene way before "Jump Around" ever got backwards-baseball-cap-wearing future bankers to do just that. While attending Taft High School with some guy who would eventually become Ice Cube, Everlast became a graffiti artist, and started hanging out with **Divine Styler** and DJ/

producer Bilal Bashir. Soon enough he was a member of Ice-T's Rhyme Syndicate crew and released *Forever Everlasting* (1990) for Warner Brothers. With a single called "I Got The Knack" that sampled **The Knack**'s "My Sharona", the album understandably stiffed, even though (because?) it was really close to **Vanilla Ice** territory.

With **House of Pain** though, Everlast found an image that resonated. With the goatee, Boston Celtics gear and drunken thuggishness, the "shit-kickin' Irish beat jacker" embodied a certain kind of Northeast white boy, just as **DJ Quik** and **Dr. Dre** represented Compton. Beginning with the timeless horn intro from **Bob & Earl**'s "Harlem Shuffle", the DJ Muggs-produced "Jump Around" (from their 1992 debut album *House of Pain*) was one of those records that you knew would be a hit from the second you heard it. The sax squall, bagpipe drones and damnably catchy lyrics only reinforced that impression. "Top O' The Morning To Ya" followed with more shillelagh-pounding, as did "Shamrocks And Shenanigans", although the original paled in comparison to Butch Vig's rock reconstruction.

*Same As It Ever Was* (1994) was exactly as its title professed, only less catchy and without a hit. *Truth Crushed To Earth Will Rise Again* (1996) followed suit, then House of Pain broke up amidst problems with the IRS and rumours of substance abuse. Just when you thought you would never hear from them again, **DJ Lethal** showed up as a member of rock-rap nightmare **Limp Bizkit** and Everlast released the surprise hit, *Whitey Ford Sings The Blues* (1999). Trying to remake hip-hop as folk and blues, *Whitey Ford* found Everlast adopting the persona of a beat-literate troubadour, cataloguing urban ills on "The Ends" and "What It's Like" like a **Woody Guthrie** hip to Rakim. *Eat at Whitey's* (2000) was more hip-hop delivered from a wandering minstrel, but this time with lame cameos from rock guitarists **Carlos Santana** and **Government Mule**'s Warren Haynes.

**House of Pain**
Tommy Boy, 1992

It's not exactly Proust, but you couldn't ask for a better soundtrack to a beer bust.

# WHITE RAPPERS

young black teenagers — stereo

Caucasians talking rhythmically to music have been around since time immemorial, or at least since country singer **Red Sorvine** started to imitate trucks, but it was only when palefaces like Edd "Kookie" Byrnes and **Lord Buckley** started to imitate the patter of black hepcats like **Jocko Henderson** and **Slim Gaillard** that the seeds of white rap were sown. After novelty records like The Pipkins' "Gimme Dat Ding" (a duet between a boy and a beatboxing grandfather clock) and **Steve Martin**'s "King Tut" set the stage, the first white proto-rap record was probably either **Steve Gordon & the Kosher Five**'s "Take My Rap Please" or possibly **The Fall**'s "Crap Rap 2/Like to Blow" (both 1979), in which Mark E Smith snarled, "We are the Fall/Northern white crap that talks back/We are not black, tall/No boxes for us/Do not fuck us/We are frigid stars".

While the New Wave was quick to catch on to hip-hop – **Blondie**'s "Rapture", **Tom Tom Club**'s "Wordy Rappinghood", **Maximum Joy**'s "Stretch", **Adam Ant**'s "Ant Rap" (all 1981) and **Wham!**'s "Wham Rap" (1982) – the only white guy of note inside the rap game at this point was producer **Arthur Baker**, who helped Afrika Bambaataa soup up his Kraftwerk spaceship. In 1983, punk outsiders **The Beastie Boys** made their first foray into hip-hop with a phony phone call on "Cookie Puss" (1983). Of course, the same year comedian **Rodney Dangerfield** released "Rappin' Rodney", becoming the first "rapper" to win a Grammy (for Best Comedy Record) and paving the way for innumerable white rap novelties like Joe Piscopo's "The Honeymooners Rap" (1985), Lou DiMaggio's "Hambo (First Rap Part II)" (1985), **2 Live Jews**' *As Kosher As They Wanna Be* (1990) and maybe the worst "rap" record of all-time, Jordy's "Dur Dur D'Être Bébé" (1993).

While the greatest white hip-hop records will probably always be **Double Dee & Steinski**'s "Lessons" mixes, the success of the Beastie Boys allowed other white rappers to get some dap, despite the crimes committed by the likes of **Vanilla Ice**, Maroon, Snow and Kid Rock. **MC Serch** got funky on "Melissa" (1986) and "Hey Boy" (1987) before forming **3rd Bass**, per-

haps the greatest honky pure hip-hop group, with **Prime Minister Pete Nice** and **Sam Sever**. Out in LA, Everlast was part of Ice-T's Rhyme Syndicate, while Eazy-E put on "the gangsta Madonna" **Tairrie B** and Afrocentric Zionists **Blood of Abraham**. Perhaps surprisingly, it was Public Enemy's production team, the **Bomb Squad**, that most significantly aided the cause of the ofay rapper, with their alliances with **Young Black Teenagers** (who attempted but failed to play confidence games with racial stereotypes on tracks like "Daddy Kalled Me Niga Cause I Likeded to Rhyme"), **Chilly Tee** (who also happened to be the son of Nike founder Phil Knight) and the truly awful **Kid Panic & the Adventures of Dean Dean**.

Aside from Eminem and the Beastie Boys, the most commercially successful white rapper is probably **Jesse Jaymes**, who released an atrocious album on Delicious Vinyl in 1991, but has found a second career providing basketball teams with raps to get their suburban fans amped during time-outs. He is the man responsible for such rhyme classics as "Go New York Go" (for the New York Knicks) and "The Bugs Are Back" (for the Charlotte Hornets). It's as underground rappers, however, that honkies have found the most critical success, with **El-P**, Aesop Rock, Non Phixion, Cage, Necro, the Anticon roster, Eyedea & Abilities and **MC Paul Barman** earning plaudits from journalists and "backpackers" alike.

# Ice Cube

**B**efore he exploded onto the scene in a hail of gangsta rap notoriety, Ice Cube (O'Shea Jackson) was part of the little-known LA groups the **Stereo Crew** and **CIA** (also featuring future associate **Sir Jinx**), who cut the shouty, drum-machine anthem "My Posse" (1987) with Dr. Dre on the boards. When Ice Cube walked out of N.W.A. in 1989 after a dispute over royalties (see N.W.A. entry) it quickly became clear who the real talent was among the gangsta godfathers. Although N.W.A. still had Dr. Dre's production talents (who wouldn't find his Midas touch until he left the group), Eazy and Ren (without Cube's ghostwriting skills) rapidly descended into straight-up sleaze peddling. Cube, on the other hand, went to New York to work with Public Enemy's producers, the **Bomb Squad**, and produced one of the most powerful hip-hop records ever.

It may have lacked the visceral force of the best tracks from *Straight Outta Compton*, but *AmeriKKKa's Most Wanted* (1990) was nevertheless a thunderous

album of alienation and rage. There was plenty of misogyny to be sure ("I'm Only Out For One Thing" and "You Can't Fade Me"), but it was contextualized within a riotous, feverish rant about life in black "Amerikkka" that distinguished it from the exploitation and gratuitousness of his former group. Daring to ask questions such as **"Why more niggas in the pens than in college?"**, over a hyped-up, funkier version of the trademark Bomb Squad sound,

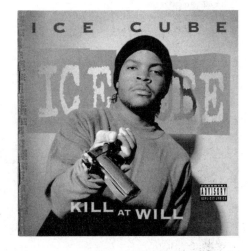

Cube managed to blend sound and fury like very few before or after. The *Kill At Will* EP (1990) may have been intended as a commercial stop-gap, but it included the remarkable "Dead Homiez", a haunting track dealing with the consequences of the gangsta lifestyle that started an entire sub-genre of "dead homie" tracks, and the great "Jackin' For Beats" which swipes rhythms from **Digital Underground**, Public Enemy, EPMD and **LL Cool J**.

Cube's jheri-curl haircut was gone for *Death Certificate* (1991), as he came under the sway of the **Nation of Islam**. Unfortunately, he also came under the sway of their bigotry and "No Vaseline" (a scathing diss of N.W.A., featuring choice epithets for their Jewish manager), "Look Who's Burnin'" and "Black Korea" all suffered from it. Nonetheless, it was still incredibly powerful stuff. Cube introduced the oft-stolen line, "Rather be judged by twelve than carried by six", into hip-hop's chrestomathy, although, as a whole, the album's more subdued production slightly deadened the impact of his rhymes.

*The Predator* (1992) continued the more streetwise, soul-based production of *Death Certificate*. Anchored by a sample of the **Isley Brothers**' "Footsteps In The Dark", "It Was A Good Day" was a stunning track that derived its stark power from what *didn't* happen ("I didn't even have to use my AK") rather than hip-hop's usual cataloguing of the streets' gruesome events. "Check

Yo Self" and "Wicked", meanwhile, found Cube collaborating with **Das EFX** to surprisingly good effect. The cinematic sweep of Cube's storytelling was matched by his appearance in the movie *Boyz 'N The Hood*. His flirtation with Hollywood, however, would eventually make his recording career increasingly irrelevant.

In between recording albums with his crew, Da Lench Mob – *Guerillas In Tha Mist* (1992) and *Planet Of Da Apes* (1994) – Cube found time to record *Lethal Injection* (1993). The work rate, not to mention the re-emergence of Dr. Dre, seemed to drain his creative wellsprings and *Lethal Injection* was little more than a re-hash of Dre's beats with the most grotesque gynophobia of his career ("Cave Bitch").

After a pointless collection of obscurities and remixes and another movie (*Friday*), Cube formed **Westside Connection** with **WC** and **Mack 10**. Despite, or maybe because of, the supergroup status, *Bow Down* (1996) wasn't notable other than as a firestarter: it did its share of East Coast baiting and tracks like "Hoo Bangin'" and "King of the Hill" continued beefs with **Common** and **Cypress Hill**. That Cube lost both of these vinyl wars proved that the fire was gone, and his *War & Peace – Vol.1 (War)* (1998) and *War & Peace – Vol.2 (Peace)* (2000) were complete duds. It came as no surprise, then, that the ensuing years saw Cube spending most of his time on movie sets (*Three Kings*, *Next Friday*,

Ice Cube back in his days of militancy and scowling.

*Barbershop*, etc.) than in the recording studio.

🔘 **AmeriKKKa's Most Wanted**
Priority, 1990

Hurling invective at everyone within earshot on top of beats that raged equally hard, this remains Ice Cube's most potent album.

# Ice-T

Ice-T (**Tracy Morrow**) is to hip-hop what Motörhead's Lemmy Kilmister is to rock: despite the fact he's not exactly the greatest at what he does, has dodgy politics and has catalyzed some of the worst aspects of the culture behind his music, you've got to love him. His unrepentance about his scabrous obsessions is disarming. He has a fierce intelligence and an accurate bullshit-detector – when Charlton Heston crawled out of the mothballs to denounce "Cop Killer" by Ice-T's metal band, **Body Count**, he responded by pointing out Heston's hypocrisy (as the chairman of the NRA, Heston had fought to keep legal a bullet called "the cop killer") – which makes Ice-T one of hip-hop's biggest icons and its most effective spokesperson.

Morrow was born in 1959 in Newark, New Jersey and he moved to LA to live with relatives as a teenager after his parents died in a car accident. His first

By the time **Eazy-E** kicked off gangsta rap, by rapping "The silly cluck head pulled out a deuce-deuce/Little did he know I had a loaded 12-gauge/One sucker dead, *LA Times* first page", on "Boyz-N-the Hood" in late 1986, the roots of gangsta rap were already well established.

Folk songs about outlaws like **Billy the Kid** and **Jesse James** have existed for at least a century. In 1965 Jamaican ska singer Prince Buster put a modern spin on this tradition when he recorded "Al Capone", which counselled "guns don't argue". In 1973, under the alias **Lightnin' Rod**, Jalal Nuriddin (a member of the militant jazz poetry group The Last Poets) recorded an album of street-corner toasts and tall tales with backing from **Kool & The Gang**, Cornell Dupree and Bernard Purdie. *Hustlers Convention* told the story of two players called Sport and Spoon who travelled to the notorious gathering of pimps, high rollers and hus-tlers at Hamhock's Hall in 1959. Complete with car-chase sound effects and crap-game skits, the album has the same cin-ematic feel and sharp details as the best hip-hop narrative, but it was the subject matter (gambling, fly threads, bitches, murder) and lines like "Everybody froze as Spoon and I rose with our pieces in our hands/Spoon scooped up the dough and we moved away slow because we had other plans" that made it the godfather of gangsta.

*Hustlers Convention* may have had more to do with the East Coast's future playa presidents

(see Jay-Z and post-*Illmatic* Nas) than the vio-lent Bloods and Crips gangs of the West Coast, but its influence on Cali rappers was obvious as soon as the scene began in the early 80s. Inspired both by *Hustlers Convention* and his surroundings, Oakland's **Too $hort** started mak-ing customised tapes for the pimps and dealers that ran his neighborhood. When Too $hort was unleashed in a real studio, his pimp and crack tales and P-Funk synths codified Left Coast hip-hop and made gangsta rap inevitable.

At around the same time, 400 miles down the road in LA, two former breakdancers were com-peting for the title of gangsta rap's OG. DJ Toddy

encounters with hip-hop culture were as a dancer (with the Radio Crew and West Coast Locksmiths) and as a graffiti art-ist. Running with LA's notorious **Crips** gang, Morrow was introduced to toasting, and to the ghetto fiction of **Iceberg Slim**. Taking the name Ice-T as a tribute to Slim, he released "The Coldest Rap/Cold Wind Madness" (1983) on Cletus Anderson's Saturn label, which had previously released the LA classic, "Bad Times" by **Captain Rapp**. Over an electro-shocked beat from Terry Lewis and Jimmy Jam, Ice-T rapped

about being "the virgin's wet dream" and wove a hustler's tale that hadn't been heard since Lightnin' Rod's *Hustler's Convention*.

"Killers" (1984) was an even starker tale of street life, but its flip, "Body Rock", was a pretty lame recitation of the elements of hip-hop culture.

Around this time, Ice appeared in the movie *Breakin'* and met the **New York City Spinmasters**, DJs Hen G and Evil E, who would become his collaborators. "Ya Don't Quit" (1985) was filled with energy (par-ticularly Evil E's stunning scratches), but

Tee's legendary *OG Batterram* tape contained tales of the po-po harassing dealers and turned UTFO's "Roxanne, Roxanne" into "Rockman, Rockman". Meanwhile, Tracy Morrow, who had rolled with the Crips when the crack epidemic turned their rivalry with the Bloods into a savage turf war, rechristened himself **Ice-T** as an homage to the ghetto fiction of Iceberg Slim. Ice's first single, 1983's "The Coldest Rap/Cold Wind Madness", was the electro-shocked tale of a hustler who hit on his mother when he got out of the womb and later bragged "I put her in the bed and she looked up at the mirror/Screamed so loud I think the East Coast could hear her." The East Coast didn't hear Ice, though, until 1986's gangsta clarion call "6 In The Mornin'". Against a slow, menacing drum-machine beat that rolled like a creeping Impala in enemy territory, Ice's first couplet was "Six in the morning, police at my door/Fresh Adidas squeak across my bathroom floor" – despite sounding a lot like Philly's **Schooly D**, gangsta rap had arrived.

Rhyming about the City of Brotherly Love's street gangs, Schooly D was the first to put "gangsta" on a record label with his 1984 single "Gangsta Boogie". His self-produced, self-released, self-titled 1985 EP featured shout-outs to Philly's notorious Park Side Killers. Meanwhile, another East Coaster had the cojones to bill himself as "the original gangster of hip-hop". **Just-Ice**'s "Little Bad Johnny" and "Gangster Of Hip-Hop" may have been only more explicit cousins of **Merle Haggard**'s country standard "Mama Tried" or Johnny "Guitar" Watson's 1950s classic "Gangster Of Love", with added Jamaican yardie-isms, but with the backing of **Cool DMX**'s beatboxing and Mantronix's drum-programming,

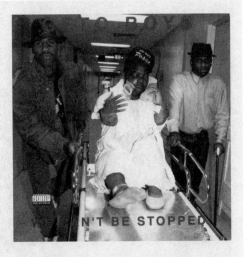

WE CAN'T BE STOPPED

Just-Ice's hard-man posturing was bolstered by the most ferocious sonic backing of all the proto-gangstas.

The Showboys' 1986 single "Drag Rap" (aka "Triggerman") took the 1960s cop show *Dragnet* out of the LA 'burbs and into the NY ghetto ("Tell him that it's time that he leaves this town/On your way back bring me his son/Lock him in the trunk, yeah, that should be fun/And so Bugs knows that he has to lose/Have his son fitted for cement shoes/Then drag him from the river, throw him back in Bugs' yard/With a note 'round his neck that says, 'Triggerman's hard'"). "Drag Rap" is notable not only because it is probably the first rap tune to mention "thugs", but also because its scattershot drums and weird xylophone break are the foundation of the New Orleans bounce style of **Cash Money** and **No Limit** – the labels that sported the colours of gangsta rap when the West fell off.

was too imitative of New York's styles to really stand out. Ice's breakthrough was "6 In The Mornin'" (1986) (the flipside of the murderous battle rap "Dog 'N The Wax"), a slow and menacing track that was the beginning of a distinctive Californian hip-hop style (despite the fact that Ice did sound quite a lot like Schooly D on it).

A new version of "6 'N The Mornin'" appeared on Ice's debut album, *Rhyme Pays* (1987). Although the album continued Ice's street narratives, it also introduced his abundant sense of humour, with rhymes like "Five freaks just to comb my hair/Monograms on my underwear" and the sample from **Black Sabbath**'s "War Pigs" on the title track. Featuring a rather scandalous cover, with Ice's wife Darlene in a V-shaped swimsuit holding a pump-action shotgun, *Power* (1988) offered more of Ice-T's gripping chronicles, a rewrite of **Curtis Mayfield**'s "Pusherman", "I'm Your Pusher", being a particularly thorny standout.

After running into trouble with the PMRC over his song "Girls LGBNAF" (i.e. "Let's Get Butt Naked And Fuck"), his

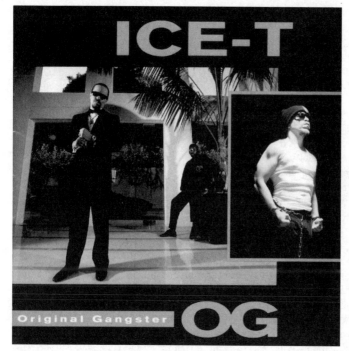

by his Rhyme Syndicate posse — **Evil E**, **Afrika Islam**, DJ Aladdin, DJ SLJ and **Bilal Bashir** — that really stood out.

This was perfected on Ice-T's best album, *O.G. Original Gangster* (1991). Ice's misogyny had largely been toned down in favour of no-nonsense, bone-rattling ghetto reportage. The relentless, jarring guitars of "New Jack Hustler", the punishing bassline of "Straight Up Nigga", and the hard-hitting drums of the title track all matched Ice's unblinking lyrics and virtuoso delivery.

Unfortunately, Ice has been unable to follow up this undeniable classic. His two **Body Count** albums would be instantly forgettable were it not for the "Cop Killer" controversy. *Home Invasion* (1993), a putative concept album about the possible implications of white, suburban kids listening to hip-hop, couldn't live up to its premise. While Ice was pursuing careers as an author, actor and TV presenter, he released *VI: Return of the Real* (1996) as an afterthought and it felt like it, especially with Ice trying to sing. *7th Deadly Sin* (1999) found Ice hooking up with web impresarios **Atomic Pop** and delivering a tired, lazy album about envious rappers, but, with his post-"Cop Killer" commercial exile and his taking on of acting roles like the kangaroo in the *Tank Girl* movie, it was hard to imagine too many rappers being jealous of his status.

Like LA's other iceman, Ice-T has since concentrated on acting (*Law & Order: Special Victim's Unit*, *3000 Miles To Graceland*, and *On The Edge*) rather than rapping.

next album, *Iceberg/Freedom of Speech... Just Watch What You Say* (1989), was an assault on the hypocrisy surrounding the First Amendment. The opener, "Shut Up, Be Happy," sampled Jello Biafra – singer of punk band The Dead Kennedys – doing one of his spoken-word routines. There were also plenty of gratuitous titty jokes, F-words and *Driller Killer* references, but more effective was Ice's straight-up gangsta shit, such the harrowing "Peel Their Caps Back". While Ice's intentions were laudable, it was the sound world created

**⊙ O.G. Original Gangster**
Sire, 1991

The best album ever made by a Black Sabbath-loving ex-Crip with a stand-up's sense of timing and James Elroy's eye for detail.

**Greatest Hits: The Evidence**
Atomic Pop, 2000

It's far from a perfect collection (where's the really early stuff?), but it was compiled by Ice himself, comes with his own liner notes and includes the best of his commercial years, so you can't complain too much.

# Intelligent Hoodlum / Tragedy

Percy Chapman (aka Percy Coles) is the original Queensbridge thug. As a thirteen-year-old, Tragedy hooked up with local DJ Hot Day and released "Go Queensbridge/Live at Hip-Hop USA" (1985) under the name **Super Kids**. The single got them noticed by Queensbridge legend Marley Marl, who produced their second and third singles, "Tragedy (Don't Do It)" (1985) and "Stunts On The Block" (1986).

Marley Marl made Tragedy a peripheral member of the Juice Crew, and he contributed "Live Motivator" and "The Rebel" (which introduced the term "illmatic" to the hip-hop lexicon some six years before Nas made it famous) to Marley Marl's *In Control Volume One* (1988) compilation. After serving time in a correctional facility for robbery, Chapman converted to Islam and renamed himself **Intelligent Hoodlum**.

With Marley Marl producing, his debut album *Intelligent Hoodlum* (1990) featured underground classics like "Arrest the President", "Black And Proud" and "Party Pack". With lines like "I'm a walkin' sunspot, my energy is radium/A gladiator generating your stadium" and "Pickin' up a pen to put my anger on paper/Intelligent Hoodlum, I design a skyscraper", he managed to wed abstract rhymes with the vernacular of the street.

The streetwise **Afrocentrism** continued on *Tragedy: Saga Of A Hoodlum* (1993). Again Marley Marl was producing, but was now some years past his prime, and the album struggled to find its feet in a rapidly shifting hip-hop climate. "Grand Groove"

and "Street Life" were both lyrical gems worthy of his first album, but the over-production dragged the rest of the album down.

In 1995 the Hoodlum hooked up with fellow Queensbridge resident Capone, and with Noreaga and Mobb Deep, he recorded "LA, LA" (1995), a dark retort to Tha Dogg Pound's "NY, NY", under the name **Tragedy Khadafi**. It was released on his own 25 To Life label. Capone-N-Noreaga released their debut album, *The War Report* on his label, but after Capone went back to prison, Noreaga severed ties with Tragedy. Trag responded on the *Iron Sheiks* (1998) EP. On tracks like "NORE-Faker" and "Blood Type", Trag mixed wrestling metaphors to denigrate Noreaga's name and accused him of stealing his style.

**Noreaga** then responded with "Halfway Thugs Pt. II" (1998), saying, "I used to write his rhymes and let him shine/ Knowing that he old school and out of time". Tragedy attempted to turn back the clock with *Against All Odds*, but the album was much delayed and, despite some fine jail-door-slamming, work-gang-style production, singles like "Bing Monsters" (2000) sounded like they were only going to convince fans that Noreaga was right.

*Still Reportin…* (2003) found Tragedy in fighting form on the mic, but his lyrics and the production (which was often a straight bite of **Kanye West**) from Booth, Sha Self, Dart La and Scram Jones made the album about as reliable as Fox News.

**Intelligent Hoodlum**
A&M, 1990

There are a few severely wack tracks but, overall, the production from Marley Marl and the Hoodlum's lyrical finesse on "Arrest the President" eventually win out.

# Irv Gotti/Murder Inc/The Inc

Jamaica, Queens' Irving Domingo Lorenzo Jr. first made a name for himself as DJ Irv in the late 1980s as **Jaz-O**'s DJ. The Jaz may have faded into obscurity, but his sometime partner in rhyme

# HiP-HOP AND FASHiON

Hip-hop started out as a celebration of the art of survival, as an art form that sprang from the hopes and desires of kids who were damned, who had been left to rot in their ghetto, ignored by the government and corporate America. But, of course, hip-hop was equally about **style** – finding something that would make you no longer invisible, something that would make you so **fly** that eventually you would go – as every ambitious graffiti writer attempted to do by scrawling his/her tag far and wide – **all-city**. To this end, hip-hop embraced the American Dream pretty damn quick, and started endorsing fashion labels from the get-go.

Hip-hop fashion changes just as fast as the music does. From the early days when the all-girl crew **The Sequence** wore "Gloria Vanderbilt gangster jeans" and the guys wore personalized sweatshirts and **Puma Clydes**, to the ghetto superhero outfits of Afrika Bambaataa & the Soul Sonic Force to the **Cazals** and **Kangols** of the "middle school", hip-hop style has never remained stagnant for very long. "Calvin Klein's no friend of mine/Don't want nobody's name on

Sartorial iconoclast Ghostface Killah and fellow Wu-Tang warriors, hard at work customizing their Clarks Wallabies with pastel-coloured spraypaint.

was a young man named Shawn Carter – the fledgling **Jay Z**. DJ Irv again found himself at the right place at the wrong time in 1992, when he co-produced the first single for an aspiring rapper signed to Ruffhouse by the name of **DMX**. These early connections may have amounted to nothing at the time, but they certainly did the aspiring CEO no harm in later life.

In 1993 he discovered Queensboro MC **Mic Geronimo** at a talent contest and produced his debut single "Shit's Real". The single got Geronimo a deal with Blunt/TVT and Irv again produced several tracks from his albums *The Natural* (1995) and *Vendetta* (1997). While working with TVT, Irv got the **Cash Money Click** (a group which included a young Ja Rule) signed to the label, but only one single, "Get The Fortune" (1995), ever came of the deal.

Irv's old connections began paying dividends in 1996 when Jaz-O was producing Jay-Z's "Ain't No Nigga". Irv mixed the track and produced the remix of "Can't Knock

The Hustle". Maybe even more importantly, it was around this time that Jay-Z dubbed the former DJ **Irv Gotti**, giving him a name that matched his ambitions. Gotti got an A&R job at Def Jam thanks to his work with Jay-Z and promptly signed his old pal DMX. His debut album, *It's Dark And Hell Is Hot* (1998), went quadruple platinum. Gotti's second signing was **Ja Rule**, whose *Veni, Vetti, Vecci* (1999), sold a million and a half. Gotti further confirmed his hit-making abilities by producing Jay-Z's "Can I Get A…" in 1998.

To repay him for his success, Def Jam gave Gotti his own label, **Murder Inc**. The label's first release, *Irv Gotti Presents The Murderers* (2000), introduced the Murderers crew – Ja Rule, **Black Child**, Tah Murdah (aka **Caddillac Tah**) and Vita – but it wasn't the smash that his previous efforts had been. Nevertheless, he kept on churning out hits with Ja Rule as a solo artist. Then **Ashanti** came onto the scene. Her little-girl-lost voice first showed up on **Big Pun**'s "How We Roll" (2001) and by the following my behind", Run-DMC rapped in 1984, but only months later Slick Rick and Schooly D were flashing their **Guccis** and **Filas**. And only two years later, Run-DMC themselves were writing paeans to their Adidas, and schooling the world in the width a shoelace ought to be.

Afrocentricity briefly brought in the black medallions, kente cloths and t-shirts with "Back to Africa" slogans, but hip-hop fashion has pretty much always been about label fetishization, whether it was the Raiders caps as worn by N.W.A. or Lil' Kim "rock[ing] the Prada, sometimes Gabbana". But hip-hop's extreme brand-consciousness isn't always about being nouveau riche and flaunting and flossing. The early 1990s trend for preppy wear – Tommy Hilfiger, Timberlands, Nautica, Perry Ellis, Gant – was a bold act of reappropriation: a bunch of former pariahs donning the threads of America's blue-blood ruling class

...and again Ghostface Killah demonstrates his fashion daring, rockin' a dressing-gown that is crazy baroque while he cooks French toast. Truly, the man is a visionary.

and, essentially, demanding their piece of the American Dream.

year she was an inescapable presence on urban radio. She appeared on three top ten hits in one week – her own "Foolish", Fat Joe's "What's Luv?" and Ja Rule's "Always on Time" – and her self-titled debut album (2002) sold some 500,000 copies in its first week. Ashanti helped Gotti (and co-producer **7 Aurelius**) hold the top spot in the American charts for 16 weeks in a row with "Foolish", "Always on Time" and J-Lo's "Ain't it Funny". Renaming his crew, Gotti then released *Irv Gotti Presents the Inc* (2002), which featured more r&b, more live instruments and new rappers in the form of **Charli Baltimore**, Merc and Ronnie Bumps.

Along the way Gotti had gathered more than a few enemies, most notably **50 Cent** and **P Diddy**. Perhaps inevitably, Gotti's fame and notoriety soon attracted the attention of the Feds, who were particu-

larly interested in his financial connections with **Kenneth "Supreme" McGriff**, a notorious drug dealer from his old neighborhood in Queens. In June 2003 Gotti was busted for possession of Ecstasy (found alongside some Viagra), but he was also indicted on more serious charges of income tax evasion in 2004. Gotti was also being investigated for firearms violations.

**Irv Gotti Presents The Inc**
Murder Inc/Def Jam, 2002

However it got there, Murder Inc was the dominant label in hip-hop in 2002. Gotti's willingness to make a hit by any means necessary – even if it meant using vocalists as noxious as Ja Rule and Ashanti – ensured that his label would be a success. His main formula – rubbing sandpaper against honey – is well in evidence here, and while you can't deny its effectiveness on radio, it's not as easy to digest in one huge dose on CD.

# Ja Rule

Even though the grammar and spelling were hopelessly incorrect, the title of Ja Rule's debut album, *Venni, Vetti Vecci*, was unfortunately very prescient. After coming onto the scene in 1999, Ja Rule saw and conquered the rap world with a strategy as deliberate and as unpalatable as Julius Caesar's.

Ja (pronounced Jah, real name **Jeff Atkins**) made his debut on **Mic Geronimo**'s "Time To Build" (1995), the B-side of "Masta IC". The producer of that record was one **DJ Irv**, who took a liking to Ja and got his group, Cash Money Click, signed to Blunt/TVT. The group released one single, "Get Fortune", which was moderately successful due to exposure on Hot 97 and *Video Music Box*. Over the next couple of years, DJ Irv metamorphosised into Irv Gotti, got an A&R job at **Def Jam** and signed Ja Rule in 1998. Ja really came to public attention with his appearance on Jay-Z's "Can I Get A…" (1998) talking about how easy it was to pimp a ho.

"Holla Holla" (1999) followed in a similar style: Ja throwing his wad in your face while sounding just like **DMX** (another Gotti signing) on top of an admittedly funky synth beat and the most annoying hook in living memory. *Venni, Vetti Vecci* (1999) was largely more of the same post-**2Pac** champagne nihilism – notably on "It's Murda" with Jay-Z and DMX, and on "World's Most Dangerous" – plus a couple of truly awful introspective tracks

("Only Begotten Son" and "Daddy's Little Baby") to keep his hollering style from getting too wearing.

"Daddy's Little Baby", a duet with **Ronald Isley**, and Ja's cameo on the Blackstreet/Janet Jackson duet, "Girlfriend/Boyfriend" (1999), had given Gotti his one big idea: combining Ja's gruff vocals with the honeyed tones of an r&b vocalist (sort of like the **Temptations** but without the talent). This crucial crossover strategy was deployed to its fullest on *Rule 3:36* (2000) on which Ja duetted with **Christina Milian** ("Between Me & You"), **Lil' Mo** ("I Cry") and **Vita** ("Put It On Me"), all of which were fairly sizeable hits. The thug-ballad blueprint reached its apex on *Pain Is Love* (2001), where Ja duetted with **J-Lo** (on the execrable "I'm Real"), Missy Elliott and Tweet ("X"), **Ashanti** ("Always On Time") and, most blasphemously, a recording of **2Pac** ("So Much Pain"). The follow-up – *The Last Temptation* (2002) – was a word-for-word, beat-for-beat copy and proved that there was such a thing as way too much of a not so good thing.

*Blood In My Eye* (2003) found Ja reeling from his label's legal trouble and from constant taunting from **50 Cent** and **Eminem**. There were no r&b crossover duets, just Ja trying to get thuggish and ruggish to limited effect. Of course, any blows that Ja managed to land were cancelled out by him doing exactly what 50 Cent accused him of: ripping off 2Pac. He quotes Shakur on "The Inc Is Back" and

then proceeds to rap with **Outlaw Hussein Fatal** on the album's last four tracks.

**Pain Is Love**
Def Jam, 2001

If you must, then this is the album to go for, the album that made Ja Rule an inescapable presence on the radio for two years. It's the same wretched mix of thuggism and grotesque sentimentality that made 2Pac such a star, but without his charisma or self-loathing, just unfelt tales of struggle and strife mixed with even more unfelt tales of sex and partying.

# Jay-Z

Displacing the claims of Biggie, Nas and Christopher Walken as the king of New York, **Shawn Carter**'s status is such that both the streets and the charts have followed his lead in calling himself "Jayhova". **Jay-Z** is a hip-hop John Woo: he chronicles violence and drug dealing with often breathtakingly vivid detail one minute, but the very next moment he's sobbing uncontrollably about his Mum. He's not exactly an original stylist, but his relaxed flow and observance of hip-hop punctilios make Jay-Z the most influential, if not the best, MC around. If his records don't convince you, then his ghostwriting for the likes of **Foxy Brown**, Puffy and **Dr. Dre** should.

The former drug dealer from Brooklyn's Marcy Projects debuted on **Big Jaz**'s "The Originators" (1990) with a high-top fade and a tongue-twisting style radically dif-

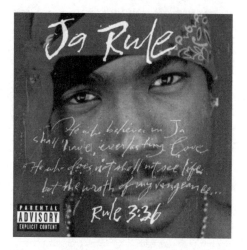

ferent from what he would become known for.

After spending a few years establishing a rep, both on the group **Original Flavor**'s second album, *Beyond Flavor* (1993) and on his own, he hooked up with Damon Dash and Kareem Burke and set up **Roc-a-Fella Records**. The new label released, "Can't Get With That/In My Lifetime" (1995) which created an underground buzz in New York. Jay-Z then blew up with his next single, "Ain't No Nigga/ Dead Presidents" (1996). "Ain't No Nigga" was a hip-hop remake of the **Four Tops**' "Ain't No Woman (Like the One I've Got)" set to the **Whole Darn Family**'s "Seven Minutes of Funk" break with production by his old mentor, **Big Jaz**. Introducing Foxy Brown, "Ain't No Nigga" was a pretty grotesque take on the battle of the sexes theme, but Jay-Z redeemed himself by being simply awesome on the mic.

"Ain't No Nigga" and "Dead Presidents" both featured on "Jigga"'s debut album, *Reasonable Doubt* (1996). Filled with tales of hustling and fashion-label fetishism, *Reasonable Doubt* dominated New York by carefully balancing underground concerns with the garish livin' large fantasies that were beginning to dominate the mainstream: "Can't Knock the Hustle" had **Mary J Blige** belting out the hook, while "Brooklyn's Finest" had **Biggie** going one on one with Jigga. *In My Lifetime, Vol.*

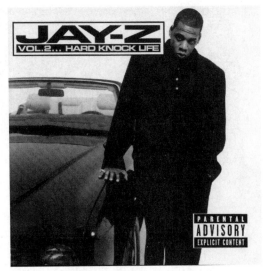

1 (1997) wasn't as striking, but on the remarkable "You Must Love Me" he created a gangsta tear-jerker out of a tale of him selling crack to his mother.

*Vol. 2... Hard Knock Life* (1998) had more tales of mercenary capitalism such as "Can I Get A..." set to futuristic beats from **Timbaland** and Irv Gotti and party-rockers like "It's Alright" set to **Talking Heads** samples. It also featured guest verses from Roc-A-Fella up and comers like **Memphis Bleek**. Once again, though, the pivotal track was schmaltzy, the **45 King**'s *Annie*-sampling "Hard Knock Life". On one level, sampling *Annie* was the crassest commercial gesture hip-hop had yet conceived of; on the other hand, though, combining Broadway's saccharine sentimentalizing of poverty with hip-hop's reality tales was a stroke of genius.

*Vol. 3... Life and Times of S. Carter* (1999) contained the awful sequel to "Hard Knock Life", the *Oliver*-sampling "Anything", but featured some choice Timbaland and **DJ Premier** beats to compensate. However, Jay-Z's work rate and his cul-de-sac themes meant that, despite his undoubted presence and charisma, he was getting tired (in both senses of the word).

*The Blueprint* (2001), however, was Jay-Hova's moment of ascension. Nothing had changed very much – he was still capitalism's biggest cheerleader since Adam Smith (although he did contextualize it

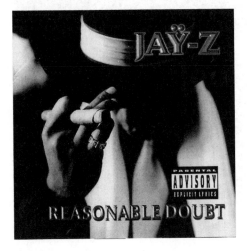

The one and only JayHova: Mr Jay-Z.

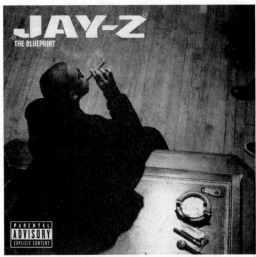

a bit this time around with lines like "I'm representin' for the seat where Rosa Parks sat/Where Malcolm X was shot/Where Martin Luther was popped" and "I'm overcharging niggas for what they did to the Cold Crush/Pay us like you owe us for all the years that you hold us") and wallowed in distasteful sexism – but, revved up by battles with Nas and Mobb Deep, and fresh production blood in the shape of **Kanye West** and Just Blaze, Jay-Z was at the top of his game. On the irresistible "Izzo (H.O.V.A.)" – which flipped one of Nas's freestyle disses – he introduced himself as "the flow of the century" and it was hard to argue.

If you thought Jay-Z's pre-eminence was simply will to power – that he had merely bigged up himself so much that it had to be true – one listen to *Unplugged* (2001), on which he recreates most of his classics with **The Roots** providing live backing, would convince you of his mic prowess. But once again all the plaudits and shifted units went to his head and *Blueprint 2: The Gift & the Curse* (2002), a 110-minute double CD, was hip-hop's most severe case of megalomania yet. He even went so far as to compare himself to Rembrandt and to sample Sinatra's "My Way".

There were some great moments – the startling Timbaland beat of "What They Gonna Do", off-handed insults ("You rappers are noodles/I got more ziti to bake")

and the heartfelt verse on "Diamonds Is Forever" – but unlike volume one there were too many guest appearances, too many different styles and at least thirty too many minutes. *The Blueprint 2.1* (2003) was a slimmed-down, single-disc version, but strangely they excised perhaps the album's best track. The collaboration with **R. Kelly**, *The Best of Both Worlds* (2002), was frankly awful – the kind of album that only bankers think is a good idea.

*The Black Album* (2003) was his self-declared swan song (but he'd been saying that for years) and was an appropriate way to bow out.

A return to *The Blueprint*'s mix of bravado and soul searching, *The Black Album* found Hova admitting "If skills sold, truth be told, I'd probably be lyrically Talib Kweli/Truthfully I want to rhyme like Common Sense/But I did five mil, I ain't been rhyming like Common since" at the same time as he was spitting "Rap critics that say he's 'Money, Cash, Hoes'/I'm from the hood stupid, what type of facts are those?/If you grew up with holes in your zapatos/You'd celebrate the minute you was havin' dough". It probably won't be too long until people are singing "Welcome back Carter".

⊙ **Reasonably Doubt**
Roc-a-Fella, 1996

Back when Jay-Z was a hungry MC and not a bloated corporate mogul living out his own raps, he was one of the most forceful mic personas in hip-hop.

⊙ **The Blueprint**
Roc-a-Fella, 2001

Yes, he's got the biggest ego this side of Sting, but that's what hip-hop has always been about. And, he's got much, much better music.

# Jayo Felony

Jayo (Justice Against Y'all Oppressors) Felony started rapping as a kid in San Diego, California. After an adolescence spent as a Crip and mostly in juvenile hall, Jayo self-released the "Livin' For Them Fo' Thangs/Piss On Your Tombstone" single (1994) which caught the attention of

**Jam Master Jay**, who signed him to his JMJ label. Jayo's debut album, *Take a Ride* (1995), was a strange combination of West Coast gangsta lyrics with East Coast production. It was most effective on "Sherm Stick", an ode to smoking **PCP**. "Can't Keep a Gee Down" ("If you dissin' gangsta rap/You get the pipe/It ain't time to preach fool/It's time to fight") foreshadowed what would become Jayo's main claim to fame – being the most outspoken defender of gangsta rap.

While the album dropped from sight almost immediately, he continued to defend the gangsta faith on records like **South Central Cartel**'s "Sowhatusayin'" (1995): "Fuck Oliver Stone, he made *Colors*/Gettin' paid off gangbangin', I want my money, muthafucka". With production from E A Ski, T-Funk and Jayo himself, *Whatcha Gonna Do* (1998) had more traditional West Coast beats, particularly on the title track (a collaboration with **DMX** and **Method Man**) and "JAYO" (a collaboration with **E-40** and **Ice Cube**). The album was an obvious bid for stardom, but with Jayo stealing hooks from **Right Said Fred**, that was always unlikely.

After guesting on Snoop protégés **Tha Eastsidaz**' "Got Beef?" (2000), Jayo got into a scuffle with Snoop on the set of *Baby Boy* because Snoop apparently used the term "Crip-hop" for an Eastsidaz song. Jayo claimed that he invented the phrase. Of course, it was also the title of his album that was released around the same time. The album was most notable for the numerous disses of both Snoop and **Jay-Z**, whom he accused of disrespecting the West Coast. If these attacks were a bid for notoriety, they didn't work because, aside from a couple of appearances on tracks by **E-40**, **Kam** and Spice 1, Jayo's crip walk hasn't been seen in a while.

⊙ **Crip Hop**
Loco/American Music, 2001

It may be the beef with both Snoop and Jay-Z that will bring you in, but it's the production (by DJ Silk and West Coast veteran Battlecat) and Jayo's forceful delivery that will hook you. While it's mostly fairly solid newfangled gangsta rap, the crossover bid "She Loves Me" is a nice change of pace.

# Jeru The Damaja

In the mid-1990s **Jeru the Damaja** (aka **Kendrick Jeru Davis**) was hailed as one of hip-hop's most innovative MCs. Although the truth is that Jeru's unorthodox flow and gruff, stentorian vocals allowed producer **DJ Premier** to be his most radical, creating some of hip-hop's wildest sonic experiments, Jeru was at least partially responsible for two of the most compelling hip-hop albums of the decade.

Jeru first appeared on Gang Starr's "I'm The Man" (1992) from their *Daily Operation* album. Riding a really fucked-up Premier jazz deconstruction (a welcome harbinger of things to come), Jeru dominated the track and made both Guru and Lil' Dap (less of a feat) sound like street-corner cipher amateurs by comparison. The following year, Jeru proved his status with one of the all-time classics, and certainly the 1990s' most outrageous single, "Come Clean". Over a beat culled from a **Shelley Manne** record that sounded like Chinese water-torture gamelan, and which ran counter to Dre's all-conquering G-Funk, Jeru reminded you that the West Coast was about metaphor, not "reality".

Nothing on *The Sun Rises in the East* (1994) could match "Come Clean", but a lot of it came close. Premier was making beats out of out-of-tune pianos, **Stockhausen** samples, backwards **Tom**

Jeru not damaging anyone at all, and being really rather cheerful.

**Scott** loops, scything horror-movie strings and, most unbelievably, **static**. Jeru never regained the absolute authority he had on "I'm The Man" or "Come Clean", but on "Statik", "Ain't The Devil Happy" and "D. Original" he was imposing, and managed to ride Premier's beats without ever sounding too awkward.

*Wrath Of The Math* (1996) was a slight disappointment. Instead of trying to boggle the mind, Premier tried to ruffle feathers: "Ya Playin' Ya Self" flipped (cleverly, granted) the beat from **Junior M.A.F.I.A.**'s "Player's Anthem" to accompany Jeru's wax war with Cream Puff and his ilk. Although he aimed at the right targets, Jeru's lyrics didn't move much beyond standard battle rhymes. When things did work, though, as on "Black Cowboy" and "Invasion", it really did sound like Jeru could save hip-hop from its worst instincts.

After four years of silence, Jeru returned with a self-produced album on his own KnowSavage label, *Heroz4hire*

(2000). Jeru's conscious rhyme style was a bit dated, but he had learned enough lessons from Premo to make the production pleasantly rootsy in a climate dominated by slip-sliding, futuristic drum machines. The production on *Divine Design* (2003), however, was basic and bland, framing Jeru's rhymes nicely, but not propelling

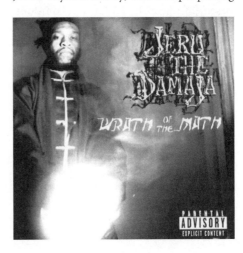

him forwards the way Premo had.

◉ **The Sun Rises In The East**
Payday, 1994

Jeru's focus on the mental side was honourable at the crux of the G-Funk/Bad Boy era, but it was Premier who was the real hero.

# Jigmastas

Despite having the entire history of recorded music at their fingertips, most hip-hop DJs are hopelessly blinkered and rarely venture outside very strict parameters. One of the few hip-hop DJs to embrace the entire musical spectrum is **DJ Spinna**, one half of the Brooklyn duo **The Jigmastas**. Unfortunately, while Spinna is willing to go off on dance-music tangents, The Jigmastas pretty much toe the underground hip-hop party line.

The duo of Spinna and **Kriminul** grew up together, but didn't show up on wax until 1994, when their track "Execution" appeared on the *Bomb Hip-Hop Compilation*, one of the earliest standard-bearers of the underground aesthetic. The following year they released the **Kraftwerk**-sampling "Beyond Real" (1995) on their own label of the same name. Apart from their own singles, over the next few years Beyond Real would release records by **The Basement Khemists**, IG Off & Hazardous, Mr Akil and **The Jet Black Ha**. Perhaps the best of the Jigmastas' early singles was "Hip Hop" (1998), on which Kriminul dropped some fairly average anti-materialistic lyrics over a truly anthemic loop of **Rotary Connection**'s "Burning the Midnight Lamp".

In between Jigmastas singles, Spinna would produce and mix for everyone from **Mary J Blige** and Shaun Escoffery to MC Eiht and **De La Soul**. His production work started to generate some buzz for his group and The Jigmastas signed to Tommy Boy Black Label. Label problems, however, meant that their debut album, *Infectious*, wasn't released until 2001. Spinna's skills were amply demonstrated throughout the album and Kriminul didn't get in the way, dropping rhymes that just rode the beat and didn't do much else.

Aside from numerous mix-albums (*Strange Games And Things*, *Raiding The Crates*, *Mix The Vibes*), Spinna produced his own slightly underwhelming *Heavy Beats Volume 1* (1999) album. Among the highlights were "Rock", a serious party-rocker encapsulating breaks both old and pre-school, and "Watch Dees", featuring a *Jaws* bassline, a **Madness** sample and **Thirstin Howell III** almost outduelling Eminem with the very special couplet "I hit you harder than Foreman landing both gloves on a low blow with no cup/Leave you speechless like when Arrested Development broke up". Spinna was also manning the boards for the **Polyrhythm Addicts**' (Mr Complex, Apani B Fly MC and Shabaam Sahdeeq) *Rhyme Related* (1999) album. His contribution to BBE's "Beat Generation" series, *Here To There* (2003), was as wide-ranging as you'd expect from a guy who can produce both gangsta rap and deep house.

◉ **Infectious**
Landspeed, 2001

Spinna doesn't quite pull out all of his production tricks here, but more than enough to let you know that he's easily one of the most talented beatsmiths working on the underground scene. "Don't Get it Twisted" (constructed from a dance instruction record) and "CSS" (based on a sped-up Brazilian loop) offer ample evidence of Spinna's easy-on-the-ears skills behind the boards. Shame about Kriminul, who's about as dull as his name.

# JJ FAD

Like their name, **Just Jammin' Fresh and Def** epitomized a long-lost era of hip-hop history. Like most girl groups from any era of pop history, **JB**, **Sassy C** and **Baby D**, with **Lady Anna** on the ones and twos, were all about an infectious camaraderie and a bubbly innocence. They rocked spandex biker shorts, oversized sunglasses and sweatshirts, and were entertainers at a time when you didn't have to be hardcore to get radio play.

With simple but effective production from **Dr. Dre**, their one hit "Supersonic" (1988), went gold and peaked at number 30 on the US pop chart. It may have been a novelty dance hit, but it made *Supersonic* (1988) Ruthless Records' first platinum album. "Way Out" was the second single, but it failed to capture listeners' imaginations the way that "Supersonic" did. Far more notable was the nasty diss track "Anotha Ho", which used a **Queen** snippet and dirty nursery rhymes to savage **Roxanne Shanté** ("A is for apple, J is for jack/Roxanne Shanté got no hair in her back/She's bald"), Salt-N-Pepa, the Real Roxanne ("Howie Tee had an MC and Roxanne was her name-o/E-i-e-i-ho, E-i-e-i-ho") and Sparky D ("Sparky D, she's so fat/When she sees food she will attack/So with a hip-hop body rock give the cow a bone and send that hippo rolling home").

Fully engaged in a cat fight with Shanté after her "Wack It" thoroughly disrespected LA's finest, JJ Fad retaliated with "Ya Goin' Down" (1990), a title which questioned Shanté's sexuality. Unfortunately, "Ya Goin' Down" was the only decent track on *Not Just a Fad* (1990) which included the abysmal hip-house disaster "We In The House". The album failed to

live up to its title, and the group quickly faded into obscurity as Ruthless became more successful and paid more attention to the likes of **Michel'le**.

**Supersonic**
Ruthless, 1988
This has all the JJ Fad anyone could ever need or want, and then some.

# J-Live

The purist's choice, J-Live is quite simply one of the best MCs around. He attacks the beat with the laidback ferocity of **Rakim**, has the vocabulary of Ezra Pound and the breath control of **Ornette Coleman**. As he himself says "The exhale's volcanic/The inhale is seismic". Unfortunately, just as he was blowing up, his career was shattered by industry machinations.

While still studying English at SUNY-Albany, J-Live took an internship at indie hip-hop label **Raw Shack**. While there he released one of the most promising debut singles in hip-hop history, "Braggin' Writes/Longevity" (1995). Over huge stabs, J-Live dished out an extraordinary verbal beating to any MC who dared to cross his path: "The ends stay revealed while the means I conceal/And those who try to steal get decapitated/You wanna snatch my $H2O$-type flow, but it evaporated... And my potential increases at a rate that's exponential/It's detrimental questioning my thesis/The penetration's exact, like amniocentesis/I rip your rhyme to pieces after draining out your fluid/My vocab is fluent, yours is evident of being truant". "Can I Get It/Hush The Crowd" (1996) followed, and while it wasn't as stunning, it nevertheless firmly established J-Live as the hottest underground MC around.

He signed with **Payday** in 1997 and recorded *The Best Part*. The album was never released and J-Live jumped ship to a Universal-affiliated label. He re-recorded *The Best Part*, but a label buyout meant that he was lost in the fray and once again the album was never released. J-Live retreated from the rap game and became a junior high-school English teacher, but the album was widely bootlegged and the dozens of versions that came out were an underground sensation.

He re-emerged on the scene with *All of the Above* (2002) which had an honest-to-goodness legitimate release. Thankfully, his skills, wit and humanity were as fresh as ever: "'Cos life can take a turn for the worse/ And have you switchin' from the coupe to the hearse/You better peep this verse/The streets ain't no joke, but man, the sidewalks might get you first". A latent political commitment was also evident on the excellent "Satisfied?": "But now it's all about NYPD caps and **Pentagon bumper stickers**/But yo, you're still a nigga/It ain't right them cops and them firemen died/That shit is real tragic but it damn sure ain't magic/It won't make the brutality disappear/It won't pull equality from behind your ear".

The *Always Will Be* EP (2003) wasn't quite as committed, but J-Live's imagination still shone through on tracks like **"Car Trouble"**, an extended metaphor for his trials and tribulations in the music biz that revolved around him being a cab driver and being recognized by one of his fares who wondered what happened to him.

**Always Has Been**
Triple Threat, 2003

An EP that contains J-Live's classic early singles "Braggin' Writes", "Longevity", "Can I Get It?", "Hush the Crowd" and "School's In". These are the records that established his reputation as one of the best MCs either above or below ground. The production is a bit rough and ready, but J-Live's awesome mic skills rise above any musical limitations.

# Jonzun Crew

While New York DJ **Afrika Bambaataa**'s "Planet Rock" (1982) was indisputably the track that kicked off the electro craze, the real roots of electro lay not in the Bronx housing projects, nor in – as is often claimed – **Kraftwerk**'s Dusseldorf studio, but in distinctly unfunky Boston, Massachusetts. In 1981 aspiring "Beantown" musicians **Michael Jonzun**, **Maurice Starr** and **Arthur Baker** collaborated on a record that combined a hip-hop sensibility with the drum machines and synthesizers of late disco – **Glory**'s "Let's Get Nice" (1981).

The following year, Starr, Jonzun and his brother Soni recorded "Pak Man (Look Out For The OVC)" (1982) as The Jonzun Crew for the short-lived **Boston International Records**. The eerie ode to the strange video-game critter was a minor club hit and its sound fitted in perfectly with the new direction being explored by Bambaataa and Arthur Baker, so **Tommy Boy** licensed the track and released a rerecorded version entitled "Pack Jam (Look Out For The OVC)" (1982). The new version, recorded by a boosted line-up that included

Steve Thorpe and Gordon Worthy, was even freakier, thanks to sub-bass that torpedoed your ears down to previously unheard depths, and some of the best drum-machine programming ever.

More funky videogame dystopian sounds followed in the form of "Space Is the Place" (1983) – a nod to otherworldly jazz visionary **Sun Ra** – but the group shifted from Ra to George Clinton's P-Funk music and suitably camp Mozart garb for the wonderfully silly "Space Cowboy" (1983).

Even two decades after its initial release, the group's debut album, *Lost in Space* (1983), remains an unheralded "afronaut" classic. Unfortunately, although Jonzun and co continued to release singles such as "Time Is Running Out", "Lovin'" (both 1984) and "Red Hott Mama" (1985) – and the patchy *Down To Earth* (1984) album – Michael Jonzun amd Maurice Starr were diverted by their discovery of teen r&b group **New Edition** and later, shudder to think, the boy band **New Kids on the Block**. Jonzun continued to release albums like *Cosmic Love* (1990), but his space cowboy shtick was long gone, replaced by a stolid professionalism.

**Lost in Space**
Tommy Boy, 1983

Including all of the group's great singles – "Pack Jam", "Space Is the Place" and "Space Cowboy" – this is perhaps the best electro album ever made. There are a couple of duff moments (most notably "Ground Control") where the group sinks into Gary Numan territory, but mostly this is an endearingly goofy and wholly funky (especially when they get the Latin percussion moving) exploration of a mind warped by both video games and George Clinton.

# JT The Bigga Figga

Pretty much all rap artists think of themselves as CEOs, but only one has written a manual that shows you how to become the Donald Trump of your block – San Francisco's **JT The Bigga Figga**. Like many of his albums, *Black Wall Street: The CEO Manual* (2002) was a self-produced instruction book for the big hustle.

JT came out of the Fillmore section of San Francisco and initially made a name for himself selling his self-released records out of the trunk of his car. *Playaz N The Game* (1993) was the most successful record on his **Get Low** label, largely thanks to "Game Recognize Game", a low-budget version of LA G-Funk (that ironically presaged Dre's productions with Eminem, and his *2001* album) that had JT making like E-40 with his novel slanguage.

The album got JT signed to Priority, who released *Dwellin' In The Labb* (1995). Despite the major label production values, the album wasn't as fresh as *Playaz* – it just sounded like regular ol' gangsta rap. The one exception was probably "Scrilla, Scratch, Paper" which featured San Fran hip-hop legends **Coughnut** from **Ill Mannered Posse** and **Tay-da-Tay** of **11-5** bringing back lingo from the 1970s: "I'm sick of niggas smiling in my face but don't like me/Jealous of my game and my fame but won't fight me". That same year, JT's **Straight Out the Labb** label released *Legal Dope*, a compilation of "Yay Area" rappers which also featured appearances from **Master P** and **TRU**, Brotha Lynch Hung and Houston's **ESG**. *Don't Stop 'Til We Major* (1996) followed in the same style, but *Game Tight* (1997) concentrated on an upwardly mobile, more r&b style of production that didn't suit his flow terribly well.

After a three-year hiatus, Get Low flooded the market with product in 2000. *Operation Takeover*, *Puttin' It On The Map* (a collection of early tracks), *Something Crucial*, the *Beware of Those* soundtrack (with **Mac Mall**) and *Longbeach 2 Fillmoe* (with **Daz Dillinger**) were all released that year with unsurprisingly mixed results. 2001 was relatively quiet, with only *Game For Sale* (with Daz Dillinger again) and the *Bay Area Bosses* compilation with protégés **San Quinn** and **Tha Gamblaz**, plus **Yukmouth**, Mac Mall, C-Bo and **Killa Tay**. 2002 saw another flurry of product, most notably *Gotta Get It* (with Juvenile) and *Hustle Relentless*, an honest-to-good-ness solo album. *Project Poetry* (2003) featured more collaborations with Juvenile and more production and hooks that were reminiscent of Dr. Dre's work with Eminem.

⊙ **Playaz N The Game**
Get Low, 1993

The subject matter doesn't go too far beyond dank (marijuana), dosia (marijuana again) and dirt (low-grade marijuana) and it sounds like your younger brother put it together in half an hour on his Casio VL Tone, but it's a classic of grass-roots Bay Area hip-hop nevertheless. Tracks like "Game Recognize Game" and "Mr Millimeter" put enough of a spin on the LA G-Funk formula to put the Fillmoe on the map.

# Juice Crew

In the mid-1980s, Queensbridge ruled hip-hop: Run DMC, LL Cool J, Salt-N-Pepa and Def Jam's Russell Simmons all repped for the borough. Although the **Juice Crew** didn't achieve anywhere near the success of their neighbours, they were perhaps the best and most important of the Queens rappers. A measure of their status was that no one has been involved in more wax wars than the Juice Crew.

In fact, the Juice Crew had its roots in an answer record – **Dimples D's** "Sucker DJs" (1983) – a response to Run DMC's "Sucker MCs". "Sucker DJs" was the first record produced by Queensbridge native **Marley Marl** (**Marlon Williams**), who had previously worked as an intern for "Planet

Rock" producer Arthur Baker. While Marley Marl produced other old school landmarks like **Just Four**'s "Games Of Life" (1983), he would have to wait for another answer record, and another female MC, to really make a name for himself.

Marley Marl had landed a gig as the engineer for Mr Magic's hip-hop show on WBLS. When **UTFO** reneged on a promise to record a promo for Mr Magic, and did so for his arch-rival DJ Red Alert instead, Marley Marl teamed up with 14-year-old **Roxanne Shanté** to record "Roxanne's Revenge" (1985), which answered UTFO's "Roxanne, Roxanne" with gum-snapping sass. Kicking off the biggest answer record craze in pop history, "Roxanne's Revenge" – rather than "Roxanne, Roxanne" – inspired over 100 records that ripped on Shanté. While the rap community was obsessed with the Roxanne saga, Shanté moved on, dropping admittedly lame social commentary on "Runaway" (1985), but returning to what she did best – remorseless disses – on "Bite This" and "Queen Of Rox" (both 1985). While her "The Def Fresh Crew" (1986) introduced the Juice Crew's clown prince **Biz Markie**, "Payback" (1987) featured Shanté "getting wild" and spitting harder rhymes than just about anyone, male or female. While Shanté had more spunk than a fertility clinic, it took the rhymes of the Juice Crew's poet laureate **Big Daddy Kane** to produce her greatest record, "Have a Nice Day" (1987). Quite simply, records, hip-hop or otherwise just don't get any better: Shanté was "a pioneer like Lola Folana/With a name that stands big like Madonna", "like Hurricane Annie she [blew] you away" with lines like "Now KRS-One you should go on vacation/With a name sounding like a wack radio station/ And as for Scott La Rock you should be ashamed/When T La Rock said, 'It's Yours', he didn't mean his name".

The Juice Crew was blessed with awe-some mic talents, but Marley Marl was still the ringleader. Marley was perhaps the greatest producer in hip-hop history, almost single-handedly responsible for bringing the sampler into hip-hop with his production on **Eric B & Rakim**'s "Eric B Is President" (1986). But even when he

(1988) was one of the best of that landmark year. *Wanted: Dead Or Alive* (1990), meanwhile, included such vivid narratives as "Streets of New York", "Money In The Bank" and "Rikers Island". *Live And Let Live* (1992), with the title track and "Ill Street Blues", completed a staggering triptych of albums that revelled in the dark demi-monde of New York.

Based on a piano loop from Otis Redding's "Hard to Handle", Marley Marl's "The Symphony" (1988), featuring Kool G Rap, Big Daddy Kane, **Masta Ace** and **Craig G**, was most likely the greatest posse cut ever. "The Symphony" was the best track on Marley's *In Control* (1988), making Marley Marl the first hip-hop producer to release an album under his own name. However, the album's title was a misnomer. Despite orchestrating LL Cool J's comeback on *Mama Said Knock You Out* (1990), Marley was becoming the victim of the more sophisticated production techniques that he pretty much originated, and the name of his House of Hits studio was now more optimism than undeniable fact, as it had been a few years earlier.

Ten years after his last album – 1991's utterly forgettable *In Control Vol. 2* – Marley Marl returned with *Re-Entry*. Of course, he had still been producing – most notably

was still using Linn drums, as he did on "Marley Marl Scratch" (1985), he brought it harder and funkier than anyone else.

The MC on "Marley Marl Scratch" was **MC Shan**, whose "The Bridge" (1986) started the second most famous battle saga in hip-hop. Rocking the beat from the Honey Drippers' "Impeach the President" and a loop of fearsome dissonance, Shan bragged about Queensbridge being the home of hip-hop, infuriating a crew from the Bronx named Boogie Down Productions, who shot back with "South Bronx", thus in turn inspiring Shan's "Kill That Noise" (1987).

Ducking the inter-borough crossfire, Marley introduced James Brown's "Funky Drummer" breakbeat into hip-hop on **Kool G Rap & DJ Polo**'s "It's A Demo" (1986). Although he was perhaps overshadowed in the crew by Big Daddy Kane (whom Kool G Rap accused of biting his style on "Ain't No Half Steppin'"), Kool G Rap was one of the great MCs of all-time. With an awesome, multi-syllabic, intensely rhythmic flow, his mic skills were on a par with Kane and Rakim, and the darkside tales he rapped helped usher in hip-hop's hardcore age. Featuring "It's A Demo", the ferocious battle rhymes of "Poison" and the prototypical criminology rap "Road To the Riches" the duo's debut album, *Road To The Riches* for **Capone-N-Noreaga** and **Rakim** – but he was so far off the radar that this had to be released on a British label. After the opening history lesson "Do U Remember?" attempted to re-assert his place in history, Marley Marl proved that he still some studio chops, even if he no longer had the clout to bring in some MCs who could match them on the microphone.

 **Droppin' Science: The Best Of Cold Chillin'**
BBE, 1999

There are many Marley Marl compilations floating around, but this fine collection was compiled by the man himself.

# Jungle Brothers

With their first three albums, the **Jungle Brothers** probably did as much as any other crew to expand the language of hip-hop. While using classic old school breakbeats to maintain connections to the block parties that nurtured the hip-hop aesthetic in the early days, **Afrika Baby Bambaataa** delved in the depths of his sampler and **Sammy B** played Twister on the turntables to create a more musical hip-hop. At a time when rap was ruled by fierce regional feuds, the rhymes and delivery of **Mike G** and Afrika suggested an open-ended camaraderie that hadn't existed since the **Treacherous Three** and **Funky Four Plus One**. Unlike the verbal virtuosity of Rakim and the clinical turntable precision of Mantronix, the Jungle Brothers made rich, numinous music that was connected to the world outside the hip-hop community. Of course, in a genre whose hardcore underground protects itself with an armour every bit as arcane as free-improv music, this broad outlook is heresy. So, with the arguable exception of their late-career forays into the poppier end of the UK's breakbeat scene, the Jungle Brothers never saw their innovations translate into big sales.

Their debut, *Straight Out The Jungle* (1988), was a strikingly original album that grafted loose-limbed funk onto the angular geometry of mid-1980s hip-hop beats. The single "I'll House You" was the foundation of the short-lived hip-house craze; elsewhere, **Marvin Gaye** and **Charles Mingus** samples crept into the mix. Complementary to their music, the Jungle Brothers' raps were rare examples of political and sexual democracy. "Jimbrowski" poked fun at macho posturing about sexual

The Jungle Brothers are known for their fondness for scratching "air turntables" from time to time.

prowess, while "Black Is Black" attacked racism and black-on-black violence.

*Done By The Forces Of Nature* (1989) was even better. The spirituality and fraternity of the first album remained and were bolstered by fatter bass and better hooks. Samples ranged from **The Coasters** to Bob Marley to **South African township jive** and the funkier feel created an album that married hip-hop's oblique verbal dexterity to pop's more demotic language. With big-budget but never too slick production values, jokes that were actually funny, and an overall feel that was almost sweet, *Done By The Forces Of Nature* was and still is hip-hop's most inclusive album.

In a genre obsessed with being hard, the JBs' unthreatening masculinity made them relative outcasts outside their Native Tongue posse (**De La Soul**, A Tribe Called Quest, and **Queen Latifah**). Aside from a brilliantly bleak re-reading of Cole Porter's "I Get a Kick Out of You" on the *Red, Hot And Blue* (1990) AIDS benefit album, the JBs kept a low profile until *J. Beez Wit The Remedy* (1993). The Afrocentricity and

embrace of pop were gone. In their place, a hazed and phased experimentalism had developed. Drowned in a narcotic fog, *J. Beez* was far from the generous, funky jam of old, but no less brilliant. Radically different from the blunted hip-hop of **Cypress Hill** or the grim mysticism of the **Wu-Tang Clan**, *J. Beez* was nonetheless obscurantist black psychedelia at its best.

Needless to say, this couldn't have been further from the hip-hop mainstream if it had been made by Celine Dion, and the Jungle Brothers disappeared for another four years. *Raw Deluxe* (1997) was stripped-down, yet sadly overproduced, and showed that while hip-hop had been moving on, the Jungle Brothers had been treading water. At around the same time as New York label Black Hoodz was releasing the *Crazy Wisdom Masters* EP of out-takes from *J. Beez Wit The Remedy*, the group was, bizarrely, aiming for the British pop market with the appalling *VIP* (1999). The ultimate indignity, though, was when the group opened up for – wait for it – the **Backstreet Boys**.

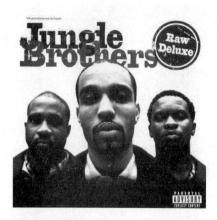

All *That We Do* (2002) was a similarly odd move which saw the group work again with house-music titan **Todd Terry**, who had produced their hip-house landmark "I'll House You". While on the one hand they seemed to be forsaking the mainstream, and even the underground, hip-hop scene with this choice, most of Terry's beats were uninspired facsimiles of the "crunk" style, and pop-rap formulas.

### ⊙ Done By The Forces Of Nature
Warner Brothers, 1989

A spectacular pop album and a great hip-hop record, this should have been as big as De La Soul's *Three Feet High And Rising*. Less self-conscious and less oblique than their Native Tongue brethren, this contains the most all-embracing hip hop ever made.

### ⊙ J. Beez Wit The Remedy
Warner Brothers, 1993

A hip-hop record that samples The Stooges? Taking a snippet of off-hand noise from Iggy and turning it into a hook, the Jungle Brothers manage to create a whirling, disjunctive sound from a conglomeration of infinitesimal details.

# Jurassic 5

It doesn't sound like anyone in hip-hop has more fun than LA's **Jurassic 5**. Formed from the fusion of two SoCal crews, Unity Committee and Rebels of Rhythm, Jurassic 5 (DJs **Cut Chemist** and **Numark** and MCs **Chali 2na**, **Zaakir**, **Akil** and **Mark 7even**) are all about recreating the inclusive, joyous vibe of the first Sugar Hill and Enjoy records. Their vinyl debut was the "Unified

Rebelution" 12" (1995) which was a combination of the **Harlem Underground Band**'s "Cheeba Cheeba", **Kraftwerk**'s "Trans-Europe Express" and the theme to *Different Strokes*. The flip featured Cut Chemist's old-school throwdown "Lesson 4", which later appeared on the album *Return Of The DJ*. Encompassing snippets of radio station IDs, **Indeep**, Harlem Underground Band, Bob James, **Dan Ackroyd** and Spoonie Gee jigsawed together, "Lesson 4" was a tribute to both **Double Dee & Steinski**'s pioneering cut 'n' paste records "Lessons 1, 2 And 3" and to the days when hip-hop was about the simple pleasures of finding a new sound and grooving to it.

1997's *Jurassic 5* EP, released on their own Rumble/Pickaninny label, perfected their back-to-the-future sound. Tracks like "Concrete Schoolyard" and "Action Satisfaction" were similar in vibe to the first two **Jungle Brothers** albums, but the highlight was Cut Chemist's follow-up to "Lesson 4", "Lesson 6", which sounded like **Magnus Pike** had been caught in a breakbeat tape loop. When the *Jurassic 5* EP was released in Europe in 1998 with the inclusion of "Jayou" (a flute-driven groove with the sterling couplet "With malignant metaphors and ganja-stained herbs/We conjugate verbs and constipate nerds like you") as an album, the group blew up and they became stars.

With this success, Jurassic 5 signed to Interscope in the US and released the *Improvise* EP (1999). With the excel-

Jurassic 5 are very proud of their disposable cameras and dictaphones.

lent title track and a brilliant remix of "Concrete Schoolyard", "Concrete and Clay", *Improvise* didn't exactly break any boundaries, but it did reaffirm them as prime exponents of underground hip-hop. *Quality Control* (2000) suffered a bit from the typical underground trap: they spent too much time trying to answer their critics, and not enough just doing their thing. There was an odd line here and there that slapped you upside the head like a can of Tango, but their interaction wasn't as joyous as on their EP. Perhaps they ran out of **Cold Crush Brothers** routines to borrow.

While there was still plenty of old school reminiscing ("What's Golden", "A Day At The Races"), *Power In Numbers* (2002) found the group expanding their palette. Guests like **Big Daddy Kane**, Percee P, Nelly Furtado, Kool Keith and JuJu from The Beatnuts forced both Cut Chemist and Numark and the rappers to change their styles a bit, to stop using the old school archaeology as a crutch. The result was that Jurassic 5 could now stand on their own 12 feet.

**Jurassic Five**
Pan, 1998

In terms of quantity, it's a bit skimpy to be called an album, but the breezy vibe, old school reminiscing and easy grooves are so joyous that you don't mind.

# Junior M.A.F.I.A.

See *Notorious BIG; see also Lil' Kim*

# Just Ice

Calling himself "the original gangster of hip-hop", **Joseph Williams** was bound to court controversy. In 1987 he was the victim of lazy reporting and was accused of murder in sensationalized newspaper and television coverage which denied him precisely what his mic name demanded. **Just Ice** was more than just tabloid fodder, however. He was one of the best old school MCs and his gruff voice was a perfect match for the booming drum machines of the day.

Recorded with **Mantronix**, Just Ice's first album, *Back To The Old School* (1986), was

201

into one. "Moshitup" featured KRS and Just trading lyrics, and it did exactly what it said on the label.

While it had the savage "Welfare Recipient", *The Desolate One* (1988) was most notable for Just's version of Jamaica's "Sleng Teng" beat, "Na Touch Da Just". With production that imitated a Kingston selector constantly rewinding, "Na Touch Da Just" was part of hip-hop's burgeoning love affair with dancehall.

By the time of *Masterpiece* (1990), hip-hop had matured considerably and Just's old school disses and boasts sounded decidedly behind the times. Neither *Gun Talk* (1993), *Kill The Rhythm (Like a Homicide)* (1995) nor *VII* (1998) could bring Just's vision of hardcore up to date either.

a perfect example of the sound that made unprepared New Yorkers fear for their lives. Filled with the kind of drums that seemed like they could make skyscrapers crumble at thirty yards and Just Ice's fierce lyrics and violent cadences, *Back to the Old School* was hip-hop made with punk rock attitude. The key track was the stunning "Cold Gettin' Dumb". Filled with plain-speech lines like "So try to make me believe all of your stupid nonsense", and chest-puncturing beats, "Cold Gettin' Dumb" was the record **Slayer** wish they could've made.

*Kool And Deadly (Justicizms)* (1987) saw Just Ice team up with **KRS-One** for an equally devastating album. Simply put, Just Ice and KRS-One tore shit up. "Going Way Back" was an old school history lesson, but with the drum-machine thunder and Just's breathless rasping, it became a threat, an exercise in self-actualisation and a subtle diss of the Juice Crew all rolled

### ⊙ Kool And Deadly
Sleeping Bag/Fresh, 1987

Officially out of print, this stunning record of old-fashioned b-boy attitude does occasionally show up on bootleg versions.

# Kam

An intriguing blend of Nation of Islam sensibilities and gangsta rhythms, the woefully underrated LA rapper Kam was born Craig Miller in 1971. He was one of Ice Cube's earliest protégés and first appeared on the *Boyz N the Hood* soundtrack (1991) on the track "Every Single Weekend". A spot on the posse cut "Colorblind" from Cube's *Death Certificate* (1991) followed soon afterward.

Kam really made a name for himself, however, with "Peace Treaty" (1992), the first single under his own name. The song was a celebration of the short-lived cease fire between LA's warring gangs following the uprising in the wake of the **Rodney King** trial. The production, both "funk-dafied" and menacing, caught the mood of the times perfectly, and Kam's eloquent and forceful rap showed what gangsta rap was capable of. *Neva Again* (1993) combined Ice Cube's rage (if not his nihilism) and funk with the Afrocentric didacticism of groups like **X-Clan**. It was a superb album, but even the bumpin' beats of **DJ Pooh**, Solid Scheme and **Torcha Chamba** couldn't disguise Kam's stridency.

He toned down the politics (he even went so far as duetting with MC Ren) for *Made In America* (1995), but even though an all-star line-up of West Coast producers (**DJ Quik**, DJ Battlecat, Warren G, E A Ski, **Big Hutch**) brought some serious heat it was lost in the post-G-Funk fray. Sadly, but typically, Kam got far more attention for his appearance on DJ Pooh's *Bad Newz Travels Fast* (1997) album – "Whoop Whoop", which savagely dissed **Ice Cube** – than for his more positive music. Admittedly, though, "Whoop Whoop" was pretty hot: a clipped but impossibly fat bassline, Bruce Lee sound effects and choice lyrics such as "It's a shame you got rich off of our stress and strife/And you ain't never gang-banged in ya life/Ya wife the one that really wear the pants in the house/So answer this, is you a man or a mouse?"

After laying low for a few years, Kam appeared on **The Eastsidaz** album in 2000 and then really returned to the fray with *Kamnesia* (2001). The politics were toned down even further, and with producers like **Jazze Pha** on board, it seemed as though Kam was aiming at the crossover success which had always eluded him. A follow-up album, *The Self*, was slated for release in 2002, but still hasn't seen the light of day.

**◉ Neva Again**
Eastwest, 1993

The best moments on this underrated record ("Peace Treaty", "Y'all Don't Hear Me Dough") rank with the most fiery tracks from Ice Cube's Bomb Squad period. The only problem came in the disconnection between the hydraulic bumpin' funk and Kam's didactic, pleasure-forsaking lyrics.

# Kid Capri

Bragging in your official press bio about spinning at private parties for **Martha Stewart** and N'Sync isn't usually the path to hip-hop glory, but when you're Kid Capri you can get away with it. In the early 1990s Kid Capri was known as the DJ who became a millionaire off his mixtapes, but more than the money, his success was his entry into the world of sneaker lines, Burger King endorsements and $15K an hour to play at some kid's bar mitzvah.

The Kid was born **David Anthony Love** in the Bronx, and according to legend, he was scratching records by the time he was eight. He eventually worked his way up the DJ ladder to a regular gig at a late incarnation of **Studio 54**. He would make tapes of his sets and sell them, along with tapes he made at home at a spot on 154th Street in Harlem. Capri's style was basically a party mix of new hits with old school classics, topped off with Capri shouting out various ghetto celebrities with his distinctive and energetic voice. Tapes like the legendary *52 Beats* (1989), a 90-minute breakbeat mix, allegedly made Capri $2,000 a night and earned him the title of **"Minister of Mixtapes"**.

His enormous reputation landed him a record contract with **Cold Chillin'**, for whom he recorded *The Tape* (1991) with **Biz Markie** manning the boards. Trying to recreate a wholly grassroots experience in a commercial recording studio wasn't exactly a recipe for success, but somehow Capri

Kid Capri waits behind in detention after school.

joke's on you jack

kid Capri

and Biz made it work. Capri inevitably moved into production, working on tracks for **KRS-One** ("Stop Frontin"), **Heavy D** ("Nuttin' But Love"), **Grand Puba** ("Back It Up") and **Big L** ("Put It On").

During his stint as DJ for *Def Comedy Jam*, Capri released *Soundtrack To The Streets* (1998), another attempt at replicating the mixtape environment, but this time with marquee rappers. By this point, the mixtape aesthetic (particularly the one developed by **DJ Clue** which this disc emulates) was thoroughly mainstream and there were no surprises to be gained from the format, even if some of the tracks, most notably Snoop Dogg's duet with Slick Rick, "Unify", were undeniably real coups. He DJed on the Puff Daddy and the Family tour in 1998 and appeared in seemingly countless advertisements for everything from Sprite to Fubu. In 2004 he was given his own imprint, No Kid'n, by Def Jam, which debuted with "I Don't Like To Dance" by Red Handed.

### ● The Tape
Cold Chillin', 1991

Recreating a mixtape in the studio may have been a pointless exercise, but it was the only way for the artform to gain any legitimacy in the industry. As a display of studio trickery, the album was pretty nifty. The problem was that mixtapes of the time worked by playing with your expectations in their novel blends and juxtapositions, and since these tracks were all newly recorded and featured no big-name rappers, there was no familiarity to play with.

# Kid Frost

Kid Frost (aka **Arturo Molina, Jr.**) will always be known more for the novelty aspects of rapping in Spanish, and bringing a Hispanic perspective to hip-hop than for the quality of his music. While this pigeonholing may be a little unfair to Frost, who is a more than competent rapper and producer, it is also testament to the fact that he has yet to make a record that's solid all the way through.

Frost spent the early part of his career hanging out with **Ice-T** and performing at low-rider car shows throughout LA. Although he debuted in 1985 duetting with a vocoder on top of a severe drum machine on "Terminator", he wouldn't come to prominence until 1990 and his hit "La Raza". Understated but unmissable, "La Raza" might not have been the first hip-hop track about Hispanic pride, but it was certainly the best. Frost's subtle rap style evaded the pop novelty territory of someone like, ulp, Gerardo, while the congas, bongos and the weird synth break that sounded a bit like an Andean pan-pipe group made his Latin roots just as clear as his words. "La Raza" was so good that it both opened and closed *Hispanic Causing Panic* (1990). Unfortunately, what came in between – with the exceptions of the unity call "Come Together" and the Spanish lesson "Ya Estuvo" – couldn't live up to it.

In 1991 Frost founded the **Latin Alliance** with fellow Hispanic hip-hoppers **ALT**, **Lyrical Engineer**, **Astronaut**, **Mellow Man Ace** and **Markski**. Their self-titled album produced a hit in the form of the inevitable cover of War's "Low Rider", but more original were "Latinos Unidos" and "Valla En Paz".

Frost's *East Side Story* (1992) was a loose narrative about a Chicano victim of LA chief of police **Darryl Gates**' policing policies. Its *mise-en-scène* was strictly old soul samples (Bill Withers and The Persuaders) and wasn't terribly original, but like, say, **Michael Mann**, Frost managed to make the utterly generic seem insightful. Tracks like "Mi Vida Loca", "Another Firme Rola (Bad 'Cause I'm Brown)" and "Raza Unite" make this Frost's best album.

Signing to **Eazy-E**'s Ruthless label, however, seemed to bring out the worst in Frost. *Smile Now, Die Later* (1995) was Frost's attempt at going hardcore, and was filled with the same gangsta clichés (both musically and lyrically) that the label boss had been trying to pedal for the past several years. *When Hell. A. Freezes Over* (1997) was more of the same and pushed Frost's **2Pac** fetishism to the fore. There was more Tuplacation on *That Was Then, This Is Now* (1999), but there was plenty of low ridin' funk and guest appearances from the likes of **Rappin' 4-Tay**, Kurupt, Jayo Felony and Roger Troutman.

*That Was Then, This Is Now, Vol. 2* (2000) was more of the same, which became evident when Thump records released both volumes as a single package in 2001. Losing the Kid, and renaming himself Frost, Molina pretty much ditched any remaining traces of his old Chicano sound (except for the collaboration with Latin rock group **Tierra** on "I'm Still Here") for *Still Up in This $#*T* (2002), which had a surfeit of generic Cali funk rollers on top of which Frost waxed earnest about a decade in the business.

⊙ **East Side Story**
Virgin, 1992

Tackling racism, prison life and what it means to be Hispanic, this is Frost's most conceptually satisfying and well-executed album.

⊙ **Frost's Greatest Joints**
Thump, 2001

Starting with "La Raza" and ending with "Diamonds and Pearls" from *That Was Then, This Is Now*, this is a solid career overview of one of hip-hop's most undersung MCs.

# Kid 'N Play

Although they were decent pop rappers, **Christopher Reid** (**Kid**) and **Christopher Martin** (**Play**) will not be remembered for their music. Far more crucial to the development of hip-hop were their contributions both sartorial (Kid's sky-scraping high-top fade, the leather jackets that Play designed for Salt-N-Pepa) and cinematic (their starring roles in the *House Party* flicks).

Kid 'N Play were originally known as **Fresh Force** and debuted with "Oh Sally" (1985). "She's A Skeezer/All Hail The Drum" (1986) was an answer record to **Run DMC**'s "My Adidas", but the group first came to attention when they changed their name and released "Last Night" (1987). Based on **Esther Williams**' "Last Night Changed it All (I Really Had a Ball)", "Last Night" was a corny tale of a double date gone wrong. Produced by Hurby "Luv Bug" Azor, the duo's debut album, *2 Hype* (1988), featured more innocuous, wholesome raps such as the title track, "Gittin' Funky" and "Do This My Way". Inevitably, there were also parent-placating messages like "Don't Do Drugs". The best track, however, was probably the go-go-esque "Rollin' With Kid 'N Play" which gave Kid and Play plenty of room to rock their dance moves. Needless to say, *2 Hype* didn't move many units on the streets.

After starring in *House Party*, Kid 'N Play tried to up their street cred slightly with *Kid 'N Play's Funhouse* (1990), which featured 'harder' raps, but it was peppered with dialogue from *House Party* and just served to prove that these guys were nothing but slumming showbiz types. Far better was the *House Party OST* (1990), which had the good sense to include other rappers' tunes alongside "Funhouse" and "Kid Vs. Play". In 1990 Kid 'N Play had the ultimate honour bestowed on them – they were the "stars" of their own Saturday-morning cartoon show on NBC, with voices by **Martin Lawrence** and Tommy Davidson. By the time *Face the Nation* (1991) came out, it was clear that the duo's future lay squarely with *House Party 2*, *House Party 3* et al.

⊙ **2 Hype**
Select, 1998

Cornier than a big plate of succotash, this nevertheless remains an enjoyable piece of pop fluff.

Redneck rock rapper, Kid, er, Rock.

# Kid Rock

Only in America. It's a story that would make **Horatio Alger** proud: white loner from the northern-most suburb of America's blackest city immerses himself in hip-hop, grows one of the world's great hairstyles, releases several albums that go nowhere, reinvents himself as a redneck rocker who also happens to like **Miami Bass**, and becomes the biggest thing since Oxycontin.

Bob Ritchie was born in 1971 in Dearborn, Michigan and rasied in Romeo, a rural town about 30 miles north of Detroit. An adolescence spent breakdanc-ing, rapping and telling dirty jokes in the schoolyard landed him an opening slot for a **Boogie Down Productions** show in Detroit. He was spotted by a Jive talent scout and inked a deal with the label who released *Grits Sandwiches For Breakfast* (1990). In true Michigan style, the Kid was a cartoon: the "Super Rhyme Maker" pimping hoes; sporting a haircut that was the the caucasian equivalent of the Kid 'n Play hi-top fade (a kind of grav-ity-defying cubist brick of an afro); "Yo-Da-Lin" in their valleys; and "shining that booty like Turtle Wax". The production from **Too $hort** and Detroit legend **Mike Clark** was a suitably ridiculous pastiche of the Beastie Boys. There were a couple of hints of his future persona, though: on "New York's Not My Home" he plays the Midwestern hick lost in the city ("I

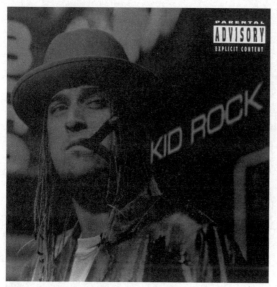

(1998) hit the streets, Atlantic's gamble paid off. "Bawitdaba" was the perfect fusion of **Pantera** and **Onyx** that frat boys had been waiting for ever since the Beastie Boys' *Licensed To Ill*, while "Welcome To The Party" had rhymes like "I don't like small cars or real big women/ But somehow I always find myself in 'em" that showed that he had developed a sense of humour. The album caught the prevailing meathead zeitgeist to the tune of 11 million copies.

*The History Of Rock* (2000) was a time-biding exercise in which the Kid rerecorded and remixed tracks from *The Polyfuze Method* and *Early Mornin' Stoned Pimp*. Of course, the production wasn't really the problem with his old tracks. It was the lyrics and the rapping, and only the new track "American Bad Ass" stood out. Kid Rock then accomplished the ultimate feat for him and his audience – he bedded **Pamela Anderson**. With nothing else to prove, or even live for, *Cocky* (2001) and *Kid Rock* (2003) lacked energy, desire, creativity or humour – the very things, in other words, that made *Devil Without A Cause* even bearable.

see a set of nice legs within my sight/But it's a fuckin' transvestite") and "With A One Two" has a sample of **The Doobie Brothers'** "China Grove".

Jive promptly dropped Kid Rock after this car-crash of a record. He then moved to Brooklyn and started to really craft his redneck trailer-park mack persona. *The Polyfuze Method* (1993) had more rock 'n' roll, particularly on "U Don't Know Me" and "Killin' Brain Cells", but the raps were still pretty pitiful. After the *Fire It Up* EP (1994), Kid Rock realised he was never going to make it in the straight hip-hop world and set about forming a live band which he called **Twisted Brown Trucker**. Recruiting DJ **Uncle Kracker**, diminutive (because of celiac disease) hypeman **Joe C**, guitarists Jason Krause and Kenny Olson, keyboardist Jimmie Bones and drummer Stefanie Eulinberg, Kid Rock recorded *Early Mornin' Stoned Pimp* (1996), a further refinement of his cracker rap-rock aesthetic. The album didn't do much, but it was noticed by Atlantic, who gambled that Kid Rock's shtick would stick in the same way as **Limp Bizkit** and **Korn**.

In typical style, Kid and his crew celebrated in a bar in Romeo, only to be locked up in a county jail after a fight broke out, but they managed to continue partying behind bars nevertheless. A few months after *Devil Without A Cause*

⊙ **Devil Without A Cause**
  Lava/Atlantic, 1998

The perfect soundtrack to killing a few brain cells – not even the Beastie Boys or House of Pain have made frat-hop this definitive. With enough Cuervo in your system, "Bawitdaba" is the best record ever. The rest of the album is nowhere near as good, but it is thoroughly agreeable background music for skeet shooting.

# King Sun

Todd Turnbow transmogrified into King Sun in the mid-1980s after being exposed to the Five Percent sect of the Nation of Islam. His rap style – strictly in that late-1980s fast-spitting (but with supreme breath control) manner – debuted in 1987 on the Zakia label. "Hey Love", a duet with **D-Moët**, was a love jam over a large portion of **Art of**

Noise's "Moments In Love" that was a medium-sized hit in the summer of 1987.

"Hey Love"'s flip, "Mythological Rapper" was much more typical of King Sun's style, which was amply displayed on *XL* (1989), his debut album for Profile. A collection of mostly uptempo beats like "Heat Up" and the supremely funky "The Fat Tape", *XL* featured some excellent production from **The 45 King** and Sun's commanding mic presence. The problem was that most of the beats were two years old, because Profile had sat on the album while waiting for a second single, which ended up being the rather awful "On The Club Tip".

*Righteous But Ruthless* (1990) followed in a similar style, with Afrocentric tracks like "Be Black" and the Five Percent throwdown "The Gods Are Talking Heads", with **Poor Righteous Teachers** sharing space with lame club and skeezer tracks such as "Big Shots", "Undercover Lover" and "Stunts". King Sun wasn't happy at Profile and shortly after his album was released he bought out his contract with the label. He hooked up with **Fat Joe**, appeared on "Another Wild Nigger From The Bronx" from Fat Joe's first album in 1993, and set up his own label with help from Joe and his crew. "Sippin' Brandy" (1993) – a low-key, downtempo, jazzy track that's oddly mixed, with Sun stringing together some pretty forced metaphors with a pretty decent, if faintly mealy-mouthed, flow – was the only record that ever came out on his Big Boss label.

During this time King Sun had sent a tape to **Ice Cube**, but never heard a response. He forgot about it until he heard Cube's "Wicked" and accused him of biting the chorus from his tape. In October 1993 King Sun rushed the DJ booth at an Ice Cube concert in New York, grabbed the mic and accused of him of stealing his music. Cube called him up to the stage, but the security guards prevented King Sun from making it. King Sun talked about the situation on "Suck No Dick" from his *Strictly Ghetto* (1994) EP on Cold Chillin'. Produced by the **Boiler Room**, the EP couldn't match

the best moments of his earlier albums, even if a truly amped-up King Sun (now calling himself **The Jeweler Sundulah**) was often a "sound to behold" on the mic. More Cali beef was aired on "NY Love" (1996) on which the Jeweler savagely attacked **2Pac**, but, apart from an appearance on Funkmaster Flex's *Mixtape Vol. III* (1998), the Sun hasn't been seen above the horizon since.

**XL**
Profile, 1989

It was two years old when it was originally released, but the time-lag doesn't matter anymore. *XL* is a good, if not great, example of the late 1980s fast rap style, with tracks like "Heat Up", "Snakes" and "The Fat Tape" showing King Sun spitting with a venom to match the tempo.

# King Tee

While his peers catalogued the ills of their Compton surroundings to multi-platinum success, South Central's **King Tee** attempted to blunt the reality of his environment with wine, women and song, but no one was interested. Despite having one of the purest flows on the Left Coast, "Tila" has been unable to translate his skills into ducats.

Tee started out as a radio DJ in the early 1980s and he soon hooked up with LA impresario Greg Mack, who released Tee's fine debut single, and West Coast classic, "Payback's A Mutha" in 1987 with DJ Keith Cooley on the ones and twos cutting up the James Brown breaks, on his **Techno-Hop** label. Tee then bragged about being "the cool Wop dancer" over a **Meters** sample on "The Coolest" (1987). The wall-quaking and rump-shaking collaboration with **DJ Pooh**, "Bass" (1988), followed and Tee landed a contract with Capitol. Although "Bass" and "Payback's a Mutha" both appeared on *Act a Fool* (1988), Tee's lyrics about 30-inch "duke-ys" (gold chains) and "Casanova fly guys" paled next to the monumental albums being produced 3,000 miles to the east in New York.

*At Your Own Risk* (1990) was better – particularly the fearsome collection of battle verses on "Ruff Rhyme (Back Again)", the cheating tale "Skanless" and the drunkard's anthem "Jay Fay Dray". Still, Tila's embrace of harmless pleasures and unintimidating music couldn't match the sheer force of neighbours **N.W.A.** and Ice-T, and King Tee was relegated to the background. *Tha Triflin' Album* (1993) found the St. Ides pitch man cold rockin' the party with gratuitous shout-outs to his favourite brand of malt liquor, and introducing his protégés **Tha Alkaholiks** on the great "Got It Bad Y'All". The album also found Tee embracing LA's ruling "Funkadelicised" sound, finally matching his mic skills to state-of-the-art production.

Mr.Hood Mr.Hood Mr.Hood Mr.Hood Mr.Hood

*IV Life* (1994) sounded hung over, after the party antics of *Tha Triflin' Album*. "Dippin'" was all bloodshot and queasy, but the great "Super Nigga" updated the old Richard Pryor comedy routine for Compton "set-trippers". *Thy Kingdom Come* (1999) came and went with little fanfare; unfortunately the lack of response was justified. While not releasing an album since, Tila has been anything but silent, popping up on tracks with Cypress Hill, Dr. Dre, Xzibit, Tha Liks, Frost and Masta Ace.

**◉ Ruff Rhymes**
Capitol, 1998

This retrospective takes most of the best tracks from his first three albums (although the inclusion of "Diss You" is unconscionable) and should go some way towards rescuing the reputation of one the West Coast's forgotten pioneers.

# KMD

Originally given a leg-up by 3rd Bass, **KMD** were like an Islamic De La Soul. Screwing around with narrative, following a logic all their own, toying with the received art of making records, KMD delivered black pride lessons with a wit and originality rare in hip-hop, or indeed any other form of popular music.

**Zev Love X** made his debut on 3rd Bass's Beastie Boys diss "Gas Face" (1990), but it was KMD's debut album *Mr Hood* (1991) that marked him out as one of hip-hop's great maverick talents. With his brother **Subroc** and childhood friend **Onyx**, Zev created a Five Percent Nation version of *Sesame Street* on the album. Détourning snippets from a found language instruction record, *Mr Hood* found KMD taking the uptight (white) title character on a tour through the ghetto, interrogating black stereotypes along the way. It was far from preachy or teachy, however, as the language was anything

but direct, the metaphors skewed and the beats mellow but trippy, like a Monet

Zev Love X, in his rather scary King Geedorah guise.

painting of the corner of 125th and Lexington.

KMD tried to continue what one of their tracks called the "humrush" on their second album, *Black Bastards* (2000), which was originally scheduled to be released in 1994. During the making of the album, Subroc was hit by a car and killed. When the album was finally completed, Elektra refused to release it because of the album's controversial cover art (a cartoon of Little Black Sambo in the gallows). Although the album had been bootlegged numerous times, and bits and pieces had emerged on Fondle 'Em, when the full album was released it proved to be another masterpiece. On "It Sounded Like a Roc", Subroc poignantly said, "If I be a ghost, expect me to haunt". The rest of the record relied on snippets of some **Last Poets** albums for its emotional and intellectual weight, creating a heavier, less quirky atmosphere than *Mr Hood*.

On "Gas Drawls" (1997) Zev mutated into **MF Doom**, a comic book persona based on the metal-faced villain from *Fantastic Four*. His *Operation Doomsday* (1999) followed the KMD tradition, by twisting comic-book records and 1980s r&b such as **Atlantic Starr** and the **SOS Band** into a disorientating aural haze, creating a sci-fi hallucination set in East Harlem, but without all of the lame futuristic trappings. Doom's lyrical flow was about as graceful as his steel mask, but it was effective – like he was freestyling to passing car radios. *Operation Doomsday* evoked loss and, well, doom better than any hip-hop in years: as he rhymed on "Rhymes Like Dimes", "Only in America could you find a way to earn a healthy buck/And still keep your attitude on self-destruct".

With all of his comic-book personas that he proceeded to adopt on his recordings Zev became a one-man **Justice League Of America**. There was the scientist **Viktor Vaughn**, Japanese movie monster **King Geedorah**, and the composer **Metal Fingers** (who has released a series of instrumental albums, *Special Herbs & Spices*). Viktor Vaughn's *Vaudeville Villain* (2003) was a putative concept album about a time traveller being stuck in the 1990s, having to defeat MCs at open-mic nights, and having his **Donkey Kong** game stolen. King Geedorah's *Take Me to Your Leader* (2003) was basically Doom and friends rapping over the top of Japanese horror movie soundtracks, with a dystopian sci-fi concept just about keeping it all together.

Madvillain was a collaboration between Doom and Madlib, and their *Madvillainy* (2004) was perhaps his best album yet. Madlib's creaky, but relatively straightforward, jazz production kept Doom's feet on planet earth, reining in his worst instincts, but not his gift for bizarre non sequiturs and non-human syntax: "Hey bro, Day Glo, set the bet, pay dough/ Before the cheddar get away, you best to get Maaco". Say what?!

### KMD

🅟 **Mr Hood**
Elektra, 1991

Like De La Soul without the hooks, this was one of the most challenging and rewarding albums of hip-hop's avant-garde golden age.

### MADVILLAIN

🅟 **Madvillainy**
Stones Throw, 2004

This Frankenstein's monster combining two of the biggest names in the hip-hop underground was one of the genre's most unlikely success stories.

# Kool DJ Herc

The center of hip-hop's prevailing creation myth, Kool DJ Herc is credited as the first DJ to isolate the breakbeat, the DNA of hip-hop music, as well as being the originator of the phrase "b-boying". The former Clive Campbell was born in Jamaica and moved to the US in 1967. His family settled in the Bronx and

Campbell started running with a graffiti crew called the **Ex-Vandals**, taking the name Kool Herc. In the early 1970s the gangs were running the Bronx and making the clubs intolerable with their menacing presence. Disco was also starting to coalesce around this time, which meant that the uptown DJs were catering to an older crowd, and were no longer playing the hard funk records that Herc and his friends loved. In response, Herc rented the community centre in his building at 1520 Sedgwick Avenue and started throwing parties. Using a guitar amp and **two turntables** as his soundsystem, Herc played records like **Jimmy Castor Bunch**'s "It's Just Begun", **James Brown**'s "Give it Up or Turnit a Loose", Aretha Franklin's "Rock Steady" and **Booker T & the MG's**' "Melting Pot".

The parties were so successful that Herc soon moved to a club called the Hevalo, improved his soundsystem to replicate the ones that he had seen on the lawns in Jamaica and got **Coke La Rock** to work the microphone. Soon Herc's posse grew in number and became known as the Herculords: **DJ Clark Kent** and breakdancers the Nigger Twins. Herc's reputation throughout the borough, and his parties at the PAL on 183rd Street and the Executive Playhouse, would attract hundreds of people. Herc's most adoring legion of fans were the breakdancers, or "b-boys" as Herc called them, who went berserk to the music he played.

Herc focused on the "break" – the short section where all the instrumentalists dropped out except for the percussionists. The break was the part of the record that the dancers wanted to hear anyway, so he isolated it by playing two copies of the same record on two turntables – when the break on one turntable finished, he would play it on the other turntable.

Herc's breakbeat style of DJing was in such demand that other DJs like **Grandmaster Flash**, **Afrika Bambaataa** and **Grand Wizard Theodore** emerged, playing a similar style of music, but with greater skill and more technological sophistication. Herc was quickly consigned to the dustbin of history, but hip-hop's dumpster-diving aesthetic has meant that Herc has never been forgotten, even if the only record he's ever appeared on was **Terminator X & the Godfathers of Threatt**'s *Super Bad* album (1994).

# Kool G Rap & DJ Polo

With an awesome, multi-syllabic, intensely rhythmic flow, Kool G Rap's mic skills were on a par with **Kane** and **Rakim**, and the darkside tales he rapped helped usher in hip-hop's hardcore age. **DJ Polo** could scratch with fury when called upon, but even from early on it was clear who was just along for the ride in this duo.

The Queens duo debuted on the first track to sample James Brown's "Funky Drummer", "It's A Demo" (1986). Featuring "It's a Demo", the ferocious battle rhymes of "Poison" and the prototypical "criminology" rap "Road to the Riches", the duo's first album, *Road To The Riches* (1988), was one of the best of that landmark year, even if it sampled **Gary Numan**'s "Cars".

*Wanted: Dead or Alive* (1990), meanwhile, included such vivid narratives as "Streets of New York", "Money in the Bank" and "Rikers Island", and "Talk Like Sex", a song so raunchy Larry Flynt would probably balk at publishing the lyrics. Kool G Rap was at his best, however, on "Kool Is Back", a lightspeed display of skills that shows off his superhuman breath control. The Kool Genius was less convincing on "Erase Racism", where he sounded truly out of his element rapping about social issues with **Big Daddy Kane** and **Biz Markie**.

*Live And Let Live* (1992), with the title track, "On The Run" and "Ill Street Blues", completed a staggering triptych of albums that revelled in the dark demi-monde of New York. The album was supposed to be co-released with Warner Bros., but the cover art – Rap and Polo feeding raw meat to a pack of dogs with two white men hanging from the ceiling in the background – had the major label running scared amidst the hysterical anti-rap furore generated by Ice-T's contemporaneous song "Cop Killer". The pressure was too great for the duo, which broke up shortly after the album was released (by Cold Chillin' on its own).

While Polo went to record such "classics" as "Freak Of The Week" (1996) with **Ron Jeremy**, Kool G Rap went on to release a couple of mediocre albums – *4, 5, 6* (1995) and *Roots Of Evil* (1998). Just as he was on the verge of falling off the edge of the rap universe, a string of collaborations with **MOP**, Nas, **Mobb Deep**, Talib Keli and **Big L** rescued his reputation. *The Giancana Story* (2002) was a much delayed return to form, largely because the hip-hop mainstream had finally caught up with him and his tales from the dark side, rather than any growth of his own. It wasn't up there with his trio of classics with DJ Polo, but it was better than anyone expected from a guy who should be boring youngsters with old war stories.

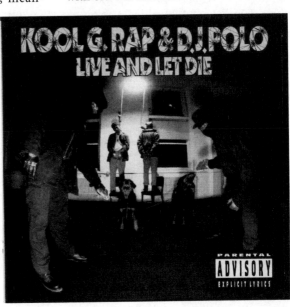

⊙ **The Best Of Cold Chillin'**
Landspeed, 2000

An absolute classic. The album moves more or less chronologically from their relatively conventional first single, "It's a Demo/I'm Fly", to the crime narratives that made the Kool Genius of Rap one of the ten greatest MCs in hip-hop. Unfortunately, it doesn't include the mind-boggling "Kool Is Back", but the rest represents the pinnacle of New York hip-hop and created the blueprint for Nas, Biggie and everyone who followed in their path.

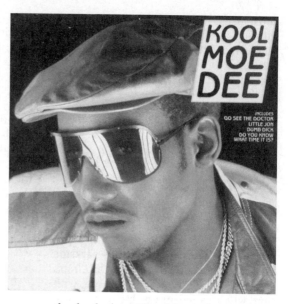

# Kool Moe Dee/ Treacherous Three

Along with Spoonie Gee, **Kool Moe Dee** (aka **Mohandas Dewese**) was the only member of the original old school to graduate into the new school. As part of **Treacherous Three** with **Special K** and **LA Sunshine**, he helped move hip-hop from the confines of the New York City Parks Commission into uptown and Bronx clubs such as Disco Fever and T-Connection. With their matching red silks and upturned collars, the Treacherous Three were the old school's sophisticates, a position they reinforced by teaming up with hip-hop's original loverman, Spoonie Gee, for their debut record. "The New Rap Language" (1980) was the flip of Spoonie's "Love Rap" and, against a beat courtesy of **Pumpkin** and **Pooche Costello**, it introduced freestyling to wax and introduced the world below 125th Street and west of the Hudson River to Kool Moe Dee's rapid-fire rhyming style.

"At The Party" (1980) rocked a synth beat that imitated the kazoo beat Grandmaster Flash had lifted from **Freedom**'s "Get Up and Dance", while Kool Moe Dee ordered everyone up by shouting out the zodiac signs just like Rahiem and Melle Mel. "Body Rock" (1980) had boasts like, "I got more rhymes than Mother Goose" and a chorus that went "Rock the body-body/Rock the body-body/Rock

the body-body/Rock" — shame about the sub-**Eddie Van Halen** guitar line and lumbering bassline. The group's biggest record, though, was "Feel The Heartbeat" (1981) which used New York's second favourite beat of all time, **Taana Gardner**'s "Heartbeat". Treacherous Three's earlier records had suffered from awkward production, but here they had music that was sleek enough to accomodate their sophisticated rhymes and vocal interplay. A true classic.

After the seriously lame "Put the Boogie in Your Body" (1981), the group moved from Enjoy to Sugar Hill. Their first Sugar Hill single, "Yes We Can-Can" (1982), was a cover of Allen Toussaint's New Orleans classic and featured a vocodered intro presaging socially conscious rhymes that "Hit your head and made your body rock". But, as Sugar Hill was eclipsed by Def Jam and Profile, the Treacherous Three's fortunes went similarly south after "Action" (1983).

In 1986 Kool Moe Dee went solo with the "skeezer"-hating (disguised as an STD awareness track) "Go See the Doctor" and an eponymous debut album produced by **Teddy Riley**. With the title track of his next album, *How Ya Like Me Now* (1987), he achieved considerable notoriety by dissing **LL Cool J**, whom he accused of biting his style. On top of Riley's cutting-edge production, Moe Dee also bragged about his elder statesman status on "Way Way Back" and gave **Will Smith** an idea or two on "Wild Wild West". Cool J responded with "Jack the Ripper" and Moe Dee followed suit with "Let's Go", claiming that "LL" "stood for lousy lover". The best moments of *Knowledge Is King* (1989), however, had Moe Dee espousing black pride rhetoric ("Pump Your Fist") and claiming that he was anything but a lousy lover ("I Go To Work"). With Riley, Moe Dee had gone platinum, but when Riley left, Moe Dee lost the commercial and creative battle to LL. "Death Blow", from his 1991 album *Funke Funke Wisdom*, didn't live up to its title, and Moe Dee had long since faded into the background by the time of *Interlude* (1994). A reunion with the Treacherous Three, *Old School Flava* (1994), didn't help matters any.

**Knowledge Is King**
Jive, 1989

With producer Teddy Riley at the height of his powers, it almost didn't matter what Moe Dee said, but he managed to keep pace with the beats.

# Kris Kross

To the chagrin of hardcore hip-hop heads everywhere, 12-year-olds Chris "**Daddy Mack**" Smith and Chris "**Mack Daddy**" Kelly were discovered in an Atlanta shopping mall in 1991 by aspiring impresario **Jermaine Dupri**, himself only 19 at the time, who was out shopping for shoes. Dupri took the duo under his wing, styled them in backwards clothing and shaved patterned eyebrows, hand-tooled a couple of undeniably catchy kiddie-rap anthems and got them signed rather bizarrely to the throughly credible and fairly hardcore **Ruffhouse** label.

Their first single, "Jump" (1992), rode a chunky sample of **The Jackson 5**'s "I Want You Back" to become one of the best-selling singles of all time. Establishing what would become Dupri's signature style, the record used obvious, readymade hooks and borrowed liberally from styles that were hot at the time (the "Miggedy-

miggedy-mack" schtick was straight from **Das EFX**). *Totally Krossed Out* (1992) contained the less convincing but similarly styled "Warm It Up", the schoolboy antics of "I Missed The Bus" and ridiculous disses of playground foes **Another Bad Creation**.

On their next album, *Da Bomb* (1993), it wasn't a bomb that dropped but their balls. No longer the cute and huggable teddy bears they were on their first album, they inevitably succumbed to the disease that plagues all teenie-boppers – they wanted to be taken seriously. On *Da Bomb* they say "nigga" a few times, sample **Dr. Dre**'s *The Chronic* and even wore their clothes the right way around. Somehow, they managed another gold single with "Alright" which featured some dancehall rhymes from **Supercat** and a really obvious sample of **Slave**'s "Just a Touch of Love".

They tried to go all the way hard on *Young, Rich and Dangerous* (1996), with very mixed results. Somehow, the album's love jam, "Tonite's the Nite" (with **Trey Lorenz** on backing vocals), went gold yet again and just missed the American top ten. Some pact with the devil must have allowed them to get **Aaliyah** on board for the almost listenable "Live And Die For Hip Hop", but the deal must have expired, because they haven't been heard from since.

**Totally Krossed Out**
Ruffhouse, 1992

It was pretty awful at the time, but "Jump" wasn't really any worse than Sir Mix-a-Lot's equally big and equally preposterous hit, "Baby Got Back". This is pretty exemplary kiddie-rap, but you'd still be better off buying any one of the thousands of comps that has "Jump" on it.

# K-Solo

K-Solo (**Kevin Madison**) is Redman's cousin and got his start as a member of EPMD's Hit Squad. He was featured on "Knick Knack Patty Wack" from EPMD's *Unfinished Business* (1989), and debuted his signature gimmick: he "S-P-E-L-L[s] very W-E-L-L". As well as making like an elementary school teacher, K-Solo also dropped science about his name, which stood for "Kevin Self, Organization Left Others".

As his name suggested, K-Solo struck out on his own soon afterwards, with *Tell The World My Name* (1990). The album featured a moderate hit in "Your Mom's In My Business", which had decent rhymes like "But it's your wife mister, she don't think that I'm charming/She thinks she's Mr Whippit and she thinks I'll squeeze her Charmin", the excellent "Tales From The Crack Side" and its meta-rap ("I wrote a rhyme it was funky/I broke in a race/'Cause the rhyme that I wrote, tried to run off my page") and the impressive "Real Solo Please Stand Up". However, K's workmanlike raps made more impact than his moments of inspiration.

K-Solo's inelastic style also undermined *Time's Up* (1992). Songs like "Who's Killing Who?", a plea to stop black-on-black violence, and the self-explanatory "Premonition Of A Black Prisoner" were laudable efforts that tried to expand K's parameters, but he presented them with no élan or verve. "Letterman", on which he resurrected his spelling-bee shtick, wasn't a lot better.

A bid in jail prematurely curtailed his career, but he re-emerged in 1997 on "It's Like That (My Big Brother)" from **Redman**'s *Muddy Waters* album. He had also hooked up with **Death Row** records, and was scheduled to release an album, but the label's legal troubles meant that the album was shelved indefinitely. K-Solo was next heard from when he unleashed lyrical blows on **DMX** on a number of mixtapes in the late 1990s and early 2000s. He accused the Dark Man of stealing his spelling style while they were both in prison together. DMX largely bowed out of the battle and Solo faded into obscurity once again. He had recorded an album tentatively titled *There Will Be Hell to Pay*, but it has yet to see the light of day. Solo appeared on **PMD**'s *The Awakening* (2003) on "Back to Work", trading verses with Parrish and Fat Joe, and also on an underground single by **Earatik Statik** called "Illstatik" (2004).

**Tell The World My Name**
Atlantic, 1990

When he wasn't wasting time spelling words that slow four-year-olds could spell, K-Solo was a very competent, if a bit leaden, MC with a decent narrative eye and ear. These are to the fore on his best records (both included here), "Your Mom's In My Business" and "Tales From The Crack Side".

# Kwamé

When was the last time you saw a rapper wearing polka dots? While you could get away with that sort of stuff in the late 1980s/early 1990s, never has an MC's choice of dress so affected his career as that of East Elmhurst, Queensbridge's **Kwamé Holland**. Perhaps his dress sense had something to do with growing up around New York's bohemian jazz scene – Kwamé was, according to legend, given his first set of drums by **Lionel Hampton**.

Although a lot of attention was lavished on his brightly coloured polka-dot shirts and geometrically challenged hi-top fade haircut, Kwamé was a fine rapper in the **Big Daddy Kane/Slick Rick/Dana Dane** mould. His mic skills, as well as a personality as colourful as his shirts, were amply demonstrated on his debut album *Kwamé the Boy Genius: Featuring A New Beginning* (1989). **The New Beginning** was Kwamé's live band who fleshed out the sample-based grooves from producer Hurby "Luv Bug" Azor. Although "Sweet Thing" was the album's first single, the best track was the very Slick Rick-styled "The Man We All Know and Love", which stole moves from **Louis Jordan** and Minnie Ripperton. Even though Kwamé was lumped in with the positivity and goofiness of the Native Tongues and their ilk, he often "held the mic with an Uzi grip".

*A Day in the Life: A Pokadelic Adventure* (1990) was a concept album about high school. It was an OK album, but it was restrained by the somewhat stupid concept, and by production that owed a bit too much to **Soul II Soul**, particularly on tracks like "Ownlee Eue". By the time of *Nastee* (1991) Kwamé's eccentric persona was already passé and he tried to compensate by getting harder and hornier. Needless to say, it didn't work. For *Incognito* (1994), Kwamé had traded in his polka dots for a leather jacket and black Tims, but the damage had already been done. Earlier that year, **Notorious BIG**'s "Unbelievable" had dropped and the line "Your style is played out like Kwamé, and those fuckin' polka dots" had killed his career in one fell swoop.

Nevertheless, Kwamé's name popped up every so often in album credits for **LL Cool J** and **Mary J Blige** (perhaps because a young P Diddy danced in one of his videos). Ten years after Biggie's insult, Kwamé got the last laugh – he was the producer of **Lloyd Banks**' monster hit "Fire".

Fortified Live featuring Mos Def & Mr. Man b/w 2000 Seasons

**Kwamé the Boy Genius: Featuring A New Beginning**
Atlantic, 1989

Yes he quotes Louis Jordan and *Sesame Street*, but it's not all sweetness and light. "Pushthepanicbutton!!!" was a pretty hot track in the vein of Big Daddy Kane's "Raw", and the Meters sample on "Boy Genius" lent funky gravitas to Kwamé's exemplary middle school battle rap.

# Talib Kweli

Talib Kweli was born Talib Greene in 1975 in Flatbush, Brooklyn. His mic name is a fusion of Arabic and Swahili meaning "seeker of truth". As his name indicates, Kweli is an "intelligent" rapper beloved of "backpackers" and critics, but Kweli is more than merely an MC who uses multisyllabic words swathed in a jazzy bohemianism. While Kweli imparts plenty of lessons and delivers a lecture or two, he tempers his teaching and eccentricity with straight-up battle raps.

Kweli debuted on "Hustle On The Side" (1995) by **Mood**, a fairly outré group from Cincinnati, Ohio, whose DJ and producer was **Hi-Tek** (Tony Cottrell). Kweli also appeared on **Sunz of Man**'s *Doom* (1997) album. Kweli and Hi-Tek then formed a partnership and called their duo **Reflection Eternal**. Their "Fortified Live" (1997), also featuring Mos Def and Mr Man, was pretty

conventional on the surface, but it was still far out enough for Mos Def to utter lines like "Sipping wishing-well water imported from Pluto", on top of icicle-like pianos and ultra-processed guitar.

Mos Def and Kweli teamed up for *Black Star* (1998), which quickly became one of the most celebrated albums of hip-hop's alternative strain. While staying true to the eternal verities of hip-hop, *Black Star* skewered the myth of "keeping it real" ("He was out chasing cream and the American Dream/Trying to pretend that the end justifies the means") and savage "Hater Players" ("You should retire, get that complimentary watch, be out"). More importantly, as their name implied, *Black Star* gave hip-hop some of roots reggae's liberation morality and some of dancehall reggae's guitar licks. The bass sounds – dyspeptic rumbles, snapping elastic thwacks, busted woofer flatulence – would have satisfied Jamaica's low-end theorists, while **Shawn J. Period**'s toy Casio keyboards sent the UK's beatmaking 1970s kitsch aficionados back to the schoolyard where they belonged.

On **Reflection Eternal**'s "The Express" (2000), Talib Kweli didn't just spit, he hocked loogies on frontin' MCs. Helping him do this was a beat from Hi-Tek that sounded like, well, a hocked loogie. The fazed and faded guitar flourishes, or synth washes, or whatever they were, were thick and mucoid, while the dragging beat sounded like the echoes in your throat when you cough up some snot. The flip, "Some Kind Of Wonderful", referenced neither the **Soul Brothers Six** nor **Grand Funk**. Instead, Kweli caused "collisions on the highway of information" and dropped some battle rhymes over a beat that was like a NY version of the **Goodie Mob**'s "Cell Therapy" cyber-work-gang rhythm.

With cameos from **Xzibit** and **Rah Digga** and quasi-jiggy production reminiscent of Q-Tip's *Amplified* album, Reflection Eternal's *Train of Thought* (2000) seemed at first to be little more than a cynical attempt to capitalise on Rawkus's recent commercial successes. However, Hi-Tek's ingenuity and sheer sense of musicality – deracinated reggae ("Soul Rebels" with **De La Soul**), fractured Sade ("Love Language"), hip-hop John Sousa ("Move Somethin") and "*Alfred Hitchcock Presents* meets The Meters" stabs ("Down For The Count") – made pop semi-crossover seem like the perfect compromise.

There was more mainstream baiting on *Quality* (2002), with beats from **Kanye West** and DJ Quik and appearances from Bilal, Pharoahe Monch and The Roots' Black Thought. While the music was exceedingly well-produced – warm and motivational in the right places – the album never generated any heat. It was merely likeable, even if there were occasional couplets such as "The President is Bush, the Vice President's a Dick/So a whole lot of fuckin' is what we gonna get".

Kweli's *The Beautiful Struggle* (2004) was delayed for several months after the album was leaked on the Internet. He addressed the situation on a mixtape, *The Beautiful Mix* (2004), which featured a harder side of Kweli than seen on his albums.

**Train of Thought**
Rawkus, 2000

There are times when they get too heavy-handed and when your attention will wander, but Hi-Tek's production is uniformly superb and Kweli's raps manage to stay on the right side of boho self-righteousness and experimentation.

# Labtekwon

L abtekwon is an MC from Baltimore who used to breakdance with the actress **Jada Pinkett** in high school. His flirtation with stardom ended there. Although he has released something like twelve albums on his own Ankh Ba label since 1993, his prodigious output is known only to a select few underground cognoscenti. Unlike most hip-hoppers who have their own label, though, Labtek hasn't just been wasting away in indie land holding out for a real record deal to come along. Instead, he's been content to issue his mumblings and musings from the margins, with all the independence and consistency of vision that implies.

Labtekwon's style is an uncompromising blend of strict Five Percent teachings (laced with plenty of post-**Sun Ra** Egyptology and outer space hoodoo), and an ascetic's version of **A Tribe Called Quest**'s jazzyness. Those under the spell of the mainstream's gaudy baubles may

say that he lacks craft and hooks and production values. While it's hard to argue with the last two, his singular, defiantly minimalist sense of purpose (seemingly untreated drum loops that don't snap or boom-bap, but kind of itch and scratch from the edges of the soundfield) was fairly compelling, even if there was no discernible growth from the early tracks, such as 1993's "CSD", to 2002's *Hustlaz Guide To The Universe* (2002). As for the craft, there were the battle rhymes of "King Of Kings" from *Nile Child* (1998) where the parameters of his usual flow, reminiscent of **Lyrics Born**, expand, with more personality than thirty MCs put together.

**Song Of The Sovereign**
Mush, 2001

This career retrospective is the easiest of Labtekwon's numerous releases to find and also the best introduction to his work. The unadorned beats and his ambiguous relationship with pleasure can be wearying, but his intelligence and commitment do shine through.

219

# Mike Ladd

Avant MC Mike Ladd has been mixing things up since he discovered hip-hop, dancehall and the Bad Brains at roughly the same time while growing up in Cambridge, Massachusetts. At the same time as he was rhyming and breakdancing, Ladd played drums for a punk rock band called **Uncle Fester**. Influenced by Divine Styler and the poetry of the Black Arts Movement, Ladd moved to the Bronx, started writing poetry with people like Tony Medina and won the Nuyorican Poets Café Slam in 1996. After purchasing some basic equipment, he made his first record, the lo-fi *Easy Listening 4 Armageddon* (1997).

*Live From Paris (The Iran-Contra Scandal Memorial Album)* (1999) was indeed a live album, but unlike the ego-stroking triple albums from the prog rock era, this was a compact, politically charged record. The music – bass-heavy, filled with space-age samples and tape loops – was as original and committed as Ladd's words. *Welcome*

*To The Afterfuture* (2000) followed, in similar, but studio-based, style. Ladd's sonic environment was a compressed, claustrophobic, dysfunctional world not dissimilar to that of compatriots **Company Flow**: synthethiser brutalism, dizzy drum 'n' bass rhythms, ornery horn fanfares, **Eddie Hazel** guitars, loops that funked like Lurch from the *Addams Family*, and thick keyboard jalopies.

If Rammellzee had ever shot a blaxploitation flick, it might have felt like Ladd's album *Gun Hill Road* (2000), which was a collaborative effort with Saul Williams, Antipop Consortium, Rob Smith from Sonic Sum and others, under the name **The Infesticons**. A satirical concept album about commercial versus underground hip-hop, it was an epic in the grand style with a sci-fi plot: an army of robots (The Majesticons) created by the evil scientist **Poof Na Na** attempt to "jiggify" the universe, only to meet resistance in the form of the Infesticons. But it was influenced by P-Funk, and, as heroic epics go, it was pretty discursive and non-linear – less *The Iliad* than a series of doodles in its margins: "beats talk like Nick Cave, but they don't get you laid", or "Like Rin Tin Tin was German/Like Mengele was killing kin/Like PM Dawn in sequined thongs/Like singing songs by Celine Dion".

After releasing the *Vernacular Homicide* EP (2001), Ladd returned to his *Gun Hill Road* narrative, this time letting The Majesticons have their say on *Beauty Party*

Mike (foreground) at Infesticons photo shoot.

Mike Ladd, in pinstripes, flossing - satirically of course - with his (anti-) jiggy crew, The Majesticons.

(2003). In many ways this was hip-hop's version of **Funkadelic**'s savage *America Eats Its Young*, but with its bad acid bitterness and lack of energy replaced by a righteousness tempered by an infectious *esprit de corps* and a sly wink. Ladd's musical imitations of commercial hip-hop were perhaps not quite as dead-on as they needed to be, but it was wonderful satire nevertheless: "Alan Greenspan get your hands up/Billy Gates, get your hands up/Malcolm Forbes, get our hands up", and "I used to read *The Nation* till I changed my mind/I used to study Marx, now I'm studying wine/As the times get worse, the worst go blind".

**Gun Hill Road**
Big Dada, 2000

Ladd's Clintonian epic is not only an attack on Cream Puff and his ilk, but an attack on contemporary culture's obsession with beauty, shiny things and glamour: it's a plea for dirt and impurity. In the putative battle between "jiggy" and left-field hip-hop – Majesticons versus Infesticons – you know who's going to win, but the pleasure is in the way the ritual slaughter is played out. There are splashes of Bollywood strings, suitably heroic beats and even a shout-out to J Mascis (of indie rock band Dinosaur Jr.): "I like rhymin' like Mascis/My beats are like molasses/Sweet and slow like Jackie Onassis/With Alzheimer's/Social climbers slip on my diarrhoea/MCs sound the same like onomatopeia".

# Lady of Rage

R obin Allen left her Farmville, Virginia home at age 17 for New York with dreams of making it as a singer. She took the name of Lady of Rage and soon hooked up with the **LA Posse** (Big Dad, Muffla, Big Ill the Mack, Breeze, DBL and Malika) and recorded a couple of tracks on their *They Come In All Colors* (1991) album. Her appearances got her noticed by **Dr. Dre**, who used her on several tracks on *The Chronic*, most notably on "Lyrical Gangbang" and "Stranded On Death Row". Her lyrics weren't great, but she had an impressive, aggressive flow and fitted in perfectly with the vibe of the album.

"Afro Puffs" (1994), from the *Above The Rim* soundtrack, was her solo debut, and it displayed her war-chant rapping perfectly. Against the backdrop of one of Dr. Dre's best productions – ominous bass gurgles and a piano sample, what sounded like a grandfather clock going berserk, P-Funk synth squiggles, and Snoop Doggy Dog on the hook – Lady of Rage spat lines like "I flow like a monthly, you can't cramp my style/For those that try to punk me here's a Pamprin, child".

"Afro Puffs" was a moderate hit, but neither an album nor a single followed until 1997, largely because of Dre's conflicts with the label's top brass. In the meantime, she dropped rhymes for **Buckshot LeFonque** and Tha Dogg Pund. The original tracks that she made with Dr. Dre for *Necessary Roughness* (1997) were eventually scrapped after Dre left the label, and the album that was finally released was produced by **DJ Premier**, Dat Nigga Daz and Kenny Parker among others. None of them, however, managed to come up with a sound that suited her as well as Dr. Dre and the fairly generic album was largely passed by.

Premo took a shine to her rhyming, and featured her on the "You Know My Steez" (1999) remix. Premier then produced the fantastic "Unfucwitable" (2002) for her. The contrast between its sped-up, childlike vocal riff and Lady of Rage's fearsome battle raps was startling, and proved that she was a commanding mic presence if given the right beat to bless.

**Necessary Roughness**
Death Row, 1997

Lady of Rage has impressed two of hip-hop's greatest producers – Dre and Premier – but she has never made an album befitting of her skills. There are some good moments on this, most notably "Some Shit" and "Microphone Pon Cok" which were both produced by Premier. Still, you're better off finding her two utterly superb singles, "Afro Puffs" and "Unfucwitable".

# Leaders Of The New School

N ow remembered only because the group introduced **Busta Rhymes**, Leaders of the New School burst onto the hip-hop scene in 1991 with all the infectious energy of **Our Gang** and the mischievousness of **The Boondocks** (without the politics). Charlie Brown, Dinco D, Cut Monitor Milo and Busta Rhymes hailed from Uniondale, Long Island, and their music was characterized by the same suburban lightheartedness that initially distinguished neighbours **De La Soul**. LONS' debut album, *A Future Without A Past* (1991), took the terminology of old school and new school quite literally, and the record was divided into "Homeroom", "Lunchroom" and "Afterschool" sessions (you could get away with stuff like that back then). Despite this, lifting routines from the **Cold Crush Brothers** and rhymes like, "Causing aggravation, I'll never pause/ Pushing out spit balls with plastic straws", *A Future Without a Past* managed to make such schoolboy antics very agreeable, due largely to production by the Bomb Squad's Eric Sadler and an irrepressible group energy on tracks like "Case of the PTA" and "International Zone Coaster".

"Case of the PTA" was a minor hit, but it was a show-stealing cameo on **A Tribe Called Quest**'s "Scenario" that made Busta a star. His lion roar soon popped up on tracks by everyone, and the Leaders' second album, *T.I.M.E. The Inner Mind's Eye* (1993), suffered from both group dissension and the changing times. The playfulness that made the first album such a joy was largely gone and replaced by some kind of murky cosmic hoo-ha. The group disbanded later that year, minutes before a scheduled TV appearance.

While Busta was busy becoming one of hip-hop's most iconic presences, the remaining Leaders of the New School, who hadn't been heard of since the group broke up, attempted a comeback with *That's How Life B* (1999), but sadly they remained unheard by just about everyone.

⊙ **A Future Without A Past**
Elektra, 1991

Reversing the two nouns in the album's title would, sadly, give you an accurate summing-up of LONS' career but, while they lasted, LONS offered a charming mix of Afrocentric positivity and schoolboy pranks.

# Lil' Flip

Lil' Flip, a laconic but charismatic rapper from Houston's Clover Land projects, first came up with his **Hustlers Stackin' Ends** crew freestyling on DJ Screw tapes in the late 1990s. Flip claims that Screw dubbed him the "Freestyle King" before he died in 2000. On his debut double album (the second disc, like all of his albums, was "screwed and chopped", on which the tracks were slowed down and messed around with, in order to make it the perfect soundtrack to the South's favourite pastime – "sippin' syrup"), *Leprechaun* (2000), Flip audaciously claimed the title if anyone had doubted it with his acceptance speech on the first track, "Freestyle King". The album cover was designed like a box of **Lucky Charms** cereal, but it got most attention for "I Can Do Dat", a single with the catchphrase repeated after every line that teetered perilously on the fine line dividing irresistibility and sheer annoyance with lyrics like "If you see it, you want it/Buy it, own it/Drive it, flaunt it/Factory chrome it" and interpolations of synth lines playing Ravel's *Bolero*.

*Undaground Legend* (2002) was another double-disc set and featured another monster single in "The Way We Ball" which had a little boy drawling "And we like to floss, all my diamonds gloss". But it was Flip's

humour and mesmerizing arrogance that made the record: "I'm still independent cause Jive couldn't afford me/The meetings were boring, for real I was snoring/The VP was fine, yeah she made me kinda horny/But that's another story". Lil' Flip's best so far, though, may have been his appearance on **David Banner**'s "Like A Pimp" (2003). On top of a bassline that made you shudder, and cowbells that brought out your inner b-boy, Flip rhymed "They like the way me and Banner pimp/You can catch us at Pappa Deaux's eatin' steak and shrimp".

*U Gotta Feel Me* (2004) was his mainstream moment. The lead single, "Game Over", was built on some Pac-Man noises, hand claps, a bass belch and understated percussion, with the catchphrase ("Flip") chanted over and over again. Elements from Kingston's dancehalls ("Check (Let's Ride)") crept into the mix, as did some "crunkdafied" Tennessee funk from **Three 6 Mafia**'s DJ Paul and Juicy J ("Represent").

⊙ **U Gotta Feel Me**
Sony, 2004

Perhaps the hip-hop sensation of the year, Flip's pre-eminence even made the *New York Times* take notice of the Dirty South style of "codeine rap" and preoccupation with "sippin' syrup" – perhaps the ultimate symbol of the Dirty South turning the tables on the Big Apple. At 87 mintues and two discs, it's way too long and there are a lot of duff tracks, but when Flip hits on a good hook he'll never let you forget it.

# Lil Jon

If you need a club to get rowdier than an Onyx video, you've got two options. If you're in New York you've got **MOP**, but if you're below the Mason-Dixon Line, the only choice is Atlanta's **Lil Jon**. The patron saint of "crunk", Lil Jon makes more out of limited sonic materials than anyone this side of Steve Reich. A Lil Jon track is rarely more than ribcage-rattling bass tones, a few synth peals and a couple of guys shouting, but nothing gets a club as amped.

Jonathan Smith was raised in stalwartly middle-class southwest Atlanta, the son of an aerospace engineer and hospital supervisor. Naming himself according

Lil Jon crunks up the volume.

to his diminutive stature, Lil Jon began DJing in high school, garnered a reputation in Atlanta for spinning hip-hop and dancehall, and landed a gig at the Phoenix nightclub. The Phoenix happened to be **Jermaine Dupri**'s favourite haunt and, when he noticed the crowd's response to Lil Jon, he offered the DJ a job at his **So So Def** label. Lil Jon quickly rose through the ranks of the organization and became the label's A&R VP.

One night, Jon and his crew went to a nightclub, and when the DJ played a track by Eightball and MJG, they all went wild, chanting "Who you wit muthafucka? Who you wit?" over the top. When the rest of the club started chanting along with them, the phenomenon of "crunk" was born. Lil Jon went to the studio with the **East Side Boyz** (Big Sam and Lil Bo) and recorded "Who You Wit?" (1996), which became a big regional hit. The record is one of the most remarkable in all of hip-hop. Strangely reminiscent of work-gang chants, "Who You Wit?" is nothing but some sub-bass, skipping cymbals, handclaps and the guys shouting over the top – literally nothing else. As well as recalling slaves working in the cotton fields, the track reached back to

the early days of New York, specifically the extremely minimal records of early Def Jam, such as T La Rock's "It's Yours" – no wonder Rick Rubin was a fan. The single anchored the album *Get Crunk – Who U Wit: Da Album* (1997).

With the profits, Lil Jon formed **Black Market Entertainment** with Dwayne Searcy. As well as producing The LG's (Lyrical Giants), Lil Jon and Black Market released *We Still Crunk!!* (2000). It was the follow-up, *Put Yo Hood Up* (2001), however, that put Lil Jon on the map, and made him the butt of countless routines from comedian Dave Chappelle, caricaturing Lil Jon's already exagerrated hollering. The title track and "Bia Bia" both introduced a slightly more fleshed-out sound than "Who You Wit?" – not that it could get any more minimal – with dramatic synth lines and percussion swiped from The Showboys' "Drag Rap".

*Kings of Crunk* (2002) continued in more or less the same style, notably on "I Don't Give A @#&%" (with **Mystikal**) and "Throw It Up" (with **Pastor Troy**). However, it was "Get Low" with the **Ying Yang Twins** that was the true anthem. For the first time, Lil Jon filled up the entire soundfield rather than just the bottom end. The skidding synths fast became his trademark, reappearing again on Usher's "Yeah" (2004). On the remix, Lil Jon reached back to his DJ roots and connected the dots between New York, Atlanta, Miami and Jamaica by working with **Busta Rhymes** and **Elephant Man**, even working in a merengue beat.

The "Get Low" remix was included on the *Part II* EP(2003), a rush release mostly of remixes, to capitalize on Lil Jon's enormous popularity. In addition to his own records, around this time he produced hits for **Too $hort** ("Shake That Monkey"), Ying Yang Twins ("Naggin'"), **Youngbloodz** ("Damn!") and **Usher**. With his enormous success, Lil Jon was soon spreading crunk across seemingly all of popular music. **Ciara**'s "Goodies" (2004) was the crunk answer to the bubblegum rap of Lumidee; Usher's "Yeah" was what he called "crunk & B"; and Lil Jon even found himself producing two tracks for nu-metal band **Korn**.

⊙ **Part II**
TVT, 2003)

It may have been a quickie cash-in release, but it contains some of Lil Jon's best work. Lil Jon's anti-song approach is great in short doses (which was what this is anyway), but Big Sam and Lil Bo's extremely limited lyrical content gets pretty boring pretty quick. So the presence of rappers like Busta Rhymes, Eightball, Petey Pablo, Jadakiss, Pastor Troy, Pitbull and TI, and dancehall don Elephant Man, makes this EP the best choice for both home and party listening. Plus it has the mind-blowing merengue mix of "Get Low".

# Lil' Keke

Like seemingly every rapper from Houston who wasn't in the **Geto Boys** or **Eightball & MJG**, Lil' Keke got his start dropping freestyles on **DJ Screw** tapes in the mid-1990s. His flow and tone aren't that dissimilar from Scarface's, but are slightly more laidback, and occasionally even deeper. What definitely isn't laidback about Keke, however, is his workrate, dropping something like fifteen albums (not counting "screwed and chopped" versions) in the seven years since he began making solo albums.

His first solo record was *Don't Mess Wit Texas* (1997) – a mediocre Southern gangsta album that had derivative production and really lame female choruses crooning crap like "Something about the Southside makes me wanna act bad". *Commission* (1998), however, was significantly better, largely due to "Southside", a monster hit that interpolated **Whodini**'s "Friends", and had a monster bassline on top of which Keke bigged up his compadres below the Mason-Dixon Line. Keke also introduced his shrewd marketing ploy of including the remix of his previous album's hit on the new album – in this case, DJ Screw's trademark "screwed and chopped" mix of "Still Pimping Pens" and a slightly different version of "Don't Mess Wit Texas".

Following Keke's master plan to the letter, the "Southside" remix, featuring **Eightball**, was on *It Was All A Dream* (1999). The remix wasn't all that different from the original version, except that Eightball's personality and wicked drawl showed up Keke's deficiencies on the mic, in particular his flow, which can become a drone. "Make 'Em Break It" was another big club track with **Juvenile** and the **Hot Boys**, while "Superstars", with **Big Hawk** and DSD, was a funky H-Town throwdown. *Featured From Coast To Coast* (2000) was something of a posse album, with tracks from Archie Lee, Ice Lord and **Da Black Side Brown** as well as Keke.

*Peepin' In My Window* (2001) found Keke treading water, with yet another rewrite of "Southside" in the form of "On Da Southside" and, of course, a screwed mix of "Superstars". *Platinum In Da Ghetto* (2001) was Keke's crossover move: higher production values, more interesting beats and lots of female choruses. "Coast 2 Coast" was the best beat aside from "Southside" that he had yet come up with.

*The Big Unit* (2003) was a collaboration with **Slim Thug** that largely sounded like Keke was phoning in his raps, even on the tracks also featuring Tela and Bun B. *Changin' Lanes* (2004) was more bass-heavy flossin', but Keke sounded a bit more interested, particularly on tracks like "When We Ride" and "Get Paid".

⊙ **Platinum In Da Ghetto**
Koch, 2001

It doesn't contain Keke's best record, "Southside", but it does have the best production of any Keke album. "Coast 2 Coast" had what sounded like African percussion underneath synth stabs that echoed both early Def Jam and Depeche Mode. Keke also brought the instrumental heat on tracks like "Cowgirl", "Callin' My Name" and "Where Da South At?". He turned in perhaps his best microphone performance as well, changing up his flow at regular intervals and including proper hooks, rather than just repeating the song title a few times.

# Lil' Kim

Millie Jackson called herself "The Queen of Rap" long before anyone but locals had ever heard of Kool Herc, but in nearly thirty years she's had very few heirs apparent to her throne. Although **Kimberly Jones** often seemed like nothing more than a succession of

The typically understated Lil' Kim.

costume changes and ludicrous wigs, the potty-mouthed, pint-sized rapper better known as Lil' Kim is perhaps the closest anyone's come. Abandoned by her parents while still in her early teens, Jones started hanging out on Bed-Stuy street corners with a gang of drug dealers led by Christopher Wallace. When Wallace transformed himself into the **Notorious BIG** and signed to Bad Boy, he signed his crew to the Atlantic imprint he had started with Lance "Un" Rivera, Undeas.

As **Junior M.A.F.I.A.**, the crew exploded on to the scene with their debut single, "Player's Anthem" (1995), which became exactly that. Aside from Biggie's cameo, **Lil' Kim** dominated the track, forcing other M.A.F.I.A. members (**Klepto**, **Lil' Cease**, **Larceny**, Chico, Trife, Nino Brown, **D-Roc**) into the background. The group's second single, "Get Money" (1995), based on a sublime **Sylvia Striplin** loop, was a duet between Biggie and Kim that found Kim threatening to "come down your throat" with some of the most ferocious vagina dentata imagery since the Middle Ages.

Kim was linked both romantically and artistically to Biggie and she later admitted to sharing both his bed and his ghostwriting pen. Whoever was responsible for the rhymes on *Hard Core* (1996), the arrogant pose, piercing sexuality and sheer bitchiness were exhilirating. The self-styled Queen Bee "kick[ed] shit like a nigga do/ Pull[ed] the trigger too" and "[did] shit to you Vanessa Del Rio be ashamed to do". The album went platinum, making the r&b diva no longer the sole role a woman could play in urban music, ushering in the age of the self-proclaimed hip-hop bitch.

Aside from providing the hook for **The LOX**'s "Money, Power, Respect" (1998), Kim laid low for a while (on the recording front, at least – no one in hip-hop attracts more press without new product, apart from Puffy) in the wake of Biggie's death and amidst troubles with her record label. She re-emerged in 2000 with Puffy now replacing B.I.G. as her mentor on *The Notorious K.I.M.* As befitting her status as one of the inaugural players in hip-hop's Ice (jewellery) Age, Kim kept the same focus on mercenary materialism and sex that had some dubbing her the Anti-Lauryn Hill. On the other hand, she had songs such as "Suck My D!#k", a castration anthem that would have Gloria Steinem nodding in appreciation.

Where *The Notorious K.I.M.* was a bid for pop crossover success, *La Bella Mafia* returned to her original hardcore gangsta queen image, with Timbaland, Swizz Beatz and Kanye West creating blinging beats that were far more appropriate than P. Diddy's over-polished, cubic zirconia productions.

⊙ **Hard Core**
Undeas/Atlantic, 1996

Despite some pretty appalling production, the Queen Bee proved she was the baddest bitch since Millie Jackson.

# Lil' Troy

Even though no one outside of H-Town had heard of him until his 1999 breakout hit, "Wanna Be A Baller", Lil' Troy Birklett (not to be confused with the Lil' Troy from Philly's **2 To Many**) had been a presence on the Houston rap scene since the late 1980s. Alongside producer Bruce "Grim" Rhodes, Troy worked with DJ Akshen, aka a pre-Geto Boy **Scarface**, on his solo record for Rap-A-Lot.

A deal with Payday amounted to nothing, and after a few more years of nothing but local fame, Troy resorted to using nefarious means to secure the money to put out *Sittin' Fat Down South* (1999) on his own **Short Stop** label. The album's lead single, "Wanna Be A Baller" (1999), was reminiscent of Warren G's "Regulate", in its ultra-laidback jazzy production and slightly remorseful lyrics, and it became a big hit. Elsewhere, though, it was all lacklustre gangsta posturing and ideas and lyrics borrowed from everyone from 2Pac to Too $hort to Run DMC. Thanks to "Wanna Be a Baller", though, the album sold a million and a half, and Troy seemed to be on his way to stardom. The problem was that Troy's financing had caught up with him and he was in jail doing eighteen months for the misuse of a communications device to commit a felony.

When he got out, Troy released the unrepentant *Back to Ballin'* (2001). The

PARENTAL ADVISORY
EXPLICIT CONTENT

surprisingly uptempo "We Gon' Lean" was an ode to the peculiar Houston "dance" in which the dancer leans left and right due to being knocked senseless on codeine cough syrup. He sampled the **Bee-Gees** on the title track and **Kool & the Gang** for the really stupid "Lesbians' Night", but the syrup provided the album's only other decent track, a "screwed" version of "Wanna Be A Baller", which was one of the last mixes that **DJ Screw** did before he passed away in 2000. Unfortunately, *Back To Ballin'* was also the last thing that Troy has done in a while.

⊙ **Sittin' Fat Down South**
Short Stop, 1999

"Wanna Be A Baller" was undoubtedly a great track, but how many times can you listen to tired lyrics about blades and "20-inch crawlers"? And how many times do you need to listen to yet another 2Pac manqué?

# LL COOL J

There may have been brighter hip-hop supernovas – MC Hammer, Tone Loc, Vanilla Ice and Coolio – but **LL Cool J** (Ladies Love Cool James) is hip hop's biggest, most enduring and greatest pop star. **James Todd Smith** first came to the attention of Def Jam co-founder Rick Rubin after one of the Beastie Boys heard the 14-year-old's self-produced demo tape. He then exploded onto the scene with his first single, "I Need A Beat" (1984), a withering

drum-machine breakdown that hit with the force of a Harlem wrecking ball. As Def Jam's first 12" release, it provided the minimalist blueprint that would become the label's stylistic hallmark for the next couple of years.

The follow-up, "I Can't Live Without My Radio" (1985) , remains the ultimate b-boy anthem: the lines, "Terrorizing my neighbours with the heavy bass/I keep suckers in fear by the look on my face" and "My name is Cool J, I devastate the show/But I couldn't survive without my radio", say everything you need to know about the hip-hop aesthetic. Both singles were contained, along with the dozens cut "That's A Lie", on his immortal debut album, *Radio* (1985). The album's best cut, though, was "Rock the Bells", a devastating collage of urban noise, b-boy attitude and overmodulated bass. *Radio* and Run DMC's debut were the first hip-hop albums on which the music bragged as hard as the raps.

LL Cool J was the neighbourhood kid made good, but the celebrity went to his head and his next album, *Bigger And Deffer* (1987), was a muddled attempt to keep up with the musical advances that he and Run DMC had made possible. Although it contained pure hip-hop like "Go Cut Creator, Go" and the okay bragging cut "I'm Bad" (which suffered from music that had nowhere near the power of his debut), the album will be remembered for his first ballad, the utterly wretched "I Need Love".

"I Need Love" was a huge hit – the first hip-hop record to top the r&b charts – but LL quickly became a metaphorical punch bag. Kool Moe Dee savaged him on "How Ya Like Me Now" and LL hit back with the awesome "Jack the Ripper" (1988). However, LL didn't learn his lesson, and his ego got even bigger on *Walking With A Panther* (1989), the smarmy ballads of which suggested that he actually believed everything he rapped. Aside from "Jack the Ripper", the album's other highlight was the slow, moody, eerie "Goin' Back To Cali", written for the *Less Than Zero* soundtrack, which sounded like a slowed-down Miami Bass track.

With the burgeoning conscious hip-hop movement, the hip-hop community no longer loved Cool James, but producer **Marley Marl** stepped in to solve the problem. Preceded by the seriously hype "Jingling Baby", *Mama Said Knock You Out* (1990) saw Cool J going back to his roots and, not surprisingly, it provided him with his biggest record. *Mama Said* is probably hip-hop's greatest pop album: it's not

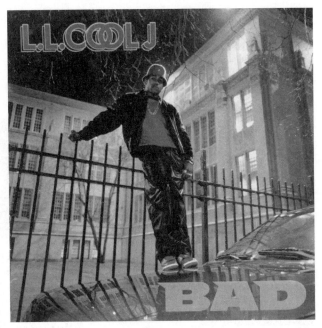

innovative in the slightest, but it nails every generic convention on the head, even Cool J's quiet-storm pillow talk ("Around The Way Girl", "Milky Cereal" and "Jingling Baby"). Most of all, though, it was LL back to doing what he did best: "Rolling over punks like a redneck trucker". The title track was the best song he ever did, and it remains one of hip-hop's best singles.

Inevitably, *14 Shots To The Dome* (1993) was a huge let-down. *Mama Said* was all about Cool J coming back, but having successfully come back he now had nothing to rap about. Cool J's second, and probably permanent, slide into irrelevance worsened with the execrable *Mr. Smith* (1995) and *Phenomenon* (1997). Slicker than Hammer's big-budget fiasco albums, these represented the worst excesses of Cool J's obsession with his sexual prowess.

When **Canibus** attacked LL on 1998's "Second Round KO", it looked like it might revitalise Uncle L's career. He gave as good as he got on "The Ripper Strikes Back" (1998), but Cool J quickly settled back into his comfortable middle-age acting career and churned out dull action flick after dull action flick. With Cool J spending more time in Hollywood than Queens, **G.O.A.T.**

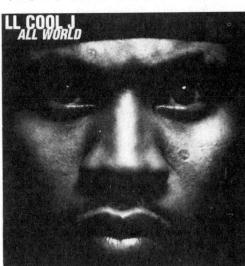

(2000) (standing for "Greatest Of All Time"), despite beats from Timbaland and DJ Scratch, was the hip-hop equivalent of those 1980s albums from holidaying screen actors Bruce Willis, Don Johnson and Eddie Murphy.

*10* (2002) was, including his greatest hits album, Uncle L's tenth album and provided further proof of his slip into mic senility. Even if he did rap about needing love, LL was once the hardest motherfucker on the block. Now he just wants to rap to the ladies, with tracks such as "Luv U Better" seemingly designed to once and for all quell the whisperings about his sexuality that have sometimes dogged him.

**◉ Radio**
Def Jam, 1985

As loud as any heavy metal, but a lot funkier.

**◉ Mama Said Knock You Out**
Def Jam, 1990

It's not as sonically innovative as PE, rhythmically dextrous as De La Soul, or smart as Eric B. & Rakim, but as a consolidation of hip-hop's turf, it's damn near perfect.

**◉ All World**
Def Jam, 1997

This has too many of his ego trips to be a perfect greatest hits package, but given the chart success of his recent output, which is as crass and idiotic as anything by P. Diddy, this is probably the best we'll get.

# Lootpack/ Madlib

Growing up in Oxnard, an unremarkable beach community up the coast from LA, distanced from any major hip-hop scene, the members of Lootpack were forced to come up with their own take on the music and culture. As with most outsiders, history, digging and documentation became more important than the current flavour of the month. Unlike many indie hip-hop outsiders, though, Lootpack weren't just torch bearers of the traditionalist "true school", they reinterpreted and reinvented it with a healthy sense of humour and a quirky sense of the bizarre.

Madlib (Otis Jackson Jr, son of soul/gospel singer Otis Jackson Sr), **Wildchild** (Jack Brown), **DJ Romes** (Romeo Jimenez) and **KanKick** got together at the dawn of the 1990s, and recorded a demo that eventually fell into the hands of **Tha Alkaholiks'** Tash. KanKick soon left the crew, but the rest of Lootpack became part of the Likwit Crew and appeared on Tha Alkaholiks' *21 & Over*, *Coast II Coast* and *Likwidation* albums.

In 1996 they recorded the *Psyche Move EP* (which has since been re-released, along with other early Lootpack nuggets, on *The Lost Tapes* (2004)) which led to a link up with Peanut Butter Wolf's Stones Throw label. On *Sound Pieces: Da Antidote!* (1999) the group wasn't afraid to admit that they still went to open mic nights to keep their flows tight; they turned the "Crate Digger" (the obsessive producer who buries his head in the secondhand record racks looking for breaks) into a superhero; and they claimed to "break MCs on contact" by using the "laws of physics", promising to "carbonate your flow because it sounds flat".

*Sound Pieces'* "Weeded" introduced one of Madlib's many alteregos, the ultra-nasal, helium-voiced **Quasimoto**. On the psychedelic rap landmark *The Unseen* (2000), Quas/Madlib sounded like a Q-Tip record being played a touch too fast – about, say, 39 rpm – while the production was a fazed, dubby take on **A Tribe Called Quest**-style jazz beats (if the legendary Berlin techno label Chain

Reaction had been based in the Bay Area it might have sounded like this). Quas emerged from his belltower once again for the less inspired three-track EP, *Astronaut* (2002).

Madlib then turned his attentions to the jazz that he had made a career out of sampling. The phantom combo **Yesterdays New Quintet** put out the album *Angles Without Edges* in 2001: a fairly straight-ahead tribute to all the jazz cats that had made post-Tribe hip-hop possible. Donning four new aliases – Ahmad Miller, Monk Hughes, Joe McDuffrey and Malik Flavors – Madlib played all the instruments himself. The peripatetic Lib then knocked together a rather wonderful mix of vintage reggae from the Trojan label for *Blunted In The Bomb Shelter* (2002).

Next, Madlib teamed up with Slum Village's Jay Dilla for *Champion Sound* (2003), released under the name **Jaylib**, on which one rapped over the other's beats. It was a huge underground sensation before it was released, but the strange relationship between the over- and undergrounds that they both tried to

straddle failed to move the album beyond the marquee billing. **Madvillain** was a similar, but much more successful collaboration – between Madlib and MF Doom (see KMD entry). The resulting album *Madvillainy* (2004) was a different story entirely, as they both reined in each other's worst instincts.

Meanwhile, **KanKick** released his first solo LP, *From Artz Unknown*, in 2003 with DJ Romes on the turntables. **Wildchild**'s *Secondary Protocol* (2003) was a fine underground album, with Wildchild getting seriously nice on the microphone, though not saying a hell of a lot. Why wasn't "Make Them Clap" (2002), a monstrously funky number courtesy of Madlib, on it?

 **Quasimoto – The Unseen**
Stones Throw, 2000

Avoiding the twin pitfalls of boho smarm and excessive abstraction, Madlib delivers a classic of psychedelic rap. His voice was processed so it was helium high, but without the Chipmunk speed. The contrast between his alien voice and the dusty, crusty beats produced a weird but funky-as-hell discombobulation.

# Lord Finesse

Rarely has a mic name been so appropriate as the one adopted by **Robert Hall**. Upholding the traditions of The Bronx, **Lord Finesse** is one of the great pure MCs in hip-hop. Despite being blessed with an abundance of skills, however, Finesse hasn't been blessed with an abundance of great records and his reputation doesn't match his ability.

He has made one undeniably classic record, though. "Funky Technician" (1990) began with a brilliant scratch of Craig G's "Mmm-Mmm-Mmm ain't that somethin'" line from "The Symphony" by DJ Mike Smooth, and which then settled into a groove based on a choked guitar line. Finesse proceeded to drop rhymes like "Now I'm the man with intellect/Know when to disrespect/I kick a rhyme and make MCs want to hit the deck", "Keep the crowd listening, I'm so magnificent/It even says 'Finesse' on my birth certificate" and "Using bad words/Pronouns and adverbs/Puttin' English together just like a mad nerd".

*Funky Technician* (1990) featured similarly styled mellow grooves such as "Strictly for the Ladies", over which Finesse showed off his mastery of the mic device. While the album is notable for his freestyling skills and funky wordplay, it also marked the beginning of one of East Coast hip-hop's most enduring partnerships, the **Diggin' In the Crates Crew** (see entry). **AG** matched Finesse verse for verse on tracks like "Keep It Flowing", produced by Diamond D, and "Back To Back Rhyming", which was produced by AG's partner Showbiz.

*Return Of The Funky Man* (1992) was more of the same, but the grooves were less inspiring. While Finesse was as good as ever on tracks like "Show 'Em How We Do Things", "Isn't He Something" and "Return of the Funky Man", the production wasn't as bright as the debut and, as a result, Finesse just didn't sound as imposing. *The Awakening* (1996) compounded the problem with sparser beats and a hardcore vibe that didn't do Finesse any favours.

**Funky Technician**
Wild Pitch, 1990

With beats by the cream of the New York scene (Diamond D, Premier, Showbiz), this is the one time Finesse has had production equal to his rhyme skills.

Lord Finesse.

# Lords of the Underground

The Lords of the Underground – **Doitall**, **Mr Funke** and **DJ Lord Jazz** – first got together at Shaw University in North Carolina, which is entirely appropriate given their frat-party antics and pep-rally rhymes. They toured with Cypress Hill, but their big break came when **Marley Marl**'s cousin became their manager.

Thanks to his relative's involvement with the group, the legendary producer signed up to produce their debut album, *Here Come The Lords* (1993). Featuring five monster club tracks – "Flow On", "Chief Rocka", "Psycho", "Funky Child" and "Here Come The Lords" – the album was a textbook example of the 1993-4 East Coast sound: heavy mid-tempo drums with lots of sax drops. Neither Doitall nor Mr Funke were up to much on the mic, but their chant-along verses didn't trip up on Marley Marl's production.

*Keepers Of The Funk* (1994) was a significant step down. Even though Marley Marl and **K-Def** were behind the boards again, the production wasn't as consistent, especially since Bad Boy had now changed the sound of New York. Suffering from the changed climate, the group headed back underground for five years before they re-emerged once again with *Resurrection* (1999). The album was released on Queen Latifah's **Jersey Kidz**

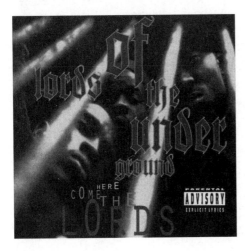

label and, fittingly, there was more than a little resemblance to Latifah protégés **Naughty By Nature**. While the music and their rap styles were up to date, the lyrics weren't: "Take your bills like Clinton/ Nigga I ain't bullshittin'", "Cook niggas in a minute like rice", and so on. It was little wonder that they vanished straight back underground after *Resurrection*.

⊙ **Here Come The Lords**
Pendulum, 1993

It ain't much in the lyrics department, but it is one heck of a party album. "Chief Rocka" and "Flow On", especially, will get just about any party moving, especially if your crowd was anywhere near a club or a more enlightened frat party in 1993.

# Lordz of Brooklyn

"Hey goombah, where ya at?" Picking up where House of Pain left off, the Lordz of Brooklyn made what they called "goombah rap", remaking hip-hop for the stickball-playing mooks from their neighborhood. You could tell by the way they used their walk that The Lordz of Brooklyn repped the largely Italian **Bay Ridge** section of King's County – home of Lento's pizza, Kelly's tavern, the Verrazano Narrows Bridge and the movie *Saturday Night Fever*'s **Tony Manero**.

Core Lordz, Mike "Kaves" McLeer and his brother Adam "ADM" McLeer, grew up tagging the R train that thundered through their neighbourhood. After doing a backdrop for Public Enemy, the brothers McLeer decided to try their hand at rapping and set about creating a sound that reflected their white working-class roots. They started out as the Verrazano Boys, with Kaves on the mic and ADM on the wheels of steel, but after lots of local gigs and renaming themselves after the Sly Stallone/Henry Winkler flick *The Lords Of Flatbush*, the McLeer's recruited Dino Botz, Scotty Edge and Pauly Two Times.

After Kaves toured with **House of Pain**, the Lordz got signed to American recordings and released their debut single, "Saturday Night Fever" (1995), an ode to a rowdy weekend of drinking, fucking and fighting that was based on clever samples of **Schooly D** and **The Guess Who**. *All In The Family* (1995) followed in much the same way, with meathead raps on top of rough drum loops and rock samples. While many of the songs sounded like *Sopranos* episodes, on "Tails Fom the Rails" they dusted off old school legend **Rammellzee** for a graff reminiscence.

The album didn't exactly set the world on fire and the Lordz were promptly dropped from American. Over the next few years it seemed as if the Lordz had gone into the witness relocation programme, with only sporadic appearances like the *Gravesend* soundtrack (1997), a collabo with **Freddie Foxxx** (1998), a duet with porn star **Rebecca Wild** ("Titty Bar" (2000)) and a rock-rap cover of Run DMC's "Sucker MCs" (2000) with **Everlast**. They re-emerged in 2003 with a three-piece rock band in tow on *Graffiti Roc*. The album was very contemporary and not bad at all, but it couldn't compare with the excellent production of the band's debut. Nevertheless, the skater boys on the Warped Tour were happy.

⊙ **All In The Family**
Ventrue/American, 1995

They may have rapped like a bunch of guys with fingerless gloves busting your kneecaps with stickball bats, but the production, mostly from ADM, was as cinematic as a John Woo flick. Doo-wop, psychedelia, pool-hall banter, head-knocking drums and Kiss all combined for a rowdy but very funky thrash-around.

# Lost Boyz

The **Lost Boyz** are one of the very few hip-hop crews to have it both ways. They made their commercial breakthrough with materialistic party jams, but the bulk of their material actually deals with the flipside of the ghetto fabulous lifestyle.

**Freaky Tah** (**Raymond Rogers**) and **Mr. Cheeks** (**Terrence Kelly**) made names for themselves at hip-hop jams held in Jamaica, Queens' Baisley Park in the early 1990s. With childhood friends **Pretty Lou** (**Eric Ruth**) and **DJ Spigg Nice** (**Ronald Blackwell**) in tow, the Lost Boyz signed to Uptown and released their debut album, *Legal Drug Money*, in 1995. It went gold on the strength Of The anthems "Lifestyles of the Rich and Shameless" and "Jeeps, Lex Coups, Bimaz & Benz". Produced by **Easy Mo Bee**, "Jeeps, Lex Coups, Bimaz & Benz" had an easy flowing beat and an undeniable "throw-your-hands-in-the-air" chorus that absolutely destroyed clubs. Acknowledging that this kind of obsession with money had its dark side, "Renee" was a chilling morality tale about a lover who was lost to the kill-or-be-killed code of the streets. A corollary to

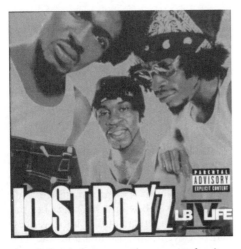

this dialectic between glamour and grime was the interplay of Freaky Tah's grating, almost screaming cadences and Mr. Cheeks' smooth, eloquent vpcals.

With tracks like "Music Makes Me High" and "Me & My Crazy World" being blasted from SUVs throughout New York, *Love, Peace And Nappiness* (1997) followed *Legal Drug Money* into gold territory. On March 28, 1999, however, Freaky Tah was shot in the back of the head outside a party in Queens. The Lost Boyz continued as a trio and released *LB Fam IV Life* (1999). Although the group desperately missed Tah, "Let's Roll Dice" was an effective anthem of the trife life, while "Only Live Once" and "LB Fam IV Life" mourned the fallen rapper with chracteristic poignance.

Mr. Cheeks emerged as a solo artist in 2001 with the massive "Lights, Camera, Action". With its chopped-up wah-wah guitar, disco strings and skittering drums during the chorus, the single tore shit up in the clubs. As he did with the Lost Boyz, Cheeks tempered his tales of club prowling with morality plays on *John P Kelly* (2001), which suffered from lacklustre production, apart from on the single. The follow-up, *Back Again!* (2003), had better beats, but lacked anything as galvanizing as "Lights, Camera, Action".

In 2004, Spigg Nice was sentenced to 37 years in prison for his part in ten bank robberies committed between 2000 and 2002.

⊙ **Legal Drug Money**
Uptown/Universal, 1995

An engaging album that managed to be both hardened and compassionate, party-hearty and chilling.

# Lovebug Starski

Sometimes hip-hop works in mysterious ways. If it wasn't for Lovebug Starski, there would be no **Kid Rock**. Starski was an old school pioneer whose catch-phrase was "Bob-a-bob-a-bob-a-bob-didda-bob-de-danga-dang-diggy-diggy-diggy-diggy-dang with the bang-bang boogie". Kid Rock shortened it to "Bawitdaba", added a crunching power chord and went multi-platinum, while Starski languished in obscurity and personal problems.

Also known as Kevin Smith, Lovebug Starksi grew up in the Bronx and joined the **Black Spades** as a teenager. Naming himself after two of the biggest cultural icons of the day – Herbie the Lovebug and Starsky from *Starsky & Hutch* – Smith started working with legendary DJ **Pete DJ Jones**, carrying his equipment and filling in for him when he didn't feel like spinning. When he struck out on his own, Starski played at clubs like the Burger King disco, Harlem World and the Disco Fever. Working with **Kool DJ AJ**, Starski made the transition from the turntables to the microphone. He claims to have both invented the phrase "hip-hop" (although that is more often credited to Spoonie Gee) and to be the inspiration for "Rapper's Delight", because he played at Sugarhill founder **Sylvia Robinson**'s birthday party at the Harlem World.

Starski finally made it to wax in 1981 on the moody "Positive Life", a collaborative rap with the **Harlem World Crew** on top of The Police's "Voices Inside My Head". Three years passed before the survivalism of "You Gotta Believe" (1984) was released on Fever Records (the label of the Disco Fever club where he was one of the house DJs). The flip, "Starski, Live At The Disco Fever", was the perfect bridge between the old and middle schools with its, by this point, old-fashioned rhymes on top of state-of-the-art drum machines from **Run DMC** collaborator Larry Smith. "Do the Right Thing/Live At The Disco Fever Pt. II" (1984) followed in nearly identical fashion.

Starski appeared on the *Rappin'* soundtrack (1985), but hip-hop fashions were changing at light speed and by the time of "House Rocker" (1985) and "Amityville" (1986), Starski was left well behind. He was arrested for drug possession in 1987 and wasn't released until 1991.

> ⊙ **"You Gotta Believe/Starski, Live At The Disco Fever"**
> Fever, 1984
>
> Lovebug Starski should nowadays be seen as being in the hallowed company of Flash, Bam and Herc as a true hip-hop pioneer. Instead, he has largely been lost to history. This blend of post-"The Message" urban realism and old school party rap is his finest recorded moment. For a truer picture of the old days, seek out the mixtapes that he did before his jail bid, which were sold alongside tapes by Kid Capri and aren't that difficult to get hold of.

# The Lox

Jason "**Jadakiss**" Phillips, Sean "Sheek" Jacobs and David Styles are three MCs from Yonkers, New York who made names for themselves on New York's mixtape circuit in the mid-1990s, but are certainly more famous for facing down the **Bad Boy** empire. Originally calling themselves the **Warlocks** and then just The Lox (an acronym for Living Off Experience, not a reference to bagel toppings), the trio were so big on the underground scene that they had a greatest hits mixtape before they had even inked a deal. In 1995 The Lox recorded "Niggaz Done Started Something" with fellow Yonkers MC **DMX** and generated an enormous street buzz. Another Yonkers native, Mary J Blige, introduced the group to P Diddy who promptly signed them to Bad Boy, initially as ghostwriters, and then as artists.

Their "We'll Always Love Big Poppa" (1997) was the slightly more rugged B-side to Puff's noxious "I'll Be Missing You", and the uncomfortable partnership between glossy pop and street-level thuggery would characterize their stint at Bad Boy.

*Money, Power & Respect* (1998) attempted to dress The Lox up in jiggy clothes, to uneven effect. The title track, based on string swoops from **Dexter Wansel**'s "New Beginning", brought the street hustlers into the boardroom without too much trouble, but tracks like "If You Think I'm Jiggy", based on **Rod Stewart**'s "Do Ya Think I'm Sexy", were just awful.

The Lox clearly weren't comfortable in Puff's shiny suits, and were unhappy that all the samples drained the profits from their gold album. The group started bad-mouthing Bad Boy and wearing "Let the Lox Go" T-shirts at public appearances. Bad Boy eventually relented and sold The Lox's contract to the **Ruff Ryders** camp. *We Are The Streets* (2000) had crunching beats from **Swizz Beatz**, Timbaland and **DJ Premier** – settings in which The Lox, and their tales of thuggery, sex and drugs, seemed very comfortable.

It was always evident that Jadakiss was the most talented of the trio and that it was only a matter of time before he went solo, which he did in 2001 with *Kiss Tha Game Goodbye*. There were some hot tracks like the **Neptunes**-produced "Knock Yourself Out" and the **Alchemist**-produced "We Gonna Make It", but, strangely, given his experience at Bad Boy, the album suffered from trying to please too many different demographics rather than sticking to what Jada did best. *Kiss Of Death* (2004) was similarly over-produced, but at least on "Why?", produced by **Mobb Deep**'s Havoc, Jada sprinkled the track with a hint of

KISS THA GAME GOODBYE

dirt by asking questions like "Why'd they come up with the witness protection, then they let the Terminator win the election?" and "You know why they made the new twenties?/'Cos I got all the old ones". A more raw Jadakiss was in evidence on the excellent **DJ Green Lantern** mixtape *The Champ Is Here* (2004) where Jada dropped ferocious battle rhymes over simple, unadorned beats.

### We Are The Streets
Ruff Ryders/Interscope, 2000

It's hardly a masterpiece – The Lox's occasionally great punchlines are almost always undermined by lazy phrasing and dull choruses – but it's a far better display of their wares than their Bad Boy outing. Jadakiss, Sheek and Styles are clearly happy to be free from the meddling of Cream Puff, and celebrate with appealing joie de vivre on "Bring it On", "Fuck You" and "Blood Pressure".

# L'Trimm

Miami's Lady Tigra and Bunny D were responsible for one of the great novelty singles of all-time, "Cars With the Boom!" (1988). The combination of the gut-churning bass and the girlish voices, of the sound of urban menace and their charming naiveté (particularly as they giggled their way through the record's first twenty seconds) was an irresistible pop confection.

**Tigra** and **Bunny** had debuted a year

earlier with "Grab It!" (1987), a more risqué retort to Salt-N-Pepa's "Push It" with lyrics like "You say you want to push it, but your pushing is through/ Girl, let's push you aside and show you what to do/You've got to grab it, grab it like you want it". Both tracks, along with another Salt-N-Pepa diss, "Better Yet L'Trimm", were featured on the bubblegum rap classic *Grab It!* (1988).

*Drop That Bottom* (1989) followed in a pretty similar style, but without any hits, and then, towards the end of the album, came a couple of ill-advised forays into hip-house. After an appearance on **Tricky Nikki**'s "Bust The Rhythm Of My ABCs" (1989), even more hip-house and some very questionable Daisy Age attire featured on *Groovy* (1991). Forgoing the bass almost entirely, they now wanted to be **Snap!**, it seemed, and the results weren't very pretty, especially on a woeful cover of **The Archies**' "Sugar Sugar" – with a couple of rare instances (Tiffany, of course, comes to mind) bubblegum was only good when it was fresh, rather than twenty years old.

### Grab It!
Atco, 1988

L'Trimm were that rarest of things in hip-hop – unrepentant bimbos – and this album's vibe is almost as rare again, one full of charm and innocence. The production was often as air-headed as Tigra and Bunny, but that only added to the album's effervescence. While thoroughly wonderful, "Cars With the Boom" had just about the most unlikely objects of lust in the annals of popular music – as they bragged "My boyfriend really knows where it's at/He's got 50-inch woofers all along the back".

# Ludacris

One of the most engaging personalities to grace the mic in recent years, Ludacris has parlayed a Cheech & Chong-meets-Richard-Pryor sense of humour, an easy flow and **Def Jam**'s marketing muscle, into winning him the title of the Dirty South's most successful solo rapper.

Christopher Bridges was born in Champaign, Illinois and grew up there

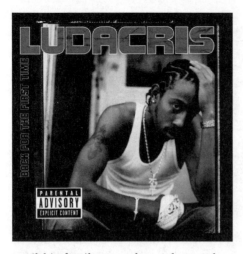

until his family moved to Atlanta when he was 14. After dropping out of Georgia State to concentrate on rapping, he made a demo tape that earned him an internship at an Atlanta radio station (where he recorded promos for every DJ on the station's roster), and which got him noticed by **Timbaland**, who put him on "Fat Rabbit" on *Tim's Bio* (1998). **Jermaine Dupri** then asked Ludacris to appear on the theme song to the *John Madden 2000* video game. With the money, Ludacris financed the recording and release of *Incognegro* (2000) on his own **Disturbing Tha Peace** label. Thanks to the maddeningly intense click-track synth line, drum 'n' bass-style bass stabs and rather frank lyrics of "What's Your Fantasy", the album became a sensation in Atlanta. *Incognegro* caught the attention of **Scarface**, who had just been appointed head of Def Jam South, and he promptly signed Ludacris. Def Jam repackaged the album as *Back for the First Time* (2000), adding four tracks: the Neptunes-produced "Southern Hospitality", a remake of "Fat Rabbit", the **UGK** collaboration "Stick 'Em Up" and the "What's Your Fantasy?" remix with **Trina** and **Foxy Brown**. With Def Jam's promotional skills, the album went triple-platinum.

On *Word of Mouf* (2001), Luda emphasized the stand-up comedy routine aspect of his rapping. Even when Luda got "crunk" and threw some 'bows (elbows), as on "Move Bitch" with **Mystikal**, there were punchlines and ingenious snaps aplenty. *Chicken-N-Beer* (2003) further established his rep as the Chris Rock of rap: "Watch out for the medallion, my diamonds are reckless/Feels like a midget is hangin' from my necklace" (from the **Kanye West**-produced "Stand Up").

### ⊙ Back For The First Time
Def Jam South, 2000

Ludacris is more of a freak than Prince, but unlike other ho-obsessed rappers, Luda isn't hateful, just dirty. He also has a sense of humour and a sly wink, making him immensely likeable on the mic. Plus, his producers always seem to come up trumps. Here, Shondrae (on "What's Your Fantasy") and the Neptunes (with the kazoo synth-lines and skeletal drum track of "Southern Hospitality") threaten to steal the show.

# Luniz

The partnership of **Yukmouth** and **Numskull** started in Oakland, California in 1992 as the Loony Tunes. After garnering a reputation in the Bay Area, the duo changed their name to

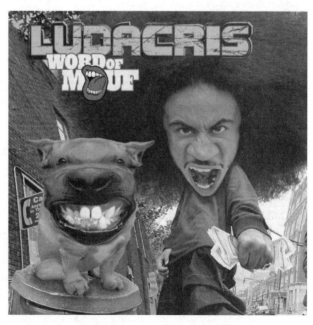

the **Luniz** and signed to Noo Trybe. Featuring super-slick, Bay Area funk production, their 1995 single, "I Got 5 On It", was one of the year's biggest hits. Incredibly hypnotic and instantly catchy, "I Got 5 On It" was based on a loop from Club Nouveau's "Why You Treat Me So Bad" and horn stabs from Kool & the Gang. Over these perfect, radio-friendly beats, Yukmouth and Numskull drawled about splitting the cost of a bag of weed, creating a ganja-smoking anthem every bit the equal of **Cypress Hill**'s "Stoned Is the Way Of The Walk" or **The Pharcyde**'s "Pack The Pipe".

Unfortunately, the Luniz's debut album, *Operation Stackola* (1995), couldn't maintain the same standards. "Playa Hata" (which was aimed straight at Too $hort's head) and "Blame A Nigga" were both OK tracks, but *Operation Stackola* was generic East Bay rap without any personality to differentiate Luniz from the rest of Oakland's hustler's convention. Marred by its desperate search for another hit, *Lunitik Muzik* (1997) was lowest common denominator gangsta rap and was even

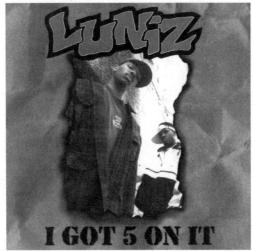

I GOT 5 ON IT

CDVUS 94
7243 8 40523 2 4

worse than their debut. It was perhaps notable only for "Funkin' Over Nuthin'" in which the Luniz and **Too $hort** made peace after the deaths of 2Pac and Biggie.

Yukmouth went solo in 1999 with a double-CD, *Thugged Out: The Albulation*, recorded for Houston's Rap-A-Lot. Harder than *Lunitik Muzik*, *Thugged Out* was a big hit with the *Muder Dog* crowd, but it also saw him broaden his range with "Revalationz", an uncompromising track about losing his parents to AIDS. Of course, the baller wasn't completely reformed and "Stallion" featured **MC Ren** remaking **N.W.A.**'s godawful "Just Don't Bite It". While Yukmouth has claimed that the Luniz are still together, "Falling" seemed to be a fairly definitive statement to the contrary: "My old record company is trying to sue me/ Is it because I quit the Luniz/And left they ass broke as fuck in the boonies?"

⊙ **Operation Stackola**
Noo Trybe, 1995

The only Luniz track worth owning is "I Got 5 On It", but if you can't track down the single, it's here.

# Mac Mall

Jamal Rocker's grandfather and Earl Stevens' grandmother were cousins, so it's no wonder that there's more than a passing resemblance between the music of **Mac Mall** (Rocker) and **E-40** (Stevens). While Mac Mall is more straightforward than the eccentric E-40, they are both equally captivating on the mic, and both specialize in spitting game over classic rolling Bay Area funk.

Mac Mall exploded onto the Bay Area rap scene as a 16-year-old. His album *Illegal Business?* (1993) was a smooth, slinky piece of post-G-Funk produced by **Khayree** and released on his Young Black Brotha label. Tracks like "Sic Wit Tis" and "Ghetto Theme" were slow-rolling Vallejo anthems that showcased Mac Mall's engaging mack tales perfectly, while on the strange "My Opinion", Mac Mall attempted to put the game in perspective by uttering lines like "I'm trying to go to school but the system wouldn't have me" in a voice processed to sound like an alien.

After sprinkling E-40's "Dusted And Disgusted" (1995) with a verse comparing himself to **Sly Stallone**, Mac Mall worked with Ant Banks, Tone Capone, Cold 187um, Mike Moseley and Khayree again on *Untouchable* (1996), and the music was often extraordinary. Khayree's "Let's Get a Telly" was nothing but an extended bass fart, a kick drum and some wah-wah guitar, while Ant Banks' "Pimp Or Die" bumped like Joe Tex's worst nightmare.

In 1999 Mac Mall started his own Sessed Out label with the rap/R&B compilation *Mac Mall Presents The Mallennium* (1999) – featuring Yukmouth, Ray Luv, JT the Bigga Figga and Dwayne Wiggins – and his own *Illegal Business? 2000* (1999). Although he was still working with Khayree, the beats on *Illegal Business? 2000* were the worst of his career, epitomized by the schlocky keyboards and forced female chorus of the crossover attempt "Wide Open".

*Immaculate* (2001) was a strange, schizophrenic, but ultimately laudable album. There were songs about the game, like "POP", "Bossin' Up" and "Some More of It", but most of the album had "Mac

Jesus" in a conversation with the man upstairs. Mac had always been aware of, and rapped about, the other side of the mack's lifestyle, but on "The Man Upstairs" he asked the big questions: "As the choir sings songs of redemption/ In the US we dyin' for religion/Out in Europe they dyin' for religion/I say this and hope the Holy Father's listenin'/Livin' in this New Age Babylon, preachers havin' telethons/Justice playin' war games, waitin' on the Red Don/And then they wonder why the kids do drugs/'Cos Uncle Sam don't show no love".

*Mackin' Speaks Louder Than Words* (2002) had Mac Mall back on the street corner pimpin' hoes and slinging game. The straight "Yay Area" funk was back as well, but it seemed forced and tired after *Immaculate*. Teaming up with another Northern California kingpin, **JT The Bigga Figga**, on *Illegal Game* (2004) didn't seem to help matters any.

⊙ **Immaculate**
Sessed Out, 2001

The production's weak, it doesn't always work, Mac's attempts to be simultaneously hard and spiritual are strained, some of the lyrics are terrible and it suffers from a split personality, but as a portrait of a game-spitter wrestling with the consequences of his actions, it's pretty fascinating. If you're looking for the pimp-strolling funk he made his name with, stick with his first two albums, but if you want to watch a mack fight his inner demons and work out the contradictions inherent in the game, get this occasionally insightful album.

# Mack 10

Gangsta rap's critics complain that it's the same ol' shit time after time, that the OG is the same as the new G. For empirical evidence, you don't have to look any further than Inglewood, California's **Mack 10**. Ever since being given his chance to shine by Ice Cube in 1993, Mack 10 has gone gold by toeing the West Coast party line and sounding a lot like his mentor.

Cube produced Mack Dime's debut album, *Mack 10* (1995), which was just like much of the second wave of gangsta

rap, in that it took the rage out of the music in favour of smooth-rolling gangsta funk and a laid-back, almost blasé delivery – lo-cal SoCal. The only notable tracks were "Westside Slaughterhouse" (which introduced the **Westside Connection** team of Mack, Cube and WC, who would make their regional pride full-length on the *Bow Down* album) and the hit "Foe Life", but Mack was largely kicking the same game Cube did six or seven years earlier.

Aside from the utterly pointless remake of "Dopeman", which only increased the accusations of copyright infringement, *Based On A True Story* (1997) managed to find some humour and fresh angles in a genre that was more tired than Rip Van Winkle, particularly on the Kool & the Gang pastiche "Inglewood Swangin'". *The Recipe* (1998), however, saw Mack trying to break out of LA with guest appearances by everyone from **Foxy Brown** to **Master P** to the late Eazy-E. The problem was that while *The Recipe* had plenty of ingredients, it didn't have much flavour.

The following year Mack introduced his Hoo-Bangin' label with the *Hoo-Bangin' Mix Tape* (1999). Aiming to fill the gap left by Death Row's absence, Mack signed **MC Eiht** to Hoo Bangin', along with artists such as the **Road Dawgs** and CJ Mac. Like his *Thicker Than Water* movie (a straight-to-video story of life in LA, in the time-honoured tradition of hip-hop movie-making patented by Master P), however, Hoo-Bangin' suffered from a lack of ideas and formulaic production. Unfortunately,

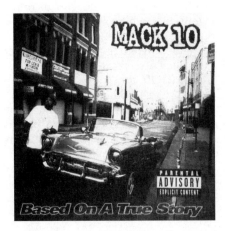

Mack's *The Paper Route* (2000) extravaganza couldn't stop the rot.

◉ **Based An A True Story**
Priority, 1997

It may not be saying much, but this might be the best G-Funk album of the latter half of the 1990s.

# ◉ Macola Records

Macola Records was the pre-eminent California hip-hop label of the 1980s. Without it, **N.W.A.**, Ice-T, MC Hammer, 2 Live Crew and **Egyptian Lover** might never have made it to the world beyond Crenshaw. The company was founded by **Don MacMillan** as a record manufacturer and distributor in 1983 and became a record label in 1984.

Macola was distributing major early West Coast hip-hop records from small California labels. Among its clientele were: **Ruthless**; Andre Manuel's (aka the **Unknown DJ**) **Techno Hop** (the Unknown DJ's very own early edit classic "808 Beats" (1984), Ice-T's "Ya Don't Quit" and "6 'n the Mornin'" (both 1986) and Rodney O & Joe Cooley's "Payback's a Mutha" (1987)); Egyptian Lover's **Egyptian Empire**; Fresh Beat (2 Live Crew); the Arabian Prince's **Rapsur** (apart from the Arabian Prince's first records, the label was responsible for launching the comedy rap of Bobby Jimmy, aka radio personality Russ Parr, and his backing band the Critters); MC

Hammer's **Bustin** Records; and Jay King's Jay label (Timex Social Club's "Rumors"). But the Macola label's own first successes were with Dr. Dre and Yella's **World Class Wreckin' Cru**'s "Surgery" and "Juice" (both 1985).

In the same year, Macola put out **Bobby Jimmy & the Critters**' "Big Butt" in 1985 – a virtuoso use of the 808 cowbell and the 303 squelch a good two years before it was discovered by chicago house producers. More idiosyncratically, Jimmy was talking about his *own* big butt, not some hoochie's. The group's other big hit, "Roaches" (1986), was a parody of **Timex Social Club**'s "Rumors" and was a bit like "The Message" sung by Eddie Murphy doing one of his Billie 'Buckwheat' Thomas impressions.

Macola introduced **Ice Cube** on CIA's "Cru In Action" (1987) and **Cypress Hill**'s DJ Muggs on 7A3's "We Will Rock You" (1987). 2 Live Crew's "What I Like" (1987) was a rare example of social relevance from the group, while World Class Wreckin' Cru's "Cabbage Patch" (1987) was a fusion of the "Peter Piper" beat and the crowd noises from **T La Rock**'s "It's Yours". With the Fila Fresh Crew's first couple of records, Macola once again introduced the world to a very talented rapper (**The DOC**), but with the enormous success of N.W.A., Macola's role as a local distributor became less and less important, as the entire world now had its eyes on LA's hip-hop scene. The label stopped trading in 1989.

**VARIOUS ARTISTS**

◉ **The Best of Macola Vol. 1**
Macola, 1987

The selection isn't as strong as it could be, especially for hip-hop fans – there are too many dance tracks (Georgio, Stacey Q, Timex Social Club) – but this is the best label overview available. The album features such classic West Coast hip-hop as the Unknown DJ's "808 Beats", Ice-T's "Ya Don't Quit", 2 Live Crew's "What I Like" and World Class Wreckin' Cru's "Cabbage Patch".

# Madlib

◊ See *Lootpack/Madlib*

# Mad Skillz

Richmond, Virginia's Mad Skillz is one of a number of very talented free-style specialists who win plenty of battles, but can't translate their skills to vinyl. Mad Skillz (born Shaquan Lewis) first came to prominence in 1993 when he finished second to another freestyle specialist, **Supernatural**, in the prestigious New Music Seminar MC Battle for World Supremacy. A legendary freestyled verse with **Q-Tip** on the Stretch Armstrong Show, on WKCR radio, cemented his reputation and guaranteed him plenty of time on mixtapes from coast to coast to coast.

He soon signed with Big Beat and released the disappointing *From Where???* (1995). There were a couple of hot tracks – the pure hip-hop of "The Nod Factor" and "Extra Abstract Skillz" (with **Large Professor** and Q-Tip) – but neither the production nor Skillz' raps were compelling enough to hold your interest for much longer. Over the course of an album, Skillz' one-dimensional topics and cadence just wore you down instead of winning you over.

Skillz returned to Virginia, where he started ghostwriting for other rappers, and then hooked up with fellow Commonwealth resident **Timbaland**. Skillz became Tim's secret weapon, appearing on tracks such as the remix of **Aaliyah**'s "Are You That Somebody" (1998) and Timbaland's "To My" from *Tim's Bio* (1998). On his own "Ghost Writer" (2000), over a loop of music that conjured images of Ashkenazis shuffling through the Lower East Side of New York circa 1920, Skillz borrowed **Jay-Z**'s flow and bragged about all the lame rappers who needed his ghostwriting talents. On the flip, "Together" was marred by the worst Timbaland production ever. It sounded like Tim had listened to Pharoah Monche's smash "Simon Says" too often, and was overall as awkward as Puff Daddy in a "hooptie" – while "One, Two" sounded even more like Jay-Z than Jayhova himself.

However, Skillz' talent for imitation would pay dividends on his infamous "Rap Up" series which began in 2000.

Often he would imitate the big hits of the previous year, whilst at other times he'd recap the year's events with the savage wit that marked his mixtape freestyles. After he dropped the excellent, Timbaland-produced "Off the Wall" (2003), "Rap Up 2003" had Skillz imitating 50 Cent's "Wanksta", as he rapped about the Kobe Bryant scandal (basketball hero Bryant had been accused of rape): "The dummy move of the year that would be Kobe Bryant/Y'all think she lyin'?/That's the second time Kobe been on TV cryin'/I'm like, 'Damn, Kobe, in high school you was the man, Kobe/What the hell happened to you?'"

In the midst of the 2004 NBA championships, a **DJ Sickamore** mixtape emerged with Shaquille O'Neal standing up for Kobe and dissing Mad Skillz with lines like "You're the fourth-best from Virginia/Guess what, I don't fuck with scrubs either". Skillz retorted with the lame "The Champ", which featured Shaq's basketball nemesis from the Detroit Pistons, Ben Wallace. Skillz was reputed to have seven more answer tracks aimed at Shaq lined up.

🅘 **From Where???**
Big Beat/Atlantic, 1995

Mad Skillz is one of the most cutting, funniest rappers around. The problem is that he can't use 90% of his best lyrics on records due to the vigilance of record label legal teams. His only album is marred by its dull focus on skills – very little of Skillz' humour or personality comes through. You are much better served by seeking out his innumerable mixtape appearances, or any of his "Rap Up" series. Of special note is his freestyle over 50 Cent's "In Da Club", on one of Kay Slay's mixtapes.

# Main Source

Main Source may be Canada's finest contribution to hip-hop, but most of the action came from Brooklynite **Paul Mitchell** (aka **Large Professor**), who has also worked on tracks for Eric B & Rakim, Nas, Biz Markie, Intelligent Hoodlum and Kool G Rap. The standing of Extra P (as he is also known) among hip-hop heads can be gauged from the fact that, next to Tupac, he's the most bootlegged hip-hop artist. While Large Professor may be hip-hop's most potent triple threat (on the decks, on the mic and behind the desk), brothers **Sir Scratch** (**Shawn McKenzie**) and **K-Cut** (**Kevin McKenzie**) both added a little something to the Main Source sound.

The group debuted on the incredibly rare "Think/Watch Roger Do His Thing" single (1989) on Actual records. They also appeared on a Canuck hip-hop comp, but it was *Breaking Atoms* (1991) that established their rep. While Extra P's production is often compared to Pete Rock's, the Prof's use of jazz is much more disorientating. Check the denuded keyboard and horn samples on "Live At The Barbeque" (1991) (the track that introduced both Nas and Akinyele) and the epic "Peace Is Not the Word to Play". "Peace ..." was a sophisticated examination of hypocrisy, a topic which would crop again on the remarkable racism metaphor "A Friendly Game Of Baseball" and the woman-trouble narrative "Looking at the Front Door".

*Breaking Atoms* sold only 130,000 copies, despite being hailed as a classic, and the critique of hip-hop commercialization, "Fakin' The Funk" (1992), was to be the original line-up's last record. Originally found on the *White Men Can't Jump* movie soundtrack, "Fakin' The Funk", thankfully, did not live up to its title, with its clever Kool & the Gang and doo-wop samples. The crew split up soon afterwards amidst recriminations, and Sir Scratch and K-Cut carried on with **Mikey D** replacing Extra P. Their album, *Fuck What You Think* (1994), was never officially released, which probably turned out to be a good thing, after some weak tracks emerged on a Japanese collection, *The Best of Main Source* (1996).

Large Professor signed to Geffen in the aftermath and released two fine (if not as good as the original Main Source material) singles – "Mad Scientist" and "I Wanna Chill" (both 1995) – but his proposed album *The LP* was shelved. Various tracks have appeared on any number of bootlegs,

but the only legit releases to feature his name as an artist have been collaborations with Chris Lowe, and the man who shared the mic with him on "Fakin' The Funk", **Neek the Exotic**. Most notable of these was Neek's excellent EP, *Backs 'N Necks* (1999).

◉ **Breaking Atoms**
Wild Pitch, 1991

After years of being unavailable, this classic was eventually reissued so it could get the props it never got the first time around.

# Mantronix

His clarion-call-cum-manifesto, "Man plus electronics equals **Mantronix**", may not have been the most promising of equations for hip-hop success, but back in his day **Kurtis Khaleel** was one of the most important producers in hip-hop. Born in Jamaica in 1965, Khaleel moved to New York from Vancouver, Canada in 1980. After the usual tale of being inspired by Bambaataa and Grand Mixer D.ST, and making pause-button cassette edits on his home hi-fi, **Kurtis Mantronik** and **MC Tee** cut a cheap demo which they gave to Sleeping Bag records' Will Socolov. Sleeping Bag promptly released "Fresh Is The Word" (1985). Mantronik's groundbreaking use of the SP-1200 sampler made it a sizeable hit in New York.

Kurtis and Tee.

In addition to "Fresh Is the Word", *Mantronix* (1985) contained the massive "Bassline", which lived up to Mantronix's name, sounding like some kind of awesome union of circuitry and flesh. Mantronik became one of the most sought-after producers in New York. Sleeping Bag's **Fresh** imprint was launched with Mantronik's drum-machine masterpiece, **Tricky Tee**'s "Johnny the Fox" (1985). Mantronik also produced **Just Ice**'s staggering *Back To The Old School* (1986) album which included the classics, "Cold Gettin' Dumb" and "Latoya", and the chopped-up "Mardi Gras" break (by Bob James) on T La Rock's "Breaking Bells" (1986). The latter also featured the mind-boggling spliced edits of **Chep Nunez** and **Omar Santana**, both of whom would contribute to the Mantronix sound in the future. Mantronik also pre-

dated New Jack Swing's combination of hip-hop and soul, with his electro-soul productions for **Joyce Sims**.

"Scream" from *Music Madness* (1986) remains one of the few hip-hop records that borrowed both Kraftwerk's synth lines *and* their icy detachment. Where **Afrika Bambaataa and the Soulsonic Force** decorated their Kraftwerk thievery with the traditional, good-time, "dance-as-transcendence" lyrics, on "Scream", MC Tee sounds as though he'd rather be at home playing **Pac-Man** on his Atari videogame console. Similarly, "Who Is It?" prefigured Mantronik's move towards full-on techno, with its withering synth stabs and subdued, streamlined beats. *In Full Effect* (1988) found Mantronix struggling to keep up with a changing hip-hop scene, but it managed to stay ahead of the times on one track, the

## The Album

# MANTRONIX
# MANTRONIX
# MANTRONIX

immortal "King Of The Beats". Aided once again by Nunez's editing, "King Of The Beats" was a cut-up of classic and soon-to-be classic breaks which managed to be both futuristic (it introduced the legendary "Amen" break, which would become the cornerstone of the drum 'n' bass scene) and still sound as close to the live experience of DJ **Kool Herc** wrecking the decks as anyone had in several years.

*This Should Move Ya* (1990) and *The Incredible Sound Machine* (1991) found Mantronix moving inexorably towards club music, a trend which continued right up to his 1998 "comeback" record, *I Sing the Body Electro*.

**The Best of Mantronix (1986–1988)**
Sleeping Bag, 1990

It's long out of print, but this really does feature the best of Mantronik's work, without the filler that ruined his early records.

# Marley Marl

◊ See *Juice Crew*

# Mase

◊ See *Bad Boy records*

# Masta Ace

In 1985 Masta Ace, from the Howard Projects in Brownsville, Brooklyn, won a rap competition, for which the grand prize was six hours of studio time with super-producer *Marley Marl*. Ace was studying at the University of Rhode Island at the time, and he didn't venture into the studio until he graduated a year later. They recorded a couple of songs, and Marley Marl was so impressed that he included Masta Ace on the legendary Juice Crew posse cut "The Symphony" (1988).

Masta Ace's first solo single was "Letter To The Better" (1989), a stone-cold classic of the late 1980s fast rap style, which was built around a clipped wah-wah guitar loop. On *Take A Look Around* (1990) Masta Ace staked his claim to be one of the great pure New York MCs. On tracks like "I Got Ta" and "Music Man" (which introduced a soon-to-be classic **Atomic Rooster** sample), Masta Ace "ripped MCs like a paper bag", but he was just as comfortable impersonating Biz Markie on "Me and the Biz".

Although Ace got a lot of love from British neo-soul groups such as Young Disciples and Brand New Heavies (both of whom he rapped with), *Take a Look Around* didn't do much commercially, and Masta Ace took out his frustrations on *Slaughtahouse* (1993), which was released under the name Masta Ace Inc. Although Ace was spitting venom throughout, the album was a bit schizophrenic. The title track was a savage parody of gangsta rap's mindless violence, but "Who U Jackin'?" had Ace and Paula Perry playing muggers cutting up fools for fun. Inconsistency aside, though, it was great to hear Ace at full flow. A remix of *Slaughtahouse*'s "Jeep Ass Niguh", rechristened "Born To Roll", became Ace's biggest hit, largely thanks to its booming bassline.

There were lots more bowel-clenching 808 beats on *Sittin' On Chrome* (1995), and Ace significantly dumbed down his lyrical

ple of high whiteys/Who had to be on mad coke and Ecstacy/To think for a second you could stand next to me/Look, don't ever again mention my name in your freestyles/Or I'll cut up your transmission faster than Lee Miles ... 'Cos ever since Heav was in Vernon, I been burnin'/Next year y'all be up in Rawkus, internin'".

*Long Hot Summer* (2004) was, conceptually, the prequel to *Disposable Arts*, and featured production from Dug Infinite, DR Period, DJ Spinna and Ace himself, as well as cameos from **The Beatnuts**, Rahzel, Ed OG, Jean Grae and Big Noyd.

◉ **Best of Cold Chillin'**
Cold Chillin'/Landspeed, 2001

This gets the nod over *Take a Look Around*, of which it is almost an exact replica, for the simple reason that this includes the original version of "Letter to the Better", rather than the remix featured on the 1990 album. Masta Ace has maintained a career because his style is flexible enough to work in both East and West Coast styles. This album, however, is pure New York hip-hop circa 1990, and his voice feels more at home here than anywhere else.

style to match. Aside from "Born To Roll", in which Masta Ace compares rollin' in your car with a boomin' system to revolution, the commitment that had marked his previous album was noticeably absent.

It reappeared, however, on *Disposable Arts* (2001), a sort of concept album which tracks its main protagonist as he goes back to school but then eventually ends up in jail. The real point of the album, though, was for Ace to once again heap scorn on the state of hip-hop. This was most apparent on the ferocious diss track "Acknowledge", where he took the group **High & Mighty** down several pegs: "One thing, who named y'all the High & Mighty/To me, you all sound like a cou-

# Master P / No Limit records

I f nothing else, you've got to admire **Master P**. Not only for his business acumen and empire-building skills, but for the fact that the Alexander the Great of hip-hop has stayed true to no-nonsense, no-pretence hip-hop. While all around him ran away from gangsta rap and ghetto sentimentality in favour of 'futuristic' beats and ridiculous space-age garb, **Master P** and his **No Limit** soldiers almost singlehandedly brought back the medallions and garish jewellery of the old school and the metaphorical meat-and-potatoes rapping of Tupac and his ilk. It may very well be nothing but "give the people what they want" pragmatism (best exemplified by **Skullduggery**'s "Where You From",

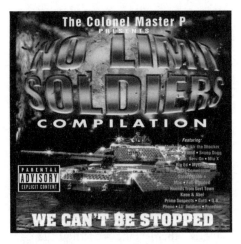

Carlos Stephens, KLC, O'Dell and **Craig B**), was slower and scarier than anything from Cali, especially when coupled with lyrical details such as dipping cigarettes in formaldehyde to get high.

As brutal as P's story-telling was, it was the cameo from **Mia X** (**Mia Kristen Young**) that stole the show. Even though she sounded a lot like Ice Cube protégé **Yo-Yo**, Mia X's precise enunciation and street-sass contrasted perfectly with P's molasses mumbling. Mia X had a local hit in New Orleans with "The Big Payback" (1993), before Master P snapped her up for No Limit and released the so-so *Good Girl Gone Bad* (1995). Far better was *Unlady Like* (1997) which included a savage remake of Salt-N-Pepa's "I'll Take Your Man". *Mama Drama* (1998) had too many "lurve" interludes, but the over-the-top theatrics of the title track made up for the poorly conceived slow ones and the duet with The Gap Band's Charlie Wilson.

With the death of Tupac Shakur, Master P saw an opening. On albums like *Ice Cream Man* (1996) and *Ghetto D* (1997), Master P combined the most saccharine, Hallmark-card sentimentality ("I Miss My Homies") with unrepentant gangsta-isms, shout-outs to the projects, and the most garish production values this side of a Siegfried & Roy spectacular ("Make 'Em

in which Skullduggery claims to be from pretty much everywhere in the US except Alaska), but P's version of the rags-to-riches Motown fairy tale – his No Limit record label is massively successful – is somehow more admirable, more likable than that of other inner-city media moguls. Shame about the music, though.

**Percy Miller** grew up in the Calliope Projects in New Orleans, but he moved to Richmond, California along with brothers **Zyshonne** and **Corey** after their brother Kevin was murdered in 1988. Percy opened a record store there and the three started making tapes which sold well in the Bay Area. The Millers moved back to Louisiana in 1994, setting up a home base in Baton Rouge. With Master P's West Coast connections, No Limit released the *West Coast Bad Boyz* (1994) and *Down South Hustlers* (1994) compilations. Although Master P released his first two albums, *The Ghetto's Trying To Kill Me* and *99 Ways To Die* at around the same time, No Limit wouldn't start attracting attention until **TRU**'s (Master P and his brothers, now known as **Silkk the Shocker** and **C-Murder**) "I'm Bout It, Bout It" (1995). Although the synth whine was lifted wholesale from the Dr. Dre songbook, "I'm Bout It, Bout It", produced by No Limit's **Beats By the Pound** team (**Mo B. Dick**,

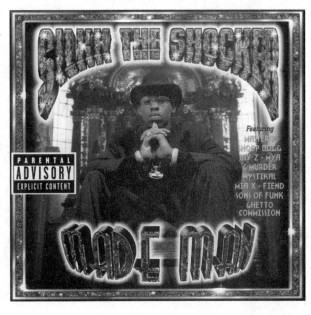

Say Uhh"). Sounding like James Brown passing a kidney stone (particularly on the abominable "I Got the Hook-Up!"), Master P's "unnggh" might just be the most unappealing catchphrase in living memory.

It's fair to say Master P's main triumphs haven't been artistic ones. In 1998 P made something like $56.5 million. With his remake of Run DMC's "Dumb Girl" ("Thug Girl"), *MP Da Last Don* (1998) went quadruple platinum; he poached the extremely bankable **Snoop Dogg** from Death Row and released his *Da Game Is To Be Sold, Not To Be Told* (1998) and *Top Dogg* (1999); his *I'm Bout It* film went straight to video, but was nonetheless one of 1997's best-seller while *I Got The Hook-Up* netted $7m from the cinemas; his sports management agency signed high-profile clients like Heisman Trophy winner Ricky Williams; he started clothing, real estate and, believe it or not, petrol station businesses; and he even had two try-outs with NBA teams.

Another commercial coup was luring **Mystikal** away from Jive records. Mystikal's No Limit debut, *Unpredictable* (1997), turned his already hyper flow into an unremitting torrent of noise. Mystikal also appeared on what is probably Beats By The Pound's least workmanlike production, Silkk the Shocker's cyberdelic Mardi Gras chant, "It Ain't My Fault" (1999).

1999, however, saw a change in fortune for No Limit. Having lost momentum to cross-town rivals Cash Money, and what with Mystikal jumping ship

and Snoop's contract expiring, "It Ain't My Fault" and TRU's *Exorcist*-sampling and OutKast-biting "Hoody Hoo" were the label's only two hits. P's sports management enterprise negotiated bad deals for its clients and was struggling, and P's *Only God Can Judge Me* (2000) extravaganza, featuring the most blatant Tupac rip-offs of his career, and sub-Cliff Richard version of the Lord's Prayer, limped to gold sales. One measure of just how far the No Limit empire had fallen could be found on the *WWF Aggression* (2000) wrestling tie-in album, where C-Murder had the awful task of recording the third-rate wrestler Gangrel's theme song – Method Man got the biggest star, The Rock, and comparative nobodies Dame Grease and Meeno got The Undertaker. Master P tried a change of nomenclature with the **504 Boyz** (basically TRU plus Mystikal and newcomer **Krazy**), but their *Goodfellas* (2000) was riddled with remakes and a paucity of ideas. It seemed like only God could save P now.

Instead, it was his 11-year-old son, Lil' Romeo. With the underage Lil' Bow Wow all over the charts and his empire in tatters, Master P, who's never seen a formula he couldn't exploit, took the me-too-ism he applied to gangsta rap, and turned it to kiddie rap. Lil' Romeo's self-titled debut album (2001) was an enormous hit thanks to its US number-one lead single "My Baby", which – surprise, surprise – sampled the Jackson 5.

Still, as much as Master P and his marketing team might have wished otherwise, you can't pin a record-label's hopes on a pre-adolescent. On *Good Side, Bad Side* (2004), a fairly ridiculous double-disc concept album, Master P turned to the producer who has supplanted him as the linchpin of Southern rap, Lil Jon. Jon's "Who Them Boyz" (featuring a verse from C-Murder that was recorded in prison – living up to his name, he was doing a bid for attempted murder) and "Act a Fool" were the best tracks on an otherwise patchy and overlong album. Adding real tragedy to Master P's commercial fall from grace, former No Limit rapper **Soulja Slim** was murdered outside his mother's house in November 2003.

**True**
No Limit, 1995

The album that put No Limit on the map is probably the label's most palatable, and the rallying cry which anchors "I'm Bout It, Bout It", makes it certainly No Limit's best track.

# MC Breed

Unlike fellow Flint, Michigan rappers the **Dayton Family**, gangsta rapper MC Breed (Eric Breed) isn't so hardcore that he doesn't care about selling records. While the Dayton Family wallow in their rep as the hardest mo-fo's to come

out of the hardest city in America, Breed wants to be all things gangsta to all people. While obviously owing more than a substantial debt to Too $hort and 2Pac, he also gives it up to his peeps down South, and to **Erick Sermon**.

Remarkably, considering he came from the boondocks, he exploded onto the national scene with his first single, "Ain't No Future In Yo' Frontin'" (1991). Bumpin' along on samples of **Zapp**'s "More Bounce To The Ounce", Ohio Players' "Funky Worm" and **Flavor Flav**, on top of the whining synths that were just starting to come out of Compton, "Ain't No Future…" was an absolute monster and even influenced artists on the West Coast. There was nothing else even remotely as galvanizing or as gangsta on *MC Breed & the DFC* (1991), with his **Da Flint Crew** – Alpha Breed and T-Double E. The rest of the album was strangely characterized by East Coast beats that were a year or so old already, and something of a social conscience, even if it wasn't terribly well articulated.

*20 Below* (1992) dispensed with any lingering East Coast-isms in favour of straight-up **Ice Cube**-apeing. The trend continued with *The New Breed* (1993), which Breed recorded in California with **The DOC** and Warren G, and featured a cameo from **2Pac** on "Gotta Get Mine". *Funkafied* (1994) took the West Coast's fascination with P-Funk one step further by using primarily live musicians and even had Dr Funkenstein himself, **George Clinton**, guesting on a couple of tracks. Easily Breed's best album, *Funkafied*, with almost no airplay, made the top ten of the r&b charts.

Despite the album's success, Breed once again changed his style for *Big Baller* (1995). As the title might suggest, Breed had headed south to Atlanta, where he hooked up with **Too $hort** and tried but failed to replicate the Dirty South sound of Organized Noize and co. *To Da Beat Ch'all* (1996) faired slightly better and was notable for featuring some of Dirty South kingpin **Jazze Pha**'s earliest production work. *Flatline* (1997) continued along the same lines, but added **Ant Banks** to bring some smooth rolling Bay Area mackin' music to the mix, alongside the Southern fried "pimp-trick-gangsta-clique" shit.

After leaving the Wrap/Ichiban record label for Power/Roadrunner, Breed seemed to lose his way with a series of awful albums: *It's All Good* (1999), *2 For The Show* (1999) and *MC Breed Presents The Thugz Vol. 1* (2000). Breed moved back to Michigan in 2001 and *The Fharmicist* (2001), on Detroit indie Fharmacy, found him rejuvenated. "Let's Go To The Club" had a vaguely menacing tick-tock beat that bore a passing resemblance to Eminem's "Lose Yourself" from the following year.

**The Best of Breed**
2001, Ichiban

Originally released in 1995, this greatest hits package was rereleased after "Let's Go to the Club" became a regional hit in the Midwest. Even though it only includes material from his first Southern album, this has just about all the Breed anyone could need.

# MC Eiht / Compton's Most Wanted

Of all the groups that followed in N.W.A.'s bullet trail, **Compton's Most Wanted** might have been the best. Formed by former Crip member **Aaron Tyler** (aka **MC Eiht**), ex-World Class Wreckin' Cru member **The Unknown DJ** and **DJ Slip**, CMW's first single was "Rhymes Too Funky" (1988) which appeared on the Sound Control Mob's *The Compton Compilation*. Signing to Orpheus, CMW dropped the landmark *It's A Compton Thang* (1990). While the album featured the debut of Eiht's trademark "geeyaahh" catchphrase and his unique, oddly

punctuated flow, *It's a Compton Thang* is perhaps most notable as the instigator of hip-hop's most notorious and brutal beef, with its DJ Quik disses on "Duck Sick".

Now signed to Epic, the group continued to make gangsta tales of surprising emotional depth, thanks to Slip's slick production on *Straight Checkn' 'Em* (1991). But for all of Eiht's harrowing tales of ghetto alienation and Slip's graceful pimp limp on "Growin' Up In The Hood" and "Compton Lynching", *Straight Checkn' 'Em*'s best track

was another DJ Quik bitch-slap, "Def Wish". The dark, edgy and cinematic *Music To Driveby* (1992) was CMW's best album, and a bona fide street classic, thanks to "Hood Took Me Under", "Compton 4 Life" and "Dead Men Tell No Lies".

In 1993 Eiht starred as A-Wax in the Hughes Brothers' *Menace II Society*, and provided the soundtrack's best moment on "Streiht Up Menace", which managed to overcome its saccharine production with a precisely detailed narrative. Getting used to seeing his name up in lights, CMW became MC Eiht featuring CMW for *We Come Strapped* (1994). Despite largely uninspiring production that resulted from Slip's downplayed role, *We Come Strapped*

went gold and was Eiht's biggest hit.

*Death Threatz* (1996) and *Last Man Standing* (1997), however, were both artistic and commercial disappointments. In the wake of the deaths of Tupac and Biggie and his own commerical death, Eiht quashed his beef with DJ Quik and dropped his gang affiliation by signing to former Blood gang member **Mack 10**'s Hoo Bangin' label. *Section 8* (1999) marked a decade in the industry for Eiht and it sounded like it: the production was a pale imitation of the dark jazz Slip used to provide for him, and Eiht sounded positively octogenarian on tracks such as "Hood Still Got Me Under". *N' My Neighborhood* (2000) similarly lacked the intensity of his earlier joints and sounded like an old, reformed G sitting on the porch, sipping lemonade and telling little Gs stories of the good old days.

⊙ **Music To Driveby**
Epic, 1992

Probably the best West Coast gangsta rap album not produced by Dr. Dre.

# MC Lyte

Embodying both gum-snapping sass and gun-clapping blasts, **MC Lyte** is, apart from her one-time rival Roxanne Shanté, hip-hop's nicest-on-the-mic female MC. Of course, the erstwhile **Lana Moorer** borrowed a trick or two from Audio Two's MC Milk – close your eyes and that could easily be her on "Top Billin'" – but considering he is her half-brother, it isn't much of a crime. In fact, Lyte's wax debut was an inspired summit with Milk and his partner in Audio Two, Giz: "I Cram To Understand U (Sam)" (1987) was a scathing indictment of a crackhead ex.

"I Cram to Understand U" featured on her superlative debut album, *Lyte As A Rock* (1988). The fearsome "10% Dis" was a savage response to Antoinette's "I Got An Attitude" which included the devastating couplet, "30 days a month your moon is rude/We know the cause of your bloody attitude". "Paper Thin" was even better: "Ooohs" from a male chorus, grinding guitars, menacing minimalist beats and more choice epithets for the luckless former paramour Sam.

*Eyes On This* (1989) was just as good and more popular. On top of more fleshed-out beats and some of the best scratching of the era (courtesy of **DJ K-Rock**), Lyte continued the Sam saga on "Not Wit' a Dealer", warned against rising above your station on "Cappuccino", and got raucous on "Cha Cha Cha". However, for her next album, *Act Like You Know* (1991), Lyte didn't heed her own message on "Cappuccino" and got a make-over, swapping the b-girl attitude for cosmetic air-brushing and sonic sweetening. Aside from the **Toto**-sampling "Poor Georgie", the album was a commercial and critical bomb.

With hardcore ruling the roost, she returned to her tough chick image on *Ain't No Other* (1993). While the move was a commercial success (the single "Ruffneck" was the first gold single by a female solo rapper), all the expletives and bad behaviour seemed forced. Strangely, she abandoned the mack-slapping for slow jamming on *Bad as I Wanna B* (1996), which

featured production by **Jermaine Dupri** and R Kelly. Despite the effort, the album's only hit was Puffy's remix of "Cold Rock A Party" which made liberal use of a sample of **Diana Ross**'s "Upside Down" and became Lyte's biggest hit. *Seven & Seven* (1998) was even worse, particularly the remake of Audio Two's "Top Billin'" which was just paper-thin.

⊙ **Lyte As A Rock**
First Priority/Atlantic, 1988
Classics like "10% Dis", "I Cram To Understand U" and "Paper Thin" make this one of the finest albums of the era, by a male or female.

# MC 900 Ft Jesus

Like many artists working the fringes of hip-hop in the late 1980s/ early 1990s – Disposable Heroes of Hiphoprisy, Consolidated, Meat Beat Manifesto – Dallas native **Mark Griffin** came to the music from the Industrial scene. Unlike most artists, Griffin took his nom de disque from a sermon by TV evangelist Oral Roberts in which a vision of Jesus, 900 feet tall, told him not to worry about his financial straits.

With turntablist **DJ Zero** in tow, the skyscraper messiah debuted on the

The lift's broken. The light bulb's gone. It really is *Hell With The Lid Off* being MC 900 Ft Jesus.

*MC 900 Ft Jesus With DJ Zero* EP (1989). On *Hell With The Lid Off* (1990), 900 Ft sounded like Beastie Boy Ad Rock with a drawl, and a cosmic **William Burroughs** jones. He took pot shots at Shirley MacLaine, blamed being late for work on Bigfoot stealing his car and insisted that UFOs were real. The album was a strange mix of stilted jazzy/funky middle school hip-hop, and rigid acid house and techno.

*Welcome To My Dream* (1991) was less synth-driven, even if it was still a bit strained, giving DJ Zero more room to shine on the wheels of steel. "Falling Elevators" was more than a little reminiscent of **Miles Davis** circa *Jack Johnson*, while "Killer Inside Me" was somewhere between the Stone Roses and **James Chance & the Contortions**. Griffin's lyrics, though, were less quirky, and more hamfistedly "poetic".

*One Step Ahead Of The Spider* (1994) had a full live band (including **Vernon Reid** on guitar on "Stare and Stare"), but the music still felt brittle. Nevertheless, the album included his biggest hit, "If I Only Had A Brain". "Stare And Stare" was

a Curtis Mayfield cover that was undone by the fact that Griffin couldn't sing, but there were still moments when Griffin impressed you with his imagination. Despite its mild commercial success, this was to be the last MC 900 Ft Jesus album, as Griffin – possibly uniquely in post-hip-hop-career paths – became a flight instructor.

**Hell With The Lid Off**
Nettwerk/IRS, 1990

The other 900 Ft Jesus albums are probably more interesting musically, but the richer music only makes Griffin's deficiencies as a lyricist more obvious. With the more industrial tone of this album, his beatnikisms sound more sinister, more relevant and less like, well, beatnikisms.

# MC Ren

◊ See *N.W.A.*

# MC Serch

◊ See *3rd Bass*

# MC Shan

↷ See *Juice Crew*

# Mellow Man Ace

Ulpiano Sergio Reyes was born in Cuba in 1967, and moved with his family to Los Angeles four years later. He (now calling himself Mellow Man Ace) and his brother Senen (aka Cypress Hill's **Sen Dog**) were raised in LA's Southgate section on Cypress Ave. The two formed a group called DVX (Devastating Vocal Excellence) with **DJ Muggs** and **B-Real**. When Ace got a solo deal with Delicious Vinyl, the rest of the group became Cypress Hill.

Ace hooked up with producers **Def Jef** and the Dust Brothers and recorded *Escape From Havana* (1989). The album's lead single, "Mentirosa" ("Liar"), eventually became a huge hit (number fourteen on the US charts) on the strength of its catchy samples of Santana's "Evil Ways" and its even catchier "Spanglish" rapping. Ace was the first Hispanic rapper to go gold and, what with the similar success of **Kid Frost**'s "La Raza", the two pooled their resources and formed **Latin Alliance**. The group released one album, *The Latin Alliance* (1991), and one pretty decent single, a cover of War's "Low Rider".

Ace's *Brother With Two Tongues* (1992) followed in a similar style, but the gimmick had run its commercial course and he was promptly forgotten about. After laying low for several years, with only the odd appearance on a couple of obscure Latino hip-hop records, Ace reunited with Cypress Hill for their Spanish language album *Los Grandes Exitos En Español* (1999). Ace co-wrote and rapped on several of the songs on the album, which was a huge hit in Mexico.

Ace returned as a solo artist on *From the Darkness Into the Light* (2000), which featured production from DJ Muggs. The album played like your typical redemption story, with Ace charting his discovery of "The Truth" during his years in the commercial wilderness, only it was punctuated by withering verbal tirades against haters and suckers from Ace and Sen Dog. *Vengo A Cobrar* (2004) (*I Came To Get Paid*) had Ace making a bid for recompense for all his years out of the limelight.

**Escape from Havana**
Capitol, 1989

Chunky, catchy, witty production from the Dust Brothers (similar in style to their work with Young MC) is the highlight of this fine commercially-minded album. Mellow Man Ace spends too much time rapping about the ladies, but his "Spanglish" rapping often hits the target.

# Memphis Bleek

On "Coming Of Age" from his *Reasonable Doubt* (1996) album, Jay-Z says of protége Memphis Bleek, "I see myself in his eyes". Well, whatever the King of New York saw, it hasn't become apparent to anyone else, because Memphis Bleek has yet to escape the charge of coat-tail riding.

He debuted on "Coming of Age", echoing Al Pacino's Scarface in proclaiming that "The only thing I got in this world is my word and my nuts/And I won't break 'em for nobody". Bleek then appeared on the next two Jay-Z albums before releasing *Coming Of Age* (1999). Despite being surrounded by some of the best producers (**Swizz Beatz**, Irv Gotti, and Buckwild) and some of hip-hop's biggest names (Jay-Z, **Noreaga**, Ja Rule, **Beanie Sigel**), Bleek was flat and just didn't live up to the billing.

*The Understanding* (2000) followed in the same style: the top producers in the game (**Timbaland**, Just Blaze), marquee cameos (Jay-Z, Carl Thomas) and juvenile raps about the streets, bitches and guns. Unlike his CEO, or Nas, who both rhyme about the same subjects Bleek does, Bleek had no insights, sense of pathos, journalistic chops or plain old mic skills to elevate his raps above ghetto pornography.

Despite three years on the down-low, Bleek hadn't grown or changed at all for *M.A.D.E.* (2003). He was once again outshone by his guests (particularly MOP, who show up on "Hood Muzik", which might be the only truly affecting track of Bleek's career) and couldn't keep up with top-drawer beats from **Just Blaze**, Scott Storch and **Kanye West**. The lead single, "Round Here", even had to rip off the Dirty South technique of repeating the catchphrase every single line in order to produce anything memorable out of Bleek.

**M.A.D.E·**
Roc-A-Fella, 2003

This album gets the nod over Bleek's others only because it has the most contemporary beats – lthough "contemporary" might not be quite the right word, because "We Ballin'" is nothing but a remake of "Big Pimpin'" and "I Wanna Love U" is an interpolation of Michael Jackson's "PYT". Aside from the intense "Hood Muzik" with MOP, the best track here is "Just Blaze, Bleek And Free" which rides a strangely arrhythmic beat from, as the title suggests, Just Blaze.

# Method Man

◊ See *Wu-Tang Clan*

# MF Doom

◊ See *KMD*

# Mic Geronimo

Mic Geronimo was raised in Flushing, Queens and started rapping at the age of 15. A few years later he was discovered at a talent show by **DJ Irv**, who was Big Jaz's DJ at the time. The two went into a studio together and recorded "Shit's Real" (1993) and pressed it up themselves. The track's mournful piano line and Geronimo's chronicling of the "trife life" in Queens made it an underground hit in New York.

On the strength of "Shit's Real", Geronimo signed to Blunt/TVT and released *The Natural* (1995). He bragged that he had "the greatest vocabulary in any era", but the reality was that Geronimo had a smooth, graceful flow, but not the analytical eye that made Nas (to whom he was frequently compared) such a sensation.

Nevertheless the album got some attention on New York's underground scene.

With his mentor DJ Irv now going by the handle of Irv Gotti, *The Vendetta* (1997) was much more friendly, Gotti having now raised the commercial stakes. Calling in favours, Gotti assembled a roster of production talent and guest stars that even megastars would have been envious of: **Pete Rock**, Buckwild, Jay-Z, **Marley Marl**, The Lox, **Tragedy**, Black Rob, **DMX**, Ja Rule, **Havoc** and one Sean "Puffy" Combs. Diddy produced "Nothin' Move But The Money" (which was a pretty big hit), and its smoothness dominated the album. *The Natural* had Geronimo's "butter" flow working against gritty New York beats, but this time around Geronimo had nothing to work from – there was no tension.

After two disappointing albums, Geronimo returned underground to continue guerilla operations against the forces that kept him down. "Criminal Warfare '99" (1999) was a Queens posse cut, with Noreaga, Tragedy, Hurricane G and **Hedrush Napoleon** produced by DJ Premier. *Long Road Back* (2003) showed that his effortless flow remained undiminished by years out of the game, but once again, it was the lack of interesting observations or characterful beats that undid him.

**The Natural**
Blunt/TVT, 1995

Mic Geronimo has one of the smoothest flows in the business, and while he has never received truly sympathetic beats, the sparse New York underground sound here is more successful than any other of his attempts. The bass-heavy music sets off Geronimo's flow nicely, but it's Geronimo's lack of anything to say, and the constant apeing of Nas (check out "Masta IC", for instance), that makes the album mediocre.

# Mobb Deep

With their drug-dealing, beatdown-delivering thug tales from the Queensbridge housing project, **Mobb Deep**'s Havoc and **Prodigy** are the poet laureates of the trife life. But while no one would ever be foolish enough to question the veracity of their rhymes, **Kejuan**

The infamous Mobb Deep.

**Muchita** and **Albert Johnson** actually got together as students in rather different environs, the Manhattan School of Art and Design. The duo was signed to 4th & Broadway while they were both still students, and both just 15 years old. Despite production from **DJ Premier** and other A-list beat makers – and a bona fide underground classic in "Hit It From The Back" – *Juvenile Hell* (1993) was held back by the duo's youth and fell like the proverbial tree in the forest.

Undeterred, the Queensbridge pair took the means of production into their own hands, and unleashed "Shook Ones (Pt. II)" (1995). Against a Wu-Tangy loop that sounded like a zither, Havoc and Prodigy

turned some fairly average battle-rhymes into a gruesome parable about needing to be numb to survive the streets. "Shook Ones" was the Mobb Deep appeal in miniature: not particularly original, but doggedly savage rhymes, delivered by MCs with ice water in their veins who didn't have to resort to any gimmicks to make you believe them.

*The Infamous* (1995) was the same formula writ large: minor-chord piano loops, Grim Reaper strings and brutal lyrics that reflected the bleakness of their surroundings. In addition to "Shook Ones", the album included such classics as the collaboration with **Raekwon**, "Eye For An Eye (Your Beef Is Mine)".

*Hell On Earth* (1996) was no great (perhaps not even any) stylistic leap forward and was similarly teeth-grindingly intense. "Animal Instinct", "Drop A Gem On 'Em" and the title track were all brutally effective and followed the style established by *The Infamous* letter for letter. *Murda Muzik* (1999) was a comparative disappointment. Instead of the unflinching tales of old, much of *Murda Muzik* was marred by a kind of sentimentality on tracks like "Streets Raised Me" and "Spread Love". Of course, the fact that the rest of the album was the same album they'd been making for the previous four years didn't help matters any. "Quiet Storm", however, managed to be everything you'd expect from them, while pushing their sound to new dimensions with an eerie, gurgling-synth bassline and a big, dark space in the track where their hearts should have been.

Perhaps sensing they were stagnating, Prodigy went solo for *HNIC (Head Nigga In Charge)* (2000) which expanded on the standard Mobb Deep sound with tracks produced by **Alchemist**, Rockwilder and Bink, as well as beats from **Havoc**.

They may have called their fifth album *Infamy* (2001), but it was anything but the sound that originally made them infamous. With the exception of the adrenalizing "Burn", the album seemed preoccupied with the clubs and pop charts, as it drifted absent mindedly between Neptunes-lite beats and weak duets with r&b groups.

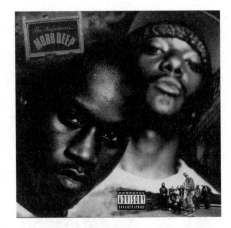

The independently released *Free Agents – The Murda Mixtape* (2003) took them out of the penthouse and brought the group back to the grimy Queensbridge projects, but while the style certainly suited Prodigy and Havoc more than the unseemly r&b experiments, the streets turned out to be nothing but cul-de-sacs in terms of keeping the Mobb Deep name known. "Got It Twisted", the lead single from *Amerikaz Nightmare* (2004), pointed the way out of the doldrums, with a killer sample from the unlikely source of **Thomas Dolby**.

 **The Infamous**
Loud, 1995

The no-nonsense deliveries and forbiddingly bleak arrangements make this a bone-chilling classic of Rotten Apple hardcore. There's no sunshine, and there are no hooks to draw you into their world, only all-consuming paranoia and vivid details that are grimly fascinating.

# M.O.P.

Perhaps the most revealing statistic about Brownsville, Brooklyn's **Mash Out Posse**, and their status among real hip-hop heads, is that their *First Family 4 Life* album was the most stolen album from New York City's HMV stores in 1998. With so many boosted units, **M.O.P.** have yet to translate their rep into sales but, with their cathartic tales of violence, they probably have more respect on the streets of the Rotten Apple than any other hip-hop artist. **Lil' Fame**

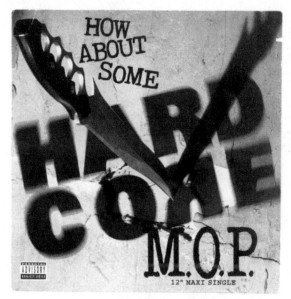

*First Family 4 Life* (1998) was even better, but it was equally slept on. The single "4 Alarm Blaze" sampled Survivor's "Eye of the Tiger" (!) and an unrelenting siren sound to paint a savage picture full of urban clautrophobia that, amazingly, wasn't compromised by Jay-Z's cameo. "Breakin' The Rules" had what may be the scariest line in all of hip-hop – "Before you test me/Know that I feel that the impact from a gat when it kicks back is sexy" – while "Real Nigga Hillfiguz" was a more introspective Premo track that had Billy Danze admitting uncharacterically "I've always been afraid to die".

Unlike so many of their peers, MOP just kept on getting better, and *Warriorz* (2000) was their best yet. Featuring the hyper-amped inner-city war chants that were their trademark, *Warriorz* proved that you didn't have to cozy up to Mariah or J-Lo, or have Ashanti sing your hook, to cross over to the pop charts. Bizarrely, the album's two singles, "Cold As Ice" and "Ante Up", were both top ten pop hits in Britain, where the pop charts are rarely home to hardcore hip-hop. While "Cold As Ice" may have been a slight nod to mainstream acceptance, with its sped-up Foreigner sample (chipmunk vocal samples being a hallmark of chart success from Babylon Zoo to **Kanye West**), Fame and Danze

may be like an "orthopedic shoe/[He's] got mad soul", but it's **Billy Danze** and his Son of Sam-inspired alias, William Berkowitz, who epitomizes M.O.P.'s approach.

While they first appeared on an underground comp called *The Hill That's Real* (1992), they really burst on the scene with the awesome "(How About Some) Hardcore" (1993). The track, produced by **Laz-E-Laz**, featured a galvanising horn riff, a dirty bassline and no-nonsense drums, which created a stark background over which Lil' Fame and Billy Danze spat (literally) ferocious battle lines like "I used to pack slingshots, but now I'm packing heavy metal". "(How About Some) Hardcore" was included on their debut album, *To The Death* (1994), which also included the similarly brutal "Rugged Neva Smoove" and the mean and moody bell-ringer "Downtown Swinga".

Although it didn't have a single as devastating as "(How About Some) Hardcore", *Firing Squad* (1996) was a better album. Their verbal gunplay was adorned with more fully-realised tracks, and the album featured production by the one and only DJ Premier. "Dead & Gone" and "World Famous" took their weapon-fetishism-as-battling-technique to the absolute limit of metaphorical plausibility and proved that no one, not even **Mobb Deep**, was as hard as they were.

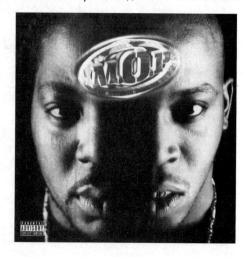

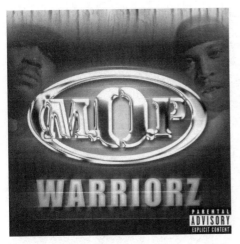

were as brash and brutal as ever. In 2004, the Mash Out Posse started hundreds of mosh pits with *Mash Out Posse*, a collaboration with heavy metal group **Shiner Massive**. Including classics such as "Ante Up" and "Nine & Two Clips" and new material, the album proved that MOP are the very avatar of true hardcore, everyone else is just Zalman King. While waiting for Roc-A-Fella to release their next album, Fame and Danze recorded "Bloody Murder" (2004), featuring a classic DJ Premier beat, as **Marxmen**.

**10 Years And Gunnin'**
Columbia, 2003

An excellent greatest hits package of violent, uncompromising, frightening rhymes that epitomise underground, street-level hip-hop.

# Mos Def

Inevitably compared to the Native Tongue rappers he sometimes hung around with, Mos Def was hailed by many critics as the herald of a return to the conscious rap of the late 1980s. While Mos Def's politics were often front and centre, what Mos Def really represented was a return to hip-hop's roots as an all-embracing movement, and a form of music that had ears wide open to everything, rather than just being a marketing tool.

Mos Def was born Dante Terrell Smith and his career in showbiz started in high school when he appeared in some made-for-TV movies and in a short-lived sitcom with Nell Carter and Roger Mosley. In 1994, he was a regular on *The Cosby Mysteries*. That same year Mos Def formed a rap group, **Urban Thermo Dynamics**, with his older brother DCQ (from **Medina Green**) and his younger sister Ces. They self-released a self-titled album in 1994. It wasn't bad, but Mos Def hadn't developed his own style yet – his flow was very reminiscent of **Grand Puba** and his voice was overly declamatory.

The project got him noticed, though, and Mos Def appeared on **De La Soul**'s "Big Brother Beat" and **Da Bush Babees'** "Love Song" and "SOS" (all 1996). A verse on **Reflection Eternal**'s "Fortified Live" (1997), in which he was "Sipping wishing-well water imported from Pluto", had the underground buzzing. He lived up to the hype on his solo debut "Universal Magnetic" (1997). After reminiscing about *Ten Speed And Brown Shoe* and "Planet Rock", Mos Def mumbled like a depressed Craig Mack with a cold and "kept it raw-boned like Skeletor" on top of a sublime Fender Rhodes loop courtesy of producer **Shawn J Period**.

With Reflection Eternal's **Talib Kweli**, Mos Def recorded *Mos Def & Talib Kweli Are Black Star* (1998). As their name indicated, Black Star was as much about reggae as it was about hip-hop. Both the teachings of Marcus Garvey and roots reggae's liberationist drive played a large part in the record's momentum, as did the guitar lick from **U-Roy**'s "Tom Drunk" (on "Definition") and Jamaica's own low-end theory. Jiggy stardust it wasn't, but it was cider from Mars to wash down with his previous year's wishing-well water from Pluto.

After some fine examples of b-boy hip-hop purism – "Body Rock" with **Q-Tip** and **Tash** (1998) and "B-Boy Document" with **High & Mighty** and Mad Skillz (1999) – Mos Def released *Black On Both Sides* (1999). While he set himself up as the hip-hop messiah with admittedly excellent lines such as "Hip-hop will simply amaze you/Craze you, pay you/Do whatever you say do/But black, it can't save you", the album was less of a lyrical manifesto and more of a musical tour de force. One of the richest, most tactile hip-hop albums ever, *Black On Both Sides* had production from **Diamond**, 88 Keys, **DJ Premier**, Ali Shaheed Muhammed, Psycho Les and **Ayatollah** (the **Aretha Franklin** sample on "Ms Fat Booty" might well be the precursor for the whole high-speed sample trend).

As the coda of "Rock N Roll" suggested, Mos Def went on to become involved in the

Black Rock movement, and concocted a supergroup called **Black Jack Johnson** with P-Funk's **Bernie Worrell**, Bad Brains' Dr Know, Living Colour's Will Calhoun and Sugar Hill bassist **Doug Wimbish**. The group was slated to release an album in 2002, but it never came out. During the confusion with Black Jack Johnson and with Rawkus Records's troubles, Mos Def returned to acting, appearing in movies such as *Monster's Ball* and *The Italian Job*. Signing to Geffen, Mos Def released a low-key 12" in 2004 featuring the tracks "Jump Off" (with Ludacris) and "Magnificent" (with Vinia Mojica).

**Black On Both Sides**
Rawkus, 1999

You should always be wary of albums that claim to make hip-hop more "musical" – as if hip-hop wasn't musical to begin with. "Musical" usually means more melodic – never one of hip-hop's strengths, and nor should it be. This, however, is one album where "musicality" is nothing to be scared of. Making A Tribe Called Quest's sonic template even richer and simultaneously more current, the production here compensates for Mos Def's occasional mis-steps.

# Mr Complex

A long-time presence on the underground, Queens MC Mr Complex (aka Corey Roberts) graduated from New York's High School of Art & Design with ambitious aspirations to be a filmmaker, illustrator and rapper. He first made a splash in the hip-hop scene in the mid-1990s with the duo **Organized Konfusion**, whom he had met during high school. Pharoahe Monch and Prince Po Along produced both his demo – which got him featured in *The Source* magazine's "Unsigned Hype" column – and then his first single, "Against the Grain" (1995). Complex sounded more than a little like Pharoahe, only with a less stentorian voice.

Complex then hooked up with **DJ Spinna** for the consummate 1990s underground single, "Visualize/Why Don't Cha" (1997), released on the Raw Shack label. Thanks to its preposterously funky bassline, "Visualize" was a monster hit on the underground hip-hop scene. After a single produced by Lee Stone, "I'm A Kill It/Big Fronter" (1998), Complex once again hooked up with DJ Spinna for the **Polyrhythm Addicts** project with **Apani B Fly MC** and **Shabaam Sahdeeq**. They initially came together to record what was essentially a Complex posse cut, "Not Your Ordinary" (1998), but Nervous records liked it so much that the group ended up recorded an entire, inspired album for them. Named *Rhyme Related* (1999), it featured Spinna laying down simple and choppy beats that offset the MCs' often tricksy styles perfectly.

The title of Complex's solo "Stabbin' You" (1999) single referred both to his lyrical darts and producer Lee Stone's SP 1200 chops. The horn stabs on it were absolutely vicious, and the angular but head-nodding drums danced a tarantella around sharp corners. Meanwhile, Complex lived up to his name, spitting lines about his "hare-brained schemes" like he was Elmer Fudd, and warning sucker MCs that they'd end up "in the jars on the counters with the pickles and pig's feet" like he was Yosemite Sam.

"Stabbin' You", along with all of his other solo singles, was included on the retrospective *Complex Catalog* (2000), released on his own Corerecords. The Pharoahe Monch-produced "Divine Intervention" (1999) and "I'ma Kill It" also appeared on *Hold This Down* (2001), a fine album full of good, if not great, battle rhymes and plenty of punchlines.

*Twisted Mister* (2004) was a bit of a letdown, with the wack love-jam "Glue" which featured **Biz Markie** imitating Austin Powers, and the flaccid sex rap "Scrape Your Back Out", with **El-Fudge**, taking up far too much space.

⊙ **Complex Catalog**
Corerecords, 2000

A collection of the underground 12"s that made Mr Complex's reputation. Despite his name, Complex is like a less complex, less charismatic Pharoahe Monch. That's not necessarily a bad thing, particularly as Complex generally rhymes on beats that are choppier and more straightforward than Monch's "organized confusion".

# Mr Lif

↻ See *Definitive Jux records*

# Keith Murray

It really says something when a rapper thinks he's so nice on the mic that he can go by his government name. For Long Islander **Keith Murray**, though, it wasn't always that way. He made his recording debut at the dawn of the 1990s with a ridiculously obscure single under the name of **Keefy Keef**. But it was only when he was given a platform by his neighbour **Erick Sermon**, of EPMD, that Keith Murray really shone.

Murray's debut under his real name was on "Hostile" from Sermon's *No Pressure* (1993) album. His own *The Most Beautifullest Thing In This World* (1994), displayed Murray's smooth, smoky skills on the mic to fine effect, going gold on the strength of the superb title track. In the course of the song, Murray professed to be "inter-planetarian like Doctor Who", and informed us that he was "shakin' the membrane of Encyclopedia Brown" (whatever that means) as he delved into the furthest reaches of Roget's Thesaurus while still riding Sermon's fluid beats

elegantly.

*Enigma* (1996) was less startling. Murray's flow wasn't as tight, his vocabulary wasn't as imaginative and the production was a bit lifeless. Murray, Sermon and **Redman** joined forces for **Def Squad**'s *El Niño* (1998). While the album was largely dull, there were occasional great lines like "You're soft like CD 101.9", to keep your interest.

On May 24, 1995 Murray and his crew were involved in an altercation with a Connecticut promoter. The promoter's 16 year-old brother alleged that Murray had hit him over the head with a bar

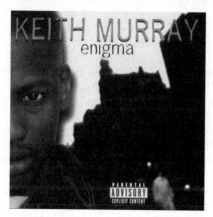

stool. Murray was found guilty of second-degree assault and sentenced to three years in prison. He began his jail term at around the same time his thrid album, *It's a Beautiful Thing* (1999) was released. Despite his legal troubles (or maybe because of them), the album was more of the same, even if "Secret Indictment" explicitly addressed his run-in with the law.

When he had served his sentence, Murray returned with *He's Keith Murray* (2003). The contemporary production (from **Just Blaze**, Clark Kent, Jazze Pha and **Khalil**) didn't suit Murray's flow, and he often sounded like Redman without the charisma and hyper energy (especially on the lead single "Yeah Yeah U Know It").

### The Most Beautifullest Hits
Jive, 1999

Yeah, it was a crass commercial cash-in on Murray's notoriety during his jail term, and a stop-gap measure, but his albums always suffered from sameness, making such a collection ideal. Everything from "Hostile" to the remix of LL Cool J's "I Shot Ya" (in which Murray appears along side LL, Foxy Brown, Fat Joe and Mobb Deep's Prodigy) is included on this collection.

# Mush Records

The Mush label began releasing downtempo instrumental hip-hop in 1998. Since its first release, **Boom Bip & DJ Osiris'** *Low End Sequence* EP (1998), Mush has gone on to become one of the standard-bearers for experimental hip-hop.

It doesn't get any more experimental than the label's first full-length release, **Dose One** & Boom Bip's *Circle* (2000). At first listen, the album appeared to be little more than a self-indulgent curio, but its surrealism turned out to be far more than contrariness for contrariness's sake. It was antique and scratchy, yet totally ahead of its time – very similar in overall effect to the opening credits sequence of the movie *Seven*.

This feeling of a dialogue between the past and the future was largely down to the contrasts and juxtapositions within Boom Bip's music. Wires shorted on top of tribal Brazilian percussion; head-nodding beats circumcised a **Louis Armstrong** trumpet riff; Dose One rhymed to an electro beat, while the ghost of a children's TV show theme played in the background; accelerating guitar feedback drowned out an icicle-like marimba; *musique concrète* rubbed up against chimes twinkling like mobiles above a baby's cot; **Ennio Morricone** harmonicas shadowed Wendy Carlos Moogs; and submarine-depth dub reminiscent of **Pole** or **Plastikman** was filled out by *Phantom Of The Opera* church organs. The music framed Dose One's regression therapy lyrics perfectly. Dose's logorrhoea – different overdubbed conversations ran parallel to each other on several tracks – and his oscillation between his mic persona and his 'real' incarnation as a guy named Adam, turned *Circle* into hip-hop from the lunatic fringe, both touching and touched.

The *Ropeladder 12* compilation (2000) effectively served as the label's manifesto. With tracks from many members of the **Anticon** records crew – **Aesop Rock**, Lulu Mushi, **Fat Jon The Ample Soul Physician**, Labtekwon, **Radioinactive**, Nickodemus

Mush recording artist Radioinactive.

and **DJ Osiris** – the album remade hip-hop as an artefact of Outsider Art. It tried to fashion an emotionally direct medium out of scribbles, bottle caps, pop culture detritus, and rhymes scrawled in crayon.

This aesthetic took many shapes: from the lonely, urban bedsit curmudgeon persona exhibited by Aesop Rock on his album *Float* (2000), through the exotic casbah on Mars created by **Radioinactive** (one Kamal de Iruretagoyena) on his lo-fi, Sun Ra-influenced album *Pyrimidi* (2001), to the schizophrenic doodles and impressionistic reveries of cLOUDDEAD's self-titled collection of 10" releases (2001).

**Fat Jon**'s *Wave Motion* (2001) album stayed true to the label's roots, with an instrumental selection that harked back to early 1970s "afrodelia". Jel's *10 Seconds* (2002) was an ode to the SP1200 sampler – more specifically, to its ability to make all beats sound characteristically dusty and grainy. It also paid homage to the detached, fazed, elegiac quality that **DJ Shadow** first coaxed from the sampler's decay and truncate functions, and its drum-machine-like pads.

**Awol One** and **Daddy Kev** injected the energy and sounds of free jazz into hip-hop on *Slanguage* (2003), while rappers

Busdriver, **Radioinactive** and **Daedelus** turned it into a State Fair on their carnivalesque *The Weather* (2003) album, with song titles like "Weather Locklear" and zingy lines such as "You are confusing that Mercedes emblem for a peace sign/And I'm mistaking that peace sign for a crosshair". Radioinactive and Antimc indulged in more sub-Sun Ra outer-space schtick on *Free Kamal* (2004). The production, especially on "With Light Within" (which is basically a **King Sunny Ade** track), was often superb.

## BOOM BIP & DOSE ONE

**Circle**
Mush, 2000

It won't make a club get "crunk", the girls get jiggy or even your head nod, but this is one of the most extraordinary hip-hop albums ever made. A collection of stream-of-consciousness poems about childhood, set to music that sounds like an imaginary calliope whirling in a schizophrenic's mind, *Circle* is also one of the most challenging albums hip-hop has thrown up. But with madman boasts like, "I can write anything I want ... 70% of all Episcopalian blue-collar jewellers don't believe in such a thing as collective church and state/I can write Mother Teresa in binary code and 'BOOBLESS' on a calculator", the effort is repaid in spades.

# Mystikal

With an old Southern soulman's grunt delivering the rapid-fire rhyming styles of Jamaican dancehall, New Orleans rapper Mystikal (aka Michael Tyler) will never need a Ritalin prescription. One of the most intense rappers in the business, Mystikal's high-octane, full-throttle growl is the direct precursor of **Lil Jon**'s simple "crunk" barks.

Tyler served in the army during **Operation Desert Storm** as an engineer looking for landmines, and then did eight months in a military prison for going AWOL. When he got out, he started rapping in earnest and recorded a self-titled album for local label **Big Boy** in 1995. While he was recording the album, his sister Michelle was murdered, and he recorded the song "Y'all Ain't Ready Yet" by way of catharsis. Both the song and the album were huge hits in the fiercely supportive local Louisiana music scene, winning Big Boy a distribution deal with Jive. *Mind of Mystikal* (1996) was a reissue of his debut album, but with a couple of extra tracks. One of them, the impressive "Here I Go",

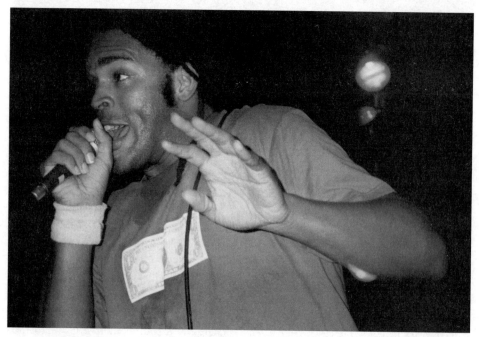

Project Blowed and Mush records stalwart, Busdriver.

Mystikal lays on the warm Southern charm.

had Mystikal coming across like a preacher filled with a not-so-holy spirit, on top of ominous blaxploitation funk.

His debut for **No Limit** records, *Unpredictable* (1997), turned his already hyperactive flow into an unremitting torrent of noise. The title track had him just hurling tirades at sucker MCs without regard for the beat, which was constructed from a sample of **Parliament**'s "Sir Nose D'Voidoffunk".

*Ghetto Fabulous* (1998) followed in the same style, but it was his appearance on **Silkk the Shocker**'s "It Ain't My Fault" (1999) rapping "We ain't gonna fall for the banana in the tailpipe" that was his most impresive rap during his stint at No Limit.

On *Let's Get Ready* (2000) Mystikal distanced himself from No Limit and finally showed what he was workin' wit', most impressively on the Neptunes-pro-

duced "Shake Ya Ass" and "Danger (Been So Long)". The inspired lunacy of the **Neptunes** and **Earthtone III** (aka OutKast) production was a perfect fit with Mystikal's throaty eccentricities, and brought more out of him than than the workmanlike beats of No Limit's **Beats By the Pound**

crew.

The Neptunes reappeared on *Tarantula*'s (2001) "Bouncin' Back" – Duke Ellington meets DJ Jimi uptown in the Calliope Projects. Mystikal kept up his **Mr Excitement**/gumbofied DMX persona, and became one of the biggest names in the biz, even gracing **Mariah Carey** records with his bayou bark. The relaese of his *Prince of the South* (2004) album was over-shadowed by his six-year jail sentence for sexual battery.

### ◉ Let's Get Ready
Jive, 2000

Although Beats by the Pound produce much of this album under their new moniker, Medicine Men, it's on the Neptunes and Earthtone III tracks that Mystikal really shines. Mystikal's at his best barking out non-sequiturs about twerking and women's asses, but he's also fairly compelling when exploring the dark side/light side dichoto-my in time-honoured Tupac/DMX/David Banner fashion.

# Nappy Roots

The Southern rap sensation of 2002, Kentucky's Nappy Roots (**Skinny DeVille**, **B Stille**, **Big V**, **R Prophet**, **Scales** and **Ron Clutch**) began when the group's members were all students at Western Kentucky University. They started releasing tapes that circulated throughout the campus and became so popular that they self-released three albums, *Country Fried Cess* (1998), *Uglyforthehometeam* (1999) and *No Comb, No Brush, No Fade, No Perm* (2000), which were recorded at the studio/record store that they opened in Bowling Green.

Their grassroots efforts got the group signed to Atlantic, who included their "Riches to Rags (MMMKay)" on the *South Park* movie soundtrack (1999) before releasing their *Watermelon, Chicken & Gritz* (2002). Coming of age in the hip-hop desert of western Kentucky, Nappy Roots had a take on the music that was relatively untainted by genre pigeonholing or commercial considerations. Their debut album was consequently fresh and

unspoiled, managing to be simultaneously elegaic ("Awnaw"), uplifting ("Kentucky Mud") and innervating ("Sholiz").

The album was a huge success – the governor of Kentucky even went so far as to declare September 16 **"Nappy Roots Day"**. The group approached their new-found fame with characteristic homespun even-handedness on *Wooden Leather* (2003): "Been all around the globe from Monday to Sunday/Y'all the same folk we see in Kentucky/It must mean … the whole damn world is country". Their success meant that the group could afford to bring in superstars like **Raphael Saadiq**, **Kanye West** and **Lil Jon**. But, unlike many hip-hop artists, the rigours of sudden success did not leave them cynical, jaundiced and ornery – Nappy Roots were still sensitive and intelligent enough to be sick and tired of being sick and tired.

**⊙ Watermelon, Chicken & Gritz**
Atlantic, 2002
Amongst the flood of "crunk" saturating the charts, Nappy Roots stood out by adhering to the Southern virtues first laid out by OutKast and Goodie MOb. Like the best blues records, this album is bacchanalian, profound and demotic at the same time.

# Nas

Main Source's "Live At The Barbeque" (1991) may have marked the debut of Akinyele, but no one remembers it for that. Instead, everyone knows "Live At The Barbeque" for the lines, "When I was 12 I went to hell for snuffing Jesus/**Nasty Nas** is a rebel to America/Police murderer, I'm causin' hysteria". One of the most powerful MCs ever to bless a mic, **Nasir Jones**, the son of jazz trumpeter Olu Dara, is hip-hop's chosen one. After several false messiahs, the Queensbridge standard-bearer was anointed Rakim's successor when he dropped one of the greatest albums ever, *Illmatic* (1994).

Nas had also released "Half Time" (1992) on the *Zebrahead* soundtrack and appeared on **MC Serch**'s "Back To The Grill Again" (1993), but it was *Illmatic* that heralded the coming of New York hip-hop's saviour. Not since N.W.A.'s *Straight Outta Compton* had there been such a potent evocation of life on the street; not since Public Enemy's *Fear of a*

*Black Planet* had there been such a devastating match between lyrics and production; and not since Eric B and Rakim's *Paid in Full* had there been a new MC who so fully commanded the microphone. Over an unbearably tense beat from DJ Premier, "New York State Of Mind" was an intense, visceral tale of a hustler who "never sleep[s], because sleep is the cousin of death". On the album's other tracks, **Pete Rock** ("The World Is Yours"), Q-Tip ("One Love"), LES ("Life's A Bitch") and **Large Professor** ("It Ain't Hard To Tell") all contributed some of the best beats of their careers, and Nas moved from chilling nihilism to moving neighbourhood newscasting with ease.

*Illmatic* was the work of a precocious man-child (he was only 19 when it was made), but, unfortunately, Nas seems to have regressed ever since. Although his remake of Kurtis Blow's "If I Ruled The World" made more of the implied politics of the "Imagine that" hook than the original, most of the follow-up album *It Was Written* (1996) was a garish celebration of the thug life, rather than a forensic examination of it. His intensity on the mic made *Illmatic* vital, but

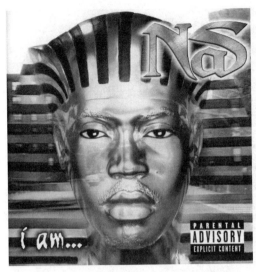

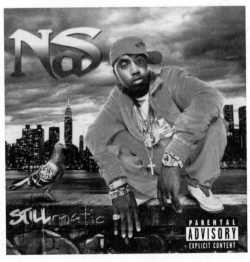

QB Finest gathered together such illustrious MCs as **Roxanne Shanté**, Craig G, Prodigy and Havoc from **Mobb Deep**, Cormega, and **Big Noyd** for a roughhouse posse party. While thuggery was the order of the day, the album was most notable for Nas's "Oochie Wally", a track that sampled the prog rock band Gong, and gave **RZA**'s signature eerie Chinese zithers a breezy tradewind lilt.

While "Oochie Wally"'s production was terrific, the rapping was a complete embarassment. After Nas had questioned **Jay-Z**'s sexuality on a mixtape, Jayhova hit back with "Takeover", which declared "your [i.e. Nas's] bodyguard's 'Oochie Wally' verse better than yours". On *Stillmatic* (2001) Nas seemed at least to have been recharged by the conflict, if not to be the poet of old. He tried to walk a thin line between the fiercely intelligent and sensitive kid of yore and the flashy star that he had become, but on the extraordinary "One Mic", where he starts out softly and slowly gathers momentum until he explodes, it was almost as if hip-hop's messiah had returned.

*The Lost Tapes* (2002) compiled some of the much-bootlegged material that Nas had recorded while he was sipping out of **P. Diddy**'s brandy snifters, but which had never been released. Again, it was not a patch on the fusion of words and music on *Illmatic*, but tracks such as the nostalgic "Doo Rags", the political "Black Zombies"

here he sounded complacent, moving into a comfortable middle age at 21, resting on his laurels, and clinking champagne flutes with Prada-clad honeys in the club's VIP room. His album with his **The Firm** posse (Foxy Brown, Cormega and AZ), *The Firm* (1997), was even worse, bringing label whoring to new heights of excess.

He toned down the flossin' to more everyday Johnson & Johnson levels on *I Am...* (1999), which had a couple of OK tracks in the form of Primo's "Nas Is Like" and the ridiculously over-the-top "Hate Me Know", but it felt like a schizophrenic battle between the Nasty Nas of old and his Nas Escobar persona. *Nastradamus* (1999), too, suffered from an obsession with shiny things and a lack of interesting subjects for his beat journalism, now that he'd moved out of the projects. "Big Girl" and "You Owe Me" (with singer **Ginuwine**) were both unseemly r&b-esque ballads, while "God Love Us" was so saccharine it could have been a 2Pac track. Not even DJ Premier could rescue *Nastradamus*, contributing the tired "Come Get Up". Like its near-namesake's millennial predictions, *Nastradamus* was a bit of a non-event.

Nas stepped down from his ivory tower in 2000 for the *QB Finest* project on his own **Ill Will** label. A celebration of the hip-hop legacy of Queensbridge (the world's largest housing project),

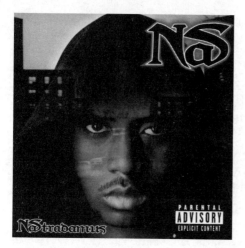

and the superlative murder narrative "Blaze A 50" showed that Nas hadn't lost his imagination or humanity during his fur-coat era. Sadly, the label brass kept it under wraps.

The death of his mother, Ann Jones, marked *God's Son* (2002), making it Nas's most inward-looking album. "Book Of Rhymes" had Nas looking back at his notebooks – reminiscing, but full of criticism and self-loathing at the same time – while "The Last Real Nigga Alive" worked the *Scarface* theme into a confessional about his various beefs. "Made You Look" and "Get Down" were both back-to-basics old school tracks that were positively anthemic. The rest of the album, however, was pretty weak, especially "Hey Nas", where Nas became a loverman, the anemic "The Cross" (produced by **Eminem**), and the sickly sweet "I Can".

"Thief's Theme" (2004), a mean and moody slow burner that had Nas spitting over a slowed-down "Inna Gadda Da Vida", was another one of those teaser singles that made everyone think that the old Nas was back, only to be disappointed by the album. But one classic Nas cut per album is still better than *I Am*.

**Illmatic**
Columbia, 1994

On 1999's "Hate Me Now", Nas bragged that he was the "most critically acclaimed/Pulitzer Prize winner/Best storyteller/Thug narrator". This album is why.

# Nate Dogg

Single-handedly making the r&b hook cool and masculine, Nate Dogg has one of the most recognizable voices in hip-hop. The **Teddy Pendergrass** of rap was born Nathaniel Dwayne Hale, the son of a preacher, in Long Beach, California. He went to high school with Warren Griffin III and Calvin Broadus, and when Hale returned from four years in the marines they formed a group called **213**. By that time, his two younger friends had metamorphosised into **Warren G** and **Snoop Doggy Dogg**. Warren played a 213 tape for his half-brother, Dr. Dre, who promptly asked Snoop and Nate Dogg to join Death Row records.

Nate Dogg was one of the key players in the G-Funk sound. His seemingly sweet but definitely rugged hooks perfectly fit Dre's vision of pimped-out swagger, casual violence and smooth *sang froid*. His macho crooning style could be heard on almost the entirety of the G-Funk canon: *The Chronic, Doggystyle, Regulate… G Funk Era, All Eyez On Me* and the *Above The Rim* soundtrack. His own *G-Funk Classics* album was scheduled to be released in 1995, but the gathering storm at Death Row meant that it was shelved indefinitely. Nate left the label shortly after Dr. Dre and eventually released *G-Funk Classics Vols 1 & 2* (1998) on Breakaway Records. The three-year delay was evident, as the now double-disc set sounded dated and uninspired.

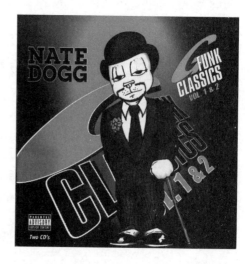

The Prodigal Son (2000) didn't suffer from any label problems, but the results were nonetheless the same.

His albums had tanked, G-Funk was dead, but somehow Nate Dogg salvaged his career by appearing on seemingly every other rap record. He sang with everyone from **Ludacris** to **Mos Def** and **Pharoahe Monch**, from **Eminem** to Eve, from Shade Sheist to **Fabolous**. *Music & Me* (2001) had far better production than his previous albums – especially the contributions from **Mike City** and West Coast veteran **Battlecat** who gave him almost-songs that suited his style far more than the straight-ahead hip-hop beats that he had previously tried to sing over.

**Music & Me**
Elektra, 2001

This is Nate Dogg's best album by far, but hip-hop's favourite singer will probably never make a great album. His voice works best as added colour, rather than as the main feature, when prolonged exposure reveals the flaws.

# Naughty By Nature

At first glance, East Orange, New Jersey's **Naughty By Nature** seem little more than no-frills professionals in a genre filled with ego-trippers, divas and big willies. Dig deeper, though, and NBN quickly reveal themselves as perhaps the finest pop-rap group of the 1990s. They certainly had all the ingredients: a sex-symbol lead MC in **Treach** (**Anthony Criss**), whose rapid-fire mic style was capable of delivering both simple hooks and minor epiphanies; a decent hype-man in **Vinnie Brown**; and a producer, **Kay-Gee** (**Keir Gist**), supplying Puffy-inspiring production comprised of easy to digest, easy to recognise samples.

Vinnie and Kay-Gee were in a group called **New Style** until they joined forces with Treach and rechristened the crew **Naughty By Nature**. Coming under the wing of Queen Latifah, NBN signed with Tommy Boy and released one of the most auspicious debut singles ever. "OPP" (1991) was an enormous pop hit, largely thanks to its sampling of a sizeable chunk of the **Jackson 5**'s "ABC", and an aggressive stickering campaign in the New York metropolitan area. Of course, the sly, cleverly constructed cheating tale didn't hurt either – the lyrics intimated that the titles's coy initials stood for either "Other Peoples' Property" or "Other Peoples' Pussy". Similarly chunky piano samples and easy-rolling drums featured on "Guard Your Grill" and "Uptown Anthem" from *Naughty By Nature* (1991), which proved that Treach was capable of twisting metaphors as well as tongue-twisting hooks.

*19NaughtyIII* (1993) featured the mind-numbingly facile hit "Hip Hop Hooray", but, with the inclusion of tracks like "The Hood Comes First", it was hard to hate them. By this time, NBN had become

Naughty By Nature chain themselves to the counter in protest about how long their ice-cream sundaes are taking to arrive.

one of the first hip-hop groups to start their own line of clothing, **Naughty Gear**, and Treach's acting career started to take off, with roles in *Juice* and *Jason's Lyric*. On *Poverty's Paradise* (1995), however, the group seemed to lose their focus and, despite a moderate hit in "Feel Me Flow", it was their least successful album. Nevertheless, *Poverty's Paradise* won them the largely irrelevant rap Grammy that year.

After a four-year absence, NBN returned with more hip-hop cheerleading on *Nineteen Naughty Nine: Nature's Fury* (1999). The Buppie production hadn't changed at all, but what once sounded fresh and invigorating was now lazy and as tiring as a vat of relaxer.

**Naughty By Nature**
Tommy Boy, 1991

With simple, chant-along hooks, this drew the blueprint for crossover hip-hop in the 1990s.

# Nelly/St Lunatics

Hip-hop has always been more about how you say it than what you say, but no one has taken that dictum to such absurd lengths as **Nelly**. The St Louis rapper became one of the biggest stars of the new millennium on the strength of unforgettable hooks based on schoolyard songs, double-dutch chants and nonsense rhymes. In fact, Nelly stumbled upon *the* formula for hip-hop crossover success: making hip-hop's adult preoccupations (blunts, bitches, riches, mackin' and stackin') sound as innocent as a game of patty-cake (see also **Jay-Z**'s "Hard Knock Life", **Ashanti**'s little-girl-lost voice, **Lumidee** et al).

Nelly was born Cornel Haynes, Jr. in Austin, Texas. His father was in the air force, so he moved around a lot until his parents divorced and his mother settled in St Louis. Inspired by the success of local rappers **Sylk Smoov**, **Domino** and **JCD**, Nelly and his St Lunatics crew put out a single, "Gimme What You Got" (1996), that was a big local hit. St Lunatics followed with a second local hit, "Who's the Boss" (1997) and a self-titled EP (1998 – later reissued in 2003), but due to label shenanigans their album was never released. The group stayed local until they hooked up with **Mase**'s former manager and a track called "Hot Shit" (1999) became a regional sensation.

Soon Universal came calling and the song was rereleased as "Country Grammar". The mildly bouncing beat, concocted by comrade-in-arms Jason "Jay E" Epperson, and the singsong hook were irresistible. Even though Nelly was actually saying stuff like "I'm fucking lesbian twins now", the record became a huge hit, propelling Nelly's debut album, *Country Grammar* (2000), to nine-times platinum status. The rest of the album was in very much the same style – in fact every song was damn-near identical – but the kiddie funk was so disarming that you didn't mind all that much.

The St Lunatics (**Murphy Lee**, **City Spud**, **Ali**, **Kyjuan** and **Nelly**) released *Free City* (2001), an album which followed in pretty much the exact same style, blending New Orleans bounce, Cleveland double-time and Missouri twang. Nelly's second solo move, *Nellyville* (2002), found Nelly moving away from Jay E's signature beats on a few occasions, with mixed results. "Dilemma", featuring Destiny's Child's **Kelly Rowland**, was as drab and forced as most r&b crossover moves are, while the **Neptunes**' "Hot in Herre" was even more undeniably catchy than "Country Grammar".

While Nelly was releasing retreads and pointless remixes, *Da Derrty Versions: The Reinvention* (2003), the St Lunatics were making their own solo moves. Ali's *Heavy Starch* (2002) merely proved that the crew was right in choosing Nelly as the group's first solo artist. **Murphy Lee**'s *Murphy's Law* (2003) fared better, mostly thanks to killer beats from Jay E, **Mannie Fresh** and

**Jazze Pha**, but he didn't have anything like Nelly's charisma either.

Nelly's *Iz U* (2004) album was previewed by "Flap Your Wings", a Neptunes-produced cyberdelic afrobeat groove that showcased Nelly at his least cornball and possibly most appealing since "Country Grammar" went atomic.

**Nellyville**
Universal, 2002

On the surface, Nelly's second album is interchangeable with his first. But the outside production talent called in for his sophomore effort freshens things up a bit, because his usual collaborator Jay E has only one groove. Nelly also moves beyond the party raps on "Roc the Mic" (with Freeway, Beanie Sigel and Murphy Lee), where he defends himself against KRS-One, who was upset that Nelly called himself number one: "I strike a nerve in old MCs wantin to come back/ I got the strength that he's lost and that's fact".

# Neptunes / N*E*R*D*

It had been a long time since Gary "US" Bonds, Jimmy Soul and Swamp Dogg put Virginia on the soul/r&b map, so it was little short of astounding when the contemporary hip-hop and r&b scene started to be dominated by two producers from the Old Dominion in the late 1990s. First, **Timbaland** exploded onto the scene in 1997 with Missy Elliott riding his dancehall-inspired digi-beats. Then, the **Neptunes** emerged out of VA with a new slant on Timbaland's off-kilter bounce and cowbells.

School friends Chad Hugo and Pharell Williams began producing tracks together in the early 1990s. Their big break was **SWV**'s "Use Your Heart" (1996) which gave the girl group a more mature sound. Later that year, they produced the Bee-Gees-sampling "When Boy Meets Girl" for Bad Boy girl group **Total**. The duo really got noticed, however, with **Mase**'s "Lookin' At Me" and **Noreaga**'s "Superthug" (1998). "Superthug" was their star turn: a sample of **Blondie**'s "Heart Of Glass", a synthesized guitar

N*E*R*D*

line that sounded like a rubber band snapped across a cake tin, kick-drums that managed to have a bit of shuffle in them as well as boom, backing vocals from **Kelis** and the most annoying hook from Noreaga ever ("What what what what what what").

Another big hit from a rapper not accustomed to chart placings came in the form of **Ol' Dirty Bastard**'s ferociously catchy "Got Your Money" (1999), while Kelis's "Caught Out There" (1999) once again displayed their gift for hooks that were annoying but completely unforgettable, with her shouted "I hate you so much right now". The following year, though, was the year planets aligned for the Neptunes: **Beenie Man**'s "Girls Dem Sugar", **Jay-Z**'s "I Just Wanna Luv U", Ludacris' "Southern Hospitality", **Mystikal**'s "Shake Ya Ass", **Cuban Link**'s "Still Telling Lies" and **Philly's Most Wanted**'s "Cross The Border" (all 2000) were all big radio hits and established the 'Tunes as the biggest producers in the game.

Their reputation was cemented when they were tipped to steer **Britney Spears** into the adult market with the vastly underrated "I'm A Slave 4 U" (2001). More hip-hop hits followed with **Jadakiss**'s "Knock Yourself Out", P Diddy's "Diddy", Fabolous's "Young'n", Mystikal's "Bouncin' Back", Tha Liks' "Best U Can" and **Usher**'s "U Don't Have to Call" (all 2001).

Along with another school friend, **Shay Thornton**, Hugo and Williams formed **N*E*R*D*** (No One Ever Really Dies) and recorded *In Search of...* (2001). The instrumentation on the original version of the album was almost all electronic, with snarling synth lines and ominous beatbox rhythms. Tracks like the biting satires "Lapdance" (featuring lyrics such as "the government's soundin' like strippers to me") and "Rock Star Poser" were seethingly political, and fitted the vibe created by the ugly production perfectly. Despite the album's evident brilliance, Hugo and Williams weren't happy with it and it was only ever

released in the UK (despite their objections). They rerecorded the album with a band called **Spymob** and released it in 2002. It was still a great album, but the brighter sound didn't fit the message as well.

As the Neptunes, Hugo and Williams continued to churn out hit after hit: **Nelly**'s "Hot in Here" (2002), **The Clipse**'s "Grindin'" (2002), Noreaga's "Nothin'" (2002), Jay-Z's "Change Clothes" (2003), Snoop's "From Da Church To Da Palace" (2002) and "Beautiful" (2003), **Kardinal Offishall**'s "Belly Dancer" (2003), Busta Rhymes' "Pass The Courvoisier" (2002) and "Light Your Ass On Fire" (2003), Kelis' "Milkshake" (2003), **N'Sync**'s "Girlfriend" (2002), Justin Timberlake's "Like I Love You" (2002) and Pharrell's own "Frontin'" (2003). *The Neptunes Present... Clones* (2003) was uneven, but on tracks such as "Frontin'", "Light Your Ass On Fire" and **Rosco P Coldchain**'s "Hot" it still brought the heat.

N*E*R*D* reunited for another maddening album, *Fly Or Die* (2004). Part hip-hop, part prog rock, *Fly Or Die* was a bit too **Prince** for comfort, but it proved what enormous talents Hugo and Williams are. If only they could learn how to rein it in a bit. Far better than the album was the Native Tongues remix of one of its tracks, "She Wants to Move"

(2004), in which the original's "her ass is like a spaceship I want to ride" was replaced with often sparkling verses from **Q-Tip**, Common, Mos Def and **De La Soul**. In 2004 Snoop Dogg signed with the Neptunes' Star Trak label, with Hugo promising that they would bring him back to the G-Funk golden age.

---

N*E*R*D*

◉ **In Search Of...**
Virgin UK, 2001

It was never supposed to have been released in the first place, and it has now been deleted, but the extraordinary original version of this album is the best work the Neptunes have been involved in. (The version that was released is still a fine substitute.) Angry and sardonic but still bumpin', this is the album that hundreds of disgruntled, jaded afrodelic stars have tried to make and failed. It is perhaps the closest anyone has come to making a contemporary version of Sly Stone's *There's a Riot Goin' On*.

# New Kingdom

With their love of feedback, rhythms that were dusted rather than dusty, and psychedelic lyrics, **New Kingdom** never exactly endeared themselves to the hip-hop hardcore – or even to the **Beastie Boys**/Cypress Hill-loving skatepunks who you'd have thought would be their only possible audience. Instead, New Kingdom found a small audience amongst the avant-garde cognoscenti, who flew their freak flag high.

**Jason Furlow** and **Sebastian Laws** first met in 1987 while both were working at New York's legendary used-clothing emporium

## RAP-ROCK

The merger of rock and rap is as old as hip-hop itself. One of Afrika Bambaataa's favourite breaks, and one of the most famous in all of hip-hop, is "The Mexican" by British prog-rock group **Babe Ruth**. Beats from **The Monkees** ("Mary Mary"), **Friend & Lover** ("Reach Out in the Darkness"), **Mountain** ("Long Red"), **Thin Lizzy** ("Johnny the Fox") and **The Rolling Stones** ("Hot Stuff") were all important early breakbeat records.

The first hip-hop record to acknowledge rock was probably **Kurtis Blow**'s sort-of-cover of Bachman-Turner Overdrive's "Takin' Care of Business" (1980). "The Mexican" would be interpolated, along with Kraftwerk, on Bambaataa's "Planet Rock" (1982), while **The Fearless Four** would use Cat Stevens' electronic oddity, "Was Dog a Doughnut", on their stab at electro glory "It's Magic" (1982). Around this time, hip-hop took off in downtown clubs like The Roxy and Danceteria, introducing punk to uptown, and vice-versa. The following year the Sugar Hill house band reworked **Liquid Liquid**'s "Cavern" for Grandmaster Flash and Melle Mel's "White Lines" (1983). This was, of course, the same year that recovering hardcore punk kids **The Beastie Boys** recorded "Cookie Puss", their first foray into hip-hop, and **Cold**

**Crush Brothers** recorded "Punk Rock Rap". While Bambaataa recorded with Sex Pistol **John Lydon** as Timezone in 1984, and UTFO's "Roxanne, Roxanne" (1984) brought the drums from Billy Squier's "Big Beat" into vogue (to be revisited twenty years later by the UK's **Dizzee Rascal**), it would be LL Cool J's "Rock The Bells" (1985) and its sample of the guitar line from AC/DC's "Let's Get It Up" that brought the snarling guitar into hip-hop, thanks to metal-head producer **Rick Rubin**. It was Rubin who made rap-rock inevitable with his production of The Beastie Boys' *License to III* (1986), and by introducing Slayer to Public Enemy.

It took Run-DMC's collaboration with Aerosmith to bring hip-hop back to the pop charts after the initial success of "Rapper's Delight", and as hip-hop started to grow in prominence, rock bands were soon forced to incorporate hip-hop to remain relevant. **The Red Hot Chili Peppers** had laid the foundations with their embracing of funk in the mid-1980s, but when thrash metallers Anthrax covered Public Enemy's "Bring the Noise" (1991), the first rock cover of a hip-hop song, rock's future path was set, and the nu-metal histrionics of Limp Bizkit and Kid Rock were only a few short years away.

Canal Jeans. For them, a union between the punk rock of Laws' adolescence, Furlow's love of **Curtis Mayfield** and the hip-hop that was turning them both on seemed perfectly natural. Enlisting the help of engineer/producer **Scotty Hard**, the two recorded a demo that got them signed to Gee Street.

Their debut album *Heavy Load* (1993) began with the words "Talk to me now/ Pouring no lies, no suits and ties/No need to rush, we love to fuck time", Nosaj sounded like a b-boy Howlin' Wolf with delerium tremens, while the beats sounded like the Beastie Boys' *Check Your Head* covered with grime and chip grease, or **Tricky**'s *Maxinquaye* a couple of years early.

*Paradise Don't Come Cheap* (1996), the follow-up, was even more uncompromising. "Mexico Or Bust" was a spaghetti western set in John Shaft's New York, while "Horse Latitudes" was Kid Rock's "Cowboy" as recorded by the **Southern Death Cult**. The song titles and vibe were more goth than hip-hop, and the music recalled nothing so much as 1970s heavy rock on downers, especially on "Terror Mad Visionary" and "Unicorns Were Horses" – which featured a humorous cameo from jazz musician **John Medeski** on organ that recalled Deep Purple's Jon Lord.

The group temporarily dissolved when Gee Street was swallowed up by Virgin. Nosaj went on to work with **Morcheeba**, Pitch Shifter and **Bill Laswell,** before morphing into his new persona **Nature Boy Jim Kelley**, under which name he recorded three albums, *Jump Out The Window Music Vols. 1-3*, while Sebastian worked with Kevin Martin's dub-noise band **Ice,** and continued working with Scotty Hard on some releases for the Wordsound label. Seb and Scotty then put together the band **Truck Stop**, which has continued to plough New Kingdom's scuzzy, stoner-rock furrow over extensive tours and two EPs.

⊙ **Paradise Don't Come Cheap**
Gee Street, 1996

Your head probably won't nod, but your gut will definitely churn. This is dirty hip-hop, not as in Bubba Sparxx or the Dirty South, but as in the bilge from the bottom of the East River. Thick, gloopy and processed to hell, this is psychedelic hip-hop at its most challenging and, occasionally, most rewarding.

# Nice & Smooth

Singing back-up for New Edition and Bobby Brown might not be the most promising of starts for a career in hip-hop, but **Darryl Barnes** (aka **Smooth Bee**) rose above his r&b origins to become a mainstay on the early 1990s hip-hop scene with his partner in rhyme **Gregg Mays** (aka **Gregg Nice**). Like labelmates EPMD, **Nice & Smooth** specialized in light-hearted party rhymes that balanced out the hardcore politics and self-righteous consciousness which dominated New York hip-hop of the time.

Nice & Smooth debuted on wax as Greg Nice and Smooth Bee on "Dope On A Rope" (1987) which has since become a highly prized hip-hop treasure. The duo's eponymous debut album of 1989 was the last record to be released on Sleeping Bag's **Fresh** subsidiary. Despite virtually non-existent promotion and distribution, the album had two semi-hit singles in the **Mary Jane Girls**-sampling "More And More Hits" and the great "Funky For You", which has probably featured in more DJ routines than any other record this side of the *Kung Fu* soundtrack. With their exaggerated, cartoonish deliveries (they sounded not unlike butlers on American sitcoms) and **Partridge Family** and Tommy Roe samples, Nice & Smooth managed to stay just on the right side of the novelty artist line.

Moving to **Russell Simmons**' Def Jam empire, Nice & Smooth released *Ain't A Damn Thing Changed* (1991). While "Hip Hop Junkies" and its great "I dress warm so that I won't catch pneumonia/My rhymes are stronger than ammonia/I'm a diamond, you're a cubic zirconia" line showed that their style hadn't changed much, the **Tracy Chapman**-sampling, anti-drug track, "Sometimes I Rhyme Slow", betrayed a creeping maturity. Although "Sometimes I Rhyme Slow" was a big hit, the group's finest moment came as guest stars on **Gang Starr**'s "DWYCK", the stoopidest posse cut of them all.

While *Jewel Of The Nile* (1994) had Smooth Bee going back to his r&b roots on the truly awful "Cheri", the deep funk production and a cameo from **Slick Rick** saved the album from congealing into a smarmy ooze. Not even a truncated version of "DWYCK", however, could prevent **Blazing Hot Vol. IV** (1997) from being as wack as its ageing (ungracefully) lover-men cover. Tellingly, it was released on Scotti Bros., former home of groups such as Survivor.

⊙ **Nice & Smooth**
Fresh, 1989

Like many things from this period, it now sounds hopelessly dated, but age hasn't dulled its effervescence. Tracks like "More and More Hits", "Funky For You" and "Dope On A Rope" are classic upbeat middle-school party jams that don't pale at all in comparison to the work of their more serious contemporaries.

# Non Phixion

As they describe themselves on "There Is No Future", Non Phixion "mix consciousness with a twist of profanity". They have a paranoiac's political sensibility, but they combine it with **Biohazard**'s energy and Al Goldstein's appreciation of the good life.

**Ill Bill**, **Goretex**, **Sabac Red** and **DJ Eclipse** grew up in the Glenwood Projects in Canarsie, Brooklyn and came together as a group in 1995. The group hooked up

with **MC Serch**, who signed the group to his Serchlite label. Singles like "Legacy" (1996) and "5 Boros" (1997) generated considerable hype in the underground, but the quartet really gained attention with the extraordinary political fantasy "I Shot Reagan" (1998), released on their own Uncle Howie label.

The group was signed to Geffen, but they were far too uncompromising for a major label and the deal amounted to nothing. They moved to Matador for the stunning "Black Helicopters" (2000), surely the first hip-hop track based on a klezmer sample. Thank Yahweh, the rest was just as original. Ill Bill, Sabac and Goretex ripped shit like an over-caffeinated Mohel, rhymed "shiksa" with "whisper", and hallucinated CIA and UN conspiracies, having beheld a good herd or two of William Cooper's pale horses.

An aborted deal with Warner Bros followed, but it wasn't until Uncle Howie hooked up with Landspeed records that they released their debut album, *The Future Is Now* (2002). While much of the production was handled by Ill Bill's brother, **Necro**, the highlights (aside from "Black Helicopters") were provided by big-name outsiders such as **Large Professor** ("Drug Music"), **Pete Rock** ("If You Got Love"), **Juju** of the Beatnuts ("Suicide Bomb") and **DJ Premier** (the seriously funky "Rock Stars").

*The Green CD/DVD* (2004) was

essentially a mixtape with freestyles from Bobbito's WKCR show interspersed with new songs. The DVD, though, included a pretty funny parody of cult classic TV show **Graffiti Rock**, with Bobbito hosting. Necro's Psycho+Logical label released Ill Bill's solo album, *What's Wrong With Bill?* (2004), as well as a collection of his early pre-Non Phixion tapes, *Ill Bill: The Early Years* (2004).

⊙ **The Future Is Now**
Uncle Howie/Landspeed, 2002

Non Phixion are a strange combination of conspiracy theory, backpacker wordiness and mosh-pit thuggery. It doesn't always work, but when it does (on "Black Helicopters", "Rock Stars" and "The CIA Is Trying To Kill Me") it results in some of the best underground hip-hop there is.

# Notorious BIG

L ike Tupac – the yin to his yang – **Christopher Wallace** was a bundle of contradictions. The former Bed-Stuy drug dealer was a gregarious court jester who used his quick wit to camouflage a heart of darkness. **Notorious BIG** made his money with MTV-friendly, overweight-lover party raps, but earned his rep with his pure mic skills: cinematic details, a hardcore sensibility tempered by a remorseful pathos, and a voice that enveloped the beat.

Biggie's vinyl debut was on the remix of **Mary J Blige**'s "Real Love" (1992). His solo debut was the uproarious "Party And Bullshit" (1993) from the *Who's The Man* soundtrack. After seemingly endless remix appearances, Biggie dropped *Ready To Die* (1994) on Puffy Combs' newly formed **Bad Boy** label. Showcasing his skills on the smoking, **Premier**-produced "Unbelievable", rocking Mtume's "Juicy Fruit" on the hopeful "Juicy", and blowing his brains out on "Suicidal Thoughts", Big Poppa embodied hip-hop's new "playa" lifestyle, tempered by the fear of death, and the knowledge that it could all come

Notorious BIG

crashing down at any second. Amassing platinum sales, *Ready To Die* was the album that put New York back on the map commercially, and the subsequent beef with Death Row would haunt the rest of Biggie's short life.

Biggie's commercial instincts were confirmed with the success of his **Junior M.A.F.I.A.** crew, and his guidance of Lil' Kim's career. His second album, *Life After Death* (1997), was released just days after he was murdered outside of a music industry party. It was a sprawling double album that tried to be all things to all people. While Big Poppa proved that he had "been smooth since days of Underoos", an MC – no matter how great – was often only as good as his producer's beats. *Life After Death* was, like Biggie himself, too padded out. Tracks like "Kick In The Door", and those produced by Premier, were gritty East Coast underground hip-hop that

could hold their own against any of New York's all-time greats. Elsewhere, though, he rode Hammer-sized chunks of **Diana Ross** on "Mo Money Mo Problems", tried to out-mack **Too $hort** and attempted **Bone Thugs-N-Harmony**'s tongue-twisting cadences on "Notorious Thugs". While this wasn't much different from the formula of his first album, this time round it just sounded like a bunch of tracks – there was no tension, no pathos and not enough humour.

Like other pop-music martyrs, Notorious BIG had his musical carrion picked bare by scavengers out to make a quick buck, on *Born Again* (1999). Unlike **Bob Marley**, **Jimi Hendrix** or **2Pac**, who all left behind mountains of unreleased

material, Biggie's master-tape estate was blessedly small. In fact, in order to turn the scant amount of material featured on *Born Again* into a full-length album, Bad Boy had to call in favours from **Juvenile**, Mobb Deep, **Sadat X**, Redman, **Nas**, Missy Elliott and, amazingly – since he had been banished from the Bad Boy fold – **Craig Mack**. There were so many cameo appearances here that Biggie sounded like a guest star himself. There was little of the sense of humour, or the insights of a man wrestling with his demons, that made Biggie such a star and, with a couple of exceptions, *Born Again* was as crass as you'd fear it would be.

**⊙ Ready To Die**
Bad Boy, 1994

The reason that this album revitalised New York hip-hop was that Biggie managed the trick that Dre had perfected on *The Chronic*: he tempered an unremittingly bleak vision with hi-jinks and *joie de vivre*.

# N.W.A.

H ip-hop in 1988 was a lot like rock in 1970. While many rock critics were championing artier, "progressive" groups like Genesis and King Crimson, the real action (which would prove far more influential) was happening with the reviled Black Sabbath. In 1988, music critics were lauding the political rage of Public Enemy, and denigrating **N.W.A.**'s apolitical nihilism. However, ultimately, it was not PE's radical soundscapes and politically-engaged rhymes but the hardcore rap that N.W.A. more or less pioneered which ended up becoming the *lingua franca* of hip-hop.

In 1986 **Eric Wright** decided he wanted to start a record company as a way to get paid. Hooking up with the World Class Wreckin' Cru's **Dr. Dre (Andre Young)**, **DJ Yella (Antoine Carraby)**, and former CIA rapper **Ice Cube**, Eazy-E recorded "Boyz 'N The Hood" as a demo. Written by Ice Cube, produced by Dre

**the notorious** BIG

**r e a d y** t o d i e

A post-Ice Cube N.W.A. psych themselves up for yogalates and a nice swim at Brixton Recreation Centre.

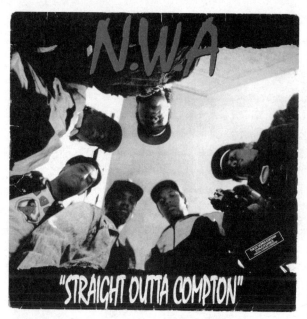

"STRAIGHT OUTTA COMPTON"

*Outta Compton* and *Eazy Duz It*) left the group in 1989. In 1990 N.W.A. returned with the *100 Miles and Runnin'* EP, which found Dre and Yella imitating the sound of the **Bomb Squad**, who had just produced Ice Cube's *AmeriKKKa's Most Wanted* (1990). "Real Niggaz", a savage diss of Cube, however, was a breakthrough: Dre's drums were funkier and the track was dominated by an eerie wah-wah riff that presaged Dre's future G-Funk direction.

While Ice Cube responded with the equally no-holds-barred "No Vaseline" (1991), N.W.A., and particularly Dre, would get the last laugh. *Efil4zaggin* (1991) defined the sound of popular music for the next decade. With its whining synth lick and rolling rhythm, "Alwayz Into Somethin'" was the blueprint for G-Funk, while "Just Don't Bite It" laid the foundation for the wave of blue raps and skits that would mar hip-hop in the future.

After another dispute over publishing rights, Dre left N.W.A., leaving Eazy-E to pursue an uninspiring solo career. He joined up with his protégés **Above the Law** for a series of brutal Dre disses contained on the *It's On (Dr. Dre) 187um Killa* EP (1993). While his own albums became increas-

and rapped by Eazy-E (the first time he ever took the mic), "Boyz 'N The Hood" took LA by storm, and soon Eazy-E's Ruthless Records got a distribution deal with Priority. With **MC Ren** (**Lorenzo Patterson**) and **Arabian Prince** (**Kim Nazell**), **Niggaz With Attitude** recorded a compilation album, *N.W.A. And The Posse* (1987), whose highlight was Ice Cube's "Dopeman". Most of *N.W.A. And the Posse*, however, was, like Eazy-E's solo debut, *Eazy Duz It* (1988), made up of unnoteworthy party raps.

*Straight Outta Compton* (1988), on the other hand, was the most uncompromising vision of life that popular music had yet produced. Unlike heavy metal's cartoon depictions of the dark side, N.W.A. sounded like they had first-hand knowledge of everything they talked about. They never flinched, never embellished – they even called it "reality rap". The first three tracks of *Compton* — "Straight Outta Compton", "Gangsta Gangsta" and "Fuck Tha Police" — were the most powerful records hip-hop had produced. And not only lyrically, but sonically: Dre's drum machines knocked you in the solar plexus like a gun butt.

After a contract dispute, Ice Cube (who had written most of *Straight*

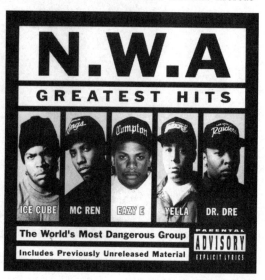

ingly irrelevant, Eazy-E kept releasing solo albums by Ren (*Kick My Black Azz* (1992), *Shock Of The Hour* (1993), *The Villain in Black* (1995) and *Ruthless For Life* (1998)) and introduced **Bone Thugs-N-Harmony**. Ruthless records stayed relatively healthy until Eazy-E's death from AIDS in 1995.

In 2004 Ren signed with Paris's Guerrila Funk label, and was scheduled to release an album in 2005.

**◉ Greatest Hits**
Ruthless/Priority, 1996

While *Straight Outta Compton* is unquestionably N.W.A.'s best album, all of its great tracks are here along with some choice moments from *100 Miles And Runnin'* and *Efil4zaggin*.

# EAST COAST VS. WEST COAST

Once upon a time, an east-west feud in hip-hop would have meant the **Crash Crew** from West Harlem battling the **Tantalizing 4 MCs** from the East Side for supremacy at the Harlem World. In the late 1980s, though, thanks to N.W.A., California started to blow up, and New Yorkers who believed hip-hop supremacy was their birthright started to feel insecure.

The first trans-continental beefs were fairly mild: **Roxanne Shanté**'s walkover against **JJ Fad** in 1987 and 1988, and **3rd Bass**'s diss-fest against **MC Hammer** in 1989 and 1990. Things started to get ugly with Tim Dog's *Penicillin on Wax* (1991) album, which included such challenges to the West Coast's primacy as "Fuck Compton", "Step to Me", "DJ Quik Beatdown" and "Michel'le Conversation". It didn't take long for both **Dr. Dre** and **DJ Quik** to respond with tracks like "Fuck Wit Dre Day" and "Way 2 Fonky" (both 1992).

Aside from a flare-up between **Ice Cube** and **Common** in 1994 and 1995 (which was a West Coast-Midwest beef anyway), things remained relatively quiet until **2Pac** started to blame his shooting on former friend **Notorious BIG** and then signed to Death Row while he was in prison on sexual assault charges. With 2Pac continuously talking about the incident whenever he got the chance, Death Row released **Tha Dogg Pound**'s "New York, New York" (1995). While the track only really attacked the Big Apple in the chorus ("New York, New York big city of dreams/And everything in New York ain't always what it seems/You might

get fooled if you come from out of town/But I'm down by law, and I'm from tha Dogg Pound"), it incensed the East Coast. **Mobb Deep** responded with "LA, LA" (1995), a far better record, and the intensity really started to crank up.

When he got out of prison, 2Pac released three of the most scathing diss tracks ever – "Hit 'Em Up", "Against All Odds" and "Bomb First (My Second Reply)" (all 1996), the last two as **Makaveli**. 2Pac savaged Mobb Deep, as well as Notorious BIG, Puffy, Lil' Kim, Jay-Z and West Coaster Chino XL with *bons mots* such as "I'm a Bad Boy killa, Jay-Z die too/Lookin' out for Mobb Deep, nigga when I find you/Weak motherfuckers don't deserve to breathe" and "That's why I fucked your bitch, you fat motherfucker" (directed at Notorious BIG).

A free-for-all then ensued, with records from **Mobb Deep** ("Drop a Gem on 'Em"), **Westside Connection** ("Bow Down"), **King Sun** ("New York Live") and **E-40** ("Record Haters") (all 1996) entering the fray. With the murders of Tupac Shakur and Biggie the beef pretty much fizzled out. Many commentators, most of them completely unfamiliar with hip-hop culture, blamed the East Coast-West Coast rivalry, and hip-hop music itself, for their deaths. This was, of course, as preposterous as blaming Johnny Cash, Spade Cooley, David Allan Coe or Merle Haggard for a Saturday-night brawl at a Tennessee roadhouse. Competition and violence are among American popular culture's favourite subjects – it's only fools who act on them.

# Onyx

Don't let their origins as a dance troupe fool you. Jamaica, Queens' **Onyx** weren't about genie pants, funny haircuts and pickaninny grins. Instead, with their black hoodies, shaven heads and roughneck scowls, Onyx brought hip-hop into the mosh-pit. While groups such as **UTFO** and **Public Enemy** collaborated with thrash-metallers Anthrax, N.W.A. displayed a punk-rock nihilism, and Esham camouflaged his rhymes in corpse make-up, Onyx brought a slam-dancing, locker-room-bragging male camaraderie reminiscent of **AC/DC** into hip-hop.

**Stickyfingaz**, **Fredro Star**, **Big DS** and **Suave Sonny Seeza** were discovered and signed by Run DMC's Jam Master Jay, who also produced their first album, *Bacdafucup* (1993). Filled with shouty, sing-along choruses, lame sexual innuendo and a drunken primitivism, *Bacdafucup* could have been an Oi! punk album if it had been made by ale-swilling British dolies in the early 1980s. But

Peter & The Test Tube Babies were never funky enough to sample The Mohawks' "Champ", as Onyx did on their mega-hit, "Slam". The thrashy testosterone fest continued on tracks such as "Throw Ya Gunz" (a very funny take on hip-hop's worst cliché "throw your hands in the air and wave 'em like you just don't care"), "Bichasniguz" and the really dumb "Blac Vagina Finda".

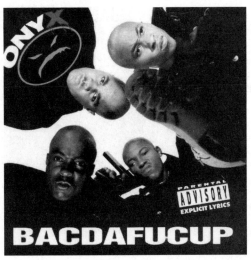

Losing both Big DS and Jam Master Jay, Onyx applied their self-proclaimed "grimee" rhyming style to their own beats on *All We Got Iz Us* (1995). Without Jay's simple but effective production, or the soccer terrace *esprit de corps*, however, the album failed miserably in its attempts to tell "shocking" stories from the naked city – it was totally outclassed by their neighbours from Queensbridge such as Mobb Deep. *Shut 'Em Down* (1998) went back to the raucousness of the first album and wasn't a bad attempt at recovering lost ground, but by this point people like **Limp Bizkit** and **Kid Rock** had reclaimed Onyx's territory for skate punks and bored suburbanites.

The group soon disbanded and **Sticky Fingaz** went solo with *Black Trash: The Autobiography Of Kirk Jones* (2000), but he wasn't making anyone "bacdafucup" any more.

With this in mind, the group reunited. *Bacdafucup, Pt. II* (2002) was a desperate

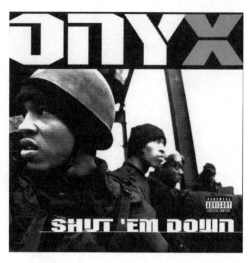

grasp at former glories – they remade their old hits, only this time with choruses that would have embarassed Kriss Kross. To wit, "Slam Harder"'s rousing hook was "Slam harder than Vince Carter". D'oh!

# HiP-HOP AND THE MOViES

Ever since **Ice-T** made a cameo appearance in 1984's *Breakin'*, it's been a truism that almost every rapper who attains any sort of success wants to be an actor. **LL Cool J**, Queen Latifah, Will Smith, Sticky Fingaz and **Ice Cube** have pretty much turned their backs on hip-hop in favour of Hollywood, while rappers such as **DMX**, Method Man, Redman, Fredro Starr, Ja Rule and **Mos Def** look like they're heading that way. The irony, however, is that despite the rap influx, Hollywood and hip-hop tend to mix as badly as oil and water.

While documentary has always treated hip-hop well – *Style Wars*, *Breaking And Entering*, *The Show*, *Rhyme & Reason*, *Scratch*, *Battle Sounds* and so on – feature film has been as unkind to hip-hop as it has been to rock. Thanks to its indie aesthetic, the first hip-hop film is still perhaps the best. *Wild Style* (1982) certainly has its flaws – weak acting, thin plot, no budget – but its flaws are also its strengths: it isn't a Norman Rockwell version of the streets, so there are no schmucks like Lorenzo Lamas posing as breakdancers, and it feels raw and real. In contrast with the grotesque racism of films such as *Fort Apache The Bronx*, *Wild Style* was a rare glimpse of humanity in Hollywood's filmic portrayals of the Rotten Apple. In the rash of movies capitalizing on the vogue for breakdancing in the mid-1980s – *Breakin'*, *Beat Street*, *Body*

GRANDMASTER MELLE MEL & THE FURIOUS FIVE

BEAT STREET
from the motion picture
BEAT STREET

INTERNATIONALLY KNOWN
Part 1 & 2

12" SINGLE
SH-32019

⊙ **Bacdafucup**
RAL/Columbia, 1993

Given the success of Run DMC's collaboration with Aerosmith, it's a wonder no one thought of this sooner, but fitting that Jam Master Jay was behind it all.

# Organized Konfusion

Originally protégés of legendary producer Paul C, calling themselves **Simply II Positive** (and recording a so-so, Meters-sampling demo, "International Arrival", and a 12" called "Memories of Love" on Solid Sound), Pharoahe Monch and Prince Poetry thankfully changed their name and became one of hip-hop's greatest and most radical groups. Due to the duo's uncompromising complexity in a climate that demanded "realness", **Organized Konfusion** languished in obscurity until

their split, and Monch blew "the fuck up" with judicious use of the F-word and a monster Godzilla sample on "Simon Says" in 1999.

As their name would suggest, Organized Konfusion's self-titled debut album (1991) was a schizophrenic mishmash of styles that didn't do them any favours in finding them an audience. "Fudge Pudge" found Prince Poetry imitating both an answering machine and the *Hong Kong Phooey* theme over a mellow, jazzy beat, while Monch bragged about his dick and fucking Heather Hunter. "Who Stole My Last Piece of Chicken?" found Monch making like **Marcel Proust** and reminiscing on things past. The album's highlight, though, was the mind-boggling "Releasing Hypnotical Gases". Based around a crazy **Weather Report** sample, "Releasing Hypnotical Gases" was a collection of sci-fi battle rhymes that would have left Einstein dumbfounded ("It's ironic when a demonic government uti-

---

*Rock* and, of course, everyone's favourite film title, *Breakin' 2: Electric Boogaloo – Krush Groove* (1985) stood out for the quality of its performances, a vaguely believable storyline (it was originally commissioned by **Russell Simmons** to be his biopic) and decent direction from the woefully underrated Michael Schultz. It would be the last decent hip-hop movie until **Spike Lee's** *Do The Right Thing* (1989), in which Lee managed to create a filmic language that approximated the funky edits of hip-hop itself.

Gangsta rap was always destined to play in the cinemas and in the early 1990s *Boyz 'N the Hood* (1991) and *Menace II Society* (1993) gave the cinematic narratives of gangsta rap the celluloid sweep they always begged for. *Juice* (1992) featured a star turn from Tupac Shakur, and was the first movie to have an actual hip-hop score (rather than just a soundtrack), courtesy of the **Bomb Squad**. This brief golden age of hip-hop filmmaking was quickly interrupted by video directors thinking they could move easily to the big screen (**Hype Williams'** 1998 flop *Belly*) and by just about every

other rapper making their own straight-to-video vanity project thanks to the startling success of Master P's *I'm Bout It* (1997). Just as hip-hop and cinema looked set to be nothing but a string of DMX and Steven Seagal collaborations, along came Eminem in *8 Mile* (2002), which although mired in the usual biopic problems, was certainly the best hip-hop movie in a decade.

lises bionics in a six million dollar man/ To capture me, clever, however, you can never, ever begin to apprehend a hologram") that predated a decade of self-conscious, avant-garde black futurism from the likes of Antipop Consortium.

*Stress: The Extinction Agenda* (1994) found Monch recovering from the death of his father and the duo wrestling with their label. On tracks such as the intro, "Stress", and "Maintain", they vented their anger by "crush[ing], kill[ing] and destroy[ing]" racist cab drivers and indeed anyone else who walked into their path. As Monch says, "[he] like[s] the taste of radioactive waste", and the music was thick, fetid, and noxious, more like electric-period **Miles Davis** than the cool

bop favoured by most hip-hop producers. "Black Sunday" used a loop also used by **A Tribe Called Quest**, but they elongated it, stretching it to breaking point, replacing Quest's languid insouciance with an enervated survival instinct. "3-2-1" was a joyous celebration of skills, but the album's defining track was "Stray Bullet": a gruesome narrative written from the viewpoint of a bullet that gets lodged in a six-year old's head.

*Equinox* (1997) was perhaps their most challenging album. Although, in its concept album format, it veered perilously close to Yes and ELP territory, *Equinox* just about succeeded despite itself. The story, about two characters named Life and Malice, was pretty lame, but the songs themselves were often extraordinary, particularly the stunning "Hate", in which Monch and Prince Po adopted the personas of two white supremacists.

Tired of earning respect but no cream, Monch changed tack, adopting a more straightforward approach on his solo debut *Internal Affairs* (1999). Instead of trying to move butts, the production of "Simon Says" tried to bludgeon you into submission, a plan which came to fruition when the track blew up in New York. The rest of the album was equally brutal and unforgiving. While it's hard to begrudge this most underrated of MCs' success, *Internal Affairs* was disappointingly one-dimensional and strangely bleak.

*Inner Visions* was scheduled to be Monch's follow up, but Rawkus's problems meant that the album was indefinitely shelved. One track, "Agent Orange" (2002), a post-9/11 follow-up to "Releasing Hypnotical Gases", did trickle out, and it suggested a return to his Organized Konfusion style. At press time, there were rumours floating around that Monch had signed up with Eminem's Shady Records.

**Prince Po** released his solo album, *The Slickness* (2004), on indie hip-hop label Lex. An uneven affair, the album was as all over the place as its producers and cameos: **Danger Mouse**, J-Zone, Richard X, Raekwon, MF Doom and **Jemini**.

⊙ **Stress: The Extinction Agenda**
Hollywood Basic, 1994

It may be challenging, but even people who want their music to be as easy as a Jackie Collins novel can appreciate the pure skills of "Bring it On" and "Let's Organize" and the chilling story-telling of "Stray Bullet".

# OutKast

A partnership, originally called **2 Shades Deep**, that began at Tri-Cities High School (Atlanta's version of the Julliard), OutKast (**Antwan "Big Boi" Patton** and **Andre "Dre" Benjamin**) are one of the most impressive acts in hip-hop. Without sacrificing hip-hop's main pleasure principle, Dre and Big Boi have managed to grow and shift directions over the course of their career – a unique feat in hip-hop. They celebrate the good life with all the verve of Jay-Z and the big-ballers, and their music is as flashy and shiny as a set of 20-inch rims on a new BMW. However, unlike just about everyone else working in similar territory, they never shy away from the consequences of their chosen lifestyle, and their music, while crowd pleasing, is also rich, deep and detailed, never succumbing to the cheap hook or easy way out.

The duo's first appearance on wax was a verse on a remix of TLC's "What About Your Friends" (1993). However, it was "Player's Ball", originally recorded for *A LaFace Family Christmas* (1993) that really caught people's attention. With its Curtis Mayfield-styled falsetto underpinning its depiction of "black man's heaven", "Player's Ball" went gold when it was released as a single in early 1994.

Their debut album, *Southernplayalisti cadillacmuzik* (1994), sought to subvert the Southern stereotype of playa music. The gangsta-leaning production provided by Organized Noize (**Rico Wade, Pat "Sleepy" Brown** and **Ray Murray**)

was rich, deep and detailed, but never as seductive or crowd-pleasing as Dr. Dre's: the album's sonic trademark was a truncated homunculus of the 808 clavé sound so characteristic of booty music. *Souther nplayalisticadillacmuzik* was a melancholy depiction of "the game", which never shied away from its consequences: the chorus of "Crumblin' Erb" went "There's only so much time left in this crazy world/I'm just crumblin' herb"; "Call Of Da Wild" was the story of a G who heard voices in his head, like the **Geto Boys**; and the spoken "True Dat" had the brusque put-down "If you think it's all about pimping hoes and slammin' Cadillac doors/You probably a cracker or a nigga who think you a cracker".

*ATLiens* (1996) was probably more "mature", but their acquired wisdom was never thrown in your face and it didn't shackle their vision, fun or grooves. With lines such as "I live by the beat like you live cheque to cheque/If you don't move your feet, then I don't eat, so we like neck to neck", the slow, bluesy creep of "Elevators (Me & You)" was one of the first Southern singles to go nationwide. Elsewhere, **OutKast** got more explicitly political on tracks like "Babylon" and "Mainstream".

Their masterwork, however, was *Aquemini* (1998), for which they largely handled their own production, as **Earthtone III** (with their former DJ, **Mr DJ**).

OutKast delve deep into the space-age-P-Funk-dandy-pimp-mack-graduation-ball wardrobe.

Opening with a song called "Return of the 'G'", *Aquemini* set you up for some time-honoured hip-hop big-ballin' and shot-callin', but then hit you with lyrics such as "Return of the gangsta thanks to/ Them niggas who got dem kids, who got enough to buy an ounce/But not enough to bounce dem kids to the zoo/Or to the park so they grow up never seein' the light/So they end up being like your sorry ass/Robbin' niggas in broad-ass daylight". Other highlights included the hoedown

"Rosa Parks" (complete with harmonica break from Dre's pastor) and the mind-blowing "Liberation".

On *Stankonia* (2000), Dre and Big Boi moved away from the Southern-fried, mystical, mumbo-jumbo gumbo of *Aquemini* towards a more space-age, P-Funk flava. Giving futuristic funk some good ol' Southern "stank", Dre and Big Boi laid down some morality tales along the way, revelled in the pleasures of the flesh and registered the inevitable emotional toll, bemoaned life in Babylon, and asked what makes so many people do so much fucked-up shit. And, as ever, there were no easy answers.

After four platinum-selling albums, and

the biggest critical consensus for any hip-hop group since Public Enemy, if any contemporary crew deserved a greatest hits album it was OutKast. While it would be pretty difficult to come up with a better selection of tracks, the usual 'greatest hits' problems applied on *Big Boi And Dre Present... OutKast* (2001). Their studio albums may not exactly be 'concept albums', but they do tend to work as an organic whole. On the original albums, tracks like "Crumblin' Erb", "Git Up, Git Out" and "Aquemini" – moving, frightening, occasionally beautiful songs that showed the flip side of the player lifestyle – were sequenced towards the end, where they became epiphanies, visions

# THE DIRTY SOUTH

For nearly all of the 20th century the South was the cradle of American music. Everything from jazz to the blues, from gospel to country, from rock 'n' roll to soul was born south of the Mason-Dixon Line. It was also, for a long time, the "sick man of America", the region that represented everything that was wrong with the American experiment. In the 1970s, however, that all changed. The South was "rising again", as the civil rights movement excised the worst of the South's racial extremism, and new investment made the Sun Belt a magnet for new hi-tech industries. At the same time, the industrial cities of the North were crumbling thanks to white flight and post-industrialism. Suddenly, it was the Rust Belt that was articulating America's zeitgeist in music: punk rock, disco, house, techno and, of course, hip-hop were all invented in the North.

That said, though, Southern involvement in hip-hop is almost as old as hip-hop itself. The third record released by Sugar Hill was by a group of three women from Columbia, South Carolina, **The Sequence**, who bragged that they were going to "Funk You Up" (1979) with distinctively downhome accents. The following year, Sugar Hill licensed a record from the Big Bad Wolf label by Tennessee radio **DJ Super Wolf**, "Super Wolf Can Do It" (1980). Aside from the rappers' hayseed tones of voice, there was nothing particularly Southern about these records, and that held true for other early Southern rap records like **The Pied Piper of**

**Funkingham**'s "Blow Some Funk This Way" (1981), **Sandy Kerr**'s "Thug Rock" (1982), **Gee Crew**'s "Freakenstein" (1983) or **Starting Five**'s electro tribute to the Memphis State basketball team, "MSU" (1983).

A mutation of electro gave the South its first distinctive rap style – Miami Bass – beginning in 1984. While Bass shone the spotlight on the South's strip-bar culture, it strove for the universality of booty rather than anything specifically regional. The same could be said for the late 1980s roster of **Payroll Records**, which featured rappers from North Cackalacka like **Supreme Nyborn** and the **Bizzee Boys**, who made fast-rap classics like "Versatility" and "Hype Time" (both 1988) respectively, but could have been from Queensborough just as easily as Greensboro.

Houston's **Geto Boys** may have began their career ripping off Run-DMC, but they soon started to depict the dark side of Houston's murderous Fifth Ward. At around the same time, New Orleans' **DJ Jimi** helped pioneer the Crescent City's Bounce sound and put the "dirty" into the Dirty South on records like "Where They At?" (1992). With groups like **Eightball & MJG, 5th Ward Boyz, The Convicts** and **UGK** emerging in the early 1990s, the South was perhaps merely waiting for California's gangsta rappers, who almost all rhymed with a distinctly country flow, to legitimize Southern-fried hip-hop.

of humanity in a culture that tries its damnedest to bury it under a veneer of harder-than-thou poses. Here, out of context, there was no logic to the sequencing and nuances tended to get lost.

For the two-disc *Speakerboxxx/The Love Below* (2003) Big Boi and Dre largely recorded their discs separately, with Big Boi in Atlanta and Dre working and living in LA. Left to his own devices, Dre sounded like **Prince** did when he was spreading himself thin trying to get out of his record contract, while Big Boi, on the other hand, seemed to grow as an artist. *Speakerboxxx* bumped like hell and bordered on genius at points, but there were no moments of transcendence; *The Love Below* simply overreached itself.

⊙ **Aquemini**
LaFace, 1998

It's contradictory, and drags in places, but this is nevertheless one of the most impressive hip-hop records ever recorded. One of the few hip-hop epics to succeed on its own terms, *Aquemini* explores OutKast's emotional and lifestyle quandaries critically, rather than wallowing in them, and has music that equals, and perhaps even surpasses, its lyrical ambitions.

# Petey Pablo

One of the most promising rappers from the Dirty South, Petey Pablo grew up in Greenville, North Carolina. He left home at age 13 and got involved with the street life in Baltimore and later in Raleigh, North Carolina.

After serving six years in jail, Pablo moved to New York, where he hooked up with **Black Rob** and **Busta Rhymes** (almost becoming a member of the Flipmode Squad). According to legend he was in a club's bathroom rapping with Black Rob and **Doug E Fresh** when the A&R director of Jive walked in, heard him and signed him on the spot.

Pablo first appeared on the remix of Black Rob's "Whoa!" (1999) and then on **Mystikal**'s "Come See About Me" (2000). Pablo made a lot of noises about not rapping about his cars, or how many people he had shot, but by the fourth line on his first single, "Raise Up" (2001), he was rapping "I'm a superstar, bought me a big ol' car/4.6 black 54 from the front to back/And got a button in the middle, make the trunk go 'eh-eh'".

Contradictory or not, "Raise Up" was a thunderous **Timbaland** production with an equally powerful performance from Pablo and the collaboration anchored *Diary of a Sinner: 1st Entry* (2001). The real highlight of the album, though, was another Timbaland beat, "I Told Y'All", an Afro-Delta juju fusion that ranks as one of Tim's best.

*Still Writing In My Diary: 2nd Entry* was scheduled to drop in 2002, but the only thing Pablo released was "Blow Your Whistle", with **Mannie Fresh** behind the boards. His second album was finally released in 2004. Instead of Timbaland , it was Lil Jon that dominated this time around (even though there were a couple of nifty Timbo beats in "Get On Dis Motorcycle" and "Break it Off"). "Freak-a-Leek" may have been about as sexually explicit a song ever to be played on American radio, but thanks to a hideously catchy beat from the king of "crunk", it would have been a hit even if he'd rapped about wart medication.

Petey Pablo.

**Still Writing In My Diary**
Jive, 2004

"Freak-a-Leek" was one of *the* singles of the year that crunk really broke, and Pablo was at his most charismatic and least imitative on it. Throw in a couple of Timbaland zingers alongside it and you've got a strong, if not great, album of Southern-fried hip-hop.

# Paris

Born in San Francisco and raised in Oakland, **Oscar Jackson** has tried to uphold the Bay Area's tradition of radicalism in rhyme. While an economics student and radio DJ at University of California-Davis, he became influenced by both the Black Panthers and the Nation of Islam, renamed himself **Paris** and started his own label, Scarface. He released his first single, "Scarface Groove" (1988), which got him signed to Tommy Boy.

His first single for Tommy Boy was "Break The Grip Of Shame" (1989). Housed in a sleeve picturing a white cop grabbing a screaming black boy in a choke hold, "Break The Grip Of Shame" had all the lyrical poses of black militancy, but didn't actually say all that much. Instead, the message was in the music: fearsome, plastic-funk synth stabs, scathing guitar riffs and devastating scratching from **DJ Mad Mike** (not to be confused with Underground Resistance's techno rabble-rouser of the same name). His debut album, *The Devil Made Me Do It* (1990), was a bit uneven skills-wise, but it was uniformly intense, making it one of the classics of the short-lived black nationalist trend in hip-hop.

*Sleeping With The Enemy* (1992) kept the message confined to the lyrics. While the production was fairly standard and dull West Coast funk, his rhymes on "Guerillas In The Mist", "Conspiracy Of Silence" and "Make Way For A Panther" were scathing. The album, however, only attracted notoriety for "Bush Killa", an interlude in which Paris dreams of assassinating President Bush, and the cop-killing fantasy, "Coffee, Donuts & Death", which forced the Time-Warner-owned Tommy Boy to drop the album in the wake of the hullabaloo over **Ice-T** and **Body Count**'s "Cop Killer".

*Guerrilla Funk* (1994) saw Paris trying to make G-Funk explicitly political, with mixed results, especially on the title track which was little more than watered-down rapping over a Puff Daddy-sized chunk of Funkadelic's "(Not Just) Knee Deep". Paris continued to provide funk for the trunk with his production of the **Conscious Daughters**' *Ear To The Street* (1993), which featured the bumping, if not very conscious "Something To Ride To (Fonky Expedition)". Paris's much delayed *Unleashed* (1998) followed the same formula to even more disappointing, increasingly

irrelevant effect. Perhaps this was because, in the meantime, Paris had worked as an investment banker.

Maybe it was the Shrub's ascent to the presidency or the aftermath of 9/11, but Paris returned recharged and reanimated with the controversial *Sonic Jihad* (2003). The album's cover depicted a plane crashing into the White House, while the album's first single, "What Would You Do?", had Paris twisting a classic Public Enemy rap into a conspiracy theory rant about what Bush knew about 9/11.

⊙ **The Devil Made Me Do It**
Tommy Boy, 1990

It's not perfect by any means – the music rarely lives up to the message, and Paris isn't as nice on the mic as you'd like – but it's still a ferocious blast of righteous rage nonetheless.

# Pastor Troy

Micah LeVar Troy grew up as a pastor's son in the College Park section of Atlanta. Like many rappers from down South, Troy was torn between the vision of life presented on his gangsta rap albums (which he wasn't allowed to play at home) and that of his father's church. While Troy often makes allusions to his faith on his albums, and took his father's title as a show of respect, he has yet to explore this contradiction as convincingly as fellow ATLiens **OutKast** or Mississippi's **David Banner**.

After dropping out of Payne College, Troy and his clique, the **Down South Georgia Boys** (**Lil Pete**, **Pin Head** and **Black Out**), recorded *We Ready – I Declare War* (1999), a seriously lo-fi album of grassroots Southern-fried gangsta that featured a lot of yelling over tinny beats. If you could hear past the bluster and his triple-time "flow", though, there were a few interesting moments, like when Troy rhymed "assault rifle" with "Holy Bible", and when Troy mocked and hurled invective at **Master P**, with whom he had a long and drawn-out feud.

Troy recorded the album *Book I* (2000) with Memphis producer

SMK and rapper 11/29 as Pastor Troy & the Congregation. While Troy wasn't exactly fulfilling the family legacy with his chorus on "Ghetto Raised" ("Ghetto raised, ghetto paid/Ghetto muthafuckas are everyday/ Ghetto muthafuckas don't like to pray/ Ghetto muthafuckas just like to spray"), the album, with its pan-Dixie line-up and production that didn't scream "this was sold out of the back of my car", was Troy's breakthrough.

Such a breakthrough, in fact, that Troy signed with Universal. *Face Off* (2001) included several tracks that were remastered from his debut, most notably "No Mo Play In GA" and "Rhonda", but it was "This Tha City" and its electric guitar line and skittering hi-hats that got the most attention. Down South Georgia Boys' *Last Supper* (2001) followed in a similar style, with "Playing God" being one of the biggest and messiest dog's dinners ever to appear on chromium oxide.

At long last, on *Universal Soldier* (2002), Troy had some decent beats. **Jazze Pha** contributed a couple of good tracks and **Lil Jon** threw down for the "Peach State" on "Who, What, When, Where". **Timbaland**'s beat for are "Are We Cuttin'" – synth stabs somewhere between Emperor Nero pomp and darkcore drum 'n' bass, secondary rhythms that sounded like someone hyperventilating – would have been one of the singles of the decade if he had given it to Missy Elliott or Bubba Sparxxx, or even Kingpin Skinny Pimp.

DSGB's *Til Death Do Us Part* (2003) had some more solid beats, courtesy of **David Banner** and Pastor Troy himself on "Sittin' On Thangs" (which used large portions of **Loose Ends**' "Hanging on a String"). *By Any Means Neccessary* (2004) had a monster "crunk" anthem in "Ridin' Big", but very little else going for it.

**Universal Soldier**
Universal, 2002

This is the best Pastor Troy album by some distance, probably because he himself has so little to do with what makes it good. Timbaland, Lil Jon and Jazze Pha give him sometimes incredible

# CHRISTIAN RAP

With its concern with the here and now, and its focus on the pleasures of the flesh, hip-hop would seem to be an awkward match for Christianity. Like the blues, but unlike the soul and r&b that were its immediate antecedents, hip-hop has no roots in the church, no umbilical cord always pulling its greatest performers back to the flock no matter how far they strayed.

However, hip-hop does have deep ancestral roots in the West African griot and the tradition of praise singing that exists right across the African diaspora, and its gift for delivering messages and self-aggrandisement makes hip-hop the perfect proselytising vehicle. Of course, hip-hop has also long had a connection with the Five Percent sect of Islam, so religion and rapping have never been far away from each other.

The first hip-hop record that explicitly tried to spread the gospel was probably **MC Sweet**'s "Jesus Christ (The Gospel Beat)" (1982). Although the blending of the good word and the rap lexicon was ungainly at best ("Jesus Christ entered into my life/He washed away all of my sins/Gonna make me chilly nice"), the production was a rather wonderful admixture of gospel keyboards and handclaps with the late disco that early hip-hoppers loved.

When rap started to become big business beyond New York, numerous preachers jumped onto the bandwagon in order to try to reach the youngsters who were foregoing the church in favour of the street-corner cipher. The best of this series of records was "I Ain't Into That" (1985) by **The Rappin' Reverend Dr. C. Dexter Wise III**. Similar to "Jesus Christ (The Gospel Beat)" in its fusion of hip-hop beats and gospel stomp, "I Ain't Into That" transcends its novelty record origins with lyrics such as "Pushers and pimps tryin' to make me stray/Servin' me death on a silver tray".

In the 1980s, paralleling the emergence of the Moral Majority, the stadium churches and the commercialization of religion, contemporary Christian musicians started aping popular styles down to the last detail but inserting material to work with, and he mostly stays out of the way of the beats. "Bless America", however, may be one of the ten worst hip-hop songs ever.

# The Pharcyde

Representing the LA underground, the **Pharcyde** managed to see the funny side of hip-hop while all around them lay the aftermath of Darryl Gates' policies, smashed St. Ides bottles and endemic crack. The nucleus of the group — **Imani Wilcox, Tre "Slimkid" Hardson** and **Romye "Booty Brown" Robinson** — met while they were working as dancers and choreographers, and they even briefly featured on the TV show *In Living Color*. Hooking up with **Derrick "Fat Lip" Stewart**, the Pharcyde signed a deal with Delicious Vinyl in 1991.

The group's debut album, *Bizarre Ride II The Pharcyde* (1992), was a carnival of silliness, group camaraderie, goofy gags, dusty samples and inventive flows. "Ya Mama"

was an update of the traditional street-corner pastimes of snapping and the dozens. On top of a neat organ riff, the Pharcyde dropped a series of classic snaps ("Your Mama's got a peg leg with a kickstand" and **"Your Mama got a glass eye with a fish in it"**) alongside original insults detined to become standards ("Your Mama's got an afro with a chin strap", and "You was beatboxin' for Lou Rawls"). However, when the carnival left town, these hip-hop nerds got all introspective and self-deprecating, talking disarmingly honestly about sexual frustration on the awesome "Passing Me By" and "Oh Shit".

In time-honoured fashion, however, the Pharcyde suffered from hip-hop's blight of becoming more sombre, and trying to be more "real" on their follow-up, *Labcabincalifornia* (1995). On "Somethin' That Means Somethin'" and "Devil Music", they recounted their difficulties with their record label and moaned about the dark side of fame over subdued jazz samples. The single, "Runnin'", continued the bad

Christian-themed lyrics. Towards the end of the decade, with hip-hop well on its way to becoming the lingua franca of pop music, contemporary Christian musicians began doing the same with hip-hop. This resulted in some of the worst music ever committed to chromium oxide, and a gross series of heresies against the glorious tradition of religious music. The worst offenders were undoubtedly **dc Talk**, a group who jumped on more passing bandwagons than the Bee-Gees. When they weren't sounding like U2 with stolen Public Enemy samples and decided to concentrate on rapping, they were less funky than **Vanilla Ice** over beats that were simply paper-thin. The Almighty will undoubtedly strike me down for saying this, but they sucked.

Bringing slightly more flava to the saviour were groups such as the Nashville-based **Grits** (who tried to clean up the Dirty South), **Gospel Gangstaz** and **Str8 Young Gangstaz** (who tried to turn West Coast gun-clappers into West Coast happy-clappers) and **T-Bone** (who tried to put the "hug" back into "thug"). However, in an apparent contradiction to the dictum that says one should render to Caesar what is Caesar's and to God what is God's, the Christian rap

machine keeps churning out identikit copies of popular groups and styles. **Lil' iROCC** (I Rely on Christ Completely) is a thirteen-year-old who's the sanctified equivalent of Lil' Bow Wow. **KJ-52** is an admittedly more-talented-than-usual Christian rapper who is a parallel-universe replica of **Eminem**, right down to a pair of recordings called "Dear Slim", which copy Eminem's "Stan" (only without the Dido sample) and which urge him to let Christ into his life.

With the emergence of **Kanye West** and his professed love of Jesus, perhaps the musical scourge that is Christian rap will heal itself and become a bit more creative.

MC SWEET

**Jesus Christ (The Gospel Beat)**
Lection Records, 1982

You'll have to pay a king's ransom for this, but the first Christian rap is probably the best. The rapping is a little square (even by 1982 standards), but the production – sublime Sugar Hill-style disco, holy roller piano, handclaps and exhortations from the congregation – is little short of inspirational.

The Pharcyde.

trip, and was accompanied by a **Spike Jonez** video that shot the band moving backwards with the tape running in the reverse direction, giving it an off-kilter, slightly queasy feel that fitted the music perfectly.

The Pharcyde were troubled by internal strife as well as record-label troubles and Fat Lip left the group shortly after *Labcabincalifornia* was released. Slim Kid, Imani and Booty Brown re-emerged in 1999 with the *Testing the Waters* EP on the tiny Chapter One Records. The title was disappointingly accurate, as it found the group rapping tentatively and hesitantly, albeit in a similar style to *Labcabin*.

Fat Lip, meanwhile, grew self-conscious, and rapped about the plight of the MC who fell off on "What's Up Fat Lip?" (2000): "Yeah I'm a brother but sometimes I don't feel black/My girl is white/My game ain't tight/Niggas who ain't seen me in a while be like, 'Dude, you aiight?'". Delicious Vinyl are scheduled to release his solo album, originally titled *Revenge Of The Nerd* but now rechristened *The Loneliest* *Punk*, though the absurdly long delay (four years and counting) does not inspire confidence.

Without Fat Lip, the remaining members of Pharcyde recorded the half-hearted and half-witted concept album *Plain Rap* (2000). They returned with *Humboldt Beginnings* (2004), a sort-of-concept album about weed that was pleasantly bright and cheerful, but didn't do much beyond that.

**Bizarre Ride II The Pharcyde**
Delicious Vinyl, 1992

Taking hip-hop on a ride through the funhouse, the Pharcyde made one of the best, most original albums of the 1990s.

# PM Dawn

Just how hip-hop can a group that has recorded with both Elton John and Boy George be? Even if the most hardcore thing they ever did was getting tossed off a stage by KRS-One, PM Dawn (**Prince Be** and **DJ MinuteMix**) represented the last gasp of hip-hop as an open-ended, open-minded form that embraced anything and everything, as long it bumped. PM Dawn's problem was that they swooned more than they bumped.

**Attrell** (Prince Be) and **Jarrett Cordes** grew up in a musical family in Jersey City, New Jersey – their stepfather was a member of **Kool & the Gang**. After getting their musical start at family parties, the two brothers recorded a demo, "Check the Logic", which got them signed to Gee Street as Prince Bee and DJ MinuteMix. Taking the name PM Dawn (inspired by the expression "from the darkest hour comes the light"), the duo released "Ode To A Forgetful Mind/Paper Doll" (1991) before scoring a minor hit in the UK with "A Watcher's Point Of View" (1991) which reached number 36. It was "Set Adrift on Memory Bliss" (1991), however, that really brought the group to prominence. Based on a large chunk of **Spandau Ballet**'s "True", "Set Adrift" tried to unite New York's two great street-corner musics – hip-hop and doo-wop – with an 1980s synth shimmer and a Prince come-on. It was an admittedly clever pop song, but *Of The Heart, Of The Soul And Of The Cross: The Utopian Experience* (1991) was as lousy as its title. When the album was released, its psychedelic escapism and introspection was novel enough to cut through its abiding air of joss sticks and fluttering kaftans. But, listening to it now, the hippy-dippy schtick is as annoying as Madonna's embrace of the Kabbalah, and The Beatles-derived pop hooks don't hold up as well as they once seemed to.

*The Bliss Album... ? (Vibrations Of Love And Anger And The Ponderance Of Life And Existence)* (1993) featured another b-boy-baiting sample (a fragment of **George Michael**'s "Father Figure" on "Looking Through Patient Eyes"), more dreamy pop set to breakbeats, and a cover of The Beatles's "Norwegian Wood". "Plastic", however, contained an oblique retort in its lyrics ("What's hard at first, but melts in the heat, they call that plastic") which was directed at KRS-One, who had crashed the stage during the group's performance at New York's Sound Factory in 1992, pushed Prince Be into the crowd and performed "I'm Still #1".

*Jesus Wept* (1995) – perhaps the group's most bearable title, but worst record – found Prince Be sampling **Deep Purple** instead of the new-wavers, singing even more and becoming even more self-indulgent. *Dearest Christian, I'm So Very Sorry For Bringing You Here. Love, Dad* (1998) featured yet more singing and even less rapping than *Jesus Wept*, but this time around Prince Be did at least deign to throw in a few melodies.

In 2000, the group released two limited-edition albums, *F*cked Music* and *Unreleased*, via their website. Aside from the sweet r&b of "Amnesia" (2002), they haven't been heard from since.

**The Best Of PM Dawn**
V2, 2000

Perhaps not the best selection of their tracks, but on the songs collected here their fey spirituality, half-baked "philosophy", and Prince Be's moaning flow are toned down in favour of hooks. It may be more pop than hip-hop, but at least it does it more creatively than Candyman did.

# Pooh-Man

Hailing from Cokeland (aka Oakland), the main claim to fame of Pooh-Man (aka Lawrence Thomas) is to have introduced the word "dank" as a slang term for marijuana into the hip-hop phrasebook. On "Fuckin' Wit Dank" (1991), released under the name of **MC Pooh**, he sounded like a combination of **Too $hort** and **Eazy-E**, with his pronounced Bay Area drawl laid on top of a huge synth bassline courtesy of producer **Ant Banks.** The rest of *Life Of A Criminal* (1991) was similarly formative NorCal gangsta funk with Pooh spinning classic "game" yarns such as "Oakland" ("Down here we say fuck the politicians/Because dealing drugs is a family tradition").

Changing his name to Pooh-Man, the rapper released the more fully realized *Funky As I Wanna Be* (1992). With Ant Banks again manning the boards, the album had better, richer production values, and collaborations with **MC Breed** ("Don't Cost a Dime") and **Too $hort** ("Racia"), but Pooh spent most of the album trying to out-$hort the $hort, to limited effect.

After a small role in *Menace II Society*, Pooh-Man released the unrelentingly savage *Judgement Day* (1993). After a negative remark from Ant Banks on a radio programme, Pooh-Man parted ways with the **Dangerous Crew** (Banks, Spice 1, Goldie, Too $hort) and *Judgement Day* was a non-stop diss fest: "Another nigga turned traitor/He wanna be a rapper, fool stick to the crossfader"; "The 'Peace to My Nine' bullshit I just couldn't bear/Here's my glock, listen to me cock it"; and "I'm leaving three corpses behind me/Mhisani, Banks and that nigga named Randy".

After some equally nasty responses from Banks and Too $hort (especially "Fuckin' Wit Banks" which remade Pooh's biggest hit), *Ain't No Love* (1994) continued where *Judgement Day* left off. The title track was a withering attack on Too $hort ("Stop spendin' all your cash and fix your teeth") whom he accused of snitching on him in court – around this time Pooh was sentenced to five years in San Quentin for robbing a bank, during which time he nevertheless managed to release *State Vs. Poohman Straight From San Quentin* (1997). A sappy, cloying record full of nostalgia and **Junior** samples, the album did introduce a new form of rap song – the going-to-prison ballad – on "Sentenced To Five", with **JT the Bigga Figga**.

When he was released from the pen, Pooh-Man recorded *Fuckin' Wit Dank 2001* (2001) and reunited with Ant Banks and Spice 1.

● **Judgement Day**
Scarface, 1993

*Life of a Criminal* is in many ways a better album – and is certainly more important in showcasing an early icon of Oakland "game spitting", but this now hard-to-find album is nonetheless winningly breathtaking in its relentless venom. Pooh ain't much of a lyricist, and the production is only so-so, but the metaphorical murderousness is often thrilling.

# Poor Righteous Teachers

Spiritual descendents of Clarence 13X, the **Poor Righteous Teachers** were, along with Brand Nubian, among the best of the wave of Five Percent Nation rappers that emerged at the beginning of the 1990s. Formed in Trenton, New Jersey, the trio of **Wise Intelligent**, **Culture Freedom** and **Father Shaheed** attempted to tackle ignorance by dropping moral lessons into their raps, unsurprisingly attracting a great deal of controversy with their belief in the godhood of black men.

Despite their commitment to the Koran, and to the teachings of Clarence 13X (a former Nation Of Islam member who established the splinter group Five Percent Nation), it was the profane art of hip-hop production that initially attracted attention their way. "Rock Dis Funky Joint" from their debut album, *Holy Intellect* (1990), was a supremely groovalicious cut-up of **War**'s "Slippin' Into Darkness", the body-rockin' rhythms of which made a potentially tedious lesson much more interesting and effective than memorising the times tables with Miss Crabtree. Most of *Holy Intellect* followed suit: the combination of Wise Intelligent's ragga-styled chit-chit-chatter and producer **Tony D**'s ricocheting funk ultimately championed inclusive pop values rather than strict dogma.

*Pure Poverty* (1991) was nearly as good, with a more pronounced dancehall flavour, and it produced another semi-hit in the r&b-tinged, but still pretty decent, "Shakiyla (JRH)". *Black Business* (1993) had more nods to Kingston deejays in the form of "Nobody Move", but the didacticism which had always threatened to rear its ugly head finally did so, and made the album less fun than Ramadan. Released after Wise Intelligent's ill-conceived solo move, *Killin' U For Fun* (1995), *The New World Order* (1996) was a slight return to form (particularly the storming "Gods, Earths And 85ers", which turned a recital of the Five Percent creed into a street anthem), but it was bogged down by too many awkward cameos (from **KRS-One**, Miss Jones, **Junior Reid** and The Fugees, who were to borrow the singjay style of "Shakiyla" for their own tracks) and too many crap skits. PRT remained quiet until a poorly selected best-of, *Righteous Grooves*, appeared in 1999.

*Losin' My Religion* (2001), on their own Exit 7A label, downplayed Wise Intelligent's reggae influences in favour of weak stabs at the post-**Timbaland** style that were undermined by the lack of a big budget. And yes, the title track did kind of manage to work the REM song in there.

⦿ **Holy Intellect**
Profile, 1990

Too many Five Percenter hip-hoppers didn't seem to understand that nation-building requires a populist vision, but, on this album at least, PRT balanced their pedantry with galvanising grooves.

# ⦿ Profile records

S tarted by **Steve Plotnicki** and **Corey Robbins** in 1981, **Profile Records** is probably the most important independent label of the last 25 years. Not only was Profile the label that graduated hip-hop from the old to the new school, but, while all of its contemporaries sold out to the corporate dollar, Profile remained firmly independent until its demise.

Plotnicki and Robbins were both established players on the Big Apple club scene, and the first releases on their label were so-so disco records. Their first hip-hop signing was **Lonnie Love** (**Alonzo Brown**) who released "Young Ladies" (1981) to little fanfare. With the label rapidly running

out of money, Lonnie Love mutated into **Mr Hyde** and teamed up with **Dr Jeckyl** (**Andre Harrell**), for "Genius Rap" (1981). One of the first hip-hop records to jack the beat from Tom Tom Club's "Genius of Love", "Genius Rap" featured Brown and Harrell bragging about being in *Jet* magazine and having "jazz, pizzazz, razamatazz". It became the label's first hit.

Profile continued to have moderate success with tracks such as **Disco Four**'s "We're at the Party" (1982), **Fresh 3 MCs**' "Fresh" (1983), **Pumpkin**'s awesome "King of the Beat" (1983) and **Rammellzee Vs. K-Rob**'s all-time great, "Beat Bop" (1983). However, with the release of **Run DMC**'s "It's Like That/Sucker MCs" (1983), the label changed the face of hip-hop and, subsequently, all of popular music. Enveloped in a brittle, mechanic, absolutely booming drum-machine armour, "Sucker MCs" had none of the call-and-response, dance-floor-rallying "yes, yes, y'alls" of Sugar Hill Gang and the like. Instead, it was pure b-boy braggadocio, calling names with savage aggression, and even bragging with a defiantly inverted snobbery about eating "chicken and collard greens" – this was no fantasy, this was "reality".

While Run DMC continued to redefine hip-hop, Profile had hits with novelty records such as **Dana Dane**'s Slick Rick-aping "Nightmares" (1985) and "Cinderfella Dana Dane" (1987), and **Spyder D**'s "Buckwheat Beat" (1985). However, with **Word Of Mouth Featuring DJ Cheese**'s mind-boggling early scratch record, "King Kut" (1985), the label proved that it was here for the duration. K-Rob returned in 1986 with the in-your-face "I'm a Homeboy", which featured DJ Cheese on the cuts, the Latin Rascals on the edits and Duke Bootee behind the boards. It may have been based on James Brown, but **Sweet Tee & Jazzy Joyce**'s "It's My Beat" (1986) was as loud and as angular as any drum-machine anthem by Run DMC.

**Rob Base & DJ E-Z Rock**, **Special Ed** and **Poor Righteous Teachers** kept the label's profile high as hip-hop became more sample-based. Profile mined the New York underground to put out records from

King Sun and **Twin Hype**, reached out to the West with **DJ Quik**, and even bogled in the dancehall with records from **Daddy Freddy** and **Asher D**.

Due partially to legal wrangles between Robbins and Plotnicki, the label lost its footing in the early-to-mid-1990s, and records from **Nine**, **Smoothe Da Hustler** and **Camp Lo** couldn't fully stop the rot. In the late 1990s, Profile was bought out by Arista and ceased to exist.

### VARIOUS ARTISTS

⊙ **Diggin' In The Crates**
Profile, 1994

An impeccable collection from the label's glory days featuring Run DMC, Rammellzee, Pumpkin and DJ Cheese.

# Public Enemy

Hip-hop fundamentalists may think otherwise, but **Public Enemy** were unquestionably hip-hop's greatest group. No other hip-hop crew has had such an impact on both popular music and popular culture in general. Before PE, hip-hop only ever flared up in the mainstream consciousness when the **Beastie Boys** got busted for their outrageous frat-boy antics or when **Run DMC** shared the stage with Aerosmith. PE made hip-hop the most vital cultural form of the last 25 years and made everybody – be they college professors, newspaper columnists or lunkhead

guitarists – come to terms with hip-hop. PE attracted the most controversy for their embrace of the teachings of the Nation of Islam, but with **Chuck D**'s forceful delivery and the **Bomb Squad**'s radical sonics, they would have attracted notoriety even if they'd been supporters of Billy Graham.

Public Enemy came together in the early 1980s around **Bill Stephney**'s radio show on Adelphi University's WBAU. Stephney was joined by the Spectrum City DJ crew – **Hank** and **Keith Boxley** (later renaming themselves **Shocklee**) – and graphic design student **Carlton Ridenhour**. The crew would mix tracks on air, with Ridenhour (aka **Chuck D**) rapping over the top in a stentorian boom. The crew recorded one 12" as Spectrum City on the Vanguard label, "Lies" (1984). A sparse drum-machine track with tinkling bell interludes, it had Chuck D and **Butch Cassidy** (Aaron Allen) trading lines such as "You say Reagan's chill – Lies!". The track is also notable for its very early James Brown piano sample. But it was one of their on-air jams that eventually found its way to Def Jam's Rick Rubin, and the abrasive "Public Enemy No. 1" chimed immediately with Rubin's rabble-rousing aesthetic.

With DJ **Norman Rogers** (**Terminator X**), Minister of Information **Professor Griff** (**Richard Griffin**) and hype man **Flavor Flav** (**William Drayton**), an expanded Public Enemy signed to Def Jam in 1987. Produced by the Bomb Squad (the Shocklees and **Eric Sadler**), their first single, "Public Enemy No. 1" (1987), proved Rubin's instincts correct. Looping the buzzing Moog intro from the JB's "Blow Your Head" into a fierce dissonance, "Public Enemy No. 1" sounded like nothing else. With their very first record they had achieved their ambition: to hit like a Led Zeppelin power chord. *Yo! Bum Rush The Show* (1987) was the sound of a group just finding its feet. Nevertheless, tracks like "Public Enemy No. 1", "Miuzi Weighs A Ton" and "Rightstarter (Message To A Black Man)" hinted that the group had prodigious talent. It would be realised on their next album.

Like many of hip-hop's biggest acts, PE were wracked by paranoia, but instead of wallowing in it like Notorious BIG or

to the controversy was "Welcome
To The Terrordome" (1990).
Perhaps the most radical single
ever to achieve significant sales,
"Welcome To The Terrordome"
was the Bomb Squad at their most
unmelodic, intense and seething. *Fear of A Black Planet* (1990),
which included the two singles,
was just as incendiary, and in its
own way just as awesome as *It
Takes A Nation...*, even if it lacked
its head-spinning sonic invention.

*Apocalypse 91 ... The Enemy
Strikes Black* (1991) was a tangible
retreat. The dissonance had been
replaced by a streamlined funk
that, while it still walloped, didn't
have anywhere near the force of
their previous albums. The group,
reeling from media scrutiny, personnel
strife and Flavor Flav's personal problems
released the poorly conceived *Greatest
Misses* (1992) and the messy, trying-too-
hard *Muse Sick-N-Hour Mess Age* (1994).
Hip-hop is ruthless: if you miss a step and
fail to keep up for even a second, it swal-
lows you whole, and the music's standard-bearers fell victim to the very thing
that made the music so vital. The group
fell apart and Chuck released a poorly
received solo album, *The Autobiography Of
Mistachuck* (1996).

After they reunited to work on the
soundtrack to Spike Lee's movie *He Got
Game*, they released *There's a Poison Goin'*

2Pac, they projected it outward, on hip-
hop's greatest album and one of popular music's true masterpieces, *It Takes A
Nation Of Millions To Hold Us Back* (1988).
It was hip-hop as urban noise, as black
rage, as punk rock, as revenge fantasy, as
community activism, as intellectual rigour: the album was organised chaos. On
it, Chuck D embraced the teachings of
Louis Farrakhan, criticised urban radio
for backing away from the group's pro-
black politics, slammed drug dealers,
declared he was "an un-Tom" and sprayed
militant graffiti over the FBI building.
With a sound swarming with feedback
drones, James Brown horn riffs turned
into air-raid sirens, and shards of thrash
metal guitar, no group had so perfectly
matched words and music since the **Velvet
Underground**. But for all the agit-prop it
was still as funky as hell: "Louder Than A
Bomb" sampled and borrowed the dynamics of **Kool & the Gang**'s "Who's Gonna
Take The Weight", while Flavor Flav threw
around surrealist comic asides like Richard
Pryor in a Dali landscape.

The homophobic and anti-semitic
bullshit of cohort Professor Griff got the
group in trouble with the media, and
the spotlight on them only intensified
with the release of the incredible Elvis-
dissing "Fight The Power" (1989), which
many commentators read as an incite-

On... (1999). They may not have had the millennial fervour of old but, like John Pilger, Chuck D was pointing the finger and naming names, and it wasn't pretty. Everyone from Puffy to **Funkmaster Flex** and Def Jam came under the gaze of Chuck's rhetorical cross-hairs, and no one survived intact. No wonder it was available almost exclusively on the internet. Being pissed-off at the industry will never produce music as great as being pissed-off with the world, but then again there is no more awesome sound in the world than a pissed-off Chuck D, no matter what the reason. As Chuck said, quoting fifteen-

time world heavyweight champion **Ric Flair**, "If you want to be be the man, you got to beat the man." No one has yet.

*Revolverlution* (2002) was a strange mix of new material (most notably the self-explanatory "Son Of A Bush"), remixes of old tracks, live recordings and interview snippets. It was a mish-mash to be sure, but when they hit the right targets, it was still pretty devastating.

**It Takes A Nation Of Millions To Hold Us Back**
Def Jam, 1988
Quite simply the best hip-hop album ever.

# Hip-Hop Video

When it first started broadcasting, MTV was all but a closed shop to black artists. One of the few black acts to be shown on the network in its early days was **Musical Youth**, a group of unthreatening kids from England singing about a cooking pot (if the brass knew that their hit, "Pass the Dutchie", was a cover of a song about a ganga pipe, not even they would have got on). Even **Michael Jackson** was deemed inappropriate for the network. According to legend, when MTV refused to air the video for "Billie Jean", Walter Yetnikoff (the president of Jackson's label) threatened to cut off MTV from all of CBS's artists. MTV relented, and Jackson's *Thriller* soon became the biggest-selling album ever, thanks to constant MTV exposure.

While MTV regularly aired videos by **Lionel Richie**, Prince and Billy Ocean, rap was still a no-go area. Other video programs like *Night Tracks*, *Night Flight* and New York's *Video Music Box* and *New York Hot Tracks* stepped in to pick up the slack, but hip-hop video remained a decidedly underground concern until Run-DMC teamed up with an over-the-hill Aerosmith on "Walk This Way" in 1986. Another well-past-their-prime white group, The Beach Boys, allowed **The Fat Boys** to break through to MTV with their version of "Wipeout" in 1987. The first rap group to appear on MTV without rock chaperones were the Beastie Boys.

However, by 1988 rap was becoming an una-

voidable force, and MTV begrudgingly granted some airtime to **Public Enemy** and **LL Cool J**. In the summer, MTV began to air *YO! MTV Raps*, hosted by longtime scenester **Fab 5 Freddy**. The show quickly became one of the network's most popular and critically lauded shows. If there was one single factor behind hip-hop becoming mainstream, it was probably *YO! MTV Raps*, and the exposure it provided hip-hop in areas of the US without "urban" radio.

The explosion of gangsta rap at the beginning of the 1990s ruined *YO!*, but paradoxically made hip-hop the ultimate video genre. While MTV baulked at playing such violent music, an upstart channel called **Video Jukebox** jumped into the fray. It operated via a 900 Number that viewers called to choose the video they wanted to watch. Without any advertisers to appease, the network could show anything they liked, and they dared to play all the videos that MTV refused to program.

Very quickly, MTV realised it looked distinctly behind the times, and so when Dr. Dre released *The Chronic* it jumped all over the videos. Hip-hop artists and labels started to spend lavishly on videos, in the hopes that MTV would put them into heavy rotation. The ploy worked: MTV was dominated by hip-hop videos in the mid-to-late 1990s, with auteurs like **Hype Williams**, **Spike Jonez** and **Paul Hunter** creating a visual language to match hip-hop's sonic flights of fancy.

# Quannum Collective

The San Francisco Bay Area's **Quannum Collective – DJ Shadow**, **Latyrx** and **Blackalicious** – had their lives saved by hip-hop and want to save yours too. Recognising the limitations of throwing their guns in the air à la Onyx, the Quannum crew try to get their transcendental groove on, with their only weapons being mics and the wheels of steel.

The main Quannum players – Shadow, **Lyrics Born**, **Lateef**, **Chief Xcel** and **Gift of Gab** – first got together in the early 1990s while most of the members were attending the University of California at Davis. Turning the college radio station, KDVS, into their own personal clubhouse, the crew raided the record library for rare grooves, and spent endless hours in the booths freestyling to the latest instrumentals. While Shadow had

already had material released on Dave Funkenklein's Hollywood Basic label (his remix of **Lifers' Group**'s "Real Deal" and "Lesson 4" in 1991, and the "Legitimate Mix" for **Zimbabwe Legit** in 1992) as well as work for Tommy Boy, Wild Pitch and Big Beat, the crew really started making moves in 1993, when they formed their own label, **Solesides**. Their first record was by Lyrics Born (then known as Asia Born), entitled "Send Them", with Shadow's "Entropy" on the flip, a 17-minute discourse on why hip-hop culture was dying.

Blackalicious (comprised of Gift of Gab and Chief Xcel) followed in 1995 with the *Melodica* EP, which featured the classic "Swan Lake", an almighty rumination based upon **The Stylistics**' "People Make the World Go Round". After some detours on Mo' Wax (Shadow's "Hardcore Hip-Hop" b/w Blackalicious' "Fully Charged On Planet X", and Shadow's landmark *Endtroducing* album (both 1996)), Latyrx (Lateef and Lyrics Born) followed with

Quannum Collective.

their self-titled album, featuring wonderful lines like "Suckas steer clear of me like feminists do car shows", and the *Muzapper's Mixes* EP in 1997.

At the end of 1997, however, Solesides was shut down and the crew reorganised as the Quannum collective, with a new label, Quannum Projects. Since making this Quannum leap, they have released two albums, the label showcase *Spectrum* (1999), and Blackalicious's magnificent double album, *Nia* (1999). *Spectrum* was a sprawl of styles, encompassing the sci-fi blasts of "Divine Intervention" (complete with a stentorian rap from the black mystic Vincent Price, **Divine**

**Styler**), the dystopic claustrophobia of "Looking Over A City" with Company Flow's **El-P**, straight-up old school funk on "I Changed My Mind" and "People Like Me", the cheeky ode to the 1980s that was "Hott People", and good old-fashioned hip-hop on "Concentration" (with **Jurassic 5**) and "The Extravaganza" (with **Souls of Mischief**). All in all, it was the sound of the collective showing off its multi-faceted skills. *Nia*, meanwhile, and its accompanying *A2G* EP, were showcases for Gift of Gab, who is a walking encyclopedia of MCing styles.

Blackalicious's *Blazing Arrow* (2002) was a bit flatter than *Nia*, but it occasionally

achieved a beauty rare in hip-hop (as on "First in Flight", a duet with **Gil Scott-Heron**), and Gift of Gab was sometimes dazzling (on "Paragraph President" and "Chemical Calisthenics", a funky reading of the Periodic Table with **Cut Chemist**). Gab's solo album, *4th Dimensional Rocketships Going Up* (2004), indulged Gab's preachy side and didn't have Xcel on hand to rein in his worst instincts.

Lyrics Born's solo album, *Later That Day...* (2003), was a quasi-narrative about a lousy day-in-the-life, which had stunning production (mostly from Lyrics Born himself). It was at its best when it revelled in his love of early 1980s funk on tracks such as "Callin' Out", "Hott Bizness" and "Do That There" (dig those cowbells!).

# Queen Latifah

ana Owens' greatest strength is also, unfortunately, her weakness. With a big, engaging personality, she's a born entertainer, a fact which shines through all her performances on the mic. But she's an entertainer (and a business-woman) first and an MC second.

Owens got her start in the rap game as a beatboxer for a high school rhyme troupe calling themselves Ladies Fresh. After meeting the 45 King, she transformed herself into **Queen Latifah** (Arabic for "fine, sensitive and delicate") and quickly became the leading light of the Flavor Unit posse. She signed to Tommy Boy and released the landmark album *All Hail The Queen* (1989). With her regal mien, afrocentric dress, charisma and womanist rhymes, Latifah projected a highly original persona on tracks such as "Queen Of Royal Badness", "Ladies First" (with **Monie Love**), "Wrath Of My Madness", "Evil That Men Do" (with **KRS-One**) and "Mama Gave Birth To The Soul Children" (with **De La Soul**). It was a critically acclaimed album, but went nowhere commercially. However, Latifah clearly had made her mark on popular culture – one measure of this is how often her name cropped in comedienne **Sandra Bernhardt**'s routines.

*Nature Of A Sista* (1991), however, was a retreat into the usual roles accorded to women in showbiz, and its move into r&b

failed to provide a commercial break-through. Latifah would eventually realize her ambitions by landing a starring role in the Fox network's long-running TV sit-com *Living Single*, not to mention silver-screen appearances in *Jungle Fever*, *Juice*, *House Party 2* and *Set It Off*. *Black Reign* (1993) took Latifah out of the r&b pent-house and back on to the street. That street may have been Fifth Avenue, but at least the excellent "U.N.I.T.Y. (Who You Calling A Bitch?)" had some royal badness in it, and it won her a Grammy. *Order In The Court* (1998), however, once again clad Latifah in velvet instead of African head-wraps

as she attempted to venture into **Lauryn Hill** territory on the "Heard it Through the Grapevine"-sampling "Paper". However, the silver screen beckoned once again, and Latifah hasn't been near a recording studio since.

**All Hail the Queen**
Tommy Boy, 1989

Both righteous and bumptious, this seemed to the beginning of one of the most promising careers in hip-hop. Unfortunately, typical music biz inability to deal with a female artist who isn't pop fluff sent Latifah to Hollywood full-time. A perfunctory greatest hits compilation, *She's a Queen: A Collection Of Hits* (Motown, 2002), was released, but this remains her best record.

# ROOTS OF THE DAISY AGE

The "DAISY Age" was De La Soul's anagram for **Da Inner Sound Y'All** – their bohemian answer to the clichés and formulaic raps of the "dookie-chain era" of the mid-1980s. The arty, Afrocentric strain of rap is often specifically associated with the Native Tongue posse – De La Soul, **Jungle Brothers**, A Tribe Called Quest, **Queen Latifah** and Black Sheep – and fellow travellers such as **Brand Nubian**, Poor Righteous Teachers and **X Clan**. But "positivity" and hip-hop, in actual fact, have a far deeper relationship than brash materialism and hip-hop: this era was not merely a blip, but part of a larger progression.

Hip-hop originally grew from the gang culture of The Bronx in the early 1970s, and just as hip-hop was starting to coalesce, the gangs them-selves were becoming more politicised and com-munity-minded. The **Young Lords Party** turned their organizational skills to social programs, gangs such as the **Savage Skulls** cleared their neighbourhoods of junkies and dealers, and, of course, Afrika Bambaataa's Universal Zulu Nation turned gang warfare into musical and artistic competition.

While most of the earliest hip-hop records were simply concerned with cold rockin' the party, many contained moments of social real-ism such as Kurtis Blow's "The Breaks" or **Tanya Winley**'s "Vicious Rap" ("Look at the govern-ment/They sit back, relax, don't give a damn…"). **Brother D & the Collective Effort**'s 1980 single, "How We Gonna Make the Black Nation Rise?", was probably the first explicitly political rap

track. Afrika Bambaataa's "Planet Rock" (1982) expressed a sentiment that was positively hip-pyish – the whole world rocking to the one same groove.

The success of **Grandmaster Flash & the Furious Five**'s "The Message" (1982) paved the way for more downbeat ghetto reportage. **Treacherous Three**'s "Yes We Can Can" (1982) was a cover of an old Allen Toussaint message of racial uplift. Despite his ridiculous delivery, **Jimmy Spicer**'s "Money (Dollar Bill Y'All)" (1983) was social commentary à la vintage James Brown and Bobby Byrd tracks. Even radio DJ **Mr Magic** got into the game with "Magic's Message (There Has To Be A Better Way)" (1984). Meanwhile, while not political, the surrealism of **K-Rob Vs. Rammellzee**'s "Beat Bop" (1983) gave a new waywardness of poetic licence to every rapper who followed.

The explosion of crack turned hip-hop more hardcore and more "street" in the mid-1980s, but records such as **Spectrum City**'s "Lies" (1984 – an embryonic Public Enemy's first record) kept politics in focus. The period also witnessed the growth of the **Five Percent** sect of the Nation of Islam, who provided a disciplined alternative to the chaos of the streets, and records like **Divine Force**'s "Holy War" (1986) which, while remaining within the b-boy tradition of bragging and dissing, felt as if they somehow offered a new way to organize knowledge, and expressed a utopian vision of the world away from the projects and dealers.

# Rammellzee

Rapper, wildstyle graffiti artist, screenwriter and "garbage god cosmologist", **Rammellzee** is one of hip-hop's true originals. Nobody has taken the figurative implications of hip-hop culture as literally or as far out as Rammellzee. He is the prophet of what he calls Ikonoklast Panzerism or Gothic Futurism. These two homemade philosophies attempt to make some of hip-hop's basic tropes – obsessive sci-fi and horror imagery, ritual name-calling, "double-dutch remanipulation" of language, and the recontextualising of readymades – into theoretical bedrocks of a culture war against a society that has refused to acknowledge the existence, let alone genius, of African and Asian cultural forms. He came up with these ideas in 1979 and has doggedly pursued them in a peripatetic career that has included recording one of the greatest hip-hop jams on wax ("Beat Bop"), symbolically bombing both the New York City transit system and gallery exhibitions in New York and Europe, a stint collaborating with **Bill**

**Laswell**, and writing a screenplay for what he calls an "intellectual horror film".

Rammellzee's graffiti tag – "E.G." (Evolution Griller) – plagued the commuters of New York's IRT subway line in the 1970s, but his name first came to wider public attention in 1983 thanks to his duel with fellow rapper **K-Rob** on the classic 12" "Beat Bop". Dressed in a prototypically schematic, black-and-white record sleeve by artist **Jean-Michel Basquiat**, which proclaimed its place of origin as "New Yoke, NY", "Beat Bop" picked up thematically where Grandmaster Flash and the Furious Five's "The Message" left off. It turned their synthesis of partying and reportage into a "death, death, death jam y'all".

Simultaneously funny, frightening and indecipherable, "Beat Bop" heard rap revelling in its invention of a new way of speaking: "Like a .38 shootin' real straight/ Because I'm down like a double-dutch remanipulation on the beat/Grandmaster make a move when I'm shootin' to the boom-boom". Furthermore, like all great songs, "Beat Bop" created a new musical language as well. Where most hip-hop tracks of the time had beats that were as subtle as cement shoes, "Beat Bop" was a spongy, dubby, stringy masterpiece that made you feel like you were flitting in and out of consciousness. Off-kilter violins crept into the mix as if they were stalking the two rappers; everything was surrounded by water-drop percussion and bubbles of sound; the bongos belied, rather than shaped, the groove; Rammellzee would sound as if he was rapping from the catacombs, only to surface with pinpoint clarity for the next word. It did indeed sound like "the beat from the depths of Hell".

Ramm then worked with **Stuart Algabright** (the man behind Dominatrix's "The Dominatrix Sleeps Tonight") as part of the **Death Comet Crew**. They released the singles "Exterior St", "Scratching Galaxies" and "At the Marble Bar" (1985) on Beggars Banquet. Ramm next turned up, with Bill Laswell in tow, on his **Gettovets** project, and he provided the hip-hop element in the diasporic funkathon of Sly & Robbie's *Rhythm Killers* (1987) album.

*Missionaries Moving* (1988), the Gettovets album, was pure beatbox synergy. It took Rick Rubin's Def Jam experiments with the similarities between the booming sounds of heavy metal and hip-hop even further, by appending explicit politics to their collision, and featured Ramm, Laswell, **Bootsy Collins**, Grandmixer D.ST, Nicky Skopelitis and Shock Dell. On "The Lecture", Ramm donned his "Master Killer" mask and dropping some demented science over some patented Laswellian, industrial funk grooves.

He has since spent his time working on a screenplay/performance art extravaganza called *Letter Racers and Monster Models*. Using both graffiti's guerrilla assault on "standard" English and rap's B-movie sensibility as starting points, it created a mythology of hip-hop in which the graffiti-tagger's rhetorical bombing raids and assassin missions on subway cars acquired a tangible reality. In his imagined world, the letters of the alphabet were spaceships made

# DOUGH ON PLASTIC

Although hip-hop was essentially invented by record collectors and has its fair share of rare records, it hasn't generated anywhere near the prices that Northern Soul or doo-wop rarities fetch (regularly commanding prices of several thousand dollars). With Jean-Michel Basquiat's original art work, K-Rob Vs. Rammellzee's *Beat Bop* (number one in the list) has sold for over $2,000. If you stumble across Maggotronics' *Radio Mars*, go to Germany, where it fetches upwards of $700, to sell it.

Nevertheless, if you find any of the following in your uncle's attic, they'll keep you in polyester and beer for at least a few weeks.

### 1. K-ROB VS. RAMMELLZEE

**Beat Bop**
Tartown, 1983

### 2. MAGGOTRONICS

**Radio Mars**
4 Sight, 1984

### 3. NICE & NASTY THREE

**Ultimate Rap**
Holiday, 1980

### 4. VARIOUS ARTISTS

**Chocolate Star EP**
Chocolate Star, 1982

### 5. VARIOUS ARTISTS

**Live Convention '82**
Disco Wax, 1982

### 6. THE MARVELOUS THREE & THE YOUNGER GENERATION

**Rappin' All Over**
Brass, 1980

### 7. GRAND WIZARD THEODORE & THE FANTASTIC ROMANTIC 5

**Can I Get A Soul Clapp**
Disco Wax, 1982)

of plastic, skateboard wheels, hood ornaments, disused telephones, scrap metal and discarded clothing; a world where rappers were superhero librarians and the wordplay of comic-book characters hit with the ideological force of an Elijah Muhammed hip to Derrida.

With 2004 witnessing so many bands, style magazines and music critics fetishizing the early 1980s New York art-punk scene, it seemed fitting that Ramm should re-emerge with a new album, called *Bi-Conicals of the Rammellzee*. While he was reunited with old sparring partners K-Rob and Shockdell, the album couldn't recapture the mad genius of his original records – everything was too forced and too self-conscious.

### Beat Bop
Profile, 1983

Housed in a Jean-Michel Basquiat sleeve, this is one of the most expensive records in the world. It also happens to be one of the best, and it's available on the *Beat Classic* (DC Recordings, 1997) compilation CD.

# Rap-A-Lot records

While Houston's notorious Rap-A-Lot will probably forever be best known for its association with **The Geto Boys**, the label has one of the deepest catalgoues of any in hip-hop, even if most of it is exploitative splatter-rap. As one-dimensional as its output may have been, Rap-A-Lot deserves to be ranked alongside hip-hop's most important labels if only for the fact that it was a pioneer of Southern rap, and was one of the first regional rap labels to achieve any kind of outside success.

According to a press release, the label was formed in 1987 by James "Lil' J" Smith (now known as **James Prince**) in an effort to ensure that some of the boys from his neighbourhood (Houston's Fifth Ward) stayed in school. In exchange for sticking

### 8. DR JECKYLL & MR HYDE

**Jeckyll And Hyde Dance**
Rojac, 1982

### 9. DJ HOLLYWOOD

**Hollywood's World**
Abdull-Akbar, 1987

### 10. LIFERS GROUP/DJ SHADOW

**Real Deal/Lesson 4**
Hollywood BASIC, 1991

### 11. MAIN SOURCE

**Think**
Actual, 1989

### 12. VARIOUS ARTISTS

**Live Convention '81**
Disco Wax, 1981

### 13. FAMILY FOUR

**Rap Attack**
Tyson, 1980

### 14. ULTRAMAGNETIC MCS

**To Give You Love**
Diamond International, 1986

### 15. DOUBLE DEE & STEINSKI

**The Payoff Mix**
Mastermix, 1984

"Beat Bop" by Rammellzee Vs K-Rob: hip-hop's priciest piece of wax

with their studies, Smith/Prince provided them with the equipment to record and release a rap album. The group became the original incarnation of The Geto Boys. While their first album, *Making Trouble* (1988), was a fairly awful rip-off of **Run DMC**, it produced an almost-star in the form of lead rapper **Raheem Bashawn**. Raheem's first solo album, *The Vigilante* (1988), was produced by Smith and Karl Stephenson and was one of the precursors of the G-Funk sound, with its synthesizer melodies and low-rider funk.

Sonically, **Willie D**'s *Controversy* (1989) was a rapprochement between the two styles – synth melodies which were proto-West Coast colliding with the uptempo breakbeats of the East Coast. Willie's ultra-hardcore rhymes gave Smith a few pointers he would use to relaunch The Geto Boys and become the kingpin of the Houston rap scene. The Geto Boys's *Grip It! On That Other Level* (1989) changed the face of rap, and Smith used the formula for his other newly discovered artists. On her two albums, *The Big Payback* (1990) and *Stick-N-Moove* (1992), **Choice** applied The Geto Boys's psychopathic gangsta schtick to female sexuality, predating Lil' Kim and Trina by the better part of a decade. **The Convicts** (Big Mike and Lord 3-2), meanwhile, rapped the penitentiary blues on *The Convicts* (1991). **The Terrorists** (Dope-E and Egypt-E) politicized their violence on tracks like "Fuck The Media", from *Terror Strikes: Always Bizness, Never Personal* (1991), while posse member **Ganksta NIP** was straight-up psychotic on *The South Park Psycho* (1992), *Psychic Thoughts* (1993), *Psychotic Genius* (1996) and *Interview With A Killa* (1998).

Even when the label wasn't putting out albums that wallowed in the dark side, Rap-A-Lot still managed to innovate. Bay Area's **Seagram** rapped in the ghetto pig Latin that Snoop Doggy Dog would later take into the mainstream. **The Odd Squad** (Devin the Dude, Jugg Mugg and "Blind" Rob Quest – DJ Screw was in the original line-up but left before they recorded anything) made *Fadanuf Fa Erybody* (1994), which blended a stoned Southern boy humour with The Pharcyde's *esprit de corps* over uptempo Das EFX-style beats.

After the G-Funk onslaught, though, much of Rap-A-Lot's output sounded imitative. **The 5th Ward Boyz** (Andre "007" Barnes, Eric "E-Rock" Taylor and Richard "Lo-Life" Nash) released several albums of competent, but hardly original, gangsta rap. The best of these was probably their third album, *Rated G* (1995), which featured some classic rollers from producers NO Joe and Mike Dean. Chicago's **Do Or Die** (AK, NARD and Belo) had a huge hit with the rapid-fire rapping of "Po' Pimp" (1996), which was also notable for featuring **Twista**, but subsequent releases only showed how much they were indebted to Bone Thugs-N-Harmony. Luring Memphis rapper **Tela** away from cross-town rivals Suave House and signing Alabama's **Dirty**, Rap-A-Lot dabbled in straightforward Dirty South style too.

Devin the Dude's breakthrough album, *Just Tryin' Ta Live* (2002), and a production deal with **Juvenile** augured more creative releases for the label. It also suggested that the label was on a more secure footing, after having been the target of DEA and Congressional investigations into the label's involvement with drug-dealing – nothing ever came of them.

**VARIOUS ARTISTS**

⊙ **10th Anniversary: Rap-A-Lot Records**
Rap-A-Lot, 1996

By no means the best track listing (no Convicts or Odd Squad for starters), but it's the easiest Rap-A-Lot label compilation to find. Justifiably dominated by The Geto Boys and their solo albums, it still has a couple of rarities in Raheem's "5th Ward" and Ganksta NIP's "Psycho". *Underground Masters* (Rap-A-Lot, 1992) has more variety – Choice, Convicts, OG Style, Big Mello, Ganksta NIP as well as The Geto Boys – but quite a few weak tracks.

# Rappin' 4-Tay

The San Francisco Bay Area may have a long and illustrious hip-hop history, but all the action is in Oakland and Vallejo. San Franscico itself probably ranks somewhere between Flint, Michigan and Bowling Green, Kentucky in terms of a rap legacy. Along with **Paris**, one of the first Frisco rappers of note was Rappin' 4-Tay (Anthony Forte), who repped for the city's Fillmore section. He debuted on **Too $hort**'s "Don't Fight The Feelin'" (1988), dropping mack science about the differences between black and white women.

After a ten-month jail sentence for selling drugs, he formed Rag Top Records and released *4-Tay Is Back* (1992). 4-Tay's well-observed tales of "the game" in the City By

The Bay became something of a local sensation, and got him signed to Chrysalis. *Don't Fight The Feelin'* (1994) was an absolute classic of "Yay Area" hip-hop. "Playaz Club" had 4-Tay "working his toes on a mink rug", and the music and rapping was equally lush and smooth. The song sounded like a traditional NorCal mack's tale, but it was actually a fairly clever metaphor about the rap game. 4-Tay's recording persona had violent moodswings – one minute he was laid back

# REGGAETÓN

Reggaetón – a fusion of hip-hop, Jamaican dancehall and Puerto Rican rhythms such as *bomba* and *plena* – is currently the hottest thing in the Spanish-speaking communities of Miami and New York, not to mention its homeland of Puerto Rico. Like hip-hop and dancehall before it, reggaetón has shocked the older and more conservative factions of Puerto Rican music with its frank depiction of sex, drugs and crime.

While reggaetón itself began sometime around 1993/94 in Puerto Rico, its roots can be traced back to Panama, and artists such as **El General** (whose "Tu Pum Pum" was a huge hit across the Americas in 1991), **La Atrevida**, **Nando Boom** and **El Gringo** who toasted in Spanish over Jamaican dancehall riddims in the late 1980s and early 1990s. At around the same time, a Boricua rapper named **Vico-C** was rapping in Spanish over New York hip-hop beats, and soon began to incorporate Dominican merengue (which in the early 1990s was the *lingua franca* of Latin American pop) into his music.

Rapping in Spanish over popular Jamaican riddims such as "Fever Pitch", the group **The Noise** (**Baby Rasta y Gringo**, **Ivy Queen**, **Maicol y Manuel**, **Don Chezina** and **Las Guanabanas**) kick-started reggaetón in 1994. The Noise was the brainchild of producer DJ Negro (who had worked with Vico-C), who added timbales and congas to his mix of dancehall and hip-hop, making it more authentically Puerto Rican.

**Ivy Queen** (Martha Ivelisse Pesante) is the first lady of reggaetón. Her hits "Somos Raperos Pero No Delincuentes" (1996), "Pon Atención" and "Como Mujer" (both 1997) attracted the attention of – surprise surprise – **Wyclef Jean**,

who appeared on her second album, **The Original Rude Girl** (1998). The star of The Noise, however, was Don Chezina (Ricardo Garcia Ortiz), "The Machine Gun Rapper of Puerto Rico". Chezina's rep was earned largely after he left The Noise and worked with producer **DJ Playero** on *Bien Guillao de Ganster* (1996), reggaetón's equivalent of *Straight Outta Compton*.

Other big reggaetón artists include **Don Omar**, **Daddy Yankee**, and **Hecto y Tito**, but the biggest is probably **Tego Calderón**. While attending high school in Miami, Calderón was hooked on the politically-charged rap of Public Enemy and Boogie Down Productions. He started rapping in English, but changed to Spanish when he first heard Vico-C, and (reluctantly) climbed aboard the reggaetón bandwagon in the late 1990s. His first album, *El Abayarde (The King Of The Fire Ants)* (2002), is the biggest-selling reggaetón album to date, and perhaps the least typical. His rhyming was relaxed, owing as much to Ismael Rivera as Chuck D, and his themes were more socially conscious than the norm. *El Enemy De Los Güasíbiri* (2004) followed in much the same style.

**El Abayarde**
White Lion, 2002

Perhaps not as raucous and freewheeling as most reggaetón, this is nevertheless the best single-artist reggaetón album. The fusion of hip-hop, dancehall and salsa is never forced and, while his use of both contemporary and 1960s slang will be lost on most non-Boricua listeners, his rhyming style won't be.

and avuncular, the next he was wildin' on dank (marijuana) and gin – but it made for a compelling album.

Ironically, 4-Tay was in San Quentin when *Off Parole* (1996) was released. As smooth and funky as *Don't Fight The Feelin'*, *Off Parole* had plenty of easy-listening – and in the case of "A Lil' Some'em Some'em", not so easy-listening – party jams. It also featured tracks such as "Phat Like That", on which 4-Tay's seven-year-old daughter gets in on the action, asking, "Daddy, when do I get paid?" That bizarre combination of sentimentality and hardcore thuggery no doubt appealed to **2Pac**, who rapped with 4-Tay on "Only God Can Judge Me" from 2Pac's *All Eyez On Me* album (1996).

*4 Tha Hard Way* (1997) didn't have nearly as good production as 4-Tay's previous couple of records (although **Ant Banks** dropped some rolling funk on "Where You Playin' At?") and 4-Tay had to work harder to groove with the tracks, losing his main selling point – his buttery flow – in the process. The same problem plagued *Bigga Than Da Game* (1998), which showed 4-Tay trying to spread some consciousness on tracks like "What Ya Gonna Do?" and "All Together Now". *Introduction to Mackin'* (1999) again featured faster, more fractured flows. But his return to his favourite topic – the game – and the cameos by OG macks **Max Julien** and **Bishop Don Magic Juan**, as well as new bloods like Snoop, Kurupt and **Jayo Felony**, seemed to find 4-Tay in a better mood and on better form.

With his return to mackin', 4-Tay joined Ant Banks' Bay Area supergroup **TWDY** (**The Whole Damn Yay**) for the *Derty Werk* (1999) album. The album was underwhelming, but did have two classics: "Players Holiday" and "Cross Me Up". He left the group the following year (he was replaced by Dolla Will) and recorded *Gangsta Gumbo* (2002) with a cast of thousands including Too $hort, Coolio, Nate Dogg, Spice 1, E-40, Eightball and Kurupt.

**Don't Fight The Feelin'**
Chrysalis, 1994

Easily 4-Tay's best album. "Playaz Club" and "I'll Be Around" are Bay Area standards thanks to

Franky J's jazzy funk and 4-Tay's babbling-brook rhyme style. 4-Tay's just as good on the uptempo, more hardcore numbers such as "Keep One In The Chamba" and "Dank Season".

# Ras Kass

Naming himself after a legendary African king, Ras Kass (John Austin III) is undoubtedly MC royalty. While his flow isn't the nicest, he keeps the polysyllables rolling easily, but it's as a lyricist (clever juxtapositions, devastating boasts and put-downs and impressive conceptual conceits) that **Ras Kass** has earned his reputation. Along with Saafir and Xzibit, Ras Kass was a member of the group Golden State Warriors. Like the basketball team from which they took their name, the GSWs never fully realised their potential as, although they recorded the odd track here and there, they were prevented from releasing an album by record label wranglings.

Ras Kass debuted alongside Saafir and Ahmad on the underground favourite "Come Widdit" (1994) from the *Street Fighter* soundtrack. Ras Kass dominated the track, and his appearance generated significant hype for his debut album. Coming across like a gangsta who was hip to Frantz Fanon, Ras Kass's *Soul On Ice* (1996) had all the makings of a classic, until you paid a bit more attention to the beats. While "Nature Of The Threat" was a scathing attack on racism and "Sonset" was a clever dissection of the East-West rivalry, the production was unfocused and didn't match up to his lyrical skills. It took **Diamond D**'s David Axelrod-sampling "Soul On Ice" remix (1997) to give Ras Kass the musical backdrop he deserved.

As Ras Kass himself said, *Rasassination* (1998) was the "same shit, different toilet". Although it had some ghetto-fabulous *Sturm und Drang* production on a couple of tracks, and great lines such as "This one girl tried to Billie Jean me/But I was wearing two rubbers, so name that nigga Houdini", the intro to "OohWee!" summed up the album's main problem:

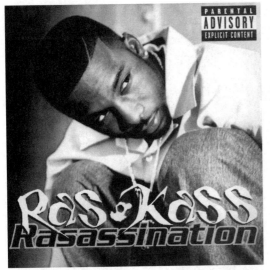

# Rawkus records

Hip-hop is no different from politics in the strange bedfellows it will often throw up. Indie standard-bearer Rawkus Records allegedly got off the ground with start-up capital from **Rupert Murdoch** and began its life by releasing records by an highly conceptual electronica artist, the mobile-phone terrorist Robin Rimbaud, better known as **Scanner**. However, after putting out records from the **Brick City Kids** (aka the Artifacts), **B-One** and **Black Attack**, Brian Brater and Jarret Myer's label hit its stride with three of underground hip-hop's biggest anthems of the 1990s.

"Fire In Which You Burn" (1997) by the **Indelible MCs** (**Company Flow** augmented by **Juggaknots**) had a beat which sounded like Ravi Shankar tuning up amidst of funkless old school drums and brutal scratching. It didn't let record-buyers forget about the label's experimental origins and it pushed hip-hop about as far as it could possibly go. "Fortified Live" (1997), by **Reflection Eternal** (Talib Kweli and DJ Hi-Tek, and featuring **Mos Def** and Mr Man), on the other hand,

"I don't give a fuck about a beat. I'm a lyricist, I just do my thing". The one element that had changed, though, was that Ras Kass didn't temper his West Coast party raps with intellectual trappings: this was pure "game spitting" that his Golden State Warriors team-mates would have been proud of.

Ras Kass recorded two follow-up albums, *Van Gogh* and *Goldyn Chyld*, but both were shelved. The rapper decided to start his own Re-Up label, but Priority blocked the release of any album. Around the time Ras Kass was trying to extricate himself from his contract, he was arrested and sent to jail for a third drink-driving conviction. Still incarcerated, Ras Kass sued Priority in 2004, charging the label with restraint of trade and breach of contract.

### Soul On Ice
Priority, 1996

Ras Kass's lyrics, charisma and delivery are often stunning on this ultmately frustrating album. The received wisdom about the set is that the music is terrible, but that isn't quite true. The beats themselves are fine and occasionally good (Battlecat's "Marinatin'", most notably). The problem is that the smooth beats and the radical Ras Kass just don't fit. If DJ Premier, vintage Large Professor – or even Dr. Dre in Eminem mode – had been let loose on the a capellas, you would have one of the all-time classics.

Talib Kweli (left) and Mos Def are Black Star.

was more conventional, but it was still out-there enough to set the underground on fire. The record that really put Rawkus on the map, though, was Mos Def's "Universal Magnetic" (1997) – consummate New York lyrical purism on top of Shawn J Period's classic Fender Rhodes loop.

12"s from **Shabaam Sahdeeq**, Sir Menelik, L-Fudge and **RA the Rugged Man** followed, along with Company Flow's boundary-breaking *Funcrusher Plus* album (1997). The committed and spiritual *Mos Def & Talib Kweli Are Black Star* (1998) album threatened to put the label in the ghetto of "hip-hop it's OK for indie kids to like", with all the concomitant hype about its Native-Tongues-revival sound. But the album had enough of an emphasis on traditional hip-hop virtues that that never happened.

*Lyricist Lounge* (1998), a composite portrait of the art of MCing (freestyl-

ing, hip-hop poetry, ciphers from MCs hustling for record deals and beatboxing) was a fine survey of underground hip-hop's unique homiletics. The most accessible track was the mightily smooth old school throwdown, "Body Rock", featuring Mos Def, **Q-Tip** and **Tash** from **The Alkaholiks**. Far less polished was the gruff "Famous Last Words" by **Word A' Mouth**, which used a Tom Waits sample to compensate for some tough-guy, numbskull rapping. The album's second disc was hosted by inspired lunatics **Kool Keith** and **Sir Menelik**, "live at Shea Stadium". The silliness was punctuated by **Lord Have Mercy & D.V. alias Khrist**'s brilliantly bizarre combination of work-song chanting and messianic delusion on "Holy Water". Typically, though, Indelible MCs stole the show with the sequel to their furiously atonal "Fire In Which You Burn": this time using a beat made out of an incredibly harsh drum machine and

the smart bomb sound from an ancient *Defender* videogame.

Rawkus blew up in 1999 with Mos Def's brilliant *Black On Both Sides* album and **Pharoahe Monch**'s "Simon Says" from his *Internal Affairs* album. After a new distribution deal with Priority, Rawkus moved away from the more radical aspects of underground hip-hop (prompting stalwarts Company Flow to leave the label), although they maintained their commitment to the streets with albums from old faves like **Kool G Rap** and **Big L**, and *Ego Trip* magazine's excellent compilation of obscure hip-hop, *The Big Playback* (2000).

However, by this time Rawkus was being courted by both MCA and Def Jam, with MCA eventually winning out. About a year into the deal, having had only one big record, Talib Kweli's *Quality* (2002), Jay Boberg (the man who brokered the deal for MCA) was fired. What was left of Rawkus withered and died, thanks, typically, to multinational malnourishment.

**Soundbombing II**
Rawkus, 1999

All three instalments of the *Soundbombing* series are essentials, but the combination of the outrageous (Pharoahe Monch's "The Mayor" and Co Flow's "Patriotism"), the funky (Dilated Peoples and Tash's "Soundbombing") and the slamming (Eminem's "Any Man" and

Sir Menelik's "7XL") makes this the best of the bunch.

# Redman

The only member of EPMD's Hit Squad to enjoy continued success and a good rep was Brick City's Redman (**Reggie Noble**). Like Das EFX, the self-professed Funk Doctor Spock came with an original style, but from the beginning it was clear that it wasn't a gimmick – Redman was truly unhinged.

The Redman psychosis was introduced on "Hardcore" ("You bet I drop heavy, so girls grab your Cotex") and "Brothers On My Jock", from EPMD's *Business As Usual* (1990). Redman's lyrics weren't up to much, but his sheer force of personality was overwhelming. So overwhelming, in fact, that he could command an entire album with only one guest appearance. *Whut? Thee Album* (1992) was produced by **Erick Sermon** (who was also the one guest) and the hard funk paralleled Redman's guttural, crazier-than-Busta Rhymes flow perfectly. While he was inspired by horror flicks, Redman never dwelt on splatter schtick. Instead he dropped rhymes such as "Snapped the neck of Michael Myers, then I freaked it/'Cause it was August when he was takin' this trick or treat shit" on "Rated

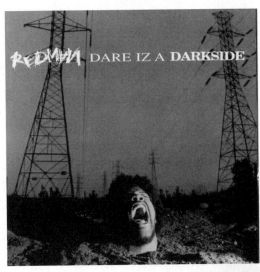

R". He told you "How To Roll A Blunt" on *Whut*, but *Dare Iz a Darkside* (1994) was stickier than Northern Lights resin, and the album's vagueness and blurriness suggested that Redman had smoked a few too many "trees". Tracks like "Tonight's Da Nite" and the Hawaiian guitar-tinged "Green Island" stood out from the haze.

Redman became a star with some of the most quoted lines in recent rap history ("Six million ways to die so I chose/Made it six million and one with your eyes closed" and "I'm bombin' you like Lebanon") on "How High" (1995), a duet with **Method Man** which sampled **Silver Convention** and reached number thirteen on the American pop charts. Despite its title, *Muddy Waters* (1996) didn't wallow in the bong murk of the previous record. Instead, Red and **K-Solo** traded verses over the beat from **Just Ice**'s "Cold Gettin' Dumb", and **E-Dub** and the Noble one got stoopid on "Whateva Man".

*Doc's Da Name 2000* (1999) was more of the same. If not quite as inspired, it marked Redman as one of the most consistent MCs around. *Black Out!* (1999), meanwhile, saw Redman duetting with Method Man again to similar effect, with great lines such as "Cereal Killer"'s "Take nuts and screws outta ferris wheels". By *Malpractice* (2001), though, his schtick was wearing a bit thin, particularly with all the remakes, rehashes and sequels of previous songs.

However, by this point Redman was more of a media personality than a rapper. The movie *How High* (2001) starred Red and Meth as two stoners who smoke a potent strain of weed that allows them to ace their SATs and get into Harvard. After hosting the lame comedy series *Stung*, the duo somehow managed to get their own series on the Fox network, *Method & Red*.

### ◉ Whut? Thee Album
Def Jam, 1992

Predating Dr. Dre's *The Chronic* by a couple of months, this was the perfect East Coast retort to G-Funk. Erick Sermon uses hefty chunks of P-Funk, Zapp and other classic funk records to construct beats that party just as hard as they flex. Redman, meanwhile, freaks every beat with inimitable flair, particularly when he breaks into, ahem, "Korean" on the song "Blow Your Mind".

# Richie Rich / 415

Not to be confused with the Richie Rich who produced "I'll House You" for the Jungle Brothers, or the Richie Rich who was 3rd Bass's DJ, Oakland's Richie Rich is one of the titans of Bay Area rap. One of the first "Cokeland" rappers to emerge from the shadow of **Too $hort**, Richie Rich first made a name for himself with the group **415** (with D-Loc, JED and DJ Darryl). 415's first album, *41Fivin'* (1989), showcased **Dubble R**'s raspy voice as he dropped lyrics bragging about his gleaming car accessories, zeniths and vogues, on Bay Area standards such as "Side Show" and "Snitches & Bitches".

The album sold around 150,000 copies and was hailed as a NorCal classic. Its greatest influence, however, may have been felt a few hundred miles south in LA. Snoop Dogg formed **213** with Warren G and Nate Dogg, based on the 415 formula, and Snoop's flow owes at least a small debt to Richie Rich's style.

After the success of *41Fivin'*, Dubble R recorded a solo album, *Don't Do It* (1990), which wasn't as good. It did at least contain the classic "Rodney The Geek", which advised kids with thick glasses and goofy teeth: "Don't attempt to be hard, be what you are, man/Be yourself, cause that's what time it is". The track was such a favourite that Rich released the *Geek's Revenge* EP (1990) soon afterwards to capitalize on its popularity.

Rich was a certified star by this point, but then he had a few run-ins with the law. He spent most of the next two years in Santa Rita County jail for cocaine possession. While he was locked up, the rest of 415 released *Nu Niggaz On Tha Blokk* (1991), a barely better than competent gangsta rap album that had none of the humour or style of their debut. Rich was disillusioned with the rap game when he was released, and returned to hustling before re-emerging on tracks with **2Pac**, Too $hort and the **Luniz**. Rich then formed his own Oakland Hills 41510 label and released *Half Thang* (1996), an album of thick, slinky Oakland funk and hustling tall tales.

Surprisingly, Rich hooked up with Def Jam for *Seasoned Veteran* (1996). While the beats (from **Mike Moseley**, Ric Roc, Lev Berlak and **DJ Darryl**) weren't quite as good as his previous record, guest appearances from 2Pac (on "Niggas Done Changed"), the Luniz and **E-40** helped round the album out. After another long sabbatical, Rich returned with *The Game* (2001), a disappointing album featuring a load of remakes of tunes by **The Fat Boys**, **Run DMC**, **Ice-T** and Rich sounding just monotonous rather than laid-back.

*Nixon, Pryor, Roundtree* (2002) didn't live up to the inventive promise of its title and was ruined by cheap and nasty production, although Rich and Too $hort sounded pretty good on top of the contemporary, choppy-stab style of "Say Bitch".

⊙ **Richie Rich – Greatest Hits**
Big League, 2000
Including hits from both the first 415 album ("Side Show", "Snitches & Bitches", "415") and Rich's first solo album ("Rodney The Geek", "Female FED"), this is the best Rich collection available. With the exception of "Rodney The Geek", the album is straight game-slanging but Dubble R's flow, and the "Cokeland" funk more than make up for the monotonous theme.

# Pete Rock & CL Smooth

" T he Chocolate Boy Wonder" **Pete "Rock" Phillips** is one of the most revered producers in hip-hop. As one of the first hardcore beat-diggers to make a name as a producer, Rock has been consistently able to perform a highwire act by precariously balancing raw beats with melodic loops. Along with **A Tribe Called Quest**, Rock helped institute hip-hop's love affair with smooth basslines and jazzy horns.

Growing up in money-earnin' Mount Vernon, New York, Rock began his career in the 1980s under the aegis of Marley Marl and his cousin Heavy D. After some run-of-the-mill remixes for the likes of Johnny Gill, and his incredible remix of Public Enemy's "Shut 'Em Down", Rock teamed up with MC **CL Smooth** (**Corey Penn**) for the *All Souled Out* EP (1991). On tracks like "The Creator" and "Go With The Flow", the easy horn stabs blended perfectly with Smooth's technically unblemished (but content-lite) delivery. On "Good Life", their style really suited their subject matter, via CL's comments on the perils of being a middle-class African-American in the US.

Dedicated to Heavy D's dancer Trouble T-Roy, who died when he fell from a rafter before a concert, "They Reminisce Over You (T.R.O.Y.)" anchored *Mecca And*

The Soul Brother (1992) and was the duo's best track. Pete Rock's jazz stylings, which could often be just too damn suave, here imbued Smooth's semi-autobiographical musings and mourning with an emotional depth that very few hip-hop tracks before or since have managed. While not as good, "Ghettos Of The Mind", "Straighten It Out", "Lots Of Lovin'" and "For Pete's Sake" showed that "T.R.O.Y." was no fluke.

The Main Ingredient (1994) was fine on the skills quotient (nasty breaks and loops complementing on-point rhymes), but it never went beyond sheer professionalism, and the sound was even slicker than before. Soon afterwards the duo split, with Smooth fading into history and Rock working with everyone from **Nas** and **Slick Rick** to **Common** and **Janet Jackson**. Rock re-emerged under his own name on Soul Survivor (1998), which found him toning down his horn samples in favour of sparser, less adorned drum beats, though he remained as funky as ever.

After contributing a fine selection of obscure funk to BBE's Funk Spectrum series (2001), Rock dropped PeteStrumentals (2001) for the label. The mostly MC-less, midtempo jazzy beats were left unembellished, becoming nothing but ambient hip-hop: music which you could either listen to intently or ignore completely – it didn't matter. Soul Survivor II (2004) was what Rock's style always threatened: to become so

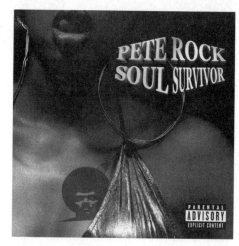

bland and pro forma that you didn't even notice when the album was over. Perhaps the only high point was "Appreciate", which reunited Rock with CL Smooth and recaptured some of the musing, melancholy feel of their best work.

**Mecca And The Soul Brother**
Elektra, 1992

The style may have been eclipsed by hardcore posturing, but this was state-of-the-art hip-hop in the early 1990s. Jazzy hip-hop may have become one of the genre's most soul-destroying ghettoes, but this album, released just as the rot was setting in, is its apotheosis.

# The Roots

The Roots are one of those groups that people respect to the hilt, but don't necessarily like. There's no doubt that they're one of the most original, consistently creative crews around, but their coffee-shop self-righteousness and talkin'-all-that-jazz arrogance alienates much of the hip-hop community, making them pretty much the exclusive property of the bohemian fringe.

The group first took, um, root when MC **Black Thought** (**Tariq Trotter**) met beat maker **Ahmir "?uestlove" Thompson** (he was originally dubbed **B.R.O.theR ?uestion**) at Philadelphia's High School for the Creative and Performing Arts in 1987. The duo originally called themselves the Square Roots and acquired a local rep by busking around the City of

Brotherly Love. Lacking money for turntables, ?uestlove would imitate classic breakbeats on his drum kit, instilling in the group a commitment to performance and live instrumentation. With MC **Malik B** (**Malik Abdul Basit**) and bassist **Hub** (**Leonard Hubbard**) on board, The Roots recorded their rough debut album, *Organix* (1993), and released it themselves on the Remedy label.

With the mind-boggling human beatboxer **Rahzel the Godfather of Noyze** and keyboards man **Kamal** coming on board, The Roots released *Do You Want More?* in 1995. Drenched in watery Fender Rhodes riffs, *Do You Want More?* perfectly caught the vibe of the jazzy, black bohemian intelligentsia. Although there were no samples, tracks like "Mellow My Man" and "? Vs. Rahzel" demonstrated that their embrace of live instruments wasn't a retrograde step. Nevertheless, they were lumped in with the likes of **Digable Planets**, a fate which they partially brought on themselves with their "we're giving you what you need, not what you want" rhetoric. The banging "Clones"

from *Illadelph Halflife* (1996), however, was the best riposte the group could have made to the charge. Unfortunately, the rest of the album didn't really go anywhere and they failed to convince that they were anything other than the best live act in hip-hop (not necessarily all that impressive a feat, given the competition).

Named after **Chinua Achebe**'s book about the effects of colonialism, *Things Fall Apart* (1999) was the group's most fully realised album and, in spite of its "death of hip-hop" theme, it managed not to sound too convinced of its own magnificence. Although The Roots couldn't escape their own arty ghetto, *Things Fall Apart* engaged more with the real world, and the production had a real emotional depth, not just a patina of cool.

Meanwhile, Rahzel released a fine solo album, *Make The Music 2000* (1999), while *The Roots Come Alive* (2000) was a good document of their fearsome prowess on stage, but was let down a little by some slightly under-par performances.

Roots sticksman ?uestlove.

*Phrenology* (2002) finally got the balance between righteousness and rage just about right. This isn't to say that the sanctimony had been completely excised, or that there weren't mis-steps (the chorus of "The Seed (2.0)", or the **Bad Brains**-lite of "!!!"). It's more that the music was hard and edgy and inventive enough to do more than just massage your ego (and theirs). Oh, and the Kool G Rap/Public Enemy homage "Thought @ Work" was the best thing they had ever done.

*The Tipping Point* (2004) followed,

# THE HUMAN BEATBOX

Human beatboxing is essentially making percussion with the mouth by imitating the sound of drum-machines and turntable scratches. Setting aside its clear antecedents, such as scatting or sound poetry, no one is really certain when human beatboxing actually started. The first beatboxer on record was Darren "Buffy" Robinson, who claimed that he started beatboxing in 1981, when he huffed and puffed on **Disco 3**'s "Human Beatbox" in 1984, before the group became known as the Fat Boys. He was followed in short succession by **Doug E Fresh** (then called Dougy Fresh) on "The Original Human Beatbox" (1984).

1985 was the year the beatbox broke, with classic records by **Doug E Fresh** ("La Di Da Di" and "Get Fresh"), **UTFO** ("Bite It") and **The Bad Boys** ("Veronica"). Marley Marl tried to do the same thing he had done with Roxanne Shanté – getting her to record a retaliatory answer record – with the Glamour Girls, who answered "Veronica" with "Oh Veronica" (1986), featuring **Craig G** spitting into the mic. Marl's next record was Roxanne Shanté's "Def Fresh Crew" (1986) which featured **Biz Markie** beatboxing as well as imitating the old Meow Mix commercials. Biz turned in a much better performance on his own "A One Two" (1986), rocking the beat from **Nu Shooz**'s "I Can't Wait" with some ridiculous epiglottis control. Just Ice introduced the **Human DMX**, who did impressive imitations of the Oberheim drum machine, on records like "Latoya" and "Gangster Of Hip-Hop" (both 1986). Perhaps the greatest beatbox record of the era, however, was "Jockbox (America Loves The Skinny Boys)" (1986) by Connecticut's **Skinny Boys**. Beatboxer Jacques "Jock" Harrison did everything that Biz and Human DMX did, but with greater force and clarity.

Greg Nice pushed Jock's skills even further on the stunning "Three Minutes Of Beatboxing" (1987) by **T La Rock**. 1987 also saw the debut of the beatboxer who would take the skill to the next level, with **Rahzel**'s appearance on Mikey D & the LA Posse's "Dawn". Even back then Rahzel had a greater repertoire than his fellow mouth-percussionists, but the Godfather of Noyze wouldn't really come to the fore until his staggering performance on The Roots's "The Lesson (Part 1)" (1994). Rahzel's solo album, **Make The Music 2000** (1999), is perhaps too one-dimensional, but there are some mind-boggling tracks, particularly his recreation of the Wu-Tang Clan's "Wu-Tang Clan Ain't Nuthing Ta F'Wit".

In the era of bling and hoochies in hot-pants, beatboxers have taken a backseat, but a new-generation of 'boxers sprang up nevertheless: California's **Click Tha Supah Latin** (who does a ridiculous version of Salt N Pepa's "Push It"); **Kenny Muhammad** "The Human Orchestra" (who beatboxes house and drum 'n' bass as well as hip-hop); **Scratch** (Rahzel's equally talented partner in The Roots – seek out his rendition of "Planet Rock"); the French group **Saian Supa Crew** (who lend some weight to Anita Ward's airheaded disco novelty "Ring My Bell") and the UK's **Killa Kela**, whose *Permanent Marker* (2002) is one of the great documents of the art.

BIZ MARKIE
THE INHUMAN ORCHESTRA featuring T.J. SWAN

MAKE THE MUSIC WITH YOUR MOUTH, BIZ

THE ROOTS
things fall apart

with more straight-up beats and less live instrumentation. The lead single, "Don't Say Nuthin'", was a sleek **Scott Storch** number, and the chorus had **Black Thought** merely mumbling (deliberately) – perhaps the group's most effective critique yet of the state of hip-hop. Elsewhere, they covered the old breakbeat classic "Melting Pot" and shared the mic with **Mad Skillz** and **Ol' Dirty**.

**Things Fall Apart**
MCA, 1999

Melancholic but hopeful, this is The Roots' best album by some distance.

# Royce Da 5'9"

Royce Da 5'9" came out of the Motor City fuelled by more hype than any rapper since, well, his one-time compadre **Eminem**. Royce was first heard by most people as part of **Bad Meets Evil** with Eminem on songs like "Scary Movies" and "Nuttin' To Do" (both 1999). With his superb breath control and unhinged battle rhymes, Royce more than held his own next to Em.

"Boom" (2000), an underground hit with a bangin' beat courtesy of **DJ Premier**, had lyrics like "My saliva and spit can split thread into fiber

and bits/So trust me, I'm as live as it gets". The buzz around Royce was building, but his album *Rock City* was continually delayed. The next anyone heard from Royce was a shockingly awful guest verse on teeny-bopper **Willa Ford**'s "I Wanna Be Bad" (2001). When a single, "U Can't Touch Me" (2001), was finally released from his album, the pop crossover production compounded the problem, leaving him tagged as a sell-out, and his album was shelved indefinitely.

When *Rock City V 2.0* (2002) was finally released, Royce showed what all the fuss (that had by now died down) was about. With beats from Premo, **Alchemist**, the **Neptunes** and Nashiem Myrick, Royce had great material to work with, but his superb mic skills and often killer punchlines were the stars of the show.

*Build & Destroy* (2003) was a self-released collection of mixtape appearances, freestyles and tracks from the cutting-room floor. Unlike most similar endeavours, however, it was pretty awesome. The first disc consisted of material that, for one reason or another, had never made it onto the first album, but on this evidence probably should have. On the second disc Royce unleashed his verbal arsenal on Eminem and the Shady crew. After some shenanigans with **D12**, and

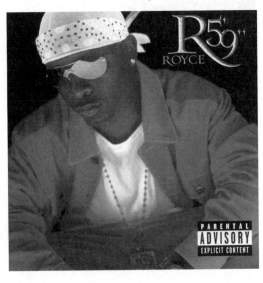

ROYCE DA 5'9"

bewilderment over Eminem's decision to sign **50 Cent** and **Obie Trice** rather than Royce, he shot back with ferocious disses on tracks such as "Malcolm X", "What We Do" and "Death Day" (the latter to 50's "In Da Club" beat).

*Death Is Certain* (2004) toned things down a bit, and suffered from the lack of high-powered beat artillery that his previous records had. There was one exception, however – "Hip-Hop" from the ever-fertile Premier – which had Royce claiming "90 percent of you niggas ain't hard/Here 'Just to Get a Rep', you not Gang Starrs/The finest flow will amaze/ Rap without me is *The Source* minus the "Quotable" page".

◉ **Build & Destroy**
  Trouble, 2003

The disc is way too long and of dubious legality, but if you can wade through all its fragments, it also features the best material Royce Da 5'9" has

committed to tape. "Nuttin' to Do" was from the Bad Meets Evil days, when Royce and Eminem were on speaking terms, but pretty much the entire second disc is devoted to D12, Eminem and 50 Cent smackdowns, most of which connect.

# Run DMC

They may have stopped rocking long before they retired, but **Run DMC** will always be hip-hop's Kings of Rock. Executing a drum-machine minimalism with the brutal economy of Bruce Lee's one-inch punch, the trio from Hollis, Queens – **Run** (**Joseph Simmons**), **DMC** (**Darryl McDaniels**) and **Jam Master Jay** (**Jason Mizell**) – made music that was as hard as New York pictured itself.

Rendering everything that had preceded it distinctly old school with one

Run DMC, back when they were tougher than leather.

fell swoop, Run DMC's first single "It's Like That/Sucker MCs" (1983) completely changed hip-hop. Previously, hip-hop records were pretty much party jams done to live funk tracks laid down by studio bands. With a spartan, loud (*really* loud), rhythm from **Orange Krush** (**Larry Smith**) and nothing else but rhymes, "Sucker MCs" redefined the b-boy as all attitude: a hard rock with his arms crossed, a scowl hidden behind his Cazal glasses, untied sneakers on his feet, and a fedora on his head, like a Hasidic diamond merchant. Their third single, "Rock Box" (1984), featured guitarist Eddie Martinez tearing off some heavy-metal shards, making

their drum machine matrix even more potent. *Run DMC* (1984) was a collection of their singles, but it was still hip-hop's first great album.

*King of Rock* (1985) was a slight disappointment, but the title track made the implicit message of "Rock Box" crystal clear: Phil Collins and Bruce Springsteen move over – this is our time now. In case anyone missed it, they found Aerosmith in the rehab clinic, dusted them off and released a cover of "Walk This Way" (1986), which would bring hip-hop back to the mainstream for the first time since the novelty effect of "Rapper's Delight" wore off. While *Raising Hell* (1986) had obvious crossover numbers like "Walk This Way" and "You Be Illin'", it was the pure hip-hop of "Peter Piper", "Perfection", "It's Tricky" and "My Adidas" that made the record the best early hip-hop album. Co-produced by Def Jam's Rick Rubin and Russell Simmons, *Raising Hell* was the first rap album to achieve platinum sales, eventually selling three million copies.

Run DMC opened the doors for hip-hop (even contributing to the album that kicked the door down, the Beastie Boys' *License to Ill*), but they were locked out almost immediately afterwards. **The Juice Crew, Boogie Down Productions**

and **Public Enemy** took hip-hop beyond anyone's expectations and Run DMC couldn't keep up. There was some pretty good music on *Tougher Than Leather* (1988) — "Run's House", "Beats To The Rhyme", "I'm Not Going Out Like That", and even the Monkees-sampling "Mary, Mary" — but it sounded like Perry Como compared to *It Takes A Nation Of Millions To Hold Us Back* or *Straight Outta Compton*.

*Back From Hell* (1990) found them lagging behind the times – ironically, they were trying to sound hard when only seven years earlier they had been meaner than anyone else. Run had become Reverend Run for *Down With The King* (1993), and the Christian themes made them hip-hop exiles, even though the Pete Rock-produced title track hit the charts.

Their *Crown Royal* (2001) album was much delayed and was doomed to make little impact, as architects were about as respected as the Mayor of New York in the hip-hop community. The former Kings Of Rock were reduced to collaborating with that bozo from **Third Eye Blind**, Fred Durst, Sugar Ray and **Kid Rock**. A whole generation ago Run DMC injected some hip-hop into Aerosmith and saved their careers, but the roles were now reversed, and it was the young

Turk (rap) rockers who were attempting to save the elder statesmen of hip-hop. It wasn't a pretty sight to behold. The other half of *Crown Royal*, however, was filled wth cameos from the likes of **Nas**, **Method Man** and Mobb Deep's **Prodigy**. Unfortunately, Run and DMC (when he appeared) seemed as equally out of their element on the hardcore cuts as they did on the MTV-friendly numbers.

In October 2002, Run DMC had just finished a tour with Kid Rock and Aerosmith and were planning their twentieth anniversary album when Jam Master Jay was murdered in a Queens studio. As of press time, the murder was still unsolved.

● **Together Forever: Greatest Hits 1983-1991**
Profile, 1991

The sequencing sucks (what's wrong with simple chronology?) and the packaging is pretty lame, but these are the records that made hip-hop hip-hop. 2002's *Greatest Hits* (Arista) has the same foibles.

# S

## Saafir / Hobo Junction

When Oakland gets hip-hop props it's almost invariably for its mackin' rappers from the Eastside. West Oakland's **Saafir**, however, was an original stylist whose hip-hop career got lost because he wasn't interested in rapping about the game, and even less in playing by New York's rules.

Saafir began rapping in a local crew called Children of Destiny in the late 1980s, but the group would soon become better known by the name Hobo Junction. Saafir hooked up with the eccentric local crew, **Digital Underground**, and appeared on their *Body Hat Syndrome* (1993). Around this time he was hanging around with **Tupac Shakur**, and through him he met the Hughes brothers, who were casting for their *Menace II Society* movie at the time. They picked Saafir to play a small role in the film.

Saafir guested on **Casual**'s *Fear Itself* (1994) and was featured, along with fellow Golden State Warrior **Ras Kass** and

**Ahmad** on "Come Widdit" (1994) from the *Street Fighter* soundtrack. Like Ras Kass, Saafir was torn between making drop-top anthems and chinstroke-friendly beats for backpackers. His debut album, *Boxcar Sessions* (1994), was impressively experimental, with both beats and syntax flying around at oblique angles. But you got the impression that his stridency was more an expression of bullish aggression than any wish to be an "MC Escher".

While recording the album, Saafir got into a feud with Casual, and the ensuing battle between their respective crews (Hobo Junction and Hieroglyphics) became one of the most intense in hip-hop's long and intense history of rivalries. After a particularly heated chapter in the war, which was played on the Wake Up Show, both crews nearly came to blows and gunshots were fired.

Two of the star soldiers in the battle – lyrically that is – were Saafir's protegés **The WhoRidas** (Mr Taylor and King Saan (Saafir's younger brother)). Their debut album, *Whoridin'* (1997), was a leftfield take on the traditional Oakland concerns of "Shot Callin' and Big Ballin'" based on clever samples of Vaughn Mason and Kraftwerk. Later albums, *High Times* (1999) and *Corner Store* (2002) weren't quite as good.

After his debut album was roundly overlooked, Saafir changed both his name and his style for *Trigonometry* (1997). Released under the name **Mr No No**, the album was a traditional ride through "Cokeland", rollin' hundred dollar bills in a 5.0, with a trunk full of funk courtesy of Digital Underground's **Shock G**. It wasn't exactly straight game-spitting, though, as Saafir dropped lyrics like "In my younger summers my moods used to spook me/I used to wonder the smell of Janet Jackson's booty". *Hit List* (1999) followed, with a mixed-up collection of rhymes both clever ("The hustlers could peep all your flavour before the aftertaste") and dismal ("You ain't killed shit so I killed your little homie and fucked your bitch").

In 1995, the Hobo Junction crew (Saafir, WhoRidas, **JZ**, Eyecue, **Big Nous**, Rashinel, Daarina, **Third Raill Vic** and **Poke Martian**) set up their own label, with "Who Riden'" (1995) as the first release. Collective albums such as *Limited Edition* (1996), *The Black Label* (1998) and *The Cleaners* (2000) featured lo-fi beats and showed MCs like Big Nous and Eyecue to be similarly abstract in style to Saafir, both lyrically and rhythmically.

**Boxcar Sessions**
Qwest, 1994

Saafir couldn't care less about riding the beat, and seems to change his flow at will, but when teamed with the right music the effect can be stunning. The jazziness here doesn't always work, but on tracks like "Battle Drill" ("Start ya engines but you look exhausted like carbon monoxide") and "Can U Feel Me?", he more or less sticks to the prevailing rhythm and drops some gems.

# Salt-N-Pepa

The careers of hip-hop's most enduring female rappers can be traced to the Sears Roebuck store on Fordham Ave. in The Bronx. Former Queensborough College students **Cheryl James** and **Sandy Denton** met co-worker **Hurby "Luv Bug" Azor** there, who persuaded them to record an answer record to Doug E Fresh's "The Show". Credited to **Super Nature**, "The Show Stoppa (Is Stupid Fresh)" was released on Pop Art three months after Doug E Fresh's tune came out in 1985. Less vitriolic than Roxanne Shanté's "Roxanne's Revenge" (the record's clear inspiration), "The Show Stoppa" was pretty lame, apart from the dissing of MC Ricky D and his "plastic Ballys and fake gold tooth".

"The salt and pepper MCs" renamed themselves **Salt-N-Pepa** (adding DJ **Spinderella** Mark I, **Pamela Greene**) for their debut album, *Hot, Cool & Vicious* (1986). Including such classics of b-girl attitude as "Tramp", "Push It" and the go-go/Grover Washington Jr. fusion of "My Mic Sounds Nice", the album went double platinum, making them the first female rappers to achieve such a commercial success. For the disappointing *A Salt With A Deadly Pepa* (1988), there was a slight change of personnel, with **Dee Dee Roper** wearing Spinderella's glass slippers, but it couldn't help such dire material as a cover of "Twist And Shout" and the ill-advised rock-rap of "I Gotcha".

salt 'n' pepa
none of your business

Abandoning the leather jackets, rope chains and basketball sweats of b-girldom in favour of the push-up bras, high heels and slinky black dresses of r&b, Salt-N-Pepa evolved into the best urban pop group of the early 1990s. *Blacks Magic* (1990) was far from a perfect album, but in "Expression" and "Let's Talk About Sex" it had two singles that out-sassed and out-sexed Madonna on her own turf. *Very Necessary* (1993) followed the same formula, but was even better and eventually sold five million copies, largely thanks to the singles "Shoop" and the inspired remake of Lynda Lyndell's "What A Man" featuring **En Vogue**.

*Very Necessary*, however, was the group's commercial and artistic peak. *Brand New* (1997) was musically anything but, and suffered from the group severing ties with Azor, who had produced all of their previous records. Salt now seems more interested in working with gospel singer **Kirk Franklin**, while Pepa has concentrated on bringing up her child with Naughty By Nature's Treach. Spinderella, meanwhile, is still waiting to release a long-delayed solo project.

⊙ **The Best Of Salt-N-Pepa**
FFRR, 2000

Predictably, but disappointingly, it has neither "The Show Stoppa" nor "My Mic Sounds Nice", yet this is the only compilation that covers both their sassy early records and their made-over union of hip-hop and r&b.

# Schooly D

Philadelphia may be known as the City of Brotherly Love, and its most famous musical export may be the lush proto-disco of the Philadelphia International label, with its theme song "Love Is the Message", but in hip-hop circles it will always be known as the birthplace of gangsta rap. Accessorizing like a b-boy Alexis Carrington and rhyming about street gangs, **Schooly D** almost single-handedly invented hardcore hip-hop and "reality rap". It wasn't just Schooly's lyrics and his matter-of-fact style of reportage that created a new genre, however, but the unrelenting drum-machine tattoo of his music, with vicious scratching from **DJ Code Money** that sounded like a jagged knife being yanked out of a freshly killed carcass.

Although he had released two singles in 1984, "Gangster Boogie/Maniac" and "CIA/Cold Blooded Blitz", the former **Jesse Weaver** really exploded on the scene in 1985 with his self-produced, self-released, self-titled EP. Giving shout-outs to the Gucci and Fila labels, as well as Philly's

notorious Park Side Killers in his trademark "dusted" style, Schooly's was the kind of endorsement that corporations have nightmares about. "P.S.K. 'What Does That Mean?'" is the ground zero of gangsta rap: its tale of casual violence and brutal sex was contained by a unbelievably loud boomscape of kick drums, rat-a-tat-tat cymbals and acidic scratching – a sheer powerhouse of sound that wouldn't be equalled until N.W.A.'s *Straight Outta Compton*.

Hooking up with engineer **Joe "The Butcher" Nicolo**, Schooly released the classic *Saturday Night – The Album* (1987). Introduced by a catchy cowbell pattern and a biting wah-wah guitar, "Saturday Night" was "better"-produced than his debut, but just as raw. Although nothing else on the album was as memorable, "Parkside

5-2" was an obvious model for the gangstas of the left Coast, "B-Boy Rhyme and Riddle" was a radical reconstruction of a Sly Stone keyboard riff, and "Housing The Joint" was a response to **Spoonie Gee**'s "The Godfather".

Schooly signed to Jive and released the disappointing, uninspired and overproduced *Smoke Some Kill* (1988). Like Philly's favourite son, Rocky Balboa, Schooly was trying hard now to keep up with the times, and *Am I Black Enough For You* (1989) managed to insinuate Schooly's gangsta persona into the vogue for black nationalism. Tracks like "Livin' In The Jungle", "Gangsta Boogie" and "Black Jesus" were hardly groundbreaking message tracks, but at least they didn't sacrifice Schooly's b-boy brio for the sake of political correctness.

# THE MIXTAPE

More than any other mainstream genre, hip-hop is the ultimate cassette music. In its earliest days, it didn't exist in recorded form on any other medium and the hip-hop virus spread through the trading of tapes of parties and shows. The "jeep-beat" style and **Miami Bass** were designed to be played on cassettes in cars over booming audio sound systems. Hip-hop's collage aesthetic meant that even people without turntables and a mixer

could replicate the DJs' cut 'n' paste antics by making their own "pause-button edits" on a home cassette deck. However, it was with the mixtape that hip-hop really gave it up for the cassette. Even now that CDs have replaced cassettes as the medium of choice, they're still called mixtapes, not mix CDs.

It was disco DJs who invented the idea of the mixtape in the early 1970s, when they would make reel-to-reel tapes of their sets (as back-ups, just in case there were technical difficulties) , which were later sold to the public on cassette by a couple of entrepreneurs. But it was hip-hop that made the mixtape an art form. Hip-hop tapes started to emerge slightly after the first disco mixes in the mid-1970s, with live performances by **Flash**, **Kool Herc** and **Afrika Bambaataa** circulating around New York City. When MC crews started to develop, tapes of their performances began to be collected and traded with fervour by hip-hop fanatics.

The mixtape came of age in the mid-1980s when **Brucie B**, the DJ at the legendary Harlem roller rink The Rooftop, started to tape his sets and sell them on the streets. Soon DJs such as **Kid Capri** and **Doo Wop** followed suit, with mixtapes

*How A Black Man Feels* (1991), however, did, and the album sucked. *Welcome To America* (1994) returned Schooly to the criminality he was happiest talking about, but although the production was good, it was clear that Schooly was well past his prime. *Reservoir Dog* (1995) found Schooly going back to producing his own damn self. The stripped-down feel of the tracks certainly framed his gruff style better than any new-fangled production methods, but the Park Side Killer was no longer a thriller – an impression that *Funk 'N Pussy* (2000), with its murky production and very average rhymes, couldn't change.

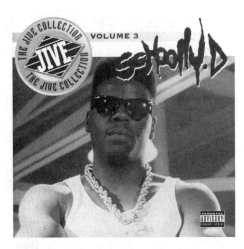

⊙ **The Best Of Schooly D**
Jive, 2003

Featuring the best of both *Schooly D* and *Saturday Night*, this is exactly the same compilation as *The*

*Jive Collection Series Volume 3* (1995), only slightly cleaned up. It remains the best available Schooly comp on the market and is an essential proto-gangsta primer.

---

that they had created at home, rather than in the club. Capri became the first mixtape superstar thanks to the party atmosphere and sophisticated cutting of his tapes. **Ron G** took over from Capri and became the mixtape kingpin in the early 1990s with his "blends": r&b acapellas over hip-hop beats, such as **Janet Jackson**'s "Alright" over the beat from Biz Markie's "This Is Something for the Radio", or **Marvin Gaye**'s "Sexual Healing" over BDP's "The Bridge Is Over".

By 1994, everyone was making blend tapes and a young **DJ Clue** was searching for a way to make a name in a crowded marketplace. He put the unreleased version of Notorious BIG's "One More Chance" on one of his tapes and in one fell swoop the hip-hop mixtape was no longer about mixing, but scoring exclusive tracks and freestyles. For a decade this has been the standard format of the mixtape, with labels and up-and-coming artists using it as a promotional tool, and established artists using the mixtape to diss other artists rather than doing it on an album.

### KID CAPRI

**52 Beats**
1989

The "minister of the mixtape" cuts up some of hip-hop's greatest breaks.

### RON G

**Blends 1**
1992

Ron G changed not only the mixtape game but contemporary r&b as well with blends such as After 7's "Can't Stop" on top of EPMD's "So Whatcha Sayin'", and Tevin Campbell's "Goodbye" over the beat from Steady B's "Use Me".

### TONY TOUCH

**Power Cypha**
1996

Doo-wop may have started the trend for having nothing but back-to-back freestyles, but Tony Touch took it to the next level by having fifty of the hottest MCs in the business freestyle.

### KAY SLAY

**Streetsweeper Series**
1999-

Kay Slay hit upon the idea of collecting together diss tracks in 1999, and ever since, his *Streetsweeper* tapes have become the main venue for the airing of disputes.

### DJ IVORY

**Hear No Evil**
2001

A collection of super-rare late 1980s tracks mixed with venom and vigour. To date, no one has met the challenge of naming all 27 tracks.

# Roxanne Shanté

Her rhymes may have been ghost-written, her voice may have wavered uncontrollably, her calling-card may have been a novelty record, but Roxanne Shanté (Lolita Gooden) was just about the most vicious rapper alive, male or female. With more gum-snapping sass than Madonna and Rosie Perez combined, and a quick wit that could make a would-be suitor's dick shrivel at twenty paces, Roxanne Shanté was the undisputed mistress of the diss.

According to legend, Gooden was walking through the Queensbridge projects when she overheard three guys (**Marley Marl**, **Mr Magic** and **Tyrone Williams**) talking about how UTFO had reneged on a deal to record for Magic's radio show, and she offered her services for a record that would answer their biggest hit, "Roxanne, Roxanne". The 14-year-old took the name of Roxanne Shanté and pretended to be the Roxanne they were talking about on "Roxanne's Revenge" (1985). "He wears a Kangol and that is cute," she said about UTFO's **Kangol Kid**, "But he ain't got no money and he ain't got no loot". To make matters worse, Marley Marl used the instrumental version of "Roxanne, Roxanne" for the record, which became a huge hit and kick-started an enormous wave of answer records that numbered close to 100.

While the rap community was obsessed with the Roxanne saga, Shanté moved on, with the social commentary of "Runaway" (1985), but returning to what she did best – remorseless disses – on "Bite This" (aimed straight at the heads of **The Real Roxanne**, **Run DMC** and **Kurtis Blow**) and "Queen of Rox" (both 1985). "We came here tonight to get started/To cold act ill or get retarded," Shanté announced on "Def Fresh Crew" (1986), a duet with **Biz Markie**, and she proceeded to rhyme about her Filas while Biz meowed like a cat while he was beatboxing.

"Payback" (1987) featured Shanté "getting wild" and spitting harder

rhymes than just about anyone. While Shanté had more spunk than a fertility clinic, it took the rhymes of **Big Daddy Kane** to produce her greatest record, "Have A Nice Day" (1987). Quite simply, records – hip-hop or otherwise – just don't get any better. Shanté claimed she was "a pioneer like Lola Folana/With a name that stands big like Madonna", and that "like Hurricane Annie she [blew] you away" with lines such as "Now KRS-One you should go on vacation/With a name sounding like a wack radio station/And as for Scott La Rock you should be ashamed/When T La Rock said, 'It's Yours', he didn't mean his name". In 1988 she added her inimitable touch to Rick James's r&b number one "Loosey's Rap".

Unfortunately, her first album, *Bad Sister* (1989), was a big disappointment – her breathtaking arrogance and attitude reined in by the constraints of making a proper album. *The Bitch Is Back* (1992) was more fearsome, with tracks such as "Brothers Ain't Shit", "Straight Razor" and "Big Mama" which dissed every female MC around and included these choice barbs aimed at for **Yo Yo**: "Now as for that West Coast slut/With fake-ass hair, contacts, and a padded butt/Instead of stompin to the '90s, use your brain/And stomp your ass down to Jack Lelane".

Shanté retired from rap in the mid-

1990s, gained a PhD in psychology and set up her own practice in New York.

◉ **The Best Of Cold Chillin'**
Landspeed, 2002

Hardly the model of a well thought-out package – the credits are insultingly incorrect – this is nevertheless the best available Shanté album. The only major omission is "Queen of Rox". Otherwise, this is an outstanding collection of withering put-downs, transcendent obnoxiousness and "cold-clocking", in other words, everything that made hip-hop itself great in the first place.

# Sir Mix-A-Lot

Anthony Ray transformed himself into Sir Mix-A-Lot when he began spinning discs at parties in Seattle's Central District projects. He went nationwide with his first record, "Square Dance Rap" (1985), on the Nastymix label. Owing more than a little to **Malcolm McLaren**'s do-si-dos with the **World Famous Supreme Team**, "Square Dance Rap" was an electro-shocked hoedown that fitted in perfectly with the novelty-hit nature of mid-1980s rap.

"I Want A Freak" (1986) and "Rippin'" (1987) followed, but it was with "Posse on Broadway" (1988) that Mix really blew up. One of the all-time classic low-end creepers, "Posse On Broadway" shattered the lower reaches of the American top 100 with its potent Roland 808 bass. "Posse On Broadway" featured alongside with "Square Dance Rap" on the million-selling *Swass* (1988). With the exception of "Posse", the album was undermined by the preponderance of schlocky keyboards (think Dana Dane, or Doug E Fresh's "The Show") with the exception of the surprisingly decent rap remake of Black Sabbath's "Iron Man" with local mullet-rockers **Metal Church**.

The bass was just as pronounced on *Seminar* (1989), but Mix had developed a sense of humour (as if covering "Iron Man" hadn't already let you know), and a rare self-deprecating one at that. He bragged about his "hooptie", and poked fun at the hip-hop fraternity's over-reliance on beepers. Even when

he was mackin' on "I Got Game", it was with tongue firmly in cheek: "Roll to the hotel, game was strong/She thought I spent bank, but I really spent coupons". On "National Anthem", however, Mix brought us commentary about the **Iran-Contra** scandal and the plight of Vietnam vets.

While Mix was in the lab preparing for the song that was to be his monster crossover hit, his DJ, **Kid Sensation**, was making moves of his own, getting on the mic for the bass-heavy single "Back 2 Boom" (1989). Sensation went on to release two so-so albums, *Rollin' With Number One* (1990) and *The Power Of Rhyme* (1992), but was perhaps most (in)famous for introducing baseball great **Ken Griffey Jr.** to rapping on "The Way I Swing" (1992), the B-side to "Ride The Rhythm". In 2001, Sensation returned to the ballpark, under the name **Xola Malik,** to record an ode to another member of the Seattle Mariners team, "Ichiro" (2001).

Thanks to an outrageous video and an unforgettable catchphrase, "Baby Got Back" (1992) went double-platinum and spent five weeks at the top of the US pop chart. While the female posterior is perhaps not the first subject you'd think to base a pro-black anthem on ("36-24-36, huh, only if she's 5'3" ... To the beanpole dames in the magazines/You ain't it, Miss Thing/Gimme a sista/I can't resist her"), the record was pretty damn irresistible. The rest of *Mack Daddy* (1992) kept up his signature mix of humour (on "Swap Meet Louie", unpleasant Korean stereotypes aside) and mighty bass (on "One Time's Got No Case").

The X-rated video for "Put 'Em On The Glass" (1994) was far more scabrous than the tongue-in-cheek "Baby Got Back" and prevented *Chief Boot Knocka* (1994) from reaching its full potential. It was the same old formula, with Mix talking about booty and the occasional social issue over huge basslines, but the beats were perhaps better than on *Mack Daddy*. *Return Of The Bumpasaurus* (1996) was less original, with Mix adopting Bay Area and **Bone Thugs** styles and beats. *Daddy's Home* (2003) just went to show that the mack daddy doesn't always know best.

⦿ **Beepers, Benzos & Booty: The Best Of Sir Mix-A-Lot**
Rhino, 2000

Pretty much all the Sir Mix-A-Lot anyone could need, although his serious side isn't terribly well represented (only "Society's Creation" and "One Time's Got No Case"). Still, it isn't for messages that you put on a Sir Mix-A-Lot record; it's to get the party started, and there are plenty of floor-fillers and low-rider woofer-testers on offer.

# Slick Rick

Born in the London suburb of Wimbledon in 1965, **Ricky Walters** moved to the Bronx in 1979, where he became immersed in hip-hop culture. Five years later he met beatboxer extraordinaire Doug E Fresh, and the following year Fresh and **MC Ricky D** changed hip-hop forever with the greatest double-sided single since "Hound Dog/Love Me Tender" – "The Show/La Di Da Di" (1985). While "The Show" largely belonged to Fresh's raspberry percussion, it was clear even in his short rhymes that the real mic talent was Ricky D. The flip, "La Di Da Di", also featured Fresh spittin' like Gene Krupa, but was more impressive for being the greatest rap since "The Message". While Rick introduced us to such immortal lines as "La di da di, we like to party/We don't cause trouble, we don't bother nobody", "La Di Da Di" was important because of its narrative structure and Rick's understanding of how crucial little sonic details – such as his use of a female voice and his yawning rap – were to hip-hop style.

After splitting with Fresh, Ricky D reinvented himself as **Slick Rick** and reinforced his reputation as one of hip-hop's greatest MCs with *The Great Adventures of Slick Rick* (1988). Speaking the Queen's English with a gangster lean, Rick told stories like a Homer decked out in an eyepatch, a Kangol hat and Mr T chains. Most of his mini-epics were dodgier than a

Bernard Manning stand-up routine ("Treat Her Like A Prostitute", "Indian Girl (An Adult Story)", and "Mona Lisa"), but when he broke into impromptu impressions of King Pleasure and **Dionne Warwick** he was funnier than Rudy Ray Moore or Redd Foxx. The album's most enduring track was "Children's Story", a cautionary tale that was hip-hop's equivalent of Johnny Cash's "Don't Bring Your Guns To Town".

Unfortunately, Rick didn't heed his own words and on July 3, 1990 he was arrested for attempting to shoot his cousin, who he thought had shot at him two months earlier at a club in The Bronx. He was sentenced to three-to-ten years, but Def Jam's **Russell Simmons** posted his bail and, in marathon recording sessions, recorded *The Ruler's Back* (1991). Understandably given its circumstances, the album wasn't a patch on his debut. *Behind Bars* (1994) was largely recorded while Rick was on work release, but Rick was better at relating the comic-book strips that ran in his head than at telling the reality tales the album showcased.

While Rick was on lockdown (he was eventually released in 1996), hip-hop narrative grew in sophistication from Rick's urban Brothers Grimm style to something more akin to Alain Robbe-Grillet, so when *The Art Of Storytelling* arrived in 1999 it sounded as archaic as dixieland jazz. With

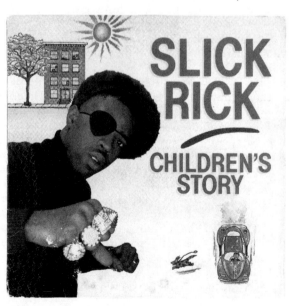

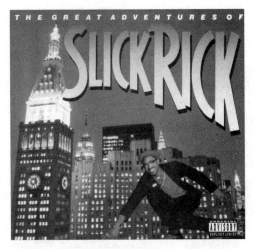

a glittering cast of thousands, including **OutKast**, Nas, Snoop and **Raekwon**, *The Art Of Storytelling* was built around simple, Morse-code drum loops that juxtaposed Rick's narratorial straight lines against the new blood's non-planar geometry.

Slick Rick had never changed his citizenship when he moved to the US, so his time in jail became grounds for deportation. Although the INS had been trying for a decade to get him deported, they seized him in 2002 and held him in prison for a year. Rick won his case and was released in late 2003.

⊙ **The Great Adventures Of Slick Rick**
Def Jam, 1988

Perhaps the ultimate example of hip-hop's golden rule: it's not what you say, but how you say it. The album largely introduced the art of narrative into hip-hop, for better or for worse: none of the spinners of picaresque rhymes who followed did it with the same grace or humour.

# Slum Village

Detroit's Slum Village are one of those groups that have turned rumour and myth into a career. **Jay Dee, Baatin** and **T3** first got together in the late 1980s at Pershing High School in Detroit, but made a name for themselves on the local club circuit in the early 1990s. Jay Dee formed a duo, 1st Down, with Phat Kat and released "A Day Wit The Homiez" (1995) on Payday. Jay started to get attention for his production work, particularly for his production

of **The Pharcyde**'s "Runnin'" (1995) and **De La Soul**'s "Stakes Is High" (1996). He joined the Ummah production crew (A Tribe Called Quest's Q-Tip and Ali Shaheed Muhammed) and had a hand in producing records by ATCQ, **Common**, Q-Tip, Macy Gray and **D'Angelo**.

During this time Slum Village released a couple of underground singles, "Fan-Tas-Tic" (1996) and "All I Do" (1997). Their *Fan-Tas-Tic* demo became a *cause célèbre amongst* the boho hip-hop set, prompting Q-Tip to rap the baton-passing lines, "This is the last time you hear me/I'm out now ... I'ma leave it in the hands of the Slum now" on Slum Village's 1998 track, "Hold Tight".

After supporting ATCQ on their final tour, Slum Village signed with A&M and were scheduled to release *Fantastic Vol. 2*, but the album was shelved due to corporate restructuring, and the group was dropped by their new multinational bosses. After much bootlegging, the album finally came out on Goodvibe in 2000. Slum Village created that ultra-jazzy, bohemian hip-hop that people who don't really like hip-hop love. The entire album was buried underneath a patina of watery Fender Rhodes licks and dragging beats. It was the same kind of thing you'd heard on a hundred records from **Black Eyed Peas** to Digable Planets, from King Britt to **LTJ Bukem**, only a few years too late and with more smugness than the rest of them combined.

After the album was released, Jay Dee left the group and released "Fuck The Police" (2001), with **Frank N Dank**. His *Welcome To Detroit* (2001), heard him woken from his Jay Dee torpor on "BBE", a rewrite of Kraftwerk's "Trans Europe Express" as a big booty anthem. After changing his name to Jay Dilla, he collaborated with West Coast producer Madlib on Jaylib's underwhelming *Champion Sound* (2003).

**Elzhi** was chosen to replace Jay Dee on the mic for Slum Village's *Trinity (Past, Present And Future)* (2002). Jay Dee still produced a couple of tracks, but whatever novelty the first album may have had, it had disappeared completely in the totally uninspired raps and Native-Tongues-by-numbers production. Appearances by Jay

Snoop Dogg and his entourage are known for their love of (a) smoke.

Dee, Kanye West and Ol' Dirty Bastard didn't change matters any for *Detroit Deli* (2004), which saw the group reduced to a duo of T3 and Elzhi.

**Fantastic Vol. 2**
Goodvibe, 2000

The only reason to listen to this ridiculously over-rated album is for Jay Dee's production, which is OK if you like somnolent "jazzy" beats that you can nod out (rather than nod your head) to. However, Jay Dee is far better and less monotonous elsewhere. Baatin and T3's rhymes are even more boring than the beats.

# Snoop Dogg

A nnouncing his arrival on the scene by bragging about killing an under-cover cop, Snoop (aka **Calvin Broadus**) burst onto the hip-hop scene fully formed. While he had been in the group 213 with Warren G and Nate Dogg, **Snoop Doggy Dogg** – unlike so many of his MC peers – was not a local mixtape legend who had been paying his dues for years before he blew up. Dre had heard one of the group's demos and put Snoop on one of hip-hop's true landmarks. "Deep Cover" (1992), from the Jeff Goldblum movie of the same name, was a menacing track built from an off-kilter piano stab, stunted James Brown horns, a grimly insistent drum beat, a monotonous bassline and Snoop's shockingly original flow – which sounded like a Slick Rick born in South Carolina instead of South London.

Snoop was also the star of Dr. Dre's monumental *The Chronic* (1992). Where "Deep Cover" was all tension and no release, *The Chronic*'s brutality and anger hid behind a smooth camouflage – a strategy characteristic of much African-American music.

"Deep Cover" was the heart-stopping, water-rushing-to-the-mouth moment of violence; *The Chronic* was the day leading up to it. Snoop's *Doggystyle* (1993), on the other hand, was the night afterwards. On its rhymes, Snoop cruised around sipping on gin and juice, smoking chronic and hitting skins to blunt his pain and blot out his surroundings. On "Who Am I (What's My Name?)", "Doggy Dogg World", and the G-Funk remake of P-Funk's "Atomic Dog", Snoop put his gangsta persona aside in favour of the simple hip-hop pleasures of talkin' shit. Elsewhere, he showed where his style came from by covering Slick Rick's "La Di Da Di" (as "Lodi Dodi") and descended into juvenilia on "The Shiznit" and the truly atrocious "Ain't No Fun". Despite its abundant failings, *Doggystyle* was the best-selling debut album ever, even outselling *The Chronic*.

*Doggystyle*'s best track, the **2Pac**-style death fantasy "Murder Was The Case", was remixed and its narrative turned into a pointless short movie, with a soundtrack by Dre. Notable only for Dre's reunion with **Ice Cube**, *Murder Was The Case* (1994) sold two million, proving just how absolutely Snoop and Dre ruled the roost. However, when his label Death Row started to fall apart and Dre left it, Snoop floundered. *Tha Doggfather* (1996) was an absolute mess. Produced by a gang of producers such as **DJ Pooh** and **Dat Nigga Daz**, the album lacked the consistency and quality of Dre's boardwork. Despite the end of the G-Funk era and an abominable cover of Biz Markie's "The Vapors", *Tha Doggfather* still went platinum.

In 1998 Snoop escaped Death Row for a ride in Master P's No Limit tank. With his molasses drawl, Snoop, now abbreviating his name to **Snoop Dogg**, seemed a perfect match for the Beats By the Pound production team's bayou gumbo, but *Da Game Is To Be Sold & Not Be Told* (1998) had too much filler, and lame rhymes – "Still A G Thang" showed just how much Snoop needed Dre's effervescence. *No Limit Top Dogg* (1999) was equally tired, the only highlights being the scandalous "B Please" with **Xzibit** and the remake of Dana Dane's "Cinderfella Dana Dane", "Snoopafella".

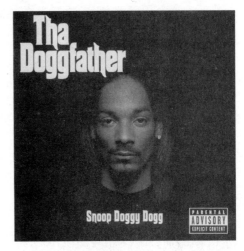

He reunited with Dre on *Dr. Dre 2001* (1999), killing it on the album's only good track, "Still D.R.E.". His Doggystyle Records label introduced the platinum-selling **Tha Eastsidaz**, while his *The Last Meal* (2000) featured a track made in gangsta heaven, a Death Row reunion with both **MC Ren** and **Lady of Rage** on top of a Timbaland beat. This was Snoop's best album since his debut, with monster beats from Timbaland, Scott Storch, Battlecat and Soopa Fly, and Snoop at his mackin' best.

Even more super-producers graced *Paid Tha Cost To Be Da Bo$$* (2002). The Neptunes stole the synth stabs from Joey Beltram's "Mentasm" (which had kicked off hardcore techno in Europe) for "From Tha Church To Da Palace", while **Premier** forced Snoop out of his languid drawl on "The One And Only" with a banging East Coast beat. Elsewhere, though, his remakes of Eric B & Rakim's "Paid In Full" ("Paper'd Up") and **Robert Palmer**'s "I Didn't Mean To Turn You On" ("Wasn't Your Fault") were less successful.

In a move bound to have huge repercussions throughout the industry, Snoop signed to The Neptunes's Star Trak label. His new bosses promised to bring him back to his *Chronic*-era prime. *R&G (Rhythm And Gangsta): The Masterpiece* (2004) didn't quite manage that, but over the economically funky beats produced by the Neptunes – and over those which aped the Neptunes pretty convincingly – Snoop sounded effortlessly suave.

**Doggystyle**
Death Row, 1993

Though it's nowhere near as good as *The Chronic*, this is still Snoop's funkiest and best solo album by some distance. Dr. Dre and Snoop are both at the top of their game. The two from-the-vaults recordings packages from Death Row – *Dead Man Walkin'* (2000) and *Death Row's Snoop Doggy Dogg's Greatest Hits* (2001) – are seriously flawed, particularly the former. Snoop's solo debut remains your best bet.

# Bubba Sparxxx

I f in 1985 you had told a hip-hop fan that before too long one of hip-hop's biggest stars would be a good ol' boy who grew up on a dirt road in southern Georgia, they would've told you to lay off the crack. Yet in 2001, on the strength of one of the hottest tracks of the year, the erstwhile **Warren Anderson Mathis** became one of hip-hop's most marketable commodities.

Mathis was turned on to hip-hop by a neighbour who had a collection of New York mixtapes. He began rapping in high school when he wasn't at football practice, and in 1996 he hooked up with Shannon Houchins, a producer for **Jermaine Dupri**'s So So Def label. He was dubbed Lil' Devil and was placed in a group called One Card Shi with rapper Jason Brown. None of the duo's tracks was ever released and they broke up in 1998. Changing his name to Bubba Sparxxx, Mathis recorded a dozen tracks with Houchins and released

them as *Dark Days, Bright Nights* (1999) on their own Noncents label. The album came to the attention of Gerardo Mejia (aka Gerardo of "Rico Suave" fame), who was an A&R man at Interscope. The label promptly signed Sparxxx and paired him with producers **Timbaland** and **Organized Noize**.

The new version of *Dark Days, Bright Nights* (2001) was impressive, and not just because of the producers. While Bubba had as much flavour as Brunswick Stew, he also brought some of **Lynyrd Skynyrd**'s Southern pride and "don't mess with us" sensibility to hip-hop: "It's funny how you look at us as nothin' more than crumbs of dust/That's scattered on your wall, when just like y'all in guns we trust ... Bouncin' beats all down the street out them Buicks on chrome 'n' blades/And even though it's Christmas Day we still eatin' on foamy plates". Bubba was more than capable of lacing Timbaland's most futuristic beats with a redneck philosophy, and tracks such as "Ugly" and "Bubba Talk" were perfectly representative of the New South.

Bubba didn't squeal like a pig on *Deliverance* (2003) either. In fact, it was even better, and more representative of his region, than his debut. "Comin' Round" had Bubba rapping lines like "There's a portion of the South in the spirit of this song/Keep followin' the fiddle, it'll never steer you wrong" over a sample of an old- time string band and Timbaland's gurgling digital funk; the title track had more echoes of hill-billy music blending with Timbaland's soul claps. Trouble lurked on the horizon, though, as word came through that Bubba had been hanging out with nu-metallers **Korn** and **Blink 182**.

**Deliverance**
Beat Club/Interscope, 2003

It will never be talked of in the same breath as the legendary country-soul records created by integrated bands in Memphis and Muscle Shoals, but this is just as symbolic. The new hi-tech South was represented by Timbaland's futuristic computer funk, while Bubba brought the moonshine and back-porch attitude. Symbolism aside, tracks like "My Tone", "Deliverance" and "Comin' Round" are simply bumpin'.

# Special Ed

**E**dward Archer may have taken his mic name from US slang for the learning-difficulties kids' classes, but his rhyme skills are anything but remedial. Ever since he burst on the scene as a precocious sixteen-year-old in 1989, **Special Ed** has been regarded as one of hip-hop's most gifted MCs. Ed not only had a flair for boast-rhymes, but, against sterling competition from Kid (of Kid 'n' Play), he had the definitve hi-top fade haircut (complete with racing stripes).

His debut album, *Youngest In Charge* (1989), was produced by **Hitman Howie Tee** and featured at least four stone-cold classics. "I Got It Made" was a minimal masterpiece of braggadocio, as was "I'm The Magnificent", which sampled Dave and Ansel Collins. "Taxing" liberally sampled The Beatles' "Sgt. Pepper's Lonely Hearts Club Band" and featured a pretty ridiculous rhyme-scheme, while the title track cemented Ed's arrogant reputation. The only weak cut on *Youngest In Charge* was the truly abysmal "Club Scene".

*Legal* (1990) saw Ed celebrating the fact that he had reached voting age. While the title track and the spy fantasy "The Mission" showed that he was as fresh as ever, the production and lyrics of numbers such as "Come On Let's Move" were stagnant at a time when hip-hop was moving forward in leaps and bounds. After a couple of years of bit-part acting roles on *The Cosby Show* and in the movie *Juice*, Ed re-emerged as part of the **Crooklyn Dodgers** – who also featured Masta Ace, Buckshot and, later, Chubb Rock. Their classic first single, "Crooklyn" (1994), was taken from the soundtrack to the Spike Lee film of the same name. "Return of the Crooklyn Dodgers" followed in 1995, and was featured in another Lee film, *Clockers*.

With the success of the Crooklyn Dodgers project, Ed released the solo album, *Revelations* (1995). Although it was met with resounding indifference, the album was a decent attempt at offering an alternative to the prevailing thug-life manifestos of the time. The only problem was that Ed's flow, once among the dopest in hip-hop, was now as old-fashioned as a Louis Armstrong scat. Undeterred, Ed forged ahead with his own label, Sure Shot, and got some underground props for "Think Twice" (1997), but he has done little of note since, apart from a brief cameo on the **Doggy Style All-Stars**' "Don't Make A Wrong Move" from *Snoop Dogg Presents: Welcome To The House* (2002).

**Youngest In Charge**
Profile, 1989

Special Ed's flow is hopelessly dated now, but at the time it was the pinnacle of mic skills, and its unswerving braggadocio remains thrilling. Countless MCs owe their styles, if not their careers, to this album.

# Spice 1

**C**alling his brand of hip-hop "suicide rap", **Spice 1** is one of the best gangsta rappers around. Although he has only really made one innovation (his rapid-fire delivery), Spice 1 deserves gangsta canonisation for consistency and staying-power. He may have been born in Texas, but by chronicling the horrors of the streets in Hayward and Oakland, California, Spice 1 ranks just below Too $hort as an East Bay original.

It was in fact Too $hort who gave Spice (when he was still calling himself MC Spice) his start, by signing him to his Dangerous Music label in 1987. Although Spice appeared on a Dangerous records

compilation, it wasn't until 1991's *Let It Be Known* EP that he made a name for himself. Over the top of trademark slippery, East Bay funk from producer Ant Banks, Spice 1 unleashed a ragga-tinged, faster-than-light-speed, tongue-twisting flow that would become a key weapon in gangsta rap's arsenal, influencing such artists as **Bone Thugs-N-Harmony** and **Three 6 Mafia**. The EP's hit, "187 Proof", reappeared on his debut album, *Spice 1* (1992), alongside the equally influential "East Bay Gangster", "Peace To My Nine" and "Money Gone".

*187 He Wrote* (1993) didn't push his style into any new directions, but it did feature one of the all-time gangsta classics, "Trigga Gots No Heart". Over a whining synth and

a dramatic blaxploitation strings and bass beat, Spice relates a tale of carefree murder with a chilling flow that was the diametric opposite of the cartoonish excesses of most West Coast street-bards. The track was so brutally effective that it was later chosen to appear on the soundtrack to *Menace II Society*. Elsewhere on the album, "The Murda Show" saw Spice and Compton's **MC Eiht** prove that G-Funk was a universal language throughout California.

*Amerikkka's Nightmare* (1994) followed pretty much the same formula. Nonetheless, it had one classic moment in the collaboration with his long-time friend **2Pac**, "Jealous Got Me Strapped". *1990-Sick* (1996) continued along the same lines as he collaborated

# MIAMI BASS

The gut-churning rumble emitting from the neon-lit IROCs and Cherokees that crawl the malls in the Southern US is **Miami Bass**. The guiltiest of guilty pleasures, Miami Bass is about one thing, and one thing only – booty (butt). With more unrepentant ribaldry than Rudy Ray Moore, Redd Foxx and Blowfly put together, the collected works of Miami Bass serve as a *Satyricon* for the late 20th century. What's interesting about booty music, though, is not so much that it's lasted for some fifteen years, with its only subject-matter being the female posterior, but that its earthiness is expressed exclusively through the most purely electronic sound this side of Iannis Xenakis.

The preponderance of thongs in south Florida perhaps made Miami Bass inevitable, but the obsession with the bottom end didn't start until the electro-bass sound cruised down the I-95 autobahn from New York in the jerry-rigged Kraftwerk hooptie known as Afrika Bambaataa's "Planet Rock" (1982). While "Planet Rock" introduced the sound of the Roland TR-808 drum machine, **Juan Atkins**, the kingpin of Detroit techno, and Richard Davis, aka **3070**, truly dropped the boom with Cybotron's "Clear" (1983).

As if kids from the Bronx and Detroit grooving to Teutonic man-machine music wasn't bizarre enough, **MC ADE (Adrian Hines)** tried to imagine what sort of music Kraftwerk's Ralf and

Florian would make if they had to soundtrack a cruise round south Florida's strip malls in a bass-booming ride. Basically a cover of "Trans-Europe Express" with additional 808 claves, archaic scratching, a vocodered voice listing the equipment used to make the record, a snippet of the *Green Acres* theme and an overmodulated synth bassline, "Bass Rock Express" made booty bounce all over the South in 1985 and became one of the founding records of Miami Bass (even though it actually originated from Fort Lauderdale).

From even further afield, Riverside, California's **2 Live Crew** relocated to Miami and defined the sound and subject-matter of Bass with "Throw the D" (1986). With *DJ Mr Mixx*'s primitively scratched Herman Kelly break and its megaton bass, "Throw the D" was probably the Crew's best record, but it was 1989's "Me So Horny" from *As Nasty As They Wanna Be* (1989) that brought the group, and bass music in general, to public attention. Based around samples of Mass Production's "Firecracker" and *Full Metal Jacket*, "Me So Horny" got exposure on MTV and embroiled the group in a whirlwind of controversy. As a solo artist, 2 Live Crew's **Luke** (originally **Luke Skyywalker**) released the all-time classic, "I Wanna Rock" in 1992, which set Luke's scurrilousness to a beat with so much relentless forward momentum that you'd forgive him for spending the rest of the record talking

again with MC Eiht on the gruesome title-track and removed the metaphors from Run DMC's "Sucker MCs", remaking it as the no-holds-barred "Sucka Ass Niggas". *The Black Bossalini (aka Dr. Bomb From Da Bay)* (1997) didn't go anywhere new either, but "Playa Man" at least found Spice getting pimp-silly over a Curtis Mayfield-esque beat from its producer, **Paris**. Although the production from Rick Rock was somewhat dated, his sixth album, *Immortalized* (1999), attempted to keep up with the East Coast sound with a cameo from **Noreaga**, and Spice was now describing his rhymes as "thug poetry".

Like that other purveyor of pro-forma NorCal gangsta rap, **JT The Bigga Figga**, Spice 1 started to flood the market with rap-

by-numbers albums: *The Playa Rich Project* (2000), *Hits Vol. 2: Ganked & Gaffled* (2001),

about his favourite position from the **Kama Sutra** (which, in fact, he does).

**Afro-Rican**'s "Give It All You Got" (1988) and "Just Let It Go" (1989), and **DJ Magic Mike's** *Drop the Bass* (1989) followed "Me So Horny" as commercial successes for bass, but the genre's biggest hits came from up north in Atlanta and Jacksonville. With less of an emphasis on the 808 sound, tracks like **Tag Team**'s "Whoomp! There It Is" (1993) and **Quad City DJs**' Barry White-sampling "C'mon N' Ride It (The Train)" (1996) had more fluid basslines and cleaner catchphrases than their Miami rivals, becoming two of the best-selling records of the 1990s.

While bass might have had its commercial apotheosis elsewhere, Miami is still the undisputed center of a sub-genre called Boom 'n' Bass. The overlord of this bizarre sub-culture is **The Dominator**, who is responsible for arming a militia of Camaros, Jeeps, vans and drop-top Cadillacs with bowel-damaging infrasound riffs. Played almost exclusively at competitions that serve to test the lower limits of automotive bass bins, Boom 'n' Bass is the ultimate example of music as a boys' toy.

While Miami producers like **Beatmaster Clay D** (responsible for **MC Cool Rock & Chaszy Chess**'s "Boot the Booty" (1988)), **Tony Mercedes** (**B-Rock & the Bizz**'s "My Baby Daddy" (1996), **69 Boyz**'s "Tootsie Roll" (1994) and **Duice**'s "Dazzey Dukes" (1993)), **DJ Smurf** and **Peter "Shy-D" Jones** perked up their spartan 808scapes with light-speed scratching and party-hearty samples, bass music's position as

a quintessential postmodern genre was realised a thousand miles to the north. Picking up from where **Dynamix II**'s mind-boggling, genre-bending throwdown "Just Give The DJ A Break" (1987) left off, Detroit's **DJ Assault** christened his brand of Bass "ghetto tech" and unleashed a flurry of supersonic samples and scratches on his awesome *Straight Up Detroit Shit* mix compilations.

Bass may be known for its limp, too-fast MCs such as Shy-D and **Prince Rahiem**, but in **Poison Clan** (**JT Money**, **Uzi**, **Debonaire**, **Trigga** and **Drugzie**), Miami had a group as hardcore as anything coming from Compton. On their debut album for Luke Skyywalker Records, *2 Lowlife Muthas* (1990), they rapped about busting caps at anyone for any reason, and bitch-slapping hoes up and down South Beach with lines such as "It's too late to straighten up because you blew it/If smoking crack makes you feel good, do it!", making them perhaps the kings of the ignorant rhyme. Nevertheless, *Poisonous Mentality* (1992) gave the group two hits with "Dance All Night" and "Shake Whatcha Mama Gave Ya". In 1999, JT Money was to have a solo hit with "Who Dat?", perhaps signalling a Miami renaissance, following the success of *Trick Daddy*'s "Nann Nigga" (1998).

## VARIOUS ARTISTS

**Booty Super Party**
Lil' Joe, 1999

A fine compilation of down-South booty hits, from "Throw the D" to "Dance All Night".

The Playa Rich Project Vol. 2 (2002), Hits Vol. 3 (2002), Spiceberg Slim (2002) and The Ridah (2004). The best of these was probably Hits Vol. 2, which contained okay tracks such as "Strapped On The Side", "Mobbin'", "Playa Man" and the "Bay Ballas Remix" of The Luniz's "I Got Five On It" with **Shock G**, **Dru Down**, **E-40** and **Richie Rich**.

⊙ **Spice 1 Hits**
Jive, 1998

Featuring all his hits from "187 Proof" to "Sucka Ass Niggas", there's really no reason to buy any other Spice 1 album. It's not elegant, it's not artful and it's certainly not pretty, but it's a fine example of "Cokeland"-style criminology.

# Jimmy Spicer

Long since consigned to the dustbin of history, Jimmy Spicer was one of the most influential early MCs. While his rhyme style was more like the overwrought theatrics of **DJ Hollywood** or **Eddie Cheeba** than streetwise MCs such as the **Funky Four** or **Furious Five**, Spicer's true legacy is that he brought the narrative structure of the old street-corner boasts into hip-hop.

Spicer's first record was "Adventures of Super Rhymes" (1980). Spicer related his tale of a black, toasting superhero in a voice not unlike **Big Bank Hank** from the Sugarhill Gang (with a brief interlude in which he recalled Bobby "Boris" Pickett), but it was an epic update of tall tales such as Stagger Lee and John Henry, spread over a remarkable fourteen minutes. Without this precursor there would be no Slick Rick.

Spicer became one of the first artists to be managed by **Russell Simmons**. Simmons produced Spicer's Casio-heavy, novelty-ish "The Bubble Bunch" (1982) in which he sounded like the Cookie Monster on the chorus and rapped lines such as "They might've been fat, but they wasn't slow/ And now they're known as the Bubble Bunch/And if they wasn't eatin' dinner, they was eatin' lunch". "Money (Dollar Bill Y'All)" (1983) was far better. Spicer was still sticking to his passé flow, but the beat (what sounded like an electro-balafon and **Doug Wimbish**-style bass) and the survivalist lyrics were unique, and presaged what

was to come on the hip-hop horizon.

Simmons brought Spicer over to Def Jam, but he was well past his prime by the time "This Is It/Beat The Clock" (1985) was released. An attempted comeback in 1990, "I Rock Boots", was as bad as its bungled title. He worked with Mad Cobra and Beenie Man in the late 1990s, but hasn't been heard from since.

◉ **Adventures Of Super Rhymes**
Dazz, 1980

Part heroic epic and part street-corner shit-talkin', the tale Spicer tells is of an MC errant and his run-ins with Howard Cosell, Count Dracula at Studio 54, Aladdin and Fred Flintstone. The original record will set you back a pretty penny, but it's available on Mantronix's That's My Beats! (Soul Jazz, 2002) compilation.

# Spoonie Gee

As Cheryl the Pearl from The Sequence said, "MC **Spoonie Gee**/Ain't a man quite like he". Credited with inventing the term "hip-hop" along with staples such as "yes, yes y'all" and "One for the trouble, two for the time/Come on y'all, let's rock that rhyme...", Spoonie Gee was perhaps the first great MC. Even though his specialty was crowd-rocking nonsense rhymes, he saw himself as a loverman in the tradition of Marvin Gaye, and his extensions of the tradition of street-corner boasting brought sex-talk into hip-hop.

**Gabe Jackson** was twelve when his mother died and he was raised by his uncle, Bobby Robinson, who was head of the Enjoy label. Although Spoonie (his nom de mic was his childhood nickname, derived from his habit of eating only with a spoon) inspired Robinson to start releasing rap records, Spoonie's own debut was on the Sound of New York USA label. "Spoonin' Rap" (1980) was a dense layering of percussion over which Spoonie introduced many of early hip-hop's catch-phrases. Spoonie's next record was released on Enjoy and is one of the true landmarks of the genre. "Love Rap" (1980) found Spoonie telling tall tales about his prowess on top of **Pumpkin**'s drums and congas by Spoonie's brother, **Pooche Costello**.

Unlike just about every other hip-hop record of the period, "Love Rap" was nothing but beats and rhymes, and it helped inaugurate the minimalism that would characterize the music over the next several years. The flip, "New Rap Language", featured Spoonie trading rhymes with **LA Sunshine**, **Kool Moe Dee** and **Special K** – aka the Treacherous Three – and it too, with its rapid-fire, freestyle feel, changed the face of hip-hop.

The following year Spoonie moved to cross-Harlem rivals Sugar Hill, re-recorded "Spoonin' Rap" and teamed up with The Sequence for "Monster Jam" (1981), one of the great old-school throwdowns. After "Spoonie's Back" (1981), Spoonie moved once again to Aaron Fuch's Tuff City label and released Davy DMX's masterpiece, "The Big Beat" (1983). After a few more tracks produced by DMX and Pumpkin, Spoonie laid low until re-emerging with *The Godfather* (1987). The title track was produced by Marley Marl and the rhymes – which attacked Schooly D for biting his style – showed that Spoonie had made the transition from old to new school with ease. While nothing else on the album could match "The Godfather"'s rumbling bassline and JB-guitar-lick sample, "Take It Off" had sprightly production backing Spoonie's slightly stale chat-up lines, while "Hit Man" featured behind-the-boards work from a young **Teddy Riley**. Unfortunately, Spoonie's been in and out of jail ever since.

⊙ **The Godfather of Hip-Hop**
Tuff City, 1997

This compiles almost all of Spoonie's early and best hits. It is an essential old school document, and unquestionably belongs in your collection next to the Grandmaster Flash and Afrika Bambaataa reissues.

# Spyder D

One of the first rappers from Hollis, Queens, **Spyder D** (Duane Hughes) was one of the old school's greatest talents, as both an MC and a producer. Unfortunately, neither his reputation nor his catalogue truly match his skills.

Spyder's first record was "Rollerskaterrap" (1980), a rap on top of the groove from **Vaughan Mason**'s "Bounce Rock Skate" that is now one of the rarest hip-hop records. Mason himself helped out with the session and became Spyder's mentor.

With college friend Tito Lewis, Spyder formed Newtroit Records and released the great (and very rare) "Big Apple Rappin' (National Rappin' Anthem)" (1980). More discofied than many of the earliest hip-hop records, "Big Apple Rappin'" shouted-out disco king **Larry Levan** (as well as Grandmaster Flash and **Pete DJ Jones**), which wasn't entirely a surprise when you heard the keyboards (reminiscent of Levan's mix of Inner Life's "Ain't No Mountain High Enough") about two-thirds of the way through.

"Smerphie's Dance" (1982), produced by Vaughan Mason in his studio in New Jersey, was perhaps the first record to follow "Planet Rock"'s lead and make use of the 808 bass. Spyder then produced cult classics such as **DJ Divine**'s "Get Into the Mix" (1983), with its forbidding Linn drums, the vocodered "Beat Classic" (1983) by **B+**, **Spyder C**'s "Unity (In The Place To Be)" (1983) and **The Playgirls**' "Our Picture Of A Man" (1984). The Playgirls' **Sparky D**, along with DJ Divine, **DJ Doc** and **Spyder C** appeared on his posse cut "Placin' The Beat" (1984). "Rap Is Here To Stay" (1985) followed, but its flipside, the less interesting "Buckwheat Beat", got more attention. *Spyder D Presents... Battle Of The Raps* (1985), on his own Fly Spy imprint, featured more of his crew members, most notably a young **Diamond D**. Around this time Spyder was managing the famous Power Play studios, the breeding ground for Teddy Riley and Herbie "Luv Bug" Azor.

Spyder was convinced that **Kool Moe Dee** had stolen the title of his second solo album from Spyder's "How Ya Like Me Now" (1987) and released the minimalist "Try To Bite Me Now" (1988) in response. He then moved to LA and became a regular disc jockey on the first all-rap station, KDAY. The dated *Gangsta Wages* (1990), in which Spyder tried to remake his old hits while sounding hard, was released on fading West Coast label Macola, which at the time was struggling to keep pace with the gangsta rap revolution spearheaded by N.W.A.

Spyder re-emerged with *True Dat* (2000), an album which didn't exactly recapture the glories of the old days, but wasn't embarrassing either, featuring appearances from **Doug E Fresh**, **Mr Cheeks**, **Craig G** and **Peter Gunz**.

**"Big Apple Rappin' (National Rappin' Anthem)"**
Newtroit, 1980

An original copy will cost you somewhere in the neighbourhood of $200, but you can find it on *Harlem World: The Sound Of The Big Apple Rappin'* (Heroes & Villains, 2001). Perhaps the best fusion of hip-hop and disco aside from "Rapper's Delight", the record was such a perfect portrait of the Big Apple that it might have changed New York City's fortunes if it had been used by the chamber of commerce.

# Steady B

Lawrence Goodman's Pop Art records was one of the first hip-hop labels to hold it down for Philadelphia. Most of the label's early releases, though, were actually by New York outsiders such as **Marley Marl**, **Roxanne Shanté**, **Craig G** and **Supernature** (aka Salt-N-Pepa). The first major artist from the City of Brotherly

Love that recorded for Pop Art was **Steady B** (Warren Sabir McGlone), who just happened to be Goodman's cousin.

He debuted at the tender age of 15 (not that he sounded very tender) on the Marley Marl-produced retort to **LL Cool J**, "Take Your Radio" (1985). Far better was his second single, "Just Call Us Def/Fly Shanté" (1985). "Just Call Us Def" remains one of the most startling productions from hip-hop's second wave: absolutely crushing drum machines that sounded as though they had been recorded in an echo chamber, acidic scratching, and snarling guitar stabs. Steady B could have just rhymed the phone book over the top and it would've been great; thankfully he didn't. After a couple of records as **MC Boob**, including the great "Bring The Beat Back" (1986), Steady B signed to Jive.

*Bring the Beat Back* (1986) was a typical "middle school" album in that it combined battle raps and shattering drum-machine production (in this case, complete with scratches from **DJ Tat Money** and **Grand Dragon KD**) with somewhat corny novelty tracks such as "Do The Fila" and "Yo Mutha". The title track, "Stupid Fresh" and the Marley Marl-produced "Get Physical" were worth the price of admission.

*What's My Name?* (1987) was more gangsta than his first, with two more Marley Marl tracks ("Use Me" and "Believe Me Das Bad"), "Don't Disturb This Groove" and "The Hill Top" standing out.

With the money from his Jive deal, Steady B started the **Hilltop Hustlers** label as a vehicle for his Hilltop Hustlers crew. Steady produced the label's first record, "Juice Crew Dis" (1987), a ferocious exposé of Steady's old allies the Juice Crew, by Cool C (aka Christopher Roney). Cool C's "Down to the Grissle" and "Crushin' and Bussin'" by **3D** (soon to become **Three Times Dope**) followed the same year. Cool C later released two lame albums, *I Gotta Habit* (1989) and *Life In The Ghetto* (1990), on Atlantic. Steady B's change of allegiances in the Bridge battle led him to hook up with KRS-One and Scott La Rock for *Let The Hustlers Play* (1988). The album's best track, "Serious", was remixed by KRS-One into a jam that fused dixieland jazz with **Dr John**.

*Going Steady* (1989) went back to the mix of his first album, with novelty cuts like "Nasty Girls" and "Mac Daddy" co-existing alongside political raps such as "Analogy Of A Black Man" and gangster tracks like "Stone Cold Hustler". *Steady B V* (1991) was too little too late and it was clear that he was on the way out. With Hilltop Hustler Cool C and Ultimate Eaze, Steady founded the group **CEB** (Countin' Endless Bank) and adopted a strictly gangsta pose on their eponymous debut of 1993, notable only for the **BT Express**-sampling "Goes Like This". In an attempt to count endless bank, Steady B and Cool C staged an armed bank robbery, during which a police officer was murdered. They were both convicted, and are serving life sentences without parole.

● **Bring The Beat Back**
Jive, 1986

It's definitely a period piece; Steady B's flow may be a bit forced; and it has a lot of filler and some lame-ish novelty tracks. But this is still a pretty great album. The title track has the first appearance of the transformer scratch on record, while "Get Physical" is one of Marley Marl's most unfairly overlooked beats.

# Stetsasonic / Prince Paul

From the time **Prince Paul Houston** started DJing for fellow Long Islander Biz Markie aged just thirteen, it's been clear that he is one of hip-hop's true originals. Comprised of rearranged ready-mades, hip-hop is the ultimate post-modern artform, but it took the boy-genius from Amityville, Long Island to bring a playful self-consciousness and a flirtatious stylistic promiscuity to the music. Taking his inspiration from the deranged cinematic sweep of **George Clinton**'s Parliafunkadelicment Thang, Prince Paul viewed hip-hop as his own playground, and is one of the few producers to make hip-hop hit as hard conceptually as it does sonically.

Prince Paul first caught the attention of **Stetsasonic** (**Daddy-O**, **Delite**, **Fruitkwan**, **DBC** and **Wise**) during a DJ battle in Brooklyn in 1984, after which they asked him to be the group's DJ. Stetsasonic had just won the Mr. Magic talent contest and with Paul on turntables they recorded "Just Say Stet" (1985) – a showcase for beatboxer Wise – for Tommy Boy records. *On Fire* (1986) advertised the group as "the world's only hip-hop band" and with an infectious group camaraderie fleshing out the sparse 808 beats on tracks such as "Go Stetsa 1", "My Rhyme" and "A.F.R.I.C.A.", they helped usher in hip-hop's most creative period.

*In Full Gear* (1988) was the group's masterpiece. Using the bassline from **Lonnie Liston Smith**'s "Expansions", "Talkin' All That Jazz" was not only the best apologia for sampling this side of Public Enemy, but it anticipated the jazzmatazz of **Guru**, **US 3** and the **Dream Warriors**. "Sally" was just as musically rich and became a big radio hit, while Paul's "Music For the Stetfully Insane" was stunningly abstract, prefiguring his mind-bending productions for **De La Soul**. "Freedom Or Death" followed "A.F.R.I.C.A." as a revolutionary message that would inspire a mini-generation of "conscious rappers". Most New

Prince Paul, such a handsome boy, hatching a plot with his henchmen.

York-based hip-hop acts had an outlook similar to the famous *New Yorker* cartoon showing the Manhattanite's world view ending at the Hudson River. Stetsasonic, on the other hand, ventured into the Jamaican dancehall on "The Odad" and gave props to the producers down south on "Miami Bass".

Although it was pleasant enough, *Blood, Sweat And No Tears* (1991) suffered from Paul's commitments elsewhere with De La Soul, and was achingly complacent at a time when the best hip-hop was all about breaking paradigms. At the time Paul had become the most in-demand producer in hip-hop, working with **MC Lyte**, **3rd Bass**, **Big Daddy Kane** and **Boogie Down Productions** as well as his famous partnership with De La Soul. Stetsasonic soon dissolved, with Daddy-O going on to work with Mary J Blige and the Red Hot Chili Peppers, among others.

In 1994 Prince Paul joined up again with Fruitkwan, alongside The RZA and Poetic, to form the **Gravediggaz**. Ingesting all-round bad vibes, splatter flicks and Grim Reaper tales, Paul spat out the Gravediggaz's debut album, *Six Feet Deep* (1994), as an act of catharsis. Finding himself suddenly a bit of a hip-hop outcast after the commercial failure of De La Soul's *Buhloone Mindstate* and enduring a custody battle over his son, the album sounded as if Paul was trying to rewrite the black American experience as a shoddy horror flick with really bad special effects. *Six Feet Deep* was shunned by critics as a "horrorcore" gimmick. *The Pick, The Sickle And The Shovel* (1998) followed in a similar style, but this time it really was a gimmick.

With the hip-hop skit he had invented on De La Soul's first album, and the cartoon gothic imagery of the Gravediggaz, Paul's individual signature as a producer was the sight gags and scenarios that he manages to conjure from purely sonic information. This was writ large on *Psychoanalysis (What Is It?)* (1996). It evoked raunchy **Rudy Ray Moore** party albums and distilled every crap skit from every hip-hop album of the previous six years into a handful of comic gems and an unhealthy obsession with bad sex, bodily fluids and stoopid wordplay. *Psychoanalysis* was one of the more successful explorations of scatalogy since N.W.A.'s *Straight Outta Compton.*

Paul's widescreen vision achieved its fullest expression on his *A Prince Among Thieves* (1999) album. Although hailed in many quarters as a work of genius, the narrative of this hip-hop musical (conceived as a film soundtrack) was a bit forced and a bit trite. The music, however, was anything but and there were some good moments (particularly De La Soul's "More Than U Know").

His next project, **Handsome Boy Modeling School**, saw him team up with the producer **Dan "The Automator" Nakamura**. The fashion-lounge-lizard concept of *So... How's Your Girl?* (1999) may have been a bit pointless, but the music was as suave, stylish, sophisticated and lovely as the Handsome Boys thought they were. With gorgeous torch-songs, wild turntable cut-ups, mondo bizarro sci-fi references and a glittering line-up of cameos, *So... How's Your Girl?* showed that the catwalk was just as vital as the streets to hip-hop, and that Prince Paul's imagination knew no bounds.

*Politics of the Business* (2003) was Paul's

response to Tommy Boy's inability to comprehend *A Prince Among Thieves* and to industry "politricks" in general. Like *A Prince Among Thieves*, though, it was pretty forced and the concept was pretty thin. Paul and Dan reopened the doors of the Handsome Boy Modeling School in 2004, with their second album *White People*, featuring appearances from alumni such as De La Soul and Del, but with a whole new class having enrolled including Cat Power, Barrington Levy, the Mars Volta and many more.

### STETSASONIC

⊙ **In Full Gear**
Tommy Boy, 1988

Aside from the awful remake of The Floaters' "Float On" with Full Force, this is one of the most influential (and most slept-on), albums in hip-hop's history.

### HANDSOME BOY MODELING SCHOOL

⊙ **So... How's Your Girl?**
Tommy Boy, 1999

Not one for the hip-hop purists, but as an expansion of boundaries it was Paul's best since De La Soul.

# ⊚ Stones Throw records

Chris Manak, then going by the name of DJ Crisscut, received his first exposure on vinyl as a producer for a group called the Slobs on their contribution to the Roxanne saga, "Roxanne's Brother" (1985). He later co-produced "You Can't Swing to This" (1989) with an MC called Lyrical Prophecy. Changing his *nom de disque* to **Peanut Butter Wolf** (a name he got from an old girlfriend's kid brother's name for the bogeyman), he then hooked up with **Charizma** (Charles Hicks) and the duo signed to Hollywood Basic. They were just about to release an EP when Charizma was shot and killed in December 1993.

After gaining some notoriety for his *Peanut Butter Breaks* (1995) breakbeat record, the Wolfman really made a name for himself on his contribution to the *Return of the DJ* (1995) compilation. "The Chronicles

A MUSICAL CURRICULUM FROM THE
**HANDSOME BOY MODELING SCHOOL**

Peanut Butter Wolf, big cheese of Stones Throw records, rocking the *paysan* look.

(I Will Always Love H.E.R.)" was a hip-hop collage moving from Mr. Magic to Jeru the Damaja which was an optimistic response to **Common**'s "I Used to Love H.E.R.". Given his upbringing in the suburban wasteland of San Mateo, California – the traditional catchment area for Van Halen and Slayer fans – it is perhaps surprising that he produced "The Chronicles", which remains the definitive hip-hop history lesson on wax.

He garnered more attention for his production work, particularly from Europe's trip-hop fraternity, most notably for his *Peanut Butter Breaks* LP and the *Lunar Props* EP (1996). These collections of fleshed-out beats were the remnants of his premature-

ly halted collaboration with Charizma. He then kicked-off his Stones Throw label in 1996 with "My World Premier", a track he'd recorded with the late Charizma. The label really established itself with MC **Rasco**'s big indie hit, "The Unassisted" (1996). With minimal production based around a stunted guitar stab, "The Unassisted" led the way for underground hip-hop's challenge to the jiggy good-life fantasies of the mainstream. Rasco's fine album, *Time Waits For No Man* (1998), showed him to be a gravel-throated battle-rhymer capable of smoking over just about any kind of beat. Even better was his *The Birth* EP (1999) (released on the UK's Copasetik label) on which Rasco forsook Peanut Butter Wolf's beats for the more direct, more neck-snapping rhythms of **His-Panik** from the Molemen. The more streamlined, less adorned beats on *The Birth* highlighted Rasco's awesome skills. Not much of a wordsmith, Rasco got over solely on the strength of one of the purest flows in the business. Teaming up with **Planet Asia** as **Cali Agents**, Rasco bit the hand that fed him on the backpacker-baiting *How The West Was Won* (2000): "I'm telling your ass that I'm out to make cash/I'm a revoke your little hip-hop pass ... I'm not in the game for tryin' to break my neck/My little baby girl can't eat your respect".

While the label was developing some fine MCs, it also gave plenty of time to the turntablists. It released **Babu**'s *Super Duck Breaks* and **Rob Swift**'s *Soulful Fruit* (1997), and PBW included a veritable Technics summit, "Tale of Five Cities", on his *My Vinyl Weighs A Ton* album (1999). The Likwit Crew's **Lootpack** released the fine *Sound Pieces – Da Antidote* (1999) album, while Lootpack member **Madlib**'s alter-ego **Quasimoto** released the excellent *The Unseen* (2000) unveiling a flow that sounded like Q-Tip on helium.

In 1999 Stone's Throw instituted a 7" series with the E-40/electro piss-take, **El Captain Funkaho**'s "My 2600", **Breakestra**'s revivalist "Getchyo Soul Togetha" and **A-Trak**'s "Enter Ralph Wiggum". The revivalist streak really took hold when the label started reissuing rare funk records, beginning with **The Highlighters**' "Poppin' Popcorn" 7" (2000) and the stellar compilation *The Funky 16 Corners* (2001). Along with rare funk, Stones Throw started disinterring ultra-rare hip-hop with *The Third Unheard: Connecticut Hip-Hop 1979-1983* (2004), which showed that the storehouse of obscure hip-hop was just as deep and just as rewarding as rare funk. On the tenth anniversary of Charizma's death, Stones Throw released *Big Shots* (2003), a collection of tracks that he and PBW had made together that left you wistfully thinking of what might have been.

The label continued to innovate with new music as well. Madlib became the star of the label with eclectic and occasionally brilliant releases under a number of guises: Quasimoto, **Yesterday's New Quintet**, Jaylib (with Jay Dilla), Madvillain (with MF Doom) and **Monk Hughes & The Outer Realm**.

### CHARIZMA & PEANUT BUTTER WOLF

⊙ **Big Shots**
Stones Throw, 2003

Regardless of the tragic story behind the album, this is a fantastic slice of early 1990s hip-hop. Charizma's rhyming is fast and furious, whilst PBW's production is loopy, punchy and chunky.

### VARIOUS ARTISTS

⊙ **The Third Unheard: Connecticut Hip-Hop 1979-1983**
Stones Throw, 2004

Stones Throw, and its affiliates Now Again and Soul-Cal, have always produced impeccable reissues, and this, its first trawl through the hip-hop crates, is no different. The irrepressible energy and joy of the music from Mr Magic, Rappermatical 5 and Pookey Blow collected here is little short of intoxicating.

# ◉ Sugar Hill records

Housing many of the most prominent African-Americans, the Sugar Hill area of Harlem was once known as America's most influential black community. The neighbourhood may have declined somewhat, but the name still has a powerful resonance within black culture. Growing out of a soul/disco label called All Platinum, Joe and Sylvia Robinson's **Sugar Hill** label was hip-hop's most important early label. The irony of Sugar Hill's position, however, was that many of its artists were not really part of the early hip-hop scene and its use of an admittedly awesome house band pushed hip-hop away from its roots as a genre based on breakbeats.

Sugar Hill was not the first label to release a rap record (that was Spring, who released **The Fatback Band**'s "King Tim III

(Personality Jock)" a few months earlier), but their October 1979 release of **Sugar Hill Gang**'s "Rapper's Delight" was truly when hip-hop moved outside the South Bronx and Harlem. Based on the groove of Chic's "Good Times", it remains one of the most infectious records ever made, more than two decades after its initial release. The record's success, however, had very little to do with **Big Bank Hank Jackson, Guy "Master Gee" O'Brien** and **Wonder Mike Wright**: it was largely the product of Nile Rodgers' guitar riffs, Bernard Edwards' bassline and lyrics lifted from the Cold Crush Brothers' Grandmaster Caz's rhyme book.

Sugar Hill's next release was **The Sequence**'s "Funk You Up" (1979). They wrote their own lyrics (well, sort of – a lot of them were based on nursery rhymes and classic street-corner toasts) and were, along with Paulette and Tanya Winley, among the first women to record hip-hop. But The Sequence – **Cheryl "The Pearl" Cook, Gwen "Blondie" Chisholm** and **Angie B. Brown** – were, strictly speaking, interlopers from outside the core hip-hop scene. The group had been discovered in South Carolina by the Sugar Hill house band (bassist **Doug Wimbish**, guitarist **Skip McDonald**, drummer **Keith LeBlanc**, percussionist **Duke Bootee**, keyboard-player **Nate Edmunds** and the **Chops** horns) and brought to New York to record such classics as "Funk You Up", "And You Know That" (1981) and "Monster Jam" with **Spoonie Gee** (1981).

With the release of **Grandmaster Flash & the Furious Five**'s "Freedom" (1980), Sugar Hill had put out a record by one of hip-hop's true innovators. On Sugar Hill, Flash & the Five released some of hip-hop's greatest records: "Adventures Of Grandmaster Flash On The Wheels Of Steel" (1981), "The Message" (1982), "Flash To The Beat" (1982), "Scorpio" (1982), "It's Nasty (Genius Of Love)" (1982), "New York, New York" (1983) and "White Lines (Don't Do It)" (1983). With the defection of Flash and crew from the Enjoy label, others soon followed: **Spoonie Gee,**

**Treacherous Three** and **Funky Four Plus One**.

With their use of a live band to back MCs up, Sugar Hill's records actually had more in common with Washington DC's go-go scene than it did with hip-hop. One of go-go's leading bands, **Trouble Funk**, recorded such classics as "Pump Me Up", "Drop The Bomb" and "Hey Fellas" (all 1982) for Sugar Hill. Members of Trouble Funk had previously been part of Chuck Brown's Soul Searchers, whose "Ashley's Roach Clip" is one of the all-time great hip-hop beats.

The Incredible Bongo Band's "Apache", however, is *the* hip-hop beat and it appeared on **West Street Mob**'s b-boy scratch fest, "Break Dancin' – Electric Boogie" (1983). By this time, though, Run DMC had emerged and Sugar Hill's style was rapidly becoming passé. They managed to postpone the inevitable with records such as **Crash Crew**'s Bob James cut-up "Breaking Bells (Take Me To The Mardi Gras)" (1982), and "We Are Known As Emcees (We Turn The Party Out)" (1983), **Busy Bee**'s Kid Rock-inspiring "Making Cash Money" (1982), Reggie Griffin's fearsome "Mirda Rock" (1982) and **Kevie Kev**'s Jones Girls pastiche, "All Night Long (Waterbed)" (1983).

With the possible exception of Treacherous Three's "Turning You On" (1984), however, Sugar Hill was quickly replaced at the top by Profile and Def Jam in the mid-1980s and the label faded into irrelevance. Still, with their innocence and charm, Sugar Hill's records remain some of the greatest pop music ever made.

## VARIOUS ARTISTS

**The Sugar Hill Story – Old School Rap To The Beat Y'All**
Sequel, 1992

Compiled by old-school-chronicler David Toop, this three-CD set is pretty much definitive. The album has everything from the radio commercial accompanying "Rapper's Delight", through rare promo-only songs such as Crash Crew's "Scratching" to all the hits.

t

# 3rd Bass

MC Serch (Michael Berrin) had recorded two solo singles, "Melissa" (1986) and "Hey Boy/Beware of the Death" (1987), for the Idlers and Warlock labels when he was encouraged to join forces with fellow Rush Management client and Columbia University graduate **Prime Minister Pete Nice** (Peter Nash). Along with DJ **Sam Sever**, they formed the group Three The Hard Way in 1987.

Adding DJ **Richie Rich** (Richard Lawson), the group was renamed 3rd Bass and recorded the unfairly overlooked *The Cactus Album* (1989), the best hip-hop album recorded by a (predominantly) white group that wasn't The Beastie Boys. In fact, right off the bat they dissed their caucasian brothers, on "Sons Of 3rd Bass": "Counterfeit style, born sworn and sold out with high voice distorted/If a Beast wish to play foetus, I'd have him aborted". They dissed **MC Hammer** and South African prime minister **P.W. Botha** too on the fabulous, Prince Paul-produced "The Gas Face", dropped some ill battle-rhymes

on "Steppin' To The AM" and created one of hip-hop's cleverest sex rhymes in "Oval Office". In addition to Prince Paul, the production was handled by Sam Sever and the **Bomb Squad** and, as you'd expect, the beats were seriously slammin'.

After a rather pointless remix EP, *Cactus Revisited* (1990), the group dissed another ofay rapper (**Vanilla Ice**) on "Pop Goes The Weasel" (1991). The lightweight song, especially when compared to "The Gas

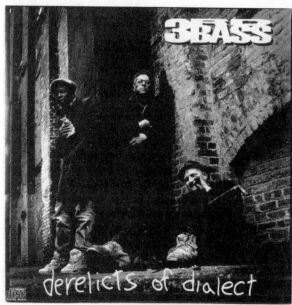

Face" and "Sons of 3rd Bass", was the lead single from the disappointing *Derelicts of Dialect* (1991). Both the hooks and the wit were in shorter supply here than on their debut, although "Portrait Of The Artist As A Hood", "Herbalz In Your Mouth" and "Ace In The Hole" managed to rise above the morass.

Sam Sever left halfway through the recording of the album to form **Downtown Science** with rapper **Bosco Money** (Ken Carabello). The duo released one self-titled album (1991) which featured some excellent production from Sever on tracks such as "Room To Breathe" and "Topic Drift". 3rd Bass split up during the *Derelicts Of Dialect* tour, with both Serch and Nice becoming solo artists. Serch's *Return Of The Product* (1992) was notable only for the debut appearance of **Nas** on "Back to the Grill". However, that was more than you could say for Pete Nice and Daddy Rich's *Dust To Dust* (1993), even though it featured production from **The Beatnuts**, **KMD** and **Sam Sever**.

Serch worked for a spell as an executive at Wild Pitch before founding Serchlite Management, which counted Nas and **OC** among its clients. Nice also went into artist management, but soon quit to become a baseball historian and memorabilia dealer. In 2001 Serch and Pete Nice reunited for

a couple of gigs and were set to release an album, *Ichabod's Cranium*, but it was never released.

**The Cactus Album**
Def Jam, 1989

An album that ranks up there with the best of any of their compatriots, whether white or black. The production from Prince Paul, Sam Sever and the Bomb Squad is often inspired (especially the loop from "Spinning Wheel" on "Sons of 3rd Bass") and the lyrics are complex, detailed and often very funny.

# Three 6 Mafia

New Orleans aside, Memphis is the cradle of American music, but ever since Al Green went gospel M-Town hasn't had a lot to shout about. Although their success is strictly regional, **Three 6 Mafia** and their **Hypnotize Minds Crew** (**Gangsta Boo**, **Indo G**, **Project Pat**, **Pastor Troy** and **Killa Klan**) are just about the only names Memphis has had to brag about recently (unless you count lo-fi indie rockers The Grifters). And while their moral-guardian-baiting tales of pimping, ho-slapping and murder don't exactly take the high road, their subject matter isn't really all that different from the group that originally put Memphis on the map, The Memphis Jug Band.

Three 6 Mafia started courting the devil when **Juicy J** met **DJ Paul** in the early 1990s. With Paul's brother **Lord Infamous** in tow, they formed the **Triple Six Mafia** and quickly became local mixtape legends. Early tracks such as **Kingpin Skinny Pimp**'s "One Life 2 Live" (1995) were largely imitative of the Cali sound, but with even more brutal fatalism. In 1995 Triple 6 changed their name to Three 6 Mafia and released their first album, *Mystic Styles*, which featured more uninspiring remakes of the West Coast gangsta/mack formula such as "Throw

Your Set". After two more underground albums, *Live By Yo Rep* (1996) (the title track was a savage diss of **Bone Thugs-N-Harmony**) and *The End* (1997), Three 6 blew up with *Chapter 2: World Domination* (1997). A remix of "Tear Da Club Up" (which had first appeared in 1995, and was to reappear again and again) epitomised the new sound emerging from the Dirty South: Juicy, Paul, Infamous and Gangsta Boo rapped in rapid-fire cadences that mirrored the skittering drum-machines firing off in the background, while the slow and low bassline was aimed at Memphis dancers doing the gangsta walk. With its mournful piano line and huge, victorious synth washes, "Tear Da Club Up" was more garish than Siegfried & Roy, but it was also "crunker" than anything **Master P** could come up with. Even bigger in the clubs was "Hit A Muthafucka" which has surely the most outrageous murder/killing-a-crowd metaphor ever: if you weren't listening close it sounded as if they were bragging about literally murdering the audience – even Sid Vicious never went that far.

Capitalising on their success, the Mafia renamed themselves **Tear Da Club Up Thugs** for the *Crazyndalazdayz* album (1999), but the real action was on the solo joints: Indo G's *Angel Dust* (1998) and Gangsta Boo's *Enquiring Minds* (1998). Recalling **Organized Noize**'s productions for Outkast and Goodie Mob, Indo G's "Remember Me Ballin'" was a gangsta's prayer to rank with **Ice**

Cube's "It Was A Good Day" and "Dead Homiez", while Gangsta Boo's "Where Dem Dollars At" was a slow-rolling Southern bounce track which was a big hit in strip-clubs. **Project Pat**'s *Ghetty Green* (1999) featured "Ballers", which was produced by Cash Money producer **Mannie Fresh,** and an ill-advised sample of The O'Jays' "Back Stabbers". Throwing taste out of the door altogether, *Three 6 Mafia Presents Hypnotize Minds Camp Posse* (2000) was a collection of blue humour and truly dirty jokes ("Azz & Tittiez" and "Dick Suckin' Hoes", for instance) that were so nasty that they would have been bowdlerised by Blowfly. *When the Smoke Clears – Sixty 6, Sixty 1* (2000) took their Southern-gothic style to even more outrageous levels. After some Bible verses and a **Portishead** sample came "Sippin' On Some Syrup", an ode to the most bizarre tipple since formaldehyde: syrup (a concoction of cough syrup, vodka and – wait for it – milk of magnesia).

Like that other Southern impresario, Master P, Juicy and Paul made their own straight-to-video movie, *Choices*, in 2001, and released a sprawling soundtrack album to accompany it with appearances from **Ludacris** and Project Pat. Pat had a huge hit with "Chickenheads", from his *Mista Don't Play: Everythangs Workin'* (2001), a battle of the sexes cut with new Hypnotize Minds crew member **La Chat**. Unfortunately, Pat lost momentum after running into legal problems for parole

violations.

On *Da Unbreakables* (2003) the Mafia's bragging was as flamboyant as their music. "Ridin' Spinners" had lines such as "My rims [are] so shiny they clear like flat-screen plasma/Gals faint when they see 'em, it's hard to breathe like they got asthma" and a guest appearance from **Lil' Flip**. Da Headbussaz was a collaboration between Three 6 Mafia and **Fiend**. Their album *Dat's How it Happen to Me* (2003) had one extraordinary song in "Get The Fuck Out My Face", based on a field-holler/old-time spiritual sample to send **Moby** back to his penthouse. *Choices 2* (2004) was the lowest common denominator version of their style, particularly on the grotesque "Squeeze It".

**Chapter 2: World Domination**
Hypnotize Minds/Relativity, 1997

As they warn, should you be easily offended, "We ain't talkin' about bustin' pimples", but this violent, misogynist and bouncing album nevertheless epitomised Southern hip-hop. If Lil Jon is a bit too staid for you, this'll be right up your alley.

# Three Times Dope

Philadelphia's Three Times Dope (rapper **EST** (Robert Waller), producer/programmer **Chuck Nice** (Walter Griggs) and **DJ Woody Wood** (Duerwood Beale)) got their start as part of Steady B's Hilltop Hustlers crew. Their first two records, "Crushin' and Bussin'" (1987) and "From Da Giddy Up" (1988), were released on Steady B and Lawrence Goodman's Hilltop Hustlers label under the name **3D**.

The group changed their name to Three Times Dope and signed to Arista. Their first single for the major was the superdope "Greatest Man Alive" (1988), an almighty boast built on a great Muddy Waters sample and punchy guitar stabs. The cautionary tale about gold-digging females "Funky Dividends" (1989) followed, but it was hard to be mad at it: it had a sample of Delegation's "Oh Honey" and the drums from "Synthetic Substitution". And it at least allowed "Michelle" – the money-hungry villain of the story – to get her own back with lines such as, "When I was with Steady B, I had it all: Gucci, Louie Vuitton, gold, Liz Claiborne. I had it all". The two singles were the best tracks on *Original Stylin'*(1989), but the featured remakes of "From Da Giddy Up" and "Crushin' And Bussin'", Woody Wood's showcase "Who Is This?" and the ridiculous boasting of "Improvin' the Groovin'" held the album together.

*Live from Acknickulous Land* (1990) took its name from the B-side of "Crushin' And Bussin'" and had improved production from Chuck Nice. Apart from the great uptempo title track, though, the album never really caught fire, with love jams such as "Weak At The Knees" and comedy numbers like "10 Lil' Sucka Emceez" falling flat. The group disappeared soon afterwards, but, surprisingly, reunited some eight years later for *The Sequel 3* (1998) which hardly recaptured past glories.

**Original Stylin'**
Arista, 1989

A solid, if not terribly inspired, late-1980s album. The so-called "sinister prime minister" EST is best when he's cocky and bragging, as on "Improvin' The Groovin'", and the production from Chuck Nice and Lawrence Goodman excels when it accelerates to higher tempos. The one inspired moment is "Greatest Man Alive" which fulfils both of the above criteria, and has loony spoken word interjections.

# TI

On his first album. Atlanta rapper TI called himself "the king of the South", demanded to be compared to **Biggie**, **2Pac** and **Jay-Z**, and flossed like he was Paris Hilton. It was the kind of arrogance that hip-hop legends are made of. It quickly became clear TI wasn't even the king of his city for his debut album didn't come close to living up to his own hype – his stature was ultimately more like "the viceroy of the South". You can't blame a guy for trying, though.

Especially when his first single had the **Neptunes** on board. "I'm Serious" (2001) had woofer-taxing synth bass, an acoustic guitar figure, **Pharrell** and **Chad**'s trademark syncopated shuffle beat and **Beenie Man** on the hook. TI wasn't bad on the mic either, with perhaps the best "pure" cadence of any rapper from down south and a breathtakingly abundant arrogance. *I'm Serious* (2001) also featured Neptunes' production on the pimptastic "What's Yo Name?" Elsewhere, though, tracks such as "Dope Boyz" and "Do It" were strictly formulaic Dirty South, if not out-and-out rip-offs of his more imaginative peers.

The follow-up was *Trap Muzik*'s (2003), which had a secret weapon in **David Banner**, who produced the weirdly anthemic "Rubberband Man". On top of Banner's loopy kid's chorale, TI claimed he was as "wild as the Taliban" and was going to "Treat these niggas like the Apollo and I'm the Sandman". **Kanye West** and **Jazze Pha** also produced a couple of tracks, but the other highlights belonged to **DJ Toomp** ("24s", a roller about cars that sounded like the theme to a horror movie) and **San Holmes** ("No More Talk", a moody track which had TI rapping, "No more chains and rings that go bling bling/And no more passionate rapping so it seems/It's just these talentless rappers – they're all acting").

**Trap Muzik**
Grand Hustle/Atlantic, 2003

TI undeniably has a great mic skills and presence, but like all rappers he still needs decent beats. The production here is much better than that of his debut – despite the presence of the Neptunes

on *I'm Serious*. Who knows, on the evidence of "Rubberband Man" and "No More Talk", maybe one day he might just become the king of the South.

# Timbaland

If hip-hop was all about the lyrics then **Timbaland** (aka **Tim Mosley**) would be somewhere between one-hit-wonder **Candyman** and **Father MC** in the queue to get into this book. However, while Timbaland has made most of his noise in the r&b world, he's still the most important and influential producer of the last half of the 1990s – perhaps even one of the all-time best. Contemporary hip-hop's signature sonics of space-hopper beats and digital ticks – what journalist Sasha Frere-Jones has christened "Typewriter Funk" – is all down to Timbaland.

The Virginian **Björk** fan – he's sampled her work several times – got his start in Da Bassment, a posse of producers, songwriters and MCs who worked in the background behind hot-tub lover-men **Jodeci**. He stepped out on his own in 1996 on two r&b albums that kicked tired slow-jammers out of the penthouse: **Ginuwine**'s *The Bachelor* and **Aaliyah**'s *One in a Million*. Then, Tim dropped the album that would change r&b forever, Missy "Misdemeanor" Elliott's *Supa Dupa Fly* (1997). The wild futurism – hyper-syncopated beats, almost surreal digital

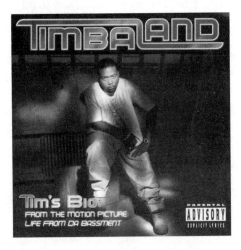

sheen and cyberdelic Kingston dancehall feel – on tracks such as "Hit 'Em Wit Da Hee" and "The Rain (Supa Dupa Fly)" has since been appropriated by every producer in the business.

On his debut album as an artist in his own right Timbaland & Magoo's *Welcome to Our World* (1997), he camouflaged his awful lyrics by layering skittering hi-hats, Gothic synth-string stabs and liquid-mercury keyboards on "Up Jumps Da Boogie" and by restyling James Brown as the protagonist of *Tron* on "Luv 2 Luv U". *Tim's Bio: Life From Da Bassment* (1998) found him mining funk from the themes of *Spiderman* and *I Dream of Jeanie* and disguising his mic incompetence with guest appearances from **Nas**, **Jay-Z** and **Mad Skillz**.

It was his outside productions, though, that made Timbaland's name in 1998. Aaliyah's "Are You That Somebody?" was a stunning record constructed out of bionic human beatboxing, gurgling babies and a rhythm track with more holes on it than a swiss cheese, while "Paper Chase" and "Jigga What, Jigga Who" from Jay-Z's *Vol. 2... Hard Knock Life* album took him out of the ghetto and into orbit. Tim reappeared on Jay-Z's *Vol. 3... Life and Times of S. Carter* (1999), contributing the black hole of "It's Hot" and the synthesizer Gulf-of-Mexico zephyrs on "Big Pimpin'". Missy Elliott's *Da Real World* (1999) was disappointing, apart from its incredible trio of singles, "She's A Bitch", "All In My Grill" and "Hot Boyz", but Timbaland changed hip-hop once again with the bhangra madness of "Get Ur Freak On" (2001) and the space-age cracker opera of **Bubba Sparxx**'s "Ugly". Tim's own *Indecent Proposal* (2001) was, as usual, less startling than his work for other artists.

After some fine records with **Petey Pablo**, another epochal Missy Elliott single, "Work It" (2002), and **Pastor Troy**'s monstrous "Are We Cuttin'?" (2002), Timbaland started to lose his way a bit. Elliott's *This Is Not a Test!* (2003) and Tim and Magoo's *Under Construction Part II* (2003) were both

flat, and seemed to suggest that either he'd run out of ideas or that the rest of the world had finally caught up to him. But Timbaland's so creative it's entirely likely he'll reinvent both r&b and hip-hop again before he's through.

◉ **Tim's Bio: From Da Bassment**
Blackground, 1998

Eventually Tim will get a greatest hits retrospective, but until that time this only half mind-boggling album will have to do. Still, you're probably better off burning your own CD of his hits for other artists.

# ◎ Tommy Boy records

Like a surprisingly large number of New Yorkers at the time, in 1979 **Tom Silverman** was the publisher/editor/writer of a dance music 'zine – one called *Disco News*. Stumbling across the nascent hip-hop culture in a Times Square record store, Silverman journeyed up to White Plains Road in The Bronx to hear **Afrika Bambaataa** spin at the T-Connection club. After his conversion experience, Silverman quickly set up his own label, **Tommy Boy**, which he ran from his apartment on the Upper East Side.

His first signing was Bambaataa and his Cosmic Force MCs who released their first record for the label under the name of **Cotton Candy** – "Havin' Fun" (1981). The group had previously record-

ed for the Winley label, but the record that established both Bambaataa (outside of The Bronx at least) and Tommy Boy was "Jazzy Sensation" (1981), credited to Afrika Bambaataa & the Jazzy 5. The record was produced by **Arthur Baker** and mixed by **Shep Pettibone** and although it was based on Gwen McRae's "Funky Sensation", its Casio clave and synth-dominated instrumental B-side marked the turn away from the live instrumentation of the Sugar Hill sound. Even more of an upheaval, however, was Bambaataa & Soulsonic Force's "Planet Rock" (1982): electro-funk which single-handedly started the **Miami Bass** and **Electro** genres, and which was to become one of the most important records of the 1980s.

With records by Planet Patrol ("Play

# B-BOYING

Despite worldwide successes from the Sugar Hill Gang, Grandmaster Flash & the Furious Five, Afrika Bambaataa and Run DMC, you've got to wonder if hip-hop would have really made it out of New York if it wasn't for the infectious athleticism of the **b-boys**. The phrase may have been brought to mainstream attention by **Run DMC**'s "Sucker MCs" ("Cold chill at a party in a b-boy stance"), but b-boying actually had nothing to do with cold chillin'. "B-boy" is short for "break boy", Kool Herc's term for the dancers who went crazy when he dropped the breaks (segments of records where all the instruments drop out to let the drummers do their thing) of records such as **The Incredible Bongo Band**'s "Apache" and **Mandrill**'s "Fencewalk". In fact, without the b-boys (and b-girls) reacting the way they did to Herc's records, there wouldn't be any hip-hop at all.

Like all aspects of hip-hop culture, b-boying is ultimately a form of competition – a facet that was crucial to its original popularity, since b-boying began when New York's ghettos were run by street gangs. **Afrika Bambaataa**'s Zulu Nation organisation helped channel violence into dancing competitions: where b-boys would uprock (criss-crossing their arms and Pro-Keds-69ers-clad feet, while keeping everything else still) and then drop and scuff the floor with their creased Lee jeans while performing backspins (spinning on your back) and turtles (a bizarre-looking manoeuvre executed in a quasi-yogic crouch).

While breakdancing (a term disowned by all true b-boys) began with crews like the **Nigger Twins**, the **Zulu Kings**, the **Salsoul Crew**, the **City Boys**, **Freeze Force**, **Starchild La Rock**, **The Disco Kids** and the **KC Crew**, the most influential was undoubtedly the **Rock Steady Crew**. Formed in 1977 by **Jo-Jo Torres**, **Jimmy Lee**, **Mongo**

**Rock**, **Spy** and **Jimmy Dee**, the Rock Steady Crew gathered together the best of the second wave of Latino b-boys who had come to dominate the field since it migrated out of the Bronx in the early 1970s. The RSC's main innovation was to make b-boying more athletic and more gymnastic. Many of these moves were pioneered by the two b-boys who are generally considered as the greatest: **Richie "Crazy Legs" Colón** and **Ken "Swift" Gabbert**. Moves such as the windmill, the whip, the 1990, the chair and the spider are credited to Crazy Legs and Ken Swift , who helped the RSC become the dominant crew in legendary battles against the **Dynamic Rockers**, the **Floor Masters** and the **New York City Breakers**.

Meanwhile, in Los Angeles, a kid called **Don Campbell** invented locking (freezing in between moves). The dance became so popular that he formed his own troupe in 1973, the **Campbellock Dancers**, which included such minor celebs as **Fred "Rerun" Berry**, **Toni Basil** and **"Shabba-Doo" Quiñones**. The style was expanded upon by **The Electric Boogaloos** (**"Boogaloo Sam" Solomon**, **Timothy "Popin' Pete" Solomon**, **Skeeter Rabbit**, **Twisto Flex Don**, **Creepin Cid** and **Tickin' Will**) who invented moves like poppin', boogaloo, tickin', twisto-flex and the old man while dancing to Zapp records. Less of a Mitch Gaylord floor routine than the East Coast style, poppin' and lockin' emphasised upper body movements in almost geometric patterns. Thanks to **Pop'N Taco**, **Mr Wiggles**, **Sugar Pop** and **Loose Bruce**, the style continues today and continues to influence the legions of Europeans and Japanese b-boys who have helped keep breakdancing alive while American hip-hoppers ran from its *Flashdance* associations.

At Your Own Risk") and **Jonzun Crew** ("Pack Jam" in 1982, and Jonzun's "Space Cowboy", the **Force MDs** ("Let Me Love You") and **Keith LeBlanc** ("No Sell Out" – featuring a sampled Malcolm X) in 1983, Tommy Boy quickly replaced Sugar Hill as the leading hip-hop label. Despite its pre-eminence, the label's greatest record was never released, being the victim of corporate copyright robber-barons. The winner of a contest held by Tommy Boy to remix **G.L.O.B.E. & Whiz Kid**'s 1983 single "Play That Beat Mr. DJ", **Double Dee & Steinski**'s "The Payoff Mix" (1984) became an enormous cult hit in New York by virtue of its prescient reading of sampling as the modern equivalent to the call-and-response that character-ised African-American music. The work of studio engineer **Doug DiFranco** and advertising jingle producer **Steve Stein**, "The Payoff Mix" was the result of end-less hours in the studio literally cutting and pasting together tapes. It spliced Spoonie Gee, Bobby Byrd, Funky Four Plus One, the World Famous Supreme Team, Incredible Bongo Band, Little Richard, exercise routines, Humphrey Bogart, Herbie Hancock, The Supremes, Grandmaster Flash, Chic and about 100 other things – not to mention, of course, "Play That Beat Mr. DJ". "The Payoff Mix" was scheduled to be released on an EP with the equally mind-boggling "Lesson Two: The James Brown Mix" and "Lesson Three: The History Of Hip-Hop", but they have only ever appeared on bootlegs.

As hip-hop matured Tommy Boy kept pace, releasing landmarks by **Stetsasonic**, **De La Soul**, **Queen Latifah**, **Digital Underground**, **House of Pain**, **Naughty By Nature**, **Paris**, **Coolio**, **Screwball** and a number of **Prince Paul** projects. Tommy Boy celebrated its twentieth anniversary in 2001 and started the Tommy Boy Black imprint to showcase underground tal-ent such as **The Jigmastas**, **Self Scientific**, **Natural Elements** and **DV Alias Khrist**. In 2002, Joel Silverman bought back the portion of the label that had been bought by Time-Warner in 1986, and started to branch out into releasing soundtracks and television shows.

⊙ **Tommy Boy's Greatest Beats**
Tommy Boy, 1998

Housed in a mini milk crate, this four-CD, 56-track compilation is easily the best label overview available, and has everything from "Planet Rock" to Coolio's "Gangsta's Paradise".

# Tone-Loc

Although these days he only gets played whenever *Surf Ninjas* or *Ace Ventura: Pet Detective* pop up on late-night cable television, Tone-Loc was once the biggest rap star in the world. "Wild Thing" (1988) was one of the ten best-selling singles in US history, and his follow-up, "Funky Cold Medina" (1989), wasn't all that far behind.

Although you'd never guess it from his music, Tone-Loc (Anthony Smith) was once a Westside Tribe Crip gang-mem-ber, who had moved to LA from Texas. His mic name came from the nickname given to him by the local *vatos*, "Antonio Loco". Rather than exploiting his vio-lent past, when it came time to rock the mic, Tone-Loc went straight for the party jams. His debut was the first single to be released on Matt Dike's Delicious Vinyl label – "Cheeba Cheeba"/"On Fire" (1987). Surfacing in the midst of the crack epidemic, "Cheeba Cheeba" was one of the first hip-hop tracks to celebrate (soft) drug use, as Loc rapped in his charcteristic rasp "I might get ill and roll an eighth in one hooter" in between the inevitable punctuations from the **Harlem Underground Band**, whose "Smokin' Cheeba Cheeba" (1976) was the rap's inspiration. Producers the **Dust Brothers** got truly inspired for "Wild Thing", however. Using a snippet of **Van Halen**'s "Jamie's Crying", they conjured a beat that was simultaneously tough and geared for maximum crossover potential, a successful formula which won "Wild Thing" double-platinum sales. At the time, only "White Christmas" and "We Are the World" were bigger-selling singles in the US, but somehow "Wild Thing" never made it to number one. *Loc-ed*

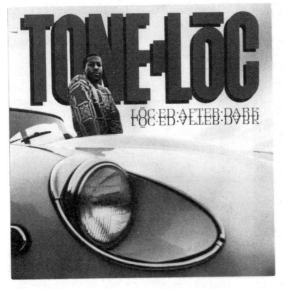

# Too $hort

He may have only one subject, but no one in hip-hop has had a longer career than Oakland's **Too $hort**. Despite the East Coast bias of most hip-hop histories, Too $hort will eventually go down as one of the three or four most important hip-hop artists of all time, for better or worse. The entire West Coast style can be traced back to Too $hort's obsession with P-Funk, synth hooks and, of course, "beeeyitches".

**Todd Shaw** was born in 1966 and raised in Los Angeles, but at age 14 he moved to Oakland to escape LA's gang culture. The Bay Area may not have had gang problems, but it was awash with crime and prostitution. Inspired by his surroundings, Shaw invented a character called Too $hort (aka $horty the Pimp, $hort Dog, etc.), a "game"-talking, bitch-slapping, "dank"-smoking mack. With schoolmate **Freddy B**, $hort made like an African praise singer or court poet, and made personalized tapes for specific customers which glorified their customers' deeds in music. Soon enough, $hort and Freddy could be found on buses selling their tapes for $5 a pop, and the two quickly became Bay Area celebs.

In 1983, $hort released *Don't Stop Rappin'* and *Players* on the tiny 75 Girls label. Nothing coming out of New York sounded anything like them: although "Don't Stop Rappin'" had booming drum machines and Bambaataa-styled vocoders, with whining synths straight out of the **Bernie Worrell** songbook, it nevertheless sounded closer to **Prince** than Grandmaster Flash. At the same time, $hort's blue lyrics couldn't have been further from the social commentary and call-and-response "Yes, yes y'all"ing coming from the Rotten Apple.

*Raw, Uncut and X-Rated* (1985), however, really set Too $hort apart. Over a bass-heavy groove, "Flat Booty Bitches" laid out $hort's nightmare: he crosses over the border into Berkeley and "sees

*After Dark* (1989) did, however, and Loc was the first African-American rapper to top the album chart (the Beastie Boys were the first rappers to acheive the feat). Although it was certainly lightweight and Loc's flow was often so stiff it sounded as if he was rapping to a metronome, it was easy to see why it topped the charts. The comedic "Funky Cold Medina" was based on more rock samples – this time from **Free** and **Kiss** – and was as catchy as "Wild Thing".

The Dust Brothers weren't on board for *Cool Hand Loc* (1991) and it showed. Loc's wooden and raspy flow only worked initially because of the hooks and beats; here, Loc just sank into the murk, and not even El DeBarge can pull him out. It didn't matter much because Loc was already a pop culture icon and his voice was so distinctive that a career as an animation voice-over artist beckoned.

**Loc-ed After Dark**
Delicious Vinyl, 1989

Loc had the croakiest voice since Clarence "Frogman" Henry, but the Dust Brothers turned this toad into a Prince Charming with their witty and catchy production. "Wild Thing" and "Funky Cold Medina" had beats constructed by the Dust Brothers and raps written by Young MC, but wouldn't have been nearly as huge as they were without Loc's voice and sly humour.

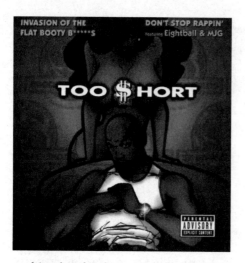

nothing but bitches with no ass". "She's A Bitch", "The Bitch Sucks Dick" and "Blow Job Betty" continued the theme. Not only had no one heard such language on vinyl since Blowfly and Lightnin' Rod, but the George Clinton-style synth-funk had become even more pronounced, and was to pave the way for **N.W.A.**, **E-40**, **Ant Banks**, **Spice 1**, **Eightball & MJG** and an entire generation. $hort released his first 12" in 1985. "Girl" was the best drug song since Melle Mel's "White Lines", and proved that $hort was more than just **Rudy Ray Moore** without a sense of humour. *Born To Mack* (1986) was originally released on his own Dangerous Music label. When $hort signed to Jive Records, the album was re-released and it introduced the rest of the world to $horty the Player. Entirely self-produced, the album nailed the $hort formula, and tracks such as "Freaky Tales" and "Dope Fiend Beat" became landmarks of Californian hip-hop. *Life Is... Too $hort* (1988) saw $hort work with Oakland producer **Al Eaton**, who fleshed out $hort's signature sound, and tracks like "City Of Dope" and "Don't Fight The Feeling" benefited from the higher production values.

*$hort Dog's In The House* (1990) followed with a more LA-influenced sound (courtesy of co-producer **Sir Jinx**) and featured his biggest hit to date: a chilling, Last Poets-sampling update of **Donny Hathaway**'s "The Ghetto". *$horty The Pimp* (1992), *Get In Where You Fit In* (1993) and

the appropriately named *Cocktales* (1995) all followed in a similar style, helping $hort notch up his sixth platinum album along the way.

$hort claimed that he was retiring after *Gettin' It (Album Number Ten)* (1996), but it was merely a clever ploy to renegotiate his contract with Jive. The album was pretty much business as usual, but it was notable for the title track, which saw $hort working with **George Clinton**. *Can't Stay Away* (1999) was $hort's "return" and, sure enough, things hadn't changed a bit. He even resorted to remaking "Flat Booty Bitches" (admittedly, "Invasion Of The Flat Booty Bitches" was pretty good) and "Freaky Tales". His eleventh album, *You Nasty* (2000), was the same old concoction of pimpin' tales and funk beats. Then again, after eighteen years of singing pretty much the same song, no-one was exactly expecting any revolutionary changes.

The repetition, however, began to get a little wearing. Too $hort became akin to a doddering old great-uncle in the corner, telling the same old war stories to a dwindling circle of listeners on albums such as *Chase the Cat* (2001), *What's My Favorite Word?* (2002) and *Married to the Game* (2003).

**Greatest Hits Volume 1: The Player Years 1983-1988**
In-A-Minute, 1993

Were it not for this double-CD package, nobody outside the Bay Area would be able to hear his 75 Girls material. Love him or hate him, this is the Rosetta Stone of West Coast hip-hop, defining both its sound and its subject matter.

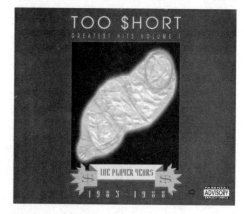

# A Tribe Called Quest

Starting off by playing second fiddle to the Jungle Brothers and De La Soul as the junior members of the Native Tongues, **A Tribe Called Quest** quickly outstripped both in terms of commercial and artistic success. Quest simplified De La's oblique logic, and hardened the Jungle Brothers's breezy jazziness to produce hip-hop that managed to be both abstract and pop-savvy. With **Q-Tip** (**Kamaal Fareed**, né **Jonathan Davis**)'s legendarily vast record collection and **Ali Shaheed Muhammad**'s equally legendary production shine, A Tribe Called Quest redefined the art of crate-digging, establishing late 1960s and early 1970s jazz as *the* motif of East Coast hip-hop in the 1990s.

Q-Tip first established himself with introductory cameos on the Jungle Brothers and De La Soul albums, but Tribe's debut album, *People's Instinctive Travels and the Paths of Rhythm* (1990), displayed a talent, effervescence and vibe that Tip's guest appearances didn't even begin to hint at. Filled with morality plays, allegorical journeys, slice-of-life vignettes and comedic asides, *People's Instinctive Travels* was a coming-of-age document. Tip, Ali Shaheed, **Phife** (**Malik Taylor**) and **Jarobi** spoke of trying to find their way in the

hip-hop game, thumb-wrestling with role models, avoiding cholesterol (on "Ham 'N' Eggs"), and chiding friends who had stepped out of line, whilst not neglecting the hip-hop tradition of calling-out fools. With rich, sprightly production based on samples which ranged eclectically from Lou Reed to Roy Ayers, and an infectious levity and sense of humour, the album was never bogged down by its worthy intentions.

Losing the largely dead weight of Jarobi, *The Low End Theory* (1991) found the new trio brimming with confidence. Tip's delivery, with its nasal timbre and heavy New York accent, had developed into one of the best flows in the business. The exuberant jazziness of the first album had become more measured and self-assured, falling just the right side of arrogance. Rather than merely using snippets of jazz as a flavour enhancer, Tribe attempted to live up to jazz's precedent as a *process* – one facilitating freedom via improvisation. The "low end theory" of the album's title was more than just a use of sub-zero frequencies to move butts (although it certainly was that), but a claim to history and heritage. Giving a rap the same aesthetic weight as a Coltrane solo, *The Low End Theory* went platinum on the strength of "important" hip-hop that realised it was only truly important if it was "boomin' in ya, boomin' in ya, boomin' in ya jeep".

After the classic, elastic "Hot Sex" (1992) from the *Boomerang* soundtrack, the Tribe attempted to perfect their aesthetic on *Midnight Marauders* (1993). Following the same blueprint as *Low End* but with a greater density, *Midnight Marauders* was more of a production showcase, letting the message be transmitted through the beats rather than lyrics. Beat junkies were justifiably astounded by the album, but the whole thing didn't quite cohere as well as the previous two.

Before *Beats, Rhymes and Life* (1996) Phife moved to Atlanta from New York — a bad omen considering only **Cameo** ever survived that journey with their brains intact. Perhaps as a result of this move to America's home of slight urban contemporary pop, *Beats, Rhymes and Life* was glossy, high-contrast hip-hop that aspired to the sheen of r&b. Typically for Tribe, the music was lazy and sleepy, but the bleariness was gone. The hazy film of old had been replaced by impossibly crisp beats and razor sharp snares. Q-Tip's flow was still impeccable, however, and Phife's talent for juxtaposition remained refreshingly unfettered: "Watch me stab up the track as if my name was OJ Simpson/I packs it in like Van Halen/I work for mine; you, you're freeloadin' like Kato Kaelin".

*The Love Movement* (1998) was even more of a disappointment, drowning in the lifeless bohemia they had set the parameters for on *The Low End Theory* and *Midnight Marauders*. There were highlights such as "Find a Way", but this was the sound of a group that had run out of ideas. *The Love Movement* was Tribe's last album.

On *Amplified* (1999), Q-Tip's solo album, he was very much his own man, and he had a new vitality as a result. The loping, jazzy beats of old were gone, but the in vogue, stop-start production style gave Q-Tip a new lease of life. With tracks as hot as "Breathe and Stop", "Vivrant Thing", "Let's Ride" and "Moving With U", *Amplified* was the acceptable face of jigginess. On "Bend Ova" (1999) Phife Dawg thought he was Blowfly and tried to fuck his way across Atlanta over seriously hot production (sparse drums and chicken-scratch guitar) from The Ummah's **Jay Dee** (who had produced Tribe's last two albums). Meanwhile, Ali Shaheed formed the boho soul group **Lucy Pearl** with exiles from **Tony! Toni! Tone!** and **En Vogue**.

Scheduled to be released in 2002, Q-Tip's *Kamaal the Abstract* was a 180 degree turn away from the shiny jigginess of *Amplified*. The album was all clavinets and Fender Rhodes licks, soul-jazz spiritualism and D'Angelo/Common/The Roots black bohemianism. It sounded nothing like contemporary hip-hop and Arista churlishly kept

it in the vault. In 2003 A Tribe Called Quest reunited for the track "(I C U) Doin' It" from the *Violator 3* album. The following year they played some live performances together and there were rumours that they had recorded a couple of tracks for an album.

**The Low End Theory**
Jive, 1991

Less joyous than their debut, this deep, serious album redefined the sound of East Coast hip-hop. It sent every crate-digger from here to Timbuktu scavenging through the second-hand-record bins for CTI records to sample. But more importantly, the album demonstrated that hip-hop was an aesthetic every bit as deep, serious and worth cherishing as any in a century-plus of African-American music.

# Obie Trice

The first time most people heard Detroit rapper Obie Trice was on the intro to **D12**'s *Devil's Night* (2001) album. Millions more heard him on the opening few bars of **Eminem**'s "Without Me" (2002), in which the phrase "Obie Trice – real name, no gimmicks" was scratched in, but Trice had been a presence on the underground Detroit scene since the late 1990s. Singles like "Dope Jobs Homeliss" (1999), "Respect" (2000) and "Well Known Asshole" (2001) won him a rep in the Motor City and the attention of Eminem who signed him to Shady Records.

While Shady was concentrating on promoting **50 Cent**, Trice made numerous mixtape appearances. When his debut album, *Cheers* (2003), finally came out after all the 50 Cent brouhaha had died down a bit, Trice even poked fun at his own much humbler status: "He ain't shit 'cos he rap for Mr Mathers/Plus 50 Cent is, like, ten times badder". Trice, indeed, was more workmanlike and less flamboyant than any of his labelmates. Rather than glorify his days spent hustling on Motown's hard streets with lurid crime tales, Trice presented himself as a Victor Hugo-like everyman just trying to make ends to meet. Of course, having Eminem, **Dr. Dre** and **Timbaland** on hand to help with the beats

didn't exactly lend credence to his "man of the people" schtick. Nor did tracks such as "Shit Hits The Fan" and "We All Die One Day", in which Trice got himself dragged into Eminem's high-profile beefs with **Ja Rule** and *The Source* magazine. Still, Trice was a fairly engaging personality on the mic, and he had enough skills not to fumble the state-of-the-art beats handed to him.

**Cheers**
Interscope, 2003

Trice is a fairly nondescript rapper, but agreeable tracks such as "Got Some Teeth" and unflubbable beats from Dr. Dre and Timbaland make this a better than average commercial rap album.

# Trick Daddy

While Liberty City's Trick Daddy (Maurice Young) certainly doesn't skimp on the meat-and-potatoes of Miami hip-hop – booty – he's more often concerned with getting his fellow thugs rowdy. Which probably isn't surprising considering that he learned how to rap during two terms in juvenile lock-up.

Trick Daddy got his start under the name Trick Daddy Dollars, rhyming on Miami legend **Luke**'s "Scarred" (1996). Hooking up with Ted Lucas's Slip-N-Slide Records, Trick Daddy Dollars released *...Based on a True Story...* (1997). The cover pictured a Trick Daddy food stamp; "Pimp" was

Trick Daddy makes the blingingest, angriest shadow-puppet rabbit ever to be projected onto a wall.

a duet with fellow Dade County charmer **JT Money**; and "Kill-A-Head" had lyrics such as "The graveyeard is my home/ Tombstones and bones/Murder weapons is the case now, don't hearse my bone/ Headhunting is my hobby, who the victim be/And who's next on my everyday headless spree".

Trick Daddy dropped the "Dollars" in his name for *www.thug.com* (1998), and the album's platinum sales more than filled the gap. "Nann Nigga", perhaps the bluest battle-of-the-sexes song ever recorded, was a huge hit on the strength of its scattershot beat and **Trina**, the Sunshine State's version of Lil' Kim, giving as good as she got. There were more playboy tales and pimp-

ing on "Suckin' And Fuckin'", but a degree of introspection was displayed on "Hold On": "Marijuana got me coping with my problems/Hennessy got me hoping I can solve them/My baby mama full of drama trying to start me/But unlike my sorry-ass father, I try harder".

*Book of Thugs (Chapter AK, Verse 47)* (2000) tried to recapture the success of "Nann Nigga" with "Shut Up", another big club hit featuring Trina sparring with Trick over what could be the Florida A&M university marching band. "Boy" might have been the first track to use the term "throwing 'bows" – rowdy dancing (that's 'bows as in elbows) – while "Amerika" borrowed a groove from **R Kelly** to diss the

Land of Liberty.

*Thugs Are Us* (2001) was slightly more commercial and featured a remake of **Ice-T**'s "99 Problems", the reggae-ish "I'm A Thug" and the posse cut "Take it To Da House" sampling the horns and beat from Hialeah neighbours **KC & The Sunshine Band**. The rest of the album, though, was little more than a collection of beats that ripped off **Swizz Beatz**. *Thug Holiday* (2002) was a significant improvement. While the title track was unpleasantly saccharine, the flute-driven "Gangsta" was the beat of Trick's career and **Jazze Pha**'s "In Da Wind" featured **Big Boi**, Goodie MOb's **Cee-Lo** and Trick's self-deprecating lines "I'm a ol' sneaky, ol' freaky, ol' geechy-ass nigga/Collard green, neckbone-eatin'-ass nigga/Always wearin' my jeans baggy saggy/You know Florida, Georgia, South Cackalacky/Growed up eatin' Spam sandwiches".

**Thug Holiday**
Slip-N-Side/Atlantic, 2002

Trick tones things down in deference to his more sensitive side and makes the best record of his career. That's not to say that Trick doesn't get low down and dirty (check out "Get That Feeling" and "All I Need"), it's just that he "drop[s] the top and let[s] the sun shine in". Uniformly good beats don't hurt either.

# Trina

Miami's Katrina Taylor exploded onto the rap scene with one of the filthiest verses on record since Lucille Bogan's "Shave 'Em Dry". On **Trick Daddy**'s 1998 hit "Nann Nigga", Trina made Lil' Kim look like Mary Whitehouse and Foxy Brown like Phyllis Schlafly. Another spunky verse on Trick's "Shut Up" (1999) landed the Liberty City vixen a solo deal with Ted Lucas's Slip-N-Slide label.

*Da Baddest Bitch* (2000) was a relentless collection of sleazey rhymes. On top of a beat that recalled Isaac Hayes's "Theme From Shaft", the title track was often breathtakingly over-the-top: "See I fuck him in the living room while his children home/I make him eat it while

my period on… See if I had the chance to be a virgin again/I'd be fucking by the time I'm ten". "Down With Me" had more *bons mots* such as "Never let a nigga hit the coochie raw/Might bust a nut on my Gucci bra". While the beats were okay, Trina was definitely best listened to in short doses, so that her potty-mouthed lyrics actually shocked. After about four songs, her punani dentata posing grew boring. However, "Niggas Ain't Shit" was a pretty decent belated response to Dr. Dre's "Bitches Ain't Shit", even if Trina was upstaged by featured MC **Lois Lane** ("You that same old nigga/With the same low figures/'Cept the lies gettin' bigga/And the sex lacks the vigour").

The "pussy power [was] still in control" on *Diamond Princess* (2002), but the beats were way better this time around. **Kanye West** strolled by with a gypsy violinist for "B R Right", **Missy Elliott** stole some tricks from Timbaland for "Rewind That Back" and "No Panties", and **Just Blaze** dropped the minimalist "How We Do?". Trina's lyrics explored the same old territory, but the parade of guest stars gave the album more variety.

Just Blaze and Kanye West returned, along with Jazze Pha, for *Glamorest Life* (2004). The lead single was a remake of **LL Cool J**'s "Big Ol' Butt" entitled "Leaving You (Big Ol' Dick)", in which she blithely informs her paramour she's leaving him because he doesn't measure up to various named rappers. If she had come up with the some true dirt à la **Bebe Ruell**'s *Groupie Central* memoirs, perhaps it would've been interesting, but the lyrics and the beat were cheesier than a sports jockstrap.

**Diamond Princess**
Slip-N-Slide, 2002

One of the rare albums where you don't mind the cavalcade of featured guest-stars because, like a bad porno flick, Trina's lyrics are titillating for about five minutes before boredom sets in. Missy Elliott, Tweet, Ludacris and Fabolous all provide respites from the opportunistic tales of head-for-cash exchange, with Ludacris sparkling brightest on "B R Right".

# ⊙ Tuff City records

Tuff City began in 1982 when long-time record-collector and *Cash Box* journalist **Aaron Fuchs** decided to join fellow doo-wop enthusiasts **Bobby Robinson** and **Paul Winley** in the hip-hop game. Operating out of Long Island City, Queens, **Tuff City** and its subsidiary **Smokin'** released dozens of near-classics in its mid-1980s heyday, but now serve the hip-hop community best as a reissue label, preserving old school and funk rarities.

The label didn't begin terribly auspiciously. **Vertical Lines**'s "Beach Boy" (1982) was a light and not very good electro-pop number produced by Barry Michael Cooper, the man who would later coin the term New Jack Swing and write the screenplays for both *New Jack City* and *Above the Rim*. Far better was Cooper's second incarnation – **The Micronawts** – whose "Letzmurph Acrossdasurf" (1983) was a bass-heavy minimal electro number with an Afrika Bambaataa dub mix. The label bore the inscription, "The Sound of Young New York", and when the label earned itself a distribution deal with CBS, it seemed like Fuchs might realise his Motown-esque ambitions. Sadly, even though Tuff City records such as **Cold Crush Brothers**'s "Punk Rock Rap", **Spoonie Gee**'s "Big Beat" and **Davy DMX**'s "One for the Treble" (all 1983) became hip-hop classics, the label's relationship with the CBS proved to be short-lived.

Part of the label's problem was that it had an over-reliance on old school legends like Cold Crush, Spoonie Gee and members of the Fearless Four, all of whom were swept aside by the ascendant **Run DMC**. Still, the old codgers managed to produce some good records: Cold Crush's "Fresh, Wild, Fly & Bold" (1984), **Grandmaster Caz**'s "Yvette" (1985) and "Get

Down Grandmaster" (1987), Spoonie Gee's "Get Off My Tip" (1984), "That's My Style" (1986) and "The Godfather" (1987), and **Traedonya**'s "The Boogaloo" (1986), which featured a verse from **Spyder D**. The man behind most of these records was the one and only Pumpkin, who even in the era of Linn drum-machines and DX-7 synths was still as funky as ever.

With his caveman vest, heavy metal bracelets and comedically violent battle-rhymes, The Bronx's **Funkmaster Wizard Wiz** was one of the middle school's most unhinged personalities. His borderline dementia was unleashed on records such as "Put That Head Out" (1985), "Crack It Up", "I Stink 'Cause I'm Funky" (both 1986) and "183rd & Grand Concourse" (1987). **Freddy B & the Mighty Mic Masters** gave the music one of its greatest anthems (and one of its strangest choruses – all echoed-out like a dub mix) with "It's The Hip-Hop" (1985). The *Smokin' Raps* and *Smokin' Beats* (both 1986) albums are highly collectible collections of tracks unavailable elsewhere, such as **Sir Fresh & DJ Critical**'s superb "Sally & Dee" and **Marley Marl**'s awesome "The Man Marley Marl".

In 1988 Tuff City hooked up with **The 45 King**, and released the epochal "The 900 Number" (1988). The 45 King helped define the sound of the late 1980s and

early 1990s with his productions for **Lakim Shabazz**, *Pure Righteousness* (1989) and *The Lost Tribe of Shabazz* (1990), and his own *The Lost Breakbeats* (1990). Poor Righteous Teachers's producer **Tony D** dropped the bomb on **YZ**'s amazingly funky "Thinking of a Master Plan" (1989). **YZ**'s *Sons of the Father* (1990) and *The YZ EP* (1991) were similarly funky, particularly on tracks such as "Taggin' It Up" and "Mixel Plic Remix".

With hip-hop becoming ever more corporate, Tuff City began to concentrate on Fuch's first love, old r&b records, and started to reissue obscure funk and old school hip-hop records.

---

### PUMPKIN

● **The Tuff City Sessions**
Ol' Skool Flava, 1995

The sound quality sucks – a problem with a lot of Tuff City releases – but the album more than makes up for it by shining a deserved spotlight on one of hip-hop's true unsung greats. Disappointingly, it doesn't have his classic "King of the Beats", but it does have Pumpkin getting loose on various productions for Grandmaster Caz, Funk Master Wizard Wiz and Spoonie Gee.

# Tuff Crew

One measure of the esteem in which the Tuff Crew are held by hip-hop fanatics is that no omission in the first edition of this book generated more response than that of the Tuff Crew. So, without further ado, the *Tuff Guide To Hip-Hop*...

The Northside Illadelph crew – MCs **LA Kid**, **Tone Love**, **Monty G** and **Overlord Ice Dog**, and the mighty DJ **Detonator Too Tuff** – got together in the mid-1980s. They released their first two singles, "Get Smart" and "Philly Style" (both 1986), on their own So Def label. Adding an O to their label's name, Tuff Crew released the epochal "My Part Of Town" (1987) on the rechristened Soo Def, now distributed by New York's Warlock Records. They may not have been the first to use the break from **Lyn Collins**' "Think", but the way they combined its speedy drums with a once-a-bar sub-bass tone was rev-

olutionary, particularly when Detonator went crazy on the transformers at the end of the track. It was indeed as they proclaimed: "So damn tuff!"

*Phanjam* (1987) was an EP shared with the **Krown Rulers** (**MC Grand Pubah** and **DJ Rocker**) from across the Ben Franklin Bridge in Camden, New Jersey. The Krown Rulers's "B Boy Document" showcased a more forbidding version of the 1986/87 Marley Marl sound (especially with its ominous bass piano riffs that cropped up every so often), with Pubah dropping lines such as "dual modulation like Radio Shack" in a voice very reminiscent of **Eazy-E**. Tuff Crew's "Def Joun" featured Detonator doing ridiculous things to **Chuck Brown & the Soul Searchers**, while the rest of the crew dropped a group rap that still had residue of Cold Crush Brothers's dynamics. The Krown Rulers released the highly underrated *Paper Chase* (1988) album ( with the duo pictured in full mediaeval knight regalia on the cover), produced by LA Kid. They faded into obscurity only to return in 2003 (Pubah now going by the name **Gambino**) with the very run-of-the-mill *The Delegation*.

According to legend, when the Tuff Crew toured in Florida in support of their *Danger Zone* (1988) album, riots broke out because their booming bass sound was so popular. With tracks such as "Smooth Momentum", "Let It Rip", "Born To Ike" and the extraordinary DJ cut "Deuce Ace Housin'", it wasn't hard to see why. *Back to Wreck Shop* (1989), however, was even better. "Gimme Some" was a seismic thank you to their fans in South Florida; "What You Don't Know" was a thick, humid remake of a **Dennis Coffey** groove featuring plenty of Detonator's DJ skills and subtle 808 bass; "Wreck Shop" and "Show 'Em Hell" were the group's best vocal performances; and Detonator was stupid fresh once again on not one, but two, DJ cuts – "Behold the Detonator" and "Soul Food".

The Deuce Ace, Tone Love and Monty G had all jumped ship by the time of *Still Dangerous* (1991). The group's dancer **Smooth K** made the leap to the microphone – an indicator of the album's poor quality. While the lyrical content was harder than ever, the beats were thin. Thankfully, Ice Dog and LA Kid were pretty nice on the mic on cuts such as "Robbin Hoods". In 1993 Ice Dog addressed the dissension in the ranks that had destroyed the group on his underground single, "Shootin' Deuces", on 4X4 Records. He seems to have got the last word.

⊙ **Back to Wreck Shop**
Warlock, 1989

If there was an award for most slept-on hip-hop album of all time, this might just walk away with the honours. With the exception of the awful "She Rides The Pony", the album is chock full of sublime mic control from LA Kid and Ice Dog, and devastating scratches from Detonator. His two showcases, "Soul Food" and "Behold the Detonator", rank among the finest DJ tracks ever.

# Twista

Ever since its inception, hip-hop has been the ultimate triumph of form over content, so it was only a matter of time before someone like Twista came along. Under his original rap name, Tung Twista, the Windy City rapper is in the *Guinness Book Of Records* as the world's fastest rapper. He doesn't have a lot to say but says it very, very quickly and with astonishing clarity, which marks him out as hip-hop's version of flashy guitar bores Yngwie Malmsteen or Al DiMeola. All that he needs now is for someone to start publishing *Mic Wrecker* magazine, and he'd be on the cover every month for the rest of his life.

He announced his presence on the hip-hop scene in 1991 with "Mista Tung Twista" rapping lines such as "Let the cavalier Tung kiss ya, it's the Mista Tung Twista/ Pumpin' a rhythm, a lyrical styler/My tongue'll be flingin' a funky pile of lyrical rhymes that's breakin 'em off in the mind" at faster-than-light speed. *Runnin' Off at Da Mouth* (1992) had even faster raps in the form of "Ratatattat" and "Razzamatazz/ Jazzamatazz". When he slowed down a bit, as on "Say What?", you could tell that even if he was flawless on the mic, he had absolutely nothing to say.

*Da Resurrection* (1995) saw him collaborating with Dres of **Black Sheep** and moving into a slightly more hardcore style of rapping. After the success of Bone Thugs-N-Harmony and the now-renamed Twista's appearance on **Do Or Die**'s "Po Pimp" (1996), he fully embraced the gangsta style on *Adrenaline Rush* (1997). When he and his producer Traxster actually moved beyond imitating Dr. Dre and Bone Thugs, Twista managed to hit a nerve or two on tracks such as "Unsolved Mystery" (which attacked the police's apathy about murder victims in the 'hood) and "Overdose" (a nice twist on G-Funk's whining synths).

For *Mobstability* (1998) Twista gave some space to his **Speed Knot Mobstaz** protégés – the smooth **Mayz** and the 2Pac-alike **Liffy Stokes** – to provide some contrast for his machine-gun rapping. There was nothing new about the record, but Traxster's beats were better (even if he did rip-off Dr. Dre again) and the Mobstaz provided some respite for weary ears. *Twista Presents Legit Ballin'* (1999), on his new Legit Ballin' label, was more of a posse album than a Twista record, with the speed demon showing up on only eight tracks (out of 24). The rest of the crew had even less to offer than Twista. His *Twista Presents Legit Ballin' Volume 2* (2001) didn't change matters.

Twista's waited until 2004 to put out his next solo album, but he certainly wasn't out of the limelight. He appeared on dozens of tracks – **Puff Daddy**'s "Is This The End?" (1997), **Memphis Bleek**'s "Is That Your Chick?" (2000), Ludacris's "Funky Thangs" (2001) and **R Kelly**'s "Ignition (Remix)" (2003) among others – and built up his reputation to marquee status. With the bulk of the production handled by Kanye West, *Kamikaze* (2004) was a huge hit. The problem was that Twista was consistently outshone by the production. On the inescapable "Slow Jamz" his lyrics were so bad that – despite the song being tongue-in-cheek – he was schooled by comedian **Jamie Foxx**, who was guest-crooner on the hook .

**Kamikaze**
Atlantic, 2004

Easily the best beats of Twista's career (from Kanye West, Eightball and Jazze Pha) and the only reason to put up with his gimmicky style. R Kelly, Cee-Lo, Too $hort, TI and Ludacris all show up to lend some weight and prevent the album from buckling under Twista's escape-velocity flow.

# 2Pac (Tupac Shakur)

Never much more than an adequate rapper, **Tupac Amaru Shakur**, like so many pop stars, was a man whose contradictions made him larger than life. With his movie star eyelashes, "Thug Life" tattoo, saccharine odes to women of the ghetto, X-rated lothario tales, self-destructive impulse, sexual assault conviction, near-death experience and eventual matyrdom, 2Pac was all things to all people.

2Pac first appeared on **Digital Underground**'s "Same Song" from *This Is an EP Release* (1990), uttering the inauspicious line, "Now I clown around when I hang around with the Underground". He also cropped up alongside fellow Undergrounders **DJ Fuze** and **Money B** on Raw Fusion's *Live From the Styleetron* (1991) album, before the release of his own debut single, "Brenda's Got a Baby" (1991). This simplistic and overly dramatic morality tale was just about the only halfway decent track on his first album, *2Pacalypse Now* (1991).

After his role playing the violent character Bishop in *Juice*, 2Pac started turing into a star. *Strictly 4 My N.I.G.G.A.Z.* (1993) was more fully realised. 2Pac was improving on the mic, and the album helped consolidate his histrionic, self-destructive, crazy persona. "Holler If Ya Hear Me" gave **Master P** most of his ideas, although P never picked up on 2Pac's fairly well-articulated black rage. "Keep Ya Head Up" was a Hallmark card addressed to all the women he would later viciously disrespect on "I Get Around".

After more film roles in *Poetic Justice* and *Above The Rim*, and a few run-ins

The late Tupac Shakur.

with the law, *Me Against The World* (1995) was released while he was in prison on a sexual assault charge. The sequel to "Keep Ya Head Up", "Dear Mama", was more inner-city Norman Rockwell sentiment and seemed calculated to counteract the reason for his incarceration in the minds of critics. The "bitch-slapping" elsewhere on the album, however, didn't do his cause any good. The title track summed up both his paranoia and his attractiveness as an outlaw figure.

Rescued from New York's Clinton Correctional Facility by Death Row CEO **Suge Knight**, who paid his $1.4 million bail, 2Pac signed to the label and released hip-hop's first single-artist, double-disc album, *All Eyez On Me* (1996). Signed to the most notorious label in the world, 2Pac proceeded to spontaneously combust: a scandalous, scabrous gangsta no longer dwelling on a morbid sense of doom, but determined to party until the "2Pacalypse" arrived. The seven-times platinum album was over-long by at least one disc, and contained more than its fair share of irredeemable misogyny, but it did contain his best track, "California Love".

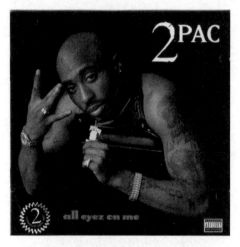

*All Eyez on Me* would be the last album he released while he was alive. With savage tracks such as "Hit 'Em Up" aimed at the **Bad Boy** stable, who 2Pac claimed were responsible for his shooting in 1995, he was blamed by many for fanning the flames of the ongoing East Coast-West Coast hip-hop feuding. On September 13, 1996 Tupac was murdered in a drive-by shooting in Las Vegas, and the recriminations have been flying around ever since. Like that of **Notorious BIG** in March 1997, 2Pac's murder remains unsolved.

Since his death, there has been a flood of 2Pac material: *Don Killuminati: The 7 Day Theory* (1996, as **Makavelli**), *R U Still Down?* (1997), *Greatest Hits* (1998), *Still I Rise* (1999) and some fifteen Makavelli bootlegs.

2Pac has never been allowed to rest in peace – only Jimi Hendrix has a comparable posthumous career. Many fans are convinced that he faked his own death and that he recorded clues to his future whereabouts. And so the 2Pac gravy train just keeps on a-rollin'. Interview discs, collections of his poetry read by other rappers, and appalling remixes packaged to look like new material appear on the shelves every other week. *Better Dayz* (2002) and *Tupac: Resurrection* (2003) were the two best – or perhaps least offensive would be a better description – of these cynical, necrophiliac efforts.

**All Eyez on Me**
Death Row, 1996

Way too long and way too unpleasant – without any redeeming features – this is nevertheless the most convincing argument for 2Pac's legendary status. The production, mostly from Johnny J and Dat Nigga Daz, is the best of 2Pac's career, although the remix of "California Love" included here is a travesty. 2Pac himself is at his most compelling, if only because he is more riddled with contradictions on this record than anywhere else in his catalogue.

# u–v

## UGK

Kickin' what they call "trill ass lyrics", dem boys from Port Arthur, Texas UGK (aka the **Underground Kingz**) manifest the filthiest aspects of the Dirty South. **Pimp C** (**Chad Butler**) and **Bun B** (**Bernard Freeman**) are big-ballin', shot-callin' playas who like "big birds and tight herb", and when they're packing heat, you don't want to "squab" with them.

Pimp C was originally in a group called Mission Impossible, which put out a song called "Underground Kingz". He eventually hooked up with Bun B after several personnel changes. Taking the song's title as their new name, UGK put out a couple of local tapes (including *The Southern Way* in 1991) before signing to Houston's Big Tyme Records for the release of *Too Hard To Swallow* (1992). The title pretty much told you all you needed to know, with the album featuring lyrics such as "I don't trust the dugout [i.e. vagina] 'cause I'm scared of the disease/'Cause she's passin' out the skins like government cheese", on top of samples of **Rufus and Chaka Khan**.

*Super Tight* (1994) was more of the same, but with Pimp C combining live instruments with obvious samples, and Bun B's down South flow notably improved. "Feds In Town" and "Protect And Serve" also expanded their lyrical concerns beyond aimless gunplay and the pursuit of punani. Before their best album, *Ridin' Dirty* (1996), was released, the duo collaborated with Houston's **DJ Screw** on the *Volume I* and *Volume II* compilations

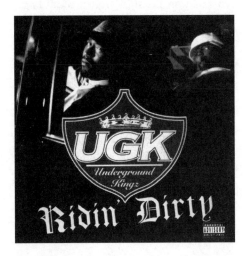

(both 1995), which found the Kingz laying down their Lone Star State pimp lyrics alongside the like-minded **Point Blank** and **PSK-13**. *Ridin' Dirty* featured more tales about rollin' down Interstate 10, but Pimp C and Bun B managed to flesh out their somewhat cheap received gangstaisms on the politically-slanted title track, in the carefully observed details of "Pinky Ring", on the moderately funny "Diamonds and Wood" and on the DJ Screw collabo, "3 'N The Mornin'". It was "Murder", however, which broke the duo outside south Texas. Its bouncy, skittering drums and ominous gangsta-leaning synth riffs backed Bun B viciously rhyming "Pelle Pelle", "smelly red jelly" and "belly" together, in a hip-hop aural equivalent of John Woo's choreographed screen violence.

*Ridin' Dirty* got UGK noticed by **Jay-Z** who invited them to contribute to "Big Pimpin'", the **Timbaland**-produced hit from his *Volume 3... The Life And Times of S. Carter* album (1999). With their newfound notoriety, *Dirty Money* (2001) was greatly delayed and widely bootlegged, but the album was a hit when it was finally released thanks to "Pimpin' Ain't No Illusion", with its cameos from Too $hort and **Kool Ace**, and the E-40-style "Choppin' Blades". *Side Hustles* (2002) documented Pimp C and Bun B's guest appearances and soundtrack contributions, recorded while they were in dispute with their label.

With Pimp C in jail on charges of aggravated assault with a handgun, Bun B concentrated on his side project **Mddl Fngz**, who released the three albums *Trouble* (2000), *Live From Da Manjah* (2001) and *No Apologies* (2004). Somewhat bizarrely, Mddl Fngz opened for UK rap/garage sensation **Dizzee Rascal**, who named UGK as one of his biggest influences, at some of his shows down south. In 2004 Bun B released his first solo album, *The Trillest*.

**⊙ Best of UGK**
Jive, 2003

Including most of their best records from "Pocket Full of Stones" to "Choppin' Blades", this is the best introduction to the Texas titans. UGK's trill-ass lyrics and beats to lean to are the cornerstones of not just Lone Star hip-hop, but pretty much the entire region south of the Mason-Dixon Line.

# Ultramagnetic MCs

The intro to **Ultramagnetic MCs's** first demo, "Space Groove" (1984), spelt out in no uncertain terms the ethos of the group that practically invented underground hip-hop: "Space, the final frontier. These are the voyages of the Ultramagnetic MCs: to boldly go where no other rapper has gone before; to examine the universe and reconstruct the style of today's hip-hop culture."

Before **Kool Keith Thornton**, **Ced Gee** (**Cedric Miller**), **Moe Luv** (**Maurice Smith**) and **TR Luv** (**Trevor Randolph**) became hip-hop's first afronauts, they were break dancers with the crews New York City Breakers and People's Choice. However, breaking didn't allow the highly individualistic Kool Keith (allegedly a sometime patient at the Creedmore and Bellevue mental hospitals) to "travel at the speed of thought", and the Bronx residents came together to form one of the greatest crews in hip-hop history.

After a thoroughly uncharacteristic first single, "To Give You Love" (1986), Ultramagnetic began to make their mark with the mind-boggling "Ego Trippin'" (1986). It featuring epochal production by Ced Gee: with a loop of Melvin Bliss drums and some vicious synth stabs, it was the best kind of minimalism – one that managed to fill the entire sound field. "Ego Trippin'" had Keith freestyling rhymes such as "As the record just turns/You learn plus burn/By the flame of the lyrics which cooks the human brain, providing overheated knowledge/By means causing pain/Make the migraine headaches..." It sounded like nothing else at the time, except for perhaps **Eric B & Rakim's** "Eric B Is President" – which was hardly surprising given that Ced Gee helped out on the beats for both *Paid In Full* and **Boogie Down Productions'** *Criminal Minded*.

"Funky" (1987), the flipside of the Keith showcase "Mentally Mad", was another radical Ced Gee production (based on a **Joe Cocker** piano sample) that was so ahead of its time it would only enter the

public consciousness nearly a decade later when the beat was swiped
wholesale by Dr. Dre on Tupac's
"California Love". People only had
to wait a few months for the full
implications of Ultramagnetic's
debut album, *Critical Beatdown*
(1988), to reach mass consciousness: the **Bomb Squad** have
often said that *Critical Beatdown*
was a major influence on Public
Enemy's *It Takes A Nation Of
Millions To Hold Us Back* (check
out "Ease Back" for proof). It
may have been a stunning exposition of early sampling technology, but *Critical Beatdown* remains
a devastating album even in an
age of 32-bit samplers and RAM-
intensive sound-editing software.
The music jumped and snapped

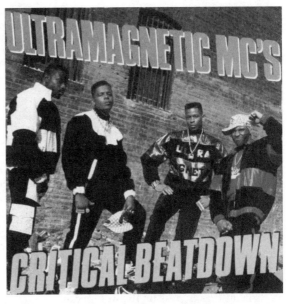

with an energy reminiscent of the **Cold
Crush Brothers**, while Kool Keith dropped
rhymes so abstract (and with cadences so
bizarre) they made a Rothko canvas look
like a Titian still life.

The flip of the amazing "Travellin' At
The Speed Of Thought" (1988), "Chorus
Line Pt. 1" was a sinister, bass heavy battle-
rhyme which introduced the rapper **Tim
Dog**. He would later release the savage
*Penicillin On Wax* (1991) which dissed eve-
ryone in sight, most notably **N.W.A.** and
**DJ Quik** on tracks like "Fuck Compton"
and "Step To Me".

The Ultramagnetics' delayed follow-up,
*Funk Your Head Up* (1992), was largely disappointing. The sex fantasies and rhymes
in general were regressive at best. The only
real highlight was the wild "Poppa Large",
which had a bassline and horror strings to
match Keith's dementia. *The Four Horsemen*
(1993) was a return to the energies that
which had fuelled their debut and had
a range that took in the rousing ("Raise
It Up"), the combative ("One Two One
Two") and the poignant ("Saga Of Dandy,
The Devil And Day").

Unclassifiable and unruly, the group
broke up in 1994, but Keith hasn't faded
away. In 1995 he released an underground
landmark, the *Cenobites* EP, with **Godfather
Don**. In 1996 Keith reinvented himself as

**Dr Octagon**, a gynaecologist from outer
space. Teaming up with the producer Dan
"Automator" Nakamura and DJ Q-Bert,
Dr Octagon released the absurd, scabrous,
but completely original *Dr Octagon* album
(1996). With influences ranging from the
*Love Story* soundtrack to Mantronix, *Dr
Octagon* had a beatscape that was as crazy
as Keith's new persona. The lyrics were a
pile-up of medical, scatological and often
zoological near-sequiturs, with stream-of-
consciousness imagery such as "can't fine-
tooth a dead ex, but the skin don't match"
and "a paramedic foetus of the East".

Without the deranged concept, Kool
Keith's *Sex Style* (1997) was more awkward.
All it proved was that he was a connoisseur
of some freaky porn. Around this time,
Keith reunited with Tim Dog as **Ultra** for
*Big Time* (1997), which was mostly a col-
lection of rants about how crap the indus-
try was.

*First Come, First Served* (1999) was just
another day at the office for Kool Keith in
his new guise, Dr Dooom: cannibalism,
keeping vermin as pets and body parts in
his car, "kicking your intestines like Ric
Flair", listening to Slayer and the Staple
Singers, borrowing toilet paper from his
neighbours, "taking your dick for ransom",
hanging with Jim Jones, eating raw steak,
"putting used diapers on your windshield
wipers", and smoking embalming fluid.

*Black Elvis/Lost in Space* (1999) continued his skewering of roach MCs with more sci-fi beats, but working on his own he wasn't as challenged as he was by the Automator or the Diesel Truckers (who produced the Dr Dooom album).

The same problem plagued *Matthew* (2000), in which his psycho routine was getting pretty boring, even if he did manage occasional zingers like "You's a dru-glord?/I don't believe you – you pay your mortgage". *Spankmaster* (2001) had Keith collaborating with shock-rapper **Esham** in an effort to spice things up, but to no avail. "Game is game," Keith reflected on *Game* (2002), released under the name KHM (with H-Bomb and Marc Live), whilst the pundits countered with "lame is lame". *The Lost Masters* (2003) should have remained that way. Not to mention Keith's involvement in **Kutmasta Kurt**'s Masters of Illusion project (2000), the Analog Brothers' *Pimp to Eat* (2000) – in which Keith teamed up with Ice T for an odd, space-age take on hip-hop's pimpin' and mackin' tropes – and Thee Undertakerz self-titled album (2003).

Lost in the flood of Kool Keith product were a couple of singles from Ced Gee ("Long Gev" (1998)) and Moe Luv ("Slaughter House" (2000)), as well as the *Diabolique* (1999) album from longtime associate Godfather Don.

**⊙ Critical Beatdown**
Next Plateau, 1988

"Taking your brain to another dimension", this is quite simply one of the greatest hip-hop albums ever. Recorded at a time before "street" and "experimental" were mutually exclusive terms, it ushered in hip-hop's sampladelic golden age and laid the foundation for several generations of underground rap.

# UMCs

A couple of years before it became the seat of the Wu Tang Clan empire, Staten Island was ruled by **Kool Kim** and **Haas G**. Originally calling themselves the **Universal MCs**, the **UMCs** made their wax debut at the height of the D.A.I.S.Y. Age on a compilation on the tiny Rough Justice label. "Invaders Of My Fruit Basket" (1989) was a sprightly, jazzy record very much in the **De La Soul** style.

Their bright, effervescent sound would reach its apex on the crew's debut album, *Fruits Of Nature* (1991). "Blue Cheese" epitomised their approach with its shuffling rhythm, cartoonish horn and flute break and abstract raps with complex metaphors. The anthemic "One To Grow On" sounded like it was based on every Blue Note record ever released, while "Swing It To The Area" had a Memphis/Hi Records funk. While the lyrics of Haas G and Kool Kim were clever – sounding almost like a freestyle in their spontaneous nature and conception – *Fruits Of Nature* belonged to producer **RNS** who, along with A Tribe Called Quest, defined jazzy hip-hop at the beginning of the 1990s.

However, at the turn of the 1990s hip-hop was becoming ever more hardcore and the UMC's ditched their Native Tongues-styled image for their next album, *Unleashed* (1994). Track titles such as "Evil Ways", "Ill Demonic Clique" and "Staten Island Comes First" told the story. While most of the tracks were clearly in thrall to the Wu-Tang Clan, "Time To Set it Straight" had fierce, organ-driven production (from Haas G and Kool Kim) that retained connections to their old sound even as it pushed in a new direction. While they tried to front at being hard, lines like "You're an anal wart" wouldn't have scared a 99-pound weakling and their uncomfortable role-playing made the UMCs seem like nothing but bandwagon jumpers. Little was heard from the pair until, out of nowhere, Kool Kim returned in 2001 with *The Haz Been*, a title which was, disappointingly, rather apt.

**Fruits Of Nature**
Wild Pitch, 1991

It might have been everything hip-hop was running away from at the time— effervescence, eclecticness and abstraction — but this is nevertheless a great, imaginative album undeserving of its pariah status.

# UTFO

The **Kangol Kid** and **The Educated Rapper** were originally a Brooklyn-based breakdance crew called the **Keystone Dancers** who pop-locked and body-rocked for Whodini. Meanwhile, UTFO's third member, **Doctor Ice**, had released "Calling Doctor Ice" (1981) for Enjoy before joining up with Kangol and Educated.

Their debut single, "Beats And Rhymes" (1984), introduced the nonsense-language style that would hit the big time with Fankie Smith's "Double Dutch Bus". But **UTFO**'s second is the more notable for being perhaps the greatest novelty record of all time, if only for the fact that it spawned more answer records than any other single in history. Produced by **Full Force**, "Roxanne Roxanne" (1984) was the tale of a beautiful woman who moves into the neighbourhood and inexplicably resists the advances of the three East Flatbush lotharios.

While "Roxanne Roxanne" was an enjoyable piece of pop fluff, it and UTFO probably remain in the memory only because of the hullabaloo that followed it. Upset at its unflattering portrayal of women, a fourteen-year-old rapper calling herself **Roxanne Shanté** recorded "Roxanne's Revenge" (1985) with Marley Marl. Using the same Billy Squier "Big Beat" rhythm, Shanté proceeded to lyrically demolish UTFO, and established herself as one of the most fearsome battle-rappers in the business. In response, UTFO teamed up with a waitress called **Joan Martinez** and released their own answer record, "The Real Roxanne" (1985). Then, producer **Spyder D** and his protégée, **Sparky D**, released "Sparky's Turn (Roxanne You're Through)" (1985) which attacked both Shanté *and* the Real Roxanne. 100 records later, after Roxanne's mother and even her shrink had been heard from, the craze was finally over.

UTFO's response to all this was "Leader Of The Pack" (1985). The implication of the title was that UTFO were the originators, but the star of the record was really their new DJ, **Mix Master Ice**. While the scratching was pretty def, UTFO proved themselves to be rappers who were clunkier than their acronym (UTFO apparently stood for Untouchable Force) and their self-titled debut album was generic at best.

Over the next few years, they tried to perk up their act with gimmicks such as rock licks on *Lethal* (1987), new jack swing on *Doin' It* (1989) and, finally, blue humour on *Bag It and Bone It* (1991). In 1989, Doctor Ice went solo with *The Mic Stalker*, a fairly thin Full Force production, although, to be fair, the title track was pretty mean in that typical late-1980s style. The doctor released "Phenomenon" in 1997 and Mixmaster Ice was last seen working as a radio DJ in Ohio.

**The Best of UTFO**
Select, 1996

You can find "Roxanne Roxanne" on innumerable old school compilations, so it's really only anoraks and trainspotters who need to seek this out.

# Vintertainment records

Started by promoter/producer Vincent Davis, Vintertainment was one of the best and is now one of the most collectible of the early hip-hop labels. During its short heyday between 1983 and 1986, the label released several classic records which have been endlessly sampled and which created the template for instrumental hip-hop.

# BREAKBEATS

Although breakbeats have probably existed since jazz pioneers **Jelly Roll Morton** and **Bunk Johnson** first started to play with drummers in New Orleans at the turn of the century, the idea of isolating the part of the record where the rest of the band "gives the drummer some" didn't occur to anyone until **Kool DJ Herc** threw his first party at the Community Centre at 1520 Sedgwick Avenue in The Bronx.

The only part of the records that Herc would play was the short section where all the musicians dropped out except for the percussionists. The "break" was the part of the record that the dancers (whom he dubbed "b-boys" or "break boys") wanted to hear anyway, so he isolated it by playing two copies of the same record on two turntables – when the break on one turntable finished, he would play it on the other. Herc's breakbeat style of DJing was much in demand and soon enough other DJs such as Grandmaster Flash, Afrika Bambaataa and Grand Wizard Theodore emerged playing a similar style of music, but with greater skill and more technological sophistication.

The breakbeat was music's great equaliser – nearly every record, no matter how unsavoury its provenance, had two or three seconds that made it worthwhile. Herc's biggest record was a 1973 cover of Jörgen Ingmann's "Apache" by Michael Viner's **Incredible Bongo Band** that featured the cheesiest organ and horn fills ever recorded, on top of a chorus of massed bongos. Apparently, Viner was a friend of the music industry's most notorious right-wing zealot, Mike Curb, and was the director of entertainment for **Richard Nixon**'s second inaugural party. So what was to become hip-hop's national anthem and the most celebrated breakbeat of all time was not only originally a hit for **Cliff Richard & the Shadows**, but was also based on a record probably designed to appeal to family values crusaders such as Mary Whitehouse. Hip-hop's cult of the break could redeem anything: breaks by neanderthal heavy metal acts like **Billy Squier**, **Aerosmith** and **Thin Lizzy** and schmaltzy jazz-lite artists such as Bob James became the basis of records by everyone from **Run DMC** to the **Wu Tang Clan**.

Two and a half decades after its development, the term "break" has come to signify any short instrumental passage, drums or otherwise, that can be sampled and chopped up. However you want to define it, the logic of the breakbeat is Hip-Hop's gift to the world and perhaps the most crucial development in popular music since Chuck Berry showed the world how to play an electric guitar.

The most sampled break of all-time is probably The Winstons' "Amen Brother", which has been used on literally hundreds of drum 'n' bass records, but the ten most sampled beats in hip-hop are:

**James Brown**: "Funky Drummer"
**Sly & the Family Stone**: "Sing A Simple Song"
**Honey Drippers**: "Impeach The President"
**Lyn Collins** : "Think"
**James Brown**: "Get Up, Get Into it And Get Involved"
**George Clinton**: "Atomic Dog"
**Melvin Bliss**: "Synthetic Substitution"
**Kool & the Gang**: "NT"
**Skull Snaps**: "It's A New Day"
**Bob James**: "Nautilus"

## VARIOUS ARTISTS

 **Ultimate Breaks And Beats Vols. 1-25**
Street Beat, 1985-1990

They may be of questionable legality, but these 25 volumes are collectively the Bible of breakbeat and represent some of the greatest and most vital musical scholarship ever undertaken. Volume 1 features the "Amen" beat.

## VARIOUS ARTISTS

 **Kurtis Blow Presents The History Of Hip-Hop Vol. 1**
Rhino, 1997

One of the few entirely legal collection of classic breakbeats, this excellent collection features "Apache", Jimmy Castor's immortal "It's Just Begun", Baby Huey's "Listen to Me" and Dennis Coffey's "Scorpio".

The label's first release was **The B Boys'** "2, 3 Break" (1983), a sliced-and-diced cut-up of Cerrone's "Rocket In The Pocket" break and Chuck Brown & The Soul Searchers' "Bustin' Loose", with DJ **Chuck Chillout** scratching them both to buggery. While the Bronx-based B boys also featured the MCs **Donald D** and **Brother B**, their second record, "Rock The House"/"Cuttin' Herbie" (1983), was once again pretty much a showcase for Chillout. These records have resonated throughout hip-hop, their most familiar echoes being heard on the **Beastie Boys'**s "The New Style" and "33% God".

Chillout's real star move, though, was on the truly amazing "Hip Hop On Wax Volume 1" (1984) in which he cut up **The Mohawks'** "Champ", **Jimmy Castor's** "It's Just Begun", **The Incredible Bongo Band's** "Apache" and a **Marvin Gaye** vocal snippet with flurries and percussive volleys of scratches and bold splashes of cymbals. "Hip Hop On Wax Vol. 2" (1984) followed, with **Red Alert** scratching up Bobby Byrd, Cymande, M and air-raid sirens in a similar style.

Vinterntainment then unleashed both **Doug E Fresh** (as Dougy Fresh) and human beatboxing to the world on "Original Human Beatbox" (1984). The B Boys's "Girls (Part 1)"/"Stick Up Kid" and "Girls (Part 2)" (both 1985) were shockingly hardcore for the time, even if Donald D and Brother B sounded very much like Run and DMC. A classic rhyme from "Girls (Part 2)", itself a play on the theme song from the cartoon *Magilla Gorilla*, would later show up in the Beastie Boys' "Hey Ladies": "I know a girl named Priscilla who looked just like Magilla/ She hangs with the crew just drinking Miller/Take my advice, at any price a play from Priscilla is mighty nice". The track's break would also later show up on **Public Enemy's** "Fear of a Black Planet".

The label's one and only hit was **Joeski Love's** "Pee-Wee's Dance" (1986), based on comedian Pee Wee Herman's television show. The record was co-released with Elektra, and Vintertainment faded into the background soon afterwards. Donald D released a couple of solo releases, "Here We Go" (1985) and "Outlaw"/"Dope Jam" (1988), before hooking up with **Ice T** and becoming a member of his Rhyme Syndicate. With the Rhyme Syndicate Donald recorded two solo albums, *Notorious* (1989) and *Let the Horns Blow* (1991) and, over a decade later, Donald D released the *Hip-Hop – Return of the Culture* (2003) on the German Hot Shit label. Chuck Chillout, of course, went on to become one of hip-hop radio's leading DJs. In 1989 he hooked up with Kool Chip and released *Masters of Rhythm* before working for both Kiss and WBLS in New York, introducing his former record boy **Funk Master Flex** and discovering **Black Moon** along the way.

## CHUCK CHILLOUT

**Hip-Hop On Wax Vol. 1**
Vintertainment, 1984

"He's the Chuck Chillout – whatcha gonna do?" An absolutely electric cut-up record. All the instalments of the *Hip Hop On Wax* series are turntable classics, but the first remains the best. Today's turntablist groups such as the Invisbl Skratch Piklz, X-ecutioners, Beat Junkies and Scratch Perverts owe their existence to this record.

# WC and the Maad Circle

With over a decade in the business, **William Calhoun** – the Maad Circle's WC – is one of the most underrated players in the rap game. Born in Texas, Calhoun's parents moved to LA in the early 1980s, where he started rapping in high school. Hooking up with the mighty **DJ Aladdin**, WC formed **Low Profile** and the duo dominated Ice T's *Rhyme Syndicate Comin' Through* (1988) compilation with "Think You Can Hang". Signing to Priority, they released the collector's item, *We're in This Together* (1989). At the time they were overshadowed by N.W.A., but *We're In This Together* is nevertheless a smoking album of classic late-1980s hip-hop. "Dub" (as in "Dubya Cee") reminisced about the old days over a rumbling LA beat on "Pay Ya Dues", and got truly nice-on-the-mic over fast tempos on "The Dub BU Just Begun". DJ Aladdin showed untouchable turntable skills on "Funky Song" and "Aladdin's On A Rampage", not to mention his jaw-drop-

ping scratch solo on "The Dub BU Just Begun".

After *We're In This Together* failed to make any noise, the duo split and WC formed the MAAD Circle (Minority Alliance Against Discrimination) with **Big Gee**, his younger brother **Crazy Toones** and **Coolio**. With seemingly all around them in caught up in in the violent glamour of gangsta rap, on *Ain't a Damn Thing Changed* (1991) the MAAD Circle rapped about absentee fathers and record label whores and on "Back To The Underground" WC bragged "I'd rather go down in the book as a brother who ripped clubs/And who told it how it was". Unsurprisingly, it too went nowhere commercially.

After industry difficulties and the departure of Coolio, the MAAD Circle finally returned with *Curb Servin'* in 1995. The highlight was the George Duke-sampling "West Up!" which, given that it featured Ice Cube and Mack 10, was basically a prototype **Westside Connection** track – Westside Connection being the supergroup the trio convened the following year. *Bow Down* (1996), the Connection's album, was

WC AND THE MAAD CIRCLE
*curb servin'*

straight-up, East Coast-baiting, gangsta material that went double platinum and finally gave WC the success he deserved. It's just a shame he had to pander to the lowest common denominator in order to do it. Without the market imprimatur of Ice Cube, WC's *The Shadiest One* (1998) was overlooked, despite its semi-classics of West Coast street funk such as "Just Clownin'" and "Fuckin' Wit Uh House Party".

WC then signed to **Def Jam**, but the fate of the much-delayed *Ghetto Heisman* (2002) was typical of the East Coast label's star-crossed forays into West Coast hip-hop territory. Despite boasting some hot jams such as "The Streets", the album was largely pro forma crip walkin'.

## LOW PROFILE

◉ **We're in This Together**
Priority, 1989

You'll have to look high and low to find it, but this is timeless, classic hip-hop. It was the perfect marriage between the samples and turntables of the East Coast and the West's love of deep 808 bass. Aladdin, one of the all-time greats on the wheels of steel, is on scintillating form throughout.

# Kanye West

The UK has understood the power of a sped-up sample for a long time. Ever since the 'Ardkore scene approached escape velocity with the likes of The Prodigy using toytown samples,

the helium voice has been a staple of both the UK pop charts (anyone remember Babylon Zoo?) and the dance underground (the early days of UK garage). The US, on the other hand, largely forgot about the pleasures of hyper-speed voices after one too many Chipmunks records. It took producer/rapper **Kanye West** to remind them.

While West wasn't the first to use the pitched-up sample, he was the first to be successful in the US with it. Of course, West is more than just a one-trick pony. He can rap – a bit like **Grand Puba** – but more importantly he was one of the first artists to span the great divide between the underground "backpackers" and the mainstream "flossers". West doesn't bust caps in his raps and even talks about God, making him potentially the ultimate hip-hop crossover artist.

West grew up in Chicago and started working with Windy City producer **No ID** while he was still in high school. West then came to the attention of Deric "D-Dot" Angelettie, one of Bad Boy's chief hitmakers, during the label's 1990s apotheosis, and worked on albums by **Harlem World**, **Foxy Brown** and the **Madd Rapper**. West's rise to prominence really began, however, with his work on Jay-Z's *The Blueprint* (2001). West was responsible for the record's two best tracks: the Jackson 5-sampling "Izzo (HOVA)" and The Doors-sampling "The Takeover". **Talib Kweli**'s gospel-flavoured "Get By" (2002) and **Scarface**'s triumphant "Guess Who's Back" (both 2002) further established West as one of hip-hop's premier beatmakers. Monster grooves for **Ludacris** and **TI** proved without doubt that West was one of the very few hip-hop producers who was comfortable in any style.

In October 2002, however, his career was almost cut short by a car accident that left his jaw fractured in three places. Soon afterwards, with his jaw still wired shut, West recorded his debut as a rapper, "Through the Wire" (2003). Using a pitched-up sample of **Chaka Khan**'s "Through the Fire" as a backdrop, West rapped, "I look back on my life like the Ghost of Christmas Past/Toys R Us where I used to spend that Christmas cash/And I

still won't grow up/I'm a grown-ass kid/ Swear I should be locked up for stupid shit that I did". The track was the centrepiece of *College Dropout* (2004), perhaps the hip-hop sensation of the year. "All Falls Down" was an extraordinary examination of hip-hop materialism: "It seems we living the American dream/But the people highest up got the lowest self-esteem/The prettiest people do the ugliest things/For the road to riches and diamond rings/We shine because they hate us, floss cause they degrade us/We trying to buy back our 40 acres/And for that paper, look how low we stoop/Even if you in a Benz, you still a nigga in a coop". Elsewhere, he rapped, "You can rap about anything except Jesus/ That means guns, sex and videotapes/But if I talk about God my record won't get played" and lampooned both gangstaism and quiet storm singers. Yet, for all of West's skewering of the ills of hip-hop culture, he was still very much trapped by it and part of it.

**College Dropout**
Roc-A-Fella, 2004

No one in the hip-hop underground has managed a parody of the mainstream as biting and accurate as this. That it was made by a super-producer who has worked for both Bad Boy records and Jay-Z, names Mase as his favorite rapper, and is signed to the mighty Roc-A-Fella empire only makes it signify more. Of course, it also means that Kanye is ultimately no less of a wage-slave and label whore than everyone he mocks.

# Whodini

With the help of pioneering hip-hop radio DJ Mr Magic, **Whodini** – Brooklynites **Jalil Hutchins**, **Ecstacy** (**John Fletcher**) and **Grandmaster Dee** (**Drew Carter**) – became the first act to be signed to Jive records. Returning the favour, Whodini's first single was an homage entitled "Magic's Wand" (1982). Following in the wake of "Planet Rock", "Magic's Wand" was co-produced by **Thomas Dolby** and featured synthesizer riffs, a chugging "Trans-Europe Express"-like intro and drum-machine beats. Rather than the supernatural weirdness of "Planet Rock", however, "Magic's Wand" had a slap-bass groove and luxurious keyboards, easily slotting into place alongside disco records of the time such as D-Train's "You're The One For Me"or The Peech Boys' "Don't Make Me Wait".

Working with Larry Smith, producer for **Run DMC** and **Kurtis Blow**, Whodini recorded their self-titled debut album in 1983. Whereas Run DMC had production which could level a skyscraper at 20 paces, Smith styled Whodini as upwardly mobile, suit-wearing suave cats who could stride into the lobby of that same skyscraper without receiving a second glance. Aside from "Magic's Wand", the biggest hit from the record was "Haunted House Of Funk", a pretty lame reworking of **Bobby (Boris) Pickett**'s "Monster Mash".

Smith's vision really came together on *Escape* (1984). Preceded by the awesome double-sided single, "Friends"/"Five Minutes Of Funk", it is often said that *Escape* was the first rap album to go platinum – though this has never been certified. Whatever the case, *Escape* was one of the best early hip-hop albums, with biting electro-funk production, unoffensive r&b vocals, tasteful vocoders and clever songwriting. Aside from "Five Minutes", the album's best track was "Freaks Come

Out At Night", a tale of Brooklyn meeting Greenwich Village at The Danceteria told to a video game beat.

Unlike AC/DC's triumphant album of the same name, *Back In Black* (1986) showed Whodini to be in terminal decline. Unable to escape the sylistic constrictions of the old school, tracks like "Funky Beat" and "One Love" were okay, but in 1986 the action was definitely elsewhere. *Open Sesame* (1987) were clearly not the magic words, and not even Mr Magic's wand could prevent Whodini from sounding like they were in a different century to Eric B & Rakim, Boogie Down Productions and the rest of the new generation. *Bag-A-Trix* (1991) was even less notable. An attempted comeback on **Jermaine Dupri**'s So-So Def label, *Six* (1996), was little short of an embarrassment, and caused a lot of friction when Dupri, a former dancer of theirs, had to drop his one-time mentors from his label.

**Jive Collection Series, Vol. 1**
Jive, 1995

Containing almost all of the excellent *Escape* album, whilst mopping up the only good tracks off *Whodini* and *Back In Black*, this is more Whodini than anyone will ever need.

# Winley Records

Paul Winley was one of the most famous and notorious characters on the early hip-hop scene. Winley had been involved in r&b since the early 1950s, when he began writing songs for his brother Harold's group, **The Clovers**. He soon began a lifelong partnership with organist Dave "Baby" Cortez, who would later play on many of the hip-hop records Winley would release, and started his own label specialising in doo-wop, recording groups such as **The Paragons** and **The Jesters**.

With the hip-hop scene in full swing, Winley released two records that would have profound implications for hip-hop. One was a collection of speeches by Malcolm X, *Black Man's History Volume 1* (1978); the other was a compilation called *Super Disco*

*Brakes* (1979). Collecting records such as **Bob James**'s "(Take Me to the) Mardi Gras", **Magic Disco Machine**'s "Scratching", **Pat Lundy**'s "Work Song" and **Dennis Coffey**'s "Scorpio", the album was one of the first, if not *the* first, breakbeat compilation. The series eventually ran to six volumes, with the last released in 1984. While these compilations were a formative influence on hip-hop culture, their dubious legality and poor sound quality would, regrettably, come to characterize his rap recordings.

Winley's first rap record featured his two daughters, **Paulette** and **Tanya** alongside longtime associates, the **Harlem Underground Band** (Cortez, George Benson, Willis Jackson and Sterling Magee). The rapping on "Rhymin' And Rappin'" (1979) wasn't great, with the sisters Winley sounding very unsure of themselves on the mic. On the musical front, the Harlem Underground's backing was straightforward r&b, without the percussive explosions that were hip-hop's raison d'être. Far better was Tanya "Sweet Tee" Winley's "Vicious Rap" (1980). The label claimed that the track had been recorded in 1978, but Sweet Tee's performance was noticeably better than on her record with her sister, suggesting that this in all likelihood came later. She still sounded like she was rapping over the top of a traditional band jamming, but at least they threw in a break this time.

Harlem Underground Band provided the backing for "Zulu Nation Throwdown" (1980), but they had changed their style to keep up with **Pumpkin**'s crew at Enjoy and the grooves laid down by the **Sugar Hill** house band. The record was more significant, however, for marking the first appearance on wax by one of hip-hop's most crucial figures, **Afrika Bambaataa**. While his role was mostly arranging and producing, his influence was certainly felt in the Harlem Underground Band's improved performance. **The Cosmic Force** were responsible for the rapping, with **Lisa Lee** absolutely destroying all the male MCs. "Zulu Nation Throwdown 2" (1980) found the renamed **Soul Sonic Force** getting loose over a mellow keyboard groove.

Bambaataa's *Death Mix* (1983), a recording of Bambaataa and Jazzy Jay DJing at a party at a Bronx high school, remains the best commercially-available snapshot of hip-hop's earliest days. The sound was awful, however, and it was essentially a bootleg released without Bambaataa's consent. Once the **Run DMC** revolution flared up, defining a harder style of both lyrics and music, Winley's days were numbered. After another record by Tanya and Paulette, "I Believe in the Wheel of Fortune" (1982), and one by Rap Dynasty, "Street Rock" (1985), the label folded.

## AFRIKA BAMBAATAA / COSMIC FORCE

🔘 **Zulu Nation Throwdown**
Winley, 1980

It may not be Bambaataa's best record, or even his best on Winley, but this is nevertheless a wonderful slice of charming, exciting grassroots hip-hop. This is the first time that Harlem Underground Band understood hip-hop – no doubt thanks to Bambaataa, who is credited with the arrangement. The record really belongs to Lisa Lee, though, who turns in one of the greatest early raps.

# Wu-Tang Clan

U tilizing a remarkable arcane mythology fashioned from fortune-cookie versions of ancient Chinese philosophy, Five Percent Nation mathematics and chess-master Gary Kasparov's Sicilian defense stratagem, the **Wu-Tang Clan** talked loudly and brandished a big shtick. For all of hip-hop's "keep it real" rhetoric, the Wu's chimerical demimonde demanded more suspension of disbelief than a James Cameron movie. The principal weaponry in the Clansmen's bag of tricks was camouflage and intimidation: from the labyrinthine obfuscation of the Wu-Tang's 36 chambers (both album title and philosophy), to quoting Sun Tzu's *The Art of War*.

Ringleader **RZA** and his charges (**Method Man, Ol' Dirty Bastard, Raekwon the Chef, Ghostface Killah, Genius/GZA, U-God, Masta Killa** and **Inspectah Deck**) know that in one important way, hip-hop is no different to Steven Seagal in an action flick: it's not necessarily possessing the skills, but the façade of invincibility that counts. Fully inhabiting a fantasy world, the Wu made more out of low culture inspiration – Hong Kong kung-fu movies, comic books, Hanna-Barbera cartoons, professional wrestling (not even the WWF, but the old school NWA) – than anyone since the George Clinton in the glory days of P-Funk.

More than just providing comic relief, though, this cultural bottom-feeding was a survival tactic for those caught in hip-hop's metaphorical cross-fire. The Wu Tang's members delighted in adopting more aliases than a Mossad agent. Not content with just one *nom de plume* Method Man

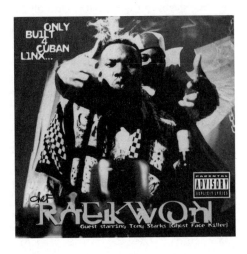

Wu-Tang Clan's RZA.

(aka Clifford Smith) referred to himself as Johnny Blaze, The Ticalion Stallion, John-John McLain, Iron Lung, the Panty Raider, and Johnny Dangerous. You could say that this name game is emblematic of **W.E.B. DuBois**' famous model of the double-consciousness of African-Americans, forced to juggle identities as a consequence of being slaves in the so-called land of the free, given the surname of their "owner" and treated like beasts in the age of so-called Enlightenment humanism. But it was also a very useful ploy in hip-hop's rhetorical war games: as Meth himself says on "Dangerous Grounds" (from *Tical 2000*), "I had to kill a schizophrenic nigga twice".

The Wu-Tang Clan and their multiple personas dwelt in a paranoiac, claustrophobic, and hallucinatory world where the city streets crawl with visible contagion, unseen creatures scuttle and scurry in the sewers and the pimps, hustlers and money-makers whisper about you behind your back in backwards Satanic verses. Producers RZA, **True Master**, **4th Disciple** and Inspectah Deck surrounded the MCs with swarms of hornet-like zithers, stinging atonal guitar licks and trademark urban-underbelly piano nocturnes.

The Wu's unique conceptual and sonic worlds were first unveiled on a self-pressed single called "Protect Ya Neck" (1992). Its enormous impact on the underground caused a record label bidding war, resulting in the Clan signing a deal with Loud which allowed each individual member to sign their own solo deals with other labels. The Clan's debut album, *Enter the Wu-Tang (36 Chambers)* (1993), is one of hip-hop's true landmarks. As hip-hop appeared to becoming more relaxed than a Compton jheri curl, *Enter the Wu-Tang* brought a whole new style. After a snippet from a **Shaw Brothers** kung-fu flick, the album began with Ghostface Killah spitting deranged verses over a distorted kick drum, detuned zithers, reversed horns and one of the most dangerous-sounding voices ever encountered on vinyl shouting, "Bring the motherfuckin' ruckus". Elsewhere on the album, RZA relocated Southern soul horns to make them rallying cries for the Rotten Apple, turned **James Brown** samples into an aural psychosis, transformed the piano loop into 1990s hip-hop's signature sound and recontextualised the songs of **Gladys Knight** and **The Charmels** as ghetto elegies. If you weren't convinced by the production, there were always incredible battle-rhymes such as "What's that in your pants? Ahh, human faeces/Throw your shitty drawers in the hamper/Next time come strapped with a Pamper".

For a couple of years RZA's production was like the Colt.45 slogan: it worked every time. Method Man's *Tical* (1994) was musically cleaner than *Enter*, but with Meth's iron-lung gust of a flow its tales of the dark side were as engaging as the Wu's debut. Ol' Dirty's *Return to the 36 Chambers: The Dirty Version* (1995) was a collection of scatology that would have made Petronious and Chaucer blush (although it was nothing compared to his gloriously outrageous follow-up of 1999, *Nigga Please*), while Ghostface Killah's *Ironman* (1996) featured the awesome interpretation of Bob James's "Nautilus" break, "Daytona 500", and the frighteningly intense "Winter Warz". The best Wu solo joints, however, were GZA's *Liquid Swords* (1995) — perhaps the only Wu album to win you over purely on skills rather than the whole concept — and Raekwon's *Only Built 4 Cuban Linx...* (1995) which ditched the pseudo-Asian mysticism for straight-up street tales that were as grim, nasty and heartbreaking as anything **Mobb Deep** ever came up with.

However, as with their inspiration – the P-Funk empire – the prolific workrate eventually caught up with the Clan. The sprawling *Wu-Tang Forever* (1997) was a double-CD with only one or two good ideas, while most of the ensuing solo albums have been nothing but the same old same old. Method Man's *Tical 2000* (1998) and Ol' Dirty's *Nigga Please* were the best of these, but where the Wu's tales

of brutal social Darwinism used to be deployed as a street-survival metaphor or as a mystic, poetic Armageddon prophecy, by the late 1990s it had become nothing but an end in itself.

Instead of downsizing to cut their losses, *The W* (2000) featured more cameos than a Robert Altman film: Nas, **Busta Rhymes**, **Redman**, **Snoop Dogg** and **Isaac Hayes**, among others. Not only did it expand the Wu brand across the marketplace, *The W* did what no recent Wu album had done: expand the Wu sound. Sure, there was plenty of the RZA's trademark – varnishing Memphis soul with a Rotten Apple patina ("Hollow Bones" and "I Can't Go To Sleep"). But he also broadened his palette on the Kraftwerkian "Careful (Click Click)" and on the Wu's first shimmy-shimmy go-go number, "Gravel Pit" – the sound of the RZA going to Far Rockaway Beach and imagining what the Beach Boys would have sounded like if they came from Shaolin (the Wu's pet name for Staten Island). *Iron Flag* (2001) kept up the momentum with the astounding "Uzi (Pinky Ring)", the vintage Wu of "Radioactive (Four Assassins)" and the ferocity of "In the Hood".

As good as the Wu was as a unit, however, the real killer bee-stings were reserved for Ghostface Killah, who had matured into one of hip-hop's lunatic geniuses on *Supreme Clientele* (2000), *Bulletproof Wallets* (2001) and *The Pretty Toney Album* (2004).

Hip-hop lost one of its most engaging personalities in November 2004 when Ol' Dirty Bastard collapsed in the studio and died. The cause of death was a heart attack precipitated by his having taking cocaine and Tramadol, a prescription painkiller, in combination.

## WU-TANG CLAN

### ⦿ Enter the Wu-Tang (36 Chambers)
Loud, 1993

Startlingly original, conceptually and sonically daring, and absolutely ferocious, this album almost single-handedly rescued New York hip-hop. It stands as one of the genre's greatest albums.

## GHOSTFACE KILLAH

### ⦿ Shaolin's Finest
Epic, 2003

It may have been released after Ghost jetted for Def Jam, but Epic finally managed to release a package worthy of the music within – after album after album of shoddy promotion and shocking packaging (who was responsible for all those aberrant tracklistings?) You'll often have absolutely no idea what Ghostface is talking about, but his imagery is so vivid that he'll suck you into his world regardless. Some of the best production in the Wu's illustrious history doesn't hurt either.

## X-CLAN

Once upon a time, Egyptology in pop music meant the anodyne spirituality of **Earth, Wind & Fire**. In the hip-hop era, however, Egyptology made itself manifest in the authoritative bassos and "vainglorious" grooves of **X-Clan**. Sure, they were riddled with contradictions and their 'Nubian' garb of nose rings, ankh jewelry, wooden canes and black leather fezzes was only about as African as afros, but their embrace of the red, black and green was at least more complex and better thought-out than many of their Afrocentric contemporaries. Though they came perilously close to Leonard Stern territory, they were skilful enough MCs to never put their feet in their mouths.

Part of the Blackwatch group, which also included YZ (of "Thinking Of A Master Plan" fame) and X-Clan satellites **Isis** and **Queen Mother Rage**, X-Clan made a lot of noise with their debut single, "A Day Of Outrage, Operation Snatchback" (1989), and album, *To the East, Blackwards* (1990).

On top of the funkin' lessons and production of **Rhythm Provider Sugar Shaft** and **Grand Architect Paradise**, rappers/lecturers **Professor X** (**Lumumba Carson**, son of activist Sonny Carson) and **Brother J** dropped some dubious pseudo-science about racial politics, but they did so with panache and style. X-Clan's catchphrase "The red, the black and the green, with the key, sissy!", still resonates throughout

X-Clan show off their fancy walking sticks.

hip-hop (check out Redman and Method Man's 1999 *Blackout* album).

Laudably, the group practiced what they preached and they organised protests against the murder of Yusef Hawkins (an African-American killed at the hands of a racist mob) and voter registration drives. *Xodus: The New Testament* (1992) was funkier than the debut and found Professor X and Brother J dissing the "humanism" of **KRS-One** and taunting **3rd Bass** with an amusing baseball metaphor on "Fire & Earth (100% Natural)". "ADAM" heard them dropping some Five Percent Nation

knowledge over **Grover Washington Jr.**'s "Mr Magic". However, the album got lost as the Afrocentric tide went out and the group soon dissolved. Professor X released the patchy *Puss 'N' Boots... The Struggle Continues* (1993) to little fanfare and Brother J re-emerged in 1996 with even less fanfare with a new group, the **Dark Sun Riders**, on *Seeds of Evolution*.

**Xodus: The New Testament**
Polydor, 1992

Funkier and less pedantic than many of their ilk, X-Clan made their pro-black medicine go down as easily as palm wine. While the P-Funk-heavy first album provided an interesting corrective to the emerging G-Funk sound, built on the same foundation, their sophomore effort managed to bump even more, and was more effective as a result.

# Xzibit

Long before Xzibit acheived fame as the host of MTV's reality-TV, automobile makeover show *Pimp My Ride*, the erstwhile Alvin Joiner was a relatively uncelebrated member of Tha Alkaholiks' **Likwit Crew**. After attracting attention during Tha Liks' 1995 tour and an appearance on **Tha Mexicanz**' "The Wake Up Show" (1996) alongside Chino XL, Mr X-to-the-Z signed to Loud.

Xzibit's debut, *At The Speed Of Life* (1996), featured "Plastic Surgery", a Golden State Warriors posse cut with **Saafir** and **Ras Kass**. The album, however, was more notable for the killer cut "Paparazzi", which cleverly attacked fake thugs. Unlike most West Coast albums, *At The Speed Of Life* was introspective, *suggesting* menace rather than shoving it down your threat. *40 Dayz & 40 Nightz* (1998), on the other hand, was a lyrical tempest, with his "Olde English leav[ing] you broken with a Crooked I". The highlight was the moody, flute-driven "Los Angeles Times", while "Three Card Molly" had barnstorming lines such as "Picture yourself crushin' Xzibit with your tough talk/That's like Christopher Reeves doin' the Crip walk". Even though "What You See Is What You Get" was a medium-sized hit, Xzibit didn't really break through until 1999 when he made some thirty guest appearances. Most notable of these was

## HIP-HOP AND ISLAM

Hip-hop and the Muslim faith have gone hand in hand ever since **Afrika Bambaataa** played **Malcolm X** speeches over the top of Kraftwerk's "Trans Europe Express" at park jams. Way back in 1983, Sugar Hill's (white) drummer **Keith LeBlanc** put some drum-machines behind Malcolm snippets on "No Sell Out", but it wasn't until the late 1980s that the influence of Islam would become pronounced in hip-hop.

Public Enemy gave shout-outs to **Louis Farrakhan**, and a sect of the Nation of Islam formed by **Clarence 13X** called the Five Percenters (aka Nation of Gods and Earths) started to become prominent in the rap world. Five Percenters such as **Rakim**, **Big Daddy Kane**, **Stetsasonic**'s Daddy-O, **Divine Force**, **Poor Righteous Teachers**, **Brand Nubian**, **Wu-Tang Clan**, **Divine Styler**, **Busta Rhymes**, **KMD**, **King Sun** and **Movement Ex** espoused a doctrine that was even further removed from Muslim orthodoxy than Elijah Muhammad's teachings: 85% of the world is the uncivilized masses, ten percent are slave-owners ("bloodsuckers of the poor") and five percent are black men "with knowledge of self" – the "poor righteous teachers" whose duty it is to spread the word and liberate the black man from the tyranny of the white devil. Once a black man attains this knowledge, he becomes divine – members call themselves "Gods".

Of course, these teachings are so far outside classical Islam as to be heretical. Yet the sect's teachings, which are heavily based on numerology, have a strong appeal to rappers who can put the religion's code-like complexities to good use in their rhymes. The Five Percenters also put an emphasis on proseletyzing, demanding that its followers be good orators – another reason for its popularity in hip-hop. The relationship between the Nation of Islam and hip-hop became so strong that by the early 1990s the NOI's youth minister was himself a rapper, **Prince Akeem**.

However, by the late 1990s, the influence of the NOI and Five Percenters was waning. Perhaps this is because of the contradictions inherent in Five Percent teachings – if you are God, you can set up your own laws. Or maybe it was because, with the rise of materialism, flossin' and expensive cars, clothes and videos, being able to dress like a god increasingly appeared to be more important than actually being one. To pose a philosophical question, what's uglier – shoving an iced out Rolex in someone's face or chanting, as **Brand Nubian** did in 1990, "drop the bomb on the Yakub crew/Drop the bomb on the caveman crew"?

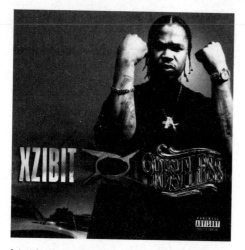

his show-stealing verse on **Snoop Dogg**'s "Bitch Please" (1999) on which "Xzibit [was] ready to scrap/Like Mike Tyson with his license back".

On *Restless* (2000), his breakthrough album, X "[stood] behind the mic like Walter Cronkite" and "rearrange[d] the game with his rugged sound". While X wasn't as devastating as he had been on *40 Dayz & 40 Nightz*, the beats managed to appeal to the radio and MTV without watering down X's roughneck flow and lyrics. "X" (produced by **Dr. Dre**) and "Get

Your Walk On" (produced by **Battlecat** and **Mel-Man**) presented X as a charming thug, as a guy who would knock your block off if you stepped to him, but would do so with wit and style. The superfly "Rimz And Tirez" had a **Curtis Mayfield**-style hook and saw Xzibit rolling as smoothly as a '62 Bonneville, presaging his star-making turn on *Pimp My Ride*.

*Man vs Machine* (2002) was a big disappointment. While it largely followed the same formula as *Restless*, the beats were weaker and more wishy-washy, and consequently X was too. Lightweight tracks such as "Losin' Your Mind" and "Heart Of Man" (which sampled 1980s pop-rockers **Toto**) just didn't gel with X's crush-kill-destroy style. Unsurprisingly, it took **MOP** ("BK To LA") and **DJ Premier** ("What A Mess") to remind Xzibit of what he did best.

**40 Dayz & 40 Nightz**
Loud, 1998

Not as easily digestible as *Restless*, *40 Dayz & 40 Nightz* is nevertheless Xzibit's finest album. Like his previous album, *At the Speed Of Life*, this is more of a mood piece than the straight-up splattercore that usually characterises the West Coast underground. "Los Angeles Times" and "Three Card Molly" are dark, grimy tracks that display Xzibit "livin' life like a bull inside a china shop".

# Ying Yang Twins

Hip-hop's relationship with the mainstream is often epitomized by the unlikely partnerships formed by the collision between underground rap and overground pop – **Run DMC** and Aerosmith, **Mariah Carey** and Ol' Dirty Bastard, Mariah Carey and Mystikal, or Jay-Z performing with **Phish**. However, surely no pair-up was as unlikely as once-wholesome pop princess **Britney Spears** and Atlanta's club hooligans **Ying Yang Twins**, who seem to talk about nothing but "coochie poppin".

The long road leading up to collaborating with America's sweetheart began in 1995 when **D-Roc** (D'Angelo Holmes) had a big Southern club hit with "Bankhead Bounce". "Bounce Shorty Bounce" (1995) followed – a strip-club anthem – and *Englewood 4 Life!* (1995) was a moderate hit in the Atlanta area. He returned with his **2 Tight Click** on *True Dawgs* (1997), a pretty run-of-the-mill Southern gangsta album with a cou-

ple of club tracks like "Just Dance" and "Booty Drop", notable only for the outrageously low megahertz count on the bassline of "Beef". D-Roc hooked up with **Kaine** (Eric Jackson Jr) for a remix with **DJ Smurf**, and the duo became the Ying Yang Twins.

After several appearances on regional bass compilations and mixtapes, the Ying Yang Twins released their first album, *Thug Walkin'* (2000), for the Collipark label, owned by **DJ Beat-In-Azz** (the new name Smurf was now going under). The album's big hit was "Whistle While You Twurk", a filthy club track which borrowed a synth shimmer from **Kraftwerk** and a whistling hook from *Snow White*. As the single was breaking nationally, though, Disney stepped in and sued over the whistle – apparently the entertainment company wasn't happy about the juxtaposition of a wholesome family song with lyrics such as "make that pussy fart".

*Alley... Return of the Ying Yang Twins* (2002) featured another ridiculous bass hit, "Say I Yi Yi". The Twins really went nationwide, though, with their appearance on **Lil Jon**'s "Get Low" (2003). *Me & My Brother* (2003) was essentially twelve sequels to "Get Low", with Lil Jon showing up again for the admittedly hot "Salt Shaker". "Naggin'" was in the great battle-of-the-sexes and playground-chant tradition, while "Georgia Dome" did at least own up to what it was in its subtitle – "Get Low Sequel". The Twins tried to get socio-political on "Calling All Zones" and the title track, but both were pretty unconvincing, even with the presence of Goodie MOb's **Khujo** on the former. It was a short road from the success of "Salt Shaker" to nuzzling with Britney on "(I Got That) Boom Boom" (2003).

◉ **Me & My Brother**
TVT, 2003

Kaine may sound like a cross between his WWE namesake and Captain Beefheart, and the Twins may steal most of their hooks from the schoolyard, but the formula gets a party real "crunk". The misspelling and mispronunciation (rhymes with "thang") of their name should be signposts enough that the only thing spiritual about this album is all the Grey Goose vodka they drink.

The Ying Yang twins: so crunk, they can't even flick a V-sign without getting it the wrong way round.

# Yo Yo

Discovered by **Ice Cube** in a shopping mall while she was still a high school cheerleader, **Yolanda Whitaker** went on to become one of the most respected women in hip-hop. Treading the fine line between pop starlet, gangsta bitch, feminist role model and good-time girl, **Yo Yo** transcended her terrible *nom de disque* and managed to convey a female perspective in hip-hop without becoming a stereotype or pandering to male fantasies.

Unfortunately, Yo Yo's talent has never really lived up to her image, and she's never been able to outdo her first appearance on wax. Acting as the feminist foil to Ice Cube's rampant misogyny on "It's A Man's World" (1990) on his *Amerikkka's Most Wanted* album, Yo Yo spat enough schoolyard insults to make Cube's dick shrivel up like a tortoise retreating into its shell. Yo Yo's debut album, *Make Way for the Motherlode* (1991), featured the excellent single "You Can't Play With My Yo Yo" and managed to make the gangsta production of Ice Cube and **Sir Jinx** bounce with Alice Walker's womanist brio.

*Black Pearl* (1992), on the other hand, was a more considered, more mature statement, but it lacked the vitality of *Motherlode*. *You Better Ask Somebody* (1993) remedied this with female gangstaisms such as "The Mackstress", an inspired remake of **Serge Gainsbourg**'s "Bonnie and Clyde" with Ice Cube, and the liberating "Girl With a Gun". *Total Control* (1996), however, repeated the mistakes of *Black Pearl* and went in for heavy-handed messages at a time when most hip-hop was concerning itself with delivering vicarious thrills. Her *Ebony* album was scheduled to be released in 1998, but its mix of r&b beats and largely East Coast-lite sound prompted the label brass to shelve it, and

## THE BOOMING SYSTEM

In this age of the iPod and MP3 players smaller than your thumb, the sight of someone lugging around an enormous boombox on their shoulders is little short of ridiculous. However, in the early days of hip-hop, before the Walkman became widespread, boomboxes were the only personal audio systems available.

In New York, boomboxes became a central part of hip-hop culture, so much so that they were called **"ghetto blasters"**. To mainstream white New Yorkers, boomboxes became as emblematic of hip-hop culture and its uncivility as **graffiti**. In a sense, boomboxes were the aural equivalent of graffiti, in effect saying, "if you're going to continue to ignore me, I'm gonna blast my music down your throat until you have to pay attention." It may have been a sentiment as old as teen culture itself, but no other youth movement terrorized subway riders and pedestrians to such an extent that New York was forced to write a clause into the city's noise codes stating that "No person shall operate or use any radio, phonograph, or tape recorder in or on any rapid transit railroad, omnibus or ferry in such a manner that the sound emanating from such sound reproduction device is audible to another person." It was the first such provision in the world.

Of course, the **Walkman** largely put a halt to the boombox, but soon enough car audio systems started to replace the boombox as an object of noise terrorism. The "trunk of funk" or "booming system" was a car stereo decked out with huge subwoofers that made the guts of passers-by churn, and were capable of shaking the foundations of small buildings. In the late 1980s they became so ubiquitous that not only did producers start tailoring "jeep beats" specifically for bumping on car stereos, but a whole subgenre of music developed that was designed to test the limits of a car's subwoofers.

But thanks to the "quality of life" campaign instigated by New York City Mayor **Rudy Giuliani**, which has since been imitated around the country, the monster car audio system is now a relic confined to the competitions run in Florida. Instead, hip-hop's latest way of getting in the face of innocent by-standers is the custom car: 24-inch spinning rims, an XBox and PlayStation hooked up to the multiple video screens inside, and a gleaming Louis Vuitton paint job.

Yo-Yo hasn't been heard from since.

# Young MC

**Y**oung MC's 1997 comeback album may have been titled *Return of the One-Hit Wonder*, but **Marvin Young** had at least three certifiable mega-hits to his credit. The only problem was that two of them were recorded by **Tone-Loc**. Young was an economics student at the University of Southern California when he met fellow students Michael Ross and Matt Dike, who had just set up a label called Delicious Vinyl. His single, "I Let 'Em Know" (1988), was the label's first release.

In 1989 Young wrote hip-hop's biggest pop hit thus far, and one of the best-selling singles of all-time – Tone-Loc's "Wild Thing". Almost as huge was the follow-up, "Funky Cold Medina", which Young also wrote. With "Bust A Move" (1989), Young MC had a platinum-selling single in his own right. While "Wild Thing" and "Funky Cold Medina" were hits because of Loc's absurd voice and great production by the **Dust Brothers**, "Bust A Move" climbed the pop charts on the back of Young MC's gentle wit and inclusiveness. Of course, the **Ballin' Jack** sample and a monstrous bassline from Red Hot Chili Pepper **Flea** didn't hurt either.

While "Bust A Move" was easily the best track on Young MC's double platinum debut album, *Stone Cold Rhymin'* (1989) may well be the best hip-hop album ever to be made by a commerical flash-in-the-pans. "Principal's Office" was a minor hit with a **Chuck Berry**-ish narrative about school mischief, while on "Got More Rhymes" Young proclaimed he had more rhymes than **Elizabeth Taylor** had husbands. Although "I Come Off" saw Young MC trying to be hard, he compared himself to ice-skater Dorothy Hammill – an indicative blunder from which he would never recover. "I Come Off" also highlighted his propensity to roll his "r"s, a gimmick he repeated on the club hit "Know How", which was built on large chunks of **Isaac Hayes**'s "Theme From Shaft" and the Incredible Bongo Band's "Apache".

*Brainstorm* (1991) saw Young MC wearing black medallions and trying to be socially relevant. His previous records had captured the pop zeitgeist, but *Brainstorm* was about a year-and-a-half too late and on tracks such as "Keep It In Your Trousers" he sounded pretty ridiculous. Despite production from **A Tribe Called Quest**'s Ali Shaheed Muhammad, *What's the Flavor* (1993) and its jazzy vibes fared little better. With the title *Return of the One-Hit Wonder*, his comeback album didn't promise much. It didn't deliver much either.

Still, two more albums followed – *Ain't Goin' Out Like That* (2000) and *Engage The Enzyme* (2002) – which were perhaps only notable for the latter's "Crucial", a relatively unsanctimonious 9/11 track. Nonetheless, he *was* going out like that.

# YoungBloodz

**A**tlanta's YoungBloodz are something like Tha Alkaholiks of the Dirty South – as if Dixie had a shortage of hedonistic, inebriated crews that liked nothing more than getting the club "crunk". The **YoungBloodz**, however, are less intense than **Trick Daddy**, less monomaniacal than **Ying Yang Twins**, less profound than **David Banner**, less spiritual than **OutKast**, less charismatic than **Ludacris**, and they throw fewer 'bows than **Lil Jon**. In other words, the YoungBloodz are content to just sit in the corner of a club getting their drink on, while all hell breaks loose around them.

**Sean Paul** (Sean Paul Joseph) and **J-Bo**

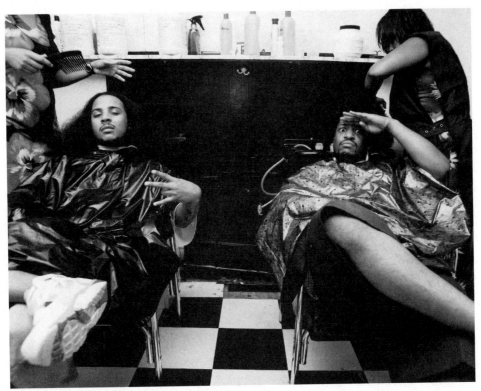

The Youngbloodz, mortified to be disturbed by a photographer whilst having their hair done. Is nothing sacred?!

(Jeffrey Ray Grigsby, the cousin of Dre from OutKast) met each other in high school in Atlanta. Being aspiring rap artists, they decided to leave home and move in together with a friend in the College Park section of Atlanta. The apartment was the unofficial headquarters of the **Attic Crew**, a group of producers and musicians who took the youngsters under their wing. The YoungBloodz soon made a name for themselves and were signed by **LaFace**. Their debut album, *Against Da Grain* (1999), had the duo getting "slizzard" over smooth beats from Organized Noize and the Attic Crew. Regional hit "85" featured an awkward acoustic-ish guitar beat from Organized Noize and a cameo from OutKast's **Big Boi**, while "U-Way (How We Do It)" was a Colt .45 anthem based on a popping popcorn synth and the dramatic undertow of a low-end piano riff. Instead of talking about how many fools they popped or how much weight they sold, they rapped about getting drunk and driving slowly on the highway to their girl's house because their license had been revoked.

A move to Jermaine Dupri's **So So Def** brought *Drankin' Patnaz* (2003), a more straightforwardly crunk album than their debut. "Damn!" was a Lil Jon beat that sounded like, well, Lil Jon and it worked fine if you weren't sick to death of his synth sound, while "Lean Low" was produced by the **Trackboyz** but sounded just like Lil Jon. The album served its purpose, though: it was perfect for pumping while cruising down highway I-85, or for tearing the club up.

**Drankin' Patnaz**
So So Def, 2003

Their debut album was marginally more interesting lyrically, but the beats here are far superior – and anyway, listening to groups like The YoungBloodz for the lyrics is like reading *Playboy* for the interviews. "Damn!", "Lean Low" and "Mud Pit" all sound great over a big system and are guaranteed party-rockers.

# Hip-Hop Slang

With hip-hop's emphasis on the word, it's hardly surprising that rappers have added more words and phrases to the English lexicon than anyone since Noah Webster. From Sugarhill Gang's "death OJ" (a nice car) to Lil Jon's "get crunk" (get rowdy, a mixture of "crazy" and "drunk"), hip-hop slang changes constantly and from region to region. Here are some of the nouns, verbs and adjectives close to hip-hop's heart that you will frequently encounter:

affirmative: aiight, fasheezy, fashizzle, fo sheedo, true that, word is bond

authenticity: realness, bout it, to come correct, furilla, hardcore, OG, trill, represent

bad: wack, bammer, bootie

big man on campus: don, don dada, don gorgon, big tymer, hot boy, big-baller, playa

car: hooptie, ride, bubble, mobie, bucket, drop, 'lac, whip, 98, Ac

car hubcaps: rims, chrome, newborns (factory rims), spinners, twankies, dubs, gold feet, blades, D's, Daytons, 20s, 24s

cocaine: yola, cake, hubba, blast, rock

diamonds: ice ("iced-out' being the look), bling bling, high beams

disrespect: diss, playa-hating, baller-blockin', cock-blockin', mack-murderin'

drug dealing: slanging, coming up, grinding, baking cake

fake: buster, shook one, faulty, ho cake, janky, chump, peanut, front, flake, toy, wanksta

good: fresh, gravy, notch, off the hook, off the heezy, out the frame, all that, hype, phat, def, live

gun: chopper, AK, nine, chop suey, nina, calico, cap (bullet), clip (bullet), deuce deuce, dillon, gatt, glock, jammy, oo-wop, paddle, piece, Tec 9, ten, eight-plus-one, Mac

joint: blunt, wood (kind of cigar used in rolling a joint), phillie, hoota, jawn, primo, turbo, rocket, tree, zootie

marijuana: weed, cheeba, Archie Bunker, Buddha, bomb, indo, collie, doja, broccoli, dank, dub, hay, chronic, ganja, herbalz, hydro, kill, lye, tical, boom, sess

money: cabbage, cheddar, cheese, scrilla, paper, dead presidents, feddie, cream, grip, scratch, chips, ducats, ends, papes, lucci

penis: jimmy, jimbrowski, bozack (scrotum), jammy, jock

police: po-po, five-o, jake, beast

relaxing: chillin', marinating, lamping

sex: cuttin', twerkin', zeez, bag up, bonin', buckwildin', knock boots, bust a nut, dig out, get busy, lay pipe, nutt, wax, wild thing, hit skins

shoes: kicks, Tims (Timberland boots), classic soldiers (Reebok sneakers)

show off: floss, stun, bark, big Willie style, flammy, flamboastin', flex, pop collars, livin' large

woman: beeyotch, batch, whoadie, bendas, breezy, duck, hutch, pigeon, scully, swisher, boo, chickenhead, frreak, skeezer, ho, honey dip, hottie, trick, hoodrat, shorty, stunt

# How hip-hop came to be

**1925** Louis Armstrong records "Heebie Jeebies" and forgets the words, using some rhythmic nonsense syllables in place of the lyrics. The result was called "scatting" and is the ancestor of human beatboxing.

**1929** Blues pianist/singer Speckled Red (aka Rufus Perryman) records the first version of the ritualized rhyming insult game called "The Dozens".

Comedian Pigmeat Markham first performs his classic routine "Here Comes The Judge" which would later be recorded in several versions set to music and become an influence on many rappers.

**1930s** Jive-talking singers such as Harry "The Hipster" Gibson, Slim Gaillard and female impersonator Frankie "Half Pint" Jaxon start recording. Their rhythmic cadences, often punctuated with nonsense words, were halfway between talking and rapping.

**1935** Blues singer Lucille Bogan records "Shave 'Em Dry", the filthiest, most explicit song recorded until the 2 Live Crew came along.

**1950s** Jamaican soundsystem DJ Count Machuki imitated hepcat American radio DJs such as Jocko Henderson and started talking rhythmically over records at yard parties.

**1953** Willie Dixon records a version of the old street-corner rhyming toast "Signifying Monkey".

**1958** Bo Diddley records "Say Man", a profoundly goofy testifyin' match between Diddley and his maracas player Jerome Green.

**1960s** The Crips and Bloods form in Los Angeles. Gangs such as Savage Skulls, Black Spades and Savage Nomads form in the Bronx.

**1960** Jorgen Ingmann and The Shadows record the first versions of "Apache", bizarrely creating the template for what would become the b-boy national anthem.

**1964** Before his fight with Sonny Liston, boxer Cassius Clay boasts in rhyme to a befuddled largely white press, "Sonny Liston is great, but he'll fall in eight".

**1965** Jamaican ska singer Prince Buster records "Al Capone", updating the old outlaw tales of the Wild West and laying the foundations for gangsta rap.

**1969** Dancer Donald Campbell invents the Campbellock move in Los Angeles.

James Brown records "Funky Drummer" with Clyde Stubblefield on skins. The record will become the most sampled record in hip-hop.

**1970** James Brown records "Brother Rapp".

Radio DJ Gary Byrd records "Are You Ready For Black Power?" in which Byrd castigates fake revolutionaries over a militant funk groove.

**1971** *The New York Times* publishes the first article about graffiti, focusing on the tags of Taki 183.

**1972** Joe Tex records *From the Roots Came the Rapper*, an album that combines plain speech derived from both stand-up comedians and preachers and downhome soul singing.

James Brown records "King Heroin", a harrowing record in which Brown adopts the persona of heroin and brags in the style of the street-corner toasts.

**1973** Lightnin' Rod, aka Last Poet Jalal Nuriddin, records an album of streetcorner toasts and tall tales called *Hustlers Convention* which is the grandaddy of all gangsta rap.

The entertainment director for President Nixon's reinauguration party Michael Viner assembles a group of studio musicians as The Incredible Bongo Band and records a version of "Apache" that will become perhaps the most famous beat in hip-hop.

Kool DJ Herc throws his first party at the community center in his building at 1520 Sedgwick Avenue in The Bronx.

On November 12 Afrika Bambaataa forms The Organization, renamed the Universal Zulu Nation the following year.

**1974** Coke LaRock starts to get on the mic and rhyme along with records spun by Kool Herc.

**1975** Millie Jackson records "The Rap/If Loving You Is Wrong I Don't Want to Be Right".

Grand Wizard Theodore invents the scratch.

**1976** The first DJ battle – between Afrika Bambaataa and Disco King Mario – is held at Junior School 123 in The Bronx.

**1977** Jimmy Dee and Jojo form the Rock Steady Crew.

**1979** Fatback's "King Tim III (Personality Jock)" and Sugarhill Gang's "Rapper's Delight" are the first rap records.

Kurtis Blow's "Christmas Rappin'" is the first rap record released on a major label.

Mr Magic's "Rap Attack" on WHBI is the first hip-hop radio show.

**1980** The *New York Post* publishes first story on breakdancing after members of the High Times Crew are arrested in Washington Heights.

Kurtis Blow is the first rapper to appear on national television when he performs "The Breaks" on *Soul Train*. "The Breaks" becomes the first gold hip-hop record.

**1981** The first DJ record, "The Adventures Of Grandmaster Flash On The Wheels Of Steel", is released.

Disco Daddy and Captain Rapp make the first West Coast hip-hop record, "Gigolo Rap".

ABC's news program *20/20* features a segment called "The Rap Phenomenon".

**1982** With help from Arthur Baker and John Robie, Afrika Bambaataa records "Planet Rock", the first electro record.

The first hip-hop movie, *Wild Style*, is released.

**1983** The graffiti documentary *Style Wars* is released.

Afrika Bambaataa & the Soul Sonic Force's "Looking For The Perfect Beat" is the first hip-hop record to use the Emulator sampling keyboard.

The Rock Steady Crew appear in *Flashdance*.

Run DMC release their first single, "It's Like That/Sucker MCs", and the old school immediately becomes old hat.

**1984** The Fresh Fest concert tour with Run DMC, Whodini, Kurtis Blow and the Fat Boys takes hip-hop across the US.

Los Angeles radio station KDAY becomes the first hip-hop-only format station in the world.

**1986** Run DMC's *Raising Hell* is the first platinum-selling rap album. Their collaboration with Aerosmith, "Walk This Way", breaks hip-hop into the pop charts.

**1988** DJ Jazzy Jeff & the Fresh Prince win first rap Grammy.

**1989** Tone Loc's "Wild Thing" is hip-hop's first certified platinum single.

# Books

Charlie Ahearn & Jim Fricke, *Yes Yes Y'All: Oral History of Hip-Hop's First Decade* (Da Capo, 2002). Seattle's Experience Music Project is behind this definitive account of the early days of hip-hop that collects first-hand tales of Herc's parties, the Cold Crush Brothers's MC battles, the Savage Skulls gang, graffiti raids on train yards and more.

Gabriel Alvarez, *Chariman Mao, Sacha Jenkins, Brent Rollins and Elliott Wilson, Ego Trip's Book of Rap Lists* (St. Martin's Griffin, 1999). From the folks behind the late, lamented *Ego Trip* magazine comes the funniest, most insane, most ludicrously trainspotterish book ever written about music, hip-hop or otherwise.

Freddy Fresh, *The Rap Records* (Nerby Publishing, 2004). The absolute bible for hip-hop collectors. Minnesota-based producer Freddy Fresh has compiled the most complete discography yet of pre-1990 hip-hop singles.

Alan Light (ed.), *The Vibe History of Hip Hop* (Plexus, 1999). *The Vibe History of Hip Hop* aims to be hip-hop's first coffee-table book and in this it succeeds admirably. The writing is uneven and stylistically all over the place, but stand-out pieces on Run DMC, The Beastie Boys and Southern hip-hop make the book more than just a collection of pretty pictures.

David Toop, *Rap Attack #3* (Serpent's Tail, 2000). Even if Toop has run out of steam and interest for this final edition, the original book on hip-hop is still perhaps the best. Toop was keenly aware of the ironies of American society and his analysis of hip-hop placed it firmly in the context of Land of the Free's war on the urban poor. Perhaps more importantly, however, Toop showed that hip-hop wasn't simply a novelty by situating it in a century of African-American cultural practice.

Oliver Wang (ed.), *Classic Material: The Hip-Hop Album Guide* (ECW Press, 2003). A collection of essays on the sixtysomething best albums in hip-hop history. The pieces are written by such respected journalists as Wang, David Toop, Jeff Chang, Joseph Patel, Chairman Mao, Dave Tompkins, Hua Hsu, Jon Caramanica, Elizabeth Mendez Berry and yours truly.

# Magazines

## Hip-Hop Connection
This British magazine offers the best coverage of the independent and underground scenes.

## Murder Dog
While the copy-editing leaves more than a bit to be desired, if you like a bit of the old ultra-violence there is no other choice.

## The Source
Despite its shady alliances and questionable practices, *The Source* remains the standard-bearer for hip-hop journalism.

## Vibe
*Vibe* has better writing than any other hip-hop magazine, but its professionalism can too often lapse into boredom.

## XXL
It's far from perfect, but with more dirt than *Vibe* and less toadying than *The Source*, *XXL* is probably the best mainstream hip-hop magazine out there.

### Wax Poetics

Wax Poetics looks like a cross between *Dazed & Confused* and an academic poetry journal, and is dedicated to the art of beat-digging. Most collector's magazines are by collectors and for collectors in the most extreme sense (the colour of the labels, matrix numbers, and who got coffee for the band in the studio), but *Wax Poetics* actually looks good and it attempts to humanise obsessive record-collecting with humour, real scholarship and politics.

# Websites

### All Hiphop.com

http://www.allhiphop.com

It doesn't exactly live up to its billing as the world's most dangerous site, but the news pages and rumour section are daily must-reads. More daily news is available, only with more annoying design and layout, at SOHH.com (http://www.sohh.com/thewire) and Street Hop (http//www.streethop.com/home).

### Cocaine, Blunts & Hip Hop Tapes

http://multsanta.madvision.co.uk/blunts//
indexb.html

An excellent audioblog from the guys behind the DC radio show of the same name. Lots of mp3s of obscure hip-hop records, and requisite lunatic scholarship to go with them.

### DaveyD.com

http://www.daveyd.com

Bay Area hip-hop stalwart Davey D has been a longtime presence on the hip-hop scene, and his site offers a more political/activist perspective than is the norm in the bling-bling era.

### The Original Hip-Hop (Rap) Lyrics Archive

http://www.ohhla.com

As with any lyrics site there are bad errors and serious omissions, but this vast resource should be your first port of call if you're trying to catch up with Twista or decode that Sun Tzu reference on a RZA B-side.

### The Rap Dictionary

http://www.rapdict.org/

Not nearly as complete as it should be, but it's still a good place to go to avoid mistaking "sherm stick" for "scrilla".

### Rap Reviews

http://www.RapReviews.com

A very useful, comprehensive archive of hip-hop record reviews. The pieces aren't always the best written out there, but the reviews are uniformly thorough, and give you a great idea of what you're going to get for your dollars.

### The (Rap) Sample FAQ

http://www.the-breaks.com

Giving you the dirt on who sampled who and who's been sampled by whom, The (Rap) Sample FAQ is one of the most essential hip-hop resources on the Net.

### Soul Sides

http://www.o-dub.com/soulsides/index.
html

A fantastic audioblog from journalist/DJ/crate-digger Oliver Wang. A few times a week Wang posts mp3s of rare hip-hop and breakbeat classics.

### Soul Strut

http://www.soulstrut.com

The Internet headquarters of the global beat-digging community. Sure, it's nerdy as heck with all the dusty-fingered obsessives bragging about their Polish sound-library records, but if you trawl the forums you will find more information about breaks and beats than you ever wanted to know.

### The True School

http://www.jayquan.com/founmain.htm

JayQuan's superlative old school remembrance site houses interviews, histories, photos and a mouth-watering list of old school tapes available for trade.

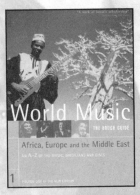

# ROUGH GUIDES TRAVEL...

## UK & Ireland
Britain
Devon & Cornwall
Dublin
Edinburgh
England
Ireland
Lake District
London
London
 DIRECTIONS
London Mini Guide
Scotland
Scottish Highlands &
 Islands
Wales

## Europe
Algarve
Amsterdam
Amsterdam
 DIRECTIONS
Andalucía
Athens DIRECTIONS
Austria
Baltic States
Barcelona
Belgium & Luxembourg
Berlin
Brittany & Normandy
Bruges & Ghent
Brussels
Budapest
Bulgaria
Copenhagen
Corfu
Corsica
Costa Brava
Crete
Croatia
Cyprus
Czech & Slovak Republics
Dodecanese & East
 Aegean
Dordogne & The Lot
Europe
Florence

France
Germany
Greece
Greek Islands
Hungary
Ibiza & Formentera
Iceland
Ionian Islands
Italy
Languedoc & Roussillon
Lisbon
Lisbon DIRECTIONS
The Loire
Madeira
Madrid
Mallorca
Malta & Gozo
Menorca
Moscow
Netherlands
Norway
Paris
Paris DIRECTIONS
Paris Mini Guide
Poland
Portugal
Prague
Provence & the Côte
 d'Azur
Pyrenees
Romania
Rome
Sardinia
Scandinavia
Sicily
Slovenia
Spain
St Petersburg
Sweden
Switzerland
Tenerife & La Gomera
Tenerife
 DIRECTIONS
Turkey
Tuscany & Umbria
Venice & The Veneto
Venice DIRECTIONS

Vienna

## Asia
Bali & Lombok
Bangkok
Beijing
Cambodia
China
Goa
Hong Kong & Macau
India
Indonesia
Japan
Laos
Malaysia, Singapore &
 Brunei
Nepal
Philippines
Singapore
South India
Southeast Asia
Sri Lanka
Thailand
Thailand's Beaches &
 Islands
Tokyo
Vietnam

## Australasia
Australia
Melbourne
New Zealand
Sydney

## North America
Alaska
Big Island of Hawaii
Boston
California
Canada
Chicago
Florida
Grand Canyon
Hawaii
Honolulu
Las Vegas
Los Angeles

Maui
Miami & the Florida Keys
Montréal
New England
New Orleans
New York City
New York City
 DIRECTIONS
New York City Mini Guide
Pacific Northwest
Rocky Mountains
San Francisco
San Francisco
 DIRECTIONS
Seattle
Southwest USA
Toronto
USA
Vancouver
Washington DC
Yosemite

## Caribbean
## & Latin America
Antigua & Barbuda
Antigua
 DIRECTIONS
Argentina
Bahamas
Barbados
Barbados
 DIRECTIONS
Belize
Bolivia
Brazil
Caribbean
Central America
Chile
Costa Rica
Cuba
Dominican Republic
Ecuador
Guatemala
Jamaica
Maya World
Mexico
Peru

Rough Guides are available from good bookstores worldwide. New titles are published every month.
Check www.roughguides.com for the latest news.

# ...MUSIC & REFERENCE

St Lucia
South America
Trinidad & Tobago

## Africa & Middle East
Cape Town
Egypt
The Gambia
Jordan
Kenya
Marrakesh
  DIRECTIONS
Morocco
South Africa, Lesotho &
  Swaziland
Syria
Tanzania
Tunisia
West Africa
Zanzibar
Zimbabwe

## Travel Theme guides
First-Time Around the
  World
First-Time Asia
First-Time Europe
First-Time Latin America
Skiing & Snowboarding in
  North America
Travel Online
Travel Health
Walks in London & SE
  England
Women Travel

## Restaurant guides
French Hotels &
  Restaurants
London
New York
San Francisco

## Maps
Algarve
Amsterdam

Andalucia & Costa del Sol
Argentina
Athens
Australia
Baja California
Barcelona
Berlin
Boston
Brittany
Brussels
Chicago
Crete
Croatia
Cuba
Cyprus
Czech Republic
Dominican Republic
Dubai & UAE
Dublin
Egypt
Florence & Siena
Frankfurt
Greece
Guatemala & Belize
Iceland
Ireland
Kenya
Lisbon
London
Los Angeles
Madrid
Mexico
Miami & Key West
Morocco
New York City
New Zealand
Northern Spain
Paris
Peru
Portugal
Prague
Rome
San Francisco
Sicily
South Africa
South India
Sri Lanka

Tenerife
Thailand
Toronto
Trinidad & Tobago
Tuscany
Venice
Washington DC
Yucatán Peninsula

## Dictionary Phrasebooks
Czech
Dutch
Egyptian Arabic
European Languages
  (Czech, French,
  German, Greek, Italian,
  Portuguese, Spanish)
French
German
Greek
Hindi & Urdu
Hungarian
Indonesian
Italian
Japanese
Mandarin Chinese
Mexican Spanish
Polish
Portuguese
Russian
Spanish
Swahili
Thai
Turkish
Vietnamese

## Music Guides
The Beatles
Bob Dylan
Cult Pop
Classical Music
Country Music
Elvis
Hip Hop
House
Irish Music
Jazz

Music USA
Opera
Reggae
Rock
Techno
World Music (2 vols)

## History Guides
China
Egypt
England
France
India
Islam
Italy
Spain
USA

## Reference Guides
Books for Teenagers
Children's Books, 0–5
Children's Books, 5–11
Cult Fiction
Cult Football
Cult Movies
Cult TV
Ethical Shopping
Formula 1
The iPod, iTunes & Music
  Online
The Internet
Internet Radio
James Bond
Kids' Movies
Lord of the Rings
Muhammed Ali
Man Utd
Personal Computers
Pregnancy & Birth
Shakespeare
Superheroes
Unexplained Phenomena
The Universe
Videogaming
Weather
Website Directory

**Also!** More than 120 Rough Guide music CDs are available from all good book and record stores.
Listen in at www.worldmusic.net